THE
PROFESSIONAL
PROTECTION
OFFICER

PRACTICAL SECURITY STRATEGIES AND EMERGING TRENDS

INTERNATIONAL FOUNDATION FOR

PROTECTION OFFICERS

ELSEVIER

AMSTERDAM • BOSTON • HEIDELBERG • LONDON
NEW YORK • OXFORD • PARIS • SAN DIEGO
SAN FRANCISCO • SINGAPORE • SYDNEY • TOKYO

Butterworth-Heinemann is an imprint of Elsevier

Butterworth-Heinemann is an imprint of Elsevier
30 Corporate Drive, Suite 400, Burlington, MA 01803, USA
The Boulevard, Langford Lane, Kidlington, Oxford, OX5 1GB, UK

Notices
Knowledge and best practice in this field are constantly changing. As new research and experience broaden
our understanding, changes in research methods, professional practices, or medical treatment may become
necessary.

Practitioners and researchers must always rely on their own experience and knowledge in evaluating and
using any information, methods, compounds, or experiments described herein. In using such information or
methods they should be mindful of their own safety and the safety of others, including parties for whom they
have a professional responsibility.

To the fullest extent of the law, neither the Publisher nor the authors, contributors, or editors, assume any
liability for any injury and/or damage to persons or property as a matter of products liability, negligence
or otherwise, or from any use or operation of any methods, products, instructions, or ideas contained in the
material herein.

Library of Congress Cataloging-in-Publication Data
Application submitted

British Library Cataloguing-in-Publication Data
A catalogue record for this book is available from the British Library.

ISBN: 978-1-85617-746-7

For information on all Butterworth-Heinemann publications,
visit our web site at www.elsevierdirect.com

Printed in United States of America

10 11 12 13 14   10 9 8 7 6 5 4 3 2 1

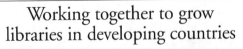

Working together to grow
libraries in developing countries

www.elsevier.com | www.bookaid.org | www.sabre.org

ELSEVIER   BOOK AID International   Sabre Foundation

Contents

5. Career Planning for Protection Professionals

CHRISTOPHER A. HERTIG AND
CHRIS RICHARDSON

II
COMMUNICATIONS

6. Effective Communications

CHARLES T. THIBODEAU

7. Security Awareness

JAMES E. SELLERS

8. Central Alarm Stations and Dispatch Operations

SEAN SMITH, JIM ELLIS, AND
RICH ABRAMS

III
PROTECTION OFFICER FUNCTIONS

9. Automation in Protection Operations

KEVIN E. PETERSON

IV
CRIME PREVENTION AND PHYSICAL SECURITY

VIII
RISK AND THREAT MANAGEMENT

IX
INVESTIGATIONS

32. Crime and Incident Scene Procedures
DENNIS SHEPP

33. Interviewing and Statements
DENNIS SHEPP

34. Foundations for Surveillance
MICHAEL STROBERGER

35. Report Writing and Field Notes
RAV-ZURIDAN YISRAEL

X
LEGAL ASPECTS OF SECURITY

36. Legal Aspects of Security
DAVID L. RAY

XI
OFFICER SAFETY AND USE OF FORCE

37. Use of Force
CHARLES T. THIBODEAU AND CHRISTOPHER A. HERTIG

38. Defensive Tactics and Officer Safety
INGE SEBYAN BLACK

39. Industrial Hazards, Safety, and the Security Patrol Officer
BRIAN D. BAKER

40. Apprehension and Detention Procedures
RICHARD P. FIEMS

XII
RELATIONS WITH OTHERS

41. Human Relations in a Global Environment
CHRISTOPHER A. HERTIG AND
DARRIEN DAVENPORT

42. Public Relations
CHARLES T. THIBODEAU,
CHRISTOPHER A. HERTIG, AND
GEORGE A. BARNETT

43. Community Relations: Making the Strategy Come Alive

MARK E. PUETZ AND K. C. POULIN

44. Networking and the Liaison Function

BRION P. GILBRIDE

45. Ethics and Professionalism

CHRISTOPHER A. HERTIG

Index   577

Foreword

The security world is constantly changing, both in the context in which it has to operate, and in terms of what it can offer as a response to a wide range of threats. This is true across the world. Indeed, globalization and the impact of technology are just two trends that have seen to that. As a consequence, security has become more complicated; or, at least, the breadth of knowledge that a good security operative, at any level, needs to draw upon has been stretched.

One of the positive signs of the march of security professionalism is that there is now more research being gathered on security-related issues. Scholars in universities, research institutes, companies, and professional bodies have helped to develop a global knowledge base. The good thing about security is that knowledge from around the world has relevance to a broad range of circumstances. After all, threats are often the same. Terrorist attacks take place globally, and the sorts of responses needed are often similar, if not the same. The principles of security apply across the board, though the contexts differ, and how the principles are applied needs to be adapted to meet local needs. This is where skill comes in. Skills are needed from those who assess risks and those who manage them, from senior executives to street-level protection officers.

It is a sad fact that offenders often move faster than response agencies. We know that many of those who commit crime adapt quickly; they share knowledge and experiences; doing so often gives them an edge. Just as people move themselves and their assets around the world with ease, offenders have tried to do so as well. Stopping them requires constant attention; as one famous terrorist agency once remarked, "We only have to succeed once."

Being on our guard, benefiting from research findings, and following good practice are crucial. Books like this one are designed to help. The coverage of this book is broad, covering domains such as communication, protection officer functions, crime prevention, safety, information security, workplace violence, risk management, investigations, private security law, and the use of force. The book provides proven knowledge to protection officers to enable them to take on the arduous tasks of asset protection and loss prevention.

This book strives to provide a foundation for improving the skill level and efficiency of protection officers. As a basic text for achieving the **Certified Protection Officer** certification, this book will be studied over and over by operatives across continents. It will also serve as a research resource for those looking to develop insight into an array of security topics. The editors are to be commended for ensuring that this edition builds positively on previous ones.

Professor Martin Gill
Director
Perpetuity Research & Consultancy
International (PRCI) Ltd
148 Upper New Walk
Leicester LE1 7QA, UK

Dr. Ona Ekhomu, CFE, CPP
Chairman
School of Management and Security
10 Turton St.
Lafiaji, Lagos, Nigeria

Contributors List

Sandi J. Davies began her career in contract security in 1980 with a primary focus on personnel administration. She became deeply involved in training and was instrumental in developing security officer training programs for a major national security guard company. Her interest in security training grew, and in 1988 she joined the newly formed International Foundation for Protection Officers (IFPO) as a program administrative assistant. In 1991, she was elected executive director of IFPO and has been a driving force in the Foundation's program development and administration. Sandi became a member of ASIS International in 1985 and served in executive positions at the chapter level.

In addition, Sandi was also a member of the Advisory Board for the Northwest Territories Security Officer Certification Committee. In 1994, Sandi was the chairperson for the Asset Protection Advisory Board for Mount Royal College in Calgary, Alberta, Canada. In 1999, Sandi agreed to serve on the Advisory Board of the International Foundation for Cultural Property Protection. Ms. Davies is also a member of the Technical Advisory Board for the Canadian General Standards Board on Security Officer Training Standards. Most recently, Sandi was chairperson for the Private Security Services Council of ASIS International.

Ms. Davies has had numerous articles published in security publications, such as *Security Management* and *SECURITY* magazine, relating to certification and training of security personnel. In the early 1990s, Ms. Davies, in a cooperative effort with the IFPO Founding Director Ronald R. Minion, coedited the *Protection Officer Training Manual* (Butterworth-Heinemann). That text is now in its eighth edition. In 1994, she contributed a chapter relating to crime prevention in Canada in the *Handbook of Loss Prevention and Crime Prevention* (Butterworth-Heinemann). In 1995, again in a cooperative effort, Ms. Davies and Mr. Minion had published a book entitled *The Security Supervisor Training Manual* with Butterworth-Heinemann. In 2008, the third edition of this text, coedited by Chris Hertig, was released entitled *Security Supervision and Management: Theory and Practices of Asset Protection*, again published by the leader in Security Trade Publications, Butterworth-Heinemann. Sandi was the editor of *Protection Officer News* published by IFPO for 13 years until it went into an electronic format.

Chris Hertig, CCP, CPOI, is a member of the Behavioral Sciences Department at York College of Pennsylvania where he teaches courses in security planning and supervision, crime prevention and physical security, legal standards of security and asset protection, ethical issues in criminal justice and criminal investigation. In addition to his regular teaching assignment, he has taught self-defense and martial arts for the education department. Prof. Hertig has also given noncredit courses in report writing, crowd management, officer survival, and public relations.

Prior to York College, Mr. Hertig spent three years as a nuclear security training administrator, developing and teaching a wide range of instructional topics for security personnel in accordance with U.S. Nuclear Regulatory Commission requirements. A Certified Protection Officer Instructor (CPOI) through the International Foundation for Protection Officers (IFPO), Prof. Hertig has given presentations to numerous professional and civic organizations. He has also consulted with instructional program providers.

Prof. Hertig has published several hundred articles, reviews, and chapters on various topics. He has been a featured columnist in several security industry publications and assisted in establishing IFPO's Article Archives, an online collection of research papers for students and practitioners. Chris served as coeditor of *Security Supervision and Management: Theory and Practice of Asset Protection* (Butterworth-Heinemann) with Sandi J. Davies, the Foundation's executive director.

Chris has been a longtime member of ASIS International, serving on the Academic Programs Council as well as the Academic–Practitioner Symposium Group. He is a charter member and past president of the Pennsylvania Association of Criminal Justice Educators and an active member of the International Association of Law Enforcement Educators and Trainers. He was also a member of the International Association of Campus Law Enforcement Administrators for many years.

Prof. Hertig began his career while in college as a student aide to the Campus Security Department. He was a member of the U.S. Army ROTC and served an internship with the Columbia County Juvenile Probation Department. After graduation, he worked for several security services firms as a security officer, investigator, and supervisor. He also spent a summer as a member of the Park Police in Mechanicsburg, PA.

Prof. Hertig holds a master's in arts (Criminology) from Indiana University of Pennsylvania, a bachelor's (Sociology) from Bloomsburg University of Pennsylvania, and an associate (Commercial Security) from Harrisburg Area Community College. He has also completed graduate courses in adult education from Penn State University, has been board certified in security management by ASIS International, and holds the designation of Certified Protection Professional (CPP).

Rich Abrams, CEM

Brian D. Baker, MA, CPP, CPO, CPOI

George A. Barnett, CPO

Colin Best, CSSM

Patrick C. Bishop, CPP, CFE, CPO

Inge Sebyan Black, CPP, CFE, CPO

Norman R. Bottom, PhD, CPP, CFE, CPO, CST

John Christman, CPP

Darrien Davenport, MS

Sandi J. Davies

David J. DeLong, CPP

Kevin T. Doss, M.Sc., CPP, PSP

Doug Durant, BA, CPP, CPO

Dr. Ona Ekhomu, CPP, CFE

Francis J. Elliott, CPP

Jim Ellis, MA, CPP, PSP, CSSM, CPO

Richard P. Fiems, MA, CPO, CSSM, CPOI

Terence M. Gibbs, MS, CPP, WSO-CSSD

Brion P. Gilbride, MSI, CSSM, CPO

Professor Martin Gill

Whitney D. Gunter, PhD., CPO

Michael A. Hannigan, CPO

Chris Hertig, CPP, CPOI

Arthur A. Holm, CPO

Robert D. Jaffin, MBS, MTS

Glen Kitteringham, M.Sc., CPP, F.Syl, CSSM, CPOI, CPO

Jenifer Lantz

Roger Maslen, CPP, CFE

Robert Metscher, CPP, CISSP, CFE, CPO, CSSM, BS, MBA

Denis A. O'Sullivan, CPP, CPO

Kevin Palacios, M.Sc., CPP, PSP, CPOI

Kevin E. Peterson, CPP, CPO, CPOI

K.C. Poulin, CPOI, CPS, CHS-III

Kevin Pound

Timothy A. Pritchard, CPP, CPOI

Mark E. Puetz, MBA

David L. Ray, BA, JD, CFE

Bethany J. Redmond

Chris Richardson, CPP

James E. Sellers, CPP, MSA

Dennis Shepp, MBA, CPP, CFE, PCI, CPOI

Sean Smith, CPO

Michael Stroberger, CPO, CLSO, CSSM,
CPOI, CLSD, CPP

Charles T. Thibodeau, M.Ed, CPP, CSSM,
CPO, CPOI

Franklin R. Timmons, CPP, CPOI

Christopher A. Vail, MS

Ernest G. Vendrell, PhD., CPP, CEM, CPO

Ted Wade

Scott A. Watson, MCJ, M.Ed., CFE

Rav-Zuridan Yisrael, MA, CPP, CPO,
CPOI, CHS-III

Introduction

A. PURPOSE

The purpose of *The Professional Protection Officer: Practical Security Strategies and Emerging Trends* is to provide "need-to-know" information for protection officers and students throughout the security industry. This resource serves as the course text for the Certified Protection Officer (CPO) program. Many security professionals also find the contents of this textbook helpful as a reference in their day-to-day security management responsibilities.

B. HISTORY OF THE TEXTBOOK

The first edition of the *Protection Officer Training Manual* (POTM) originated with the birth of the International Foundation for Protection Officers (IFPO) in 1988. Twelve dedicated security professionals from the United States and Canada had a vision: to create an organization that would provide meaningful career opportunities for line security officers throughout North America.

The newly formed IFPO Board of Directors realized that a certification program was needed, along with a professional training textbook, to make that vision a reality. Hence, the first edition of POTM was created to serve as the course text for the Certified Protection Officer (CPO) program. IFPO, the CPO program, and POTM all proved to be vital components in achieving the foundation's objectives.

Today, IFPO is the recognized catalyst in the development of professionalism throughout the private security industry. Thousands of security officers who have earned the CPO accreditation have gained knowledge and professional career enhancement; they have unselfishly provided encouragement and information to their colleagues and employers. Hence, a new dimension of opportunities has spread throughout the security industry.

The first edition was simple, short, and limited in scope, but included enough information to help the security officer better understand his or her roles, duties, and responsibilities. However, since that simple beginning, each subsequent edition has brought new and enlightening information to the security professional. The *Professional Protection Officer* is the leading text for protection officers and students. It is also widely used by those teaching in Protective Services, Criminal Justice, Homeland Security or Emergency Management courses of study.

Feedback has been the most significant factor. It has led to a standard of excellence for this new text. We have received countless letters of appreciation for the depth and quality of the seventh edition, but these same enthusiasts have been liberal with their recommendations for changes and improvements, and we have listened. Ongoing dialogue with security managers, supervisors, consultants, educators, and, of course, protection officers, has enabled us to develop and maintain a training text that will serve future learning.

C. THE EIGHTH EDITION DEDICATIONS

Norman Bottom

I first met Dr. Norman R. Bottom when I was a graduate student at Indiana University of Pennsylvania. He taught a course on executive protection on Saturday mornings that was held on the campus of Allegheny County Community College in Monroeville, Pennsylvania. Two other classes were held there on Saturdays so that people pursuing a Master's degree could take nine credits by going to class one day a week.

The class was a unique arrangement; in those days we didn't have online learning. Creative scheduling like Dr. Bottom had engineered was not the norm. The class offerings and schedule concept were a fantastic way of meeting the needs of the learner, the security industry, and the university.

It was way out in front.

The *Journal of Security Administration* was started by Norman Bottom. It was the first scholarly refereed academic journal in the security field. The journal was a major contribution to the fledgling discipline of asset protection. Norman edited it for many years, assisted by his wife, Mari, who took care of book, seminar, and video reviews. Dr. Bottom was also instrumental in founding the Academy of Security Educators and Trainers (ASET). This association included many leading trainers, practitioners, and academicians in the security industry. Some of the networking initiated through the academy is manifested in the pages of this text. Some of us met each other through ASET.

In 1982, I applied to become a Certified Protection Professional (CPP). As Dr. Bottom was a CPP, he endorsed my application.

In 1983, Norman and Professor John Kostanoski wrote a book entitled *Security and Loss Prevention*. This was an excellent text that presented the WAECUP model of loss control. This model stated that loss was attributable to

more than crime. Loss to an organization came from waste, accident, error, crime, and unethical/unprofessional practices. This was a new and important concept. Security was not just about the bad things that people do; it was much more than that. The WAECUP model is part of this text. It is part of what I teach. It is part of what we do as protectors.

In 1988, the International Foundation for Protection Officers was formed. Leading advocates of professional development helped with this organization under the direction of Ron Minion. Norman Bottom was on the Board of Directors, at one point serving as Chairman.

He was way out in front. He was always way out in front.

Now it's up to us.

Christopher A. Hertig, CPP, CPOI
Assistant Professor
York College of Pennsylvania
October 15, 2009

Fallen Officers

This edition of the textbook is dedicated to the brave officers who lost their lives on 9/11, as well as all of the other officers who have died in the line of duty. We remember and honor your sacrifice, and we salute your dedication. Our hearts and sympathies go out to your families, friends, and coworkers.

Ron Minion, CPP and IFPO Founder

Ron Minion (1938–2008) lost his battle with Lou Gehrig's Disease in 2008. He was the man behind this book, one of the founders of the IFPO, a dedicated champion of the security industry, and a tireless advocate for protection officers. His determination, and vision of professionalism through training for the industry, has resulted in a brighter future for scores of security professionals, and will continue to do so in the future.

Ron was the first examined Certified Protection Professional in Canada. He was a founding member of the Calgary Chapter of the ASIS International, where he was a chapter chair and regional vice president. As regional vice president, he earned the president's "award of merit" for establishing ASIS chapters throughout Canada. In 2006, *Security Magazine* named Ron one of the 25 Most Influential Executives.

Ron's legacy includes the thousands of line security officers he employed and mentored over the years. He knew the industry from the ground floor up, and never lost his vision of providing affordable training for security officers to help them turn their mere jobs into viable careers with brighter futures.

Ron, our friend, mentor, industry advocate, and trusted colleague, will be greatly missed.

Lee Minion, CPO

Lee Minion, son of Sandi Davies and Ron Minion, served his country in Iraq and is now embarking on a career in law enforcement. He is indeed a chip off the old block. At the Foundation, we are so very proud of him.

IFPO Team

The International Foundation for Protection Officers is supported by a team of security professionals throughout the world who, year after year, work diligently on behalf of the Foundation and what it stands for. Because of these men and women who are committed to excellence and remain steadfast in their obligation to high standards of service, IFPO continues to be successful. We thank you.

Louise Gringas

A victim of a tragic accident, our coworker, team member, and friend, Louise Gingras, brought sunshine to the IFPO Corporate Headquarters for seven years. She was taken from us far too soon, in June 2009. Louise started her tenure with the IFPO as a part-time employee in 2002, and quickly worked her way into a very valuable full-time Program Coordinator position.

Her friendly, caring nature assisted literally thousands of candidates through their desired certifications. She took pride and joy in attending to the IFPO students' and clients' needs. Her strengths were many, and her radiant smile and personality will be forever missed within our offices. She leaves behind her precious daughter, Haylee.

D. EIGHTH EDITION CONTENTS

The eighth edition has **12 units and 45 chapters**. The contributors to the eighth edition are among the best writers, academics, and practitioners in the security community. This talented group of professionals has generously provided readers of this superior textbook with unique opportunities to acquire current asset protection and life safety information. These writers are outstanding individuals who deserve recognition and appreciation for their service to the security community.

The contents of this textbook are sometimes quite basic. However, every security supervisor and manager should fully understand all of the information contained herein to provide better leadership and interpretation of officer responsibilities.

The material contained in each unit is arranged to provide the reader with a smooth flow of related security information.

At the conclusion of each chapter, there are 10 multiple choice and true/false questions. It is important to be able to answer each question correctly before proceeding to the next chapter.

E. GLOBAL CHALLENGES, NEW ROLES, AND RESPONSIBILITIES

In the late sixth century, when the Greek philosopher Heraclitus first commented that the universe is in constant flux, and the only constant is change; little could he have imagined the pace of that change in the 21st century.

Advances in medicine, science, and technology are happening at a dizzying pace, and news travels the globe in the blink of an eye. Information of all sorts is available with just a few keystrokes, and people can stay in constant touch via electronic media. Journeys that once took weeks, months, or even years now take mere hours. It is a small world these days, and economic problems and social unrest in one nation can be felt in many others.

Where once the term "security" might have referred to the lone night watchman whose greatest adversary was a burglar hoping to pick a lock, those days are long gone. The night watchman's role was viewed as merely a job that did not garner much respect in the community.

Today's private security professionals are finding their roles greatly expanded in numerous arenas worldwide, due, in part, to a much greater global threat and a reduction in public law enforcement protection. The current economic situation has caused an increase in some types of crimes. At the same time, those economic realties have also forced local municipalities to reduce public law enforcement efforts through layoffs or hiring freezes, even though the need for more protection is growing.

The threat of terrorism was spotlighted for the United States and the world on 9/11, and it is still an ever-present threat worldwide. It has and will continue to impact the industry, particularly in the areas of research and risk management methodologies.

In recent years, cyberterrorism, which threatens infrastructure and services by attacking computer networks via the Internet, has become a very serious threat. It can and has resulted in the loss of billions of dollars of proprietary information, and compromised data at a broad range of institutions, from government agencies to banks, credit card companies, and business firms. Company executives are acutely aware of the danger of data loss, and numerous laws govern what must be done if data is compromised. Cyberterrorism not only puts data at risk, it can put essential services and infrastructure at risk. Guarding against this type of threat requires continuing education about the ever-evolving risks, deterrents, prevention, and laws. Unlike the night watchman, who only worried about physical security with its fences, gates, and access points, today's protection officer must also guard against an enemy that moves at the speed of light. The protection officer must not only protect the physical premises and equipment, but must also guard against an enemy that moves silently to disrupt services, incapacitate infrastructure, and steal data.

The National Fire Protection Association's (NFPA) "Guide for Premises Security" and "Standard for the Installation of Electronic Premises Security Systems" have both caused changes that may not make news headlines, but will certainly impact the industry. The former will not affect the general public, but fire protection, security consultants, facility managers, and insurance companies will be forced to deal with it. ASIS has already begun setting standards that have impacted the industry. The latter more or less cements the impact of the former.

While the quest for mutual respect and seamless cooperation between public and private security has improved over the years, it must remain an ongoing goal for both the private and public sectors. Mutual respect and cooperation between public law enforcement and private security is essential to ensuring that security needs are met effectively.

Increasingly, security functions have been contracted out to private security firms to fill the gap between what government can do and what is needed. Private security firms are even stepping in to fill the roles that military personnel once filled on military installations and even war zones. A new type of protection officer is increasingly stepping forward to fill the need, ready to deal with new situations and challenges as they come along, thanks to ongoing education and training.

Currently, corporations that once relied on that night watchman to patrol a fence as sufficient protection are increasingly instituting their own in-house security departments. An integral part of this overall protection process is the professional security manager and supervisor, complemented with a security staff capable of attending to ongoing protection needs. Generally, corporations require their security managers and supervisors to be well educated, trained, and experienced. Private security firms are also demanding educated, trained professionals.

The night watchman might have been able to do his job with limited education, but in today's ever-changing, challenging security climate, professionals must be educated and well trained to fulfill their new, evolving, and demanding roles. This new breed of security professional is winning respect by proving it is skilled and very capable of carrying out the most sophisticated, demanding roles. They are dedicated professionals with the credentials needed to keep themselves, their employers, and their employers' assets from harm.

F. CERTIFIED PROTECTION OFFICER (CPO) PROGRAM

Professional Protection Officer: Practical Security Strategies and Emerging Trends is the course text for the Certified Protection Officer (CPO) program, an internationally recognized certification for protection officers.

The CPO designation is a professional accreditation that can be earned by completing a self-paced course based on this textbook.

In addition to having security experience or the equivalent, a candidate must complete the following stages of progression to earn the CPO designation:

- Submit application for enrollment.

- Successfully complete a midterm examination.
- Successfully complete a supervised final examination. (A proctor may be located within the candidate's organization or community.)

(Both examinations are based on the contents of this textbook.)

G. CERTIFIED PROTECTION OFFICER (CPO) FINAL CHALLENGE PROGRAM

This textbook, *The Professional Protection Officer: Practical Security Strategies and Emerging Trends*, is also the text for the CPO Final Challenge Program, which is the fast-track method of obtaining the CPO certification. The Final Challenge option eliminates the course of study and goes directly to the final exam, which is the same one that is part of the CPO program. Questions on the final exam come from the material in the textbook.

Contact the International Foundation for Protection Officers (IFPO) for more information regarding the Certified Protection Officer and/or other programs.

H. CONCLUSION

The term *protection officer* frequently appears in this textbook. What is a protection officer?

Protection officers have many titles: security guard, security officer, campus police, loss prevention officer, crime prevention officer, retail loss prevention agent, military police, and several others. They can work part time or full time. They can be assigned to protect a person, a group of people, an office building, a network, a store or factory, and many other assets in many locations. Some are armed; some are unarmed.

They can be employed as independent consultants, by a security services agency, by the military, by a state government, by the federal government, and by other organizations. The term "protection officer" is not easy to define. Titles vary, specific tasks vary, locations vary, employers vary, but the one thing that all protection officers have in common is that they are willing to take risks and put into place preventive measures to protect tangible assets, such as buildings, intangible assets, such as data, and of course, the public. They assume the risks so that others can go about their business and not have to worry about potential harm.

This textbook is written as a useful reference for security supervisors, managers, and those that teach; but the primary beneficiary is the student or working protection officer.

The editors of the Professional Protection Officer: Practical Security Strategies and Emerging Trends *are honored to work with so many academicians, researchers, and outstanding security professionals since the planning of the first edition. These talented and dedicated security professionals have worked tirelessly in supporting, promoting, and contributing to the International Foundation for Protection Officers and all of its worthwhile programs. "We could not have done it without you!"*

A special thanks goes to Alice Grime, Charles Thibodeau, and Jamie Ingram for their technical support and assistance in the production and development of this textbook.

Protection Officer Code of Ethics

The Protection Officer Shall

I	Respond to employer's professional needs
II	Exhibit exemplary conduct
III	Protect confidential information
IV	Maintain a safe & secure workplace
V	Dress to create professionalism
VI	Enforce all lawful rules & regulations
VII	Encourage liaison with public officers
VIII	Develop good rapport within the profession
IX	Strive to attain professional competence
X	Encourage high standards of officer ethics

PROTECTION OFFICER CODE OF ETHICS

Today business and the public expect a great deal from the uniformed security officer. In the past there has been far too little attention paid to the ethical aspects of the profession. There have to be solid guidelines that each officer knows and understands. More importantly, it is essential that each manager and supervisor performs his or her duties in a manner that will reflect honesty, integrity, and professionalism.

Every training program should address the need for professional conduct on and off duty. Line officers must exhibit a willingness to gain professional competency and adhere to a strict code of ethics that must include the following.

Loyalty

To the employer, the client, and the public. The officer must have a complete and thorough understanding of all of the regulations and procedures that are necessary to protect people and assets on or in relation to the facility assigned to protect.

Exemplary Conduct

The officer is under constant scrutiny by everyone in work and public places. Hence, it is essential that he or she exhibit exemplary conduct at all times. Maturity and professionalism are the key words to guide all officers.

Confidentiality

Each officer is charged with the responsibility of working in the interests of his or her employer. Providing protection means that the officer will encounter confidential information that must be carefully guarded and never compromised.

Safety and Security

The foremost responsibility of all officers is to ensure that the facility that must be protected is safe and secure for all persons with lawful access. The officer must fully understand all necessary procedures to eliminate or control security and safety risks.

Deportment

Each officer must dress in an immaculate manner. Crisp, sharp, clean, and polished are the indicators that point to a professional officer who will execute his or her protection obligations in a proficient manner and will be a credit to the profession.

Law Enforcement Liaison

It is the responsibility of each officer to make every effort to encourage and enhance positive relations with members of public law enforcement. Seek assistance when a genuine need exists and offer assistance whenever possible.

Strive to Learn

To become professionally competent, each officer must constantly strive to be knowledgeable about all aspects of his or her chosen career. How to protect people, assets, and information must always be a learning priority for every officer.

Develop Rapport

It is necessary to be constantly aware of the image that our profession projects. All officers can enhance the image of the industry, their employer, and themselves. Recognize and respect peers and security leaders throughout the industry.

Honesty

By virtue of the duties and responsibilities of all officers, honest behavior is absolutely essential at all times. Each officer occupies a position of trust that must not be violated. Dishonesty can never be tolerated by the security profession.

Prejudice

The job of protecting means that the officer must impose restrictions upon people that frequent the security workplace. All human beings must be treated equally, with dignity and respect, regardless of color, race, religion, or political beliefs.

Self-Discipline

With the position of trust comes the responsibility to diligently protect life and property. These duties can only be discharged effectively when the officer understands the gravity of his or her position. Self-discipline means trying harder and caring more.

Conclusion

The job of protecting life and property focuses much attention on the individual security officer. Hence, it is essential to be aware of the need for professional conduct at all times. By strictly adhering to each section in this code of ethics, it may be expected that we as individuals and the industry as a whole will enjoy a good reputation and gain even more acceptance from the public as well as private and government corporations. You as the individual officer must be a principal in this process.

FOUNDATIONS

1

Concepts and Theories of Asset Protection

Jim Ellis and Christopher A. Hertig

CHAPTER OBJECTIVES

- Define and explain valuation of an asset
- Provide an overall introduction to the concept of asset protection
- Discuss risks and risk management and insurance
- Explore strategies to mitigate risk
- Explore physical security measures related to asset protection
- Explain the system of Crime Prevention through Environmental Design (CPTED)

INTRODUCTION

Asset protection is the basis for everything that a protection officer does. It is the core function of the protection officer's job. Asset protection can have different meanings and functions depending on the approach to protecting the asset, its location, and even the type of asset. Asset protection has been practiced for millennia, whether it was protecting the Roman city with night sentries patrolling the streets, to placing valuables into a modern safe. The most visible and easily recognizable form of asset protection was the medieval castle. The castle was built to protect an asset, be it the king or ruler, a precious metal such as gold, or as a point from which to help protect the empire. Castles initially were quite basic, but as the risks escalated, they came to employ additional layers of protection such as a moat, drawbridge, or defensive positions.

ASSET DEFINITION

Asset protection begins with defining what the asset is. There may be one asset or many assets. An asset can be a person or people; a physical entity such as a building or plant; an object such as a painting or a gold bar; or a concept such as a formula or design. The ASIS International General Security Risk Assessment Guideline defines an asset as "Any real or personal property, tangible or intangible, that a company or individual owns that can be given or assigned a monetary value. Intangible property includes things such as goodwill, proprietary information, and related property. People are included as assets."

ASSET VALUATION

The asset must have some type of value. The value of the asset could be a real value, such as a gold bar being worth a set amount of money based on the weight of the bar and the current price of gold. The value of the asset could be based on what it would cost the company to replace it. This is sometimes difficult to calculate when discussing specialty items such as the formula or recipe for a soft drink, or the patented design for a product, the loss of which could mean the end of a company. The most intangible valuation of an asset would be in what is referred to as "reputational damage"—the loss of the image of a company or consumer confidence in a company. Reputational damage can occur through major theft of customer information, a senior executive being injured or killed, or the brand name of a company being tainted through inferior "knock-off" products. The loss of reputation is difficult to calculate because things such as unrealized sales are nearly impossible to determine. While it is not necessary to have the actual value of an asset on hand at any one time, the value of the asset must be known prior to the implementation of any protection program and reevaluated periodically thereafter.

RISKS

Criticality

Once the asset and its value are defined, it is necessary to determine what risks there are to the asset. According to the ASIS International General Security Risk Assessment Guideline, "risks or threats are those incidents likely to occur at a site, either due to a history of such events or circumstances in the local environment" (2003, p. 6). It is therefore important to have data on crime and incidents occurring in and around the site. A vulnerability assessment will include a thorough examination of the facility, personnel,

contents, materials, suppliers, and contractors, especially anything that by use or omission would damage, harm, or cause loss to the company or its personnel.

Frequency

The frequency of losses must then be determined through an examination of the types of crimes and incidents in and around the facility, with special emphasis on the dates on which they occurred. A ranking of the events should be made using a consistent scale (annually, monthly, daily, or hourly) for all such loss events.

Probability

Through an analysis of this information, trends may emerge which point to an escalation in activities that may precede a more serious crime against the company. This will help to establish the probability of such an event occurring in the future, assuming all other processes and operations at the facility remain the same. Once there is a change in the assets, the probability of loss will also change.

Impact

Finally, a ranking of the impact of any loss on the company must be made. Impact is an accounting of the tangible (real) and intangible (unrealized) costs associated with such events. All such tangible losses should be considered, from the mundane, such as the loss of power or water service, up to and including the loss of the facility including its contents and a substantial portion of the employees. Intangible losses such as the loss of current or future sales or customers should also be accounted for, to the extent that this is possible.

MITIGATION

Only after all of the factors of risk or loss have been compiled and examined can the protection officer assist with developing strategies to help mitigate the risk. All of the mitigation efforts must be designed so as not to "substantially interfere with the operation of profitability of the enterprise" (ASIS, 2003, p. 6). Mitigation efforts that do substantially impact operations are much less likely to see executive support regardless of the level of risk, as they also substantially impact the profitability of the company.

Cost/Benefit

A cost/benefit analysis must also be conducted to help assist in evaluating the mitigation measures against the costs incurred. According to the ASIS International General Security Risk Assessment Guideline, the cost benefit process "involves three steps:

- Identification of all direct and indirect consequences of the expenditure.
- Assignment of a monetary value to all costs and benefits resulting from the expenditure.
- Discounting expected future costs and revenues accruing from the expenditure to express those costs and revenues in current monetary values" (ASIS, p. 4).

If the cost/benefit evaluation determines that the cost of mitigating the risk is greater than the cost of the asset, then other measures must be employed.

ASSET PROTECTION

Layered Protection

Asset protection through risk mitigation typically involves a concept of layered protection, also known as defense in depth. In this concept, the asset is considered to be in the center, surrounded by concentric layers of protection. Each layer contributes individually, and as part of the whole, to the overall protection of the asset. The principles behind layered protection consist of deterrence, detection, delay, and defense/response. Each piece of the layered protection concept can work on its own. However, the most complete protection is afforded through combining all of the layers.

Deterrence is the practice of discouraging an individual or group from even attempting to attack the asset. This can be accomplished through a number of means such as signage, fencing, lighting, cameras, or people. Signage at the perimeter of the enterprise property would warn trespassers of the property line and the penalty for proceeding further. Further enhancements to the signage could include the addition of fencing, lights, and cameras. In a personal protection role, the deterrence would appear to be provided by the ring of protection officers, or specialists around a high-profile individual. In some rare circumstances, the illusion of additional layers of protection can be a better and more cost-effective deterrent.

Detection is the identification of a threat, preferably at the earliest possible opportunity. Alarm sensors, cameras, and even protection officers, are all means of detecting and identifying threats to the enterprise. A threat identified earlier in the asset protection process gives the remaining layers of protection more time to contribute to the overall protection of the asset.

Delaying the attacker also gives the other layers of defense a chance to work together. Sufficient layers of delay must be incorporated so that the detection and defense/response pieces of the asset protection continuum can perform their roles. Delay can be accomplished through an expansive perimeter that takes a while for the attacker to cross, fences that take time to climb, strong doors that must be breached, and interior levels of protection such as additional doors into rooms or a safe that takes even more time to enter.

A sufficiently delayed attacker allows for a defense to be mounted from within the site to repel the attacker, or for a sufficient response to be put together and proceed to the site. However, the layers of protection must delay the attacker long enough so as to be able to stop him on the way to the asset, or on his way out with the asset, but before he leaves the property with the asset.

PHYSICAL SECURITY

Physical security planning was originally based upon response to a military threat. A traditional reference for physical security is *FM 19-30 Physical Security*, published by the U.S. Army, while a modern reference is the *Facilities Physical Security Measures Guideline* published by ASIS International.

The process used to plan physical security measures is as follows:

1. Identify assets. These generally include *personnel*, *property*, *information*, and *image*.
2. Loss events are exposed. Risks are identified. This involves research rather than "seat of the pants" reasoning!
3. Probability of the loss events occurring is calculated.
4. Impact of occurrence is assessed for each loss event. This means, the effect the loss event will have in terms of *direct*, *indirect*, and *extra-expense* costs.
5. Countermeasures are selected. There can be a vast array of interventions; generally physical security utilizes target hardening techniques, such as patrols, access control, lighting, intrusion detection, surveillance, weapons detection, and so on.
6. Countermeasures are implemented.
7. Countermeasures are evaluated as to their effectiveness. Traditionally, this step has been avoided by practitioners in physical security and crime prevention.

Note: See www.securitysolutions.com and www.securitymagazine.com for products and applications.

Patrols are a key part of a physical security system. They serve as catalysts for the system, bringing all parts together. Patrols have been traditionally used by military forces to scout out the location and disposition of an opponent. They are used today by police and security forces.

While still endeavoring to locate hostile individuals (felons), modern police patrols are used to assess community environments. In a contemporary asset protection scheme, patrols are not only concerned with criminal acts but also with unauthorized activities, safety and fire protection issues, and the performance of auxiliary services. These can include delivering the company mail, checking gauges, conducting lighting surveys, assessing behavior, enforcing lease agreements, and assisting customers. Note that *community policing* or *problem-oriented policing* strategies that public police have adopted are very similar to what security practitioners have been doing for decades.

CRIME PREVENTION THROUGH ENVIRONMENTAL DESIGN

Crime Prevention Through Environmental Design (CPTED) is a system whereby territoriality reinforcement is established via barriers, access control, and surveillance. Its genesis may have been in the construction of castles and forts. The contemporary beginnings of it were through the writings of Oscar Newman (*Defensible Space*) and C. Ray Jeffrey (*Crime Prevention through Environmental Design*). CPTED theory consists of these various components:

Territoriality: Boundaries and property lines are marked. This can be the placement of barriers, shrubbery, and the use of different colors of walkways to mark areas. *Psychological* deterrents to trespass are erected to establish territoriality.
Surveillance: Observing areas makes detection and deterrence of criminal behavior more likely. There are several types of deterrence:
Natural—keeping areas open to observation, such as by clearing bushes near access points, having windows facing

out into a common courtyard, or placing a picnic area near a basketball court. All of these make for easier observation of the area to be protected. They facilitate detection of criminal or unauthorized activity.
Electronic—technological aids are used, such as closed circuit television (CCTV) and volumetric intrusion detection systems, such as passive infrared (PIR) sensors.
Organized—patrols by security personnel, police, or citizen crime watches.

Access control: Maintaining boundaries by restricting access to an area. Access is controlled via the use of locks, biometric systems, access cards, and other methods. Access control is a *physical* deterrent to trespass.

Positive activity support: In a significant departure from physical security, CPTED uses activities that divert people in the environment from involvement in crime. This may take the form of recreation, entertainment, or volunteer efforts that help society (volunteer fire companies for youth).

Maintenance: The repair of "broken windows." An environment that is not kept up properly may degenerate further. People see broken windows and believe it is acceptable to break other windows. A "snowballing" or "rolling ball" effect occurs. Prompt repair and cleaning of damage or graffiti are essential parts of CPTED.

SAFETY

Safety ushers in the more contemporary emphasis on asset protection and incorporates the WAECUP Theory of Loss Control developed by Bottom and Kostanoski in *Security and Loss Control* (first published by Macmillan in 1983).

W — Waste of time, resources, man-hours, space;
A — Accident that causes injury, downtime, increased workers' compensation costs, and so on;

E — Error in planning or execution, which results in lost funds;
C — Crime that causes loss and/or injury;
UP — Unethical/unprofessional practices, such as misrepresentation, discrimination, conflict of interest, and so on.

Accidents cost extensive amounts of *direct loss* (cost of replacement and repair) as well as indirect *loss* (downtime, investigative costs, lowered morale, legal fees, etc.) and *extra-expense loss* (advertising, rental of new rooms or equipment). Note that there are also extensive administrative law requirements under OSHA (Occupational Safety and Health Administration) and state agencies (CALOSHA and Pennsylvania Department of Labor and Industry) with which organizations must comply. Safety is a major concern to organizations for all of these reasons. Many persons in charge of security are also in charge of safety. A Director of Safety and Security has become a common title in health care, on college campuses, and in hotel environments.

RISK MANAGEMENT AND INSURANCE

"Risk management" is a term closely associated with the insurance industry. It is similar conceptually to the physical security planning process in its implementation, but it deals with risks other than "security" threats caused by humans. It is not limited to "target hardening" (*risk reduction*) approaches, such as the use of locks, barriers, intrusion alarms, and so on. Strategies for managing risk include the following:

Risk avoidance—such as completely avoiding the risk of an earthquake by avoiding geographic areas where there are active fault lines, staying out of countries that are known to kidnap people for ransom, or not making dangerous products, such as explosives.
Risk transfer—means transferring the financial impact of loss to another

organization or entity. Insurance coverage is the usual means of risk transfer. The insurance company takes on the cost of repairing or replacing the asset at risk instead of the enterprise. Of course, this comes at some cost and some delay in repairing or replacing an asset as the insurance company must investigate and process the claim. Outsourcing hazardous operations to other organizations is another example of risk transfer.

Risk assumption, risk retention, or risk acceptance—refers to accepting the risk, as it has a very low probability of occurring; the risk is extremely difficult to protect against; or the cost of changing the risk to the assets is so great or so low that any effort to change it would either be too expensive or the losses so low as to be inconsequential. For instance, it is extremely unlikely that an asteroid will strike; it is also impractical to defend against it. It would likewise be impractical to purchase insurance for a machine that has exceeded its useful shelf life and has no intrinsic value.

Risk spreading—implies using redundant systems of communication, power, or information storage. The separation of assets across some distance so that no one vulnerability can affect the entire enterprise is another example.

Risk reduction or risk mitigation—means reducing the probability of a loss-causing event through the adoption of preventive measures. That is, taking methodical, appropriate steps to lessen the risk to the organization or the frequency, probability, and impact of such risks and losses. Physical security and crime deterrence would be considered risk reduction. So, too, would the use of safety equipment.

As you can see, risks can be reduced in a number of ways, but they are never truly eliminated.

Insurance can be thought of as the "last line of defense" in a physical security system. It provides the policyholder with financial compensation from the insurance company after a loss has occurred. According to Purpura (1991), loss prevention originated within the insurance industry. Note that while the term "loss prevention" is utilized primarily within the retail sector, it is gradually being replaced with the more representative term "asset protection."

PRACTICAL EXERCISE

Pick some assets, such as vital information, that an organization needs to operate: people, works, art, and so on. Place these assets in the boxes to the left. Next, place the primary threats that may face those assets such as fire, terrorism, theft, and so on. In the column on the right, list a risk management approach, such as transfer, avoidance, or acceptance, which would be most appropriate for dealing with the threat.

Asset	Threat	Risk strategy

Insurance policies provided by an insurance company are driven by the probability of loss events occurring based on actuarial tables. The premiums and deductibles are adjusted according to the loss event probability; so, too, is the availability of insurance if insurance carriers deem a risk to be too high and refuse to write a policy. In these cases, organizations must *self-insure* or join an *insurance pool* of other organizations that pool their funds in a liquid account that is set aside in the event of a loss. There are also government insurance programs for crime and floods on the federal level, and workers' compensation on the state level.

Various types of insurance coverage have evolved, such as the following:

Business Interruption—for losses incurred after a disaster, accident, or fire while a business is not operating. Business interruption insurance helps to control indirect losses stemming from lost productivity.

Kidnap and Ransom (K & R)—for firms that have had executives abducted by criminals or terrorists. This coverage became popular in the early 1980s in response to left-wing terrorist kidnappings in Latin America. The film *Proof of Life* with Russell Crowe portrays K & R coverage.

Worker's Compensation—required by state laws to compensate workers injured on the job from the results of work-related accidents and occupational diseases (Purpura, 1991, p. 265). Rates paid for premiums by employers are based on job hazard, and in part on an employer's record of accidents.

Liability insurance—to cover legal costs and *compensatory* damage awards (punitive damages are not generally covered). Attorney's fees and associated costs can become quite high during civil litigation regardless of whether the case is settled or goes before a court.

Fire insurance—one of the first types of insurance developed; some policies mandate that the insured conduct periodic patrols of various areas on the property—the use of watch tour systems had developed as a result of this.

Burglary insurance—for losses associated with unlawful intrusion. Burglary insurance policies generally require evidence of forced entry.

Robbery insurance—coverage for forcible thefts committed in the presence of another.

Theft insurance—policies cover losses from theft; may include burglary and robbery losses.

Bonds—*fidelity* bonds require investigation of the covered employee by the bonding company (the insurer); these bonds indemnify the holder against dishonest acts committed by the employee. The holder of the bonds is exempt from financial responsibility for the dishonest acts of the employee.

Employment Practices Liability (EPL)—insures against legal costs due to unlawful employment practices such as sexual harassment, discrimination, and so on. Contemporary liability exposure for ongoing illegal employment practices is substantial, with awards and settlements running into the multimillions.

EMERGING TRENDS

An emerging new paradigm of asset protection is the consideration that must be made for an attacker who will enter a protected area with the goal of destroying an asset in place. The homicide/suicide bomber is an especially troubling trend and is difficult to provide sufficient levels of protection against. The amount of time to detect, delay, and defend is essentially reduced by half as the attacker does not have to add in time to flee. Depending on the asset to be protected and the preexisting environment in which the protection officer must operate, strengthening the ability to detect and delay the adversary must be given especially careful consideration. This may include the addition of intelligence assets that can overtly or covertly uncover the adversary's plans. Cooperative information sharing with other entities such as law enforcement or in some areas, the military, may be the best option for strengthening the detection aspect of asset protection.

Like the homicide/suicide bomber, improvised explosive devices (IEDs) are also an especially troubling trend. Not limited to areas of conflict, domestic extremist organizations have used these devices to intimidate, maim, and destroy. Special attention and alternative plans must be carefully developed for organizations that conduct work that may attract the attention of such groups, including specialized protection plans for executives. In areas of conflict where the threat of IEDs is real, options for reducing the risk include, but are not limited to, traveling covertly, using decoy vehicles, or using telephones, videos, and Internet conferencing.

Specialization in the industry is the continuation of a long-standing trend that is gaining greater acceptance outside of the business. Both large and small security businesses are finding specialties in which to focus and thrive. Some security officer companies are established as, or are establishing, separate divisions devoted to retail security in malls and protection of chemical plants or nuclear power stations. Electronic security companies may find specialization in surveillance systems for casinos or integrating various security, fire alarm, and building control systems into a cohesive platform using the client's computer network.

Professionalism is also the continuation of a long-standing trend that is finding favor by the companies and clients that security professionals work for and with. College degrees at the Bachelor's and Master's levels are an almost universal requirement for security managers at all levels, and for some security officers in specialized sectors. Certification by industry organizations such as the International Foundation for Protection Officers and ASIS International is also becoming a requisite for some companies.

SUMMARY

Being involved in the practice of asset protection is the first step toward advancement in your field and acceptance in your enterprise. The protection officer must be ready to volunteer and assist in learning this craft.

References

General Security Risk Assessment Guideline. (2003). Alexandria, VA: ASIS International.

Biery, K. D., Jr., & Schaub, J. L. (1994). *The ultimate security survey.* Boston, MA: Butterworth-Heinemann.

Broder, J. F. (1984). *Risk analysis and the security survey.* Boston, MA: Butterworth-Heinemann.

Calder, J. D. (1985). Industrial guards in the nineteenth and twentieth centuries: The mean years. *Journal of Security Administration, 8*(2).

Coleman, J. W. (1969). *The Molly Maguire riots: Industrial conflict in the Pennsylvania coal region.* New York, NY: Arno & The New York Times.

Constable, G. (Ed.). (1990). *The old west.* New York, NY: Time-Life Books.

Cote, A., & Bugbee, P. (1988). *Principles of fire protection.* Quincy, MA: National Fire Protection Association.

Fennelly, L. J. (1989). *Handbook of loss prevention and crime prevention* (2nd ed.). Boston, MA: Butterworths.

Fennelly, L. J. (1996). *Handbook of loss prevention and crime prevention* (3rd ed.). Boston, MA: Butterworth-Heinemann.

Fiems, R., & Hertig, C. (2001). *Protection officer guidebook.* Naples, FL: International Foundation for Protection Officers.

Fossum, J. (1982). *Labor relations: Development, structure, process*. Dallas, TX: Business Publications, Inc.

Garcia, M. L. (2001). *The design and evaluation of physical protection systems*. Boston, MA: Butterworth-Heinemann.

Girard, C. M. (1989). Planning, management and evaluation, Chapter 31. In L. J. Fennelly (Ed.), *Handbook of loss prevention and crime prevention* (2nd ed.). Boston, MA: Butterworths.

Gilbride, B. P. (1999). Sexual harassment. In S. J. Davies & R. R. Minion (Eds.), *Security supervision: Theory and practice of asset protection*. Woburn, MA: Butterworth-Heinemann.

Green, G., revised by Fischer, R. J. (1987). *Introduction to security* (4th ed.). Boston, MA: Butterworths.

Hertig, C. A. (2002). *Investigative concepts*. Unpublished paper. York College of Pennsylvania.

Hertig, C. A., Fennelly, L. J., & Tyska, L. A. (1998). *Civil liability for security personnel*. Naples, FL: International Foundation for Protection Officers.

Johnson, T. (2002). *Retail loss prevention management models* Unpublished paper. York College of Pennsylvania.

Kuykendall, J. (1986). The municipal police detective: An historical analysis. *Criminology, 24*(1).

Mackay, J. (1996). *Allan Pinkerton: The first private eye*. New York, NY: John Wiley & Sons.

Matthews, L. J. (1990). *Pioneers and trailblazers: Adventures of the old west*. New York, NY: Derrydale.

Nalla, M., & Newman, G. (1990). *A primer in private security*. Albany, NY: Harrow & Heston.

National Advisory Committee on Criminal Justice Standards and Goals. (1976). *Report of the task force on private security*. Washington, DC.

Peak, K. J. (1997). *Policing in America: Methods, issues, challenges*. Upper Saddle River, NJ: Prentice-Hall.

Purpura, P. P. (1991). *Security and loss prevention: An introduction*. Stoneham, MA: Butterworth-Heinemann.

Sennewald, C. A. (1985). *Effective security management* (2nd ed.). Boston, MA: Butterworths.

SECURITY QUIZ

1. The ASIS International General Security Risk Assessment Guideline defines an asset as "Any real or personal property, tangible or intangible, that a company or individual owns, that can be given or assigned a monetary value.
   a. True
   b. False

2. CPTED stands for Crime Prevention through Environmental Dedication.
   a. True
   b. False

3. Physical security planning was originally based upon response to a military threat.
   a. True
   b. False

4. Risk Management is a term closely associated with the insurance industry.
   a. True
   b. False

5. A vulnerability assessment will include a thorough examination of the following:
   a. Facility and personnel
   b. Contents and material
   c. Suppliers and contractors
   d. All the above

6. Deterrence is the practice of discouraging an individual or group from even attempting to attack the asset.
   a. True
   b. False

7. All risks can be reduced completely.
   a. True
   b. False

8. There is a theory of loss control developed by Bottom and Kostanoski in security and loss control. It is known as:
   a. WASTE
   b. WASTMGMT
   c. WAECUP
   d. WHATSUP

9. The most intangible valuation of an asset would be in what is referred to as:
   a. Liquid asset
   b. Respectful damage
   c. Punitive damage
   d. Reputational damage

10. Intangible property include things such as goodwill, proprietary information, and related property.
    a. True
    b. False

2

The Evolution of Asset Protection and Security

Christopher A. Hertig and John Christman

CHAPTER OBJECTIVES

- Discuss the importance of looking at the cycle of history
- List and define key terms
- Explore the growth of the security industry through wartime and policing units
- Compare and contrast private security and public police
- Explain how the fire protection industry developed
- Look at how commerce and economic and marketing trends are related to asset protection
- Explore how demographics, historical class struggles, and labor relations have all contributed to the protection profession
- Provide avenues toward the PATH to Professionalism
- Offer suggestions for pursuing contemporary careers in asset protection

INTRODUCTION

History is illustrative for many reasons; there are trends and themes that run throughout the march of time and that repeat themselves—to a degree. P. T. Barnum said, "All history is bunk," and he was right—to a degree. History is a *perspective*. In many cases, that perspective gets distorted, or lost, over time.

Studying history is important as it gives us perspective on where things were, where they are now, and where they may be in the future. Historical analysis can provide insight into how certain issues were dealt with. This may give guidance in contemporary or future problem solving.

Finally, history provides a laboratory for the testing of theory. Solutions that were developed in response to certain problems had positive or negative effects in addressing those problems. An example is the Prohibition Era in the United States, beginning in 1919. Alcoholic beverage manufacture or distribution was against the law. As a result, huge criminal enterprises sprang up in response to consumer demand. A black market economy was formed with gangsters seeking to profit. Some people feel that the current legal prohibition against drugs is analogous to Prohibition. This is an arguable point: drugs are not as socially accepted as the drinking of alcohol was in 1920s American society. Nonetheless, the emergence of black markets due to extensive consumer demand for illegal goods or services is something that all students of asset protection should appreciate.

THE CYCLE OF HISTORY

The security industry has a rich and varied background. "Security" implies protection: safety from attack, espionage, or sabotage. It means being able to live, work, or play free from harm, in a stable environment. Organizations must take measures to minimize disruption. These measures are dependent on a variety of factors, such as threat probability, criticality, culture of the organization, financial resources available, and so on. The measures taken have changed over time.

The historical development of "asset protection" (the broader, more contemporary term encompassing safety and fire protection) and "security" (the older term; more oriented to crime/espionage/terrorism issues) reveals several trends. These trends appear to be cyclical in nature.

1. Private initiatives generally precede public. In many cases, private protective measures are started to fill a void in services offered by governments. Private corporations are more nimble and flexible than governments. This enables them to start new programs, protection or control forces, etc.
2. Control forces may be involved in class struggles. Control forces—military, police, security—work to keep certain groups of citizens in line.
3. There is a strong relationship between commerce and protective needs. The amount and type of commerce (ships, trains, Internet, and so on) determines the threats or risks posed to the commerce system. Each risk

demands different protective strategies and tactics. These change with technological developments. Politics and economics are also factors. In 2008 and 2009, piracy on the high seas became a major issue due to large numbers of unemployed mariners.
4. Demographics—population size, density, age distribution—plays a key role in crime control and safety. Large numbers of recent immigrants who do not understand the language or customs of their newly adopted country create safety and security challenges. College students living in dormitories create another set of challenges. High-rise office buildings with business tenants have different protection needs from two-story apartment complexes for low-income families. Security measures must be relevant to the environment in which they are implemented and every environment is different.
5. Military forces and concepts are intimately involved in protection. Foreign invaders, riots that have to be contained by soldiers, and international terrorists are all addressed by military forces. Contemporary protective forces often operate on a military organizational structure. Police, security, and firefighting organizations have a paramilitary chain-of-command with sergeants, lieutenants, and captains. The military has clearly exerted an influence over police, security, and fire departments.
6. Security efforts generally are a step behind the latest methods of criminal attack. The saying *"As one hole in the net is mended, the fish swim toward another"* seems particularly relevant.
7. Protective efforts are usually initiated after serious problems have occurred. The September 11, 2001, attacks on the Pentagon and World Trade Center initiated substantial reforms in the federal government, such as the Transportation Security Administration. Wars and major natural disasters also create new protective organizations, laws, and so on.

8. Protective efforts often are spawned by the need for mutual protection. Homeland Security is a current example: governmental units at all levels coming together in partnership with private organizations to protect against terrorism. Another example is fire societies that were established in Boston in 1718, where society members helped each other to salvage goods after a fire (Cote & Bugbee, 1988).

KEY TERMS

"Assets" are tangibles or intangibles that have value. If assets are stolen, lost, destroyed, or damaged, the entity (organization or individual) owning them suffers a loss. There are four basic classifications of assets:

1. **People**—employees, visitors, clients, patients, students, and so on.
2. **Property**—real estate, buildings, raw materials, equipment, merchandise, and so on.
3. **Information**—vital information that is necessary for an organization's survival, such as employee and vendor lists, organizational plans, and other items without which the organization could not operate; confidential information such as patient records, personnel or student records; proprietary information such as trade secrets, customer lists, and marketing plans; classified information that is essential to national defense.
4. **Image**—the image cultivated through years of public relations and advertising that an organization or individual (celebrity) has established. Customer goodwill is an asset. So, too, is a positive image that will not attract the ire of extremist groups or individuals.

Security is concerned with those threats that are posed by humans. Espionage, sabotage, theft, and assault are examples.

Asset protection takes a broader view. It is also concerned with waste, errors and accidents, natural disasters, labor shortages, equipment breakdowns, fires, and so on. Asset protection covers any loss an organization suffers that is not related to marketing.

Crime Prevention through Environmental Design, (CPTED), is a theory of crime deterrence based on environmental design. Facilities are constructed—or arranged—in such a way that criminals feel uncomfortable and refrain from committing crimes.

Physical security is a plan or design developed for the purpose of attempting to eliminate or minimize the threats posed by potential loss event occurrences. It incorporates locks, barriers, access control systems, lighting, alarms, and security officers. Physical security is a vast field of study. It can be said that it is the "heart" of security. It encompasses CPTED as well as procedural controls.

Personnel security is designed to screen out undesirable employees. It is done to protect both the employer and other employees. The screening, or *vetting*, of employees to prevent probes by foreign intelligence agents originated within the military-industrial complex of the 1950s to 1980s. The old term "industrial security" (as in "American Society for Industrial Security") referred to Department of Defense (DOD) contractor firms. These companies made munitions, tanks, airplanes, and so on for military usage. While espionage—in particular economic espionage—is a major issue, contemporary personnel security also deals with workplace violence, internal theft, and terrorism. The current emphasis on terrorism could be seen as a historical cycle repeating itself—the Cold War measures concerning spies bearing some similarity to the issues of terrorism. Each era was focused on persons infiltrating facilities and information sources and causing problems.

Asset protection encompasses those threats posed by nature, accident, market, and economic factors as well as those posed strictly by humans.

Asset protection incorporates fire protection, HAZMAT, and safety within the discipline. It seeks to identify and manage all risks posed to an organization and incorporates many concepts of *risk management*. Asset protection is the approach used in addressing problems by many organizations. It is perhaps similar to the "all hazards approach" used in emergency management. In some cases, the term "loss prevention" is used. This has been particularly common in the retail security sector.

As threats change over time and involve different environments, asset protection is a truly dynamic undertaking. The history of security/ asset protection is formulated in a variety of areas. Security is influenced by commerce, war, natural disaster, economic and cultural changes.

THE WARTIME GROWTH OF SECURITY

Military defense is often discussed in the literature on the history of security. Ortmeier (1999) reveals that in prehistoric times, cave dwellers stacked rocks around perimeters in front of their caves to both mark this space and warn off intruders. The Praetorian Guard in ancient Rome were military personnel. Military threats employ military approaches. Such approaches often utilize military personnel and incorporate *military culture*.

"Defense-in-depth" is a military concept wherein assets are protected by successive lines of defense. This includes clear zones, outer perimeters, inner perimeters, and soldiers or protection officers. This is a key element of physical security plans. Contemporary facility models of defense-in-depth incorporate layers of protection. Safes and vaults, alarm systems, and insurance coverage all comprise the layers of the protection plan.

Military threats and organizations have been employed throughout history. The Byzantine empire, which replaced the Roman empire,

hired soldiers from the northern Viking regions. The Varangian Guards operated for hundreds of years, serving as bodyguards, suppressing riots and occasionally functioning as combat troops. In the American Revolution, Britain employed German mercenaries from the province of Hessia (Hessians). It was not until the rise of Napoleon that the use of standard full-time armies on active duty was typical. Privately hired soldiers and security personnel were the norm for most of history (Maggio, 2009). Today there are private military companies who provide security, intelligence, and logistical services to nations. Iraq and Afghanistan have seen expanding markets for these firms. Modern armies are too small to do all that is asked of them. As a result, private companies have stepped in to handle security and other functions that don't absolutely require soldiers.

A review of some events in history that created security problems is outlined here.

July 1916—an explosion at Black Tom Island, a munitions storage facility in New Jersey, was set off by a German saboteur. This increased War Department security measures. German agents also set fires, filled fire extinguishers with gasoline, sold heroin to soldiers to make them addicted, and even contaminated the milk supply at the Ft. Leavenworth Cadet School with nitrogenous germs. German agents also fomented strikes in key war industries to slow down production of war materials (Velke, 2004). The potential for problems caused by saboteurs, foreign intelligence agents (spies), and terrorists who are state-sponsored creates a need for increased security measures during all military conflicts. Note that in most discussions of terrorism, foreign agents are not included, although they can be a major problem.

World War II—U.S. Department of War established internal security division and swore in 200,000 security officers as military police auxiliary. State National Guard units were also activated. In some cases, states had Home Guard organizations that enabled the National Guard to engage in combat or combat support activities while the Home Guard maintained a domestic security posture. **Korean War**—The "Cold War" era began with heightened tensions between the United States and Russia. *The Industrial Security Manual* was published in 1952. This was considered the "Bible" of Department of Defense (DOD) contractor security procedures. It established information protection, personnel security, and physical security measures for DOD contractors. Since the United States was in a wartime economy until about 1975, there was heavy activity in this sector. Many security personnel worked in "industrial security."

HISTORY OF POLICING

Police in Ancient Rome consisted of the Praetorian Guards, which was a military unit. There were also cohorts who kept peace. The vigiles were civilian freemen who controlled fires and assisted in controlling crime and disorder. It is interesting to note that urban mob violence was one reason why municipal police were formed in both England and the United States.

With the Norman Conquest of England in 1066, there were several significant governmental developments:

1. The introduction of feudalism, a contractual relationship between lords of the manor, and their tenants or vassals. Feudalism was a system in which the landholder provided for the security of the tenant peasants in exchange for a portion of the harvest.
2. The centralization of government.
3. The reorganization of the church.

One protection development that was established was a community-based system of policing called the *frankpledge*. The frankpledge system required every male over the age of 12 to form into a group of 10 with his neighbors called a "tithing." The tithing was sworn to help protect fellow citizens and apprehend and deliver persons who committed crimes. Ten tithings were grouped into hundreds who were directed by a constable. The constable was appointed by a nobleman and was, in effect, the first police officer (Peak, 1997).

Note that early Roman and English—and later American—policing functions were dependent on citizen involvement. This is still true today. Homeland Security requires citizens to be vigilant for indications of terrorism. Major disasters require government, corporate, and nonprofit volunteer organizations (Red Cross) to work together. The lesson is that the need for mutual assistance spawns protective efforts.

In the early nineteenth century, London continued to have a large population with crime and disorder problems. As few organizational models were available at this time, the military model was adopted for the London Metropolitan Police (Ortmeier, 1999). What Robert Peel established in 1829 in London served as an organizational model for police and security departments. In America, cities began to develop uniformed police forces in the mid-1800s. These forces were similar to what we have today. Peel set forth a series of principles upon which a police force could be established and administered. While his specific frame of reference was public law enforcement, the principles are also adaptable to uniformed private protection forces:

1. The police must be stable, efficient, and organized along military lines.
2. The police must be under government control.
3. The absence of crime will best prove the efficiency of police.
4. The distribution of crime news is absolutely essential.
5. The deployment of police strength both by time and by area is essential.

6. No quality is more indispensable to a police officer than a perfect command of temper; a quiet, determined manner has more effect than violent action.
7. Good appearance commands respect.
8. The securing and training of proper persons are at the root of efficiency.
9. Public security demands that every police officer be given a number.
10. Police headquarters should be centrally located.
11. Police officers should be hired on a probationary basis.
12. Police records are necessary to the correct distribution of police strength.

In the mid-nineteenth century, major American cities began to develop police departments. These forces evolved out of earlier night watch systems that utilized volunteers or civilians. Some of these forces only operated at night, and they were no longer effective at controlling crime in burgeoning urban environments. Organized, paid, full-time police operating under the principles established by Robert Peel began to take shape.

State police forces also developed. The Pennsylvania State Police is generally regarded as the first modern state police department. While Texas and Massachusetts had state police forces, these were vastly different from the organizations we think of today as "state police." The Pennsylvania State Police have full law enforcement authority. They also are responsible for traffic control on state highways such as the Pennsylvania Turnpike. In some states, there are separate highway patrol forces that specialize in traffic law enforcement (California Highway Patrol, Ohio Highway Patrol).

"PRIVATE SECURITY" OR "PUBLIC POLICE"?

Policing is both public *and* private. Public policing as we know it is relatively recent. Private police forces are older in most cases. Private policing preceded public policing with merchant, parish, and dock police forces in England. Public and private were difficult to distinguish from each other. Railroad Police were, and still are, a privately employed police force with full law enforcement authority. Many states in America enacted legislation to establish railroad police forces. In many rural areas these were the only law enforcement agencies in existence. By 1914 there were 12,000 railroad police in America. During World War I they were deputized by the federal government (Purpura, 2002). The Coal and Iron Police in Pennsylvania were also privately employed and had law enforcement powers.

Current policing in the United States was greatly influenced by the Omnibus Crime Control and Safe Streets Act of 1968. This created the Law Enforcement Assistance Administration (LEAA), which funded training and education for police. Police by the thousands began to acquire college educations. Criminal justice programs were started at colleges across the country. While there were only five or so institutions offering degrees in criminal justice prior to 1968, today there are thousands. The LEAA also provided grant monies for equipment and crime analysis by police departments. The LEAA also spent massive sums on developing criminal justice.

Fees were used to pay for early police services. The Parliamentary Reward System in England paid a fee of 40 English pounds to private persons who captured felons. Both Jonathan Wild and the Bow Street Runners were early private detectives who worked under the Parliamentary Reward System. In the nineteenth century, there were private detectives who received rewards for recovering stolen property. Over time these private detectives were replaced by public police, due to criticism of their methods as well as the entry of insurance companies. Once there were insurance policies to compensate policyholders for their losses, the incentive to recover stolen property subsided (Kuykendall, 1986). This change was gradual;

U.S. police often worked for rewards. One of the notable contributions of Allan Pinkerton was that he established a code of ethics and forbade the acceptance of rewards by his men.

There are still some examples of fee systems in use today, but these are rare. Constables in Pennsylvania are private citizens with arrest powers who serve warrants and perform various court functions on a fee basis. The constable system was imported from England and is an elected office in Pennsylvania. Note that an advantage of the fee system is that the government is only paying for services rendered. There is no benefit package such as health insurance and retirement.

Some other examples of "private security" or "public law enforcement" include the following:

1. Police in major cities may serve as "ambassadors" of the city. These officers may be stationed in transportation centers or public facilities where people visiting the city are likely to meet them. This is the same role played by private protection officers in hotels, resorts, casinos, and shopping centers. The concept is the same: aid and assist visitors and preserve the quality of life for those visitors.
2. Contract security personnel patrol apartment complexes, housing developments, and shopping centers in a form of "community-oriented policing." Some firms specialize in "weeding" out the criminal element via surveillance and apprehension of drug dealers and other criminals. This helps create a safe environment for the contract officers to assume their "community-oriented" policing role. They help neighborhood children, organize community activities, and so on.
3. College campuses often have campus police who conduct more asset protection and security work than law enforcement functions. Some colleges have both police and security divisions. Almost all have some type of student patrols.

4. Federal agencies such as the Secret Service and U.S. Marshals are really more concerned with security than law enforcement functions. There is also the Federal Protective Service, National Security Agency, and Customs and Border Protection. While the officers who work for these organizations have law enforcement authority, they are first and foremost protection organizations.
5. Government agencies often have either proprietary or contract security departments. Housing bureaus, school systems, parks departments, reservoirs, and so on are protected by security personnel. Some cities and counties have their own proprietary security departments.
6. Military and federal installations have security forces. These may be either proprietary government employees or private contract officers. The U.S. federal government is a large user of contract security services.
7. Shopping centers are private properties open to the public for business. They usually have proprietary security forces. Some have police substations within so that close cooperation between mall management, the security department, and the police department is facilitated.
8. Commissioned security officers are used in some environments. These are privately employed protection officers who have police commissions. This enables them to make arrests under certain circumstances, for certain types of offenses and/or within a specified area. Large hospitals and resorts located in remote locations, and quite a few private colleges, use this model.

The *blending* of police and security was great in the nineteenth century and, it is probably safe to say, within the past 30 years or so. It will probably continue as our society becomes increasingly complex and we more frequently utilize resources on a contractual/outsourcing or task force basis. Computer crimes will necessitate contracting out for investigative expertise by government agencies. So, too, will cost considerations as police are extremely expensive employees to maintain. Police require extensive preemployment screening, training, equipment, and health and pension benefits. As a result they will have to be used more judiciously. Functions that do not absolutely require a sworn law enforcement officer can be performed by a civilian. This can be a municipal proprietary or contract employee.

Additional factors in this blending are retirement plans and an aging population. Retired police do not make enough money to cease working. Employing them as security officers or investigators may utilize their skills in a mutually beneficial manner to both employer and officer.

An area of concern is police "moonlighting" in security. This can create numerous problems, such as determining whether the off-duty police officer is a police officer or security officer when making apprehensions, and so on. There may be a temptation to use official databases for the benefit of a private employer. Preferential treatment of the employer (store, mall, theater, restaurant, hotel, etc.) by the police may occur. Off-duty work may also begin to take precedence over the full-time job. The officer may spend too many hours working off-duty and become tired. Officer survival concerns are greatly expanded with off-duty police. Employers of off-duty police may also have a hard time controlling them. Terminating their employment can create intense hostility from local police departments.

FIRE PROTECTION

Fire protection is a major issue in asset protection. Fire can destroy almost anything. It is a chemical process whereby heat, fuel, and oxygen combine in a chemical chain reaction to turn a solid or liquid into a gas. *With adequate amounts of heat and oxygen, virtually anything can become fuel for a fire.*

The threat of fire varies with the environment. The *perception* of that threat also changes. Before the Civil War, fire insurance executives generally viewed fire as good for business (Purpura, 1991). Fires were similar to airplane crashes in that they were relatively improbable events that created hysteria and spurred the purchase of insurance policies. Insurance companies made money on these policies until excessive fires—in heavily populated areas where buildings were constructed of wood—caused enormous amounts of claims to be paid.

Here is a brief overview of some major events in the development of fire protection beginning in the 1600s:

1631: A disastrous fire in Boston resulted in the first fire ordinance in the United States. This ordinance prohibited wooden chimneys and thatched roofs (Ortmeier, 1999). Wooden chimneys were banned in London in 1647 (Cote & Bugbee, 1988). Wooden chimneys were often used in American soldiers' winter quarters and the cabins of slaves.

1666: The Great Fire of London spread due to closely situated wooden buildings, wind, and dry weather. The fire initiated some interest in fire prevention by insurance companies. A complete code of building regulations was adopted but not made effective, since commissioners to enforce the regulations were not appointed until 1774 (Cote & Bugbee, 1988).

1667: Phoenix Fire Office—a private firefighting service that suppressed fires on subscribers' property. Subscribers' had a crest on their buildings to mark them. Other private fire companies also formed. Today, some industrial complexes and other facilities have their own proprietary or in-house fire brigades. Some of these are well equipped and can suppress small fires. In most cases, fire departments are paid public professionals. Volunteer firemen are also used and play an important role in providing firefighting services to many areas. Some fire departments are a hybrid of paid and volunteer firefighters.

1871: Peshtigo Fire—a logging community in Wisconsin; Peshtigo had very dry weather and this aided the spread of a forest fire that burned vast acres of land. A massive firestorm formed where the fire consumed oxygen at such a rate that it created significant draft. Firestorms occur where a fire is large enough to essentially create its own mini-weather system. The Peshtigo Fire was probably the worst fire in U.S. history. It is relatively unknown because the Chicago Fire, which occurred a few days later, received more attention from the news media.

1871: Chicago Fire. As in the Great Fire of London, closely situated wooden buildings caught fire in dry weather. The wind whipped the fire through Chicago, and the city was destroyed. We commemorate the Chicago Fire with Fire Prevention Week. Fire Prevention Week is held each year in October.

1894: Underwriter's Laboratories (UL) was formed. UL is an independent testing laboratory. It subjects products to extensive tests to see if they work as they are supposed to and if they are safe.

1896: The National Fire Protection Administration development of *standards* for fire protection. These standards are used throughout the industry and are the basis for many municipal fire codes.

1948: The National Burglar and Fire Alarm Association (NBFAA) was formed. NBFAA offers membership, publications, seminars, and professional certification programs for alarm installers.

1965: National Board of Fire Underwriters was merged with the American Insurance Association. This resulted in the development of the National Building Code for municipalities (Purpura, 1991).

COMMERCE

Commerce has a tremendous relationship to asset protection. Professional security personnel must understand the marketing of their employer's goods and services in order to be effective. A retail loss prevention agent must understand that selling merchandise is the reason for the existence of the store, not the apprehension of shoplifters. *Marketing must be balanced with security.* They are "both different sides of the same coin." It can be said, in both a theoretical and practical sense, that "marketing is the 'flip side' of security."

From the beginning of the nineteenth century until the development of the railroads, massive canal networks were constructed in the eastern United States. During their heyday, canals had asset protection concerns with accidents and labor shortages. Workers were sometimes injured and barges and canals damaged.

Railroad expansion during the nineteenth century was dramatic. Railroads were necessary to ship goods and raw materials in large quantities. Railroads had, and still have, a variety of security and safety issues. Nineteenth-century American railroads faced attacks and sabotage of tracks and telegraph lines by Native Americans, buffalo stampedes, wrecks, and labor difficulties. The labor problems included both shortages of workers and strikes. While the railroads had their own police forces and contracted with the Pinkerton Agency, they also relied on an external control force—the Union Army. The Army had nearly 5,000 soldiers patrolling along and around the tracks in 1868 (Matthews, 1990). Human resource management problems (recruitment of quality personnel), safety issues, and external threats faced by the railroads, parallel the challenges facing contemporary asset protection managers. Today's manager is concerned with personnel recruitment (hiring) and retention (keeping workers), OSHA compliance, and external threats such as terrorist attacks.

Air transport is vulnerable to theft, safety problems, terrorists, and "air rage" by emotionally disturbed passengers. In 1969, numerous airplane hijackings occurred, and in 1974, the Anti-Hijacking and Air Transportation Security Act was passed, establishing security programs at airports. "Air rage" and the September 11 hijackings as well as the shoe bomb possessed by Richard Reid are more current issues.

Shipping on the high seas has historically presented problems with piracy and labor/human resource management (HRM) issues. Contemporary cruise ships face issues such as drunken, assaultive passengers and lawsuits due to cases of sexual harassment and rapes. The threat of terrorism is also very real, be it through the commandeering of a cruise ship, the smuggling of weapons of mass destruction aboard freighters, or attacks on ports such as detonating an explosive-laden ship within a harbor. Piracy—the robbery or hijacking of ships—continues to be a problem in some areas.

Telephone communication and Internet commerce are the new fronts for security issues relating to commerce. *Disinformation* (the deliberate dissemination of false information such as "urban legends"), theft of communications services, and so on are major concerns.

ECONOMIC AND MARKETING TRENDS AND ASSET PROTECTION

The desirability of an asset has an effect on the probability of its being stolen. A fundamental component of protection is to assign a monetary value to something. Historically, the "robber barons" of the late nineteenth century needed protection of their railroads, coal mines, and steel mills. They also needed personal

protection due to their vast wealth, as do current celebrities such as rock stars, film stars, and corporate executives.

With the availability of retail store outlets and self-service shopping, shoplifting has become a major issue. It is a low-tech crime that can be carried out by juveniles, drug addicts, and so on. With the high value of some store merchandise, sophisticated professional thieves, and even terrorist groups engage in retail theft. Organized Retail Theft (ORT) incorporates theft, repackaging, and distribution of the stolen product. It is a sophisticated operation involving various entities and warehouses to store the merchandise.

Contemporary loss problems include the counterfeiting of name brand items. Cigarettes are also a prime black market item because of their cost due to tax increases. Criminal enterprises that respond to these black markets are becoming more sophisticated. The theft of information concerning the development of new toys and drugs are major issues. "Competitive intelligence" and counterintelligence are key asset protection functions today. Internet crimes ranging from harassing e-mails to viruses, diversion of funds, denial of service attacks, and espionage are also problems. The theft of phone service and credit (identity theft or credit card theft) is also a major problem. Identity theft/fraud creates large amounts of indirect loss to the victim as investigating and cleaning up the problem takes enormous amounts of time. Employers of identity theft victims are also affected by a loss of productivity as the victim must take time to straighten out the financial mess.

Criminal targets change as rapidly as economics and markets dictate. Understanding markets is crucial to comprehending and subsequently planning protective measures. Marketing is the "flip side" of security in more ways than one.

Generally speaking, criminals outpace the efforts of police and security professionals.

Historically, they have been able to create loss by being one step ahead of protective measures.

DEMOGRAPHICS

Demographics play a major role in asset protection. *Demographic* theories of crime causation focus on the changing composition of the population. *Urbanization* theories of crime causation focus on the changing of a society from rural to urban, and *cultural-difference* theories focus on cultural conflict within a society (Ortmeier, 1999).

Population shifts in London during the Industrial Revolution brought in large numbers of shop workers who had previously worked in farming. There were cultural conflicts, drunkenness, overpopulation, and rampant crime. Riots were common and police action needed to be concerted and organized (along military lines). American cities, such as New York during the 1850s, experienced similar crime and social problems.

Immigration has caused increases in crime due to cultural conflicts—for example, the rapid expansion of Irish immigration in America during the period 1845 to 1852 in response to the Potato Famine of 1847. Coleman (1969) cites census statistics from 1870 as stating that there were 8,641 Irish immigrants to the United States in 1845, 29,540 in 1847, and 157,548 in 1852. As the coal mines provided, on their face, lucrative offers of employment, numerous Irish immigrants became employed as coal miners. Irish miners who felt exploited struck back at the mine bosses and railroad owners through organized criminal activities.

The Molly Maguires were an underground organization predominantly comprised of Irish miners, who perpetrated assaults and homicides against those they didn't like. They also engaged in acts of sabotage against the railroads. They were thugs in the eyes of Allan Pinkerton, labor union activists according to revisionist historians in the 1970s, and, perhaps, to a degree, terrorists. The "Mollies" were investigated by a Pinkerton operative in a three-year undercover operation. Many of the Molly Maguires were hanged in the mid-1870s. The Molly Maguires took their name from Irish activists/criminals who dressed as women and fought the landlords in Ireland (a class struggle). See *The Molly Maguires* with Sean Connery and Richard Harris for a 1969—and perhaps "revisionist"—perspective on this.

The Molly Maguires case was important as it was probably the first use of a task force (Pinkerton men teamed with Coal and Iron Police) as well as the first major undercover investigation.

Invariably there are criminals among immigrant groups who exploit their fellow countrymen. In most cases, organized crime activity dissipates after the immigrant group becomes assimilated into the dominant culture. Common examples of this are slave trading, prostitution, gambling, narcotics, and smuggling. Extortion via protection rackets as well as criminal group infiltration of organized labor also occurs. See the movies *Goodfellas* and *Once Upon a Time in America* for some perspective on organized crime infiltration.

Current immigrant criminal enterprises are from Russian organized crime groups, South

PRACTICAL EXERCISE

List an ethnic group that is largely employed in a certain industry. Do their employers exploit that group? How? What types of actions could they take to exact revenge on their employers?

Korean groups, and so on. With the breakup of the Soviet Union, many of these immigrant groups have turned to criminal enterprises. A new wrinkle is that some organized crime today is *transnational* and crosses international borders. The more traditional organized crime groups have stayed within their own ethnic group and preyed upon the members.

Population density, culture, age, gender, and other factors also play heavily in terms of safety issues. Elder care requires certain aspects of asset protection. Government requirements for long-term care facilities and patients suffering from Alzheimer's create daily challenges. Emergency planning for a population that is not ambulatory and has failing hearing and sight is also an issue. In school security, managers must focus on drug dealing, evacuation plans, active shooters, parking, and crowd management at special events. Hotel security must be concerned with a transitory population. Issues include disorderly guests, dishonest employees, sexual assault, and fire and guest services. Each population has unique safety and security needs.

CLASS STRUGGLES AND TERRORISM

A recurrent theme concerning the history of security and that of policing is the presence of class struggles. Class struggles were apparent during the French Revolution and later with the development of terrorism as a significant security/law enforcement problem. It also relates, to some degree, to the problems encountered with the organized labor movement in America. The following discussion on terrorism relates to left-wing and right-wing terrorism that is politically and economically inspired. Left-wing terrorists are usually anti-government and have socialist leanings. Right-wing terrorists are anti-government and highly conservative. These are two basic classifications of political extremism. There are, however,

numerous other types. Note that not all terrorist activity is politically inspired. In the United States many are the acts of mentally ill individuals. Whatever the motivation behind it, each terrorist threat requires both a proactive and a reactive response to it.

Terrorism can perhaps be understood by looking at a few significant events.

1848—*Communist Manifesto* was written by Karl Marx and Friedrich Engels. This established the political theory of Marxism—often called "Communism." The bourgeoisie (ruling class of capitalists) exploit the proletariat (laborers). The proletariat should rise up and overthrow the bourgeoisie and establish a utopian society, a "dictatorship of the proletariat" where everyone shares equally. Propaganda was used to educate the masses and inspire them to revolt. Marxism was born in 1848 and left-wing terrorist groups throughout the world followed it.
1886—The Haymarket Riot in Chicago was instigated by anarchists during a rally against McCormick Harvester. A bomb was thrown and seven policemen were killed, with another 60 injured. Six workers were also killed as police and workers exchanged gunfire. Anarchists believed in the abolition of governments. This movement utilized terror tactics such as assassination (William McKinley and six other heads of state) and bombings. They were very active in France, Russia, Italy, Spain, Germany, and the United States during the later nineteenth and early twentieth centuries. There are still anarchists in contemporary American society, but their violent activities have subsided greatly since the 1880s to the 1920s. After the Haymarket Affair, local industrialists donated land to the federal government so that troops could be stationed nearby. Fort Sheridan was built for this purpose.
1969—There were numerous hijackings of airliners to Cuba by dissident individuals. There were also bombings of federal

buildings. In the Munich Massacre, Israeli athletes at the Olympics were killed by Palestinian terrorists. The Munich Massacre showed the world that terrorism was indeed a problem. It brought terrorism to the living rooms of the world via television.

1972—Patty Hearst and the Symbionese Liberation Army (SLA)—a left-wing antigovernment group. The granddaughter of newspaper magnate William Randolph Hearst was kidnapped by the SLA and later joined them. She was "underground" for 20 months, traveling across the country. The Patty Hearst case showed that fugitives could remain underground for extensive periods of time in the United States. See the film *The Patty Hearst Story* for an excellent treatment of how left-wing radicals operated in the United States during the early 1970s.

1973—Nyack Incident—several left-wing terrorist groups thought to be long dormant collaborated on a "fundraiser" (armored car robbery) in Nyack, New York. This showed that groups thought to be long dormant were still active. Note that the Vietnam War created intense antigovernment feelings in the United States. After the U.S. involvement in Vietnam ended in 1973, much of the left-wing sentiment faded. The Nyack Incident showed that there were still some virulent left-wing terrorist groups operating. That is an important lesson: that groups no longer "on the radar" can reemerge. Note that occasionally 1970s terrorists are still being caught. The Nyack Incident also showed that left-wing groups were working in concert with one another. This is a major concern with terrorism as "the enemy of my enemy is my friend." Alliances can easily and quickly form between groups.

In the 1980s and 1990s, right-wing terrorism became more of an issue than left-wing, Marxist-inspired terrorist activity. Economically disenfranchised males in rural America often believed that they were being subjugated economically by Jewish bankers and a federal government that raised their taxes and took away their gun ownership rights. Minority groups were seen as taking their jobs. In urban areas, the Skinheads formed. American Skinheads are based on a working-class movement in the United Kingdom during the early 1970s. The British Skinheads wore Doc Martens boots and close-cropped hair, and they targeted minority group members and immigrants for taking their jobs. The right-wing groups gain followers during economically depressed times. They are also inspired by government control over gun ownership and increased taxes.

In the 1990s and into the early twenty-first century, terrorism perpetrated by right-wing extremists was largely overshadowed by the activities of radical Islamic fundamentalists.

A series of terrorist events within the late 1990s and early twenty-first century include the following:

- The 1993 World Trade Center bombing by Islamic fundamentalists who planted an explosives-laden vehicle in the parking garage and detonated it.
- The 1995 Oklahoma City Bombing by right-wing terrorists who used a massive truck bomb to demolish the Alfred P. Murrah Federal Building.
- The September 11, 2001, World Trade Center and Pentagon attacks by Islamic fundamentalists associated with al-Qaeda. The attackers hijacked four airliners and crashed two of them into the World Trade Center and one into the Pentagon. One airliner was crashed in a field near Somerset, Pennsylvania, after passengers overpowered the hijackers. This alerted the United States that it had a serious problem with some of the more radical followers of Islam.

In Madrid on March 11, 2004, 192 people were killed and 1,841 wounded when 10 bombs exploded on four commuter trains. The bombs exploded within minutes of each other. Seven of the key suspects, including the alleged master mind, died in the explosion. A policeman was also killed. Twenty-one people were arrested in connection with the attacks, most of them Moroccan (http://news.bbc.co.uk/2/shared/spl/hi/guides/457000/457031/html/. Retrieved October 11, 2009). The choice of multiple targets in a simultaneous coordinated attack is a key feature of an operation by al-Qaeda. The attack appears to have been designed to inflict the maximum number of civilian casualties. This is also consistent with previous al-Qaeda operations (http://news.bbc.co.uk/2/hi/europe/3582501.stm. Retrieved October 11, 2009).

In Mumbai, India, on November 28, 2008, 151 people were killed by terrorists using automatic weapons and hand grenades. The 60 terrorists were in nine different groups with some attacking train stations and others taking hostages in a hotel (http://www.boston.com/bigpicture/2008/11/mumbai_under_attack.html. Retrieved October 11, 2009). Islamic fundamentalists based in Pakistan were behind the attack.

The 9/11 attacks in America, the 3/11 attacks in Madrid, and the attack in Mumbai all illustrate the workings of organized, dedicated terrorists. To better understand the forces driving radical Islamic fundamentalists, consider the following:

Old vs. New—there is a "clash of cultures" between traditional ideals and new, Western values. There is also a power shift away from religious leaders who formerly had much more control over their followers.

Class struggles—large numbers of unemployed or underemployed persons living in poverty.

Demographics—undereducated or *miseducated* Middle Eastern or Muslim young men who have been taught that the United States is "The Great Satan." These impressionable young men can become an army of destruction if the right conditions are met.

PRACTICAL EXERCISE

Develop a list of specific threat actions posed by terrorists, such as bombings, assassinations, cyber attacks, kidnapping, and so on. Next, list a proactive countermeasure to be used before the attack is launched. Finally, list a reactive countermeasure to be employed as the attack is taking place or after the attack has occurred.

Terrorist Threat Action	Proactive	Reactive

Culture of warfare—some areas of the world have experienced warfare for an extended period of time. This warfare may be low, medium, or high intensity. In most cases it is low-intensity guerrilla warfare or insurgency. In some cases, entire generations of people have been immersed in wars. Afghanistan, Palestine, and Bosnia are examples of this.

Religion—a perversion of Islam that emphasizes traditional values and demonizes the West has occurred. Religion is a powerful influence on people. People who are living in poverty or feel discriminated against may turn to religion as an answer to their problems. Religion also gives legitimacy to the exhortations of leaders. If a leader advocates deviant behavior—violence—it may be acceptable to his impressionable followers.

Charismatic leaders—all dynamic groups have charismatic leaders. Extremist groups thrive on them. A charismatic leader can exploit—as did Adolf Hitler—cultural, social, and economic forces in a negative way. Charismatic leaders can create large numbers of youthful terrorists.

LABOR RELATIONS

Labor relations have played a very large role in the history of both policing and security in America. It is also important for understanding the development of society as a whole. Organized labor brought together people of different ethnic groups. It established numerous changes in the workplace, such as benefit plans for employees and the establishment of disciplinary procedures based on the concept of due process.

While union membership is declining at present, many of the contemporary approaches to labor relations, physical security, contingency planning, and personnel security are a result of earlier labor issues. One must understand the historical context of "labor relations" in American society to fully appreciate the development of both labor unions and control forces.

"Labor relations" during "the mean years" of 1866–1937 (Calder, 1985) consisted of some tactics employed by management that would be unacceptable by contemporary society. These included the intimidation of labor leaders, spies, and "agent provocateurs" (persons who instigate illegal activity and then work to have the participants arrested for violating the law) in unions; assaults with machine guns; the importation of strike breakers (workers who replace those who are on strike); the subversion of attempts by workers to organize by the promotion of interethnic conflict; and the use of thugs to intimidate workers.

Note: See *Matewan* with James Earl Jones, Chris Cooper, and Mary MacDonald for an excellent treatment of this topic based on the 1920 Matewan Massacre. The Matewan Massacre was a gun battle waged between striking miners and the Baldwin-Felts Detective Agency in Matewan, West Virginia.

These are some of the key events in the struggle of organized labor within the United States.

1866—National Labor Union was formed in Baltimore—a national union was now in place rather than the previous groups. These were local or trade-specific small groups with little power. A national union could mobilize large numbers of workers. These workers could organize massive strikes and shut down factories, mines, and railroads.

1892—Homestead Strike—a labor dispute between the Carnegie Steel Company and the Amalgamated Association of Iron and Steel workers resulted in a lockout. Henry Clay Frick, Carnegie's general manager, tried to get the workers to accept a wage cut. He then locked the workers out of the plant so that they could not work. The workers assumed that Frick would do this and reopen the plant using strikebreakers (employees who replace striking workers). Three hundred Pinkerton detectives came by barge up the Monongahela River and tried to secure the plant. A battle ensued which lasted all day. The workers used a small cannon to try and sink the barges and set them on fire by pouring oil into the river and lighting it. The Pinkertons were defeated and had to surrender (Fossum, 1982). Nine strikers and seven Pinkertons were killed (Gage, 2009). The militia were called in by the governor. Interestingly enough, Frick was later shot by an anarchist who attacked him in his home.

1894—Pullman Strike—the Pullman Palace Car Company laid off half of their employees and forced the rest to take a 40% wage cut. Workers were required to live in company housing. After the wage reductions, there was no reduction in the rent for the housing. The local strike became a sympathy strike as American Railway Union (ARU) members refused to handle trains with Pullman cars. Trains were stopped and Pullman cars were uncoupled. The rail owners assembled trains so that if Pullman cars were uncoupled, mail cars would also be cut off. Interfering with the mail was a federal offense. Eugene Debs, the ARU leader was sent to jail for conspiring to obstruct the mail. President Grover Cleveland called out the Army so that the mail could be delivered and the strike was broken (Fossum, 1982).

1900—Latimer Massacre—large numbers of Serbian miners were killed by sheriffs' deputies during a strike in Latimer, Pennsylvania. The United States offered an official apology to the government of Serbia after this incident.

1905—Pennsylvania State Police—first modern state police force. Formed from the Philadelphia City Cavalry after the Great Anthracite Strike in 1903–1904.

1933—National Industrial Recovery Act insured collective bargaining rights. Wagner Act (National Labor Relations Act) created the National Labor Relations Board in 1935, giving a real enforcement function to the National Industrial Recovery Act.

1937—Battle of the Overpass. During a strike against the Ford Motor Company, labor leader Walter Reuther and a companion were severely beaten by Ford Service security officers while not doing anything illegal. This beating was not unusual except that it was photographed by newspaper reporters. The American public was not sympathetic toward unions as they were regarded as "communist" or "anarchist." With the Battle of the Overpass, however, the public was outraged at the actions of Dearborn, Michigan, police and Bennett's Ford Service men—the end of "the mean years" of labor relations.

1947—In 1946, there were a large number of strikes; organized labor reached its zenith in this period. Congress passed the Taft-Hartley Act. One of the provisions of the Act is that the U.S. president, through the attorney general, can obtain an injunction against a strike or lockout if a substantial area is affected or national security is threatened.

Today, there are specialized contract security firms that have strike security forces. These firms supply consulting and guard service to companies having labor difficulties. They generally employ persons with a military background and provide their personnel with training in labor law, crowd management, and so on. These specialized firms are able to manage volatile labor disputes with minimal harm to persons or property. Additionally, the collective bargaining rights of workers are upheld. Strikes are handled in a much more professional manner than in the past.

PRACTICAL EXERCISE

It is 1920. The Great War is over and you are a military veteran with service in World War I. You are out of work and have several children to feed. The best employment prospect is with a private security firm that is doing strike security work. How do you feel about this?

LAW

The first codification of law in Western civilization is generally attributed to Hammurabi who served as king of Babylon from 1792 B.C. to 1750 B.C. The Code of Hammurabi specified offenses and punishments for each. While the popular view is that the Code consisted of "an eye for an eye," this may not be completely true. There were differing punishments based on the social class standing of the victim and offender. More important, much of the Code deals with what we would refer to today as "civil law." There is discussion of the granting of receipts, husbandry, town planning, commerce, divorce, regulations for certain occupations, and slavery (Bottero, 1973).

Another major legal development occurred in 1215 with the Magna Carta ("Great Charter") in England. The document specified the responsibilities of the state were to its subjects regarding individual rights, privileges, and security. The Magna Carta established the concept of *due process*. This means that everyone should be treated fairly and according to uniform procedures. It is the basis for most law and disciplinary procedures. Due process was incorporated into the Fifth Amendment of the U.S. Constitution: "no person shall be deprived of life, liberty or property without due process of law." Perhaps most important, the Magna Carta implied that the king was not above the law.

Law can be divided into *statutory law*—established by legislative statute, *case law*—established by a court decision, and *common law*—passed down through tradition. All relate heavily to asset protection. Protection professionals must be well versed in legal concepts. In many cases, security managers, safety directors, and consultants develop policies and procedures based on legal obligations. Protection managers are also occasionally asked to give upper management advice on general legal issues (specific legal concerns should *only* be addressed by an attorney after careful research of similar cases). Protection officers and investigators must also make legal determinations during the course of their duties. Protection officers must be "legal consultants" well versed in legal standards relating to privacy, property rights, and governmental mandates.

Laws are authored in response to social changes, which apply political pressure. Areas of the law relating to asset protection/security include the following:

1. Criminal law with offenses such as trespassing, various types of thefts (retail theft, theft of trade secrets, and so on), vandalism, assault, burglary, robbery, rape, and so on. Criminal offenses that an environment is most likely to encounter vary with that environment. Schools have different legal challenges than shopping centers; manufacturing facilities face their own unique legal issues, as do hotels. Protection officers should become familiar with the criminal laws that are most commonly violated in the environment they are assigned to protect. *Note:* See www.looseleaflaw.com or www.gouldlaw.com for state criminal codes in the United States.

2. Civil law relates to legal standards, which govern the conduct between individuals. Civil law relates to contracts that include the following.

   a) Contract security service
   b) Private investigative service
   c) Armored car service
   d) Personal protection/executive protection service
   e) Alarm monitoring
   f) Alarm response
   g) Employment contracts for management and labor
   h) Nondisclosure pacts—agreements not to disclose proprietary information, such as trade secrets
   i) Noncompetitive agreements or pacts—agreements not to seek employment with competing firms within a specific time frame and/or geographic area after termination of employment
   j) Leases between landlords and tenants—these can be individuals who rent apartments or businesses, such as in shopping centers

Civil law also involves asset forfeiture and civil demand or civil recovery. The former is a civil process used by law enforcement officials to obtain property used to commit crimes. Once a drug dealer or fence has been arrested, their home, car, and any other asset they have that has been used in the commission of the offense is taken. This is a civil process before any criminal conviction has occurred. Civil recovery is used by merchants to obtain monetary fees from shoplifters. Shoplifters are sent a civil demand letter stating that if they do not pay a certain fee they will be sued. As a civil suit will ruin someone's credit, many people simply pay the money, which is collected by a third party. This is much more effective for merchants, as they do not have to proceed with criminal prosecution, tying up time and merchandise (this must be kept as evidence and can't be sold). The processes for forfeiture and civil recovery are not encumbered by constitutional protections to the accused (as in criminal law) and the burden of proof is a preponderance (majority such as 55%) of the evidence. In a criminal case, proof beyond a reasonable doubt (99% certainty) is required. Civil laws are being used increasingly to combat criminal activity. Civil law also covers torts or private wrongs committed against another, such as defamation, invasion of privacy, assault, battery, and so on. Torts may be thought of as the civil equivalent of crimes. It must be borne in mind, however, that the definitions are different.

Negligence is a failure to exercise reasonable and due care (such as not following a recognized standard) by doing something dangerous or not doing something, which is necessary for safety. In order to prove negligence, the plaintiff (party bringing the action or suit) may have to show the following:

- The existence of a duty
- A failure to perform that duty
- Injury or harm occurring to a party to whom the duty was owed
- The harm was reasonably foreseeable
- The harm was caused by the failure of the defendant to perform the duty (Hertig, Fennelly, & Tyska, 1998)

3. Administrative or regulatory law is established to regulate technical aspects of society. Administrative or regulatory agencies are created by the federal or state legislature. These agencies have the authority to create rules and regulations. They investigate and enforce compliance with those regulations. They also adjudicate violations and mete out punishments. These agencies are very powerful. Complying with their regulations is extremely important; so, too, is complying with them and remaining in business. Federal administrative agencies in the United States include the following:

a) Occupational Safety and Health Administration
b) National Labor Relations Board
c) Environmental Protection Agency
d) Federal Aviation Administration
e) Nuclear Regulatory Commission
f) Federal Communications Commission
g) Equal Employment Opportunity Commission

Agencies also exist on the state level, such as CALOSHA or the Pennsylvania Department of Labor and Industry, Human Relations Commission, Alcoholic Beverage Commissions, Private Detective and Protective Agent Licensing Board, and so on. There are also city or municipal boards of health, building inspection, zoning, and so on. These regulate food handling in public kitchens, fire escapes and fire detection equipment, the number of parking spaces required, setback rules from property lines, building permits, and so on. For information on state security licensing, see the International Association of Security and Investigative Regulators (http://www.iasir.org).

The 1990 Campus Security and Student Right to Know Act passed in the United States requires colleges to report all crimes committed on their campuses. They must also publish crime statistics. The Act is enforced by the U.S. Department of Education, which can levy monetary penalties for noncompliance. Another important regulatory law is the Bank Protection Act of 1968. This law established security standards to be used in banks that are insured by the Federal Deposit Insurance Corporation (FDIC). Portions of the Act are enforced by different federal agencies.

4. Labor or employment law consists of statutory laws, court decisions, and administrative agency regulations (Equal Employment Opportunity Commission, National Labor Relations Board, and so on) that regulate the employer-employee relationship. Labor law also consists of contracts between employees and employers and privacy issues.

HISTORY OF SECURITY SERVICES

Security services or contract security agencies have played a large role in both public and private protection. *Outsourcing* or contracting for security makes economic sense. Flat hourly rates are charged and clients do not have to worry about benefit costs and associated human resource management issues. The client can hire as many personnel as desired for as long as desired. This provides for flexibility in protection. Additionally, contract service firms may have specialized expertise that the client does not.

There are career opportunities here for those who are adept at sales, client relations, and HRM. Security services are growing and will continue to do so. In addition to standard "guard service" there are alarm response, alarm monitoring, armored car, personal protection specialists (PPS), and private investigation. There will always be a need to understand the dynamics of the outsourcing process for both contractors *and* clients.

While contract security firms usually offer private investigative services, most firms specialize in one or the other. Early security service firms began by offering investigative services and later transitioned into contract security. This happened because there were greater markets—and profits—in providing security service. In some cases, this continues to occur, although the growth in demand for private investigation is robust enough to allow companies to be profitable while keeping investigation as their sole service. Pinkerton, a Scottish immigrant, became involved in investigation by accident. While searching for wood to make barrels, the young cooper discovered a gang of counterfeiters.

Pinkerton established the largest protective and investigative agency in the world with branch offices in many countries. By the mid-1990s, Pinkerton had 250 offices worldwide with over 50,000 employees (Mackay, 1996). Pinkerton had extensive centralized records and a code of ethics, used undercover investigation, employed the first female detective (Kate Warne—60 years before the first female police officer), and used wanted posters. Pinkerton is credited with being the first to start a security service; in actuality there were other services started before him, but none has become as well known as his was.

1858—Edwin Holmes started the first "central office" (central station) for alarm monitoring and response. Today we use the term "central alarm station" or "central station." Many central stations are contract, off-premises facilities that monitor intrusion, fire and process (temperature or pressure gauges), or duress (emergency medical or robbery) alarms. Customers pay for the monitoring services. Holmes Protection provides monitoring and alarm response services.

1874—American District Telegraph (ADT) was founded. ADT became the largest alarm company in the world. Their main product was magnetic contact switches (the little gray boxes above doors and windows in restaurants and stores). Today they provide a wide variety of electronic security equipment. They also provide CCTV, access control systems, and fire protection systems. ADT bought Holmes Protection in the late 1990s. ADT is now a unit of Tyco Fire and Security Services (Purpura, 2002).

1891—Brinks Armored became the largest armored car company in the world. Founded by Washington Perry Brinks, the firm transports cash and other valuables. Brinks also

monitors home alarm systems and has become a household name in the United States.

1909—William J. Burns—Burns was the original head of the "Bureau of Investigation," which later became the Federal Bureau of Investigation under J. Edgar Hoover in 1932. William J. Burns founded the William J. Burns Detective Agency in 1909. He was virulently antianarchist and anticommunist, believing that unions were being controlled by subversives and that unions were fronts for anarchists and communists. Burns was known for his ability to use evidence collection at the scene of a crime to capture suspects. In 1910, he apprehended the McNamara brothers, who were president and secretary of the United Iron Worker's Union, for a bombing of the Los Angeles Times building. He traced them from parts of the unexploded bomb. The McNamaras were supposedly avowed anarchists. In the 1970s and 1980s, Burns International Security Services, Inc. became one of the largest contract security firms in the world. It has since been acquired by Securitas.

1954—George Wackenhut founded the Wackenhut Corporation (wackenhut .com—see the job info on the Custom Protection Officer program). The firm provided security services in over 55 different countries backed by a staff of 70,000 employees. It also provided staffing for prisons on a contract basis. Wackenhut was acquired by the Danish firm Group4falck in 2002. The parent firm is now known as "G4S" and Wackenhut is "G4S Wackenhut." G4S Wackenhut provides access control and perimeter security to the U.S. army in various overseas locations (http://www.g4s .com/uk/uk-working_for_g4s/uk-join_us/ uk-vacancy-kosovo.htmTail. Retrieved October 10, 2009).

THE PATH TO PROFESSIONALISM

There have been some significant developments along the path toward professionalism for the Security Industry:

1955—The American Society for Industrial Security (ASIS) was formed in Washington, DC. ASIS consisted of security directors for Department of Defense contractor firms. Over the passage of time, ASIS International has grown to over 37,000 members in over 200 chapters worldwide (http://www .asisonline.org/about/history/index.xml. Retrieved October 11, 2009). Members have a diverse range of positions within private industry, law enforcement, government and security service, and supply firms. ASIS has numerous councils on such topics as health care, retail, campus, banking, economic crime, commercial real estate, gaming and wagering protection, and so on.

1971—*the Rand Report on Private Police in America*—this was a private research study by the Rand Corporation. It was important as the security industry had not been studied. The *Rand Report* found that the security industry was large, growing, and unregulated. The average security officer was an aging white male with a limited education who was usually untrained and who worked many hours to make ends meet. The *Rand Report* was useful as a reference point for the *Report of the Task Force on Private Security* in 1975.

1975—The *Report of the Task Force on Private Security* conducted by the National Advisory Committee on Criminal Justice Standards and Goals was published in 1976. The committee found a lack of training, regulation, and job descriptions within the security industry. The report advocated minimum training standards; these have been used as guides by some states in setting up mandated training and licensing requirements.

1977—Certified Protection Professional (CPP) Program established by ASIS. First envisioned during the 1950s, the CPP program acknowledged that managers must be competent in a variety of generic subjects such as physical security, personnel security, legal aspects, management, investigations, and so on. There have been thousands of persons designated as Certified Protection Professionals around the world. The CPP program has become an important credential for management level personnel. The process takes approximately 10 years to complete. Recertification is required through continuing education and contributions to the industry every 3 years.

1985—*The Private Security and Police in America: The Hallcrest Report* was published. This report was written by Hallcrest Systems under funding from the Department of Justice. The report studied the contributions of police and security to control crime as well as the relationship between the public and private sector. The report also found that the average security officer was younger and better educated than the "aging white male" in the *Rand Report* of 1971.

1988—International Foundation for Protection Officers (IFPO)—formed to upgrade the professional status of public and private protection officers. The IFPO has membership, publications, an Article Archives on their Web site, and several professional certification programs. Over 35,000 people worldwide have become Certified Protection Officers. There is also a Certified Security Supervision and Management (CSSM) designation. Over 3,500 people have attained this designation. In 2001, the Foundation launched the Certified Protection Officer Instructor (CPOI) designation for those individuals who may instruct the CPO Program in a traditional classroom environment. Certified Protection Officer Instructors must be CPOs with instructional qualifications. They must also have security industry and teaching experience. In addition, they must have professional memberships in organizations such as IFPO, ASIS, the American Society for Training & Development, or the International Association of Law Enforcement Educators and Trainers.

1988—The Association of Certified Fraud Examiners (ACFE) was started. Today, the ACFE has a membership in excess of 45,000 members, representing more than 50 countries (http://www.pacfe.org/home .asp. Retrieved October 11, 2009). Certified Fraud Examiners are employed by a host of public and private entities including District Attorney's offices, federal investigative agencies, state police, corporate security departments, private investigative firms, and accounting firms. Fraud is a concern in virtually all environments. CFEs must have experience in fraud investigation and pass an exam on Criminology and Ethics, Fraudulent Financial Transactions, Fraud Investigation, and Legal Elements of Fraud. Note that there are also student memberships available in the ACFE.

The *2008 Compensation Guide for Anti-Fraud Professionals* found that CFEs earn nearly 22% more than their noncertified colleagues (http:// www.acfe.com/about/cfe-designation.asp. Retrieved on October 11, 2009). This is similar to other professional certification programs. Studies continually find higher earnings for certified individuals.

CONTEMPORARY CAREERS IN ASSET PROTECTION

There are numerous career fields open to people seeking a challenging and rewarding career in asset protection. Every organization employs some types of protective measures. Many—if not most—have security personnel. A sampling of positions available and functions that persons holding those positions perform is outlined here. Note that information on careers in law, public safety, and security can be obtained by visiting http://www.careerclusters.org.

Fixed posts: Many protection officers work at fixed posts. These may include baggage screening at airports, vehicle gates at manufacturing facilities, emergency rooms in hospitals, access control points at concerts, in museums, or in the lobbies of high-rise buildings. Generally, fixed post duties are more rudimentary and are assigned to new officers. Once the officers master the post assignment, they may be given duties at other posts. Often, fixed post functions are contracted out to security service firms, as it is cheaper to do so. Additionally, the contract agencies can supply the required number of personnel when manpower requirements fluctuate, such as at special events, emergencies, or when facilities close for the evening. College students, retirees, homemakers, or active duty military personnel may begin their careers performing fixed post duties. *A key point in career development is to master the fixed post duties.* Persons who have not done that will probably not get additional duties assigned to them. There are generally extensive opportunities for promotion available to those who are willing to work hard, grow, and develop professionally.

Patrol officer: A patrol officer must be able to observe and report discrepancies in the protected environment. They must collect intelligence on changes, unusual situations, or suspicious persons (intelligence agent role). Patrol officers must be adept at interacting with the public in the environment be that visitors, employees, students, patients, or guests (management representative role). Patrol officers must effectively maintain compliance with organizational policies (enforcement agent role). In doing so, they must know the rules of the facility as well as legal issues relating to privacy, search and seizure, property rights, and the rights of employees (legal consultant role). Patrol officers must also be able to respond to problems that may occur, such as slippery walkways, blocked emergency exits, hazardous materials spills, fires, fights, or crimes in progress. Obviously, patrol officers need a variety of skill sets. They must be competent in many things.

Retail loss prevention agent: Positions that are available with many large firms. These jobs offer persons the ability to learn valuable investigative skills, such as surveillance and interrogation. They are readily available and often accept part-time employees. There are extensive opportunities for advancement within retail security!

Central alarm station operator/dispatcher: Security officers in many environments will act as dispatchers or central alarm station operators. They will monitor alarm panels, CCTV screens, and electronic access control systems. As technology expands, so does the job of the central alarm station operator. These central alarm stations may be either proprietary or contract. In a proprietary "in-house" setting, central alarm stations evolve over time. Many facilities develop central alarm stations in an incremental manner. They often start with a security office that has a desk, a telephone, and a radio. After a while, the organization will add additional monitoring systems. First, there is a camera observing the lobby. Next, there is a camera on the parking area. Then there may be intrusion detection systems in sensitive areas which annunciate (terminate) at the central office. Fire alarm panels may also be located there. Finally, an electronic access control system is added which has a monitor in the central office.

There are access control systems and alarm systems. The reader must bear in mind today we have various types of alarms.

1. Intrusion alarms, which are *point protection* (on a specific point, such as door or window), *perimeter protection* (fence protection, such as those that detect vibration on a chain link fence or beam-type systems, such as microwave placed along a perimeter line), or *area protection* (volumetric intrusion detection for an area such as passive infrared or PIR or ultrasonic).
2. Fire alarms that may be ionization detectors (responding to the products of combustion in the earliest phase of a fire).
3. Emergency, panic, or duress alarms, which are activated by someone in distress.
4. Process alarms that monitor equipment or utilities (temperature, water pressure, air pressure, power).

What began as a security office is now a central alarm station/dispatch center. Obviously, facility managers must plan for the eventual expansion of their security offices. Serious thought must be given to alarm response. If alarms notify property managers of problems, there must be a rapid, effective response to resolving those problems. This is a key issue in protection that has traditionally been overlooked. Contract alarm response or patrol car service is one option: what Edwin Holmes started in 1858 needs to be integrated into a contemporary asset protection system. Persons beginning careers in asset protection should seek to understand the central alarm/dispatch operation. It is "the brain" of the security operation, serving as a *command*, *control*, and *communications* center.

Auditor/investigator: Auditors check on things such as financial records (financial audits) or procedures (procedural or operational audits) to see if conditions are what they are supposed to be. Audits seek to uncover deviations from procedure, errors, or criminal behavior (Purpura, 2002). A deviation from a procedure might be documenting something that the writer did not verify occurred—taking a "shortcut." Audits may also uncover errors such as mistakes made in pricing merchandise or forgetting to record required information.

Criminal behavior may include falsifying employee attendance records or removing raw materials from the workplace. Audits may start investigations or investigations may launch audits to see the scope of the problem. Audits may detect loss stemming from waste, error, crime or unethical/unprofessional practices. In that sense they support the WAECUP Model of Loss Control.

Private investigators: They work for companies, individuals, or governments on a fee basis. They contract out to perform various types of investigative activity. Criminal investigation done by private investigators includes undercover investigation of workplace theft, sabotage, or drug abuse. Surveillance of suspected employees may also be conducted. Some private investigators are forensic accountants, trained to investigate fraudulent accounting and present a case in court. Fraud examination is a large and growing concern of all types of organizations, not just insurance carriers. Visit the Association of Certified Fraud Examiners at http://www.acfe.com for more information on fraud examination.

Specialized security functions such as K-9 handlers, crowd management specialists who work concerts in arenas, strike security personnel, and information technology (IT) specialists also exist. These persons are specialists with unique skill sets. They have prior experience, training, and education that qualify them for their positions. They have "paid their dues" and evolved in their careers.

Educational opportunities are available both online and in traditional college programs. Persons wishing to move up the ranks of management will need higher education. The Web site asisonline.org has information on careers and academic programs. There is an extensive listing of colleges that offer academic coursework in security. In addition, ASIS offers full-time college students membership at greatly reduced rates. There is also a Student Paper Competition for both undergraduate and graduate students. Winning papers are eligible for cash prizes.

The International Foundation for Protection Officers also features links to colleges on their Web site (http://www.ifpo.org). The foundation has also provided scholarships to faculty who teach security courses.

Networking is crucial to career success in security or investigation, as not all good jobs are advertised publicly. Almost all are obtained through personal contacts. There is an old saying:

"If you don't know nobody, nobody knows you."
This saying makes up for in accuracy what it lacks in English. Professional contacts can be gained through organizational membership, such as ASIS International, IFPO, or the International Foundation for Cultural Property Protection (http://www.ifcpp.org). Professional organizations usually have job placement services and membership directories. They provide members with the opportunity to meet others in their field and discuss matters of mutual concern. Attendance at seminars sponsored by professional organizations is another way to network. Management-level personnel can participate in the International Association of Healthcare Security & Safety (http://www.iahss.org) or the International Association of Campus Law Enforcement Administrators (http://www.iaclea.org).

Professional development can be obtained through a variety of sources. Professional organizations offer seminars and online programs. Some offer certification programs such as the International Foundation for Cultural Property (http://www.ifcpp.org) that offers both the Certified Institutional Protection Specialist (CIPS) and Certified Institutional Protection Manager (CIPM) designations.

"Learning never ceases."
This chapter discussed the past and present. The future belongs to those who reach out and grasp it.

EMERGING TRENDS

Security service firms are moving into new markets. Providing security at special events is one example. While contract security at concerts or sporting events has been going on for a long time, now companies are hiring specialized service firms for other types of events. The company Christmas party or picnic may be examples. Securing abandoned buildings is a new line of business where contract firms have partnered with exterminators to offer a complete package of care for a vacant property. Recovering assets in the wake of floods and other disasters is another new line. This goes with disaster recovery services where firms will take care of food, clothing, lodging, and toilets after a disaster.

Protection of government buildings and transportation of inmates are other expanding lines of business for contract firms. The federal government in the United States is probably the largest employer of contract security services.

There are also more security services for governments and armed forces in hostile areas. These services include personal protection and facility security. The clients may be government or military organizations. They may also be private companies. In war-torn areas of the world, such as Iraq and Afghanistan, contract security personnel provide personal protection for VIPs. They are also providing fixed site security in unstable areas where there is exploration and development of natural resources. Oil, gas, and minerals all require processing and they all require protection. These resources are sometimes highly valuable (such as precious metals) and can be stolen by criminal or terrorist gangs. They may also be targets of insurgents and terrorists who wish to disrupt the flow of oil or gas. As energy demands increase so, too, does the need to find new sources of fuel. Many of these sources are in remote areas where insurrection, terrorism, or banditry can be a problem.

Threats to commerce/supply chain security are necessitating more attention. Guarding drug shipments against hijacking or covert diversion is an example. As fears of pandemics grow, as does the abuse of prescription drugs, pharmaceuticals have become targets for theft.

Piracy on the high seas is rampant. This is of concern, as approximately 90% of the world's cargo travels by sea. Consulting, kidnap and ransom negotiation, and armed security officers are services that can be offered to the shipping industry. Just as the Pinkerton National Detective Agency provided protection for railroads in the nineteenth century, so, too, will contract firms offer services relating to goods in commerce.

Supply chain security efforts are not only contracted out; more and more organizations are taking steps to ensure the protection of their supply chains internally. And theft is only one source of loss for an organization. Any disruption of a supply chain, be it due to strikes, civil unrest, terrorism, or natural disasters, costs an organization money. An increasing number of organizations will have personnel on board who will work on supply chain security. These individuals will perform risk assessments, monitor various aspects of the supply chain, and investigate problems as they occur.

Along with this is an increased emphasis on international crime and loss problems. The International Foundation for Protection Officers has designated persons as Certified Protection Officers in over 50 different countries. ASIS International continues to expand with local chapters being formed in new areas of the world. There are more international security conferences with attendees from private companies, nonprofit organizations, and governments attending.

Identity theft/fraud will continue to grow. New schemes and means of acquiring personal and financial data will evolve. As a result the convergence of physical and IT security will increase. A greater use of biometric access systems for entry into databases is occurring. So, too, are educational initiatives designed to prevent the problems in the first place. Security departments in all organizations will play a greater role in educating the workforce about various types of hazards.

Investigative efforts in the wake of identity theft/fraud are also growing. These investigations require liaison between police and corporate security departments in banks and credit card companies as well as state and federal agencies. Identity theft/fraud is multijurisdictional. Perhaps a historical cycle is repeating itself; outlaws in the American West committed crimes in various jurisdictions, making it difficult to apprehend them. Filling the void were the Pinkertons and other private investigative agencies. Later on, governmental investigative agencies were formed to combat the problem.

References

Bottero, J. (1973). The first law code. In S. G. F. Brandon (Ed.), *Milestones of history: Ancient empires*. New York, NY: Newsweek Books.

Calder, J. D. (1985). Industrial guards in the nineteenth and twentieth centuries: The mean years. *Journal of Security Administration*, 8(2).

Coleman, J. W. (1969). *The Molly Maguire riots: Industrial conflict in the Pennsylvania coal region*. New York, NY: Arno & The New York Times.

Constable, G. (Ed.), (1990). *The old west*. New York, NY: Time-Life Books.

Cote, A., & Bugbee, P. (1988). *Principles of fire protection*. Quincy, MA: National Fire Protection Association.

Fossum, J. (1982). *Labor relations: Development, structure, process*. Dallas, TX: Business Publications, Inc.

Gage, B. (2009). *The day Wall Street exploded: A story of America in its first age of terror*. New York, NY: Oxford University Press.

Hertig, C. A., Fennelly, L. J., & Tyska, L. A. (1998). *Civil liability for security personnel*. Naples, FL: International Foundation for Protection Officers.

Kuykendall, J. (1986). The municipal police detective: An historical analysis. *Criminology*, 24(1), 175–201.

Maggio, E. J. (2009). *Private security in the 21st century: Concepts and applications*. Sudbury, MA: Jones & Bartlett.

Mackay, J. (1996). *Allan Pinkerton: The first private eye*. New York, NY: John Wiley & Sons.

Matthews, L. J. (1990). *Pioneers and trailblazers: Adventures of the old west*. New York, NY: Derrydale.

National Advisory Committee on Criminal Justice Standards and Goals. (1976). *Report of the task force on private security*. Washington, DC.

Ortmeier, P. J. (1999). *Public safety and security administration*. Woburn, Ma: Butterworth-Heinemann.

Peak, K. J. (1997). *Policing in America: Methods, issues, challenges*. Upper Saddle River, NJ: Prentice-Hall.

Purpura, P. P. (2002). *Security and loss prevention: An introduction*. Stoneham, MA: Butterworth-Heinemann.

Velke, J. A. (2004). *The true story of the Baldwin-Felts detective agency*. USA: John Velke.

Resources

The History Channel website has an array of information regarding history. <http://www.history.com/>.

For career information. <http://www.careerclusters.com/>. See the Career Cluster on Law, Public Safety, Corrections and Security.

The International Foundation for Protection Officers also has career information on their Web site at http://www.ifpo.org/. The Foundation offers a variety of instructional courses, memberships, and other resources for protective services professionals.

Additional career information for the retail sector can be obtained by visiting http://www.lpjobs.com/.

For information on security service firms visit http://www.g4s.com/ or http://www.securitas.com/en/. The National Association of Security Companies (http://www.nasco.org/) consists of a dozen or so of the largest contract security firms in the United States and Canada.

Training courses online can be obtained through AST Corporation (astcorp.com). Specialized topics can be studied so that new assignments or jobs can be prepared for. These courses can be used to target individual career interests and earn recertification credits for Certified Protection Officer designates. Other courses are available through ASIS International (asisonline.org).

For more information on fire protection, visit the National Fire Protection Association at nfpa.org.

SECURITY QUIZ

1. Which of these is a type of control force used in Ancient Rome?
   a. Roman chariots
   b. Praetorian guards
   c. Varangian guards
   d. Nubian mercenaries
2. In what year and country did the Peshtigo Fire occur?
   a. 1655, England
   b. 1655, America
   c. 1871, England
   d. 1871, America
3. Railroad police were, and still are, a privately employed police force with full law enforcement authority.
   a. True
   b. False
4. Which of these are reasons that are driving radical Islamic fundamentalism?
   a. Undereducated or miseducated young men who have learned that the United States is "The Great Satan"
   b. A large number of unemployed or underemployed people living in poverty
   c. Charismatic leaders
   d. All of the above
5. What is the importance of the Taft-Hartley Act?
   a. This act ensured collective bargaining rights
   b. This allowed the first labor union to be formed
   c. The U.S. president, via the attorney general, can obtain an injunction against a strike or lockout if a substantial area is affected or national security is threatened
   d. This act forced labor unions to temporarily disband until clearer regulations for labor unions could be put into place
6. Intrusion alarms are point protection only.
   a. True
   b. False
7. Which of these are lessons that have been learned by studying the history of security?
   a. The need for a chain of command
   b. An increase in professionalism
   c. The need for professional training
   d. Both B and C
8. Allan Pinkerton was known for which of the following unique innovations?
   a. Arming officers with handguns
   b. Extensive centralized records
   c. A training camp for his employees
   d. The idea of making prisoners post bail
9. The central alarm/dispatch operation is "the brain" of a security operation, serving as the command, control, and communications center.
   a. True
   b. False

3

Role of the Professional Protection Officer

Kevin Palacios and Christopher A. Hertig

CHAPTER OBJECTIVES

- Provide definition of a protection officer
- Explain levels of protection staff
- Look at the major roles of protection officers
- Discuss the core functions of the protection officer
- Explore prevention, mitigation, and response functions

INTRODUCTION

Life is all about taking risks, and so is business. If businesses were to decide not to take any risks, chances are that they would end up losing more than what they wanted to protect in the first place. Speculative risks allow us to grow and—if in a profit-making organization—gain wealth. Inherent risks where there is no potential for gain (loss events) must be managed. As we move forward in life (and business), the risks we have to take grow bigger and bigger. Every organization needs people to address those inevitable issues … risks.

DEFINITION OF A PROTECTION OFFICER

A professional protection officer is a person whose primary job function is the protection of people and assets. The protection officer is dedicated to protecting organizations, individuals, or various publics (customers, visitors, patients, the general public, etc.). Protection officers work to give everyone peace of mind. The officers focus on safety and security so that others may concentrate on their own primary concerns. Although employees need to focus on their work, they must also be concerned about safety hazards or the actions of criminals. Students in a school are there to learn. Visitors are to conduct whatever business they have in a facility (distribution center, library, park, etc.). Customers in a retail store are to have an enjoyable shopping experience. At the same time each of these groups must have a healthy concern for their own safety and security.

The professional career path of a protection officer (PO) might take him through the operational level (basic protection officer), supervisory level (Certified Protection Officer), and strategic level (management). The change in level and job title represents the addition of responsibilities, but the core of the job description remains the same. A person who chooses a career path in safety or security will never stop being a protection officer. They will never cease to protect people, information, assets, reputation, and the environment surrounding an organization.

The protection officer may be acting as the agent or representative of the landlord. They may not have any arrest authority beyond that of a regular citizen. In other cases they may have some type of police commission with specific arrest authority: they may arrest for certain offenses and/or within a specific area. They may be members of a law enforcement organization whose job assignment is protecting a public figure, coordinating crime prevention activities, or guarding government buildings. Protection officers may be civilian or military, sworn or unsworn. Job titles vary considerably; a protection officer may be referred to in different ways. While the more common titles are "security officer," "security guard," or "retail loss prevention agent," some protection officers may have the title of "police officer," "campus police officer," "special officer," "crime prevention coordinator," "loss prevention officer," "deputy sheriff," "military policeman," and so on. (In many states these titles are controlled by state law. The state statutes should be reviewed in each state to determine the words you may or may not use.)

This protection officer could have full-time, part-time, or occasional employment. Part-time security work is very common in some areas. Many security service firms are largely staffed by part-time personnel. Amusement parks that are open during the summer may employ a large seasonal staff during the busy season. The security department may be managed by a small core of permanent persons. It is not unusual for police officers to work occasional security details. This may be while they are on official police duty or it may be while off-duty for a private employer. Security service firms that provide protection during special events may use a combination of regular staff, part-time probation officers, and a few off-duty police. Sometimes persons in the military are assigned to security work temporarily within the armed forces. In other cases they work for a civilian employer as a security officer or retail loss prevention agent.

> The key is that the person's major focus is on protection of others, tangible assets such as property, or intangible assets such as information or reputation. Legal authority or job title is not the determinant of what a "protection officer" is.

LEVELS OF PROTECTION STAFF

A general framework for the design of security functions within an organization is as follows:

1. **Nonprotection employees.** They need basic information about self-protection and some method to report hazards and threats.
2. **Basic Level Protection Officer.** Includes everyone from the protection team who must follow simple orders, look after activities carried out by nonprotection employees, and work in a low- to mid-threat environment. Basic level officers don't need any previous experience and might (or might not) need operational—basic level—specialized skills. This person needs a basic training, enough to cover foreseeable situations he or she might encounter. Completion of state or provincial training, Officer Basic Training, Basic Protection Officer programs through AST Corporation, Basic Security Officer Training Series through the Professional Security Officer Training Network, 360 Training programs, and so on.

Examples include uniformed guards, doormen, patrol guards, and so on.

3. **Intermediate Level Protection Officer.** The Intermediate Level officer is related to the CPO; it includes everyone who must follow more complex orders, look after processes carried out by protection and non-protection employees, works in a mid- to high-threat

environment, and needs previous experience and specialized skills. This person needs a complete understanding of the various unexpected situations he might encounter. Therefore, training has to be very complete. This is why they should complete both the Certified Protection Officer, (CPO) certification and employer training. Examples include group leaders, personal protection specialists, retail loss prevention officers, radio operators, central alarm station monitors, contract security in high-threat zones, and so on.

4. **Advanced Level Supervisory and Managerial Protection Officers.** This level correlates with the educational and experience level of individuals who have been designated Certified in Security Supervision and Management (CSSM). It includes everyone who must give orders and make decisions regarding personnel. This person must have an understanding of how the full entity (organization) works, people management, leadership, and motivation. This is a line supervision or entry-level management position. This individual must have met all CPO certification requirements in addition to supervisory and management courses. Completion of the Foundation's Security Supervision and Management Program is recommended.

Examples include shift leaders, security supervisors, asset protection team leaders, and so on.

MAJOR ROLES OF PROTECTION OFFICERS

There are several major roles that protection officers fulfill.

1. Management representative
2. Intelligence agent
3. Compliance or enforcement agent
4. Legal consultant

Management representative—the officer acts as an agent, a representative of management to employees, visitors, and others. This is where the officer is concerned with representing the philosophies of management (employer or client). In order to do this effectively, they must thoroughly understand the mission statement of the organization. They need to know what the policies are and the underlying philosophy behind them.

The major emphasis in the management representative role is on positive relations with the various publics with which security departments deal (employees, customers, visitors, patients, vendors, local law enforcement officers, etc.). A solid background in public and customer relations is a necessity. So, too, is diplomacy when dealing with other departments, external agencies, and so on.

Another aspect of this role is educational. Security officers may be very active in educating employees, visitors, students, guests, patients, and so on about safe practices. As the officers grow professionally, they may become increasingly involved in educational efforts. As the security industry becomes more complex, requiring the protection of more intangible assets, this educational role will become more common.

Intelligence agent—in this role the officer collects information for management. The officer must have an understanding of what information is pertinent. They cannot pry into areas that are not managerial concerns related to loss. At the same time, they must be effective at gaining critical loss-related information.

While application of the Waste, Accident, Error, Crime, and Unethical Practices (WAECUP) model is useful, another point to remember is that large problems start as small ones. Issues such as terrorism, crimes, safety hazards, environmental hazards, data loss, major embarrassments, and so on generally begin as unusual or out-of-the-ordinary situations. From there, they mushroom into serious problems.

An old safety concept is that there is often "a leak before a break." That is, a major problem starts out as a small issue. A crack in a wall or floor may mean significant structural damage. It may also indicate extensive erosion of soil underneath the building. It is a small crack, but it may indicate much larger problems.

When investigating crime or misconduct, the principle of expansive significance is important to remember. *"Minor is major."* Minor criminal issues often turn out to be of major significance once they are fully investigated. Major crime problems are resolved through combating minor criminal behavior. The same is true of employee misconduct; it often turns out to be more extensive than it initially appeared.

> In short, professional protection officers must collect intelligence on changes in the environment, unusual situations, or suspicious persons.

Most, but by no means all, of the intelligence agent's role is performed while the officer is on patrol. Officers on patrol should always do the following:

1. **Look up**—see if there are any pipes leaking or water coming from another floor. Check for items improperly stacked. Look for problems with the ceiling or roof.
2. **Look down**—look for problems in footing. Look for spills on the floor from soft drinks, bottles of liquid detergent, liquid from pipes or storage tanks. Look for ice or snow. Look for carpet that is not properly fastened down. Look for tripping hazards such as items left on the floor.
3. **Look around**—check for equipment and machinery that are not turned on or off when they are supposed to be. Verify that all trash collection points are properly maintained. Trash can become a safety or fire hazard. It may also indicate attempts at theft where an employee discards something for later retrieval. It may also indicate things being thrown out that should not be. Trash collection points may relate to any or all parts of the WAECUP model.
4. Whether on patrol or on post, officers should always play the "What-If? Game." This is also known as "constructive daydreaming"

or "mental rehearsal." It is simply a process where officers construct scenarios and review how they would be handled. These could be crime, terrorism, emergency or crisis management concerns, and so on. Safety issues may include slip and falls, structural collapse, persons tripping, or the onset of medical problems (diabetic shock, heat stroke, seizures, heart attacks, etc.).

Playing the "What-If? Game" helps prepare the officer for response to the event as if *they have seen it before.* It also aids in uncovering unforeseen loss events/scenarios. **This is part of the ongoing risk assessment that protection staff perform on a daily basis.** Note that significant issues should be documented. Preferably this documentation is reinforced by personal communication with the appropriate supervisory personnel.

Obviously, proficiency in human and public relations is important to fulfilling the role effectively. Most information comes from people. Officers who are approachable learn more about what is going on in the environment they are protecting. Officers must be approachable but they cannot use the workplace as their social network. They must exhibit interest in people and processes without getting personally, romantically, or financially involved. Professional protection officers engage in short, productive interactions with people. They make every conversation an interview.

Enforcement or compliance agent—this is where the officer enforces the rules of the environment. He or she gains compliance with the rules. The officer must know the rules to be enforced. He or she must be thoroughly conversant with them. The officer modifies and manages human behavior so that the rules established by management are followed.

Sometimes the term "enforcement agent" is too strong, too law enforcement-oriented to work in a security setting such as a hotel, resort, or office complex. Protection officers must be acutely aware of the cultural expectations of their work environment. They must understand the "territory."

In some cases they will have to be very directive; in most they will be more like "compliance ambassadors." Most people simply need to be reminded about what the rules are. Diplomacy and tact are the most frequently used tools of professional protection officers.

There are two major aspects to enforcement:

1. **Procedural**—the "what" of enforcement. The officer must know what to enforce. This includes all rules and procedures. The officer must know what the rules are and review them regularly. Job knowledge in this area is a prerequisite to success. Note that in many instances the confidence displayed by a knowledgeable officer goes a long way toward convincing people to listen to them.

2. **Interpersonal**—the "how" of enforcement. This entails interpersonal skills and communications. Using the proper words, articulating clearly, and speaking at the proper volume and tone are crucial to effective communication. The remainder of human communication—about two-thirds—is nonverbal. Posture, appearance, and gestures come into play here.

Legal consultant—In this role the officer knows the relevant legal standard and applies it. The officer makes legal assessments. These assessments relate to a variety of issues: privacy, search and seizure, property rights, and compliance with administrative laws, and so on.

A related compliance concern is making sure that all organizational rules are being enforced. These rules often originate from professional standards or guidelines. They may also be in place due to insurance company requirements.

Contemporary protection officers are facing increased demands in this area. The role of "legal consultant" is becoming more important. It is also becoming increasingly complex.

Astute security professionals will learn all that they can about laws, standards, and guidelines. They will keep abreast of them and be able to apply them: knowing a regulation is the first step but understanding how to interpret it and apply it to a specific environment is what is really needed. Personnel knowledgeable about this are in demand. Those who wish to move up into leadership roles will jump at every opportunity to learn about the interpretation and application of regulations, standards, and guidelines.

WHAT IT MEANS TO BE A PROFESSIONAL

A professional protection officer distinguishes him- or herself by dedication and commitment. They are not simply performing a job in order to receive compensation. They are instead dedicated to serving their employers, clients, and the community as a whole. Because of their commitment, they stand out from others who may share their same job title and pay grade. They have achieved professional status, a few aspects of which are discussed below:

- **Follows a code of ethics.** The International Foundation for Protection Officer's code of ethics is presented in this book. Each item in the Code contains a key aspect of professionalism.
- **Shares a common history with his colleagues.** A glimpse of the professional history shared with other protection officers is displayed in various chapters throughout this text. A common history creates a bond between officers.
- **Supports and works with colleagues.** A professional protection officer respects and works with others. Officers analyze various problems and help each other address them. Effecting and maintaining productive relationships with colleagues is very important.
- **Owns a common body of knowledge.** The different chapters of this book cover the varied aspects that a contemporary protection officer must master in order to succeed in an

ever-changing world. Professional protection officers have a foundation of professional knowledge in topics such as physical security, investigation, crisis management, safety, and so on.

- **Makes his or her own decisions**. Uses discretionary judgment to solve problems. Figures out how to address certain situations and takes the appropriate action. While an entry-level police or security officer must abide by their employer or client's directions, they do act independently.
- **Is loss conscious**. Professional protection officers look for hazards—constantly. Officers continually ponder the consequences of loss events (fires, accidents, terrorist attacks, errors, etc.). They think in terms of the impact of occurrence. This separates them from practitioners in other disciplines.

A professional can't just be appointed. A professional is a person who has accepted his responsibility and embraces it with pride. Professionals have a positive outlook. Professionals know their limits, but are always looking to expand them. They learn and grow from experience, training, and education. Growth is an ongoing process; it never stops.

> One does not "be" a professional protection officer.
> One must "become" a professional protection officer.

In order to accomplish his duties, the protection officer must also be *competent*; this means that the officer must have the proper balance of knowledge, skills, and attitude. Continuous professional development through education, training, and experience is necessary to become competent. Education gives one knowledge; training provides a means of developing skills. Experience expands upon and refines those skills and helps to develop one's abilities. Attitude ties knowledge, skills, and abilities together.

A professional protection officer must also demand the authority and tools needed to accomplish his responsibilities.

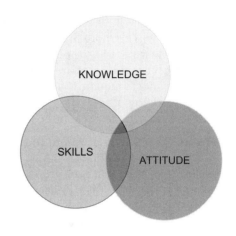

Protection Officer as an Agent

Protection officers are the employees or the agents of property owners and managers. These can be the employer of the officer or the client of the officer's employer in the case of a security service firm. As agents, officers act in the interest of the owners and managers. They also represent owners and managers of their organizations in several different ways. Every decision a protection officer makes reflects on the organization he represents. A common example is that patrol officers are often the only people on the premises during evenings and weekends. Some people have referred to this as the security officer being the "after-hours Chairman of the Board."

In a managerial position, the protection officer might have a specific role in part of a security process, or a much broader loss control role. The concept of loss control goes way beyond physical and logical security. A future trend is to expand loss control functions to coordinate enterprise-wide risk management identified as the health, safety, security, environment, and quality process (HSSEQ).

The role of the protection officer is to prevent, mitigate, and respond to intentionally created loss event occurrences as well as accidental incidents.

Of course, while fulfilling ever broader duties, the protection officer must always prioritize his attention to the most critical resources to be protected. These are (in order of priority):

- **PEOPLE.** Employees, agents, third-party workers, customers, visitors
- **INFORMATION.** Physical and digital records, proprietary info, other information to maintain confidentiality, integrity, and availability
- **ASSETS.** Those that the organization owns, manages, maintains, controls, or is responsible for (facilities, goods, assets of monetary value)
- **REPUTATION.** Hard-earned public image; everything that contributes to the desired positioning of the organization
- **ENVIRONMENT.** Surrounding the organization, natural, community, stakeholders' interests, social responsibility

Core Functions

The protection officer must become a valuable member of the organization; his participation in systems, processes, and activities must always add value. The value added by a protection officer's performance is measured in the level of improvement that his work brings into the organization's protective process and objectives:

- Vigilance of better practices and recommend state-of-the-art standards (in addition to the organization's regulator-specific requirements)
- Improving policies, procedures, job-specific instructions (not just following them)
- Always reporting adequately and keeping adequate records

It is widely accepted that every process of an organization must fulfill a *Plan-Do-Check-Act* *Cycle* (Brown & Blackmon, 2001); the protection process is no exception:

- **PLAN—Preventative Functions.** The cycle begins by planning protective measures BEFORE they are performed.
- **DO—Mitigation Functions.** All protective measures performed DURING daily operations.
- **CHECK—Loss Event.** Verification of protective systems takes place during loss events, but the effectiveness of a system could also be verified by a protection officer during audits and inspections.
- **ACT—Response Functions.** AFTER an emergency arises, the officer must respond accordingly, bring all operations back to normal, and provide the cycle with the necessary feedback.

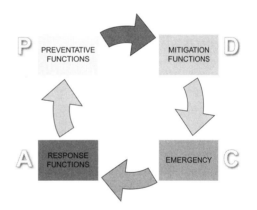

Simply stated, in any given organization, the core function of the protection officer is to ensure the continuity of the protective cycle; to prevent all possible **hazards** from becoming **threats**, to mitigate threats in order to decrease the **probability** and potential **consequences** of its occurrence, but also to respond adequately and timely to all types of loss events in order to regain control of the situation while preventing **future** occurrences (beginning of a new-improved cycle).

PREVENTATIVE FUNCTIONS

Prevention includes (but is not limited to) all actions taken before active protection measures are performed. These functions are easily remembered with the four Is:

- Investigate (Preventative and reconstructive investigations)
- Identify (Hazards and risk factors—assess risks)
- Induce (Communicate and train)
- Integrate (Countermeasures to treat risk)

MITIGATION FUNCTIONS

During an actual protection task, an adequate mix of procedures, equipment, and people reduces probability and consequences of risk. Mitigation functions are remembered with the 4 Ds:

- Dissuade (Potential aggressors)
- Detect (Hazards that are being activated)
- Delay (Separate physically or delay the aggressor from the objective)
- Detain (Stop the hazard)

RESPONSE FUNCTIONS

Ideally, risk has been mitigated before it creates loss. In cases where this has not happened, it is necessary to respond.

After a loss event occurs, all efforts must focus not only on bringing the situation back to normal but to **improving** the previous situation by **vaccinating** the organization from that, or a similar risk. Response functions are easy to remember if we use the four Rs:

- React (Act immediately in accordance with established procedures)
- Resume (Gain control of the situation)

- Reinitiate (Start operations with a view to bringing them to the normal level)
- Recuperate (Wholly recuperate the operative level and vaccinate from that risk)

Examples of protection cycles performed by the various levels of protection officers are outlined below.

BASIC PROTECTION OFFICER

- A patrol officer in a shopping center tours the facility to create an "offender-hostile" but "customer-friendly" environment. During his tour he must identify hazards and risk factors (using checklists or his own judgment). While on patrol he sees some liquid spilled on the floor and judges that this represents a fall risk **(PREVENTION)**.
- He secures the area according to his training and procedures, and stays on the spot until someone competent (i.e., general services) arrives to fix it **(MITIGATION)**.
- He reports all actions taken and recommends improvements in procedures to prevent future unsafe conditions **(RESPONSE)**.

INTERMEDIATE PROTECTION OFFICER

- A security supervisor receives reports that indicate some employees are suspiciously wandering around the company trash containers after working hours. The containers are in the back of the building. The supervisor identifies this as a theft-through-garbage risk **(PREVENTION)**.
- Starting immediately, she assigns a guard to temporarily patrol that area and gives him specific orders, explaining the nature of the risk and signs of the threat to identify,

how to act, and when to report. At the same time, the supervisor organizes a talk to employees given by the local police about crime awareness and the effects of crime in the organization (MITIGATION).

- The supervisor then initiates an internal investigation while reporting this risk to management. She recommends changes in **procedures** (employees will have to exit the premises through the front door), **equipment** (garbage containment area needs to be fenced in), and **people** (recommends changing the patrol procedures to include a more thorough check of the trash area) (RESPONSE).

ADVANCED PROTECTION OFFICER

- It has been reported to the Health, Safety, Security, and Environmental Quality manager of a petrochemical facility that someone is stealing empty containers from hazardous materials. He identifies this as a health and environmental threat, since inhabitants of poor neighborhoods in the surrounding area might be using them to store water for washing and cooking (PREVENTION).
- After assessing the risk, he sets up an awareness campaign to train the surrounding neighbors of the threat the empty containers pose. The company gives away new containers to these people, while profiting from a positive Socially Responsible Capital Campaign (goodwill from the villagers) (MITIGATE).
- As part of the campaign, the firm arranges for doctors from the closest public hospital to measure levels of contamination among villagers and the nearby river. It also

contracts to sell all empty containers of hazardous materials to a recycling plant that could treat them accordingly—this funds the whole campaign. The company revises its liability insurance to include this newly discovered risk while negotiating a premium reduction based on the calculated associated value of potential loss (RESPONSE).

Around the Globe

Financial austerity and competition among organizations show the importance of loss prevention efforts to all sizes of organizations around the globe. This has also pushed commercial organizations to seek new markets and resources in different areas of the world. Some organizations with high-risk appetites are venturing into historically inhospitable environments. Protection officers at these firms are facing broader language and cultural challenges.

Laws and regulations vary greatly in different regions of the world. Nevertheless, huge efforts are taking place to standardize procedures, training, and risk management models all over the world.

SUMMARY

A professional protection officer is dedicated to protecting people, information, physical assets, reputation and the environment surrounding organizations. As a professional, the officer follows a code of ethics, shares a common history with his colleagues, and owns a common body of knowledge.

The titles and designations given to protection officers may be insufficient when we need to express the tasks these dedicated men and women perform.

EMERGING TRENDS

Despite the fact that the basic role of all protection officers remains the same, the duties performed by protection officers are becoming increasingly specialized: health care protection, retail loss prevention, campus security, school security (elementary to secondary grades), shopping center security, high-rise building protection, banking security, and so on. These specialties, or vertical markets, continue to evolve. Some of the major contract agencies have coursework tailored to particular sectors: these providers know full well that they must take every means possible of meeting their clients' specific needs. The American Society for Industrial Security International also has a large number of councils devoted to specialty areas. In addition, there are professional associations such as the International Association of Campus Law Enforcement Administrators, the International Foundation for Cultural Property Protection, and the International Association of Healthcare Security and Safety that cater to specific sectors.

Convergence between physical and logical security is well advanced, and convergence with other risk management functions within the organizations (health, environment, safety, and quality) are quickly gaining momentum; this and the increased use of technology have demanded a new breed of highly trained/highly educated protection officers (especially at the supervisory and management levels).

Protection officers are moving into more of a leadership/ambassadorial role. While many are entry-level employees, they are also coordinators. They design and develop programs in safety and security. They are more like professionals in that they use discriminating judgment, determining their own course of action rather than being told what to do by superiors.

They continue to utilize additional technology and this technological prowess is giving them a more professional appearance. So, too, is the carrying of weapons. Contemporary protection officers are more likely to have some type of weaponry than in the past. This may not be firearms; it is usually pepper spray or some other nonlethal weapon.

There are also heavily armed protection officers in areas of the world where civil strife and warfare prevail. Hence, there is a more military emphasis than ever before. This trend will continue as energy exploration moves into dangerous areas and people's demand for security (employees at these locations) increases.

There is also a greater need for effective liaison with police, fire, emergency medical, and military organizations. Regional disasters such as massive snow storms, earthquakes, or hurricanes require close cooperation. So, too, does the provision of security at major public events: there are 50 or more different organizations providing security at the Super Bowl in the United States.

The issue of training continues to be a concern. While on paper it may appear as though security personnel are being trained, closer inspection reveals that this is often not the case. Sometimes in contract security there is a major disconnect between the corporate policy on training and what actually happens in the field. Maggio (2009) cites a 2005 study in New York City in which it was found that most security personnel reported having less training than was required. Moreover, the training that was given failed to emphasize terrorism or working with police or firefighters.

One possible solution to the training dilemma is state or provincial mandates. A state or province may require security officers to have a certain amount of training and to be licensed. Unfortunately, it takes a long time to get legislation enacted. Once it is in place the training is generally minimal. Also, the regulations rarely cover all protection officers; most state/provincial laws only cover contract security personnel.

There are some positives to this, however. In the United Kingdom, the Security Industry Authority is improving regulations for door supervisors and others. There are inspections being done to insure that protection officers in clubs are licensed. In California and Ontario, both contract and proprietary security personnel are regulated. As of this writing, the province of Alberta is also moving in that direction.

Outsourcing of police services to private contract firms continues. While public police may espouse the principles of community policing, they may not be able to practice it. The reality is that public police have budgetary concerns and limited resources. There is a movement in some areas toward having private security personnel perform order maintenance and quality-of-life patrols. A security service firm may be better equipped to do this in large shopping centers, parks, or housing developments. The public police can then focus more on investigations, drug enforcement, and the response to felonious behavior.

This shift also triggers an evolution of the protection officer from being a "private security" officer to becoming something of a public servant. Such a role may create confusion in the mind of the officer. Only thorough education, training, and highly structured socialization will prevent role confusion.

Another driver of this trend is the growth of security service providers. Some of these companies are quite large and operate internationally. Others are not as large or international but may have a major share of a local or regional market. Either scenario may lead to monopolization. Once this happens, the client has limited choice in selecting a security service provider. Should this occur, there may be both an increase in costs and a degradation of service.

University degrees and internationally recognized professional certifications, such as the ones awarded by the International Foundation for Protection Officers and ASIS International, are in great demand among quality-conscious employers all around the globe. This trend will continue as society places more emphasis on obtaining credentials.

While degrees and professional certifications are key components of professionalism, so, too, are guidelines and standards. Voluntary guidelines or compulsory standards developed by professional associations are having a major impact on the practice of protection. At the present time, standards and guidelines are being developed on an array of topics such as the Private Security Officer Selection and Training Guideline by ASIS International. This guideline establishes minimum criteria for selecting and training security officers. It is of obvious use to employers and contract agencies. It may also assist regulatory bodies in establishing state or provincial licensing requirements. (http://www.asisonline.org/guidelines/inprogress_published.htm. Retrieved October 13, 2009). In addition to employers, contractors, and governmental agencies, insurance carriers can use standards and guidelines. Policyholders may receive a premium reduction for meeting a guideline or standard.

Obviously, standards and guidelines will have a major impact on the practice of protection over time. And the professional protection officer is a key factor in compliance.

References

Brown, S., & Blackmon, K. (2001). *Operations management: Policy, practice and performance improvement*. Woburn, MA: Butterworth-Heinemann.

Maggio, E. J. (2009). *Private security in the 21st century: Concepts and applications*. Sudbury, MA: Jones & Bartlett.

Resources

Training courses online can be obtained through AST Corporation (http://www.astcorp.com). There are a wide variety of courses! Specialized topics can be studied to prepare for new assignments or jobs. These courses can be used to target individual career interests and earn recertification credits for Certified Protection Officer designates.

360 Training has a series of online instructional programs for security personnel. 360 specializes in continuous learning and recertification. Visit http://www.360training.com/.

ASIS International publishes the Protection of Assets Manual, a comprehensive online reference guide. The POA is the primary text for the Certified Protection Professional designation. It contains several chapters relating to the role of the protection officer, including Security Officer Training and Private Policing in Public Environments. Go to http://www.asisonline.org or http://www.protectionofassets.com/PDFSamples/POA_TableByVolume_Oct2008.pdf.

Butterworth-Heinemann is the premier publisher of security texts. There is a wide array of titles available on physical security, investigation, emergency management, and so on. Visit http://www.elsevierdirect.com/index.jsp.

SECURITY QUIZ

1. Which of the following best describes a protection officer?
   a. A man or a woman hired to look after an entrance door
   b. A man or a woman who concentrates on safety and security while others perform various tasks
   c. A man or a woman in charge of welcoming visitors and providing them with information
   d. A man or a woman hired to dissuade potential trespassers

2. The career path of a protection officer might take him through:
   a. Operational level
   b. Supervisory level
   c. Management level
   d. All the above

3. The Professional Protection Officer has some essential characteristics. Which of the following is *not* one of them?
   a. Follows a code of ethics
   b. Shares a common history
   c. Masters the use of lethal and non-lethal weapons
   d. Owns a common body of knowledge

4. Competency can be demonstrated through professional certifications, and consists of an adequate balance of three characteristics. Which of the following is *not* one of those?
   a. Attitude
   b. Skills
   c. Communication
   d. Knowledge

5. Every decision that a protection officer makes reflects on the organization he or she represents; for instance, patrol officers often times are the only people on the premises (during night and weekends). Which of the following tasks is most unusual to a basic protection officer?
   a. Collect intelligence on changes, unusual situations, or suspicious persons
   b. Maintain compliance with organizational policies
   c. Legal consultant role
   d. Interacting with the public in the environment

6. The basic role of the protection officer is to prevent, mitigate, and respond to:
   a. Intentionally created risks (security)
   b. Accidental and unintentional risks (safety, health, environment, and quality)
   c. Any and all risks in the WAECUP model
   d. None of the above

7. There are five types of critical resources to be protected; which of the following is *not* one of those?
   a. Time
   b. Information
   c. People
   d. Reputation

8. The value added by a protection officer's performance is measured in the level of improvement that his work brings into the organization's protective process and objectives. Examples of this can include:
   a. Vigilance of better practices and recommends state of the art standards

b. Always reporting adequately and keeping adequate records

c. Improving policies, procedures, job-specific instructions

d. All of the above

9. All actions taken before active protection measures are performed can be included in the preventative functions. Which of the following is not one of those actions?

    a. Preventative investigations

    b. Identification of hazards and risk factors

    c. Induction training

    d. Separate physically or in time the aggressor from the objective

10. One of the steps taken during response functions performed by protection officers is recovery. Which of the following is an example of it?

    a. Assets not damaged during a fire are quickly moved into a secure location

    b. A claim is filed with an insurance company

    c. Video footage from a bank robbery is given to local police

    d. All the above

4

The Protection Officer as a Leader

Franklin R. Timmons and
Scott A. Watson

CHAPTER OBJECTIVES

- Compare and contrast the words "management" and "leadership"
- List and explain 10 expectations of leaders
- Identify and explain three critical leadership skills
- List four key interpersonal communication skills and explain their importance

INTRODUCTION

In the course of this chapter, we will discuss the basic principles, skills, and characteristics of leadership. To understand leadership, we need to establish from the beginning that leaders and supervisors/managers are not one and the same. Our expectation would be that every supervisor/manager is a leader, but every leader is not necessarily tasked with direct line supervision.

Simply stated, a leader is anyone who *influences the willing actions of others in support of organizational goals and processes*. Note the word "influences" in this definition. A leader derives his or her power from the ability to inspire others to willingly follow a process or recommended course of action in support of organizational goals and objectives. Since leaders are not necessarily charged and empowered with direct authority, the "willingly" part of the definition is of critical importance. In contrast, a manager or supervisor is charged and empowered with direct authority; however, without solid leadership skills, the manager will be ineffective in meeting organizational goals and objectives (Hertig, McGough, & Smith, 2008; Johnson, 2005; Sennewald, 1985).

> ### Who should study and develop leadership skills?
>
> 1. **Managers and Supervisors:** Those entrusted with management and supervisory roles have, by virtue of their acceptance of their position, a responsibility to study and develop leadership skills.
> 2. **Team Members:** Those who wish to take on the added responsibility of influencing their

own team, and the greater organization they serve, should study and develop leadership skills.

3. **High Potential:** Those with high leadership potential should be encouraged to study the principles of leadership in order to make a career decision about their long-term goals.

It is also important to keep in mind that not everyone desires to be a leader, and that's okay. There are a great many people who are both content and effective in their roles as a team member. Still, a manager or supervisor should never assume that one is content; lines of communication need to remain open and the question needs to be asked (Watson, 2007).

DO YOU REALLY WANT TO BE A LEADER?

To some people, the idea of being a leader sounds glamorous because they immediately think of exerting influence over a team, being consulted about important decisions, and being recognized as indispensible to the organization. Indeed, leaders experience many of these benefits, but they come at a high price.

The legendary football coach Vince Lombardi said, "Leaders aren't born; they are made. And they are made just like anything else, through hard work. And that's the price we'll have to pay to achieve that goal, or any goal."

The decision to develop leadership skills and assume a role of influence within an organization should not be taken lightly. Leadership involves long-term commitment and hard work without an immediate payoff. Leadership is not about position or privilege and often involves putting one's self-interest below that of the team. Before embarking on the journey to become a leader, it is wise to answer the following ten questions about, and for, yourself:

1. Do you have a sense of mission that is greater than your own personal interests?
2. Are ethics more important to you than your career?
3. Do you have a desire to help people solve both work-related and personal problems?
4. Do you care about people enough to constructively challenge them when they are engaged in activities that are hurtful to themselves, others, or the organization?
5. Do you readily accept responsibility for your own mistakes?
6. Are you willing to accept responsibility for the mistakes of others who are following your lead?
7. Can you see potential in others?
8. Are you willing to develop potential in others?
9. Do you handle setbacks well?
10. Are you patient?

1. **Yes:** If you can answer "yes" to all of the above questions, then you should consider developing leadership skills.
2. **I'm not sure:** If you answered "I'm not sure," then you owe it to the organization you serve and yourself to study leadership in order to fully answer those questions.
3. **No:** If you answered "no" to most of the questions, then, at this point in your life, you probably wouldn't be content or effective in a leadership role.

Coach Lombardi was right; leadership is hard work!

As previously stated, leadership isn't for everyone and many people do not seek out leadership positions. Still, the seasons of a person's life change and with time, so, too, can one's desire to become a leader. Leaving oneself open to the possibility of becoming a leader is a wise choice, as some of the most effective leaders are sometimes the most reluctant to assume those roles (Hertig et al., 2008; Johnson, 2005; Sennewald, 1985; Watson, 2007).

TEAM MEMBER SKILLS: THE FOUNDATION OF LEADERSHIP

If you make the decision that becoming a leader is a worthwhile goal, the hard work begins as a team member. As team members, we all have certain understood and implied responsibilities. Much of what we do is grounded in the roles and expectations set forth by the organization we serve, but other characteristics include the values that we, as team members, possess. You cannot be an effective leader until you have first met the basic tenets of being an effective team member. Some very important attributes of being an effective team member are:

1. Communicate effectively; in fact, over-communicate.
2. Be aware of error traps in the workplace or daily work processes.
3. Ensure that firewalls or protection is in place to address the error traps.
4. Be motivated to improve operations; always strive for excellence.
5. Continuously identify ways to improve human performance.
6. Advise management when problems exist in performing work.
7. Have a questioning and supportive attitude as well as a willingness to be a proactive problem solver.
8. Embrace and practice the STAR concept (Stop, Think, Act, Review).
9. Strive for success but have a plan for failure. Continually ask, "What if?"
10. Take the time required to do the job right the first time.

(U.S. Department of Energy, 2009)

EXPECTATIONS OF LEADERS

Now that we understand what it takes to be an effective employee, let's examine what additional expectations we have of leaders. Remember, as we previously stated, a leader is any individual who *influences the willing actions of others in support of organizational goals and processes.*

Additional traits that can characterize a leader in any organization include:

1. Encourages open communication.
2. Advocates teamwork, to eliminate error traps, and strengthen firewalls.
3. Seeks out and eliminates organizational weaknesses that foster error traps.
4. Reinforces desired work behaviors.
5. Knows the importance of preventing error traps.
6. Challenges atmospheres that support complacency.
7. Works to clarify organizational and individual employee issues.
8. Champions "across the board" adherence to the highest standards.
9. Ensures all workers fully understand the potential consequences of unsafe behavior.
10. Minimizes unfamiliarity among members of the team.

Leadership involves the ability to understand the goals of the organization we serve. For the sake of our chapter, let's refer to everyone outside our sphere of influence as our customer. Our clients, our managers and supervisors, our peers and our community, no matter who that may be, are our customers. Once we understand the goals and objectives of our customers, then we can better serve their needs (Hertig et al., 2008; Johnson, 2005; Sennewald, 1985; Watson, 2007).

THREE CRITICAL LEADERSHIP SKILLS

The development of leadership skills is a lifelong process, so a complete list and detailed explanation of all the skill sets required for effective leadership could fill several libraries. What follows is an overview of three broad categories of practice that all leaders should study and strive to master.

Practice 1: Ethics. This is the cornerstone of the protection field. The organizations we serve entrust us to protect their most valuable assets. As a professional protection officer, you are likely to have access to secure areas of the facility in which you work. You are also likely to have access to confidential information, knowledge of specific security vulnerabilities, and the trust of individuals within the organization. As a result of this expanded access, knowledge, and trust, we in the protection field are held to a higher standard of behavior than the population at large.

cognizant, not only of what constitutes violations of law and organizational policy but also what *appears* to violate such laws and policies. Only by doing so can the protection officer avoid doing wrong, while engendering confidence in those he or she serves (Department of the Army, 2006; Hertig et al., 2008; Johnson, 2005; Sennewald, 1985; Watson, 2007).

Practice 2: Mission Focus. Organizations exist for a purpose. This purpose is the organization's mission or reason for existence. The role of the security department is to provide professional protective services that allow the organization to accomplish its mission. The role of the protection officer is to ensure that the security department accomplishes its mission to serve the organization. Those who wish to be leaders in the protection field must be familiar with the organization's mission and how the security department contributes to accomplishing it.

Ethics goes beyond the following concepts:

1. **Following Organizational Rules:** It is not enough for a protection officer to simply refrain from violating organizational rules; everyone is supposed to follow the rules. Since the professional protection officer is expected to enforce rules, following those same rules is expected as a matter of course.
2. **Complying with Laws:** It is not enough for the protection officer to simply comply with laws. Laws are, after all, minimal standards of behavior expected by the society at large. A protection officer should not only comply with legal requirements but also should strive to go above and beyond the minimal standards provided by law.

The Professional Protection Officer's quest to be mission oriented should include an understanding of the following:

1. The organization's mission.
2. Who the organization serves.
3. The organization's values.
4. The history of the organization.
5. The organization's structure.
6. The geographic area and economic climate in which the organization operates.
7. The image of the organization.
8. The security department's role in the organization.
9. The security department's organizational structure.
10. His or her own role in accomplishing the mission.

(U.S. Department of the Army, 2006; Watson, 2007)

Practically speaking then, ethics both encompass and surpass the minimal standards of law and the basic expectations of the organizations we serve. A protection officer should always be

Practice 3: Interpersonal Communication. Organizations consist of groups of people all working together under a common structure for a common purpose. An ability to understand and relate to people is a key element in effective leadership because it enables the leader to influence others to accomplish organizational and departmental missions.

There are four basic communication skills needed of every leader: verbal, nonverbal, listening, and writing (Figure 4-1). The optimal way to communicate is face-to-face. This allows both the sender and the receiver of information to engage in real-time verbal and nonverbal analysis. It also allows for clarification and immediate feedback.

1. **Verbal Communication:** Verbal communication is comprised of the spoken word. It is very important because it allows us to:
   a. Express ourselves in words.
   b. Ask questions and clarify nonverbal communication actions.
   c. Provide feedback to the listener.
2. **Nonverbal Communication:** Nonverbal communication is just that; communicating with your body or emotions. Some experts say that we do the vast majority of our communicating nonverbally. No matter how you or another individual communicates nonverbally, clarification is critical in checking for understanding. A nonverbal message has meaning, just as a verbal one does. The content is more difficult to "read," but it is just as important. Many actions are interpreted with specific feelings, whether or not those feelings were meant to be conveyed by the sender. By asking for clarification, misunderstandings can be kept to a minimum.
3. **Listening Skills:** Listening is oftentimes the most overlooked aspect of communication. Although more than half of our communicating time is spent listening, compared to other types of communication, we spend a small amount of time learning how to listen effectively or actively. In order to improve your listening skills, listen actively, devoting all of your concentration to the task. In fact, to be a good leader, we must be a good listener. We must understand what the expectations really are and we must align our roles and responsibilities to meet those expectations. Comprehension is the primary goal of listening. We need to understand the message being sent before we can process the information, evaluate it, and provide a response. **NOTE:** If at any time, during this process, you get confusing information—ask for clarification!
4. **Writing Skills:** Writing is another key element in communication and a skill developed over a lifetime. As a professional protection officer you may find yourself writing incident reports, daily logs, email communications, proposals, training programs, statements, security survey reports, and annual reports along with a host of other correspondence. There are many ways to enhance one's writing capability but the best teacher is direct experience and professional feedback from peers, managers, supervisors, and customers.

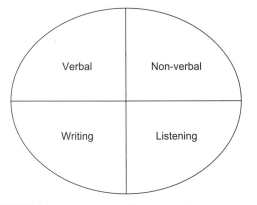

FIGURE 4-1   Four key areas of interpersonal communication.

Over time, writing tends to improve, so don't be discouraged if this is a weak area for you.

The protection officer who strives to maintain the highest standards of ethics, constantly remains aligned with departmental and organizational mission, develops solid interpersonal communications skills, and will make steady progress in developing leadership skills (U.S. Department of the Army, 2006; Elgin, 1980; Sennewald, 1985).

TEN STEPS TO BECOMING AN EFFECTIVE LEADER

The following 10 steps or precepts are provided as a guideline for the serious student of leadership.

1. **Be the Leader You Would Want to Follow:** Remember our definition of leadership: any individual who *influences the willing actions of others in support of organizational goals and processes.* Ask yourself, "What type of leader would I be willing to follow?" Once you answer that question, strive to be that leader!

2. **Accept That Conflict Is a Normal and Healthy Part of Growth:** Remember that conflict is inevitable in all areas of human endeavor. While some conflicts can have negative effects, the absence of conflict would mean that everything would always stay the same and improvement would never occur. When engaged in a conflict, ask yourself, "What progress can be made by actively listening to another point of view?"

3. **Know Yourself and Know Others:** A leader has to be completely honest about his or her strengths and weaknesses as well as the strengths and weaknesses of others. Only by doing so can the leader make significant progress toward accomplishing both the departmental and organizational goals. Train yourself to be constantly assessing your strengths, weaknesses, and motivations, as well as those of others around you.

4. **Continually Assess the Situation:** Life moves quickly and situations can change instantly. As a professional protection officer and a leader, you must prepare for whatever is coming next. This can only be accomplished by training yourself to develop and maintain situational awareness.

5. **Remember What Is Truly Important:** As mentioned earlier, ethics is the cornerstone of the protection field and an organization's mission is its reason for existence. Always keep in mind that ethics is more important than a specific job; your career is more important than a specific position and the mission is more important than pet projects or short-term gains. Remembering what is truly important will help you keep perspective.

6. **Take Action:** A leader must know when to act and when to wait. Failure to act, especially in the protection field, can be very costly.

7. **Position Yourself and Your Organization Well:** A leader must position him- or herself to be ready to take advantage of opportunities when they arise. As you move forward in any situation always be aware of potential opportunities and take the time to position yourself and your team so that you can capitalize on them when they arise.

8. **Be Adaptable:** It is easy to get hung up on ideas, but not all ideas are acceptable to the organizations we serve, nor are all ideas workable. Always be ready to adapt your plans to suit the needs of the organization. Doing so will allow you to overcome obstacles quickly and be more effective in the long run.

9. **Avoid Predictability:** The protection field requires structure and accountability, but it also requires staying one step ahead of situations and those who would victimize the people or organizations we serve.

10. **Collect and Use Information:** Information is the lifeblood of an organization and affects the functioning of an effective protection team. As a leader, it is important to collect and properly use information about the organization, threats, vulnerabilities, and a host of other matters. By being mission-focused and honing the interpersonal skills necessary to develop good relationships, the professional protection officer will find more sources of information and, in turn, be a more effective leader.

These 10 steps or precepts, if worked on, will help the professional protection officer in developing solid leadership skills (Watson, 2007).

THE LEADER AS AN AGENT OF CHANGE

As the last link between senior management and line employees or customers, it is the leader's job to assist in the implementation of change. To do this, certain obstacles must be overcome. There are several strategies for reducing resistance to change. Much resistance to change comes from lack of trust or people having to operate outside their comfort zone.

Resistance can sometimes be overcome or the impact lessened if the following are completed:

1. Fully explain the upcoming changes.
2. Make certain employees or customers fully understand the change.
3. When possible, discuss why the change is required.
4. Identify and discuss the possible effects with employees or customers.
5. Answer questions, or take the information and follow-up if you don't know the answer.
6. Build trust with your employees; they will better accept the change.
7. Be honest and be consistent.

Change can potentially create fear in the organization and paranoia in the minds of executives and managers hired to protect the status quo. Change not only drives fear, it also drives the fact that more effort is required to complete the change. This entire process means moving outside the individuals' comfort zone. Many people believe in the saying "don't rock the boat." An important point to consider is that the boat is already rocking. The question is, do we steer the organization (boat) into the wave or do we allow the organization to be broadsided? A key element to help any organization better deal with the effects of change is TRUST.

Trust can't be purchased. It is a house that must be built one brick at a time. It opens the door to the path for success. Trust is earned through the following simple steps:

- **Honesty**—Can an employee/customer believe what you say?
- **Integrity**—Can an employee/customer believe you will keep your promise?
- **Openness**—Can employees/customers believe that you will share what you know?

(Hertig et al., 2008; Johnson, 2005)

PITFALLS OF LEADERSHIP

Oftentimes, people who see themselves as leaders think that others will follow them without question. Leaders must understand that leading is more about serving, negotiating, motivating, communicating, and actively listening than the physical act of leading. Incorrectly assessing a situation and trying to be overly persuasive or dominant can bring disaster to a leader, especially one who has just assumed that role.

Some pitfalls that a leader should recognize and consider are as follows:

1. Leading is more about achieving a shared goal, not managing or supervising people.
2. A leader has to always display confidence, trustworthiness, and truth. In other words,

characteristics that make someone want to follow them.

3. Many times, other employees/customers have the answers or at least some thoughts. Leaders need to be active listeners.
4. Make certain the elements of leadership are aligned with corporate or customer goals and desires.

(Hertig et al., 2008; Johnson, 2005; Sennewald, 1985; Watson, 2007)

CONCLUSION

A leader is any individual who *influences the willing actions of others in support of organizational goals and processes.* While leadership roles can be rewarding, they come at the high cost of consistent hard work and dedication, often without a discernible return on investment. Those who wish to assume leadership positions in the protection field must be prepared to put the needs of the team above their own. They must exercise the highest standards of ethics, remain mission-focused, and develop the solid interpersonal skills necessary to motivate others (Hertig et al., 2008; Johnson, 2005; Sennewald, 1985).

References

Elgin, S. H. (1980). *The gentle art of verbal self defense.* Upper Saddle River, NJ: Prentice Hall.

Hertig, C. A., McGough, M., & Smith, S. R. (2008). Leadership for protection professionals. In S. J. Davies & C. A. Hertig (Eds.), *Security supervision and management* (3rd ed.) (pp. 219–239). Burlington, MA: Elsevier.

Johnson, B. R. (2005). *Principles of security management.* Upper Saddle River, NJ: Prentice Hall.

Sennewald, C. A. (1985). *Effective security management* (2nd ed.). Newton, MA: Butterworth-Heinemann.

U.S. Department of the Army. (2006). *FM 22 army leadership competent, confident, and agile.* Retrieved August 27, 2009, from <http://greerfoundation.org/CouncilofPromisingLeaders.html>.

U.S. Department of Energy (2009). *Human performance improvement handbook; Volume 2: Human performance tools for individuals, work teams and management.* Retrieved

August 27, 2009, from <http://www.hss.doe.gov/nuclearsafety/ns/techstds/standard/hdbk1028/doe-hdbk-1028-2009_volume2.pdf>.

Watson, S. A. (2007). *The art of war for security managers; ten steps to enhance your organizational effectiveness.* Burlington, MA: Elsevier.

Resources

Bolton, R. B. (1979). *People skills: How to assert yourself, listen to others and resolve conflicts.* New York, NY: Simon & Schuster.

Elgin, S. H. (1993). *The gentle art of written verbal self defense: How to write your way out of life's delicate situations.* Upper Saddle River, NJ: Prentice Hall.

Fujishin, R. (1993). *Discovering the leader within; running small groups successfully.* San Francisco, CA: Acadia Books.

Sawyer, R. D., & Tzu, S. (1994). *The art of war.* Boulder, CO: Westview Press Inc.

SECURITY QUIZ

1. Leaders and supervisors are not one and the same. Our expectation is that every supervisor is a leader but not every leader is necessarily a supervisor.
   a. True
   b. False
2. The key for a supervisor to get anyone to do anything is to:
   a. Threaten them to do it
   b. Get them to want to do it
   c. Bribe them to do it
   d. None of the above
3. Leadership is not about self-interest; it is about being other-person-centered. Thus, before embarking on a mission to become a leader, one should conduct a self-examination in all the following ways, except to:
   a. Assure that no one in the group will be able to pass you up and become your boss
   b. Make ethics more important than your career
   c. Have a deep desire to help others solve both work-related and personal problems
   d. Find the potential in subordinates and push those subordinates to self-actualize

4. An effective team member will display the following attributes:
   a. Continuously identify ways to improve human performance
   b. Advise upline management when problems exist in work performance
   c. Be motivated to improve operations and always strive for excellence
   d. All the above

5. Traits that can characterize a leader in any organization include all the following, except:
   a. Advocate teamwork in the ranks
   b. Encourage open communications
   c. Support complacency in the ranks
   d. None of the above

6. There are numerous critical leadership skills. A leader will display all of the following skill sets, except:
   a. High ethical beliefs and attitudes
   b. A high ability to communicate well while understanding and relating to all people
   c. Learning how the mission of the organization compares to the leader's career goals
   d. Being aware of the organization's mission and being focused on accomplishing that mission

7. There are four communication skills needed for every leader. Which of the following is not one of them?
   a. Never missing a chance to shut up (listening)
   b. Top down as a priority communications direction
   c. Complete and concise face-to-face communications

d. Reader-friendly written material, sending complete, clear, easily understood communications

8. The optimal way to communicate is written.
   a. True
   b. False

9. Some experts say we conduct a vast amount of our communications nonverbally. No matter how we or others communicate nonverbally, we must always strive for clarification if we want to achieve understanding. Which of the following is true about nonverbal communications?
   a. The content is more difficult to read than verbal and written communications
   b. The message being sent is usually just as important as other forms of communication
   c. Asking for clarification will keep the misunderstanding to a minimum
   d. All the above

10. Leaders are often called upon to institute change in a department. Change is hard to accept by many subordinates because of insecurities or lack of trust. Resistance can be overcome by all of the following suggestions, except:
    a. When possible, discuss why the change is required
    b. Inform the employees that if they cannot accept the change you will help them find work elsewhere
    c. Be honest and consistent
    d. Answer questions, or take the information and follow-up if you don't know the answer

5

Career Planning for Protection Professionals

Christopher A. Hertig and Chris Richardson

CHAPTER OBJECTIVES

- Review the importance of career planning
- Emphasize the significance of education and training
- List relevant resources for education, training, career planning, internships, and licensing/certification
- Networking
- Job search
  - Résumés
  - Interviews
- Explore opportunities for career advancement

IMPORTANCE OF CAREER PLANNING

Career planning is essential to becoming a successful security professional. This is a multistep process that evolves as experience is gained and education is obtained. The first step in this process is exploring the numerous industry segments that are available in security. A great resource to start with is the *Career Opportunities in Security* booklet, published by ASIS International. It can be found at http://www.asisonline.org/career center/careers2005.pdf

Another suggestion is to speak with a professional in a particular security field about their job responsibilities and duties. A more in-depth approach would be to job shadow the professional for a half or full day. This exposure will allow a broad overview of a particular security discipline and give a "front-line" view of the specific career.

Career centers at colleges and universities can also be beneficial. They typically have valuable resources to assist in career planning and developing a career path. Many of them have an extensive network of contacts as well.

It is important to remember several key points about careers:

1. Career planning is a continual process that may change course a few times throughout a professional's career.
2. Careers are like recipes—they consist of various ingredients—all in the proper proportion.

3. While it is usually easy to see why someone has been successful in a career, it may not be evident why someone did not succeed. *"Nobody gives you a scorecard when it comes to a career."*

EDUCATION

Education is the cornerstone of career placement and advancement. There are rare exceptions where advancement to the most senior level has occurred without advanced degrees, but for the most part, in today's market, a degree is essential. There are over 100 colleges and universities offering degrees or programs in security management and over 1,600 that offer criminal justice degrees or programs. Furthermore, many of these academic institutions offer online programs, enabling access for more "nontraditional" students.

Additionally, education enables a broader view of the industry and the various disciplines. It helps people to see how their job functions, however exciting or mundane, contribute to a larger mission. Education helps prepare students to lead others and manage the mission.

Education is an essential career component. Unfortunately, it is not always easy to determine exactly where education helps one to advance. Holding a degree or certificate may or may not aid one in getting a job. Generally, the degree experience should help prepare one for the process of preparing a résumé, researching employers, and being interviewed. Employers look favorably upon persons that have demonstrated the commitment and personal organization necessary to obtain a degree.

But in many cases, having a degree does not automatically open doors. There may be other qualifications that the employer seeks, such as experience, licensing, or certification. A degreed individual may become confused and discouraged when finding that their education does not automatically get them a position.

Persons with college degrees tend to obtain higher-paying jobs, yet this is not always easy to see. The career ladder they follow is not simple. College graduates may not see the immediate benefit of having a degree. It may take them several years and several jobs for the degree to really help them advance. After all, there are relatively few "requirements" but many "expectations," meaning that while the degree may not be required, it is expected.

The jobless rate for college graduates is much lower than the rate for non-graduates. This holds true in both boom and bust economic climates. During good times and bad, degreed persons have significantly lower rates of unemployment. Earnings are also much greater for graduates. Graduating from high school creates a wage jump of about 32%; some college experience without a degree increases wages approximately 13%. Graduation from college increases salaries around 77% (Leonard, 2009).

TRAINING

Training is a structured learning experience designed to enable one to perform a specific task. Employees who are trained can perform tasks more efficiently and more safely. Training aids employers by increasing the effectiveness of employees. Training also increases the communication between employees and management. It helps to give the employees a better idea of management's expectations.

Training also reduces the fear and frustration employees face when confronted with problems on the job. Training prepares them for the job and thus they feel more confident. As a result, training generally reduces employee turnover. Employees are more engaged when they have received adequate training.

Professional organizations such as the British Security Industry Association, the International Foundation for Protection Officers, and the Electronic Security Association (formerly the

National Burglar and Fire Alarm Association) support training efforts. The International Association of Chiefs of Police (IACP) has been a staunch advocate of training. The IACP launched various training initiatives such as the Training Keys: short instructional memos on specific topics. These keys could be easily delivered to classes of police officers by a supervisor. Finally, ASIS International launched a "Standard on Security Officer Selection and Training" to ensure that hiring standards were met and training addresses all the areas that it needs to address.

While professionals have supported training both within professional organizations and as individuals, there are many issues involved in providing training.

Training is expensive for employers to provide. Aside from the instructional costs, the employer is paying employees for their time yet not directly benefiting from it, as the employees are being paid for non-productive time while they are learning. This situation has helped to propel the growth in distance learning. Distance learning helps one avoid many of the costs associated with training as well as with scheduling problems. Distance learning also helps individuals to learn on their own; some contract security firms and police departments have embraced this concept. These organizations provide motivated employees with the option of professional growth.

Anyone serious about pursuing a career should seek out training on their own. Doing so helps them to learn important skills. It also makes them more attractive to employers. Trained individuals may save an employer money on training costs. In some areas it is becoming increasingly common for people to send themselves through a police academy so that they are more certain of landing a police job. A person who has completed training on their own also stands out as someone who is motivated and employers generally wish to hire only the most motivated of personnel.

As completing training costs time and money, taking an instructional program should

be thought through beforehand. The costs and benefits should be weighed. Finding out what employers think of the training is important. Lengthy, extensive training classes must be scrutinized before enrolling in them.

There is a common mistake made by people completing training at a police academy (which is several months in length and costs thousands of dollars) which is assuming they are guaranteed employment. While this will help one to get a police job, it does not guarantee it. Additionally, state Police Officer Standards and Training Commissions generally place a time limit on completing an academy and finding employment. A police academy graduate may have only 2 years to find a job or be decertified. The students must know themselves and the employment market before going into debt.

Another pitfall, which some young people fall victim to, is taking the wrong courses. Some people take all manner of martial arts and firearms training. While this is desirable in moderation, job seekers should beware of potential employers branding them as "Martial Arts Masters of Mayhem" or "gun nuts." In some employment settings this is the "kiss of death" for job applicants. Martial skills should be bundled with other competencies such as first aid, firefighting, customer service, writing, research, and so on.

One solution to obtaining training is through volunteer work. Volunteer fire companies and ambulance services provide training to their members. There are also occasions when agencies that offer services to crime victims or disaster relief will train volunteers. While the Red Cross is well known, there may also be local organizations that will offer training to volunteers.

EXPERIENCE

Experience in a particular field or in a position is one of the most cited criteria or qualifications for employers. A quick search through online job boards or job openings will reveal that the majority of the positions requires a "minimum" number of years of experience. If experience is not required for a particular position, there are often other qualifying criteria such as education, certification, or skills listed as a prerequisite.

Internships are an excellent way for a student to gain experience in the security and/or criminal justice industry. Employers are much more inclined to hire an intern with no or limited experience than a permanent employee with no or limited experience. The significant differences are the internship has defined employment dates, the intern is more closely supervised, and internships are often unpaid.

Two new Web sites have been recently launched to connect employers and students with internships. The Web site www.securityinternships.com provides a listing of security internships listed by employers with both a proprietary and contract security staff. The Web site www.criminaljusticeinternships.com provides a listing of criminal justice internships with local, state, and federal agencies. Both Web sites offer more than just a listing of internships. They offer résumé templates, scholarship information, career news articles, and a listing of other valuable Web sites.

There are times when career planning involves a transition into another field or discipline. For example, a security director may want to transition into audit or compliance. While these two fields are loosely related, the transition may be smoother if it occurs within the same organization. It is more difficult to transition into another field or discipline at another company or organization.

Volunteering is another approach to filling the experience void in one's résumé. Volunteer work can sometimes be performed for non-profit organizations such as churches or civic organizations. It can also be offered by different departments in one's employing organization; an employee may volunteer to perform work outside of their department. This gives them volunteer experience, something to put on their résumé, and references for future jobs.

LICENSING/CERTIFICATION

With some positions a license is required. This may be at the state, provincial, or county level. In some cases, there are also cities that license security and police personnel.

Research into career options must include licensing requirements. There are almost always licenses required for armed security personnel. It is also common to license those who offer investigative services on a contractual basis (private investigation). Some jurisdictions license alarm installers, security consultants, personal protection specialists, door supervisors in clubs, and locksmiths.

Certification is another valuable addition to the résumé and skill set of security professionals. Almost every security discipline and security society or organization has their own certification and it is worthwhile to seek out and obtain the relevant certifications.

There are more recognized certifications than others, but as with educational institutions, it is important to vet the certifying body to ensure the validity of the certification.

To be a well-rounded professional, certifications in areas other than security contribute to success. For instance, a certification in public speaking, finance, accounting, or computers can provide additional opportunities and salary increases.

NETWORKING

Networking with security industry experts can excel the progression of security professionals. Networking can begin at any career stage and is advantageous to both young and experienced security managers and executives. Networking can occur during industry conferences, through social mediums such as LinkedIn, and through professional associations. It also occurs through job experience, various job assignments, and meeting people through employment.

All too often, networking is considered a tool to find employment. Although it is advantageous to network with industry peers and colleagues to search for a security position, networking has many other benefits beyond finding the next job. It allows one to reach out to others for assistance with solving a complex problem or to benchmark a process or procedure. Networking also enables one to stay up-to-date on industry news and trends. In this respect, networking aids in finding jobs. It also helps in succeeding at those jobs.

JOB SEARCH

Online job searching has surged in the past decade. The Internet allows for an unprecedented number of jobs to be listed by employers and searched by applicants. There are large companies such as monster.com and careerbuilder.com that list job openings for every career and discipline available. There are also niche job sites that focus on specific industries.

Before a job search can be started, a résumé must be constructed. A résumé is often the first exposure an employer has to an applicant. Furthermore, the employer or recruiter spends less than 30 seconds reviewing a résumé. This signifies the importance of an impressive résumé in getting an interview for a position.

There are two formats for résumés: functional and chronological. A chronological résumé focuses on the time format of experience. It typically lists employment and other activities according to dates, with the most recent listed first. A functional résumé doesn't focus on dates; rather, it focuses on a narrative style of skill sets and experience.

A widely recognized resource for job searching and résumé writing is *Knock 'em Dead Job Search* and *Knock 'em Dead Resumes*, both written by Martin Yate.

The objective of the job search and résumé is to provide an opportunity for an interview. Arguably the most important process in landing a position, the interview is where the final decision to hire the most qualified and best candidate occurs. Nothing should be overlooked during this process.

Preparation for the interview should be thorough and well thought out. It is important to research the employer to ensure the applicant knows the history of the company and is up-to-date on any recent news such as mergers, expansion, stock price, awards, and so on. In addition to researching the company, the applicant should drive to the interview location the day before to ensure that directions are accurate and to notate the amount of travel time.

Social networking sites are being used more frequently by employers to screen applicants. It is imperative for an applicant to scour through any social networking site they are members of to ensure any pictures or videos that could be deemed inappropriate are removed prior to the application process.

CAREER ADVANCEMENT

Career progression goes beyond education and experience. Security professionals have attributed their successful climb up the proverbial "ladder" to credibility, leadership, and interpersonal skills. These qualities and skills develop over time and require an investment of time and energy devoted to a career path. There are four approaches to reaching career objectives: become a resident expert on a security topic, develop a personal brand, cultivate a mentorship, and establish a network of colleagues.

Excel at one's current job tasks. While the knowledge, skills, and abilities required for a supervisory position differ from those of a subordinate, people who don't "shine" will not be promoted.

Being visible is important. Joining committees and taking on additional projects is one way to do this. Mach (2009) states that it is advantageous to work across your organization.

Richardson (2009) states that there are four strategies that can help security professionals advance on the job: becoming an expert in some area; developing a personal brand; finding a mentor; and networking.

Become an expert in an area that is needed. A retail loss-prevention officer who masters interviewing, a casino security professional who can design camera systems, or a protection officer at a high security facility who becomes a software expert are all in demand. Becoming a reliable source of information or expertise gets one noticed. It opens up opportunities to work on special projects and meet new people.

Develop a brand. A brand is a unique style. One person may project himself as an innovator. Another may be a researcher. Still another may excel at social relationships and politicking.

Find a mentor. Mentors are important. They provide guidance and insight. They enable the person being mentored to grow on their own into new levels of competency. They aid the protégé in gaining additional areas of competence.

Sponsors are another means of helping one advance in their career. A sponsor is someone who brings along a subordinate when they themselves obtain a promotion. Sponsors may be chosen to head up a different division of an organization. Care must be taken in choosing a sponsor. Sometimes sponsors fall out of favor within an organization. A sponsor who is on the wrong side of politics is not a good sponsor to have. In a similar vein, a sponsor who is not very ethical is a liability. Ethics is crucial in this regard.

In some cases, promotion within one's employment organization is simply not happening. This may be due to a small number of positions being available. It may also be the case that the persons holding those positions are not leaving them. In these situations, one either has to be satisfied staying where they are or seek employment in another organization.

EMERGING TRENDS

Enrollment in colleges and universities is at an all-time high. Employers are streamlining processes and asking employees to do more with less. When employers hire, they have the ability to be more selective and seek out the most qualified candidate. A reduced workforce and an influx of applications for open positions increase the competitiveness of the candidates. Experience and education are two of the most important areas that set candidates apart.

Emergency management is closely related to security and homeland security. Emergency or crisis management has been a career field that has rapidly expanded over the past several years. There are many career opportunities available with government, private, and nonprofit organizations.

In addition, academia has noticed this trend and consequently there are a growing number of colleges and universities that offer a degree or program in Crisis or Emergency Management.

Job searching and applying for jobs are increasingly becoming online activities. It must be noted, however, that there is a major role for interpersonal, face-to-face interaction. The practices of investigation, asset protection, and so on, are interpersonal endeavors. They cannot be completely performed electronically. Additionally, the job search and acquisition processes require in-person abilities. One will be limited without a personal network. In addition, job candidates who don't do well in interviews will not be hired.

References

Alexander, D. (2009). *Achieving diversity: A battle for the sexes.* <http://www.info4security.com/story.asp?>sectioncode= 10&storycode=4121598&c=12 Retrieved 02.12.09.

Bixler, S. (1992). *Professional presence: The total program for gaining that extra edge in business by America's top corporate image consultant.* New York, NY: Perigee.

Choi, C. (2009, February 1). Signing up for an online degree? Know the costs. *York Sunday News*, 2E.

Cosgrove, S. (2007, January 28). Grades are great—but grads need skills. *York Sunday News.*

Ford, W. (1999). *The accelerated job search.* Walnut Creek, CA: Management Advantage.

Goulet, T. (2008). *How to get credit for your ideas at work.* <http://msn.careerbuilder.com/>Article/MSN-1692-Workplace-Issues-What-Gets-You-Through-the-Workday/?cbsid=43d7d1cf28254e729bd0131b1fb8522a-280787170-VI-4&sc_extcmp=JS_1692_advice&cbRecursionCnt=2&SiteId=cbmsn41692&ArticleID=1692&gt1=23000 Retrieved 11.23.08.

Hopson, J. L., Hopson, E. H., & Hagen, T. (2009, March 15). Speak up to your supervisor. *York Sunday News.*

Jones, L. (1992). *The encyclopedia of career change and work issues.* Phoenix, AZ: Orynx.

Leonard, C. (2009, January 25). A degree still pays. *York Sunday News.*

Mach, S. (2009). *World-class customer service: The key to York College's success.* York, PA (January 13).

Richardson, C. (2009, February 1) "Steps Toward Career Success" Security Management Magazine, 53, 91–92.

Yena, D. (1987). *Career directions.* Homewood, IL: Career directions: A special edition of Johnson & Wales University.

Resources

The Electronic Security Association (formerly the National Burglar & Fire Alarm Association; www.alarm.org) sponsors a variety of educational programs with the purpose of representing, promoting, and enhancing the growth and professional development of the electronic life safety, security, and integrated systems industry. In cooperation with a federation of state associations, ESA provides government advocacy and delivers timely information and professional development tools. There are various certification programs for alarm installers, technicians, and related electronics professionals.

The National Partnership for Careers in Law, Public Safety, Corrections and Security was initiated in 1999 with funding from the U.S. Department of Justice. The Partnership exists "to build and support career development programs and systems that ensure seamless transitions by linking and integrating secondary and post-secondary education, professional certifications, and organizational recruitment, employment, training and retention systems." The Partnership provides career information to students and others. Additional information can be accessed at www.careerclusters.org.

Internships in security can be found at www.securityinternships.com.

Internships in criminal justice can be found at www.criminaljusticeinternships.com.

SECURITY QUIZ

1. Which of the following best describes the importance of career planning?
   a. Meet with parents and friends to determine which career is best
   b. Job shadow a professional currently in the field of one's potential career
   c. Complete a self-evaluation study that can be found on the Internet
   d. None of the above

2. When earning an education what are the most important considerations?
   a. Determine if the college or university is accredited
   b. Gain work experience through internships or volunteer work
   c. Maintain a satisfactory grade point average
   d. All of the above

3. On average, how much of a salary increase do college graduates earn over noncollege graduates?
   a. 77%
   b. 58%
   c. 84%
   d. 35%

4. Why is experience such an important component of your résumé (choose the best answer)?
   a. Experience provides exposure to scenarios and interaction not available in the classroom
   b. Education is more important than experience and it is not necessary
   c. It demonstrates a high level of motivation

d. A job allows the student to earn money while in school

5. On average, how many certifications should one obtain?
   a. 8
   b. 4
   c. 9
   d. None of the above

6. What is the difference between a functional and a chronological résumé?
   a. A functional résumé lists the functions that you performed at a job
   b. A functional résumé is a summary of experience, whereas a chronological résumé lists jobs or positions by dates of employment
   c. There is no difference
   d. A chronological résumé only lists education and certification

7. When interviewing for a job, what preparation is necessary (choose the best answer)?
   a. Drive the route to the interview location the day before
   b. Research the organization
   c. Be prepared to answer standard interview questions
   d. All of the above

8. Why do employers search social networking sites for applicant information?
   a. They want to find other candidates for other open positions
   b. Searching these sites provides a quick and efficient way to learn more about the candidate
   c. To find a specific person's résumé
   d. Employers do not search social networking sites on job applicants

9. There are four strategies for developing a career; choose the one that is *not* a strategy.
   a. Develop a personal brand
   b. Network
   c. Find a mentor
   d. List one's résumé on an online job board

10. What is one of the fastest growing fields related to security?
    a. Law enforcement
    b. Homeland security
    c. Private detectives
    d. Contract security

UNIT II

COMMUNICATIONS

6

Effective Communications

Charles T. Thibodeau

CHAPTER OBJECTIVES

- Definition of effective communications
- Why effective communications is necessary
- The six essentials of effective communications
- How to address each audience effectively
- Myths and misconceptions about communications
- Proper use of communication devices

EFFECTIVE COMMUNICATIONS DEFINED

"Effective communications" is the faithful reproduction of a thought, idea, observation, instruction, request, greeting, or warning, expressed in a verbal, written, electronic alarm annunciation, or pictorial media, originated and transmitted by a communicator or communicating device to a specifically targeted receiver or receiver group. The term "faithful reproduction" means that whatever was contained in the communicator's original message is both received and understood by the targeted receiver or receiver group. The element of understanding the message is the central focus of this definition, for without that element, communications are blocked. Put another way, effective communications simply are nonexistent without a two-way, mutual understanding of the message being communicated.

DUE DILIGENCE BASED ON EFFECTIVE COMMUNICATIONS

Businesses are required by law to establish and maintain what is called "due diligence." In layman's terms, that means operating their affairs by paying particular attention to the best welfare and interest of their visitor's safety and security needs. To meet this "due diligence" requirement, businesses must focus on foreseeable real and perceived threats. Next, the law expects businesses to warn people of danger and then avoid or mitigate those threats that have a chance of materializing and causing a substantial loss of assets, damage to property, and/or injury to people.

To comply with this mandate, businesses must conduct perpetual risk analysis, vulnerability assessments, integrated countermeasure designs, security officer training, employee security awareness training, and contingency planning. However, without "effective" communications, none of these practices and procedures could exist. Thus, effective communications are a key element in assisting businesses in meeting their mandate to provide proof of compliance with required levels of due diligence.

CHANNELS OF COMMUNICATIONS

There are four channels of communications in any organization or company: top-down, bottom-up, horizontal, and the grapevine. The first three are essential for information to flow in every direction. These are the formal and official forms of communications. The fourth form of communications found in most organizations is the grapevine, which consists of an outgrowth of informal and casual groupings of employees. Effective communications in any security department requires all four of these forms. They provide maximum performance both during stable and predictable periods and during times of stress.

THE SIX ESSENTIALS OF EFFECTIVE COMMUNICATIONS

Effective communications must be:

- Timely
- Complete
- Clear
- Concise
- Factual
- Accurate

This is a bare bones list of requirements. Certainly, the complete list includes other attributes, but if these six factors are present, communications will be extremely effective.

CONSIDER THE AUDIENCE

Everyone communicates at different levels. If you are communicating with someone who is many levels below your communication level, the message you are sending stands a good chance of being misunderstood. In addition, assuming that everyone speaks and understands on your level is almost a guarantee that you will be an ineffective communicator. The midpoint between talking above your audience and talking below your audience is currently the seventh-grade level. If you want perfect clarity in your communications, then speak slowly, carefully choosing your words, using no more than five- or six-letter words, and choosing words that are commonly known. In many cases, when asked to repeat a message, the receiving person uses different words. Thus, each time you are requested to repeat a message, say it in different words.

The security officer's communications must also accommodate the language difficulties of an ever-growing ESL (English as a Second Language) population. Spanish and French are common, second to English, and there is an ever-growing Asian population whose languages include Korean, Laotian, Hmong, Mandarin, and Vietnamese. The security officer of the future may indeed need to be bilingual. Another consideration is medically afflicted people with communication impediments, although there may be nothing you can do to breach their communication difficulties. When dealing with the deaf, blind, or people afflicted with multiple sclerosis (MS), patience is your greatest asset, and a strong commitment to help these people will get you through it. Just be persistent until you can find the way each one communicates.

VERIFYING COMMUNICATIONS WITH FEEDBACK

It is of the utmost importance that the receiver of a message gives you some kind of indication that he or she received the message and the message received is the same one you sent. What I am alluding to here is the use of feedback to confirm that the receiver did in fact receive and understand the message. The initial communicator who sent the message is responsible for ensuring that the message was not only received, but was the same message that was sent. The communicator has a right to believe the message was received and understood if a confirmation message is returned. Acceptable confirmation messages among peers would be any of the following: "10-4," "roger," "good copy," or a very short verbal message repeating your message.

MYTHS AND MISCONCEPTIONS IN COMMUNICATIONS

There is one misconception that causes more errors than any other in the communications field and that is something called brevity, or keeping each communication as brief as possible. In an attempt to accomplish this one goal, the communicator uses abbreviations, personal shorthand, partial words or partial sentences, poor grammar, and a message that requires deciphering.

Being brief many times is *not* an important goal of writing. Saying as few words as possible and speaking in code is *not* always the best choice of content for verbal communications. The above list of six essentials must be present to have a clear and concise message.

The length of the message is important in many situations, such as sending duress codes or using a two-way radio. However, brevity is one of the least important factors and most destructive factors to the attempt to be "effective" with

your communications. A much better question to ask, when finished preparing a message is "Does this message have all six essentials of effective communications?" If not, fix it before the message is sent. If that fix extends the message length, it is better to violate the brevity rule than the need-to-decipher rule. Abbreviations are only valuable to the receiver who can decipher them. Shorthand is usually only valuable to the sender of the message and in many cases cannot be deciphered readily by the receiver of the message. If there is any absolute rule in effective message sending, it is this: No message other than a crypto-message should have to be deciphered by any receiver of the message.

PROPER USE OF COMMUNICATIONS DEVICES

Telephone Systems

The telephone is one of the most important tools that any security officer can have at his or her disposal. At the same time, if the telephone equipment is not properly designed for a security or emergency setting, it can be a great problem, hampering effective communications. The telephone equipment in a security program must be simple to use with the least probability of failing during an emergency.

In modern cutting-edge security control centers, there will be a 10-button phone with caller ID on it for day-to-day business. It will be a part of the facility PBX or electronic phone system, and like all phones, it will have the ability to place calls outside the facility as well as within the facility. It will also be tied into a tape recording device to record all incoming and outgoing calls.

Separate and apart from the 10-button phone, there will be a red phone used exclusively for emergencies with caller ID and tape recording device on it as well. This red phone may have a strobe light connected to it to distinguish the ringing sound from all the other phones in the room. This phone will have no dial-out capability; in fact, the face of the phone will have no dialing keyboard.

The reason for having a separate red phone for emergencies is that the security operator or dispatcher will at some point need to communicate over the regular phone lines to call for fire, police, or emergency medical assistance and for other assistance. If the emergency phone is tied into the 10-button phone, the emergency event caller at the scene of the emergency must be put on hold while public assistance is being called. Never hang up on the emergency event caller or put the emergency event caller on hold during an actual emergency. The caller under the stress of an emergency may hang up whenever they cannot hear the sound of your voice or noise in the control center.

In addition, each security station in the facility should be equipped with a red phone as well as a regular phone. When an emergency call comes in, each red phone should be picked up with the remote stations just listening in to the conversation between the dispatcher and emergency event caller.

Then, before hanging up, each station will confirm that they have received the message heard over the red phone. The emergency telephone system is not a place to skimp on cost or design when so much depends on effective communications during emergencies. In fact, just in case you lose your connection with the emergency event caller, it is best to jot down that person's name and phone number immediately at the outset of the call.

A third phone, a yellow phone, would be a single analog line separate and apart from the facility PBX or electronic telephone system. This phone will have a hardwired four-lead telephone cable inside of a conduit from the wall jack in the room where the phone is located to the street-level mainframe. The conduit will lessen the threat of the line being cut or burned through during an emergency. This line will tie directly to the mainframe of the local telephone office and it will operate on its own power. Therefore, this direct tie to the outside world will be somewhat protected from numerous threats. The conduit-encased phone line would almost assure an outside line during any power outage or computer failure that could cripple the facility's PBX or electronic telephone system.

In some facilities a fourth, black phone is physically identical to the red phone; it cannot be dialed. This phone is dedicated to panic alarm annunciation. If there is a threat on executive row, or a robbery in the credit union, certain designated employees are trained to use the black phone for "duress code" messages.

The cell phone is the newest addition to the phone systems available for security officers. In many locations, security departments are investing in cell phones that double as two-way radios. At this point, for most security departments, these telephone-radio combination units are too costly. In other locations, cell phones are used as back-up units to the two-way radios for communications where two-way radio signals are blocked by dead spots. Cell phones play an important part during patrol duties to allow emergency calls to be made from the scene, back to the control center when the two-way radio is ineffective. The cell phone can also be used for calls directly to the 911 emergency response centers.

Two-Way Radios

The two-way radio is the primary mobile communications device that almost all security officers use to communicate with the control center and between other officers, supervisors, and management. There are some problems with most two-way radio systems and that trouble includes, but is not limited to, failure to operate in dead spots, being susceptible to operator error, and having short battery life. In addition, an adequate two-way radio system is expensive; the units are bulky and take up space on a crowded utility belt. Some of these radios break down regularly and are costly to maintain. However, all of these shortcomings aside, we could not do the security job as well as we do without effective communications devices like the two-way radios.

Two-way radios are miniature radio stations and as such, something called "ground-wave propagation" makes the difference between effective communications and either broken communications with static or no communications at all. Ground-wave propagations are the scientific explanation that explains how a radio signal travels from the source antenna to the receiving antenna. It also explains that if anywhere along that path, there is an object that is so well grounded, like an I-beam or other metal object, the signal may be short-circuited and driven into the ground before the message reaches the receiver's antenna. Because the transmission antenna sends out many pear-shaped signals, not just one, to overcome this signal interference problem, the officer needs only to walk a few feet from where the transmission is garbled and the signal may be reestablished.

The two-way radio is most effective with the antenna 90 degrees perpendicular to the ground. The antenna should be pointing straight up in the air during use. By tipping the antenna sideways or horizontal to the ground, the unit becomes directional and the strongest transmission will be along the line where the antenna is pointing. If a two-way radio antenna is pointing away from the receiving antenna, then the radio is being used in a very ineffective manner.

In many systems, signal strength gets a boost by use of a repeater. A repeater is a great help but the process by which it works makes it somewhat user-unfriendly. The repeater receives the signal, turns it around, and sends it back out as a more powerful signal. That process takes time; thus, the two-way radio communicator must hold the transmission switch down for two seconds before talking in order to engage the repeater and then the communicator must hold the switch down for two seconds after the message is finished

to allow for processing. If this is not done, your message will be clipped at both ends. When holding the transceiver up to talk, hold it to the side of your mouth and speak across the microphone. Do not speak directly into the microphone or you may speak too loudly and cause distortion of the transmitted message.

The frequency of the radio also has an impact on effective communications. Most radios used by security are FM transceivers. They are either VHF or UHF. Two-way radios that are called VHF transceivers work on what is known as very high frequency. The UHF radios operate on ultrahigh frequency. The difference between these two transmission levels is the lower the frequency, the longer the wavelength. That means the VHF signal will travel a long way, but a VHF signal is a relatively weak signal and does not work as well in tall buildings with lots of steel. By contrast, the UHF transceiver is a stronger signal but has a much shorter wavelength. That means that it packs a wallop and works well in tall buildings with lots of steel, but it cannot travel too far. A UHF system with numerous repeaters in line is possibly the most effective two-way radio communications system.

Pagers

The pager takes a telephone call to respond to unless it is a voice pager or a text pager that displays messages. Pagers are nice because they are small and work just about everywhere. However, they do not allow the message receiver to respond with a message and they do not allow for verification that the signal was received and understood. Pagers should be used for back-up only. Two-way radios and cell phones are the best communications devices for portable operations.

Intercoms

In a retail setting or a hospital setting emergency, codes are sent over the intercom. We all know that "code blue" means cardiovascular problems complicated by respiratory failure. We know that "code red" means fire. In some retail companies a call over the intercom such as "Mr. Jones, please come to the front of the store" means that security is needed at the front of the store. The intercom is useful when it is working, but traditionally the intercom system is a weak link in the communications systems of any facility. There are problems with volume and static, and they seem to have more than their fair share of maintenance needs. If the intended receiver of the message is out of the area where there are no speakers, the message will not be received. In addition, there usually are no procedures to inform the communicator that the message was received and understood. Despite the problems, however, intercoms are still needed. Extra speakers should be placed in remote and hard-to-hear-in areas all over the facility to assure emergency messages reach everyone. If you work in a facility equipped with intercoms for communications and you even think that a message might have been transmitted over an intercom, call dispatch and check out your suspicion.

The mistake that a communicator can make using the intercom is to speak too loudly into the speaker. Many systems will distort if the input signal exceeds maximum input peak-to-peak frequency. You do not have to speak loudly when announcing over an intercom, as they have built-in amplifiers to adjust the sound level.

SUMMARY

Effective communications do not exist when the speaker and the receiver are not "on the same page." That is the bottom line in many contract dispute cases where the seller and the buyer failed to reach a "mutual assent to the same proposition." This means that the buyer expected to receive something that the seller was not selling; thus the contract could be declared null and void all because the buyer and seller were experiencing a lack of effective communications.

One of the situations that led to the death of hundreds of firefighters in New York City during the 9/11 terrorist attacks in 2001 was the fact that their two-way radio system failed. Poor communications turned deadly in that situation. We have to be continuously vigilant of effective communications in our security work. Failure to communicate effectively, including failure to communicate at all, can very quickly turn into serious injury or death.

EMERGING TRENDS

As states across this country continue to pass laws for mandatory security officer training, effective communications will be an important part of that training. A training curriculum authorized by a state licensing board will likely contain report writing as a mandatory component. It will be a supervisor's prerogative to assure that the officers in his or her command are following the report writing training they receive. Therefore, it will take the state licensing board and the security officer trainers and supervisors, both in contract and proprietary security, to enforce acceptable levels of effective communications in the workplace. These supervisors should not hesitate to have a security officer rewrite his or her report when that report fails the *effective* communications test. In addition, poor report writing should be rewarded with mandatory writing class refreshers taken repeatedly until effective communications improvement is observed. It is very possible that this turn around trend in effective communications will emerge over the next decade as security departments work toward ensuring that effective communications exists throughout the security industry.

SECURITY QUIZ

1. Which of the following best describes effective communications?
   a. A faithful reproduction of a message sent to a receiver clearly understood and confirmed by the receiver
   b. A message sent by a communicator who expects the receiver to understand it
   c. A message that is sent to a person with hope that it will be understood by all
   d. All of the above

2. Tort law expects every business to actively pursue the following:
   a. employee background checks
   b. due diligence regarding safety and security
   c. adequate training of all employees
   d. employee benefits

3. There are four channels of communications in most companies; which of the following is *not* a channel?
   a. Top-down communications
   b. Bottom-up communications
   c. Grapevine communications
   d. Reverse-horizontal communications

4. There are six essentials of effective communications; which of the following is *not* one of those essentials?
   a. The communications must be complete
   b. The communications must be clear
   c. The communications must be consistent
   d. The communications must be concise

5. Effective communications has built-in flexibility to facilitate the needs of the receiver or receiver groups. Which of the following characteristic is important to take into consideration?
   a. Communications grade level remembering the seventh-grade midpoint rule
   b. English as a Second Language (ESL), people with poor understanding of English
   c. Medical condition such as speech impediment, hearing loss, or poor sight
   d. All of the above

6. A very important part of effective communications is that the communicator must be able to tell which of the following? Choose the best answer.
   a. That the communications were necessary
   b. That the communications were timely
   c. That the message was received
   d. That the message has been received and understood

7. The one misconception that causes more errors than any other in effective communications is:
   a. Every message must be brief
   b. Every message requires some interpretation
   c. Every message must be clear and concise
   d. None of the above

8. The telephone equipment in a security program must be which of the following? Choose the best answer.
   a. It must be technologically rugged and capable of working under severe conditions
   b. It must be simple to use with the least probability of failing during an emergency
   c. It must be available on a 24/7 basis
   d. None of the above

9. In the security office, separate and apart from the general use telephone, there will be a red phone used exclusively for emergencies. That phone will have the following attachments to make it more effective. Which of the following is not one of those attachments?
   a. Ringer
   b. Strobe
   c. Tape recording device
   d. Beeping sound every 3 seconds

10. During some emergency situations, the phone system will be destroyed, especially when there is a building collapse. What can we do to protect that phone line?
    a. Use a separate single-cable phone line not part of the building's main phone system
    b. Place the telephone cable inside of a metal conduit
    c. Have the cable enter/exit the building at the lowest level of the building
    d. All of the above

7

Security Awareness

James E. Sellers

CHAPTER OBJECTIVES

- Explore the importance of security awareness to the overall success of an organization
- Explain how a stakeholder approach is used to create a partnership, which helps achieve a safe and secure environment
- Explore examples of "lessons learned" by an organization to help partners understand why security awareness is important personally and for the success of the organization
- Discuss how focus groups and surveys are utilized for better communication

INTRODUCTION

Security awareness has long been a goal of organizations that strive to provide a safe and secure environment for their employees, customers, and those who want to defend precious assets. The practice of security awareness operates best when a reasonable plan is put together with policies and procedures that support a comprehensive team concept. A security awareness team is crucial to sustaining a healthy corporate environment, and it should include everyone connected to corporate functions.

Managers should formulate a plan that emphasizes enlisting every employee to form partnerships with critical external acquaintances to build a diverse team. When properly launched and actively reinforced, an effective security awareness team encompasses various entities to achieve basic protective goals, which that help deter unwanted activities that threaten the organization.

Although the basic roles, skills, and knowledge of team members will vary, each should understand that he/she is an essential player in safety management and in helping the company achieve security goals. This creates an environment that reduces liability risk and loss prevention by encouraging general safety practices and strategies that produce lasting results. Whether a matter of routine or during an emergency, team members should, at least, know the most current corporate security plan, accept responsibility, and have the ability to implement program objectives.

WHAT IS SECURITY AWARENESS?

When we speak about "security awareness," we are talking about the need to focus attention on security throughout the organization and to keep security in the forefront of every employee's mind during the day. It involves a sense of duty by those who could be affected to be aware of security practices as they relate to daily activities of the organization. Although the plan can be extensive, it does not require every employee to know every aspect; many times it will apply to specialized or departmental duties.

Security awareness provides a framework of established policies and procedures that participants employ by reporting unsafe conditions, suspicious activity, and noticing general safety breaches, merely as second nature.

Team members are trained and polled regularly to heighten their awareness about changing trends in practices and rapidly advancing technology. In the past, the main concern has been on physical site security issues; focusing mostly on gates, doors, windows, and locks. Today, along with physical awareness, security initiatives must include internal matters, like avoiding workplace violence, enhancing personal safety, and being up-to-date on the latest information technology, including safe Internet practices. Greater emphasis must now be placed on these issues, more so than in the past.

EXPANDING THE TEAM THROUGH PARTNERSHIPS

To be effective, the security department should instill "security awareness" among members from all layers of the organization as well as external partners.

1. Employees should be made to feel part of the awareness team and should be solicited for their ideas to improve security. Encourage employees to report security problems and correct safety potential issues when observed. Use a double loop communication model, which means that information should not only flow from the top of the organization down, but should also flow back up to the top. It is in this way that outdated procedures are discovered and corrected.

2. Modern security techniques now involve more collaboration with external associates such as customers, venders, contractors, insurance providers, security consultants, public safety officials, law enforcement, the fire department, government emergency management operators, and others. By collaborating with associates a synergy is developed that acts as a force multiplier. Value is added to the security plan by using proven ideas from experienced external contributors.

Security departments should liaise with local, state, and federal law enforcement officials. These officials can speak with management to reinforce security and safety practices that the security department recommends including in company policies and procedures. The security manager should solicit the officials to offer advice and feedback from their observations.

The internal and external partners described above become stakeholders through common interests and shared goals that help the organization succeed. Stakeholders may be directly or indirectly related to an organization and may offer input that reflects commitment to ongoing functions. As stakeholders, managers and employees all benefit through financial or personal investment, employment, and so on. All share the belief that it is in their best interest to protect and promote the organization as if it were their very own. See Figure 7-1.

TECHNIQUES FOR REINFORCING POLICY AND PROCEDURES TO INCREASE SECURITY AWARENESS

To greatly increase security awareness, members from all layers of the organization and

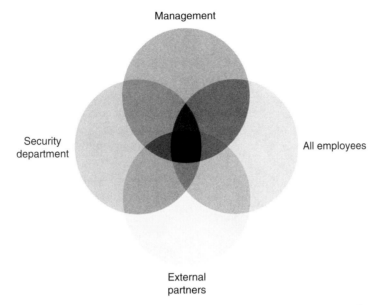

FIGURE 7-1 Security awareness with partner approach (stakeholder). *Figure courtesy of J. E. Sellers, 2009.*

external partners should be instilled with a sense of partnership through interactive activities that include orientation sessions, training, security updates via newsletters, e-mails, and informative signage.

- All employees should be apprised of the organization's policies and procedures upon entering the organization. Employee orientation should be documented and signed to indicate the rules are understood.
- Organizational policies and procedures should be clear, concise, and written correctly. They should also be reviewed and updated annually, at a minimum. Print and electronic copies should be readily available to all employees.
- Repetition of the security awareness message will lead to increased involvement.
- Repetition can be accomplished by such methods as daily exposure through the use of posters, weekly exposure via e-mails, and monthly or quarterly exposure through newsletters and handouts.

- Security awareness meetings should be held with all departments at least every quarter.

Technology such as Internet e-mail, Webcast training, and electronic newsletters, now enable security departments to easily and inexpensively communicate and distribute valuable security and safety information throughout the organization. The correspondence should focus on the positive outcomes that can be achieved if the organization's security procedures are followed. See Figure 7-2.

DOUBLE LOOP LEARNING

Management should consider the Double Loop Learning theory of Argyris and Schon (1978). In this theory the organization becomes a "learning organization" by detecting and correcting errors through questioning and modification of existing norms, procedures, polices, and objectives. According to Fiol and Lyles (1985), learning

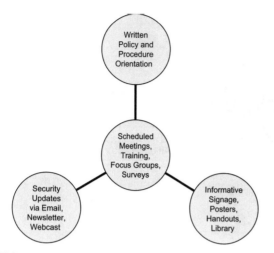

FIGURE 7-2   Developing security awareness. *From Policy and procedure reinforcement (J. E. Sellers, 2009).*

is "the process of improving actions through better knowledge and understanding." With a double loop learning security awareness communication model (Figure 7-3), a mechanism is instituted which provides feedback from employees on improving security awareness. By creating double loop communication, employees can then become stakeholders who have a vested interest in the success of the security awareness effort.

TOOLS

The tools utilized to create this valuable feedback are focus groups and surveys.

Focus Groups: Focus groups consist of individuals selected by management to participate

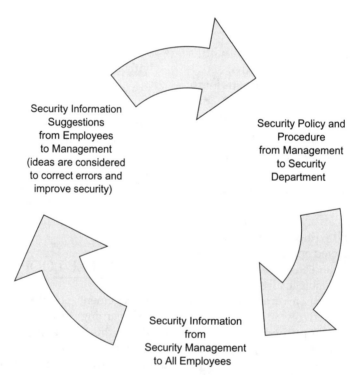

FIGURE 7-3   Developing security awareness. *Double loop learning security awareness communication model (J. E. Sellers, 2009). Adapted from Argyris and Schon (1978).*

in discussions on security policies, procedures, and other security programs. The groups consist of mostly "end users" who operate under the policies. It is this group that often can offer practical solutions for seemingly complicated "problems." Focus groups have brief scheduled meetings that have minimum interference with the company's scheduled core activities.

Surveys: Short surveys on security awareness should be included in e-mails, newsletters, and Webcasts. The surveys can be evaluated to identify what areas of the security awareness program should be adjusted to keep it on track.

Information from the focus groups and surveys should be available within the organization to lend credence to the double loop security awareness communication process and improve the management/employee partnership.

LESSONS LEARNED

The technique for obtaining greater involvement in security awareness should include a collection of lessons learned from inside the organization. This technique uses examples in which security awareness leads to a successful outcome, resulting in an increase in safety or a reduction in crime. The "lessons learned" examples show how security awareness fits into the organization's culture or even contributes to creating a security culture where one was nonexistent.

The "lessons learned" examples help employees and partners understand why strong security is important to them personally as well as to the success of the organization.

RESOURCES

Security department managers should reach out to available resources provided by professional groups when setting policies and procedures. There are a number of industry-specific organizations that provide support by sharing information with their members. There also are security organizations such as IFPO and ASIS that have established guidelines on security topics. These organizations have Websites that offer security information and provide links to other valuable sources.

EMERGING TRENDS

Ever-improving and changing technology provides business opportunities, yet at the same time creates security dilemmas for security managers. Subjects, such as information technology (IT), now occupy much of the security department's resources. Technology in the form of cellular phones, computers, digital cameras, copiers, and facsimile machines, while increasing the speed of conducting business, can also be a method for compromising valuable organizational or personal information through theft or misuse. Without safeguards, including rules regarding the use of electronic devices, severe security breaches could result. These security breaches may include computer viruses that can be introduced via the Internet. These viruses can attack the organization's computer system and result in lost productivity and expensive corrective action. It is imperative that all stakeholders know how they can be affected and be made aware of the dangers of misusing information technology. They must be vigilant, use safe Internet practices, and report any suspicious computer activity. The security director should always seek better ways to provide employees with the knowledge necessary for secure information technology use.

References

Argyris, C., & Schon, D. (1978). *Organizational learning: A theory of action perspective*. Reading, MA: Addison-Wesley.

Argysis, C. (1991). *Teaching smart people to learn.* Harvard Business Review.

Fiol, C., & Lyles, M. (1985) Briacliff, NY: Academy of Management. *Academy of Management, 10*(4), 803–813.

Figures 7-1, 7-2, 7-3 content by J. E. Sellers (2009) using Micro Soft, 2003 "drawing".

Senge, P. M. (1990). *The fifth discipline: The art and practice of the learning organization.* New York: Doubleday.

Sellers, J. E. (2002). *A study of contributing factors to job satisfaction at the Atlanta police department's crimes against property section.* Atlanta.

SECURITY QUIZ

1. Security awareness is simply letting everyone know in the organization how security impacts them and how important they are, as stakeholders and team members, to the continued success of the company.
   a. True
   b. False

2. To be effective, the security department should instill "security awareness" among all levels of the organization and external partners.
   a. True
   b. False

3. Security awareness meetings should be held with all departments at a minimum frequency of:
   a. Annually
   b. Quarterly
   c. Weekly
   d. Daily

4. Security awareness should be instilled among half of the members, from all layers of the organization and external partners.
   a. True
   b. False

5. In double loop communication, information should not only flow from the top of the organization but also a process should be in place for information to travel back to the top.
   a. True
   b. False

6. The "lessons learned" examples help employees and partners understand why security awareness is important to them personally and for the success of the organization.
   a. True
   b. False

7. Which is a method to increase security awareness among all layers of the organization and external partners?
   a. Eyeglasses
   b. Bright lights
   c. Interactive activities
   d. None of the above

8. Focus groups consist of:
   a. Organizations
   b. External partners
   c. Individuals selected by management
   d. None of the above

9. When double loop communication is used, the following employees have the opportunity to become active:
   a. Police officers
   b. Stakeholders
   c. Managers
   d. None of the above

10. Team members are trained and polled regularly to heighten their awareness about changing trends in practices and rapidly advancing technology in security.
    a. True
    b. False

8

Central Alarm Stations and Dispatch Operations

Sean Smith, Jim Ellis, and Rich Abrams

CHAPTER OBJECTIVES

- Explain the history of central alarm stations and dispatch centers and how they evolved into the technologically advanced operations of today

- Provide an overview of the various types of alarm and control systems that may be monitored by a central station, as well as computerized visitor management systems

- Introduce the numerous types of sensors incorporated into alarm and control systems that transmit messages back to the central station

- Provide an overview of the transmission media by which messages are transmitted from alarm and control sensors to their systems' central processors

- Introduce the reader to the communications equipment utilized by dispatchers in a central station, with a focus on radio and telephone systems

INTRODUCTION

In the modern world of safety and security, the necessity of a fully functional central alarm station and dispatch center must not be underestimated. According to Abrams (2003), "The control room is the nerve center of any safety and security department." Such an operation is capable of detecting nearly any emergency that could occur, 24 hours a day, 7 days a week. Such situations may include fire, burglary, major facility equipment failure, or certain natural disasters. Equally as important is the responsibility of a dispatcher to coordinate communications with protection officers in the field, as well as assist agencies and the general public. Alarm systems are powerful tools in the prevention of crime and disaster, but the observations of the field officer and the report from the customer on the telephone are also vital. Dispatchers are trained to obtain and record all the information necessary to send an appropriate response to any situation, ranging from a customer who is locked out of his or her office to a field officer being assaulted by a suspect. Thanks to sophisticated detection and communication equipment—and very quick thinking—dispatch and monitoring staff are prepared to coordinate an immediate response to all of the above and more.

HISTORY OF CENTRAL ALARM AND DISPATCH CENTERS

In the past, humans acted as both alarm sensors and transmission media. In order for a response to occur, an emergency situation had to be directly observed by a citizen, who then rushed to police or fire headquarters to notify the authorities in person (National Communications Institute [NCI], 2001). However, this process began to change when William Cooke and Charles Wheatstone invented the electrical telegraph in 1837 (Stewart, 1994). The telegraph was tailored to the public safety industry in 1852, when William Channing invented the fire alarm telegraph (Fischer, 2008a), which allowed a citizen to activate a pull box, sending a signal with the location of that box to the local fire company.

In 1853, Augustus Russell Pope developed and patented the first modern burglar alarm in Somerville, Massachusetts. It involved an open electrical circuit that connected the doors and windows in a building; when a protected door or window was opened, the circuit would close and activate an audible alarm. Pope only completed one installation, however. The patent was sold in 1858 to Edwin Holmes, who greatly expanded the business (Fischer, 2008a).

Holmes installed his first burglar alarm system in Boston in 1858 (Ellis, 2007). However, within 1 year, he chose to relocate to New York City, because at the time, it was perceived to be where "all the country's burglars made their home" (Fischer, 2008b). By 1866, Holmes's client base had grown to over 1200 residential customers. Around this time, he began marketing to business entities as well as private residences, with great success. The year 1868 brought several technological advances to Holmes's burglar

alarm systems, such as an attached clock that could activate and deactivate the system at certain intervals, as well as a latching circuit that required authorized personnel to manually reset the system prior to deactivating the audible alarm (Fischer, 2008b).

Around the year 1877, Holmes installed the first network of burglar alarm systems connected to a central station (Ellis, 2007). He sent his son to Boston to establish a second central station there. While in Boston, Holmes Jr. discovered that alarm signals could be transmitted to a central station via preexisting telephone wires, and vice versa. He set up a network of 700 telephones connected to the Boston central office, and promptly informed Holmes Sr., who set up a similar operation in New York City. In 1878, Holmes Sr. expanded his telephone interests by becoming president of the newly formed Bell Telephone Company. He sold his interest in the company 2 years later but retained the exclusive right to utilize Bell telephone wires for his alarm circuits (Fischer, 2008c).

In 1871, Holmes was introduced to direct competition when Edward Callahan formed the American District Telegraph company, which eventually became ADT. They utilized manual action call boxes connected to a central monitoring station (Ellis, 2007). When the station received an alarm, messenger boys were dispatched to the source and would immediately report their findings to local police or fire officials via preexisting call boxes. By 1875, ADT had expanded from New York City to Brooklyn, Baltimore, Philadelphia, and Chicago (Fischer, 2008d). At this time, the company offered police, fire, and all-purpose messenger boy services; however, within a few years, they began to offer a contract security patrol service known as the "Night Watch." Even so, messenger boy services initially accounted for over 70% of the company's revenue. However, use of this service declined rapidly with the development and proliferation of the telephone. In 1901, R. C. Clowery, then owner of ADT, decided the wisest course of action was to focus almost exclusively on police, fire, and security services (Fischer, 2008d).

In 1877, the city of Albany, New York, purchased the world's first police telephones and installed them in the mayor's office and five city districts (Stewart, 1994). In 1883, the Gamewell Company created a call box that could be used by the police or the public. These call box systems were installed in Washington, DC, Chicago, Detroit, and Boston within the next several years. In the United Kingdom, gas lights were installed on top of police call boxes, which could be lit by police headquarters in order to notify the officer on foot patrol to contact the nearest station (Stewart, 1994).

Radio communication for police would come many years later. The first police radios in America were utilized by officers in Detroit, Michigan, in 1928. These were only capable of transmitting from the base station to a mobile radio. Bayonne, New Jersey, became the first police department to utilize two-way radios in 1933 (Institute of Electrical and Electronics Engineers, 2009). At that time, and for many years, a dispatch center was a relatively simple operation. A typical center would consist of a telephone system, a radio system, and a record-keeping interface. The telephone system was basic, unlikely to incorporate features that were not found in residential or office telephones, other than a manual switchboard used to redirect calls. The radio system was a simple desk microphone with a "push to talk" switch. Records were kept by hand on a series of paper forms (NCI, 2001). Such an operation may be staffed by a switchboard operator, or by a police or protection officer assigned to the desk.

Currently, the core functions of a dispatch center remain the same: telephone communication, radio communication, and recordkeeping. However, the technology has changed drastically over the years. Consumer-grade telephones have been replaced with multi-line telephone terminals accompanied by features such as touch screens, enhanced caller ID, voice recording, and telecommunication devices for the deaf. Two-way radios have evolved into networks including many advanced features, such as:

- touch screen interface
- voice recording
- remote paging
- remote activation and deactivation of handheld units

Pencil-and-paper record-keeping systems have been replaced by computer-aided dispatch software, making it much easier to enter new data and retrieve archived information. These systems can be integrated with a variety of other programs, including report management software, telephone or radio interfaces, geographic mapping and tracking systems, and even alarm-monitoring software.

TYPES OF MONITORING SYSTEMS

A security officer might come into contact with any number of monitoring systems when staffing a console. Each system may control a specific action or sequence of actions if so programmed. The most complex are integrated systems that operate multiple individual operations from one software application.

Alarm Systems

At the basic, but most reliable, end of the spectrum is an alarm system that monitors areas of a facility. This would consist of sensors placed around the facility and connected to a central console. In some systems, the console might include lights and a buzzer such that a violation or alarm would cause both the light and buzzer to activate. Toggle switches connected in the circuit allow for areas to be shunted, bypassed, or silenced until the alarm can be investigated. This also allows for a sensor with a fault on it to be silenced until repaired. However, this generally leads to the assumption that any alarm on that device is usually a false alarm. It is therefore imperative to repair any part of the system that is malfunctioning as soon as possible. Depending on the type of sensor that is malfunctioning, it may be necessary to station an additional security officer in that area or conduct additional patrols.

Modern alarm systems have a keypad that operates much in this same fashion, but with the addition of a communicator that allows the signals to be transmitted offsite to another console in a neighboring facility, an alarm central monitoring station, or in rare cases, to the police. Some modern alarm systems will spell out the location of the alarm in a textual format. As long as the naming convention is consistent across the system and all officers are trained in how to locate an alarm that is spelled out, this can be a very cost-effective method of monitoring a facility.

Fixed graphical alarm panels will show an outline of the facility and critical areas being monitored within. When an alarm is generated, it is much easier to find and locate the alarm because the alarm is shown relative to the layout of the facility. Computer-based graphical alarm panels will also show the facility, but can be modified as the facility or the system expands in scope and coverage.

Access Control Systems

Access control systems are based on the premise that issuing keys to all employees who need them is generally not cost-effective. Another premise of an access control system is that it would be cost prohibitive to rekey the facility should a key be lost. Finally, an access control system can limit employee access; allowing them entry only to areas in which they are authorized, or granting entry during certain times of day.

An access control system uses a means of verification, known as a credential, to allow a person to enter an area. The credential can be something that is known, generally a personal identification number; something that is carried, such as a card or token; or something that the authorized person has, such as a fingerprint or iris (the colored part of the eye). The credential is entered, swiped, presented, or scanned, and, after some level of verification, access is granted or denied.

Access control systems come with various means of operation and scope from a single door to many thousands of doors or alarms around the world. At the small end of the access control spectrum is the single door keypad at which a person enters a code that is mechanically or electronically verified. Most access control systems use a card-based credential, which is swiped or presented to an electronic reader to gain access. These systems can be used across just a few doors to many thousands of doors and sensors connected via the company's computer network. The most secure access control systems utilize a biometric authentication process. Biometrics entails using something that is part of the person for verification of identity, such as fingerprints, hand geometry, vein pattern recognition, voice print, and iris recognition. Biometrics can be used as the sole means of verification, but are frequently used in conjunction with a card reader.

Another main component of medium- to large-sized access control systems is the distributed processor, sometimes referred to as a field controller. This computer is installed between the main computer and the card reader at the door and communicates back to the main computer only when necessary, such as to request updated information about card holders or when there is an alarm. The distributed processor makes all of the decisions as to granting or denying access to a person who presents their card at the card reader, therefore taking the processing load off the main computer and allowing the entire system to operate faster. The distributed processor also allows the system to continue to operate if the connection back to the main computer is interrupted. Typically, distributed processors control between 2 and 16 doors and allow for the connection of various sensors, just like a regular alarm system. Distributed processors can communicate to the main computer via a communications protocol such as RS-232 or RS-485, although an increasing number of systems are now being connected to a company's internal computer network (intranet). Newer systems are taking the network connection all the way down to the card reader at the door. Other systems use a Web-based interface for programming the system and can communicate down to the distributed processor via the network or through the wireless data network available from cell phone companies.

The main computer in an access control system can be a simple desktop computer for small systems up to redundant mirrored servers for very large systems, or any combination in between. In smaller systems, the computer is used for entering cardholder information and programming the system, whereas in larger systems there may be multiple computers dedicated to programming and photo badge creation or monitoring and controlling the various alarms and doors connected to the system. In the largest systems the desktops communicate to a server, which is a high-speed computer able to perform several thousand operations per second: essential for controlling the flow of data back and forth across a large access control system. In some cases, a secondary server is kept on standby to act as a reserve to the primary server should it fail or need periodic maintenance. When this secondary server is receiving the same updates at almost the same time as the primary server and can automatically take over the processing load, it is said to be redundant or mirrored.

Access control systems can be used to monitor alarms, such as door alarms, duress buttons, or environmental situations (high or low temperature, sump pump, water level). The control systems typically contain a graphical interface that allows the application to show building layout or to import floor plans from another application. Thus, all activity in the system is presented on a single screen. Automatic actions for certain events can be programmed into such a system, such as calling up a particular camera when a door goes into alarm.

Fire Alarm Systems

Of all the alarm systems, it is most critical for security officers to understand the basic operation and interaction of fire alarm systems. Fire alarm systems are regulated by building and fire alarm codes adopted by the municipality in which the facility resides. Because different municipalities may adopt different codes, how a system operates or is installed at one location might be quite different at another location. As fire alarm systems are so essential for the safety of the employees and the well-being of the facility, it is critical to have a thorough working knowledge of the operation of the system and the security officer's role in its successful use. It is also very important to understand the proper operation of the system and expectations of the fire department.

Fire alarm systems typically have a main control panel with a display. If necessary, additional displays can be installed in other areas. Larger systems may incorporate a graphical display of the facility and locations of the various sensors therein. Where the alarm must be monitored offsite, a communicator or dialer is installed to allow the fire alarm to send alerts to an alarm company central station or, in some rare cases, to the fire department.

Like intrusion alarm systems, fire alarms can be connected with a number of devices on a zone. Newer, larger fire alarm systems (and intrusion alarm systems as well) utilize a multiplex loop, where all of the devices are connected on the same loop, with each device having its own unique identifier or address. This type of system is known as a multiplex or addressable system. The largest fire alarm systems integrate dozens or hundreds of control panels across several facilities, with a dedicated main computer in the company command center for monitoring.

Building Automation Systems (BAS)

Building automation systems operate much the same, and in a similar configuration, as access control systems. Building automation systems control heating, ventilating and air conditioning (known collectively as HVAC), as well as lights. More expansive systems can assist in controlling elevators, escalators, and irrigation systems. Building automation systems may integrate with, or share the same software and hardware as, an access control system.

Closed-Circuit Television Systems (CCTV)

Closed-circuit television (CCTV) systems allow dispatchers to watch over a large number of areas at once. They provide an excellent (and cost-effective) way to monitor high-sensitivity and high-risk locations at all times, without needing to post a protection officer at those locations. The cameras used may be easily visible to the public or they may be hidden to the point of near-invisibility, depending on the needs of the organization and the locations at which they are stationed.

From the central monitoring station, a dispatcher may be able to view up to 16 separate images in real time on a single monitor (Nelson, 1999). Alternatively, he or she may view a single image at a time, and switch to other images on demand or at preset intervals. The video images may be in color or black-and-white format. According to Nelson (1999), color images are better for identification purposes, while black-and-white images have better performance in low light. Cameras may be stationary, but those with pan, tilt, and zoom capabilities can easily be installed wherever they are necessary. From

the central monitoring station, dispatchers can control these cameras at will, in order to focus on locations or individuals that require close observation at a given time. These cameras can also be set up to focus on a series of locations, one after another, each for a preset length of time.

CCTV cameras generally incorporate a method of recording the images they monitor. This allows protection officers to revisit images to verify descriptions of individuals and events, and also to retain those images for use as evidence. At particularly sensitive locations, video may be recorded on a continuous basis, but this very quickly consumes a great deal of data storage space. Cameras that are integrated with other sensors—intrusion sensors, for example—can be set up to focus on a specific area and begin recording when an alarm is received from the associated sensor. A dispatcher typically has the ability to begin and end a video recording at any time and to take a single snapshot image. Images have typically been stored on video cassettes, in either real time or time-lapse format (Ruiz, 1999). However, the current trend is for image files to be digitally stored onto computer hard disk drives either using digital video recorders, (DVR), or with several drives together, or onto large capacity storage devices known as network attached storage (NAS) or storage area networks (SANs). It is possible to connect the hard disk drives into a configuration known as a redundant array of independent disks, or RAID. Such a configuration has the capability of either manually or automatically backing up drives so that the failure of any one drive does not result in the loss of all recorded data. Other options for exporting images include CD-ROM compact disks, digital video disks, or even USB flash drives.

Integrated Systems

As security and fire alarm systems become more expansive in scope and operation, it is sometimes necessary to link the systems together under one controlling piece of software or application. Other times it is necessary to link various systems together, such as human resources systems, parking applications, and payroll systems, so that there is greater functionality and more accurate information flowing automatically between those systems. Such systems are generically referred to as "integrated systems."

TYPES OF SENSORS

All security, fire, and other alarm systems incorporate a wide variety of sensors at various points throughout a protected facility. The basic purpose of a sensor is to detect a physical change in the environment, interpret what event might be taking place, and transmit that information back to a central processor where it is translated into a format that can be read by the dispatchers in the central alarm station.

Intrusion Sensors

Intrusion sensors are meant to determine whether an unauthorized person has accessed, or attempted to access, a protected area (Garcia, 1999). Various types of sensors can be placed around the perimeter of a facility, around a smaller area within the facility, or on a particular spot or item (Morris, 2003). They typically incorporate a short delay prior to generating an alarm, in order to allow an authorized person to deactivate the system without sending a false alarm to the monitoring station. Types of intrusion sensors include:

- **Magnetic contact switches.** These are placed on doors, windows, and other potential access points. Typically, the first part of the mechanism is placed on the frame and the second part is placed on the movable portion of the access point. When the access point is opened, the magnetic signal is interrupted and the sensor generates an alarm.

- **Glass break sensors.** When a pane of glass breaks, it emits sound waves in a specific frequency. Glass break sensors are able to pick up this frequency and generate an alarm in response. They are particularly useful near windows and glass doors (J. Russell, personal communication, July 8, 2009).

- **Motion sensors.** Microwave sensors send waves of electromagnetic energy back and forth within an area. If an intruder enters, the energy is interrupted, and the sensor generates an alarm. Passive infrared sensors detect the body heat of an intruder and generate an alarm in response. Ideally, an area will be protected by dual-technology sensors. These combine microwave and infrared technology into one sensor, increasing the reliability of the system and decreasing the number of false alarms transmitted to the monitoring station (Morris, 2003).

- **Electric eye.** This type of sensor consists of a transmitter, which generates infrared light in a straight line, and a receiver directly opposite the transmitter. When the beam of light is broken by an intruder, an alarm is sent to the central processor. Electric eyes have declined in popularity due to the availability of motion detectors with greater reliability (J. Russell, personal communication, July 8, 2009).

- **Seismic sensors.** These are able to pick up vibrations on a surface and when a certain vibration threshold is reached, an alarm is generated. Seismic sensors may be placed on floors in order to detect a walking intruder, or on walls or doors, to detect an attempted break-in (J. Russell, personal communication, July 8, 2009).

- **Pressure sensors.** These detect the weight of a person or object. If an intruder steps on a pressure mat, the change in surface weight activates an alarm. Alternatively, a pressure switch may be placed underneath an object at risk of theft or removal. Again, if an intruder removes the object, the change in surface weight triggers an alarm.

- **Panic and duress alarms.** These are switches that must be manually activated by a staff member when he or she is threatened by an intruder or other emergency. Typically, they are utilized in high-risk or high-sensitivity areas and are hidden from the general public. Alternatively, handheld wireless panic alarm triggers may be issued directly to employees (Morris, 2003).

Access Control Sensors

Access control sensors may be used to detect unauthorized access to a facility, and to generate security alarms in response. However, they may also be used to grant access to authorized personnel when presented with the proper credentials. Several types of access control sensors are often used at a single entry point in order to provide multiple layers of security:

- **Magnetic contact switches.** These operate in the same manner as they do when applied to intrusion detection systems. These switches are able to detect whether a door is open or closed; if the door is opened without presentation of a proper credential, a forced door alarm will be generated (J. Russell, personal communication, July 8, 2009).
- **Request-to-exit devices.** Also known as REX switches, these are sometimes embedded into the crash bar or doorknob on the interior of a door. A motion sensor may also be used as a request-to-exit device when mounted above the door, to sense a person traveling toward the door to exit. When the door is opened properly in order to exit an area, the REX switch is triggered and bypasses the magnetic contact switch, avoiding a false alarm. However, if the door is left open for an extended period of time, a held door alarm will be generated. Unless there is a requirement to do so, REX devices should

not be programmed to unlock the door, as this allows the door to be unlocked from the outside without a key or card.

- **Keypad locks.** These devices require an employee to input a numeric code in order to bypass the locking mechanism. Because codes can be easily transferred to unauthorized persons, these locks are often used in conjunction with other access control measures.
- **Magnetic strip readers.** An employee is issued a card with a magnetic strip, which is embedded with numerical data. The employee swipes the card through the reader, which uses that data to verify his or her authorization for access (J. Russell, personal communication, July 8, 2009).
- **Proximity card readers.** Proximity cards are also embedded with a numeric identifier. The staff member waves the card near the reader, which utilizes radio frequencies to receive the data, which is sent to the field controller. The field controller verifies the card and grants or denies access accordingly (Best, 2003).
- **Wiegand card readers.** A Wiegand card contains specially treated wires with a unique magnetic signature. A sensing coil inside the reader receives the data contained within the employee's card (Best, 2003). The card can either be swiped or passed through, depending on the design of the reader.
- **Biometric readers.** These detect the unique characteristics of parts of a person's body in order to verify his or her access privileges. Biometric readers include fingerprint scanners, handprint scanners, retinal scanners, facial recognition, and voice recognition.

Fire Alarm Sensors

The ability of fire to devastate lives and property should never be underestimated. Fire alarm sensors seek to prevent significant damage by detecting fires in their earliest stages, allowing protection officers and fire officials ample time to respond. Fire alarm sensors include (J. Russell, personal communication, July 8, 2009):

- **Heat detectors.** These measure changes in a room's ambient temperature. They are programmed to a certain baseline temperature and when the room's temperature exceeds the baseline, a fire alarm is triggered.
- **Photoelectric smoke detectors.** This type of detector contains an electric eye, generating a beam of infrared light within its housing. When smoke enters the detector, it refracts that infrared light, and an alarm is triggered in response.
- **Ionization detectors.** These devices contain a tiny amount of radioactive material, which creates radiation in an ionization chamber. Any smoke that enters will absorb some of the radiation and change the electrical charge within the chamber, prompting the device to send an alarm signal to the monitoring station.
- **Air sampling detectors.** These are often used to protect rooms filled with sensitive equipment, such as computer servers. They continuously take in air from the room and analyze the air samples for smoke or combustion particles. If a positive result is received, the detector generates an alarm and in many cases, immediately causes a fire suppressant to be discharged within the room.
- **Beam detectors.** These utilize an electric eye, which extends a beam of infrared light across an entire room, rather than within the housing of a photoelectric detector. They are most often used in rooms with very high ceilings, where it would be impractical to install and maintain a smaller detector. Again, the beam of light will be refracted by smoke in the room and an alarm will be triggered.
- **Flame detectors.** These are able to spot actual flames, rather than sense smoke

or combustion particles. They typically incorporate ultraviolet light sensors, infrared light sensors, or visible light sensors.
- **Pull stations.** These switches are strategically placed throughout a protected facility, and when a person observes fire or smoke, he or she is encouraged to manually pull the nearest switch, triggering a fire alarm and speeding evacuation of the area. Unfortunately, pull stations are easily abused. To activate a pull station in order to cause a false public alarm is a criminal offense in most jurisdictions; therefore, protection officers responding to such alarms should be prepared to enforce their organization's relevant policy or involve local law enforcement as appropriate.

Building Automation Sensors

Building automation sensors are typically used to measure and adjust the heating, ventilation, air conditioning, lighting, and other environmental conditions in a protected facility. They include:

- **Gas detectors.** There are several different types of gas detectors, each of which will measure the levels of a particular type of gas in the air (such as natural gas, carbon monoxide, carbon dioxide, and radon). If the gas levels exceed a preset tolerance, an alarm is generated.
- **Level indicators.** These are often applied to tanks that hold liquids or gases that are critical to a facility's operation. When the amount of liquid or gas in the tanks drops below a preprogrammed level, a notification can be sent to the central monitoring station or to personnel who will refill the tanks (J. Russell, personal communication, July 8, 2009).
- **Temperature sensors.** As the name suggests, these measure the ambient temperature in a room. They are often utilized in rooms where

scientific experiments are being conducted and the temperature must be kept extremely hot, extremely cold, or within a specific range. If the temperature falls out of the pre-set range, an alarm is triggered.

- **Power failure sensors.** These are integrated with the electrical system of a facility. When a power failure occurs, a notification alarm can be sent to the central monitoring station. At the same time, devices such as backup generators and emergency lights can be automatically activated.
- **Integrated sensors.** Some of the same devices used to detect intruders—magnetic door switches and motion sensors, for example—can be integrated with lighting systems. In this way, lights can be programmed to turn on automatically when a staff member enters a darkened room.

Closed-Circuit Television Sensors

Closed-circuit television cameras themselves can be considered sensors because they receive visual images and transmit them back to the central monitoring station. However, human eyes alone are not the most reliable detectors when it comes to CCTV systems (Garcia, 1999), particularly when they may be focused on up to 16 images on a single monitor. For this reason, additional sensors are usually integrated into a CCTV system:

- **Integrated sensors.** The majority of CCTV sensors are not incorporated into the camera unit itself. However, CCTV systems can be integrated with a wide variety of sensors from other systems, including intrusion detection, access control, and fire detection. For example, if a bank teller triggers a panic alarm, the bank's cameras can be programmed to zoom in on his or her location and begin recording immediately. At the central monitoring station, an additional alarm may draw the dispatcher's attention to the relevant camera images.

- **Motion sensors or Video Motion Detection (VMD).** Certain types of motion sensors can be incorporated directly into a CCTV camera. These typically utilize a reference image, which is compared to the image currently being picked up by the camera, in order to detect whether the image has changed significantly (J. Russell, personal communication, July 8, 2009).
- **Facial recognition.** This biometric technology, when integrated with sophisticated CCTV cameras, can identify potentially dangerous individuals by comparing a face with wanted person lists or terrorism watch lists. They are most often utilized by law enforcement officials at immigrations checkpoints, such as airports (Best, 2003).

TRANSMISSION MEDIA

When an alarm sensor detects an event that warrants a protection officer's attention, it immediately transmits a message back to the central monitoring station. A transmission medium is simply the method by which that message is carried. Signals may be carried by a variety of solid materials, or may pass through the air itself.

- **Copper wire.** This type of material is extremely common throughout the alarm industry. Intrusion and fire alarms can be transmitted through copper cables specifically geared toward alarm systems; however, they are frequently transmitted through traditional telephone lines, which are also usually made of copper. A disadvantage of copper wire is that it can be cut or otherwise damaged, interrupting the transmission of vital signals. However, a major advantage is that it is continuously monitored by the alarm system if properly installed, so that if such damage occurs, the central monitoring station will be immediately notified (J. Russell, personal communication, July 8, 2009).

- **Optical fiber.** This type of material is increasing in popularity at a rapid pace. It was once far more expensive to install a fiber optic network than a copper one, but like most technological innovations, fiber optics are dropping in price. Copper wire carries signals in the form of electricity; optical fiber carries signals in the form of light, which is less inherently dangerous. Additionally, optical fiber is able to carry larger amounts of data at a faster rate than copper wire. Both transmission media can be cut or damaged, but like copper wire, optical fiber is continuously monitored, so the central monitoring station will be made aware as soon as this occurs.
- **Radio transmission.** This method utilizes the air as its transmission medium. Alarm signals are sent via a certain radio frequency from point A directly to point B. This solution can cover a much longer distance than copper wire or optical fiber. A drawback with some radio systems, however, is that the signal is prone to interference from trees, other objects, or competing radio signals (J. Russell, personal communication, July 8, 2009).
- **Cellular transmission.** Cellular signals are similar to radio signals; in fact, they operate within the radio frequency spectrum. The difference is that cellular signals are transmitted at a higher frequency within that spectrum. Additionally, they utilize cell towers that are capable of digitally processing, sending, and receiving the signals over a wider area than traditional radio signals. Unfortunately, this transmission medium is not continuously monitored; therefore, in fire alarm systems, it can only be used as a backup method, rather than a first line of defense (J. Russell, personal communication, July 8, 2009).

VISITOR MANAGEMENT SYSTEMS

Several organizations—large office buildings and schools, for example—receive a large number of visitors each day as part of their normal operations. Personnel at the front office or security office must fulfill two functions: first, they must determine whether or not to allow a visitor access to the building. Second, they must keep a log of all visitors who have arrived and departed.

In the past, organizations typically relied on a paper sign-in sheet at the building's main entrance. A visitor would write his or her name, time of arrival, specific destination within the building, and purpose of the visit on the sign-in sheet. Personnel at the desk would verify the visitor's identity, ensure that he or she had permission to enter the building, and in most cases, issue a temporary identification badge for the visitor to wear while on the premises. The visitor would then be required to sign out when exiting the building. This type of procedure is still in place at many organizations, especially smaller ones, due to its simplicity and low cost.

However, for many larger organizations, electronic visitor management systems prove safer and more cost-effective because staff members no longer need to spend time logging visitors in and out, and personally clearing each one through applicable unwanted person databases (Savicki, 2007). Such solutions greatly increased in popularity after September 11, 2001. A typical electronic visitor management system consists of a kiosk at the building's entrance, an attached printer, and software that links the kiosk to the front office or security office. A visitor approaches the kiosk and enters his or her personal information or presents his or her driver's license for the machine to read. The purpose of the visit must also be provided (Moorhouse, 2008). The kiosk may check the individual through applicable state and national databases—sex offender registries are typically utilized in school settings—as well as organizationally defined unwanted person databases. If the visitor is not cleared, he or she is issued a voided identification badge and appropriate staff members are notified automatically to take further action (Savicki, 2007). If the visitor is cleared, the kiosk prints an identification badge for him or her to wear on the premises, which includes a facial photograph, the date, time, and purpose of the visit (Moorhouse, 2008). An added benefit is the ability of staff members to easily search the software database for detailed information on previous visitors.

It is also possible to integrate a visitor management system with a building's access control system. For example, the card printed by the kiosk may be programmed with certain electronic credentials, which would allow the bearer to enter authorized doors by swiping the card or presenting it to an electronic reader. Alternatively, frequent visitors may be issued a permanent card or tag, which can be presented to the kiosk when entering or exiting the building, without necessitating a new identification card for each visit (Savicki, 2007).

COMMUNICATIONS

Communications equipment plays a huge role in the successful resolution of alarms, criminal and policy violations, emergency situations, and, of course, customer service. In a modern central monitoring and dispatch station, communication takes many forms. However, the vast majority of communication is performed verbally, through telephone lines and radio channels.

A modern telephone system in a central station will incorporate many technological advances available to the general public, such as caller ID, preset number dialers, and the ability to place callers on hold or transfer them to other lines. However, the system should also be tailored for use by emergency service personnel.

The system's interface may be a series of physical keys on what looks like a very large telephone base, or it may be integrated with touchscreen software, to allow the operator to switch between functions quickly and easily. Typically, the operator will be equipped with a headset, in order to move about the station and keep both hands free while communicating with a caller. The system may incorporate several incoming emergency lines and several incoming nonemergency lines, which would likely be shared by all telephone consoles at the station. Each console would also have access to its own line for outgoing calls. Alternatively, all emergency calls may be routed to a dedicated "red phone" in the station, eliminating the need to place an emergency caller on hold while briefing police, fire, or emergency medical services (Thibodeau, 2003). It is common for all telephone calls, incoming and outgoing, emergency and nonemergency, to be automatically recorded and archived for supervisors to refer to later.

In agencies with very advanced technology, telephone systems may be integrated with a variety of other systems in the central station. For example, it is possible to connect certain telephone software with certain computer-aided dispatch software and geographic mapping software. In these situations, the central station may receive an emergency call, and the location provided by the caller ID may be automatically highlighted on a computerized map. The location might then be automatically imported into the computer-aided dispatch software when a new event is created by the operator.

Organizational policy varies with regard to the usage of cellular phones by protection officers in the field. When they are permitted, they can be very useful tools for relaying information back and forth that is sensitive but nonemergency in nature. At the very least, it is common for a patrol supervisor to be equipped with an organization-issued cellular phone for this purpose.

Radio systems are equally as important as telephone systems in both emergency and nonemergency situations. They are the most frequently used method by which field officers communicate with their dispatchers and with each other. A modern radio system interface, like that of a modern telephone system, may consist of a set of keys or may incorporate a touch screen for ease of use. The same headset used by the operator for telephone communication will often be integrated with the station's radio system as well. Additionally, the central station should be equipped with software enabling an operator to see the name or ID of a handheld or mobile unit; to page, activate, or deactivate an individual unit; to acknowledge emergency signals received; and to perform maintenance functions.

The radio system will typically be capable of monitoring and transmitting on a large number of channels simultaneously. These may consist of the primary channel, an emergency channel, a tactical channel, maintenance and custodial staff channels, and many more. Direct monitoring and transmitting on local police, fire, and emergency medical channels is also possible.

A two-way radio operates in either simplex or duplex mode. In simplex mode, a radio transmits and receives messages on the same frequency and communicates directly with other radios. In duplex mode, a radio transmits and receives messages on two different frequencies. This mode also incorporates a repeater. A repeater is simply a stationary device, attached to an antenna, which receives a radio message, amplifies it to increase its range, then retransmits the message to its destination. Duplex mode is far more common than simplex mode in this day and age.

Radio equipment can be either analog or digital. Analog equipment has been in use for many years. It tends to be less complicated than digital, and is therefore less expensive to purchase and maintain. It also tends to be more compatible with existing radio systems. Digital equipment allows for a larger number of officers to talk at once on the same channel. It also allows for different types of data—for example, text

messages—to be sent and received. Certain digital radio systems can even be integrated with certain computer-aided dispatch software, which can communicate via text with individual radio units.

CONCLUSION

Remember: the most important component of a central monitoring and dispatch operation is you, the protection officer assigned to the station. Cutting-edge technology is no substitute for an individual with good communication skills, sound judgment, knowledge of department policy, and proper and up-to-date training.

After completing the initial department-approved courses and on-the-job training, it is important to continue growing as a professional. This is achieved in part by studying current departmental policy and seeking continuous feedback from coworkers and supervisors. However, in order to keep up with industry developments and open up additional training opportunities, it is often wise to turn to a professional organization.

The International Foundation for Protection Officers is an excellent starting point. Their Certified Protection Officer program is extremely beneficial to officers both in the field and at the central console. Several organizations exist, however, which provide more specialized opportunities for dispatchers and monitoring personnel. The Association of Public Safety Communications Officials (APCO) and the National Emergency Number Association (NENA) provide continuing education programs and advocacy for dispatchers in the public and private sectors. The National Burglar and Fire Alarm Association (NBFAA), the Security Industry Association (SIA) and Central Station Alarm Association (CSAA), provide similar services, but are geared toward the life safety and security alarm monitoring end of the spectrum.

EMERGING TRENDS

- As we have seen, many different types of alarms can be integrated with each other to achieve optimal results. Likewise, telephone and radio systems can be integrated with computer-aided dispatch software and a variety of other software packages. The ability to integrate is highly valued, and as technology improves, the ability will continue to become more widespread.
- Plain language radio transmission is rapidly becoming the preferred protocol for many organizations, rather than the use of 10-codes and other codes to denote certain types of events. This is because plain language makes it far easier to cooperate with other agencies during emergency situations.
- Digital radio systems are becoming more widespread, thanks to their enhanced voice and data transmission capabilities, and the potential for integration with software applications. However, for many organizations, analog systems provide plenty of functionality at a greatly reduced cost. While digital equipment is on the rise, analog equipment is far from obsolete.
- Text-based communication has been utilized among protection officers for years, incorporated into the mobile data terminals installed in many police and security vehicles. It has also been utilized in telecommunications devices for the deaf, which allow the hearing-impaired to quickly call for emergency assistance. However, very recently, a call center in Iowa became the first in the nation to accept emergency text messages to 911 (Svensson, 2009). This capability is likely to be adopted by many more emergency call centers in the near future. Whether or not similar technology will become popular in the private sector remains to be seen.

References

Abrams, R. (2003). Central alarm stations and dispatch centers. In: *Protection officer training manual* (7th ed.) (pp. 93–95). Burlington: Elsevier Science.

Best, C. (2003). Access control. In: *Protection officer training manual* (7th ed.) (pp. 96–102). Burlington: Elsevier Science.

Ellis, J. (2007). *Proprietary central alarm monitoring stations in modern security management operations* (Master's thesis, Webster University, 2007).

Fischer, J. (2008a). Who was Augustus Russell Pope? *CSAA Signals*, 14(3). Retrieved June 30, 2009, from http://www.csaaul.org/AugustusRussellPope.html.

Fischer, J. (2008b). Our father's beginning. *CSAA Signals*, 14(4). Retrieved June 30, 2009, from http://www.csaaul.org/EdwinHolmes1.html.

Fischer, J. (2008c). Protecting the protection? *CSAA Signals*, 14(5). Retrieved June 30, 2009, from http://www.csaaul.org/BirthofCentralStationIdea.html.

Fischer, J. (2008d). The central station evolves. *CSAA Signals*, 14(7). Retrieved June 30, 2009, from http://www.csaaul.org/BirthofADT.html.

Garcia, M. L. (1999). Security systems design and evaluation. In S. J. Davies & R. R. Minion (Eds.), *Security supervision: Theory and practice of asset protection* (2nd ed.) (pp. 236–254). Burlington: Elsevier Science.

Institute of Electrical and Electronics Engineers. (2009). *IEEE history center: Milestones chronological listing*. Retrieved from <http://www.ieee.org/web/aboutus/history_center/milestones_alpha.html>.

Moorhouse, E. (January 20, 2008). Kiosks guard the lobbies at Lenape district's high schools. *The Burlington County Times*. Retrieved from <http://www.phillyburbs.com/pb-dyn/news/112-01202008-1474276.html>.

Morris, C. (2003). Alarm systems fundamentals. In *Protection officer training manual* (7th ed.) (pp. 87–92). Burlington: Elsevier Science.

National Communications Institute. (2001). Carter, C. D. (Ed.). In *Basic communications officer: Student's course guide* (4th ed.). Gainesville, FL: Georgia Design and Graphics.

Nelson, L. A. (1999). Designing operations centers. In S. J. Davies & R. R. Minion (Eds.), *Security supervision: Theory and practice of asset protection* (2nd ed.) (pp. 277–279). Burlington: Elsevier Science.

Ruiz, H. C. (1999). Security technologies. In S. J. Davies & R. R. Minion (Eds.), *Security supervision: Theory and practice of asset protection* (2nd ed.) (pp. 263–271). Burlington: Elsevier Science.

Savicki, M. (April 26, 2007). School uses high-tech checkpoint for visitors. *The Charlotte Observer.* Retrieved from <http://www.lobbyguard.com/news/charlotteobserver-20070426.htm>.

Stewart, R. W. (1994). The police signal box: A 100 year history (University of Strathclyde, 1994). Retrieved from <http://www.eee.strath.ac.uk/r.w.stewart/boxes.pdf>.

Svensson, P. (August 5, 2009). Iowa 911 call center becomes first to accept texts. *ABC News.* Retrieved from <http://abcnews.go.com/Technology/wireStory?id=8259735>.

Thibodeau, C. T. (2003). Effective communications. In *Protection officer training manual* (7th ed.) (pp. 166–170). Burlington: Elsevier Science.

SECURITY QUIZ

1. Magnetic contact switches, motion sensors and glass break sensors are examples of what kind of sensors.
   a. Access control
   b. Building automation
   c. Closed circuit television
   d. Intrusion
2. Magnetic stripe, wiegand, proximity and biometric are examples of access control readers.
   a. True
   b. False
3. An advanced radio dispatch system may consist of the following:
   a. Touch screen interface
   b. Voice recording
   c. Remote paging
   d. All of the above
4. A main component of a medium to large access control system is the following:
   a. Access control
   b. Distributed processor
   c. Card data
   d. Field
5. Network Attached Storage (NAS) and Storage Area Networks (SAN) are examples of Large capacity storage devices used with video surveillance systems.
   a. True
   b. False
6. The 10-codes are used to assist with rapid transmission of radio communications.
   a. True
   b. False
7. Access control sensors may be used to detect unauthorized access to a facility, and to generate security alarms in response. Which of the following is not one of those access control sensors:
   a. Magnetic contact switch
   b. Network attached storage device
   c. Keypad locks
   d. REX or request to exit device
8. A transmission medium is simply the method by which an electronic message is carried. Signals may be transmitted in a variety of ways. Which of the following is *not* one of those mediums used to transmit electronic messages:
   a. Copper wire
   b. Fiber optics
   c. Cellular Transmission
   d. None of the above
9. A smoke detector is a device to manually initiate a fire alarm
   a. True
   b. False
10. Gas, temperature and power failure are examples of which of the following sensors:
    a. Access control
    b. Building automation
    c. Closed circuit television
    d. Fire alarm

UNIT III

PROTECTION OFFICER FUNCTIONS

Automation in Protection Operations

Kevin E. Peterson

CHAPTER OBJECTIVES

- Provide a historical perspective on automation in the protection industry
- Explain the proper application of automation in the protection officer's sphere of responsibilities
- Describe different types of technology applications that support protection operations
- Identify emerging roles for protection officers with regard to automation
- Emphasize the need for appropriate education and training in information technology and security automation as part of a well-rounded professional development strategy for protection professionals

(Note: In this chapter we mention a number of specific products and product/service providers. This is meant to present the reader with a general view of the types of products, services, and providers that are available to security and protection professionals today. We feel that this information is beneficial and supports the purpose of the book. It does not represent an endorsement of any particular product or vendor by the author, the publisher, or IFPO.)

HISTORICAL PERSPECTIVE

The security industry in the United States was born in the mid-1800s and grew rapidly with the establishment of innovative companies such as the Pinkerton Detective Agency and Wells Fargo. These companies provided a variety of services such as investigations, executive protection, guard forces, and counterintelligence. The innovations of that time included such techniques as mug shots, handwriting analysis, and criminal information databases (ASIS International, 2006, pp. 6–7).

In the late 1800s and early 1900s, security providers focused much of their attention on labor unrest. Although some changes in the industry occurred during this time, such as state and federal regulation of security companies and increased "professionalization" of these firms (e.g., the use of written contracts, sales staffs, and a formal command structure), the services themselves remained largely low-tech, focusing on armed guards and facility protection (Smith, 2003).

The next major jump in security services occurred as World War II approached and the defense industrial complex emerged. The field of "industrial security" was established to meet the needs of the federal government in managing security requirements for defense contractors. The "industrial security" era resulted in a wide array of new security-related technologies, concepts, and procedures—and an increase in the use of security officers. Existing security providers opened specialized divisions and new providers were established to meet the need.

Despite these innovations and forward-looking companies, many people viewed the security industry as nothing more than night watchmen, even up to and through the 1960s. Over the next three decades, the use of security officers became more prevalent. Ironically, one reason for this may have been the development of security technology such as electronic access control and surveillance systems. For example, these technologies led to the establishment of security operations centers (or command centers), which created a new function for protection professionals.

During these years, computer and communications technologies developed rapidly and permeated virtually every type of business as well as our personal lives. However, the security services industry is generally perceived as having been slow to embrace technology in the performance of their mission.

The terrorist attacks of September 11, 2001, brought new and intense attention to the security industry in both the public and private sectors. One of the benefits of this attention was the development and implementation of new and improved security technology applications. Essentially, it gave a "shot in the arm" to security budgets and made it easier for security professionals to justify innovations in equipment, tactics, and techniques.

A number of studies in recent years have projected massive expansion of electronic security systems employing advanced technologies, but they also concluded that the human element (i.e., security officers) will not be predominantly replaced by technology (Webster University, 2009). This conclusion is particularly interesting, and profound, since some of those studies were funded by security systems vendors.

Nonetheless, technology can and should be exploited by the security services industry—and this will require officers and supervisors who are well rounded in technology applications. Some of these applications are discussed in the remainder of this chapter, according to the primary functions they perform.

CONTEMPORARY SECURITY ENVIRONMENT

Today, an increasing number and variety of technology applications support security functions. The most relevant of these applications, from the perspective of the professional protection officer, are listed below.

Incident Management Systems

Few would argue that one of the most tedious tasks for the protection officer is report writing. Originally, incident management systems simply changed the task of writing a hardcopy report into a computer-based function where officers would enter the same data into a computer using a word-processing-like program. One of the benefits of this change was that users of these reports no longer had to deal with issues such as poor handwriting and missing pages. Data entry, however, was awkward, formats were cumbersome, and it was difficult or impossible to include attachments, diagrams, and sketches.

The functionality of incident management systems expanded rapidly and developed into more integrated tools such as IRIMS (Incident

Reporting and Information Management System), a product of a Canadian firm known as PPM 2000. The product was introduced in the mid-1990s and released as a full enterprise-wide version in 2001. During this time, a number of competing products such as iViewSystems entered the marketplace as well.

The real benefit of these tools is their ability to integrate, manage, and truly use the information not only for incident management but also for subsequent investigations, trend analysis, and strategic security planning. Unfortunately, many organizations (whether by decisions of the executive management or of security directors themselves) remained with the "comfortable" paper-and-pencil method, using hardcopy (often handwritten) incident reports.

Some of the complaints regarding automated incident management systems were a lack of user-friendliness, inability to adequately tailor the system to the particular company using it, inconvenient report generators, and, not insignificantly, that officers were not computer-savvy enough to effectively use the systems. Today, many of those problems have been solved with new versions of the software or even new product lines for incident management systems. For instance, most products now include extremely user-friendly GUIs (Graphic User Interfaces) that make data entry straightforward and officer familiarization quick. See the "Emerging Trends" box at the end of this chapter to learn about some of the trends in these systems and why they have become an invaluable tool for asset protection programs in both the public and private sectors.

Visitor Management Tools

Automated visitor management tools are widely available today and should be in use by almost all types and sizes of organization. Among the types of visitor management tools are:

- Visitor management modules within incident management systems

- Stand-alone visitor management tools that can be linked to existing incident management systems
- Stand-alone visitor management products (independent)
- Sophisticated, completely integrated visitor management tools
- Simple, low-end, affordable visitor management tools

Automated tools for visitor management have several advantages, including the ability to keep a searchable record of visitors and generate reports based on individual, company, facility, or date range. Data from these systems can also support subsequent investigations when an incident is discovered after the fact. From a life safety perspective, some systems can report who is currently in a facility, allowing protection professionals to better account for all building occupants in the event of an evacuation.

System components may include an input device that can read driver's licenses or other identification cards (including photographs), cameras, badge printers, and self-service kiosks (for larger applications). Most automated systems also allow employees to preregister expected visitors (this can usually be done through the company intranet right from the employee's desktop). Another benefit is the ability to store records of and designate frequent or repeat visitors. Both of these capabilities serve to streamline entry procedures, thereby facilitating business operations and presenting a professional security image for the organization.

Among popular product providers are EasyLobby, iTrak (by iViewSystems), TEMPbadge (the company that first introduced self-expiring paper badges), and LobbyGuard. In addition, extremely affordable packages such as one by Brother are available at popular office supply stores. This indicates that there are visitor management tools on the market for all types of users, all sizes of facilities, and at all cost levels.

There is no excuse today for using a hand-written sign-in log as a visitor management tool. In addition to the inefficiencies and inability to electronically store and access data, hardcopy visitor logs can represent a security vulnerability. Visitors can generally view the log while they are signing in and see who else (individual, company, etc.) was recently in the facility. In some environments, that may be very sensitive information—or may at least represent a privacy issue.

Crime Mapping

Another category of automation that is increasingly important to the crime prevention and security communities is that of crime mapping. The most well-known and respected provider of crime mapping services is CAP Index. They refer to their primary capabilities as crime forecasting and security risk analysis. This firm provides several products, all based on objective crime and incident data. Among the uses for this type of data are:

- Site selection—used by organizations to aid in determining where to locate new facilities or where to expand existing facilities based in part on local crime data
- Rank and compare—the ability to compare crime statistics at different locations
- Security allocation—data to assist in determining security force deployment, staff augmentation, and resource allocation
- Litigation defense—crime data can be used to justify corporate policies and procedures that may be questioned during a security-related lawsuit or other legal action
- Loss prediction—products can be integrated with corporate data such as shrinkage figures to aid in predicting losses and setting risk tolerance (thresholds) for specific retail or other sites
- Return on investment (RoI)—data can be used to justify security expenditures and projected budgets for specific sites or entire enterprises

Near-term plans for CAP Index include "… an 'ultimate dashboard' that will merge crime forecasting with site surveys and risk assessment, event history and loss-related alerts …" (Groussman, 2008, p. 63). Tools like this should be used for strategic security planning, making a business case for new policies and programs, and conducting risk assessments. It is extremely useful to track crime data for a given location over time and also be able to compare crime levels in surrounding areas.

Geospatial Information Systems (GIS)

Closely related to crime mapping, GIS provides a graphic view of various situations by leveraging the capability to layer information from different databases or inputs over a map or image. This tool is generally used for exterior spaces (e.g., a map of a city or neighborhood), but can also be used with diagrams, campuses, or even building interiors. The objective may be to review historical data (such as incidents or a particular type), identify patterns of activity, display sensitive locations or areas that warrant special security attention, support an investigation, identify traffic patterns (vehicular, foot, or product), or compare any type of data with other data sets by location.

One example of a GIS provider is ESRI, which has supported a wide variety of homeland security, law enforcement, disaster management, and public safety projects. They provide commercial-off-the-shelf (COTS) software as well as individualized consulting and project management services. The ESRI Web site states that "a geographic information system … integrates hardware, software, and data for capturing, managing, analyzing, and displaying all forms of geographically referenced information. GIS allows us to view, understand, question, interpret, and visualize data in many ways that reveal relationships, patterns, and trends in the form of maps, globes, reports and charts." Regarding force protection and security applications, the site mentions the ability to "assess security risks, develop preparedness and security plans, and understand the impact of incidents" as key benefits (ESRI, 2009).

According to an article in the Fall 2002 edition of *Energy Currents*, GIS can be used not only for security planning but also to develop exercise scenarios and to compare projected outcomes of various security solutions. Some applications suggested by the article are comparing scenarios for pedestrian traffic flow and timing for building evacuations, simulating "entire community" response to a crisis (i.e., not only how will you react, but how will your neighbors react—and how that affects your reaction), and modeling of toxic substance releases based on wind speed and direction. The article also mentions that GIS can be used to plan and/or compare different CPTED (Crime Prevention through Environmental Design) options for corporate facilities, government agencies, or communities (Shields, 2002).

The concerns of the energy and utilities industry, and the wide variety of applications for GIS are outlined nicely in the article as follows:

> When disaster occurs, data becomes critical to life and property savings. GIS shows where the gas, water, fiber optics, and power lines are (or were). Rescue teams need to know the location of buildings, stairwells, and basement facilities. Safe traffic routes that avoid probable leaks and live wires need to be drawn. Staging areas for heavy equipment are also a GIS concern **(Shields, 2002)**.

Criminal Intelligence and Analysis Tools

According to Brian McIlravey of PPM 2000, "Using information about actual and prevented incidents is essential to the development of effective security safeguards for each workplace environment ..." (McIlravey, 2009, p. 7). This quote highlights the relevance of all of the tools discussed in this chapter to the professional protection officer specifically, and the practice of security risk management in general. Criminal intelligence/criminal analysis tools are the last application we will cover.

According to Marilyn Peterson, past president of the International Association of Law Enforcement Intelligence Analysts (IALEIA), "Criminal analysis is the application of particular analytical methods to data collected for ... criminal investigation or criminal research" and is "practiced in law enforcement ... and in private security organizations around the world" (Peterson, 1998, p. 1). This field, like some of those previously discussed, originated in a manual form and has now migrated to a largely automated process.

One of several vendors that offers automated solutions for criminal intelligence analysis is i2 Incorporated. They offer an "integrated suite of products that enables investigators and analysts to quickly understand complex scenarios and volumes of seemingly unrelated data, perform analyses, and communicate the results" (i2, 2009). Their customers include law enforcement, government, military, and intelligence users as well as commercial organizations. Products like this help protection professionals "connect the dots" to uncover crime trends and conduct complex investigations. The Protection of Assets Manual (POA) lists criminal intelligence analysis as an important "force multiplier" for investigative and security professionals (ASIS International, 2006, p. 46).

Another force multiplier is the use of commercial and other online databases. According to POA:

> Anything that significantly improves the speed and efficiency of information gathering, collation, analysis, or organization is an important force multiplier. On-line resources are such a tool and are expanding at a rapid pace **(ASIS International, 2006, p. 71)**.

That document also warns, however, against two dangers in using online resources for investigative and security functions. First, there is the danger that protection professionals will get side tracked and go off on tangents, focusing more on the online environment than on the investigative or security objectives. Second, there is a natural assumption that anything extracted from databases or online sources is credible. Users must remember to validate and corroborate all sources, including those that originate in online databases or files **(ASIS International, 2006, p. 73)**.

THE ROLE OF THE PROFESSIONAL PROTECTION OFFICER

Protection professionals, whether operating in a government or private sector environment, are increasingly relying on technology and automated applications such as those described in this chapter. Individuals who embrace technology and leverage it as a tool in performing their duties—and in their own professional development—are those who will excel. In fact, the same applies to security services providers. As security business consultant Mark Gottlieb puts it:

> Due to advances in security technology, computer literate guards who understand "smart buildings" and possess an understanding of the loss prevention function will find their services in high demand. ... Technological improvements and innovation are changing the role of the security guard. Security firms must keep abreast of these changes **(Gottlieb, 2006, p. 4)**.

Only a few years ago, administrators at a college offering an associate's degree in criminal justice and security management stated that their students—those employed as, or aspiring to become, security officers—were literally "afraid" of computers. For that reason, the college was extremely hesitant to add computer skills to their learning objectives and curriculum.

Today, things have changed as people routinely use technology in their personal lives so much that they more readily accept technology in their workplace. Still, the effective use of automated security tools should be emphasized in officer training and education programs.

Two graduate students in a Business and Organizational Security Management program studied college curricula designed to prepare protection officers for a career in security. Among their findings was a distinct lack of coursework addressing emerging technology issues. They concluded that course content should include orientation on automated tools such as incident and visitor management systems as well as crime mapping and analysis. According to their report, "Security officers lacking this knowledge would be placed at a great disadvantage among peers ..." (Bolyard & Powell, 2007, p. 4).

In addition to individual officers, security service providers might consider expanding their service offerings to include items such as:

- Conducting automation-assisted risk assessments
- Providing security technology training services
- Recommending security technology solutions to clients
- Including automated crime analysis or crime mapping within security services
- Providing security services specific to IT environments (e.g., data centers)
- Providing IT security services

As systems and procedures become more integrated and technology-dependent, we must also begin to consider the "security of security systems." The Alliance for Enterprise Security Risk Management began to address this issue in a booklet entitled "Convergent Security Risks in Physical Security Systems and IT Infrastructures." One of the many recommendations presented in the booklet was:

> Connecting special systems and devices to organizations' networks introduces new and usually serious levels of risk. The trade-offs between connecting

these systems to organizations' networks and the security risks that doing so introduces thus need to be better analyzed and understood **(Alliance for Enterprise Security Risk Management, 2006, p. 15)**.

SUMMARY

The issue of automation in protection operations can be summarized nicely with the following quotations:

> ... networked computer technology and associated applications will provide enterprises with increased operational efficiencies and intelligent security" **(Open Security Exchange, 2007, p. 3)**.

and

> ... the amount and variety of security data flowing into their information systems is only going to grow ... as their corporations grow and as new technology-based security systems come online. The corresponding need to store and organize this data for meaningful use will thus become an even more pressing issue ... **(McIlravey, 2009, p. 9)**.

Technology and automation is bringing unprecedented benefits, efficiencies, and opportunities to the field of security and assets protection. From information sharing and information management to risk assessment and strategic security planning, automated tools are truly of value. One warning, from technology consultant Anton Ivanov, however, is very relevant here:

> IT ... is a tool to allow [organizations] to implement business processes ... [and] operate more efficiently.... However, it is the *business process* that makes the business more efficient, *not IT as such* **(Ivanov, 2009)**.

We need to be careful to use technology as a tool rather than allow ourselves to be used by technology. Nonetheless, professional protection officers should develop a technology-friendly mind-set, develop their skills, and incorporate high-tech thinking into their professional worldview.

EMERGING TRENDS

The driving force in today's electronic security systems is "integration." Security systems are increasingly integrated with fire and life safety systems, communications systems, and even automated building controls. This allows new capabilities such as "downstream controls" and "automatic lockdowns." In other words, a breach at an entrance turnstile might lock down the elevators or close selected interior doors. Building controls may include doors and locks, elevators, lighting, HVAC, and communications systems. Today, these controls can be integrated with CCTV, intrusion detection, and electronic access control systems.

Another important trend is toward remote monitoring and control of security systems. Electronic security systems are now routinely capable of being controlled from remote sites via the Internet (over secure connections) and even using mobile devices such as a BlackBerry or iPod (including activation/deactivation of access cards, and dissemination of threat alerts to specific audiences). This trend is expected to continue and will require security professionals to keep up on these technologies (Belfor, 2008).

Somewhat related is the trend toward greater functionality of incident management systems. Data is being collected, analyzed, and utilized in unprecedented ways. Contemporary systems can provide valuable data for corporate investigations, level-of-trust decisions, on-site incident management, evacuation management, regulatory compliance monitoring, security performance measurement, security planning, force deployment, report generation, business case analysis, and many other tasks. As stated by Brian McIlravey: "Incident reporting and investigation management software solutions ... are becoming the keystone of a well-thought-out and executed security information management program, playing a key role in the risk management and decision-making process" (McIlravey, 2009, p. 24).

Finally, the use of online sources and integration of disparate databases for information sharing will become indispensable in protection operations. At the same time, however, this information-sharing environment will raise questions about personal privacy concerns which will likely lead to data restrictions. The proper balance between security and privacy will be a key issue and will be the subject of much discussion.

The continued development of public-private partnerships that involve the private security community may influence this issue and allow special access to security-relevant data.

In short, technology is expanding rapidly and is making more and more of an impact on security operations and the way protection professionals perform their duties. McIlravey summarized the entire issue of "automation in protection operations" this way:

There is a strong trend in security management to strengthen and make more consistent the management of security information across the enterprise. This trend is driven ... by the much broader corporate interest in data analysis and knowledge-based decision making. There is also relentless pressure to improve the speed and quality of decision making, reduce costs, improve productivity, and demonstrate a commitment to best practices (McIlravey, 2009, pp. 23–24).

References

Alliance for enterprise security risk management (AESRM). Convergent security risks in physical security systems and IT infrastructures. 2006.

ASIS International. (2006). *Protection of assets manual* (Vol. II). Investigations Management. Chapter 1, Part 1, ASIS International, Alexandria, VA.

ASIS International. (2007). *Protection of assets manual* (Vol. I). Introduction to Assets Protection. Chapter 2, Part 1, ASIS International, Alexandria, VA.

Belfor, H. J. (2008, March). Chairman ASIS International Physical Security Council, "New Directions in Security Systems and Integration: An overview" (presentation).

Bolyard, D., & Powell, D. (2007, April). *An assessment of undergraduate curriculum in criminal justice and homeland security* (master's thesis), Webster University, National Capital Region.

ESRI. Web site <www.esri.com/>. Accessed October 11, 2009.

Gottlieb, M. S. (2006). *Security: An industry study.* MSG Accountants, Consultants and Business Valuators. Great Neck, NY. (white paper).

Groussman, J. (2008, May). Loss forecasting and ROI. *Security*, pp 62–63. BNP Media, Troy, MI, http://www.securitymagazine.com.

i2, http://www.i2group.com, (corporate web site), McLean, VA, accessed September 2009.

Ivanov, A. (Technology Consultant, Cambridge, UK), Internet posting on "LinkedIn Q&A Forum/Information Security," posted 12 October 2009, <www.linkedin.com>.

McIlravey, B. (2009). *Security information management—The foundation of enterprise security* (white paper). PPM 2000 Inc. Edmonton, AB, Canada.

Open Security Exchange. (2007). *Physical security convergence: What it means, why it's needed, and how to get there,* Washington, DC (white paper).

Peterson, M. (1998). *Applications in criminal analysis: A sourcebook.* Praeger Publishing Company, Santa Barbara, CA.

Shields, B. (2002). Crime and catastrophe: A GIS response. *Energy Currents,* Fall, ESRI, Redlands, CA.

Smith, R. M. (2003). *From blackjacks to briefcases.* Ohio University Press, Athens, OH.

Webster University, National Capital Region, "Business assets protection," course materials, 2009.

SECURITY QUIZ

1. Automated visitor management systems should only be used in large, complex organizations with multiple facilities.
   a. True
   b. False

2. One use for crime mapping is to help determine where to locate new facilities.
   a. True
   b. False

3. Studies indicate that security technologies will soon make security officers obsolete.
   a. True
   b. False

4. Incident Management Systems today are really nothing more than word processing systems that allow an officer to enter reports electronically.
   a. True
   b. False

5. Two dangers mentioned in this chapter that protection professionals should be aware of in using online resources are *(circle two)*:
   a. The possibility of going off on a tangent rather than focusing on the objective
   b. The possibility of introducing a virus to the system
   c. Accidentally disseminating sensitive information to unauthorized recipients
   d. Assuming that information in online databases is credible

6. Among the advantages of automated visitor management systems are *(circle all that apply)*:
   a. Ability to reduce costs by integrating with access control systems
   b. Ability to keep a searchable record of visitors
   c. Ability to better account for all building occupants during an evacuation
   d. Ability to support subsequent investigations in the event of an incident

7. A study by Bolyard and Powell concluded that "security officers lacking this knowledge would be placed at a great disadvantage...." What "knowledge" were they referring to?
   a. An understanding of basic electronic security systems and design parameters
   b. A thorough understanding of contemporary information technology (IT) security threats and risks
   c. An orientation on automated tools such as incident and visitor management systems as well as crime mapping and analysis
   d. An orientation on the historical basis for automation in protection operations as it applies to the security industry in the United States

8. Geographic Information Systems (GIS) are closely related to:
   a. Integrated security systems
   b. Crime mapping systems
   c. Automated incident management systems
   d. Graphical user interface systems

9. A number of studies in recent years have projected massive expansion of electronic security systems employing advanced technologies, but they also concluded that the human element (i.e., security officers) will not be predominantly replaced by technology.
   a. True
   b. False

10. Technology and automation is not bringing the benefits, efficiencies, and opportunities to the field of security and asset protection that was anticipated.
    a. True
    b. False

10

Patrol Principles

Christopher A. Vail

CHAPTER OBJECTIVES

- Provide a history of security patrol
- List the major purposes of patrol
- Explore issues relating to both foot and mobile patrol
- Provide techniques that enhance an officer's ability to detect unusual situations
- List factors that influence patrol effectiveness
- Identify areas of professional conduct for officers on patrol

HISTORY OF PATROL

Security work encompasses various functions; however, there is one function that is common to all security agencies—the job of patrol. In order to understand the technical aspects of patrol, it is important to see how this function came about, how it developed, and how it changes over time. Eugene O'Neill, a famous writer, once said, "The past is the present, isn't it? It's the future, too." Therefore, to gain insight and understanding of the patrol function today, it's necessary to see its genesis. The very word "patrol" is thought to be derived from the French word *patrouiller*, which originally meant "to tramp in the mud." To many, this translation may well reflect what may be described as a function that is "arduous, tiring, difficult, and performed in conditions other than ideal" (Cole, 1995).

Around 2100 B.C., the first codification of customs was written by Hammurabi, King of Babylon. Under these laws of Hammurabi, it is believed that messengers were appointed to carry out the commands of the law—the first form of patrol duty. About 1400 B.C., Amenhotep, pharaoh of Egypt, developed a marine patrol on Egypt's coast, the first recorded history of a patrol unit.

In early Greece, guard systems were established to protect the tower, highways, and the person of Pisistratus, ruler of Athens. Ancient Rome saw the establishment of *quaestores* (inquirers; also basically judicial officers) who would go to the house of the accused and blow a trumpet or horn as an indication of his arrest. In 27 B.C., under Augustus, emperor of Rome, the Praetorian Guards were formed to protect the life and property of the emperor, and urban cohorts were established to keep the peace of the city. The *vigiles* (from which we get the word vigilantes) were formed to patrol the streets and act as enforcement officers.

Although they were nonmilitary, they were armed with staves and the traditional short swords. These patrolmen were also assigned to patrol geographical precincts.

As people moved north toward England and developed collective living arrangements (the precursors to towns), a form of individual and group responsibility for policing began to emerge through the concept of local self-government. Around A.D. 700, tithings (groups of ten families) were formed for the purpose of maintaining the peace and protecting the community. Tithingmen were elected by the group, and their responsibilities included raising the hue and cry upon learning of a crime in the group and dispensing punishment. Ten tithings were called a hundred and the head man was called a reeve. Several hundreds within the same geographical area were collectively called a shire (the equivalent of our county) and the chief law enforcement officer was called a shire-reeve (what we now call the sheriff).

William, the duke of Normandy, introduced a highly repressive police system in A.D. 1066, in which collective security was deemed far more important than individual freedom in England. He divided England into 55 separate military districts and appointed an officer of his choice to be the shire-reeve in each shire, or military district. The state assumed the responsibility for keeping the peace in this system. England lived under this system until the Magna Carta (Great Charter) was written in A.D. 1215, guaranteeing civil and political rights to individuals and restoring local control to the communities.

In 1252 in England, the watch system was established. People appointed to the duty of watchman had the responsibility for keeping the peace. They were unpaid and were often the dregs of society—the old, infirm, sick, and criminally inclined. After 1285, some watches grouped together for the purpose of safety, forming a "marching watch," which may be considered the first form of patrol organization found in our present-day system. The only

paid watchmen were those paid by merchants, parishioners, and householders. In 1737, the Elizabethan Act of 1585 was enlarged to allow cities to levy taxes to pay for the night watch.

In 1748, Henry Fielding suggested that policing was a municipal function and that some form of mobile patrol was needed to protect the highways. The Bow Street Runners were formed, with a foot patrol to operate in the inner areas of London, and a horse patrol to operate in the outer areas. In 1829, the Home Secretary, Sir Robert Peel, introduced "An Act for Improving the Police In and Near the Metropolis"—the Metropolitan Police Act. This legislation forms the basis for law enforcement organizational structure in America. Setting the stage for organized patrol activity, 1 of the 12 fundamental principles of the Act stated that "the deployment of police strength by time and area is essential." By the end of 1830, the metropolitan area of London was organized into 17 divisions and superintendents were appointed. Patrol sections were created, and each section was broken down into beat areas.

Basically, Peel replaced the patchwork of private law enforcement systems then in existence with an organized and regular police structure that would serve the state and not local interests. He believed that deterrence of criminal activity should be accomplished by patrol officers trained to prevent crime by their presence in the community. Hence, modern patrol was born.

Many English systems and beliefs became the basis for American social, political, legal, and governmental systems. In New England, communities were formed around towns and villages, which relied on constables to provide protection and keep the peace by using the watch system. The South was more rural and agricultural, with smaller communities. The county was the primary form of government, in which the sheriff system was the prominent form of law enforcement. As expansion moved westward, law enforcement organizations combined the functions and roles of constable and sheriff.

Patrol activity in America can be traced to Boston in 1636, when a night watch was formed. In 1658, New York City formed a "rattle watch," so named because they used a rattle to communicate their presence and signal each other. Oftentimes, people who committed minor crimes were sentenced to serve on the watch as punishment. As can well be imagined, order discipline was a major problem, leading New Haven to create a regulation that said "no watchman will have the liberty to sleep." A 1750 Boston rule said that "watchman will walk their rounds slowly and now and then stand and listen." Following this rule—as well as making sure to look up, down, and all around—are good procedures for contemporary protection officers to follow.

Uniformed and paid police did not come about until the early to mid-1800s. In 1833, Philadelphia began paying police officers and the New York City Police started wearing uniforms around 1855. As America grew, policing took on new shapes and challenges, with the addition of technological advances, new organizational and political structures, new laws requiring more police officers, societal reliance on law enforcement, and the slow growth of private police and security agencies. However, the patrol function of police and security remains the same and is considered the "backbone" of security and police agencies.

Security patrols may be routine and boring to some; however, the patrol activity of today is much more than "tramping in the mud," sounding the hue and cry, or shaking a rattle. The officer of today who protects a facility is responsible for the safety and security of physical—and often intellectual—assets of tremendously high value. He/she is responsible for the safety and security of a workforce consisting of people who are educated, well trained, and professional—a huge investment of human worth and productivity. Today's security officer has available training, equipment, and technology heretofore unheard of. We now live in an age of more random violent criminal activity, much of which is directed toward innocent victims; of drug-related crime; of juvenile crime involving senseless violence; of overloaded legal systems; and of more civil litigation. At the same time, there is more being demanded from property and organizational managers in terms of protection from fire, disaster, and accident. Administrative agencies at the federal, state, and local level continue to enact new regulations that employers must follow. **Security officers have more responsibility now than they have ever had before.** In fact, the patrol function is more than just the backbone of security; it is also the heart and soul of a total loss control approach.

PURPOSE OF PATROL

The function of security is to prevent and control loss. As a means of accomplishing this, patrol officers make periodic checks around a facility. Therefore, patrol can be defined as the act of moving about an area to provide protection and to conduct observation. That is a fairly simplistic definition, since while protection and observation may be the major elements of patrol, there are numerous other functions that the officer may be called on to perform during his or her tour of duty. Based on organizational needs, there are several major purposes of patrol.

1. **Detection of criminal or unauthorized activity.** Contingent upon organizations' needs, this could include trespassing, noise violations, safety violations, lease violations by tenants, alcohol violations, parking violations, and so on. In order to be effective, officers must be intimately familiar with organizational rules, laws, and patterns of criminal behavior, all of which are constantly changing.
2. **Prevention and deterrence of crime and unauthorized activity.** This includes

projecting a security presence onto the environment. Making the security program visible will at least temporarily suppress criminal/unauthorized activity.

3. **Ensure compliance with organizational policy.** At the same time this is done, public/community relations are maintained by interacting with persons in the work environment. Relations with tenants, vendors, neighboring security departments, and local law enforcement certainly come into play here. Additionally, officers may help ensure compliance with administrative agency regulations such as OSHA, EPA, or U.S. Labor Department mandates.

4. **Assess, report, and record loss-causing situations or circumstances.** This could include any type of fire, safety, or health hazard, such as chemical spills, overcrowding of rooms/area, radiation leaks, coffee pots left on, leaking pipes, unsanitary conditions, congested areas, mechanical failures, and so on.

5. **Investigate as directed by the central alarm station (CAS), dispatch, or supervisor in charge.** There are a host of possible lines of inquiry that can be requested of the patrol officer by management.

6. **Test and inspect the physical security system.** This includes alarms, locks, lights, CCTV, access points, and physical barriers such as fence lines. While assuming greater importance in high-security installations, this is a function of patrols in all environments to some degree.

7. **Act as a compensatory measure during system outages.** Should there be an outage or malfunction of a physical security system component, the patrolling officer will stand by and assume a fixed post at the affected point/area until the situation is remedied. This may simply involve calling maintenance and standing by until a lock is fixed, or it may require continuous posting out in a high-security facility with an alarm or power outage.

8. **Respond to emergencies.** This is where security patrol has traditionally varied from police patrol; while security emphasizes prevention, law enforcement emphasizes response to problems. Unfortunately, security departments must be able to respond professionally to accidents, fights, fires, intrusions, assaults, thefts, HAZMAT problems, or other reasonably foreseeable emergencies. Staffing levels, response times, training, and equipment must all support the requirement for emergency response.

9. **Performance of other services required by management.** This can include opening up areas and making them ready for visitors. It could also include dispensing literature, conduction of formal or informal surveys of visitors, testing equipment, finding lost children, or acting as an escort.

Obviously, the needs of all organizations/facilities are unique. Shopping centers have different loss control needs than warehouses. Hospitals are different from power plants. Hotels are different from amusement parks. Military installations are different from college campuses. What activities occur and what activities are unauthorized vary considerably. Patrol may involve taking action against unauthorized personnel, suspicious persons, illegal activities, and suspicious automobiles. Pertinent state and local laws and company policies will dictate what security officers are to do in these situations. Depending on the officer's employer, he or she may also be required to conduct an investigation of criminal activity. The catch-all phrase of "performance of other services" may include a multitude of functions as requested by the officer's employer, the client, and/or as needed by others such as visitors, vendors, and employees. In any event, patrol is the "eyes and ears of security."

The provision of security services is not an "afterthought;" it is a business necessity. Organizations that don't take steps to protect their assets will lose them! Employers also have a legal and moral responsibility to provide a safe and secure workplace for their employees and those who visit their organization. Insurance companies require that certain security measures be enacted. There are court decisions affecting security, particularly relating to the commission of wrongful acts or the omission of required acts. Federal, state, and local laws, rules, and regulations dictate that certain security measures be placed in effect. Security, therefore, is a part of management in any company or organization. Patrol is the essence of providing those security measures.

TYPES OF PATROL

There are two basic types of patrol: foot and mobile. With each type of patrol, different methods may be used, depending on many factors. Mobile patrols include the use of automobiles, bicycles, mopeds, and golf carts. Helicopters and horses are other means of mobile patrol, but are not all that common.

Foot patrols are normally conducted by one officer "walking a beat." Areas to be patrolled are both indoors and outdoors. The major advantage to this type of patrol is that officers can learn their assigned areas well. While this is not an all-inclusive list of what a foot patrolman can learn, he or she will learn what doors and windows are normally locked or unlocked, what lights are normally left on at night, what personnel are authorized in certain areas, where emergency equipment is located, and what potential hazards exist. Such knowledge will assist the officer in determining if anything is amiss. It is also a good opportunity for the officers to become known to the employees and to establish a positive professional relationship with everyone they contact. One way to accomplish this is by discussing the above-mentioned items, or any other official matter, with the people involved. Another advantage of foot patrol is that an officer could place himself or herself at or near high security risk areas

on a frequent and random basis, making it difficult for one with criminal intent to penetrate that area. Officers on foot patrol also have as much use of their five senses—sight, smell, taste, feel, and hearing—as their physical condition allows and they can actually "patrol" a larger area using one or more of these senses.

Major drawbacks to foot patrols are the small size of the area that can be patrolled effectively, the amount of time taken to conduct one round while carefully checking everything, and getting from one part of the area to another. Other drawbacks include access to emergency equipment if needed and personnel costs involved—it takes many protection officers to provide adequate protection. Inclement weather conditions also sometimes restrict foot patrol activity.

Patrol officers can use a number of different methods of mobile patrol. The automobile is the most common form of patrol; however, many agencies find it economical, while providing other benefits, to patrol with golf carts, bicycles, or mopeds. The advantage of mobile patrol includes the very fact that it is mobile. The officer can patrol a much larger area. Depending on which type of vehicle is used, the officer has access to emergency equipment, and he/she can carry different amounts and types of equipment. Obviously, a car can carry a lot more than a bicycle, and this is a bona fide consideration when determining what type of mobile patrol to use. While a bicycle can't carry as much equipment as a car can, it can get to places a car can't, and can do it much more quietly. These are some other factors to consider in selecting what type of mobile patrol to use:

1. Initial cost of purchase
2. Ongoing maintenance costs
3. Size of the area to be patrolled
4. Need to access emergency and other equipment, such as first-aid kits, traffic control equipment, extra rain ponchos, additional radios, and so on

5. Type of facility being protected, and the organizational image and culture of the facility
6. The threat model and degree of vulnerability of the facility

Depending on the size of the patrol area and access to a car, or in some cases where golf carts are used, the officer can also carry patrol dogs. Dogs enable the officer to search a large and/or complex environment very quickly with minimal manpower. In very large areas, aerial patrols may be conducted by helicopter. In rugged terrain, horses or ATVs may be used. Each of these methods has some capacity to carry equipment.

PREPARATION FOR PATROL

Preparation for going on patrol duty is not only the physical act of putting on a uniform; it also requires mental and psychological preparation. Security officers should act and look professional not only while on duty, but also while going to work. This not only produces a positive impression on the people they serve, but it helps the officer to perform better. When they look and act like professional security officers, such demeanor demands more respect from others. This respect generates a positive attitude in the officer, and he or she becomes more confident and more competent in his or her work.

While people should not "judge a book by its cover," the fact remains that people do judge protection officers based on their first impression. Clothes "do make the man," so one's personal appearance is important. The officer's uniform should be properly tailored and in good condition—neat, clean, and pressed. There should be no holes, patches, or loose threads dangling from it. Shoes and leather equipment should be polished. Male officers should be clean shaven. Hair and fingernails should be clean. No items not authorized by the employing organization should be attached to the uniform.

The officer should have a positive attitude when going to work—his or her mind should be focused on the job ahead. No personal problems, hobbies, or business should be carried to work with the officer.

There should be absolutely no ingestion of alcoholic beverages or other psychoactive substances at least 8 hours before going on duty. The officer should have had ample rest before going to work, as he or she will need to be both mentally and physically alert on duty. Officers should have a positive attitude and an accompanying bearing that reflects courtesy, politeness, and a willingness to serve. These are basic qualities of professionalism, which instill confidence in a department.

All personal and company equipment issued or used while on duty should be checked to ensure that it is in working order. For example, making sure a pen has ink for note-taking or a radio has working batteries, which can be life-saving if the officer needs to call for help. Officers need to know all policies, rules, and regulations that pertain to the security of the facility, and particularly, the assigned patrol post. While proper procedures for performing the job should be known, many officers have their own procedures for accomplishing a task. If used, they should be in compliance with accepted practices of the security agency, the client, and certainly, the law.

It is important, when preparing to go on patrol, that the officer knows the property he or she is protecting "like the back of his/her hand." The location and condition of emergency equipment, water shut-off valves, electrical controls, fire alarms, and telephones should be known, as the patrol officer may be the first responder to a situation requiring their use. The location of any hazardous materials, or places where hazardous materials are worked with, should be firmly implanted in the officer's mind. All doors and windows, and the condition they're normally found in, should be well known. This includes knowledge of existing scratches or other marks that could otherwise be a sign of forcible entry. Also, some doors and windows are frequently left open, some partially open, and some should never be open. Knowledge of the state of these exits and entrances is very valuable to the patrolman.

The alert patrol officer will know what type of conduct, organizational behavior in this case, is considered acceptable or normal at his or her facility. Conduct that is considered abnormal in one area or section may be very commonplace in another. Examples include such things as what doors are normally left ajar; what vendors or service personnel use what doors regularly; what computers are left on; what certain smells or odors are normal; and what types of people frequent the facility. The officer must first be able to determine what is customary for his or her patrol area, and then look for actions, conditions, or patterns that are unusual. Each officer must decide in his or her own mind, and to his or her own satisfaction, what is suspicious. This will vary by experience, background, training, attitude, and type of environment in which he or she works. A successful officer is one who is able to combine logical suspicion with skillful observation and has enough natural curiosity to investigate those conditions that he or she feels are unusual.

If an officer works the night shift, it is advisable to visit the work site during the day. This will give the officer a fresh and clearer perspective of his/her responsibilities. For example, the officer might discover the existence of doors or windows that he or she didn't even know were there. He or she might discover that a part of the facility thought to be empty or unused is really full of expensive equipment. Or the officer might find that an area thought to contain valuable equipment or materials is actually empty or full of items to be discarded. It also gives the officer the opportunity to talk with and discuss security issues about the facility with other officers whom he or she normally doesn't meet.

These are some techniques that enhance an officer's ability to detect unusual situations.

- Get to know people in the patrol environment. Maintain a professional—not personal—relationship with them. Have some idea what their jobs and/or functions are. Most people will gladly elaborate on what they do if asked in a tactful manner.
- Inspect equipment. Get in the habit of checking maintenance tags on equipment. Know what the equipment does.
- Get to know maintenance personnel and procedures. Consider taking an orientation tour with the maintenance department.
- Visit the central alarm station, if possible. Become familiar with the alarms and CCTV in each protected point and area.

There are many different incidents that could occur to an officer on patrol that may require immediate action on his or her part or on the part of others. As the first responding authority to such incidents, the officer should be mentally and physically alert and able to respond, making correct decisions as to what needs to be done. The officer may have to take immediate action using his or her own professional knowledge, skills, and abilities, or he or she may have to direct others such as the police, EMS, fire, or maintenance personnel to the scene via the most expedient way.

In some circumstances, the officer may have to control a gathering group of onlookers and it is essential to know how to isolate them from the crisis point (problem area). Being able to block off an area quickly and efficiently is obviously important in emergencies. Since anything could happen at any time, the effective security officer knows his or her patrol area very well.

When arriving for duty, an officer should be briefed by a supervisor or check with the previous shift for any unusual events or occurrences; suspicious activities or persons; facility problems dealing with security, fire, or safety; orders, directives, and policies; and any expected VIPs, vendors, contractors, and so on. Determine if there are any communication "dead areas" and where they are. In other words, to be fully prepared to go on patrol, an officer must know what has happened, what is happening, and what is likely to happen.

One area of preparation often overlooked by many officers and departments is that of continuing training and education. With the many and increased demands placed on security personnel today, it is essential for the officer to stay abreast of the latest laws, equipment, products, services, and procedures in security. This information is gained only through education or training. Companies who contract out for their security services, proprietary security departments, and security companies themselves, should provide basic and ongoing training for their security officers. Companies can establish internal training programs, send officers or require officers to attend local colleges that have security educational programs, or have their officers take home-study courses.

There are also private vendors who specialize in conducting security training programs. If a local police department has a "ride-along" program, this can provide excellent training for the security officer. Another way for an officer to gain new information and knowledge is by reading security- and law enforcement–related professional journals and magazines. *Protection News, Security, Police and Security News, FBI Law Enforcement Bulletin,* and *Security Management* are all excellent sources of up-to-date professional information.

TECHNIQUES OF PATROL

As stated earlier, patrol is defined as the act of moving about an area to provide protection and conduct observation. In the security world, the majority of patrol activity is focused on the prevention of criminal behavior. A crime cannot occur unless three elements are present: the

opportunity, the desire, and the tools. Patrol officers have a direct influence over the first one and some influence over the second. An effective patrol officer, by following accepted patrol procedures, can and will hinder the first element—the opportunity to commit a criminal act. By ensuring all doors and windows are properly closed and locked, ensuring there is adequate lighting in vulnerable areas such as where safes or valuables are kept and around the building(s) proper, and making access difficult to possible targets for criminal activity, opportunities for the criminal are reduced or eliminated. This is the very essence of loss prevention.

While the patrol officer may not be able to directly influence a person's desire to commit a crime, that desire is greatly hampered by the very presence of a security officer performing his or her patrol duties in a professional way. It is indeed a rare criminal who will commit a crime in the presence of a patrol officer (although it has happened), especially one who is visible, alert, and showing confidence. The third element is not controllable by security personnel; however, security officers should know what tools are generally used by criminals. Guns are obviously a tool, but some people have the authority and permission to carry weapons. Screwdrivers and pry bars are common everywhere, but in the hands of a criminal, they become burglar tools. Information gathering equipment, such as photographic or recording devices, may be used to steal information. Radio transmitting or monitoring devices may also be used by terrorists and sophisticated professional criminals.

Patrol is never routine; anything is liable to happen at any time. Therefore, there are two major principles of patrol that guide the effective patrol officer. **The first principle of patrol is that it should always be done in a random fashion.** Never patrol by driving or walking in the same direction. Alter routes; change the pace occasionally; walk or drive for a while and then stop to look and listen. Sometimes, turn around and backtrack your route. If someone is trying to figure out where the patrol officer will be at any given time so that they may conduct some illegal act, random patrolling will keep them off guard.

The second principle of patrol ties in with randomness: **The frequency of patrol should be random.** Do not go on patrol at the same time each time; the officer's patrol schedule should always vary. Depending on the vulnerability of the facility being protected, the officer may want to patrol the area once every few hours, once every 2 hours, once an hour or more. At the very least, every facility or area should be patrolled when going on duty and just before going off-duty. Patrol should never be conducted the same way each time by timing or route; there should be nothing predictable about a patrol officer's schedule as the officer should not patrol by a set routine or pattern.

With the use of automatic monitoring systems or barcode technology, patrols are documented. These systems generally require that officers patrol in a set sequence within an established time period. Using a random patrol route with a barcode unit is still possible by approaching each patrol point from a different direction. Times may also be varied to some degree.

Another principle of patrol is communication. Patrol officers should always keep the command post, supervisor, backup officer, or central alarm station advised of where they are and what the situation is. They must follow the following proper radio procedures:

1. Listening before speaking into the radio
2. Depressing the microphone a split second before and after speaking to ensure that all syllables are transmitted
3. Speaking clearly and a little more slowly than normal into the microphone
4. Not broadcasting when not necessary
5. Avoiding the use of profanity, horseplay, or confidential information on the radio
6. Scanners abound—especially with reporters.

Patrol officers must also thoroughly document their observations. There should be detailed notes taken on any unusual, suspicious, or potential loss-causing situation. Notes must be kept professionally and observations reported up the chain of command to the appropriate management personnel. Forms designed specifically for each environment should be on hand. Whether there is a predesigned form or not, the important thing is to report all situations if there is any doubt as to their importance.

Although it is not a patrol technique in the true sense of the word, officer survival is a major consideration when on patrol. One way to survive patrol is to use "sensible" patrol methods—that is, use all five natural senses—sight, hearing, smell, touch, and sometimes, although rarely, the sense of taste on patrol. The two strongest senses the officer will use are that of sight and hearing. If riding in a motorized vehicle an officer should keep the windows opened a little, allowing him or her to detect the sound of breaking glass or other noises of suspicious origin. He or she should not play a commercial radio loudly if the car is equipped with one as it could drown out noises that require investigation. An open window will also allow the officer to use his or her sense of smell to detect smoke or other odors that should be investigated.

Often a person is known to have a "sixth sense." This means that they seem to know when something "just isn't right," or they get a "feeling" about a person or a situation. This sense is called intuition. It develops from experience, and it permits a person to sense what is abnormal or unusual. While an officer cannot testify in court that he or she performed a certain duty by using his or her "sixth sense," it can be very accurate in determining when something needs further investigation. While it can be used as a guide to determine which action or actions are appropriate, it should never be used as the sole determining factor.

Another means of patrol survival is the use of the mental "what if?" game. This game (also known as creative daydreaming or mental rehearsal) is played as an officer patrols his or her area by thinking of any possible incident, remote as it might be, that could occur at any place or time. For instance, the officer could think of what to do if someone came running out of an office or building that is supposed to be closed and locked, just as he or she gets there. The officer could think about what actions to take if he or she heard a loud explosion, or gunshots in the area. What would an officer do if he or she smelled smoke in the area or saw a fire in progress? What would an officer do if he or she saw a chemical leak in progress? The list goes on and on. Doing this might uncover a potential loss event that has occurred or is occurring. It will also keep an officer up-to-date on company rules, regulations, policies, and procedures. It is a form of self-training, as the officer can determine his or her own needs for improvement and take the appropriate steps to correct any deficiencies in his or her professional life. Finally, it makes response to the event more efficient, should it occur. It may save the life of an officer or the life of another.

Light and noise discipline should be practiced when on patrol. This means that patrolling officers should avoid making any more noise than is necessary. They should keep the radio turned down somewhat, keep keys and equipment from jangling, and so on. They should be able to "hear others before they hear you." Note that radio net discipline is also important; overuse of the radio ties up the net and depletes the battery. Extended conversations should be carried out by landline methods, such as telephones. Note, too, that backup means of communication should always be considered when on patrol or fixed post duty. Always have a contingency plan if the primary means of communication doesn't work.

Similarly, light discipline should be practiced. This means avoid being silhouetted. Never sit with lights behind you or stay in a car with the dome light on. Use a clipboard light or flashlight. If there is a glare from lights, use it to your advantage if necessary! Use flashlights judiciously; don't have them turned on more than necessary (although for walking safety they should be used if other light sources are not available). "See others before they see you."

FACTORS THAT INFLUENCE PATROL EFFECTIVENESS

As patrol is an expensive loss control technique, it only makes sense to have the officer detect the greatest number of loss-causing situations as possible. The WAECUP theory of loss control is applicable here.

Waste—Patrol officers check scraps being thrown away, look for lights, heat, and water turned on needlessly.

Accident—Officers look for spills and other slippery walking conditions. Always observe all around patrol points for fire hazards, materials stacked too high, and so on. "Look up, down, and all around."

Error—Patrol officers should be thoroughly briefed prior to their shift as to what activities are occurring in their patrol environment. They should check and double-check schedules of building openings and shipments of personnel arrivals. In many cases, the security department functions as "the grease in the machine," making things run smoothly between different departments. In most organizations, security makes sure that things don't "fall through the cracks." Patrol officers can play a key role in alleviating problems caused by simple human error.

Crime—Become familiar with criminal behaviors in the local area. Also, keep up-to-date on criminal trends within the industry. Speaking with local police and reading industry-specific management literature are good ways to maintain one's professional education. Also, patrol in a random manner and develop professional relationships with people in the patrol area so that you are approachable. If people observe something that doesn't quite seem right, and they are comfortable talking with a security officer about it, they will. This can uncover numerous potential crimes.

UNETHICAL/UNPROFESSIONAL PRACTICES

Patrol officers should be wary of fraternizing with employees ("Familiarity breeds contempt"). They should also be on guard for possible indications of collusion between employees, employees who constantly work when no one else is around, gambling between employees, racist graffiti in bathrooms and elevators, employees conducting competing businesses while using company resources, and so on.

Since observation and perception are key effective patrol techniques, the officer should be aware of certain internal factors that can influence his or her ability to perform on patrol effectively. While the officer may not be able to control all of these factors, the very realization that they exist can help the officer be more effective. Internal factors include:

- **Fatigue:** Feeling tired or worn out can affect the way an officer perceives things (with the use of all five senses).
- **Boredom:** The more often a task is performed, the more it becomes routine and boring. Boredom leads to stress; stress leads to hasty, improper decisions being made. This can be a deadly distraction if not kept under control.
- **Personal problems:** Preoccupation with personal problems distracts from keeping one's mind on the job and should not be brought to work with the officer.
- **Known facts:** Officers with security or law enforcement experience will recognize

things such as burglary tool marks or the smell of marijuana more quickly than an inexperienced officer.
- **Variety of activities:** Officers do many various things, many of which don't even appear to be connected, and things can happen very quickly. Other employment, such as an extra job, can influence an officer's work performance (see *fatigue* above).
- **Failing senses:** Age or illness affects an officer's senses; the older or sicker he or she becomes, the less quickly the body is able to respond to stimuli. Obviously, keeping in good health aids the officer in being more discerning on patrol. It also makes for better interactions with others; something that is critical to the success—and job survival—of the officer.

There are also external factors that can affect the ability to perform the patrol function effectively, including the following.

- **Environmental conditions:** These can be weather, highway traffic conditions or lighting (day patrol vs. night patrol, interior patrol and exterior patrol).
- **Distance:** Things that are closer to us are easier to perceive, and things more distant are harder to identify clearly.
- **Time:** The more intense a person's involvement in an activity, the faster time seems to go. Also, security officers may work shift hours and often an officer needs to adjust his or her "internal clock" both at work and at home.
- **Duration of the Input:** The longer a stimulus is received, the more accurate the interpretation will be.

FIXED POSTS

While not patrols in the strict sense of the word, fixed posts manned by security personnel are a part of almost every facility. In some cases, these are in designated structures like those manufactured by commercial suppliers. In others, they may consist of manning a desk in the lobby during evening hours. Many situations support the use of temporarily fixed posts such as at public events, at traffic control points during rush hour, or during heightened periods of security, such as strikes.

Regardless of the employment, fixed posts represent a substantial amount of man-hours and cost. Fixed post duties should be performed in a professional manner, bearing in mind the following:

1. **The mission or objective of the post must be clearly understood.** The reason for the existence of the post should be specified in written post orders. These orders should be readily available to the officer manning the post.
2. **Duties as mandated by the post orders should be read and understood.** A supervisor or auditor who inspects the post should be favorably impressed with how well the officer knows his or her duties.
3. **Post orders should be kept neat, orderly, and secure.** Persons without a "need to know" should not be told what the orders of the post are.
4. **Light discipline—avoidance of being silhouetted should be maintained just as on patrol.** "See others before they see you."
5. **All equipment, especially communications equipment, should be checked when first manning the post.** Simple tests of detection equipment (X-ray, metal detectors, explosive detectors, and so on) should be conducted as early in the shift as is practical. Manuals for use of the equipment should be readily available. Officers must be accountable for the presence and condition of all equipment on post.
6. **Officers being relieved on post should brief their relief officer.** Large, complex operations may have a predesigned form for this, or a simple list of things to advise might be compiled by the officer being relieved.

7. **In high-threat situations such as strikes, civil disturbances, or crowds that could trample an officer, a route of retreat should always be open to the officer manning the post.** There may also be justification for concealing the post or building cover into it. Whatever the situation, safety of the officer must be of paramount importance.
8. **Comfort—reasonable comfort—should always be afforded to officers on post.** Care should be taken to ensure that guard booths are not so hot as to induce sleepiness.
9. **Fixed posts should be visible from other posts, patrolling officers (on foot or in a vehicle), or CCTV.** This helps to ensure the safety of officers, and provides overlapping visual coverage of the area being secured.
10. **Officers should not leave the post until properly relieved.** This is of critical importance in high-security installations or where a contract firm is billing a client for a fixed post officer. Officers should stay in the immediate vicinity of the post. They should check out the area near the post for unusual or unacceptable conditions, prior to assuming it.

CONCLUSION

The need for security is not a modern requirement. The caveman was initially concerned only for his personal well-being, and then he became responsible for his immediate family's safety and security. Eventually, families became clans or tribes which evolved into communities. Security became a social responsibility. Within this responsibility, the patrol function with designated people to conduct the patrols dates to early Egypt. Despite political, legal, and other changes, the patrol function has remained the primary means of providing security services to communities, regardless of whether they are public or private entities.

Protective services in America are based on English precedents. While there have been tremendous changes in technology, society, work, political scenes, economies, and the work forces themselves, the purpose of patrol today remains as it has always been: the protection of property and lives, the prevention and detection of crime, and the performance of other services. Today's security officer has many more duties and responsibilities than his predecessors. He or she must be technically competent in patrol techniques; the laws, rules, and regulations pertaining to security; and numerous other areas of responsibility, such as firefighting and medical emergencies. Embracing the WAECUP theory and putting it into practice will go a long way toward making patrols more cost-effective and professional.

Proper training and preparation for patrol, professional work habits, and attentive patrolling techniques will enhance the patrol officer's skill and abilities. What was once considered a punishment for minor criminal offenses, or a job with little or no responsibility for the "down and out," is rapidly becoming a profession.

In conclusion, professional patrol performance may be considered using the following acronym:

P   **Preparation**
A   **Alertness**
T   **Thoroughness**
R   **Reports**
O   **Observations**
L   **Language (communication)**

References

Butterworth-Heinemann, an imprint of Elsevier Science, has books on physical security, alarms, report writing, and security in schools, hotels, colleges, office buildings, and retail stores. http://stbooks.elsevier.com/security (800-545-2522).

Cole, G. F. (1995). *The American system of criminal justice* (7th ed.). Belmont, CA: Wadsworth.

Professional Training Resources has books and videos on patrol and a multitude of other security topics (800-998-9400), P.O. Box 439, Shaftsbury, VT 05262.

Performance Dimensions Publishing provides patrol books, videos, and equipment (800-877-7453), Powers Lake, WI 53159-0502.

SECURITY QUIZ

1. Uniformed and paid police did not come around until which of the following:
   a. The early 1900s just before World War I
   b. The 1830s when Philadelphia started paying police
   c. The late 1700s about the start of the Revolutionary War
   d. 725 A.D.

2. The patrol function is the least important but necessary part of the loss control approach.
   a. True
   b. False

3. Based on organizational needs, there are many major purposes of patrol. Which of the following is not one of those purposes:
   a. To detect unauthorized activity
   b. To prevent unauthorized activity
   c. To perform an activity that creates the appearance of authority
   d. To provide emergency response in a timely fashion

4. There are basically two types of patron. Which of the following are those two types?
   a. Mobile and foot patrol
   b. CCTV Surveillance and foot patrol
   c. Canine patrol and checking ID's at the main entrance
   d. None of the above

5. Preparation for a patrol tour of duty requires more than just putting on the uniform and going to work. It also requires mental and psychological preparation.
   a. True
   b. False

6. If the officer is working the overnight shift, 2200 to 0600, it is advisable to do which of the following:
   a. Stop ingesting alcohol-laced adult beverages two hours before the shift

b. Sleep at least 10 hours before the shift to assure alertness all through the night

c. Ingest at least four cups of coffee to keep awake all night

d. Visit the work site during the day for facility orientation

7. There are numerous techniques that help an officer to detect unusual situations. Which of the following is one of those techniques:

a. Get acquainted with the people on your shift and where they should be and what they do

b. Get to know maintenance personnel and how they can help you

c. Visit the central alarm station and become familiar with the CCTV system and what the area of coverage is

d. All the above

8. One area of preparation often overlooked by many security departments is:

a. Failing to provide continuing training and education

b. Failing to perform driver license checks on each patrol officer

c. Failing to provide less-than-lethal weapons to each officer

d. Equipping the patrol vehicle with wrong colored flashing lights

9. Which of the following is a principle of patrol that every patrol person should follow:

a. A patrol should always be done in a random fashion

b. The time the patrol officer leaves on patrol each time should be random

c. Keep in communications with either internal or external backup support when needed

d. All the above

10. There are many *internal* factors that can influence a patrol officer's performance in a negative way. Which of the following is not one of those *internal* factors:

a. Fatigue

b. Preoccupation with personal problems

c. Environmental conditions

d. Boredom

11

Traffic Control

Arthur A. Holm

CHAPTER OBJECTIVES

- Provide an overview of the importance of traffic control
- Explore the elements of successful traffic control
- Describe basic traffic control hand signals
- List five general rules for traffic direction

An officer directing traffic at a busy site provides the most frequent contact between citizens and security personnel. The importance of bearing, appearance, and attitude cannot be overemphasized. Likewise, the skillful handling of what citizens recognize to be a difficult and hazardous job can generate and maintain public respect.

SIGNS AND AUTOMATIC SIGNALS

If you hold a driver's license, then you can assume knowledge of most traffic signs. The STOP sign is without a doubt the most important sign in use today. These three functions of a STOP sign are taken for granted:

1. Regulates traffic flow.
2. Clarifies the question of right-of-way at intersections.
3. Reduces motor vehicle accidents at intersections.

Generally speaking, there are two main types of automatic traffic signals:

1. Traffic lights of three colors, sometimes with an arrow for easy turning.
2. Visual and audio warning signals commonly seen at railway crossings.

Automatic traffic signals normally provide adequate intersectional control. However, there are numerous situations that must be directed by a "point control" officer, to assure safe and efficient vehicular and pedestrian movements. Construction sites, accidents, rush hour periods, special events, or any other condition that causes congestion of traffic must receive immediate attention.

Traffic duty consists of directing and supervising traffic at gates and intersections and patrolling parking areas. These duties are performed in order to keep traffic moving with a minimum of delay and maximum of safety.

Since traffic control duty may require an officer to remain at his post for hours in all kinds of weather, protective clothing must be readily available. Proper protection against the elements is an important factor in maintaining efficient traffic control. It has been observed that a wet or cold officer presents a hazard to himself as well as to motorists.

Proper clothing should also include high-visibility material to increase the safety value during nighttime assignments, whether the intersection is well lit or not.

ROADWAY POSITIONS

The position selected to direct traffic must be suited to the particular intersection and expected traffic patterns. It must command a full view of the intersection and its approaches. In turn, the officer must be completely visible to the motorists and pedestrians. In many instances, noncompliance to gestures or whistle signals is caused by the inability of the motorist to see the officer. Usually, officers assigned to traffic control will select a position in the center of the intersection or at one of the corners.

1. The center of the intersection: This position affords the greatest visibility, but it is also the most hazardous. This location is usually selected when traffic signals are inoperative, traffic is not moving at a high rate of speed, and where there is little pedestrian traffic.
2. The corner position: Intersections having heavy pedestrian or vehicular turns can be controlled by an officer standing a few feet off the curb line at one of the corners providing the greatest personal safety and better pedestrian control.

Posture serves to communicate the fact that the officer is in command of the situation. He/she must therefore assume a military bearing, with weight evenly distributed on both feet.

When not engaged in signaling motorists, he/she must stand in the "at ease" position, facing traffic, and with hands at his/her sides. When directing traffic, shoulders must be in line with the flow of traffic and attention must be directed to the vehicular movement.

HAND SIGNALS

Prompt compliance to hand signals is dependent on the officer's ability to use uniform, clearly defined, and understandable gestures. Intersectional control does not call for complicated choreography or wild arm movements.

Improper hand signals, although highly entertaining to bystanders, cause confusion, hesitation, and lead to violations and accidents. Unusual movements undermine the purpose of traffic control and direction.

Stopping traffic: Two clearly defined motions are required to stop traffic. First, select the vehicle to be stopped. Look directly at the driver, and point in his direction with the arm fully extended. The position is held until you are observed by the driver. Then raise your hand so that the palm is extended. The position is held until you are observed by the driver. Then raise your hand so that the palm is toward the driver and the arm is slightly bent at the elbow.

Maintain this position until the oncoming traffic has stopped. With the one arm still raised, turn your head and repeat the procedure with your other hand to stop the traffic moving in the other direction. The arms are now lowered until all traffic has stopped (Figure 11-1).

Starting traffic: To start vehicular movement on the cross street, pivot a quarter turn to place your shoulders parallel with the vehicles waiting to move. When the intersection is cleared, turn your head to one side facing the waiting traffic. Attract attention by pointing to the lead car.

FIGURE 11-1   Stopping traffic.

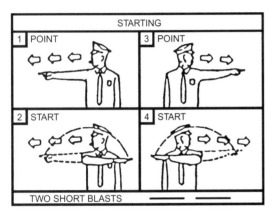

FIGURE 11-2   Starting traffic.

Then, turning the palm inward, bring the hand up and over to the chin, bending the arm at the elbow.

If the driver's attention has been properly obtained, it will only be necessary to make a few motions. After traffic begins to move, the arm is dropped to the side. The opposing traffic is then started in the same manner, but with the other arm.

Slow or timid drivers may be urged to speed up by increasing the rapidity of the arm movements. However, flailing the air with wild arm gestures and shouting at the slow-moving vehicles is unnecessary and only confuses nervous drivers and may lead to greater traffic congestion or accidents (Figure 11-2).

THE WHISTLE

The whistle, when properly used, attracts the attention of motorists and pedestrians and facilitates compliance with hand signals. Improperly used, it becomes a meaningless distraction that adds to the confusion.

To be effective, the whistle must be used in moderation. It then becomes an invaluable aid to assist in the control of the various road users. The whistle should be blown loudly and not tooted lightly. It is a means of communicating rather than a musical instrument.

One long blast is used to attract the motorist's attention to the officer's hand signals to stop. **Two short blasts** with a wave means "start." **Three short blasts** are used to give warning of unusual or dangerous conditions—turning vehicles, improper crossing, and the like. The number of warning sounds should be limited as it is in this area that most improper whistle usage occurs. Normally, **three short blasts** will suffice to warn any motorist or pedestrian.

TRAFFIC CONTROL

With the responsibility of traffic direction, you will be assigned to safely expedite the flow of traffic, with the purpose of preventing congestion and providing maximum vehicular movement. The following responsibilities must be fulfilled in order to properly carry out this assignment:

1. **Regulate the flow of traffic.** Give priority of movement to the most heavily traveled areas by allowing longer periods of running time. Traffic movements must be of equal and adequate time if the intersecting streets carry an equal traffic volume. Long runs are preferable as they reduce the loss of time from frequent changes of traffic directions.
2. **Control and assist turning vehicles.** Supervise all vehicular turns. If traffic is exceptionally heavy or a spillback is caused by another intersection, determine the preference of traffic direction. If turning vehicles increase the amount of congestion, direct traffic to continue straight ahead during the period of the backup.

Prevent improper turns; right turns from the left lane, or a left turn from the right lane, must be prohibited. Not only are they illegal, but they increase potential congestion and accidents.

Traffic backups or accidents may be caused by motorists waiting to turn left or cutting in front of oncoming automobiles. Assist vehicles wishing to turn left. Direct the waiting motorists to enter the intersection on the left turn lane. Allow approaching vehicles that present an immediate hazard to pass. Stop the other oncoming traffic and motion the vehicles turning left through the intersection (Figure 11-3).

Priority of movement is determined by the amount of traffic flow in each direction. If the number of vehicles turning left is greater than the opposing traffic flow, the turning traffic is given preference. If the oncoming traffic is heavy and there are only a few vehicles waiting to turn, these vehicles are held up until a sufficient amount of traffic has been permitted to pass through. The cross traffic is not started until the intersection has been cleared.

In heavily congested situations in which a large number of motorists are making right turns, hold back pedestrians to give precedence to the vehicular traffic.

FIGURE 11-3   Directing a left turn.

3. **Coordinate the flow of traffic with the adjacent intersections.** Whenever applicable, allow the movement of traffic at the adjoining intersections to serve as a guide. If the vehicular movement is not coordinated, traffic spillbacks may occur by reason of traffic being stopped at the next intersection.
4. **Protect pedestrians.** Immediate motorist response cannot be assured when traffic is signaled to stop. Mechanical failure, inattentiveness, or other reasons may cause failure to obey the signal. Pedestrians can then be protected only if they are held back at the curb until all moving traffic is completely stopped. Pay particular attention to children, blind or handicapped persons, and the elderly. Escort these people across the street if necessary.
5. **Assist people seeking information.** Carry a street guide or a map of the local area to assist out-of-towners or local citizens seeking directions. If an inquiry can be quickly answered, there is no need to leave the intersection. However, if a detailed explanation is necessary, direct the citizen to the curb where the answer may be given in safety. Don't leave your post unless traffic conditions permit.
6. **Assisting emergency vehicles.** Stop all vehicles and pedestrian traffic when an emergency vehicle is approaching. Give

the driver a "Go" signal indicating the intersection is clear. If the driver of the emergency vehicle signals for a turn, acknowledge by motioning in the proper direction, indicating that the way is clear.

There is no written, legal authorization that allows private citizens (security officers) to direct traffic on public land or thoroughfares. However, should you be requested or ordered by a police officer to assist him, you are obligated to do so. This includes directing traffic if necessary.

On private property, the safe movement of traffic is the responsibility of the owner or someone delegated by the owner. In most cases, the delegated authority is the security officer.

On construction sites, assistance is required to get traffic in and out of the site quickly and safely. Highway flagmen are required for the safety of the workers and for an even flow of traffic around building or repair sites.

GATE DUTY

Directing traffic from or at a gate would include such duties as checking passes, checking trip tickets, and regulating special types of traffic flow.

The position you take at a gate is determined by the design of the gate, traffic characteristics, daylight or night conditions, and the degree of control required. In taking up your position, keep these factors in mind:

a. Be visible to approaching traffic.
b. Be in a position to see approaching traffic.
c. Do not interfere unnecessarily with the flow of traffic.

EQUIPMENT

It is essential that you have the proper equipment when on traffic control.

1. **Clothing**—You must dress properly according to the weather conditions. If you are uncomfortable because you are cold or wet, you cannot perform at peak efficiency.
2. **Reflective body vests and armlets**—These aids help the motorist to see you and help protect your safety.
3. **Flashlight**—Use a flashlight with a red or orange cone on the end of it at night. This makes you more visible to the motorist and also aids in giving directions.
4. **Whistle**—The whistle is used to attract the attention of the motorist and is used in conjunction with hand signals.
5. **Radio**—The radio provides a means of communication with your supervisor or other security officers.
6. **Signs**—Stop and Go signs and flags are most commonly used on construction sites and highways.
7. **Pass or badge**—In some situations, you are required to have a pass or a badge to allow you to perform your duties at a gate, crosswalk, or building or highway construction site.

GENERAL RULES FOR TRAFFIC DIRECTION

1. Select a position best suited for the intersection.
2. Use uniform signals and gestures.
3. Keep stragglers alert and rolling in their proper traffic lanes.
4. If a spill-back begins to form, look immediately for the source of the trouble and take action.
5. Be cheerful, but firm. Do not shout or argue with motorists or pedestrians.

As a general rule, protection officers are assigned to control private parking and traffic scenes. Examples are shopping centers, parking lots, sporting events, construction sites, resort areas, and so on. Each area is different and the protection officer must exhibit sound judgment in selecting his position. For example, when an extremely heavy flow of traffic is expected at a football game, a pregame plan should be formulated.

Vehicles should be allotted space by ensuring one section is filled in an orderly fashion before rotating to another section. The signals to start and stop traffic are extremely important. **Practice them.**

SECURITY QUIZ

1. The following sign is without doubt the most important sign in use today.
   a. Yield
   b. No U Turns
   c. Stop
   d. None of the above
2. Directing traffic from or at a gate would include such duties as checking
   a. Traffic flow
   b. Entry pass
   c. Travel tickets
   d. All of the above
3. On private property, the safe movement of traffic is the responsibility of the security officer.
   a. True
   b. False
4. When signaling a driver to stop, your hand should be:
   a. Closed
   b. Palm open
   c. Finger pointed
   d. Fist clenched
5. Slow or timid drivers should not be urged forward with increased rapidity of arm motion because they may over-react and cause an accident.
   a. True
   b. False

6. Directing traffic from the corner position is safer than a center-of-the-intersection position.
   a. True
   b. False
7. Proper protection against the elements is an important factor in maintaining efficient traffic control.
   a. True
   b. False
8. The primary use of the traffic whistle is to attract the police.
   a. True
   b. False
9. General rules for traffic direction are:
   a. Select a position best suited for the intersection
   b. Use uniform signals and gestures
   c. Be cheerful, but firm
   d. All of the above
10. When on traffic control, proper equipment includes:
    a. Proper clothing
    b. Flashlight
    c. Radio
    d. All of the above

12

Crowd Management and Special Event Planning

Patrick C. Bishop,
Terence M. Gibbs, and
Jennifer Lantz

CHAPTER OBJECTIVES

- Define basic terms
- Explain causes of crowd formation
- Identify different types of crowds
- List steps to take when controlling a crowd
- Planning strategies, personal behaviors, and responsibilities of crowd control
- Explore riot control formations
- Crowd management assessment
- Alcohol serving considerations

INTRODUCTION

Whenever people gather together in large numbers, such as at athletic events, parades, strikes, peaceful demonstrations, protest rallies, and so on, there exists a potential threat for mass discord.

When disturbances do occur, it becomes the responsibility of the police, and in some instances, the responsibility of security forces, to restore order. Once a crowd has been allowed to get out of hand, through inadequate supervision or in spite of the best efforts by security personnel to prevent a disturbance, the task of restoring any semblance of order, protecting life and property, and the eventual dispersement of the crowd or mob is a tremendous one.

It is important, therefore, that police and security forces be able to quickly determine if a gathering will become uncontrollable and take immediate steps to prevent disorder. The only way this will be successfully accomplished is for the personnel of all crowd control groups to have a good understanding of the types of crowd formations that are likely to be encountered. Also, these personnel should note the different responsibilities of security officers, police, and riot control forces.

DEFINITIONS

1. **Crowd**—A concentration of people whose present or anticipated behavior is such that it requires police action for the maintenance of order.
2. **Demonstration**—A crowd that is exhibiting sympathy for or against authority, or some political, economical, or social condition.
3. **Disaster**—Any extreme or catastrophic condition that imperils or results in loss of life and/or property.
4. **Picket line**—A demonstration in which several people walk about in a public space, carrying signs that show their displeasure with a business or government policy. Often associated with strikes, picket lines are usually legal in the United States, as long as the picketers keep moving and do not attempt to harass or interfere with others in any way.
5. **Rally**—A gathering of people to show support for a common cause.
6. **Riot**—A breach of the peace committed to violence by three or more persons, in furtherance of a common cause to protest or disrupt some enterprise, venging action against anyone who may oppose them.
7. **Sit-down strike**—A form of a strike in which the workers refuse both to work or leave the workplace. This makes it impossible for the employer to bring in others to do the strikers' jobs. Sit-down strikes are illegal in the United States.
8. **Strike**—A work action in which employees withhold their labor in order to put pressure on their employer.

FORMATION OF CROWDS

A crowd may exist as a casual or temporary assembly having no cohesive group behavior. It may consist of curious onlookers at a construction site, spectators at the scene of a fatal accident, or curious citizens who are attracted to a soapbox orator. Such a crowd has a common interest for only a short time. It has no organization, no unity of purpose beyond mere curiosity, and its members come and go. Such a group will normally respond without resentment to the urgings of a police officer to "stand back," "move on," or "keep moving." There is no emotional unity and they offer little concern.

However, even in this most ordinary and routine situation, the person in authority who is lacking in good judgment and discretion may meet with resistance. Derogatory remarks, unnecessary shoving and the like cause immediate resentment in people and become self-defeating. Impartiality, courtesy, and fair play hold the key to any situation involving people.

When you instruct a crowd to "move on," it must mean everyone. If you make exceptions and allow some people to remain, strong objections may be raised. This glaring partiality may cause some people to defy you. Incidents such as these can rapidly change crowd attitudes and, if nothing else, impart a very poor impression of the security officer.

A crowd may also assemble for a deliberate purpose—spectators at a football game or a rally of some sort, or it may be a disgruntled citizen, or group of citizens, willing to be led into lawlessness if their demands are not met.

Members of these crowds have little dependence on each other, but they do have a unity of purpose; they are drawn together to share a common experience. If outside influences interfere with their purpose or enjoyment, it is possible for some individuals in the group to become unruly and aggressive. There are numerous instances of riots occurring during, or immediately following, a sporting event or rally in which emotions run high.

CAUSES OF CROWD FORMATIONS

1. **Basic cause**—The basic reason for the formation of any crowd is the occurrence of an event that is of common interest to each

individual. The nature of the crowd is largely governed by the nature of the event.

2. **Casual causes**—A large and comparatively orderly "casual crowd" may gather in a shopping area or at a sporting event. This casually formed crowd is characterized by the fact that its members think and act as individuals. There is an absence of cohesion or organization. This type of crowd is easily controlled in its formative stages, but it may develop otherwise if the event becomes alarming, or if something occurs which causes severe emotional upset to its members.

3. **Emotional causes**—Crowds that are formed due to events that incite the emotions of the members are almost invariably unruly and troublesome simply because emotion makes them blind to reason. These are the most frequently encountered emotional causes:

   a) **Social**—Crowd disturbances resulting from racial or religious differences, or excitement stemming from a celebration, sports, or other similar event.

   b) **Political**—A common political cause may result in attempts by large groups to gain political power or settle political disputes by other than lawful means.

   c) **Economic**—Economic causes of disturbances arise from conditions such as disagreements between labor and management, or from such extreme conditions of poverty that people resort to violence to obtain the necessities of life.

   d) **Absence of authority**—The absence of authority, or the failure of authorities to carry out their responsibilities, may cause people to believe they can violate the law without fear of reprisal or hindrance.

   e) **Disaster**—Disaster conditions may result in violent emotional disturbances among people in the area due to fear, hunger, loss of shelter, or injury and death of loved ones.

PSYCHOLOGICAL FACTORS

In addition to the factors that cause crowds to form and turn peaceful groups into disorderly mobs, it is important that people dealing with crowds understand that a small crowd often attracts a great many initially disinterested people, thereby rapidly increasing its size; this snowballing effect is caused by certain psychological factors:

1. **Security**—Certain individuals may be attracted to a crowd due to the feeling of security and safety it provides while associating with large numbers. This situation is most likely to arise during periods of civil unrest where large gangs are roaming the streets, looting and threatening the safety and peaceful existence of the citizens who become fearful for their well-being and join with the gang for the security it may afford them.

2. **Suggestion**—Persons joining a crowd tend to accept the ideas of a dominant member without realization or conscious objection. If the dominant member is sufficiently forceful with their words and ideas, they may be able to sway the good judgment and commonsense reasoning of those about them. There is a tendency to accept even the wildest of ideas; thus they transform the susceptible into unthinking followers.

3. **Novelty**—An individual may join a crowd as a welcome break in one's normal routine and through persuasion and suggestion react enthusiastically to what they consider proper form under these new circumstances.

4. **Loss of identity**—Similar to that of the "security" factor. The individual tends to lose self-consciousness and identity in a crowd. Consequently, one may feel safe to be neither detected nor punished for any participation in wrongdoing.

5. **Release of emotions**—The prejudices and unsatisfied desires of the individual that are

normally held in restraint may be released in an emotional crowd. This temporary release of emotions is a strong incentive to an individual to participate in the activities of the crowd. It provides the opportunity to do things he or she has been inwardly desirous of doing but hitherto has not dared.

TYPES OF CROWDS

The behavior of crowds varies widely depending on its motivational interest. Crowds are classified in accordance with their behavior patterns and it is essential that any security measures are based on recognition and understanding of the type of crowd they must deal with. The following outline is representative of most of the crowd types that might be encountered in this country.

1. **Acquisitive**—The members of an acquisitive crowd are motivated by the desire to get something. They are best illustrated by a crowd of shoppers seeking items in short supply or at an auction sale. They have no leaders, little in common, and each member is concerned with his or her own interest.
2. **Expressive**—In this type of crowd, the members gather to express their feelings such as at a convention or political rally. The expressive crowd is usually well behaved; however, some persons in it may feel that slight disorders and unscheduled demonstrations should be condoned by the officials. When they are thwarted or restrained, resentment occurs and their otherwise cheerful enthusiasm may be replaced by hostility.
3. **Spectator**—This crowd gathers to watch out of interest, curiosity, instruction, or entertainment. It is invariably well behaved and good humored initially, but since spectator sporting events, parades, and so on tend to stir the emotions rapidly, this kind of

crowd can quickly become unruly and very violent.
4. **Hostile**—Crowds of this nature are generally motivated by feelings of hate and fear to the extent they are prepared to fight for what they want. The most prominent types are strikes, political demonstrations, and hoodlums or rival mobs. Hostile crowds may have leaders who direct and maintain a high degree of hostility in their followers, but not always.
5. **Escape**—An escape crowd is one that is attempting to flee from something it fears. It is leaderless and completely disorganized, but it is homogeneous in that each person is motivated by the same desire, which is to escape. Once an escape crowd reaches safety, it will lose its homogeneity and its members must then be handled as refugees.

CROWD ACTIONS AND SUGGESTED COUNTERMEASURES

The majority of crowds do not, as a rule, resort to violence; however, any crowd is potentially dangerous or at the least, aggressive. The mood of a peaceful crowd—that is, acquisitive, spectator, or expressive—may change quickly to that of a hostile or "escape" crowd. Since most concern is caused by a hostile crowd, as opposed to the other types mentioned, a more thorough study should be made of it.

A hostile crowd is usually noisy and threatening, and its individual members may harass security personnel. This kind of crowd will hesitate to participate in planned lawlessness because it generally lacks organization and leadership in its early stages. However, it may provide the seedbed for "mob" action when it is aroused by the more forceful persons who assume leadership. It may also be triggered into violence by the undesirable actions of individual protective personnel.

Aroused crowds will often vent their resentment and hostility on those assigned to maintain order. Some individuals may try to bait security officers into committing errors of judgment, or displays of unnecessary force in order to discredit authorities, or to further incite crowd members to commit acts of lawlessness, or to oppose efforts in regaining control. Such crowd actions are usually directed toward one or two individual officers in the nature of taunts, curses and other minor annoyances. Verbal abuses must be ignored, no matter how aggressive they may become. By contrast, immediate action must be taken to those who assault, throw rocks, or attempt in any way to interfere with protective units.

In controlling a hostile crowd, sufficient manpower is basic to your success. If it appears that a peaceful demonstration or other large crowd gathering is showing hostile tendencies, do not hesitate to report and call for immediate assistance. This does not, however, mean you may or should resort to the use of unnecessary force. Such action is never justified. Potentially dangerous crowds can usually be controlled by the following methods:

1. **Removing or isolating individuals involved in precipitating an incident before the crowd can achieve unity of purpose.** This may cause temporary resentment in a very small portion of the crowd members. It is important, therefore, to immediately remove the subject from the area. Elimination of the cause of irritation will prevent an ugly incident. Remember that the injudicious use of force can well defeat your purpose and turn the entire crowd against you.

2. **Fragmentizing the crowd into small isolated groups.** The police often arrive at the scene of an incident or hastily conceived demonstration after a crowd has assembled and achieved a degree of unity. The close contact of the crowd members and the emotionalism of the situation cause the individuals in the crowd to become group-influenced and directed. Individual controls disappear and each person is swayed by

the mood and feelings of the crowd. This collective excitement is communicated to each member of the group in what is known as the "milling process."

The presence of an adequate force of men to disperse the crowd and break it into small isolated groups before it becomes hysterical and aggressive is an effective method of coping with the milling process. It is necessary for security to make a show of force, which does not necessarily mean the use of force. The mere presence of an adequate number of well-disciplined and well-trained control forces often suffices.

3. **Removing the crowd leaders.** The most excited and vocal members of a crowd establish themselves as the informal leaders. Removing or isolating the agitators contributes greatly to eventual crowd dispersal. Isolating the more boisterous individuals should only be attempted if sufficient manpower is available. A crowd is not impressed with inadequate manpower and violence may result. Individual heroics are not only foolhardy but dangerous, as well.

4. **Diverting the attention of the crowd.** The use of a public address system on the fringe of a crowd, urging the people to "break up and go home," is a successful crowd dispersal tactic. Amplifying the authoritative tone of the command attracts the attention of individuals in the crowd and breaks the spell cast by the more excited crowd members.

5. **A crowd that grows in hostility and defies orders to disperse can also be controlled by forcing the individuals to focus attention on themselves rather than the objectives of the group.** Instead of making a direct assault on the crowd, a series of random arrests is made of individuals situated on the edge of a crowd. The crowd will soon recognize that a greater number of persons are being arrested. But the fact that arrest is threatened through haphazard selection causes them to fear for their liberty and a spontaneous dispersal results.

6. **Using a recognized leader.** An effective method of counteracting the developing leadership in a crowd is by using someone having greater appeal to the crowd. A trusted labor leader, a member of the clergy, a well-known sports figure, or a well-known civil rights leader can often successfully plead for order and reason. Depending on the origin and cause of the crowd formation, an appropriate public figure or official may greatly assist in calming the excitement and emotions of the crowd.

7. **Preventing panic from developing in a crowd.** Panic is caused by fear and is most often found in the "escape" crowd fleeing from disaster or the threat of disaster or violence. The primary cause of panic is blockage of the escape route. Security actions should aim at providing an escape route, directing and controlling the progress of the crowd along the route, and at the same time dividing the crowd into small groups, if possible. The following control techniques might be implemented:
   a) Display a helpful, calm and confident attitude. Loudspeakers should be used to give directions and helpful information.
   b) Use rational members of the crowd to assist in calming or isolating hysterical persons.
   c) Provide first aid and medical attention to the injured and weak, particularly women and children.
   d) Use security to block off routes so as to channel movement in the desired direction. Care must be taken to ensure that the security forces do not panic a crowd by hasty action, arrogance, or thoughtlessness.

8. **Directing women and children.** Crowds and demonstrators may resort to having women or children wheeling baby carriages at the head of their advance. If the marchers must be stopped, an attempt should be made to divert the women and children or let

them pass through the ranks and then close rapidly behind them.

WHEN VERBALIZATION DOESN'T WORK

When verbalization is not effective, there may be a need to physically move crowd members. This should be done only as a last resort, and should include verbalization. It should be a planned action, only be done after professional instruction has been received on the proper procedures. The following are some physical control techniques that are appropriate for the movement of people in crowds:

1. "Heavy hands"—Assert your presence with your hands in front of you.
2. Be assertive! Do not take a backward step when moving the crowd.
3. Destabilize resistant persons by one or more of the following techniques:
   a) Upper torso restraint.
   b) Arm around waist with an escort hold.
   c) Belt lift with an escort hold.
   d) Bracketing with an escort hold.
   e) Pressure point control as appropriate.
   f) Wristlocks, team control position, arm bars, etc. as appropriate.

SECURITY AND DEMONSTRATIONS

Security organizations assigned to supervise demonstrations have a twofold responsibility. Regardless of individual convictions, they must first protect the peaceful demonstrators who are exercising their right to protest.

Spectators not in sympathy with the demonstration constitute a potential threat of violence. This is often aggravated by counterdemonstration whether it is organized or spontaneous.

Crowd control forces must also protect the general public from demonstrators who infringe upon the rights of others. The more common problems occur when demonstrators engage in "sit-ins" and so on, and violate the property rights of others. Fanatical members may even lie down in the path of vehicles and refuse to move. They must be picked up and carried away at once. Use of tear gas in this situation is not generally recommended in view of the passive nature of the gathering and their relatively few numbers.

Such groups may attempt to discredit security with harassment during removal, by resorting to shouts of "brutality," raising their hands as if to ward off blows, and emitting cries of pain when they are aware of the presence of news media. Such encounters will tax the patience and control of individual security officers, who must ignore all such verbal attacks.

FORMATION OF A MOB

The crowd or demonstration will deteriorate into a mob if it has been preconditioned by irritating events, aroused by rumors, and inflamed by professional agitators who appeal to emotion rather than to reason. Hostility prevails and unity replaces confusion and disorganization.

The early frustrations engendered by agitation and rumor require a climactic incident to unleash the mob and may come about for any number of reasons. It may often be influenced by the apparent weakening of the strength and attitude of security groups assigned to preserve the peace.

RESPONSIBILITY AND BEHAVIOR OF PROTECTIVE GROUPS

Protection must extend to all people. This means fair and equal treatment of all. Observe a position of neutrality—act with firmness—this is not belligerence or unreasonable force. After an order is given, it must be enforced for the preservation of the public peace and the carrying out of the traditional mission of protecting life and property of citizens to assure the basic rights of all people.

If you observe a hostile crowd gathering, never hesitate to request assistance. In these instances, it is definitely safer to overstate the number of personnel needed to restore order, than to attempt to act alone or underestimate your requirements. A show of force not only has a restraining effect on the crowd, but also provides the necessary manpower.

Order must be established. Approaching the more vocal individuals in a crowd is an effective method of dealing with a group. When addressing these persons, be firm and carefully phrase your commands. Do not become involved in an argument. Use simple language and inform the people of the violations they are or may be committing. Request that the violations stop and that the groups disperse. Allow the crowd the opportunity to withdraw peacefully without interference. If the throng defies authority and the apparent leaders make no efforts to disperse the crowd, arrests should be made and police assistance obtained.

Whenever you are dealing with an excited or hostile crowd, remember that it is potentially dangerous and may require only a slight incident to turn it into a mob—your example and your ability to maintain order are the best deterrents to mob action.

PLANNING CONSIDERATIONS

From time to time, security personnel have the opportunity to plan for large crowd control events. An example of this may be political rallies, sporting events, parades, or shopping mall events. As there is always some form of advance notice for these expected large crowd events, the following considerations should form part of the contingency procedure:

1. Is police involvement required?
2. Barriers (this includes metal fencing, ropes and stanchions, people)

3. Communications (radio and telephone, PA system)
4. First aid staff
5. Ambulance or first aid rooms
6. Doctors
7. Location of event
8. Fire procedures, equipment, personnel
9. Communications center
10. Media observation area
11. Entry and exit location for VIPs
12. Parking
13. Lavatories
14. Food concessions
15. Disabled persons areas (wheelchairs)
16. Entertainment before or after event
17. Signs
18. Timing schedule
19. Number of security personnel and degree of expertise required
20. News releases and media precoverage
21. Time of year and type of environment
22. Alternate power sources
23. Size of crowd expected
24. Vehicles for movement of VIPs, and so on

As you can see, when a large crowd control event is known and sufficient time is available for preplanning, the event should be able to take place with minimal problems for both security staff and participants alike.

PERSONAL BEHAVIOR

1. Stand your ground without yielding. Your job is to maintain order and protect life and property.
   a) Avoid all unnecessary conversation.
   b) Do not exchange pleasantries with the crowd or apologize for your actions.
   c) Do not give the impression you will not enforce orders to disperse or arrest individuals defying such an order.

2. Take lawbreakers into custody and turn over to the police for arrest.
3. Use reasonable force to enforce the law.
   a) Do not overlook violations or defiance of lawful orders.
   b) The use of unreasonable force often incites a crowd which normally would be passive or curious.
   c) Charges of brutality are often made in an attempt to discredit the security force; they will have no basis in fact if brutality is not used.
4. Remain on the fringe of the crowd. Do not get too close or mix with a hostile crowd. Remain out of reach and observant of crowd and individual activities, pending the arrival of reinforcements.
5. Assist fellow officers who may be in trouble. If one of your associates situated near you is physically attacked, go to his or her immediate assistance. Arrest the assailant. To permit such a person to escape will encourage others to assault or try to overpower individual security personnel.
6. Refrain from participating in crowd activities.
   a) An aggressive crowd will invariably throw a barrage of rocks, sticks, bottles, and so on at opposing forces. DO NOT throw them back at the crowd! This will only precipitate greater hostility and supply the crowd with more missiles.
   b) Withdraw to a safe distance until dispersal operations can be commenced.

RIOT CONTROL FORCE DEPLOYMENT PROCEDURES

Basic riot and crowd control formations used by control forces exist in the following forms (Figure 12-1):

1. **Arrowhead**—This is used to strike into and split a crowd or mob, or to provide an escort for a person(s) to a given point through a

PERSONNEL EMPLOYMENT

BASIC RIOT AND CROWD CONTROL FORMATIONS USED BY CONTROL FORCES EXIST
IN THE FOLLOWING FORMS:

a) ARROWHEAD

　　THIS IS USED TO STRIKE INTO AND SPLIT A CROWD OR MOB, TO PROVIDE AN
ESCORT FOR A PERSON (S) TO A GIVEN POINT THROUGH A FRIENDLY OR DIS-
ORGANIZED CROWD. THE USE OF AN ADDITIONAL INVERTED ARROWHEAD AT
REAR OF THE FORMATION WILL GIVE ALL-AROUND PROTECTION.

b) LEFT FLANKING　　　　　　　**AND**　　　　　　　**RIGHT FLANKING**

USED TO MOVE A CROWD OR MOB TO THE RIGHT OR LEFT, OR TO TURN A
CROWD AWAY FROM THE FRONT OF A BUILDING, FENCE, ETC.

c) LINE

USED TO MOVE A CROWD OR MOB STRAIGHT BACK UP THE STREET.

FIGURE 12-1　Riot and crowd control formations.

friendly or disorganized crowd. The use of
an additional inverted arrowhead at rear of
the formation will give all-around protection.
2. **Left flanking and right flanking**—Used to
move a crowd or mob to the right or left,
or to turn a crowd away from the front of a
building, fence, and so on.
3. **Line**—Used to move a crowd or mob
straight back up the street.

CROWD MANAGEMENT
ASSESSMENT

1. What is the officer-audience ratio?
2. Are the security personnel deployed in a way
as to maximize surveillance of the crowd?
3. What type of performance is this?
4. Are the security personnel properly trained
to handle the crowd?
5. Are the security personnel knowledgeable
in first aid?
6. Are the security personnel licensed and
armed with any weapons?
7. Are the security personnel properly briefed
on the type of crowd?
8. Is the company providing security
properly licensed?
9. Have all required permits been obtained?
10. What is the seating?
11. What is the procedure for extracting
problem people from the crowd and
ensuring that they leave the venue without
posing a threat to anyone inside or outside
the venue?
12. Is supervision present and adequate?
13. Are communications, including two-way
radios, adequate?
14. Is alcohol being served at the event?
If so, what are the procedures for
controlling access to alcoholic
beverages?
15. What are the evacuation procedures in the
event of panic in the crowd?
16. In the event of a cancellation after the
audience has been admitted to the venue,
what procedures are in place to placate the
crowd?

ALCOHOL SERVING CONSIDERATIONS

Serving alcohol at special events can create a host of safety, security, and liability issues. A few considerations regarding alcohol service are:

Are persons dispensing alcohol:

1. Properly trained in correct procedures for checking and verifying IDs of patrons?
2. Properly trained in the methods to use to control service of alcoholic beverages?
3. Properly trained in the recognition and identification of behavioral cues (TIPS program: Training for Intervention Procedures) of intoxication and the intervention techniques to use to stop

service, and therefore ensure intoxicated persons do not harm themselves or others?

Are security personnel:

1. Properly trained in the above techniques so that they can control access to the venue? They must also be able to intervene properly in matters involving intoxicated patrons, including making sure that intoxicated patrons do not harm themselves or others.
2. Properly and adequately trained in the methods of extracting problem patrons from the crowd?
3. Correctly trained and instructed to ensure that evicted patrons do not linger about the exterior of the establishment to take revenge upon other patrons or employees, or re-ignite an earlier conflict?

EMERGING TRENDS

The first and foremost emerging trend is a greater awareness by organizational management of the problems and potential liabilities associated with special events. Special events are complex undertakings and many things can go wrong. Perhaps the best way to conceptualize this is the old saying *"whatever else can go wrong, will go wrong."*

It is clear that special event security is a division of the security field that needs to be addressed. It is defined as a part of physical security, but it is not ongoing. It is occasional; only temporary. As such, it may not garner the attention that it deserves.

An interesting example of event security is at the oldest fair in the United States, the York County Fair, in York, Pennsylvania. Security at the fair is difficult because of the number of people in such a small space. The fair takes place in September, so planning must begin in March. There must be adequate EMS (emergency medical services), fire, and police in place. In fact, the fair has its own police force, a group of officers who

are sworn in for the duration of the fair. Some of the officers then joke that they are "suspended without pay for 355 days" once the fair is over.

In addition to the fair police, there are township police, and some contract security personnel. York County Deputy Sheriffs perform security at concerts held at the fair. Private investigative firms conduct surveillance and make controlled buys from vendors who sell counterfeit goods. York County Probation Department personnel search for probation violators and perform security at concerts. This is an excellent means of both apprehending probationers who are in violation as well as deterring troublemakers. Deputy U.S. Marshalls sometimes conduct sting operations for fugitives.

Gang activity is prevalent, especially on student nights when students get in for free. Nearly 100 police officers are required, and EMS needs to be prepared for possible mass casualty situations. It is evident that there is a need for even more officers, but monetarily it isn't possible.

So the trend is to reach out to the private sector and specialized service firms for security at these types of special events.

In addition to the example of the York Fair, we are seeing more varied and creative use of protection forces across the board. These include proprietary security, t-shirt security, contract security, off-duty police, and so on, all working in contact with one another. INA, Inc., based out of Harrisburg, Pennsylvania, finds that using off-duty police officers saves a great deal of money depending on the size of the venue and if the event was set up correctly. INA also utilizes probation officers who take vacation days to man special events. The probation officers are all college graduates who have had some relevant training and experience.

Another trend is having more restrictions in place as to what can be brought into an event, as well as more restrictions on tailgating parties and serving alcohol. There is also an increase in the use of dogs and horses at some special events.

Reference

Health Communications Inc. *The TIPS Program: Training for Intervention Procedures*, Alexandria, VA; 1985–2009.

Resources

The International Association of Assembly Managers is an organization of professional venue managers. The IAAM conducts and publishes research, holds meetings, and administers a professional certification program for assembly managers. Visit http://www.iaam.org/.

The Center for Venue Management Studies (CVMS) is IAAM's resource center for public assembly facility management. The Center offers a variety of books and videos. CVMS works with IAAM staff and work groups, such as the Safety and Security Task Force, to develop and distribute resource materials and practice aids for the industry. Visit http://www.iaam.org/CVMS/CVMS.htm.

SECURITY QUIZ

1. In controlling a hostile crowd, sufficient _____ is/are basic to your success.
   a. Force
   b. Manpower
   c. Time
   d. Weapons
2. The protection officer should attempt to isolate an individual troublemaker by:
   a. Taking them down
   b. Tranquilizing them
   c. Removing them
   d. Arresting them
3. If you observe a hostile crowd gathering, never hesitate to request additional:
   a. Weapons
   b. Assistance
   c. Rioters
   d. Vehicles
4. A demonstration is a crowd that is exhibiting sympathy for or against authority, or some political, economical, or social condition.
   a. True
   b. False
5. A riot means any extreme or catastrophic condition that imperils or results in loss of life and/or property.
   a. True
   b. False
6. The basic reason for the formation of any crowd is the occurrence of an event that is of common interest to each individual.
   a. True
   b. False
7. A leaderless crowd that is attempting to flee from something it fears is a/an:
   a. Spectator crowd
   b. Emotional crowd
   c. Hostile crowd
   d. Escape crowd

8. Some psychological factors in crowd formation are:
   a. Security
   b. Novelty
   c. Loss of identity
   d. None of the above
   e. All of the above

9. The protection officer dealing with crowds should:
   a. Exchange pleasantries with the crowd
   b. Give the impression he/she will enforce orders
   c. Apologize for his/her actions
   d. All of the above
   e. None of the above

10. Some riot control, force deployment procedures are:
    a. Arrowhead, left and right flanking, line
    b. Right flanking, bullet, left flanking
    c. Line, bow, arrowhead
    d. Arrowhead, bullet, left flanking

CRIME PREVENTION AND PHYSICAL SECURITY

13

Environmental Crime Control

Glen Kitteringham

CHAPTER OBJECTIVES

- Define environmental crime prevention
- Provide an overview of the main environmental crime control theories
- Explain how theory application aids in informed crime control decisions

INTRODUCTION

The private security industry has come a long way from when Allan Pinkerton created his world famous Pinkerton's Detective Agency in the middle of the nineteenth century. In the intervening 16 decades, there has been a great deal of activity. Significant steps have been taken in lock and key systems, access control hardware, the increasing ingenuity of vaults and safes, fencing systems, CCTV, increasing professionalism and training of security officers, and a host of other physical security enhancements. However, proper attention has not been given to the environmental crime control theories and subsequent practical applications behind the deployment of these human, hardware, and documentation innovations.

While the reader is likely familiar with Crime Prevention through Environmental Design (CPTED), there are several other theories that offer insight into crime control opportunities. But the question remains: Why should security practitioners know the reasons for applying particular security applications, as well as the theories behind them? Because if you are going to implement a new security application, you should understand why! Learning and applying these theories will allow you to make informed crime control decisions as to why certain security measures should or should not be carried out. Once you understand why an offender carried out unwanted activity in a particular area, you can implement security measures with a far better chance of success. As security measures cost money to implement, the wise security practitioner will not want to waste time, effort, or money. Following criminal activity, an officer may wonder: Was there an absence of a capable guardian as Felson and Cohen theorize (1979)? Did the offender make a rational choice either for or against carrying out a criminal act as Cornish and Clarke (2008) believe takes place? A deeper understanding of the offense allows the responding security professional to make keener and more analytical choices about how to respond to the situation.

Will it require a simple or a complicated fix? In some cases, simple is usually cheaper and can be just as successful as more expensive security measures.

There is a danger in thinking that once security measures have been implemented, there will never again be a crime or unwanted activity in the same area. Crime may or may not occur. Other factors may be at work, including the effects of displacement and diffusion of benefits (to be explained). This forces the security practitioner to continually review the area from many different perspectives. Has new technology made the old security solutions moot? Will an attack come from a different direction, during a different time of day? Will the attacker be forced to try new methods or bigger or better tools, or will be there be a different attacker? Continual awareness and review are necessary.

ENVIRONMENTAL CRIME PREVENTION VERSUS SOCIAL CRIME PREVENTION

A simple explanation of environmental crime prevention is that environmental crime practitioners focus their attention and energies on locations of potential criminal activity. These practitioners "look for crime patterns and seek to explain them in terms of environmental influences. From these explanations they derive rules that enable predictions to be made about emerging crime problems, and that ultimately inform the development of strategies that might be employed to prevent crime" (Wortley & Mazerolle, 2008, p. 1). Locks, doors, and other barriers, CCTV equipment, and patrolling security officers are all examples of environmental crime control measures. On the other side of the coin is social crime prevention. This area focuses upon social programs, education, employment creation, welfare, unemployment insurance, police, corrections, and other after-the-fact

follow-up measures and programs. While the intent of this chapter is not to argue the pros and cons of one theory over the other, one comment will be made. While all the programs and money spent upon social crime control can be considered laudable, it would be a foolish security manager who donated his or her security budget to a social crime control program regardless of how noble it may seem. Government and big businesses have spent billions of dollars on this issue for many years, but physical security forces are required more than ever.

Environmental crime control has not been relegated the same attention and respect as the social crime control model. Social crime control has been practiced in one form or another for hundreds of years. In contrast, environmental crime control grew from work completed at the University of Chicago in the 1920s. It was there that more attention was paid to the area in which the crime was being committed than to the people who committed the criminal acts. The theory laid dormant for several decades, but was given a rebirth by the influential writer and social commentator, Jane Jacobs, when she wrote *The Death and Life of Great American Cities* in 1961. Her work inspired both C. Ray Jeffery and Oscar Newman, both of whom took off in new directions: Jeffery, with his book, *Crime Prevention through Environmental Design*, and Newman, with his *Defensible Space*. In turn, both researchers inspired others, such as Paul and Patricia Brantingham, Tim Crowe, Ronald V. Clarke, and Marcus Felson. What follows is an overview of the various environmental crime control theories.

THEORIES

Rational Choice Theory

Rational Choice Theory was first presented by Ronald V. Clarke and Derek B. Cornish in

1986 in *The Reasoning Criminal: Rational Choice Perspectives on Offending*. As Tayler (1997, p. 293) states, the rationale behind the theory is that people will commit a crime if it is in their own best interests. Basically, the offender uses a decision-making process whereby the positive and negative aspects of committing a particular act are weighed. If the perception is that there are more reasons for proceeding, regardless of the existing security barriers, then, at the very least, an attempt will be made. If an opportunity presents itself, there is a benefit, and there is little likelihood of being apprehended, then they will commit the crime. Further, Pease (1997, p. 967) quotes Clarke and Cornish (1985), who claim that "the underlying assumption is that offenders seek to benefit themselves by their criminal behavior. This entails making decisions and choices, however rudimentary their rationality might be, being constrained by limits of time, ability, and the availability of relevant information."

Following this rationalization, it is up to the security practitioner to convince the potential offender that it is not in the offender's best interests to carry out the act. The application of situational crime prevention techniques is the result of this theory. As rational choice is the theoretical element, what follows are situational crime prevention techniques that are the practical efforts used to reduce criminal opportunities. These techniques involve increasing the effort, increasing the risk, reducing rewards, reducing provocations, and removing excuses. These five techniques are further subdivided into five subcategories to help eliminate opportunities for criminals. They can range from physical access control devices to the use of psychology to deter people's criminal tendencies. Finally, one should remember that criminal decision making is crime-specific. This means that "specific offenses bring particular benefits to offenders and are committed with specific motives in mind" (Cornish and Clarke, 2009, p. 26). The weighed actions, risks, and rewards

will be different for the laptop thief than for the arsonist, vandal, or industrial spy. In addition to these issues, even within the narrow confines of a single crime such as laptop theft, what motivates one offender (e.g., financial desire) will be different from another (e.g., a drug addict who steals to trade for crack cocaine). These situational crime prevention techniques are laid out in Table 13-1.

Rational choice theory also includes the principle that criminals are opportunistic. These opportunistic criminals are not professionals, but average people. If the reward is high enough, deterrents will not work. People will weigh the pros and cons of committing the crime, and these are centered on the specifics of the target. Finally, situational crime prevention works best with the amateur criminal and least with the professional criminal. Bearing in mind that there are different classifications of criminals, primarily amateur criminal and professional, the more security precautions taken, the more likely all but the most determined attacker will be stopped. Other factors come into play as well; two that will be discussed are displacement and diffusion of benefits.

Displacement of Crime

The basis for displacement is that a determined attacker, if stopped at or by one method, location, etc., will try other ways of committing a crime until successful. There are six elements to displacement as laid out in Table 13-2. Displacement claims that, regardless of whether a specific crime is committed at a particular location, the criminal will simply move to a more "criminal user-friendly" location until the crime can be completed. One way to remember the six elements is to consider who, what, when, where, why, and how. Coincidentally, these are also the six elements of a properly written incident report.

Research indicates that displacement is not nearly as strong a factor as many people

TABLE 13-1 Twenty-five techniques of situational prevention

Increase the Effort	Increase the Risks	Reduce the Rewards	Reduce Provocations	Remove Excuses
1. *Harden target (both premise and laptop itself)* • Steering column locks and immobilizers • Anti-robbery screens • Tamper-proof packaging	6. *Extend guardianship* • Take routine precautions: go out in groups at night leave signs of occupancy carry phone • "Cocoon" neighborhood watch	11. *Conceal targets* • Off-street parking • Gender-neutral phone directors • Unmarked bullion trucks	16. *Reduce frustrations and stress* • Efficient queues and polite service • Expanded seating • Soothing music/muted lights	21. *Set rules* • Rental agreements • Harassment codes • Hotel registration
2. *Control access to facilities* • Entry phones • Electronic card access • Baggage screening	7. *Assist natural surveillance* • Improved street lighting • Defensible Space design • Support whistleblowers	12. *Remove targets* • Removable car radio • Women's refuges • Pre-paid cards for payphones	17. *Avoid disputes* • Separate enclosures for rival soccer fans • Reduce crowding in pubs • Fixed cab fares	22. *Post instructions* • "No Parking" • "Private Property" • "Extinguish camp fires"
3. *Screen exits* • Ticket needed for exit • Export documents • Electronic merchandise tags	8. *Reduce anonymity* • Taxi driver IDs • "How's my driving?" decals • School uniforms	13. *Identify property* • Property marking • Vehicle licensing and parts marking • Cattle branding	18. *Reduce temptation* • Controls on violent pornography • Enforce good behavior on soccer field • Prohibit racial slurs	23. *Alert conscience* • Roadside speed display boards • Signatures for customs declarations • "Shoplifting is stealing"
4. *Deflect offenders* • Street closures • Separate bathrooms for women • Disperse pubs	9. *Use place managers* • CCTV for double-deck buses • Two clerks for convenience stores • Reward vigilance	14. *Disrupt markets* • Monitor pawn shops • Control classified ads • License street vendors	19. *Neutralize peer pressure* • "Idiots drink and drive" • "It's OK to say No" • Disperse troublemakers at school	24. *Assist compliance* • Easy library checkout • Public lavatories • Litter bins
5. *Control tools/weapons* • "Smart" guns • Disable stolen cell phones • Restrict spray paint sales to juveniles	10. *Strengthen formal surveillance* • Red light cameras • Burglar alarms • Security guards	15. *Deny benefits* • Ink merchandise tags • Graffiti cleaning • Speed humps	20. *Discourage imitation* • Rapid repair of vandalism • V-chips in TVs • Censor details of modus operandi	25. *Control drugs and alcohol* • Breathalyzers in pubs • Server intervention • Alcohol-free events

http://popcenter.org/library/25%20techniques%20grid.pdf. Accessed June 7, 2009.

TABLE 13-2 Methods of Displacement

		Type	Reason	Issues to Consider
1	Who	The offender changes	Quits, moves, goes to jail, retires, dies, is replaced	The next offender may have different motivations, skill sets, tools, patience, knowledge, etc. Existing security measures may no longer be adequate.
2	What	The type of offense carried out	If security measures prove to be adequate, consideration should be given to the offender changing offenses.	An addict, failing to gain access to an office to steal laptops to trade for drugs, may instead conduct a street robbery. An offender may switch from robbing banks to writing bad checks. An offender may switch from crimes of violence to Internet-based scams.
3	When	The time in which the crime was committed	Daytime, nighttime, morning, afternoon, evening, weekdays, weekends, summer, winter, etc.	The offender may change the time of their offense. If they cannot tunnel into a bank vault at night, they may rob the bank during the day. A laptop thief, if unable to defeat physical security after hours, may decide to talk their way past a receptionist to gain access.
4	Where	The location of the criminal act	Moves on to another house, store, neighborhood, city, state/province, or country, etc.	If an offender cannot gain access to one building, they may attempt to go next door to gain access. Regardless, the expectation is that they will go elsewhere. They may change locations because they have become too well known in their present area.
5	Why	The type of target which is attacked	Weaker, younger, older, less security, female, male, inability to overcome current security measures, etc.	There are a variety of reasons why the offender may switch targets. If a location is attacked and the target turns out to be removed, the offender may take other items. Retail thieves may enter a pharmacy intending to steal drugs, but if narcotics are not available and cash is, they will switch targets.
6	How	The method used to complete the crime	Gun, knife, pen, computer, vehicle, etc.	The offender may change their modus operandi. For example, the terrorists who brought down the World Trade Center towers originally used a vehicle bomb in the underground parking garage. When that failed, they used airplanes as cruise missiles.

assume. Common sense indicates that displacement increases the effort on the offender's part, which is exactly why security measures are implemented in the first place. Increasing the effort makes it more costly for the criminal (Clarke, 2008, p. 188). Displacement can also be viewed positively if the security practitioner gives thought from a planning perspective, considers how the criminal may react to existing security measures, and then creates additional security measures. This is why multiple levels of physical, IT, and procedural security measures should be implemented.

Diffusion of Benefits

Diffusion of benefits is the opposite of displacement. Just as it is assumed by critics of Rationalism that crime is simply moved to another location, there is also a belief that the benefits of situational crime prevention techniques are also moved to other locations, thereby resulting in a decrease in crime. As Pease states in reference to both issues:

The fact that displacement has been long debated, and that diffusion of benefits has been neglected suggests that displacement is dominant not because it reflects a real attempt to understand crime flux, but because it serves as a convenient excuse for doing nothing *('Why bother? It will only get displaced')" (1997, p. 978)*.

A further, somewhat controversial point to displacement is that there may be a benefit to displacing certain kinds of crimes. For example, drug and prostitution control may be made easier or more tolerable when it is away from residential neighborhoods or concentrated in one locale (Pease, 1997, p. 979).

ROUTINE ACTIVITY THEORY

Routine activity theory, developed by Cohen and Felson, revolves around three things: a "potential offender, a suitable target, and the absence of a capable guardian" (Bottoms & Wiles, 1997, p. 320). All three must come together in order for criminal activity to be realized. Routine activity theory relies on the same rational choice methodology as situational crime prevention techniques. As in any theory, routine activity theory has its criticisms. One of the primary criticisms is the assumption that criminals are rational in their decision making. They may not use the same rationale as the person implementing the security measures. They may not even be aware of the situational crime prevention techniques put into effect. They may be under the influence of drugs or alcohol or, for whatever reason, they may simply not care about the security measures.

CRIME PATTERN THEORY

Crime pattern theory, developed by Paul and Patricia Brantingham, is a rather complex amalgamation of both rational choice and routine activity theories, as well as a further introduction of sociocultural, economic, legal, and physical environmental cues. The premise is that crime does not occur randomly in time, place,

social group cohesiveness, or a host of other aspects. Acknowledging the complexity of the theory, a crime prevention response cannot come from one area alone. Instead, a multidisciplinary approach must be taken, in which responses are tailored to the situation. One must consider the criminal opportunity, the individual offender, his or her readiness and willingness to commit crime, and the combination of the previous three aspects as they impact the sociocultural, economic, legal, and environmental cues. Granted, this is not an easy theory to employ from a theoretical or a practical perspective. Some of the components of this theory are certainly beyond the security practitioner's reach to address, but knowing that a detailed examination of the environment is required may enable practitioners to view the environment from a broader perspective. Knowing that decisions to conduct criminal activity are often carried out for entirely different reasons than previously suspected gives the security officer the opportunity to view criminal activity in a new light.

CRIME PREVENTION THROUGH ENVIRONMENTAL DESIGN (CPTED)

CPTED, probably the most well known of the environmental crime control theories, was first discussed by Dr. C. Ray Jeffery in 1971. To quote Tim Crowe, a huge proponent, CPTED "expands upon the assumption that the proper design and effective use of the built environment can lead to a reduction in the fear of crime and the incidence of crime, and to an improvement in the quality of life" (Crowe, 1991, p. 1).

There are three key concepts specific to CPTED. These concepts are:

The use of natural surveillance. Natural surveillance refers to increasing the ability of legitimate place users to see farther and wider, while decreasing the ability of illegitimate place users to hide when waiting for the right time to carry out their activity. An example of using natural surveillance could be in an underground parking lot. As users leave their cars and head toward either an elevator lobby or staircase, it is often difficult to see what lies inside. By replacing cinderblock with a glass partition, the property manager increases the natural surveillance whereby legitimate users can see directly into the vestibule area instead of guessing what lies ahead. Also, it is difficult for an illegitimate user to stay in this area for long, as they are subject to increased visual scrutiny.

The use of natural access control. This concept falls under the umbrella of spatial definition. An example of natural access control is when normal place users are encouraged to use an area for legitimate purposes, and illegitimate users are discouraged from remaining in the area. How this is accomplished is determined by the particular location and imagination of the property manager. For example, if unwanted visitors remain in an area because of a design feature, such as a wall or barrier, the feature should be removed (unless required) or changed to make it less attractive, thereby reducing the overall attractiveness of the area. Another example is skateboarders who use a particular plaza because of the many attractive, flat wooden benches. Pop-up seats could be installed on the benches, making it difficult, if not impossible, for skateboarders to use them.

Territorial behavior. This concept is key to reclaiming an area if it has been taken over by illegitimate users. If design features have created a haven for illegitimate users and frightened off legitimate users, then one of the most important required actions is for the space to be reclaimed. Initially, this may take the form of enhanced security patrols to keep illegitimate users away until the area is once again seen as desirable for legitimate users. The return of high numbers of normal space users will deter the presence of illegitimate space users. A prime example is based upon the previous example of skateboarders. In one instance, an area had practically been taken over by illegitimate users, making

it a dangerous area to visit. Several CPTED strategies were employed, including design changes and enhanced security officer presence. Eventually, a large number of legitimate users returned to the area, which, in turn, further deterred the skateboarders from coming back in large numbers. While the problem has not completely gone away, it has decreased noticeably.

Further, CPTED planners should classify security strategies into three categories. The first category is the use of organized strategies. This includes the use of human resources to increase security, such as security or police officers or some other type of official guardian. The second strategy is to incorporate mechanical methods into enhanced security. This is achieved through the use of hardware such as CCTV, locking mechanisms, access control systems, fences, and other barriers. Finally, the third and probably most important strategy is to use natural enhancements to enhance security awareness. This may take the form of increased presence of legitimate place users, proper use of windows to increase surveillance, or making all users responsible for security, and so on. It is important to start with the natural methods of enhancing security, and then augment them through organized and mechanical methods.

SECOND-GENERATION CPTED

Developed in 1998 by Saville and Cleveland (2009, p. 80), second-generation CPTED includes the original emphasis on physical location and adds the newer concept of including social factors. These factors include:

1. **Social cohesion:** involves the local community in events, associations, and positive problem solving without resorting to violence, and builds positive community relationships.
2. **Connectivity:** the neighborhood has positive relations and influence with external agencies (Saville & Cleveland, 2009, p. 82).

3. **Community culture:** positive social and cultural activities.
4. **Threshold capacity:** positive community resources that do not overwhelm the area, proper land density use and zoning, and a lack of crime generators.

Second-generation CPTED focuses on the physical and social aspects of communities to minimize both criminals and criminal opportunities.

DEFENSIBLE SPACE: CRIME PREVENTION THROUGH URBAN DESIGN

This theory revolves around the public housing environment and seeks to reduce crime through the use of natural surveillance, natural access control, and territorial concern.

History of Defensible Space. While Oscar Newman has written many influential pieces on this important concept over the past 30 plus years, two of his most important works are *Architectural Design for Crime Prevention*, published in 1971 through the U.S. Department of Justice, and *Defensible Space*, published in 1972. Additional books, such as *Creating Defensible Space* from 1996, published through the U.S. Department of Housing and Urban Development, add to his significant body of work.

Concept and Strategies. While there will not be a detailed analysis of all the concepts that encompass the theory of Defensible Space, a general overview will be made. The writer encourages interested parties who seek a deeper understanding to access the aforementioned books for an in-depth analysis. Basically, Defensible Space calls for proprietors and legitimate users of residential space to act as guardians of their living areas. To quote from *Architectural Design* (p. 2):

Physical mechanisms for achieving Defensible Space are as follows:

• Those which serve to define spheres of influence of territorial influence which

occupants can easily adopt proprietary attitudes;
• Those which improve the natural capability of residents to survey both the interior and exterior of the residential space;
• Those which enhance the safety of adjoining areas such as communal facilities;
• Finally, through the judicious building materials to reduce the perception of peculiarity such as vulnerability, isolation and stigma of housing projects and their residents (Newman, 1971).

PRACTICAL APPLICATIONS

As one can see, there are some similarities between *Defensible Space* and CPTED applications. The important concept of legitimate users versus illegitimate users, the proper and effective utilization of surveillance, both natural and man-made, and creating safe havens for normal users are common to both. Knowing and understanding who belongs in an area and who does not (legitimate users versus illegitimate users of space), the importance of various types of surveillance, and encouraging legitimate users of space to use or reclaim areas for activities are recommendations that security practitioners can understand and appreciate.

SUMMARY

While this chapter has not detailed each and every theory or practice of crime prevention, it has provided an overview of the main existing environmental crime theories. Readers are encouraged to further examine the theories outlined here, as they are an important aspect of crime control. While certainly not the only theories, rational choice, routine activities, CPTED, Defensible Space, crime pattern theory, and situational crime prevention techniques comprise an important basis for explaining some of the root causes of why certain crimes may occur repeatedly in specific locations.

Not all the answers are contained here, and while every situation is unique, the security practitioner should understand that there are some basic explanations and rationales behind every criminal activity. Implementing security enhancements should be an educated decision. Hence, a detailed study of the criminal area with the accompanying rationale should reduce criminal opportunity.

References

Bottoms, A., & Wiles, P. (1997). Environmental criminology. In M. Maguire, R. Morgan, & R. Reiner (Eds.), *The Oxford handbook of criminology* (2nd ed.) (pp. 305–359). Oxford: Clarendon Press.

Clarke, R. V. (1997). *Situational crime prevention: Successful case studies* (2nd ed.). Albany, NY: Harrow and Heston.

Clarke, R. V. (2008). Situational crime prevention. In R. Wortley & L. Mazerolle (Eds.), *Environmental criminology and crime analysis* (pp. 178–194). Portland: Willan Publishing.

Cornish, D. B., & Clarke, R. V. (2008). The rational choice perspective. In R. Wortley & L. Mazerolle (Eds.), *Environmental criminology and crime analysis* (pp. 21–47). Portland: Willan Publishing.

Crowe, T. D. (1991). *Crime prevention through environmental design*. Boston, MA: Butterworth-Heinemann.

Module 1. (1999a). *Criminological theory 2: Rational choice theory: 277–304*. The Scarman Centre for Public Order: University of Leicester.

Module 1. (1999b). *Crime prevention 2: The situational approach: 305–344*. The Scarman Centre for Public Order: University of Leicester.

Module 5. (2000). *Applied crime management: Unit 3: Crime pattern analysis: 113–168*. The Scarman Centre for Public Order: University of Leicester.

Newman, O. (1971). *Architectural design for crime prevention*. National Institute of Law Enforcement and Criminal Justice.

Pease, K. (1997). Crime prevention. In M. Maguire, R. Morgan, & R. Reiner (Eds.), *The Oxford handbook of criminology* (2nd ed.) (pp. 963–995). Oxford: Clarendon Press.

Saville, G., & Cleveland, G. (2008). Second generation CPTED: The rise and fall of opportunity theory. In R. Atlas (Ed.), *21st century security and CPTED* (pp. 79–90). Boca Raton, FL: CRC Press.

Tayler, I. (1997). The political economy of crime. In M. Maguire, R. Morgan, & R. Reiner (Eds.), *The Oxford handbook of criminology* (2nd ed.) (pp. 265–303). Oxford: Clarendon Press.

Tyska, L. A., & Fennelly, L. J. (1998). *150 Things that you should know about security*. Boston, MA: Butterworth-Heinemann.

Wortley, R. (2001). A classification of techniques for controlling situational precipitators of crime. In B. Fisher & M. Gill (Eds.), *Security journal, Vol. 14*, No. 4 (pp. 63–82). Perpetuity Press.

Wortley, R., & Mazerolle, L. (2008). *Environmental criminology and crime analysis*. Portland: Willan Publishing.

Resources

Vellani, K., & Nahoun, J. (2001). *Applied crime analysis*. Butterworth-Heinemann.

Newman, O. (1996). *Creating defensible space*. U.S. Department of Housing and Urban Development.

Newman, O. (1972). *Defensible space: Crime prevention through urban design*. The Macmillan Company.

Fennelly, L. J., & Lombardi, J. H. (1997). *Spotlight on security for real estate managers*. Institute for Real Estate Management.

Jacobs, J. (1992). *The death and life of great American cities*. Vintage.

National Crime Prevention Institute (NCPI). (2001). *Understanding crime prevention* (2nd ed.). Butterworth-Heinemann.

SECURITY QUIZ

1. Environmental crime control theory focuses upon the _____ of the criminal act:
   a. Time
   b. Location
   c. Perpetrator
   d. Victim

2. Basically the offender uses a decision making process whereby the positive and negative aspects of committing a particular act is weighed. This is an example of:
   a. CPTED (Crime Prevention Through Environmental Design)
   b. Routine activity theory
   c. Rational choice theory
   d. Defensible space

3. The application of situational crime prevention techniques are the results of this theory.
   a. Rational choice theory
   b. Routine activity theory
   c. Crime pattern theory
   d. Defensible space

4. There are _____ aspects of displacement?
   a. Three
   b. Four
   c. Five
   d. Six

5. There are three key concepts specific to CPTED. Which of the following is not one?
   a. Natural surveillance
   b. Defensible space
   c. Natural access control
   d. Territorial behavior

6. There are _____ main categories of Situational Crime Prevention Techniques.
   a. Three
   b. Four
   c. Five
   d. Six

7. Further, the categories have _____ different sub-categories?
   a. Three
   b. Five
   c. Seven
   d. Nine

8. Defensible Space: Crime Prevention Through Urban Design was created by:
   a. Oscar Newman
   b. Marcus Felson
   c. Patricia Brantingham
   d. Ronald V. Clarke

9. This revolves around public housing and seeks to reduce crime through the use of natural surveillance, natural access control and territorial concern.
   a. Crime Prevention Through Environmental Design (CPTED)
   b. Crime Pattern Theory
   c. Defensible Space
   d. Rational Choice Theory

10. Routine Activity Theory, developed by Cohen and Felson, revolves around three things: which of the following is not one of the three factors?
    a. A potential offender
    b. A suitable target

   c. Acting under the influence of drugs or alcohol
   d. The absence of a capable guardian

ANSWER KEY
Manual Questions

1. Environmental Crime Prevention and Social Crime Prevention
2. Environmental, location, criminal
3. potential, criminal
4. Displacement
5. Diffusion, security
6. Location
7. Rational choice theory
8. Rational choice theory
9. Six
10. Defensible space

Interim Questions

1. Potential, target, capable
2. Crime pattern, environmental clues
3. Residential, natural, natural, territorial
4. CPTED, increase
5. Benefits, situational, techniques, decrease
6. Five
7. Five
8. Oscar Newman
9. Defensible Space
10. Acting under the influence of drugs or alcohol

Ten Final Questions

1. Defensible, guardians
2. Situational, crime, five
3. rational
4. Environmental, Chicago, location
5. Natural, illegitimate
6. Location
7. Rational choice
8. Five
9. Five
10. Defensible Space

14

Physical Security Concepts and Applications

Kevin T. Doss and
Denis A. O'Sullivan

CHAPTER OBJECTIVES

- Define physical security planning
- List five steps of the security planning process
- List three options for intrusion monitoring
- Explain the three primary objectives of security lighting
- Provide the three roles of CCTV and access controls
- Explain the value of safes, vaults, containers, fencing, and barriers

PHYSICAL SECURITY PLANNING

What is "physical security planning?" It is a recognized security process that, if followed, will result in the selection of physical countermeasures based on appropriateness. The selected countermeasures should also be justifiable from a cost point of view.

In the security planning process, the organization identifies which assets require protection and the types of risks that could compromise those assets. This critical function determines the level of appropriate countermeasure that is required based upon a formally documented process. Risks are usually categorized into three categories:

1. People—Human resources are usually the most critical asset within any organization, and as such, must receive a stronger consideration when assessing risk.
2. Property—Physical property or intellectual assets.
3. Legal liability—Legal risks can also affect people and property, but need to be considered as a separate category. This is due, in part, to the extent which lawsuits affect the security industry these days.

Additionally, the security planning process should determine the probability of such occurrences and the impact on the organization if loss should ever occur. These steps are critical to determine how to best protect organizational assets and must be performed periodically. An added benefit of the security planning process is the potential for increased security awareness throughout every level of the organization.

The security planning process consists of the following five steps:

1. Assets are identified.
2. Loss events are exposed.
3. Occurrence probability factors are assigned.
4. Impact of occurrence is assessed.
5. Countermeasures are selected.

Let's look at each of these steps.

1. Assets are identified

At first glance, this step would appear easy; however, this is not necessarily the case. Have you ever attempted to take inventory of your personal property? The major problem seems to be "how to;" that is, do we include every nut and bolt? For the purpose of following the security process, this is not necessary. It should suffice to group assets according to category except where an item is especially attractive (from a thief's viewpoint) and valuable. The following categories should encompass the majority of assets for most companies:

– land	– buildings
– heavy machinery	– production equipment
– office equipment	– office furniture
– vehicles	– cash or other negotiables
– goodwill	– public image
– raw material	– finished product

Depending on the nature of the company's activities, there may be other categories. In any event, there is one asset which has not been mentioned primarily because it is controversial: employees. Employees are a company's most valuable asset, although some people do not like to group them with all the other assets.

2. Loss events are exposed

This step consists of exposing all possible threats to the assets that were identified. Similar to how we group assets, we group threats according to their nature. All threats can be grouped under the following headings: industrial disaster, natural disaster, civil disturbance, crime, and other risks.

Industrial disasters—these should be easy to identify, associated threats related to on-site or adjacent activity. The following are typical industrial disasters that might affect most companies: explosions, fires, major accidents, and structural collapse. To correctly assess the threat, you must intimately know the nature of company activity, the nature of activity on adjacent properties, dangerous routes, flight paths, and the existence of nearby major oil or gas pipelines.

Natural disasters—the potential for a natural disaster largely rests with the geographic location of the company property. If the property is located in the southeast United States, it is reasonable to identify hurricanes as possible loss events. Similarly, if the property is located in California, it would be reasonable to plan for earthquakes. Other areas may suggest the need to identify floods or tornados as threats.

Civil disturbance—most companies can be threatened either directly or indirectly by actions that can be categorized as civil disturbances. If your company is engaged in weapons technology, or indeed any activity that might be viewed as threatening the environment, it is reasonable to expect that the company might become the target of demonstrators. All labor disputes fall under this heading.

Crime—it is relatively easy to identify crimes that might affect company operations. Any or all of the following will affect most companies: arson, assault, bomb threats, breaking and entering, theft, and vandalism. If a company is engaged in high-tech, it would be reasonable to also include espionage, extortion, and sabotage as likely threats.

Other risks—this is meant to be a catch-all for those threats that do not neatly fit the above categories. Two examples are disturbed persons and loss of utilities.

3. Occurrence probability factors are assigned

Having identified assets and exposed the threats to those assets, the next step is to quantify the possibility that the threat will occur. This is probably the most difficult step in the process. Information must be collected and carefully analyzed to determine its effect on the probability for occurrence. The following affect probability:

- The physical composition of structures—for example, wood frame or concrete block
- The climatic history of the area, such as number and frequency of tornados, hurricanes, earthquakes, and so on
- The nature of activity at the property to be protected. For example, if the products being produced are televisions and related products, then the probability for theft will likely be high
- The criminal history for the local and adjacent areas
- Is there community conflict in the area?

An analysis of the foregoing, coupled with a review of the activity and organization of the company to be protected, will enable one to make a determination with reasonable accuracy regarding the probability for a loss relative to specific assets or groups of assets.

The probability for occurrence will not be the same for all loss events. For this reason and to facilitate later correlation with impact factors, we must assign probability ratings. While the actual wording is not important, the following are suggested:

- Certain
- Highly probable
- Moderately probable
- Improbable

To make these words more meaningful, we can assign percentage weights to each: certain = 75–100%; highly probable = 50–75%; moderately probable = 25–50%; and improbable = 0–25%.

4. Impact of occurrence is assessed

This step is not as difficult or as uncertain as determining probability. Impact for almost all organizations has a bottom line of dollars and cents. The most important thing to remember is that dollar losses may be either direct or indirect and that they may be so high as to be crippling.

Direct costs are those that can be directly assigned as the value of the asset that has been lost or damaged. Indirect losses are those costs associated with the loss that would not have been incurred if the loss event had not occurred. An example is downtime.

The final task in relation to impact is to assign levels or classifications that will allow for correlation with the four degrees of probability. Again, the actual words are not important; however, the following are suggested:

- Very serious
- Serious
- Moderately serious
- Unimportant

We will see the importance of these ratings shortly. Before we move to the final step, let us recap: we have taken inventory of our assets, identified the threats to those assets, assessed the probability of occurrence for the threats, and assessed the potential impact on company operations if one of these threats were to occur.

5. Countermeasures are selected

This is the final step in the planning process. We now have to use all the data we have collected to protect our property in the most efficient manner, while also considering the cost of these countermeasures in relation to the value of our assets. The initial step is to decide on the level of protection needed; the level can range from low to very high.

When selecting physical security countermeasures, it is imperative that one use a systematic approach. By standardizing the process, mistakes are less likely to occur and more accurate calculations can be made. In addition, one must document the process and keep accurate written records of the recorded data. This allows for better-informed decisions regarding the selection and implementation of physical security countermeasures.

There are several methods or processes available to the security practitioner when selecting countermeasures; however, the simplest method to ascertain the desired levels of protection is a matrix as illustrated in Figure 14-1. For example, consider the threat of fire. The probability of a fire can be rated as "moderately probable" for most types of businesses; from a criticality point of view, we must consider fire as potentially "very serious."

Referring to our matrix, we can quickly see that the recommended level of protection is "level IV," the highest level possible. This would suggest using an effective detection system coupled with an efficient suppression system.

The large number and variety of assets and associated threats means that we will end up with a complex pattern of different levels of protection. This is not as confusing as we might expect, particularly if we think in terms of security-in-depth.

Security-in-depth, also known as **layered protection**, is a concept that means placing a series of progressively more difficult obstacles in the path of an aggressor. These obstacles are often referred to as **lines of defense**.

Threat Level Matrix

	Improbable	Moderately probable	Highly probable	Certain
Unimportant	I	I	I	I
Moderately Serious	I	II	II	II
Serious	II	III	III	IV
Very Serious	III	IV	IV	IV

Levels of Security
I   Low
II   Medium
III   High
IV   Very High

FIGURE 14-1   Threat level matrix.

The **first line of defense** is at the property line. Methods of defense at this point may be either natural, such as a river, or manmade, such as a fence. Additionally, the barrier may be psychological or physical. At the very minimum, the property boundary must be defined in some way that separates it from its neighbors. Psychological barriers, such as property definition, do not impede would-be trespassers; however, they do play an important role in the rights of the property owner.

The **second line of defense** is the exterior of buildings. Controls at this point should be difficult to overcome. It is important to remember that all six sides of structures (roof, floor, and walls) may present weaknesses that must be strengthened. Special attention must be given to the usual points of break and enters: doors, windows, and skylights. In fact, any opening greater than 96 square inches in area and less than 18 feet from grade must be protected. It is usually at this line of defense that electronic intrusion detection devices and electronic access controls are used.

The **third line of defense** is interior controls or object protection. Controls at this line of defense include electronic motion and intruder detection devices, access controls, safes, vaults, document storage cabinets, quality locking devices, and fire protection.

Applying the security-in-depth concept means more than simply establishing three lines of defense that will meet all your needs. Ideally, we would apply the principle first to the property in general terms as described above, and then to each and every asset separately. An example would be an industrial complex and an asset such as information.

The complex itself will probably be protected by a perimeter fence. Each building within will be properly secured and there will be electronic intrusion detection systems within the buildings. In addition to this general protection, we should attempt to establish protective rings around the information. For example, the information should be stored in a safe (third line of defense), the safe should be in a room that has interior motion detection (second line of defense), and access to the room should be through a door equipped with proper locking hardware and possibly a card access system (the first line of defense) (Figure 14-2).

Selecting appropriate countermeasures is a difficult task, requiring considerable practical experience and extensive knowledge of the various controls and their strengths and weaknesses. Effective planning will result in a cost-justified, integrated protection program.

An integrated protection program results from a systems approach to selecting controls. The following are two important points in relation to using a systems approach:

1. The whole, rather than its individual parts, must be considered.

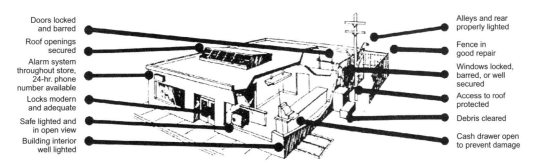

Doors locked and barred
Roof openings secured
Alarm system throughout store, 24-hr. phone number available
Locks modern and adequate
Safe lighted and in open view
Building interior well lighted

Alleys and rear properly lighted
Fence in good repair
Windows locked, barred, or well secured
Access to roof protected
Debris cleared
Cash drawer open to prevent damage

FIGURE 14-2 Defense around exterior of building.

2. Design should allow for an acceptable level of redundancy, without any unnecessary duplication of effort.

A systems approach is often referred to as "systems engineering."

The remainder of this chapter will concentrate on the physical components of a protection program. While space will not permit great detail, we will attempt to explain the major points relative to security lighting, security glazing, alarm systems, card access systems, locks and keying, closed circuit television, safes and vaults, and fencing.

SECURITY LIGHTING

Security lighting has three primary objectives:

1. It must act as a deterrent to intruders.
2. It must make detection likely if an intrusion is attempted.
3. It should not unnecessarily expose patrolling personnel.

Lighting systems are often referred to as "continuous," "standby," and "movable" or "emergency."

Continuous lighting is most commonly used. Lamps are mounted on fixed luminaries and are normally lit during the hours of darkness.

Standby lighting is different from continuous lighting in that the lamps are only lit as required.

Movable or **emergency** lighting is portable lighting that may be used to supplement either continuous or standby lighting. Light sources may be incandescent, gaseous discharge, or quartz lamps. The common lightbulb emits incandescent light.

Gaseous discharge lamps are street-type lighting and may be either mercury vapor or sodium vapor lamps. Mercury vapor lamps emit a strong light with a bluish cast. Sodium vapor lamps emit a soft yellow light. Both types of gaseous discharge lamps take 2 to 5 minutes to reach maximum intensity. They are very effective in areas where fog is prevalent. A word of caution in relation to gaseous discharge lamps is that they make color identification unreliable.

Metal halide lamps are also of a gaseous type, but due to the excellent color rendition this lamp offers, it is recommended for many security applications. Metal halide lamps can be used very effectively with color CCTV cameras due to the light properties which imitate natural daylight. The downside of this lamp is that it is expensive to use.

Incandescent lamps are typically used in residential homes for lighting. They are very inefficient and have limited use for security purposes due to the short lifecycle and expense of use.

Quartz lamps emit a very bright white light. Lighting may be classified as floodlights, searchlights, fresnels, and street lighting. The difference between floodlights and searchlights is that searchlights project a highly focused beam of light, whereas floodlights project a concentrated beam. Fresnels produce a rectangular beam of light and are particularly suitable for illuminating the exterior of buildings. Streetlights produce a diffused light and are suitable for use in parking areas and driveways.

Certain lighting intensities are recommended for specific situations.

Perimeter or property boundary	0.15 to 0.4 fc
Parking lots (open)	2.0 to 3.0 fc
Parking garage (enclosed)	5.0 to 6.0 fc
Vehicle entrances	1.0 fc
Pedestrian entrances (active)	5.0 fc
Exterior of buildings	1.0 fc
Open yards	0.2 fc

The foregoing are suggested lighting intensities only; specific circumstances may dictate different intensities. To explain the suggested intensities, "fc" means foot-candle and simply refers to the amount of light emitted within 1 square foot of a lit standard candle.

APPLICATION CONSIDERATIONS

1. When designing a protective lighting system, consider three lines of defense: the perimeter, open yards, and building exteriors.
2. All accessible exterior lamp enclosures should be in tamper- or vandal-resistive housing. This means that the receptacle and lens should be constructed of a material that will resist damage if attacked and that the mounting screws or bolts should be tamper-resistant.
3. If protective lighting is to be located in an area that may be subject to explosions, the housings should be explosive-resistant.
4. Before finalizing any decision on the installation of lighting, consider the impact that additional lighting will have on your neighbors. Failure to consult with a neighbor prior to an installation may result in costly redesign.

The foregoing is a presentation of the basics of security lighting. Prior to utilizing any of the suggested standards, please check local codes or ordinances.

GLAZING

The various uses, methods of fabrication, and overabundance of trade names make the selection of an appropriate glazing material appear very confusing. In an effort to simplify the process, we will address the subject under the following headings:

- Safety/fire
- Burglar/vandal-resistive
- Bullet resistive
- Special purpose

Safety/fire: Under this heading, we are basically looking at two types of glass: tempered and wired.

Tempered glass can be considered safety glass, as it is several times stronger than ordinary glass. It is especially resistive to accidental breakage. If it does break, it will disintegrate into small pieces with dull edges, thereby minimizing risk of injury. Tempered glass is available in different thicknesses to suit different purposes.

Wired glass is glass with a wire mesh built into it. The wire is embedded in the glass when it is still in its molten state. Wire glass resists impact because of its strength. It is also listed by Underwriter's Laboratories as a fire-retardant material.

Here are some suggested uses for safety/fire-retardant glass:

- Passageways
- Entrance doors and adjacent panels
- Sliding glass doors
- Bathtub enclosures and shower doors

Burglar/vandal-resistive: Several types of burglar/vandal-resistive glazing materials are available, including laminated glass, wired glass and acrylic, and polycarbonate plastics.

Laminated glass will resist degrees of impact proportionate to its thickness. This type of glass is particularly valuable where the quality of transparency is important and where other types of impact-resistant material may be subject to vandalism. Wired glass provides resistance of a limited nature; it will not resist prolonged attack. Acrylic plastic is particularly resistive to forced attack; however, it is not as resistive as polycarbonate. It is, however, much more transparent than polycarbonate. Polycarbonate plastic is 20 to 30 times stronger than acrylic of comparable thickness.

Bullet resistive: Bullet-resistive material is available in the form of laminated glass or acrylic and polycarbonate plastics. Bullet-resistant laminated glass consists of multiple piles of glass and plastic material laminated together. Highly transparent, bullet-resistant acrylic material is suitable for many cash-handling situations, such as those which occur in banks. Polycarbonate, consisting of several sheets of plastic laminated together, is highly resistive to ballistics; however, visibility is somewhat impaired.

Special purpose: Under this heading, we will look at transparent mirror glass, coated glass, heated glass, and rough or patterned glass.

Transparent mirror glass may be installed in a door or in a wall. From one side, it is functionally a mirror, and from the other, it permits an unobstructed view through the mirror. The primary purpose of transparent glass is for surreptitious surveillance. Flow-on or cement-on plastic coating is available for application to existing installed glass. This material may serve well as an interim measure until a more appropriate vandal-resistive material can be installed. Rough or patterned glass is available with many different designs that make it range from practically opaque to practically transparent. This type of glazing is most appropriate where there is a conflict between the need for privacy and natural light.

INTRUSION DETECTION

Every intrusion detection system is meant to detect the following:

1. Unauthorized entry
2. Unauthorized movement within
3. Unauthorized access to controlled areas or objects

There are three components to an intrusion detection system:

1. Detectors/sensors
2. System controls
3. Signal transmission

Detectors/Sensors

The design and implementation of intrusion sensors are critical for any physical security program. Intrusion sensors are typically integrated with physical barriers, such as a door or window, and must take environmental conditions into consideration to be effective. Selection of the appropriate detector, from the numerous and varied options available, is often a difficult task. The end user is well-advised to become familiar with the different types of detectors/sensors available and must evaluate both the application and environmental conditions prior to implementation. If relying on advice from a vendor for proper intrusion sensor selection, it is essential that the end user describe their objectives and make the vendor contractually responsible for meeting those stated objectives.

In the following paragraphs, we will look at different types of detectors: magnetic switches, metallic foil, audio, vibration, ultrasonic, photoelectric, passive infrared, microwave, dual technology, and video motion.

Magnetic switches: These are often referred to as door contacts. They may be either surface-mounted or recessed. The choice is largely an aesthetic one; however, the recessed ones do afford more protection from tampering. Switches are commonly "unbalanced," which means that they may be defeated by substitution of a secondary magnetic field to keep the contacts in the open position while the detector magnet is moved away from the housing containing the contacts.

For high-security applications, a "balanced" switch is available. This switch is designed to withstand defeat by creation of a secondary magnetic field. Magnetic switches have many potential uses in addition to their traditional use on doors and windows. They may be used on desk or file cabinet drawers or to secure equipment to a fixed position.

Metallic foil: This is a narrow strip of metal foil designed to break if the surface to which it is attached is attacked. It is mostly used as a glass breakage detector and is commonly seen on storefront windows and glass doors.

It may also be used as a barrier penetration detector, such as in a wall under gyprock. If properly installed, it should do its job well. A major detractor is that it is not considered aesthetically pleasing; this can also be overcome to some extent by the experienced installer.

Vibration: Vibration detectors are shock sensors. They may be used to detect persons climbing chain-link fencing, breaking through walls, or attacking safes or other containers. As glass breakage detectors, they are very effective and not too expensive.

Ultrasonic: These are motion detectors. A protected area is flooded with an oval pattern of sound waves. As the sound waves bounce off objects, they reflect a signal back to a receiver. Any movement in the protected area will cause a change in the reflected pattern, which will result in an alarm. Ultrasonic sound waves are in a frequency range that is above the capacity of the human ear. These detectors are particularly susceptible to false alarm due to air turbulence.

Photoelectric: A beam of light is transmitted to a receiver. The transmitter and receiver may be in one housing with the beam reflected. Any interruption of the beam causes an alarm. These devices are commonly used as automatic door openers or in stores to ward off a customer from entering. When used for security purposes, different methods are used to make the beam invisible to the naked eye. Either an infrared light-emitting diode is used or an infrared filter is simply placed over the light source. Either method effectively makes the beam invisible.

Infrared: These are probably the most versatile detectors currently available. Patterns of coverage are available that will protect practically any configuration of space. They can be used effectively to protect long narrow corridors, portions of rooms, or entire large rooms. Infrared detectors are often referred to as passive detectors because they are the only detector that does not monitor an environment that has been created by the detector. Infrared detectors

measure radiated energy. When activated, they simply establish the ambient temperature. From that point on, any significant deviation will result in an alarm.

Microwave: Microwave detectors use high-frequency radio waves to establish a protected area. They are particularly suitable for use in areas where air turbulence or changing air temperatures may prohibit the use of ultrasonic or infrared detectors. A major weakness with microwave is that it can penetrate beyond a protected area. Microwaves will penetrate practically all surfaces except concrete and metal.

Dual technology: Dual technology sensors combine two technologies into a single sensor. An example of this would be to combine a passive infrared sensor with a microwave sensor. An alarm signal is not generated until both sensing devices are triggered. Thus, the use of such technology should result in fewer nuisance alarms being generated if installed correctly and applied properly.

Video motion: Using CCTV cameras to initiate an alarm is another method that can be utilized for intrusion detection. Video motion technology detects changes in light brightness levels within the coverage area. It is advisable to only use video motion detection for an interior application due to the varied environmental conditions which exist outdoors. Vibrations, moving objects such as trees and bushes, and fluctuating light levels can trigger nuisance alarms when using video motion; they may render the system ineffective.

System Controls

System controls consist of components that transform individual detectors/sensors into a network of intelligence-gathering devices. System controls include data processing equipment, signal transmission equipment, on/off and reset controls, backup power supply, LED system status indicators, and any other equipment specific to a particular system.

The data processing equipment basically acts as a receiver and interpreter of signals from the sensors/detectors and reacts to these signals in accordance with preprogrammed instructions.

The signal transmission equipment is the means by which an alarm is raised. This equipment may simply activate a local siren, or it may send a signal over telephone wires to a remote monitoring location. The telephone wires may be either dedicated (the most secure system) or through the normal telephone network by use of a digital dialer that transmits to a special type of receiver/decoder.

The on/off and reset controls can be keys, toggle switches, or digital keypads. The digital keypad is recommended. The backup power supply is essential in case the electrical power supply fails or is sabotaged.

The LED (light-emitting diode) system status indicators use different colors to indicate whether the system is on or off, or if there is trouble in the system. The usual colors are red for system okay (but in the off mode), yellow for trouble somewhere in the system, and green for armed and properly functioning.

SYSTEM MONITORING

There are basically three options:

1. Local
2. Proprietary
3. Commercial

A local system is just that, a siren or bell on the outside of the protected premises. This system is not recommended due to its reliance on a passerby to actually call the police.

The proprietary system is similar to a local system in that the system is monitored on-site or remotely by employees of the owner of the protected premises. If this system is used, it is advisable to have a link from the proprietary

station to a commercial station in the event of a holdup of the monitoring personnel.

Commercial monitoring falls into two categories: monitoring stations or answering services. The answering services are useful for the economical monitoring of signals transmitted by telephone dialers; however, this is not for high security systems. Commercial monitoring stations are either Underwriters Laboratories (UL) approved or they are not. UL-approved is the best guarantee of quality service.

Note: An initial step in planning an intrusion detection system is to identify zones of protection in the building that will create a series of independent subsystems. Each subsystem should (1) be compatible with normal operations, and (2) allow for prompt response to a specific problem area.

When the functional requirements of a system have been identified, the system engineering should be left to experts.

CARD ACCESS

The decision to use, or not to use, a card access system should be based on the perceived need for accountability and the accompanying financial considerations. An objective statement for a card access system might read: "To economically eliminate the inherent security weaknesses in key access systems by electronically supervising and documenting the activities or persons authorized to access the property."

To be useful, a card access system should have the following minimum capabilities:

- Restrict access by authorized persons to certain times and/or days of the week.
- Allow controlled after-hours access to selected areas within.
- Control after-hours access to a parkade.

- Selectively control after-hours use of elevators.
- Maintain a record of all valid and invalid use of cards.
- Provide an audit trail permitting a printout of persons on the property at any one time.

There are numerous types of cards:

- Magnetic coded
- Magnetic strip coded
- Proximity coded
- Weigand coded
- Hollerith
- Optical coded

The magnetic coded card contains a sheet of flexible magnetic material on which an array of spots have been permanently magnetized. The code is determined by the polarity of the magnetized spots. The magnetic strip encoding is widely used in commercial credit cards. The proximity card is a badge into which electronically tuned circuits are laminated. The badge gets its name from the fact that it only has to be held near the reader for authorized access to be granted. The reader for this card is concealed in the wall behind drywall or paneling. The Weigand-coded badge contains a series of parallel wires embedded in the bottom half of the badge. Each wire can be assigned a logic "0" or "1;" the combination reveals the ID number.

The Hollerith badge is easy to recognize because the card has small rectangular holes punched in it. It cannot be considered a high-security badge. The optical coded badge is easy to recognize if it uses a barcode as its encoding device. The barcode is commonly used on retail goods to assist the cashier with pricing.

All of the commonly used coded cards are reliable and, with the exception of the Hollerith badge, are reasonably resistive to compromise. Although it is not recommended, many organizations like to use their access cards as both an access card and an identification badge. The information contained in the normal employee ID card can easily be incorporated into any access card:

- Company name and logo
- Details of cardholder
- Name
- Department
- Date of birth
- Signature
- Photograph
- Condition of use (restrictions)

This is not recommended, however, because if the card is lost, it will be obvious to the finder that it is owned by a particular organization, which may lead to unauthorized use of the card. There are many different card readers; the significant difference among them is the addition of a secondary method of verification or confirmation, such as the requirement for insertion of a personal identification number (PIN), through a numerical keypad.

The use of a numerical keypad usually offers the valuable option of allowing a user to signal that he is operating under duress.

Figure 14-3 shows the functional operation of a card access system.

LOCKING HARDWARE

Locking hardware can be categorized as mechanical, electrical, or electromagnetic, and as either security or nonsecurity.

Quality mechanical security locks should be used for all of the following:

- Perimeter openings
- Doors that control/restrict internal movement
- Doors to sensitive/restricted areas

Only deadbolt locks should be considered. The bolt should offer a minimum of 1-inch throw. If the door is a glass metal-framed door, the bolt should be of the pivotal type to ensure maximum throw.

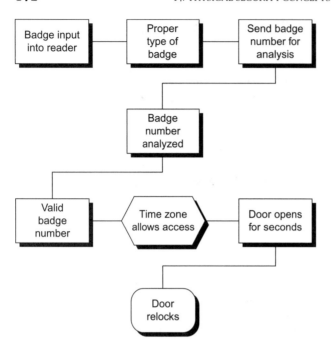

FIGURE 14-3 Functional operation of a card access system.

Electric locks are particularly suitable for the following:

- Remote control of the after-hours pedestrian entrance door
- Grade-level emergency exit doors
- Exit doors from stairwells to grade level
- All stairwell doors

Electric locks are available where the strike is normally in the locked or unlocked position. Electromagnetic locks are particularly suitable for use on emergency exit doors, as there are no moving parts that can accidentally become jammed. Several conditions must be met before this type of lock can be used on an emergency exit door:

- A manual or automated egress device to unlock door within close proximity.
- When activated, the fire alarm system must be able to automatically deactivate the locking device.
- Each location must have a fire pull station in its vicinity, and its activation must automatically deactivate the lock.

Note: It is essential that the fire department be consulted prior to any final decision on the locks of any door that may be considered an emergency exit. Get their decision in writing, and carefully consider it before compliance.

Emergency exit devices that are normally used on emergency exit doors cause justifiable security concern. If permitted, only quality electric or electromagnetic locks should be used. If electric or magnetic locks cannot be used, great care should be taken to ensure the emergency devices use such features as the following:

- Deadbolts
- Deadlocking latches
- Vertical locking bars for pairs of doors

Remember that emergency exit devices can be connected to a proprietary or commercially monitored alarm system. Loud local alarms are also an effective way to protect emergency exits.

CLOSED CIRCUIT TELEVISION

CCTV has three major roles in any physical security program:

1. To deter crime or unwanted activities
2. To allow the ability to witness an act as it occurs
3. As an investigative tool after an act has already been committed

Although CCTV is typically used to monitor a property or facility for crime prevention purposes, there are a multitude of applications with which this technology can be used to visually monitor events. CCTV is a great tool for assessing a real-time situation involving crowd control and responding to personnel movements. In addition, it can be used to capture customer movement and behavior in the retail environment as well as to monitor internal staff as they work. CCTV can also remotely watch traffic flow on highways and monitor weather activity in specific areas.

CCTV technology has progressed quickly in recent years. The advent of software-based analytics has skyrocketed the capabilities of CCTV into the future. "Intelligent video," as it is known, can offer tremendous capabilities under the right circumstances. As with any CCTV system, the surrounding environment can adversely affect the effectiveness of any CCTV program. That being stated, here are a few CCTV software feature sets that fall into the intelligent video realm:

- Video motion detection (VMD)
- People counting and tracking
- Object classification, counting and tracking
- License plate recognition
- Facial recognition
- Crowd detection
- Psychology of motion (still under development)

Intelligent video is currently used in some of the largest cities in the world to detect criminal activity and other issues, such as traffic problems, loitering, and riot activity. Among the tremendous benefits of using technology to detect certain events, intelligent video may allow for the reduction of manpower by harnessing technology to increase efficiency and accuracy of CCTV systems.

There are three main views that a standard CCTV system should provide, depending upon the application requirements:

1. Identification of any subjects
2. Identify the actions within a scene
3. Identify the scene where the act occurred

Subject identification is based on the principle that whoever or whatever is viewed must be identifiable beyond any reasonable doubt. This includes capturing specific features that could identify the person, such as nose, ears, and eye characteristics. As an example, the scene view usually will provide about 25% coverage of the person being viewed. The subject identification view is critical when used with facial recognition software, as the facial features must be captured to have a reasonable success rate in identification.

Action identification is a view that can assess what has occurred within a given area. This level of video surveillance can usually determine what has occurred. A good example might be that a painting was stolen or that an act of violence occurred. Another illustration of an action identification view would be in a retail environment to determine how a retail customer purchases specific goods while shopping, and which advertisement was most effective in gaining additional sales. The action view usually comprises about 10% of the total scene image.

Identification of a **scene view** is based on being able to identify where an act took place. An example might be in the lobby or in a specific department. Each scene must stand on its own merit and be identifiable during playback. Weather monitoring is another example of an application using a scene view.

Great care must be exercised in designing a CCTV system to ensure that the objectives are achieved. Caution is also necessary to ensure that costs do not get out of hand. This is a common problem when the system is not designed by a security expert.

The following are suggested practical applications for CCTV:

- Parkade areas, entrances/exits, shuttle elevator lobbies, stairwells, and elevators
- Shipping/receiving areas
- Main floor elevator lobbies
- Cross-over floors
- Cash handling areas

All CCTV systems are made up of several components that an end user should be, at the very least, familiar with. The following is a brief description of each component:

Cameras—a primary consideration in relation to camera selection is the available light coupled with required image quality. The two most common cameras in use today are the charge coupled device (CCD) and the complementary metal oxide semiconductor (CMOS). Both are relatively stable camera platforms that outperform older camera technology.

Lenses—there are three major types of lenses available for cameras today. They are fixed lens, varifocal lens, and zoom lens. The *fixed lens* only offers a single point of view and is best used on indoor applications due to the more consistent environment. The *varifocal lens* offers a range of views and great flexibility in application, as long as the range is within the lens capabilities, and the lens does not need to be refocused. The *zoom lens,* by contrast, is best for situations in which the lens needs to be refocused, should one change the field of view. The focus on a zoom lens is maintained either through manual or motorized adjustments.

Housings—several types of housings are available. They fall into two categories: aesthetic and environmental. Housings can also effectively disguise the existence of a camera.

Monitors—monitors are available in different sizes and in color, monochrome, or LCD. When a quality image is required, it is necessary to use a high-resolution screen.

Sequential switches—it is not necessary, or usually desirable, to have a monitor for every camera. By using a sequential switcher, the image from two or more cameras can be routinely rotated for viewing on one monitor. When required, an operator can lock on the image from one particular camera for select viewing.

Motion detectors—cameras are available with built-in motion detection capability. If movement occurs within the field of view of the camera lens, an alarm will sound at the control center, or a video recorder will be activated to record the activity that caused the alarm. This feature is very valuable when using a large number of monitors.

Pan/tilt/zoom—the need to use several cameras to cover an area or activity can be avoided by carefully positioning one camera and providing pan/tilt/zoom features.

Controls—in addition to the normal television controls, controls will be required for whatever special features are built into the system.

Consoles—the design of a control center console that houses a CCTV system is definitely an engineering task. Care must be exercised to ensure operator comfort, particularly in relation to viewing angles and ease of accessibility of controls.

Video recorders—a CCTV system should be considered incomplete if it does not have the ability to selectively record events. Recording can be done on VHS recorders; however, these are quickly being replaced by digital video recorders (DVRs) and by network video recorders (NVRs). In some cases, the recordings are sent directly to a computer server using a graphical user interface (GUI). The GUI eliminates

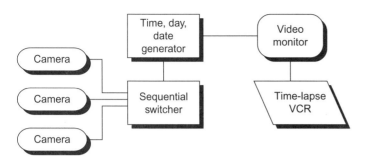

FIGURE 14-4 Typical closed circuit television system.

the need for a separate recording "box" by using software to manage the recordings.

Day/time generators—this feature has potential benefits in specific circumstances—for example, where no immediate incident response capability is available, or if the recording may be required as evidence in court.

For an example of a typical system diagram, see Figure 14-4.

SAFES AND VAULTS

Safes and vaults are designed to offer varying levels of protection from specific risks—namely burglary, robbery, and fire.

Burglary-Resistive Safes

In addition to their actual construction, burglary-resistive safes have a number of protective features:

- Locks
- Interior design
- Depository
- Time locks
- Time delay locks
- Relocking device
- Extra weight
- Floor anchoring
- Counterspy dials

Locks

Safes are available with three types of locking systems:

- Single combination
- Single key lock combination
- Dual combination

With the single combination option, an unaccompanied person with the combination can access the contents at any time. The second option, a key lock combination, requires that two persons be in attendance to open the safe. One person has the key to unlock the combination-turning mechanism, and the other has the combination to unlock the safe. The third option is similar to option two in that two persons must be in attendance to open the safe. Each person has only one of the combinations.

Interiors

Sufficient options are available in interior configurations so that the need for customization can be avoided. Available features include fixed or adjustable shelving and enclosed compartments that may be either key or combination-locked. Available options increase proportionately to the size and cost of the safe.

Depository

This feature permits the insertion of property, most often cash, without allowing access to the safe contents. The depository is usually fitted with an antifish device to inhibit retrieval of deposited property.

Time Locks

Time locks prevent access to the safe contents for predetermined timeframes by persons normally authorized for access. For example, when a bank safe is locked at the close of the business day, it cannot be opened again until the following morning. Should the bank manager be taken from his home forcibly, he cannot be forced to open the safe.

Time-Delay Locks

This feature is designed to protect against a holdup. Opening a safe equipped with this feature requires keying the lock, followed by a predetermined waiting period, before the locking mechanism will unlock. A safe with this feature is often used at late-night convenience stores or 24-hour gas stations.

Relocking Devices

These devices are designed to act as a secondary locking feature if the normal one is attacked. For example, if someone attacks the combination dial with a sledgehammer, the relocking device will activate. After this happens, only a qualified safe expert can open the safe.

Extra Weight

To prevent thieves from simply walking away with a safe, it is recommended that a safe weigh a minimum of 340 kg or 750 lbs. Most large safes do weigh 340 kg, and smaller ones can be ordered with extra weight added.

Floor Anchoring

An acceptable alternative to extra weight, where extra weight may present problems for structural reasons, is floor anchoring—provided a concrete slab is available.

Counterspy Dials

It is not uncommon for thieves to note the combination of a safe while surreptitiously viewing it being unlocked. A counterspy dial prohibits anyone other than the person immediately in front of the dial to see the numbers, and only one number is visible at a time.

Apart from the foregoing obvious security features, we can tell little about a safe by looking at it; nowhere can appearances be more deceptive. For this reason, a purchaser has to rely on a particular vendor or on independent appraisal. Independent appraisal is available from Underwriters Laboratories Inc. (UL). If a manufacturer submits a product sample to UL, they will conduct various tests and issue authority to the manufacturer to affix a specific label to the protected line. The following UL labels are available:

UL Labels	Resistant to Attack From
T.L.-15	Ordinary household tools for 15 minutes
T.L.-30	Ordinary household tools for 30 minutes
T.R.T.L.-30	Oxyacetylene torch or ordinary household tools for 30 minutes
T.R.T.L.-30 × 6	Torch and tools for 30 minutes, six sides
X-60	Explosives for 60 minutes
T.R.T.L.-60	Oxyacetylene torch for 60 minutes
T.X.-60	Torch and explosives for 60 minutes
T.X.T.L.-60	Torch, explosives, and tools for 60 minutes

Safe manufacturers sometimes assign their own ratings. An assigned rating will usually mean that the safe offers a level of protection that compares to what UL would assign if given the opportunity to test. A concern exists, however, that without an independently assigned rating or classification, a purchaser has no way of verifying the expected level of protection.

Burglary-Resistive Vaults

Any storage container specifically designed to resist forcible entry and large enough to permit a person to enter and move around within, while remaining upright, can be considered a vault. Vault construction consists of reinforced concrete walls, floor and ceiling, and a specially constructed vault door.

Any consideration to build/purchase (prefabricated vaults are available from most large safe manufacturers) must be carefully assessed to ensure cost-effectiveness. The assessment must recognize that the value of the asset to be stored in the vault will likely attract the professionally competent thief. The impact of this is that regardless of construction, the vault will only delay penetration.

In addition to applicable features as mentioned for "burglary-resistive safes," the possibility that an employee(s) may be locked into the vault accidentally or deliberately in a robbery situation must be considered. To ensure safety of employees, all vaults should be equipped with approved vault ventilators and a method of communicating to those outside the vault.

Fire-Resistive Containers

Insulated safes, filing cabinets, and record containers that offer varying degrees of protection to contents from exposure to heat are available.

The appearance of fire-resistive containers can be particularly deceptive—of necessity, the construction material is totally different from burglary safes. The insulation material used in fire-resistive containers offers little protection from physical assault.

Two very important points in relation to fire-resistive containers are:

- Paper records will destruct at temperatures in excess of 350°F (159°C).
- Computer tapes/disks will destruct at temperatures in excess of 150°F (66°C).

Underwriters Laboratories tests fire-resistive containers for their ability to protect contents when exposed to heat. Tests are also conducted to determine the container's ability to survive a drop, as might happen when a floor collapses in a fire situation.

Note: It is of the utmost importance to remember that safes and vaults are only designed to delay entry when attacked; they are not impenetrable. For this reason, safes and vaults should always be protected by a burglary alarm system. Similarly, alarm systems should be used to protect the contents of record safes from theft.

UNDERWRITERS LABORATORIES

Underwriters Laboratories (UL) is a recognized certification organization for security equipment, security systems, and security monitoring. UL criteria are important in physical security, as it helps to reduce potential litigation by conforming to specific standards. UL has created safety standards for every device, system, and monitoring center that they certify. Many jurisdictions require UL certification prior to commissioning the system, and in many cases, insurance premiums can be reduced for UL-compliant installations.

FENCING

The subject of fencing is a much more interesting and important topic than most people first realize. Fencing has been used throughout history as a defense against enemies—the walled city of Pompeii dates back to 800 B.C., and it was not uncommon for the complete frontiers of kingdoms in China to be walled (origin of the Great Wall of China). Closer to home, the old city of Quebec remains the only enclosed city in Canada and the United States.

Modern acts of terrorism and civil disturbance have resulted in innovations in the types and usage of fencing. Barbed tape (razor ribbon), a modern version of barbed wire, is a very effective (if not vicious) defensive, or should we say, offensive material. Its use is rarely justified, except where the highest standards of security are necessary—for example, in a federal penitentiary.

The use of barbed tape in industrial facilities is not common in North America. Barbed tape can be used in coils along the top of fences, instead of the conventional barbed wire overhang. In very high-risk situations, coils of barbed tape stacked in a pyramid configuration between a double conventional fence will provide a very effective defense.

Another product of modern terrorism is the freely rotating barbed wire fence topping recently developed in Ireland. When a would-be intruder grabs the overhang in an attempt to gain leverage, a second overhang simply rotates into place. This is more effective than the conventional overhang and much more acceptable for routine application than coils of barbed tape.

Fencing as used in most applications is the common chain-link type with a barbed wire, outward facing overhang. A major weakness with the chain-link fence is the ease with which it can be climbed. To overcome this problem, the British developed the "welded mesh fence." Compared to the 2-square-inch opening in chain-link fence fabric, the welded mesh fence has openings of 1.5 square inches. The openings are 3″ × ½″ and run vertically. The narrowness of the openings makes it almost impossible for a climber to gain purchase. The width of the openings also inhibits the use of wire or bolt cutters.

Prior to making any decision on the location and type of fencing, it is necessary to conduct a risk assessment. It is also necessary to gain a thorough understanding of the enterprise's operation. For the purpose of this article, we will discuss the fencing requirements for a typical manufacturing plant located in an industrial area of a large city. The objective of the fencing program is twofold—to control movement to and from the property, and to minimize the need for costly manpower at control points. The latter is to be attained by keeping the number of perimeter openings to a minimum.

While it is true that the industry is becoming ever more security conscious, it is also true that the owners of industrial facilities do not want their property to look like a prison compound or armed camp. With this in mind, the first objective is to define the boundary of the property. Most often, this will require a combination of structural and psychological barriers.

From a psychological point of view, we are only concerned with defining the boundary—mostly for legal reasons, prevention of trespass, and liability lawsuits. Property definition may be simply a change in landscaping, or indeed, anything that distinguishes the property from its neighbor.

Somewhere between the property line and the area of company activity, it will be necessary to install a structural barrier that will act as a physical deterrence to the would-be intruder. Usually, this barrier is a chain-link fence, and it should be topped with a barbed wire overhang. The following are suggested minimum specifications:

1. Minimum of 7'0" in height excluding top overhang.
2. Wire must be 9-gauge or heavier.
3. Mesh openings must not be larger than 2 square inches.
4. Fabric must be fastened securely to rigid metal or reinforced concrete posts set in concrete.
5. There should be no more than 2 inches between the bottom of the fence and the ground.

6. Where the ground is soft or sandy, the fence fabric should extend below the surface.

7. Top overhang should face outward and upward at a 45-degree angle.

8. Overhang supporting arms should be firmly affixed to the top of the fence posts.

9. Overhang should increase the overall height of the fence by 1 foot.

10. Three strands of barbed wire, spaced 6 inches apart, should be installed on the supporting arms.

11. A clear zone of 20 feet or more should exist between the perimeter and exterior structures.

12. Where possible, a clear zone of 50 feet or more should exist between the perimeter barrier and structures within the protected area.

Vehicular and pedestrian gates in the perimeter fence should be kept to a minimum—ideally, to only one common entry point for employees and business visitors. Depending on the size and layout of the site, it may be necessary to install a secondary entry point for emergency use, such as access by the fire department. However, this entry point should normally remain closed and locked.

All openings in the perimeter fence should be equipped with gates. Even if these gates are not to be electronically controlled initially, planning should provide for power to each gate location with provision for a remote control capability from the control/security center.

Typically, security control is provided at the first defensible point; however, numerous facilities allow free access beyond this point to an inner control location. This may be beneficial for many reasons, especially in large, heavy traffic plants. Once inside the initial perimeter, signs should direct employees to the employee car park, visitors to an information center, and truck traffic to shipping/receiving areas. Beyond these points, a secondary secure perimeter should be established.

The employee car park should be completely enclosed; access to the area should ideally be controlled by a card access system. Access from the car park to the plant should be through a control point (manned during shift changes).

In addition to the possible need for a secondary line of defense, there may also be a need for fenced areas to provide secure overnight storage for company vehicles, bulk raw materials, or large finished products. Waste awaiting disposal should also be stored within a fenced area. Fencing may also be required to segregate operational areas, such as stores, tool cribs, and so on.

It is important to remember that fencing is first and foremost a barrier, and that as a barrier, it does not have to be chain-link fencing. If we also remember that fencing will only delay the determined would-be intruder, it should be easy to be flexible regarding the material used. Hedging, poured concrete, solid concrete blocks, and decorative concrete blocks are all suitable fencing material.

If fencing is required to provide a very high level of protection, its use should be supplemented by fence disturbance detectors, motion detectors, and patrolling guards or surveillance by closed circuit television.

CONVERGENCE

The term "convergence" is one that is currently commonplace in the physical security arena. Simply put, convergence can be defined as the meshing of physical security, logical security, information technology, risk management, and business continuity into a seamless and integrated system and process. It would be remiss to overlook this important aspect of physical security, as the entire industry is on the road to making convergence a reality.

Organizations that take a holistic view of security and integrate their physical security program into a converged environment are finding mutual benefits within the entire organization. When an organization can integrate their video, intrusion, and access control systems into their information technology systems, there are efficiencies that can improve the entire organization.

A basic example of convergence would be using the access control system over the corporate network to transfer data and integrate with the employee time and attendance system. The human resources department can then utilize the access control database (a physical security subsystem) to track and calculate employee attendance and hours worked. Although this is a very basic example of convergence, it shows how security technology can drive business efficiency and lower operating costs through convergence.

One of the greatest challenges with convergence is due to many departments having different reporting structures, and correspondingly different missions, within the organization. Budgetary funding and political wrangling can often hinder a converged environment. Some organizations have created a Chief Security Officer (CSO) position to assist in the convergence of information technology and procedures into the physical security function. The CSO position usually has some oversight and direct accountability to make sure that multiple departments work together in a converged environment for the betterment of the organization.

CONTINUING EDUCATION

There are many benefits in continuing one's education in the security field. Continued education is part of the career planning phase and should not be overlooked as a method of differentiating oneself in the job market. It is more important than ever today to continually improve one's knowledge and education. Employers are searching for employees that are dedicated to their field and have a wide range

of exposure to concepts and theory in security management. If already employed in the security industry, an advanced degree can lead to faster promotions or an increase in salary.

Work experience is also a critical component, and when combined with the proper education, it can lead to opportunities not afforded to those without the benefit of continued education.

Universities such as the University of Leicester in the United Kingdom specialize in the compilation and distance education delivery of security-specific educational opportunities. A bit closer to home, schools such as American Military University, York College of Pennsylvania, and Eastern Kentucky University offer studies that can be tailored to one's specific area of focus. A fairly comprehensive list of universities and colleges that offer security-related degree programs can be found online at http://www.asisonline.org/education/universityPrograms/traditionalprograms.pdf/

PHYSICAL SECURITY CERTIFICATION

ASIS International offers the only board certification program for physical security professionals worldwide. The ASIS Board Certified Physical Security Professional (PSP) designation focuses on one's proficiency in three major domains of knowledge:

1. Physical security assessment
2. Application, design, and integration of physical security systems
3. Implementation of physical security measures

The course reference materials are comprised of eight publications, offering a substantial look at physical security-related topics designed to assist security professionals in their career field.

It is important to point out that the ASIS "Board-Certified" designation brings accreditation to the certification process, and thereby creates a credential that is earned through examination and not just handed out for doing coursework. As such, it has become the most respected professional designation for Physical Security Professionals worldwide.

ASIS International does have eligibility requirements, which include work experience, in order to sit for the PSP certification exam. Additional details can be found online at www.asisonline .org/certification.

EMERGING TRENDS

The physical security field is quickly developing futuristic technologies to meet developing threats. The industry is adopting automated technologies to assist in the detection and assessment phases prior to a security force response. Visual analytics, which is the science of computer-aided assessment for surveillance systems, is becoming more accurate, which has led to deployments around the world. These analytically driven solutions allow for rapid detection and assessment using facial recognition, psychology of motion, path analysis, and much, much more.

Even "simplistic" devices such as locks are becoming "smart" through the use of computer chips and RFID technology. These smart locks are almost impossible to pick and do not allow for copies of the keys to be made, except when ordered directly from the manufacturer. Surreptitious attack methods on smart locks are difficult, if not impossible, to achieve, thus making such locking devices more effective when protecting critical assets.

Currently, security professionals are being asked to do more, using fewer resources, which can make the task daunting, even for the best and brightest. Recent terrorist attacks have hastened the technology curve in order to develop robust, scalable, user-friendly physical security solutions in the never-ending effort to prevent such acts. The need for new technologies will be critical to allow these practitioners to respond and mitigate the risk. It is evident that as the threats become more sophisticated, physical security technology must improve to meet those challenges, both now and in the future.

References

ASIS International. (2009). *PSP reference* (2nd ed.). Alexandria: ASIS International.

Barnard, R. L. (1988). *Intrusion detection systems* (2nd ed.). Boston, MA: Butterworth-Heinemann.

Broder, J. F. (2006). *Risk analysis and the security survey* (3rd ed.). Boston, MA: Butterworth-Heinemann.

Fennelly, L. J. (2004). *Effective physical security* (3rd ed.). Boston, MA: Butterworth-Heinemann.

Fischer, R. J., Halibozek, E., & Green, G. (2008). *Introduction to security* (8th ed.). Boston, MA: Butterworth-Heinemann.

Garcia, M. L. (2008). *The design and evaluation of physical protection systems* (2nd ed.). Boston, MA: Butterworth-Heinemann.

Illuminating Engineering Society of North America. (2003). *Guideline for security lighting for people, property and public spaces*. New York, NY: Illuminating Engineering Society of North America.

Nilsson, F. (2009). *Intelligent network video*. New York, NY: CRC Press.

Phillips, B. (2002). *The complete book of electronic security*. New York, NY: McGraw-Hill.

Resources

Listed below are several resources that will provide additional information regarding the physical security industry:

- www.asisonline.org
- www.info4security.com
- www.siaonline.org
- www.securityinfowatch.com
- www.securitymagazine.com

SECURITY QUIZ

1. Risks are usually categorized into three categories. (Select one that does not apply)
   a. People
   b. Property
   c. Legal liability
   d. Insurance

2. Physical security planning is a recognized security process that, if followed, will result in the selection of physical countermeasures based on appropriateness.
   a. True
   b. False

3. The security planning process consists of following a selected number of steps.
   a. Three
   b. Four
   c. Five
   d. Six

4. Security-in-depth is also known as:
   a. Layered protection
   b. Concealed protection
   c. Altered protection
   d. Necessary protection

5. Microwave detectors use high-frequency sound waves to establish a protected area.
   a. True
   b. False

6. Deadbolt locks should have a minimum of a ½″ throw.
   a. True
   b. False

7. Card access systems permit accountability.
   a. True
   b. False

8. The most commonly used security fencing material is:
   a. Barbed wire
   b. Barbed tape
   c. Chain-link
   d. Welded wire mesh

9. The minimum height of a security fence should be:
   a. 7 feet
   b. 6 feet
   c. 8 feet
   d. 9 feet

10. Which of the following types of lighting are only lit on an as-required basis?
    a. Continuous
    b. Standby
    c. Movable
    d. Emergency

CHAPTER

15

Alarm System Fundamentals

Doug Durant and
Kevin Pound

CHAPTER OBJECTIVES

- Define an alarm system
- Explore the fundamentals of alarm systems and operations
- List four types of alarm monitoring
- Explain alarm sensors and how they work
- Provide effective alarm response guidelines

In many cases, alarm systems form the backbone of a facility's physical protection program. Universally used, alarms are very likely to be encountered by the protection officer or security specialist as they perform their daily duties. In fact, regardless of your industry, employer, shift schedule, or geographic location, it is likely that you will have some involvement with alarm systems.

An understanding of basic alarm systems and their operation should be considered a "core knowledge" requirement for anyone

responsible for the protection of people, property, profits, and information. This chapter provides the fundamental information you need to know to be successful at your job. It is important to point out that this material must be supplemented with specific information as it applies to the alarm systems at your duty location. While all alarm systems perform the same basic function, each manufacturer's product may operate in a slightly different manner at the location. The site may require some specific alarm system component that makes the operation of the system different from other sites that you may attend or be involved with as a security practitioner.

Starting with the basics, a definition of an alarm system is in order. Quite simply, an alarm system is used to provide early warning of an intruder. There are three components to an effective alarm system: sensor, signal, and response. The "system" can consist of a relatively simple switch that activates a local audible device (e.g., siren and/or flashing emergency lights). If the system is monitored, a signal can be sent to alert authorities or response personnel, who can then investigate the cause of the alarm. It can also be quite complex, consisting of hardware and software elements that require considerable skill and training of assigned security staff.

The most effective physical security is "layered." An alarm system should be designed to provide one or more layers of detection around an asset. Each layer is made up of a series of detection zones designed to isolate the protected property and to control the entry and exit of authorized personnel and materials.

In more sophisticated systems, sensors are interfaced with electronic entry-control devices, Closed circuit television (CCTV), alarm reporting displays (both visual and audible), and security lighting. As you can see, the alarm system can serve as a crucial "layer" in any physical security plan.

ALARM MONITORING

Your involvement with an alarm system will depend largely on how it is monitored. There are four methods of monitoring.

1. Local Monitoring

This is the simplest form of alarm monitoring. It consists of a bell or horn located near the protected door or window. In the event of an attempted penetration, the resulting sound is intended to alert nearby police, security personnel, neighbors, or company employees.

A major drawback of this approach is the fact that many people will not bother to investigate a blaring alarm. Furthermore, manpower shortages often make a security or police response impractical. Although relatively inexpensive to install, this form of alarm monitoring does not provide an adequate level of protection for most situations. Also, a potential criminal can disable these alarms relatively easily. In many jurisdictions, local municipal noise laws require the bells or horns to stop after a required period of time.

When activated, the audible alert tells the intruder his activities have been noticed. In

many cases, this will scare the criminal off before the crime can be completed. However, in other instances, a seasoned criminal may realize a response is dependent on someone in the local area not only hearing the alarm, but also taking action to investigate it. In short, the criminal may be well aware that he has a certain amount of time to "work," despite the activation of the alarm.

2. Central Station Monitoring

This is the best and most popular method of alarm monitoring. It consists of a company that is paid to provide monitoring services for a variety of clients. Typically, these alarm companies charge a one-time installation fee and then bill monthly for monitoring services. Alternatively, many larger businesses may have all of their alarm signals monitored by their own control centers and have an in-house or proprietary security force respond.

When an alarm signal is received, an employee of the alarm company is responsible for notifying the police so they can respond. In most cases, a company's security officers are also notified so they can respond as well.

Despite its popularity, central station monitoring is not without problems. There have been several documented cases where the alarm company failed to make the proper notifications. Some alarm companies will provide their own security officers to respond to and investigate alarm conditions. In these instances, the alarm company's employees must be given keys to the protected premises in order to investigate alarms. From a security and business viewpoint, this should be considered an additional risk.

3. Direct Fire or Police Monitoring

This is no longer a common method of alarm monitoring. However, in some rural or remote jurisdictions the local police or fire station will monitor alarms from their headquarters. When used, this method tends to be a relatively reliable way to monitor alarms.

4. Proprietary Monitoring

In this approach, alarms are monitored by the company's security staff. In most cases, a security control center is on the premises and serves as a focal point for all security operations. During an alarm event, the situation can be assessed by dispatching security staff to the alarm location or by using CCTV to "check things out."

In a proprietary monitoring approach, the alarm system is operated and controlled by the property owner. In most cases, this means assigned security specialists are adequately trained and are very familiar with their property and its various security systems. They have a vested interest because they are protecting "their" company.

A drawback, however, is that proprietary monitoring can be very expensive. This is because the company must not only buy the required monitoring equipment, it must also pay people to operate it. Likewise, a proprietary system may provide inferior results if it is not designed for the specific needs of a building and its occupants.

OPERATOR INTERFACE

Regardless of the type of alarm monitoring used at your current location, eventually the system's operation will come down to a human being. This person might be a monitor in a central station hundreds of miles away, or they could be one of your coworkers, assigned to the security control system on the first floor of corporate headquarters. In all cases, the operator interfaces with the alarm. He or she interacts with the alarm system through devices that can be seen, heard, or touched, as well as manipulated. In most modern systems, visual displays and printers can be used to inform the operator of an alarm or the equipment's status. Likewise, audible devices are frequently used to alert an operator to an alarm or the equipment's failure. Such computer workstations permit an operator to acknowledge and reset alarms.

Visual displays. The type of display used to visually inform the operator of the system's status is determined mostly by the system's complexity. Today, status information is usually displayed on computer workstations.

Computer workstations provide great flexibility in the type and format of alarm information that may be displayed. Both text and graphic information can be presented in a variety of colors. Multiple alarms may also be displayed. If alarms are prioritized, higher-priority alarms may be highlighted by blinking, changing colors, or by using bold print, and so on. To assist the operator in determining the correct response, alarm-specific instructions may be displayed adjacent to the alarm information.

Audible alarm devices. In conjunction with the visual display of an alarm, the system must also generate an audible alarm. The audible alarm may be produced by the ringing of a bell or by the generation of a steady or pulsating tone from an electronic device. In any case, the audible alarm serves to attract the operator's attention to the visual alarm display. Most systems have a switch to silence the audible signal before the operator resets the alarm.

Logging devices. All alarm system activity (such as arming the system, disarming the system, maintenance, and system faults) should be logged and recorded. Logged information is important not only for security personnel investigating an event, but also for maintenance personnel checking equipment. This is especially important when trying to troubleshoot nuisance or "false" alarms.

Alarm printers. Alarm printers are typically of the high-speed, continuous-feed variety. The printer provides a hard-copy record of all alarm events and system activity.

Report printers. Many modern systems include a separate printer for printed reports, which use information stored by the central computer.

Operator control. A means is required to transmit information from the operator to the system. The types of controls provided usually depends on the type of display the system uses. For example, keypads consist of a numeric or LCD display system that are generally provided with a 12-digit keypad and several function keys. These allow the operator to perform such actions as to secure, access, acknowledge, and reset alarms.

ALARM SENSORS

A basic alarm system is divided into three layers: perimeter protection, area protection, and spot protection. Perimeter protection is the first line of defense to detect a potential intruder. Alarm sensors on the perimeter are typically mounted on doors, windows, vents, and skylights. Since a vast majority of burglaries are committed using such openings, it is important that they be a priority for protection. Commonly used perimeter sensors include the following:

Glass-break sensors. These detect the breaking of glass. The noise from breaking glass consists of frequencies in both the audible and ultrasonic range. Glass-breakage sensors use microphone transducers to detect the glass breakage. The sensors are designed to respond to specific frequencies only, thus minimizing such false alarms as may be caused by banging on the glass.

Balanced magnetic switch. Balanced magnetic switches (BMSs) are typically used to detect the opening of a door, window, gate, vent, skylight, and so on. Usually, the BMS is mounted on the doorframe, and the actuating magnet is installed on the door. The BMS has a three-position reed switch and an additional magnet (called the bias magnet) located adjacent to the switch. When the door is closed, the reed switch is held in the balanced or center position by interacting magnetic fields. If the door is opened or an external magnet is brought near the sensor in an attempt to defeat it, the switch becomes unbalanced and generates an alarm.

Area protection is also sometimes called volumetric protection. The sensors used for this purpose protect the interior spaces of a business or residence. These devices provide coverage whether or not the perimeter is penetrated and are especially useful in detecting the "stay-behind" criminal. As a general rule, area sensors may be active or passive. Active sensors (such as microwave) fill the protected area with an energy pattern and recognize a disturbance in the pattern when anything moves within the detection zone.

By contrast, active sensors generate their own energy pattern to detect an intruder. Some sensors, known as dual-technology sensors, use a combination of two different technologies, usually one active and one passive, within the same unit.

Sensors used for area protection include the following:

Microwave motion sensors. With microwave motion sensors, high-frequency electromagnetic energy is used to detect an intruder's motion within the protected area.

Passive infra-red (PIR). These motion sensors detect a change in the thermal energy pattern caused by a moving intruder and initiate an alarm when the change in energy satisfies the detector's alarm criteria. These sensors are passive devices because they do not transmit energy; they monitor the energy radiated by the surrounding environment.

Dual-technology sensors. To minimize the generation of alarms caused by sources other than intruders, dual-technology sensors combine two different technologies in one unit. Ideally, this is achieved by combining two sensors that, individually, have high reliability and do not respond to common sources of false alarms. Available dual-technology sensors combine an active ultrasonic or microwave sensor with a PIR sensor.

Spot protection is used to detect unauthorized activity at a specific location. It serves as the final protective layer of a typical alarm system. Assets most commonly secured with spot protection include safes, vaults, filing cabinets, art objects, jewelry, firearms, and other high-value property. These sensors (sometimes referred to as proximity sensors) detect an intruder coming in close proximity to, touching, or lifting an object. Several different types are available, including capacitance sensors, pressure mats, and pressure switches.

Capacitance sensors. These detect an intruder approaching or touching a metal object by sensing a change in capacitance (storage of an electrical charge) between the object and the ground. A capacitor consists of two metallic plates separated by a dielectric medium (an insulating substance through which electric charges can travel via induction). A change in the dielectric medium or electrical charge results in a change in capacitance, and thus an alarm.

Pressure mats. Pressure mats generate an alarm when pressure is applied to any part of the mat's surface. For example, an alarm is triggered when someone steps on a mat. Pressure mats can be used to detect an intruder approaching a protected object, or they can be placed by doors or windows to detect entry. Because pressure mats are easy to bridge, they should be well concealed, such as hidden beneath carpeting.

Pressure switches. Mechanically activated contact switches can be used as pressure switches. Objects that require protection can be placed on top of the switch. When the object is moved, the switch actuates and generates an alarm. Naturally, in such applications, the switch must be well concealed. The interface between the switch and the protected object should be designed so that an intruder cannot slide a thin piece of material under the object to override the switch while the object is removed.

DURESS ALARMS

In addition to perimeter, area, and spot protection, alarms can also be used for specialized applications. For example, duress alarms (sometimes called "panic buttons") are frequently encountered in many business settings. They are often concealed under a desk or countertop. Duress alarms are often used by receptionists, cashiers, bank tellers, security officers, and customer service employees engaged in transactions with the general public. In short, anyone who may encounter a threatening, hostile individual in the course of his or her work may find a duress device of value.

Duress alarm devices may be fixed or portable. Operations and security personnel use them to signal a life-threatening emergency. Activation of a duress device will generate an alarm at the alarm-monitoring station. Police or security personnel are then dispatched to render assistance.

Fixed duress devices are mechanical switches permanently mounted in an inconspicuous location. They can be simple pushbutton switches activated by the touch of a finger or hand or foot-operated switches attached to the floor.

Portable duress devices are wireless units consisting of a transmitter and a receiver. The transmitter is portable and small enough to be conveniently carried by a person. The receiver is mounted in a fixed location within the facility. Either ultrasonic or RF energy can be used as the communication medium. When activated, the transmitter generates an alarm that is detected (within range) by the receiver. The receiver then activates a relay that is hardwired to the alarm-monitoring system.

NUISANCE ALARMS

A vast majority of alarms are nuisance or "false" alarms. In many jurisdictions, this places a great deal of stress on local law enforcement agencies. Each time a police officer is dispatched to investigate an alarm, valuable resources are being consumed. To make matters worse, most faulty alarms are generated by the following:

- User error
- Poor installation

- Poor maintenance
- Substandard materials
- Employee indifference
- Inadequate training and system information

Security officers and business owners must learn as much as possible about their alarm systems. Where are the sensors located? What type are they? Who monitors the system? Awareness is the first step in effective alarm management. There is simply no excuse for arming a security system only to have alarms activated because people are still in the building.

Similarly, at some larger facilities, people sometimes simply forget to turn the alarm system on. Checklists should be used to arm and disarm various parts of the alarm system as required during the business day. This will also provide documentation of who did what and will minimize the chances for oversights between shift changes.

When it comes to installation, many alarms are the result of inappropriate sensor selection or placement. Alarm installations and equipment selection are not jobs for amateurs.

Alarms are electrical/mechanical devices. As such, they require periodic maintenance. Routine operational checks should be included to ensure sensors and related components are working properly. For example, security staff should walk-test every motion detector each day. This involves physically ensuring that each detector is functioning properly.

Likewise, there is considerable truth in the saying, "you get what you pay for." Substandard materials can include sensors, mounting hardware, wiring, and even software. There is nothing wrong with going for the lowest bid on an alarm installation. However, make sure you are not chasing false economy by using inadequate materials which will break and require continual replacement and repair.

Many non-security employees have little understanding of security issues. This includes even the most basic awareness of the company's alarm system. Often, employees will think

nothing of coming into work early, staying late, or visiting the office on a holiday. There is usually nothing wrong with such activity. However, if it results in continuous alarm activations, an employee awareness program is probably in order.

Nuisance alarms consume security and law enforcement resources which could be more usefully employed in other activities. Those which come to the attention of the police can also be expensive. The nuisance alarm rate has become so bad in many areas that local governments are now assessing fines on businesses and residences. These can run into the thousands of dollars.

Your organization's ability to operate its alarm system may not only protect property but also help protect hard-earned profits as well.

ALARM RESPONSE

Earlier, the various types of alarm monitoring were discussed. In some cases, the protection officer or security specialist will be dispatched to investigate an alarm event. The alarm might be the result of an employee entering his office before the alarm is deactivated. It could have been caused by a stray cat wandering the interior of a warehouse. The simple movement of balloons, plants, or a sign from the building's air conditioning or heating system can activate a motion detector. Then again, it could be something much more dangerous.

One of the major problems with nuisance alarms is that they invariably reinforce a mindset that every alarm is a nuisance alarm. For both public law enforcement and private security, this leads to complacent attitudes and poor officer safety procedures. For the private sector protection officer, the following alarm response tactics are recommended:

- Never assume an alarm event is "nothing." Assume you are responding to an intrusion until proven otherwise.

EMERGING TRENDS

Alarm systems have and will continue to form a part of a protection plan in the foreseeable future. However, the technology and reporting mechanisms that form part of an alarm system continue to broaden. As with any technology, end users will continue to look for smarter, faster, and more economical solutions. The use of video analytics, in combination with CCTV, along with voice verification, will help to provide verified alarms. Alarm signals that generate attached video or captured images of the location of the alarm will provide the end user with a clearer picture and understanding of the situation and allow them to respond effectively. This will continue to help lower the false alarm rates and will help organizations comply with local and regional false alarm legislation.

Sensor technology continues to change, allowing for larger and more complex facilities or structures to be protected, along with new ways to send those signals. Methods of alarm notification continue to be explored with improved ways to provide mass notification alerts to large employee or student populations. Instant messaging, text alerts, and cellular messaging are some of the options being used and improved.

- Maintain radio contact with fellow officers and your security control center.
- Maintain sound discipline. Keep radio volume low. Secure noisy keys and other equipment.
- If upon arrival to the scene, you detect broken glass or other indications of an intrusion, do NOT proceed into the building. Call the police and assume a position from where you can be a "good witness."
- Evaluate all alarm information. Has there been just one alarm? Is there a series of alarms which might indicate someone is actually moving around the interior of the building? The professional evaluation of all alarms can assist you in determining where the intruder is. Relay this information to responding police units.

- Know your company's policy for alarm response. Use common sense and avoid complacency that can lead to tragic consequences.
- Know of or how to locate appropriate phone numbers and passwords for your monitoring station.
- Keep emergency call lists, updated with appropriate call-out lists, as well as local authorities.

Any alarm system is only as good as the people who operate, monitor, and respond to it. Protection officers must be properly trained to respond to alarms. They must understand how their system works and the need to treat every alarm seriously.

SECURITY QUIZ

1. In many cases, _____ _____ form the backbone of a facility's physical protection program.
   a. Alarm systems
   b. Covert surveillance
   c. Report writing
   d. Physical force

2. The primary purpose of an alarm system is:
   a. To conduct area surveillance
   b. To serve as a physical barrier
   c. To provide early warning of an intruder
   d. To lower insurance rates

3. According to the text material, the most effective security is provided with a:
   a. Technical approach
   b. Layered approach
   c. Large security force
   d. Key and lock program

4. In more sophisticated alarm systems, sensors are interfaced with electronic entry-control devices, CCTV, alarm reporting displays (both visual and audible), and _____ _____.
   a. Police patrols
   b. Aerial units
   c. Sniper teams
   d. Security lighting

5. How many different types of alarm monitoring were examined in the text?
   a. Two
   b. Three
   c. Four
   d. Six

6. Which of the following is *not* a type of alarm monitoring?
   a. Central station
   b. Direct fire and police
   c. Satellite
   d. Proprietary

7. Logging devices are used for:
   a. Recording system activities and faults
   b. Controlling CCTV cameras
   c. Recording time and attendance of security staff
   d. Access control to computer networks

8. Alarm printers are typically:
   a. Of the color laser type
   b. Of the high-speed, continuous-feed type
   c. Black and white and medium speed
   d. Extremely expensive

9. A glass-break sensor is an example of:
   a. A perimeter sensor
   b. A spot sensor
   c. An area sensor
   d. A volumetric device

10. A duress alarm is also sometimes called:
   a. A reset button
   b. A panic button
   c. Activation switch
   d. A silent partner

16

Access Control

Colin Best

CHAPTER OBJECTIVES

- Define access control
- Clarify the security professional's role in access control
- Identify various methods of achieving access control
- Emphasize the value of record keeping and data storage

INTRODUCTION

The concept of access control is relatively simple. Access control is essentially what the wording implies: the control of access to property, services, events, or information. A large part of the protection of assets, personnel, and information begins with controlling access to them and the facilities where they exist. The function and practice of access control are fundamental to the protection officer in his or her duties. The security officer will almost certainly

be expected to perform a duty relative to access control during the course of their employment. Access control is usually more than just the face at the front door. It is a combination of several things, including control, record keeping, and careful planning. In many instances, access to a given area may be by patrol and identifying any people in the area being patrolled. Other forms may involve the control and monitoring of physical security systems, such as key systems, large-scale access control, alarms, and CCTV systems.

One familiar example of access control is a security officer behind a desk at the front entrance of an office building, industrial facility, or other property. This area is often called a "checkpoint" or "guard station." This checkpoint is often a fixed post, meaning the officer is posted permanently until relieved or when policy and/or post orders dictate. The presence of the officer in this key location of common access is a deterrent to those who may be unauthorized to enter the protected area or structure. In addition to the deterrent function, an officer familiar with the protected property and its frequent occupants will recognize those who are common to the property and can challenge those who are unauthorized. This form of aiding access control is common in large apartment complexes. Recognition of regular occupants by the security officer is actually considered a very secure form of controlling access; however, this "soft" method of access control becomes less effective as the volume of traffic increases.

Achieving the task of controlling access may be considered somewhat difficult if an officer were, for example, assigned the task to control access to a property consisting of acres of land with no fences or physical boundaries. Access control could only be achieved by frequent patrols of the protected area, challenging those unfamiliar persons caught on the property. In this example, those challenges may be the accepted form of access control, with no further control necessary. However, most facilities require additional forms of controlling access, such as waste sites, storage yards, and other facilities.

In some circumstances, large properties or defensible spaces may require a softer form of physical barrier. This may be achieved through dense foliage or even through designated walkways with paint around the area of protection or defensible zone. This form of control merely implies that a certain area is off limits and offers a convenient path around the area.

Many properties cannot depend on this "soft" form of physical security. It is for this reason that it usually becomes necessary to add forms of physical security to achieve suitable access control. Fences may be erected around a property to control access and to "force" or "funnel" visitors or employees to a common entrance or "checkpoint" manned by a protection officer. Appropriate signage indicating a no trespassing order will aid in controlling access through the message that anyone trying to breach security and access the forbidden area risks arrest and trespassing charges. In situations where it is expected that the protection officer will arrest anyone caught trespassing, it is crucial that signage is in accordance with the laws concerning local trespass acts. It is also extremely important that it is within the legal rights of the protection officer to perform the arrest. The addition of locks to alternate entrances to the facility or property will also control access. Other forms of additional physical security, such as CCTV and alarm systems, will further assist in the prevention of unauthorized access, although physical security must not interrupt safe egress from the property or site in the event of an emergency.

EMERGENCY ACCESS CONTROL

One must be sure, when controlling access, that egress in the event of an emergency is not sacrificed. Local and national fire codes often present challenges to controlling access to many facilities, and it is imperative that there is no sacrifice to the safety of the occupants of a facility in order to achieve better security. In most instances, policies are drastically altered for access in an emergency. Where policy dictates, a fixed post may become a roaming position for the officer to facilitate an escort for emergency medical services or the fire department. The opposite may be true when a roaming officer will be called from a roaming patrol to a fixed position at the entrance of the protected facility to provide speedy access for dispatched emergency services.

Generally, an emergency such as fire, medical concern, hazardous spill, or gas release should result in the halt of all work in the facility to help facilitate access. Elevators and other conveyances should immediately be surrendered from casual use for use by the emergency service personnel. Parking control at a facility entrance or loading dock can be considered an access control duty where entrances are kept clear to make way for emergency personnel.

EXAMPLES OF ACCESS CONTROL

Now that a given facility or property has been equipped with fences, locks, and other barriers, access can be controlled at one focal point.

Visitors and workers can be directed to one common point of access, but still one question remains unanswered: What prevents unauthorized persons from simply accessing the facility through the front entrance, where the security officer is stationed? This is the reason to have a policy for access control. The policy should outline a clear definition of the requirements for access to the property; for instance, a facility such as a nightclub may only permit access to those of a consenting age, so persons may be required to present a valid operator's license to gain access. Some facilities may require presentation of an invitation or ticket for a public venue or private function such as concerts, large weddings, or other events. Sometimes, the officer will be assigned access control to a parking garage and handling cash, then becomes part of the assignment. The protection officer may control access to other services. For example, the officer may control access to a conveyance such as managing elevator bookings or to a loading area or entrance. The issuing of visitor and contractor badges may accomplish control of access in regard to temporary contractors. Office and industrial facilities may require contractors to present company identification. Policies and procedures regarding access control may apply only to certain people in certain areas at certain times.

The identification industry is becoming more and more advanced, and many large corporations are implementing identification systems as corporate standards for all employees. Unfortunately, the tools to replicate identification are also available to the criminal population. Dye-sublimation card printers are readily available and are compatible with most personal computers and graphics programs. It is for this reason that many companies are adding modern security features to their corporate IDs. The use of holograms and watermarking make replication of a well-designed identification card difficult by unauthorized persons. Company identification can be combined or integrated with an access card for the facility.

The above example is effective for regular occupants of a facility, but for the authorized contractor or temporary staff, the security officer may be provided with a visitor list or permits. Those appearing on permits or lists will be the only persons permitted access. Temporary or visitor badges may be issued in this case, lest a person be challenged by staff in secure areas of a facility.

AUDIT AND RECORD KEEPING

Signing a security register or muster is a common function of controlling access. The necessity of signing the security register can be considered a valid deterrent to unauthorized visitors, even if the visitor does not need to present any other credential. This form of controlling access can be applied to many facilities and areas. The security register can have two functions: it can be used as an audit trail of who accessed the facilities at any given time; it can also be used for reference by emergency services to obtain a list of "who's in" during a facility emergency, such as a fire. A register commonly contains information such as the name, employee number, work location, phone number, as well as the time in and time out and signature or initials of the individual requiring access. The officer assigned to maintaining the security register should be prepared to assist those unfamiliar with the process in order to keep neat and consistent files. Records of this nature should be archived for retrieval according to the policies outlined by the employer or the client. Once expired, the records must be considered confidential and should be destroyed prior to disposal. Maintaining confidentiality of these files can be considered part of the duty of access control.

ACCESS AUTHORIZATION

During the course of performing access control, it may become necessary to deny access to those without proper credentials. The person wishing to gain access may very well have legitimate business on the protected property, and outright denial could create losses for the facility or property being protected. It is for this reason that facilities need a clear policy for the denial of access to individuals without proper credentials.

There are some facilities that may employ a strict "No Authorization, No Access" policy that will dictate that the person requesting access without proper credentials be denied. Many facilities will have a "backup" procedure to obtain the proper authorization for access. One example may be that a facility manager or supervisor could be called to provide verbal authority for access. Another example may be to require a visitor requesting access to call an authorized occupant in the facility to provide an escort.

When the security officer is left with the decision of whether or not to allow access, it is usually best that the officer act on the side of caution and deny access until a fair approval or compromise is reached. Advising the person that he or she has to be denied access is an act best accomplished with diplomacy and respect. The event of the denial should also be documented on a report suitable for the employer or client. Policies for granting and denying access should comprise part of the protection officer's post orders or standard operating procedures.

APPLYING PHYSICAL SECURITY IN ACCESS CONTROL

For many facilities, control of access at any one point may not be practical, particularly in large facilities with many areas such as industrial and office buildings. Posting officers at these various checkpoints to control access might be an effective form of access control, but in most circumstances, would not be a cost-effective, long-term solution. These areas may

consist of executive offices, chemical rooms, file rooms, and other areas that may require limiting or curtailing access. Rather than posting an officer at every area, access is controlled by way of physical security barriers such as doors, locks, CCTV, alarms, and electronic access control. The effectiveness of physical security is further enhanced by strict key control, effective monitoring of CCTV and alarm systems by the security officer, and accurate database management in electronic access control systems. Other important tools used to aid access control are intercom, telephone, and other voice communications systems. Requests for access can be made from remote points within the facility, allowing an officer to be dispatched or to grant access remotely from an electronic access system, given proper authorization.

LOCKS AND KEY CONTROL

Locks and keys have been around for thousands of years and are definitely the standard for controlling access in many areas. Since their invention, the durability and security of locks and keys have greatly increased along with their use. Today, they help control access to almost every structure imaginable. Generally speaking, a lock is a mechanical device that consists of a cylinder, springs, and several pins or "tumblers" that prevent rotation of the lock cylinder or plug without the insertion of a correctly cut key. Higher security locks manufactured today make unauthorized replication virtually impossible. Proprietary key blanks can have a restricted issue to one distributor or end user. A restricted proprietary keyway, combined with strict key control, is an effective form of controlling access. Permanent keys should not be issued without signature or receipt. Identical keys should each have unique control numbers permanently stamped on the key to identify issue. Temporary issue of keys should be accompanied by signature on a register or key sign-out form indicating a return time.

All codes and control numbers appearing on the keys should be documented for key sign-out. All key control documentation should be considered confidential and should be subject to similar record-keeping procedures as the security register. When the need to revoke access privileges is necessary, keys should be retrieved, or if necessary, locks should be changed. Some newer generation locks can suspend or revoke access to certain keys electronically, similar to an electronic access control system. This can eliminate the costs of lock changes, as well as administrative costs of reissuing new keys to authorized people.

ELECTRONIC ACCESS CONTROL SYSTEMS

With the addition of electronic access control to a facility, the officer can gain control of many individuals in different areas of the facility at different times, regardless of traffic volume. Most access systems installed today provide ease of access for authorized parties to come and go to their authorized destinations. Access is gained by presentation of a card or other physical medium to a "reader." The reader may be connected electronically to an "interface" or "controller," or networked directly to a host computer system, a trend often referred to as "edge networked technology." Modern systems are usually configured so that the remote controller, or even the reader, will make local decisions for access control and retain history transactions locally, in the event of a host computer failure or scheduled maintenance. This feature is known in the industry as "distributed" or "field" intelligence, and the activation of this feature is often referred to as "degraded" or "offline" mode. When access is granted to a given area, the access transaction is stored electronically on disk, tape, or printed media for future retrieval as part of a "history." A person attempting to gain access where not permitted can usually be reported as an alarm

on a computer screen, directing the security officer to take a predetermined action. Specifics as to the name, ID number, time of transaction, and type of denial are also recorded electronically to histories, as well as other alarms. Histories and other system reports can be customized in various ways and can be a valuable aid in the investigation of various incidents, as well as in controlling and monitoring time and attendance. Some companies utilize data from the access control systems to trend occupancy levels and use this data to shed energy loads in order to save on rising energy prices.

The industry of electronic access systems is continually expanding in terms of technologies, manufacturers, and installations. The majority of these systems are becoming more affordable and easier to use, whereas the technology that makes the systems work is becoming more advanced. Compiling modern, easy-to-use, graphical user interface software has made the management of "enterprise" scale systems a much easier task than it was just a few years ago. Older enterprise scale systems use operating systems and software that consist mostly of typed command line interfaces, which are less user-friendly than the more recent graphical user interface-based technology. Front-end computers on these earlier systems usually require more frequent maintenance and are more costly to repair than the modern systems being installed today. Installation of an electronic access control system will also contribute to the control of keys. Master keys need only be issued in certain circumstances and may be signed out only when necessary. A daily sign-out control policy can ensure that master keys never need to leave the property. Most installed access systems use a card or similar medium to provide access in place of the key. If lost, the card can easily be voided by the operator of the system. This is a simple solution compared to the loss of a master key, which results in changing many locks and reissuing keys to all keyholders. The access card will usually have a numeric or binary code that is verified by a computer host, ensuring validity.

RADIO FREQUENCY (RF) INNOVATIONS

Most modern access control systems utilize a contactless or radio frequency card that, when merely presented near a card reader, will be read by the system and either permit or deny access. Recent innovations in access control technology have led to the use of contactless "smart" cards. In addition to providing the required data for traditional electronic access control, other information can be stored on the card, such as personal identification numbers to allow access, or even a biometric template, matching the cardholder's thumbprint or retina information to the content of the card. Other uses for the card may involve building automation or cashless vending.

Modern electronic access systems have many features to enhance the level of access control to a facility, area, or room. Turnstiles, interlocking mantraps, and parkade gates are combined with access readers to prevent passback and "piggybacking" in parking garages and high-security areas. Cards may only allow one badge in and one badge out to track the time in and out of the facility or area. Some systems have enhancements, such as the addition of "mobility impaired" access, to allow the extended opening time of a door. In the event of a stolen card, the card can be "tagged" with an alarm upon use, alerting the operator at the monitoring station to dispatch security personnel to the location of the cardholder. Meanwhile, the card remains active and permits access, so as not to alert the holder of the card.

Systems can be interfaced or integrated with other systems such as building automation, fire systems, and human resources computer databases. This allows the access holder to gain access and turn on lights or air conditioning to his or her work area with the use of the access system. With the activation of a fire alarm, an access card could be automatically validated for use by the fire department.

ACCESS SYSTEM DATABASE MANAGEMENT

Controlling the access system should have similar strict procedures to those of the key systems. Issue should be controlled by consistent and appropriate documentation. Typically, information is kept in a cardholder's file, along with a history of changes and authorizations. These files should remain easily accessible by authorized personnel until a set time has elapsed since termination of the cardholder's access. This not only assists in audits, but can also control costs, as a card with picture identification can be kept on file in the event that the cardholder returns to work in the near future. Returned damaged or defective cards should be destroyed and documented in the system database so identical cards can be reissued in the future. Equal attention should be paid to the management of electronic databases. Spelling and pattern consistency are vital to good database management. Frequent software backups may one day pay off in the event of host server failure.

BIOMETRIC TECHNOLOGIES

Biometric technology is slowly becoming more commonly used in airports and other immigration checkpoints. Facial recognition technology is integrated into CCTV systems to identify individuals who are either wanted by law enforcement or may not be permitted travel to a given country. Facial recognition technology is quickly becoming an important tool in the prevention of international terrorism, smuggling of contraband, and child abduction at points of entry in countries around the world.

ACCESS CONTROL IN THE INFORMATION AGE

Since the mid-1990s, business has migrated from the physical storefront to the Internet. We now use this medium to perform banking, manage our investments, and purchase goods and services. Companies make use of the Internet to give their employees access to the corporate network so that they may work from home. Years ago, people perceived corporate espionage as being performed by people dressed in trench coats, picking locks with crude devices, and stealing information with small cameras. Today, that image has been replaced with a teenaged computer hacker at home in his parents' basement. This sort of threat has led to an increase in the IT security field, a multibillion-dollar industry.

Another large part of controlling access is security awareness. Identifying and reporting lapses in security can prevent unauthorized access. Closing blinds in a locked office prevents access to some of the visible information held within. Paying extra attention to weaknesses in physical security, policy, and facility design can play a large part in access control. As with many processes, the policies and procedures for controlling access in facilities are sometimes subject to flaws or have "room for improvement," and should therefore be scrutinized by management. Some ideas for change and improvement can be made at the level of the protection officer, and discussion between officers concerning problems should be encouraged at shift exchanges during officer briefings and staff meetings. Tightening security should not be the only criterion for continuous improvement. In many instances, the need for faster authentication of authorized personnel may be considered essential, as losses may occur due to an unauthorized person being "held up" by security.

EMERGING TRENDS

In addition to those trends in information security, there are many new and emerging trends and tools that relate to the function of access control. These include, but are not limited to, optical high-speed turnstiles, handheld explosive and biohazard detection, and most recently, millimeter wave scanning. Millimeter wave scanning is the latest trend in pre-board screening at airport facilities. While it is an effective replacement for manually searching passengers, privacy advocates criticize the technology as unnecessarily invasive and a threat to personal privacy. The images produced by this technology for viewing by security personnel are truly vivid nude renderings of passengers. The industry insists that privacy is maintained, as there are no stored images, and the facial images are censored.

Use of these systems has not only been instituted at airports and embassies, but is becoming common in nightclubs and even theaters. The role of performing and facilitating access control continues to evolve, as does the technology that supports it. It is a vital first line of defense in the protection of people, assets, and information.

SECURITY QUIZ

1. The task of performing effective Access Control includes record_____
   a. Control
   b. Planning
   c. Keeping
   d. Destruction

2. Signing in at a security _____ is a common function of controlling access.
   a. Officer
   b. Register
   c. Course
   d. Door

3. _____ of regular occupants to a facility is considered a very secure form of access control.
   a. Recognition
   b. Harassment
   c. Interrogation
   d. Arrest

4. There needs to exist a clear policy for the denial of _____ for individuals without proper credentials.
   a. Rights
   b. Access
   c. Service
   d. Income

5. The effectiveness of physical security is further enhanced by strict _____ control.
   a. Inventory
   b. Pest
   c. Car
   d. Key

6. _____ key blanks can have a restricted issue to one distributor or end user.
   a. Metal
   b. Foreign
   c. Proprietary
   d. Expensive

7. The feature of access control systems operating off-line and not connected to a host computer is often referred to as '_____' or 'offline' mode.
   a. Upgraded
   b. Access
   c. Degraded
   d. Egress

8. Smartcards have the ability to store a biometric _____ among other types of information.
   a. Template
   b. Contemplate
   c. Record
   d. Cash

9. _____ _____ _____ is an effective alternative to manually searching airline passengers.
   a. X-Rays
   b. Facial Recognition Technology
   c. Millimeter Wave Scanning
   d. Biometric Template Technology

10. Biometric technology is slowly being removed from usage in airports and other immigration checkpoints.
    a. True
    b. False

17

Detection Technology

Kevin T. Doss,
Christopher A. Hertig, and
Bethany J. Redmond

CHAPTER OBJECTIVES

- Identify considerations for selecting and implementing detection equipment
- Metal detection
- Explosive detection
- X-ray detection
- Canine detection
- Electronic article surveillance systems
- Responding to alarms

WHICH DETECTION EQUIPMENT IS THE BEST?

It has been a long-standing practice to utilize inspections and searches to detect and prevent the introduction of dangerous articles or deter the theft of organizational assets. To better protect assets and personnel, detection equipment is used at ingress and egress points. This detection technology can enhance security personnel efforts and assist in the assessment of containers or vehicles. The selection and use of detection equipment should complement the types of inspections defined by security policy and related procedures. In addition, detection technology should be based upon the protection level required, as well as the sophistication and type of threat.

To determine which detection technology is most suitable for organizational needs, it is essential to consider the durability and reliability of the equipment, the area of detection, and volume of traffic or articles to be screened, and the aesthetic effect on and cultural fit with the work environment. It is also necessary to evaluate the life-cycle cost of the detection equipment when purchasing the proper technology. The life-cycle cost estimates include more than the initial cost of the equipment, as it is necessary to factor in the cost to install, operate, maintain, and adjust for other fees, such as applicable taxes.

After the selection of the detection equipment has been made, it is necessary for the supplier to assist in developing training material for the protection officers who will operate the equipment. This training should be developed in accordance with the manufacturer's specifications and comply with the organization's security policy and procedures. Such training should address all organizational requirements and related expectations regarding the implementation of the detection systems. The training phase will also assist in the promotion, awareness, and compliance for employee and visitor alike.

METAL DETECTION

Devices used for the detection of metal vary by application (walk-through monitors or handheld devices) and composition sensitivity (what type of metal it can detect). A manual inspection, using a handheld metal detector, may be necessary to locate objects on an individual if a larger, automated detector is triggered when the individual passes through the field of detection. It is essential that the protection officer conducting the manual inspection displays the utmost level of professionalism and courtesy to the individual subject to the screening. If possible, the gender of the officer conducting the screening should be the same as the individual being screened.

Non-portable, or "fixed," metal detectors are being used at airports, courthouses, prisons, mailrooms, and even in public schools. Moreover, high-security facilities, such as laboratories, nuclear plants, and chemical facilities, deploy such technology for both security and safety purposes. Many mineral companies have also deployed such technology to track employees who handle precious metals, such as gold or silver, due to the high value these metals have on the open market.

Another application for metal detection technology is being used by police investigative units that operate portable (often handheld) metal detectors at crime scenes to locate guns, knives, bullets, and casings for investigative purposes.

The following are several metal detection technologies in use today:

Magnetometers

A magnetometer is a device that detects changes in a magnetic field caused by the presence of ferromagnetic materials, or materials attracted by a magnet. Metals such as copper, aluminum, and zinc cannot be detected by a magnetometer.

Continuous Wave Devices

These devices generate a magnetic field of low strength. A difference in the signals sent and received by the transmitter and receiver from the introduction of a metallic object in the magnetic field will cause an alarm. Continuous wave devices can be calibrated to optimize detection of ferromagnetic or nonferromagnetic metals.

Pulse-Field Detectors

Pulse-field detectors operate by complex frequency waves that induce an eddy current in the metal introduced in the field of detection. The signal resulting from this reaction will generate an alarm when it exceeds a certain threshold. As with the continuous wave device, the pulse-field detector's phase detection permits form optimization for detection of ferromagnetic and non-ferromagnetic metals. If paired with digital technology, a pulse-field detector produces an enhanced analysis of the signal, allowing for better discrimination between different types of metals, as well as between prohibited items and harmless metal objects passing through the detection field.

X-RAY

X-ray detection technologies are also used to detect dangerous or prohibited items when screening packages, containers, or vehicles. The type of substance detected by the X-ray detector is dependent upon the energy transmitted by the device. X-ray detection devices are capable of detecting drugs, metallic items, explosives, and some food items. An example is a portable X-ray detector used in a mailroom to check packages for explosives or other dangerous items.

Standard X-ray units can only scan objects, but not people, due to the amount of radiation produced. However, low-dose X-ray units are being tested at several airports. These low-dose machines utilize backscatter technology, which allows for safe use of X-ray detection on humans. This type of detector will show the human body underneath clothes and requires a front and back scan to properly assess the individual. A note of caution must be exercised when using these devices, as there have been several lawsuits involving "invasion of privacy" charges by individuals who have been scanned. In response, one airport has started to "black out" private areas on individuals being scanned to protect their privacy.

There are a few concerns when using X-ray technology as a detection method. First is the fatigue that operators experience when looking at an X-ray monitor for extended periods of time. This can be mitigated by rotating shifts routinely based on 20- to 30-minute intervals between operators. Another important issue to operators is the assessment interpretation during image analysis. Individuals can make mistakes and often misdiagnose items or overlook dangerous objects. Mistakes can be reduced through proper training of staff and by use of corrective measures.

EXPLOSIVE DETECTION

Like metal detectors, devices used to detect explosives may vary based on method of detection or application. Some devices are suitable for screening people, while other technologies can only be used to search containers or vehicles. Security officers involved in the inspection process are responsible for preventing the introduction of hazardous materials into the area and should be able to recognize the five basic components of an explosive device:

- A power source such as a battery
- An explosive material such as TNT, dynamite, or C-4
- A detonator or blasting cap
- A triggering device such as a clock or switch
- Connecting wires

When viewing the detection equipment monitor, it is important to observe the shapes of objects being screened. Some dangerous articles will be more obvious than others. Sometimes a dangerous or hazardous item may be disassembled. In this case, a package or container may be classified as a possible threat even if only two components of an explosive device can be identified.

Chemiluminescence Detectors

Chemiluminescence detectors can detect explosives such as RDX and PETN through photochemical means. Vapor samples collected from the subject being screened are separated into components by a gas chromatograph. After the sample is heated and the existing nitrogen compounds decompose, the residual nitrogen oxide (NO) will react with ozone, creating nitrogen dioxide that emits a photon detected by the device.

Backscattering Technology

Backscattering technology utilizes a detection process which can detect organic compounds with a low atomic number using X-ray reflection. This type of sensing technology is also very effective in detecting narcotic drugs.

Computed Tomography

Computed tomography (CT) uses a computer program to automatically scan packages for explosives. CT technology uses X-ray scanners that provide 3D images of the potential explosives. The costs to operate CT technology are comparably higher than other explosive detection technologies.

CANINE DETECTION

Dogs can be very effective instruments of detection and offer great portability in a variety of security applications. Research indicates that a dog's olfactory system is 10,000 to 10,000,000 times greater than that of a human. A dog's keen sense of smell can be developed and used in a variety of detection and security applications:

- Explosives
- Human concealment and tracking
- Drugs
- Patrol services
- Chemical weapons of mass destruction
- Dual-trained as detection and bite dogs
- Defense and protection of the handler

Dogs trained for detection purposes may be more reliable than other methods of detection because they are not very susceptible to false alarms. Dogs are reliable and selective when detecting sources of chemical vapors and are able to distinguish between very similar chemical compounds. Machines used in detection are adjustable and can be altered by users to reduce the occurrence of false positives. However, if the threshold of the detection equipment is changed too much, the equipment may no longer be effective in detecting these substances.

A well-trained dog and handler team can typically work effectively for 8–10 hours. However, there are other variables to take into account to determine how long a dog can work, such as volume of work, temperature, and amount of rest. Consistency must be established during the training regimen, and every handler and dog should be trained under the same conditions. Such consistency and uniformity make it possible for dogs and handlers to be interchangeable among teams. This also allows for additional flexibility among handlers should someone be out on sick leave or take vacation time.

Typically, canine olfaction is used to detect explosives at military bases or airports, or during special events. What's more, they are very effective in tracking down illegal substances at border crossings, public schools, and correctional institutions. Dogs are also effective in detecting both live humans and/or dead bodies during environmental disasters such as Hurricane Katrina.

Additionally, the presence of a detection dog can provide a deterrent value to individuals considering entering the area with prohibited items or dangerous articles. Dogs are also of high value when used to disarm or distract dangerous subjects.

It is worth mentioning that improper behavior by the dog and handler can ruin the reputation of the company or organization. Management should consider the potential reputation damage resulting from unprofessional behavior by the handler or dog and must ensure compliance with any legislation pertaining to the use of guard dogs. Indemnity against harm or damage arising from the use of guard or detection dogs should be provided by the contractor. Another downside to using dogs is the lengthy initial training period required for both dog and handler. Such training equates to cost, and many organizations do not have the patience or funding to support it.

ELECTRONIC ARTICLE SURVEILLANCE

Electronic article surveillance (EAS) is a technology that typically uses magnetic, VHF/microwave, or barcode sensors to detect fraudulent activity. An EAS system is a protection system that uses electronic sensors and detectors that create a field of detection or surveillance. The electronic sensors, also known as labels or hard tags, are secured directly to the merchandise or asset. If the label or tag is not properly removed from the item, the detector will sound an alarm when the article passes through the zone of surveillance.

In the past, EAS technologies were generally used only in retail establishments to prevent the theft of merchandise. Today, EAS systems can be found wherever there is a need to protect assets from loss, including libraries, long-term care or assisted living facilities, and pediatric units in hospitals.

Another technology which has gained ground recently is radio frequency identification (RFID). Retailers have been at the forefront of this technology curve, using RFID to detect fraudulent activities. However, RFID technology allows for more than just theft protection at the retail outlet. Products can be tracked from the raw material stage, through the manufacturing/production stages, all the way to the end user. Thus, RFID technology provides real-time data which can assist the organization in efficiency and productivity, while protecting assets from theft or damage.

In addition to electronic EAS tags, there are a few other technologies which are currently in use. Value deprivation tags make the item more difficult to steal, but usually do not initiate an alarm. Tags such as the "gator" tag actually tear the clothing they are attached to if an attempt to remove them without the proper tool is made. Another similar tag is the infamous "ink" tag, which explodes stain onto the clothing if an attempt is made to remove it without the proper removal tool. The retailer must place such tags on clothing so they are visible, since these are considered to be deterrent devices. Moreover, additional training and funding are required to implement such technology storewide. The tags can also reduce cashier efficiency level, as the cashiers must remove the tag at the time of purchase.

RESPONDING TO ALARMS

A systematic process for the investigation, isolation, and handling of the person, item, or area being screened is necessary when responding to an alarm. The detection and identification of a dangerous or prohibited item are the first steps of incident prevention. During an inspection, a protection officer must be on the lookout for indicators of dangerous articles, unusual series of events, and abnormal behavior. After a suspect article is discovered, it is crucial for the protection officer to proceed rationally and calmly to take control of the situation. Officers and responders must act decisively, in accordance with policy and procedures, while taking into account the circumstances, the environment, and the detected material or article itself. Report the situation to the controller or supervisor and take action to reduce the threat and protect life. Be sure to control and limit access to the immediate area and direct people safely to a designated muster area, away from the suspected article. Do not attempt to move or disrupt the suspect item. Make note of any details of the article and report them to the supervisor and response personnel. When the response personnel arrive, work with them to maintain control of the area and situation.

Hands-on inspections of people are to be used only as a last resort, in concurrence with security policy, and under the direction of supervision. A manual inspection may be necessary to locate objects on an individual if an automated detector alarms. If an individual refuses to cooperate with the protection officer's request for an inspection, the officer should remember that physical force is used as a last resort and refusal to comply with the request is not a crime. Force should only be used under severe circumstances and if the protection officer reasonably believes that the individual poses a threat to others. In the event the inspection reveals the presence of a prohibited or dangerous article, the protection officer should contact law enforcement and hand the person over to them.

EMERGING TRENDS

Emerging trends in detection technology include the possible use of MRIs in airports to scan and differentiate hazardous liquids from nonhazardous liquids. Researchers at national laboratories, who developed "MagViz" to take enhanced pictures of the brain, believe that this technology might also be helpful in airport security screening. Another detection technology that is becoming more prominent is quadrupole resonance (QR) or nuclear quadrupole resonance. (NQR), which is an MRI technology used to detect hidden explosives. This technology uses radio waves (low energy type) to determine if any nitrogen-rich materials are present. The cost of these QR scanners is relatively inexpensive compared to other bulk explosive detection technologies on the market today. One potential application for QR is the detection of land mines in combat zones.

As technology advances and security demands increase, the capabilities and uses for detection equipment will also increase. Furthermore, it is anticipated that the adversary will become even more sophisticated, and detection technology will need to improve as new threats develop. In addition, both criminals and terrorists are devising unconventional methods and techniques to destroy or compromise assets. Such advancements will require a more educated and aware operator, along with an effective training program.

SUMMARY

It is evident that no single detection technology is properly suited for all applications. The detection technology must be matched to the organizational objectives and applicable threats. As with most security technologies, human interaction and assessment capabilities drive the effectiveness of detection technology. Total cost of ownership for the technology system, along with operator training, is a critical component in choosing a detection system. A security professional should consult with an attorney to discuss potential liabilities and concerns prior to implementing any of these technologies, as some may be considered "invasive." It is also critical during the planning phase to determine the threat basis and design the detection system based upon the needs and culture of the organization. Detection technology is here to stay and will become more sophisticated to meet security requirements in the future.

References

Association for Automatic Identification and Mobility. (n.d.). *Electronic article surveillance.* Retrieved October 14, 2009, from http://www.aimglobal.org/technologies/eas/.

Cannon, J. C. (2008). *MRI at the airport?* Retrieved October 15, 2009, from http://www.innovation-america.org/archive.php?articleID=447.

Fischer, R. J., Halibozek, E., & Green, G. (2008). *Introduction to security* (8th ed.). Boston, MA: Butterworth-Heinemann.

Garcia, M. L. (2008). *The design and evaluation of physical protection systems* (2nd ed.). Boston, MA: Butterworth-Heinemann.

Patterson, D. G. (2004). *Implementing physical protection systems: A practical guide.* Alexandria, VA: ASIS International.

U.S. Department of Energy. (2008). *Contractor protective force,* DOE M 470.4-3A.

SECURITY QUIZ

Detection Equipment

1. How many suspect components of an explosive device are needed to warrant a possible threat?
   a. Five
   b. Three
   c. One
   d. Two

2. Which component is not considered a basic component of an explosive device?
   a. Explosive material
   b. Detonator
   c. Connecting wires
   d. Projectile

3. Which of the following is considered to be a downside to using detection dogs?
   a. A dog's keen sense of smell can be developed and used to detect drugs and explosives
   b. Unprofessional behavior by a dog and its handler may ruin the company's reputation
   c. An individual may be deterred by the presence of a detection dog from entering a facility with a dangerous item
   d. A detection dog may be an effective tool for detecting lost or missing persons after an environmental disaster

4. A magnetometer is a kind of metal detector that detects:
   a. Zinc
   b. Aluminum
   c. Ferromagnetic material
   d. Nonferromagnetic material

5. Which of the following is not a metal detection technology used prominently in security applications?
   a. Continuous wave device

   b. X-ray
   c. Pulse-field detector
   d. CT scan

6. Which chemical compound does chemiluminescence technology detect?
   a. Carbon dioxide
   b. Nitroglycerin
   c. Nitrogen dioxide
   d. PETN

7. The selection of detection equipment should be based on:
   a. Life-cycle cost of the equipment
   b. Reliability of the equipment
   c. Type of threat
   d. All of the above

8. Electronic article surveillance (EAS) systems are used to detect:
   a. Electrodes
   b. Merchandise surplus
   c. Fraudulent activity
   d. Retail invoices

9. When responding to an alarm, it is important to:
   a. Use physical force
   b. Remove the suspected article from the area
   c. Control access to the detection equipment
   d. Abide by company policy and procedure

10. Which of the following is not a consideration when using X-ray detection technologies?
    a. Taking necessary precautions to protect one's personal privacy
    b. Implementing shift rotation for security personnel to mitigate operator fatigue
    c. Training new operators is lengthy and expensive
    d. Implementing proper training and corrective measures to reduce mistakes made in assessment interpretations

SAFETY AND FIRE PROTECTION

18

Fire Prevention, Detection, and Response

Michael Stroberger

CHAPTER OBJECTIVES

- Identify the three components of a fire triangle
- List typical hazard areas where fires may occur
- Identify the four types of fires
- Explain the use of five types of fire extinguishers
- Emphasize the necessity of developing a fire plan

Fire has long held a position as one of the most feared threats to life and property. Fires not only destroy homes and buildings, but they can also consume vast expanses of wilderness or entire neighborhoods, and take the lives of people within their area of effect. Once initiated, fires spread rapidly and become extremely hard to control or extinguish.

Our best defense is the prevention of fire before it begins. Through effective controls and inspection, this threat can be significantly reduced to the benefit of everyone. In all fire situations, the protection of human lives must be the most important factor. Property can be replaced, information recompiled, and other materials remade. Protection of human lives must be the overriding consideration in every prevention and response plan.

FIRE BASICS

Fire is, in its basic mechanics, nothing more than an extremely rapid conversion from one state to another. This reaction requires three components to occur and must continue to utilize these three components to be sustained. As such, in looking at the prevention and response to fires, it is essential that everyone understand these parts, known as the "fire triangle."

1. **Fuel**—for a fire to exist, there must be some materials available that are capable of combustion. The material could be as simple as paper or wood, or as complex as magnesium. In every case, fuel is the component that undergoes the conversion from its current state to a different state. In most cases, conversion is from a solid to a gas, with some solid materials remaining.

2. **Oxygen**—the conversion of states in a fire situation requires an interaction with available oxygen. In most cases, fires are entirely dependent on the oxygen in the surrounding air; in other, fairly rare, cases the material that is being consumed may produce oxygen as a result of this process.
3. **Heat**—the final component required to cause the fuel in an oxygenated environment to begin the process of conversion is some source of heat.

Without the presence of all three components, a fire cannot begin or be sustained. This leads us to the basic concept that cleanliness is a major contributor to the prevention of accidental fires. If all available fuels are stored in a manner consistent with fire prevention practices, they will be sufficiently removed from identified sources of heat, and the chance of combustion is almost eliminated. This means that all identified sources of fuel must be identified and properly utilized and stored, to prevent exposure to heat (Figure 18-1).

For example, one of the more common fire locations in the hospitality industry is the laundry area. The operation of industrial dryers requires the production of heat. When processing cloth, there is a certain amount of lint that is produced. As a result, there is a ready supply of fuel (lint is very combustible) in close proximity to a heat source. The prevention practice is extremely simple: remove and clean the lint filter after each load, or at least on a regular basis.

Other typical hazard areas to inspect could include the following:

- Boilers, heaters, and furnaces
- Cooking areas
- Electrical equipment and breaker rooms
- Storage areas for flammable liquids
- Vehicle storage areas
- Work areas that utilize oils, paint thinners, and other combustible liquids
- Smoking areas

As a general rule, areas that are cluttered tend to have an increased chance of fire hazards and should be frequently inspected until they are properly cleaned.

When inspecting for fire hazards, which should be a constant aspect of every patrol, it is also essential that identified hazards be

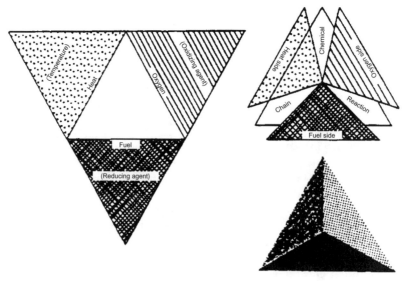

FIGURE 18-1   The fire tetrahedron.

corrected, documented, and prevented from reoccurring.

DETECTION METHODS

If prevention methods fail and a fire begins, the specific hazard must be detected so that the response program can be effective. The two methods of fire detection are human observation and electronic systems.

Human observation is often more effective, since it allows for the use of reasoning and judgment to determine the nature of the actual situation. In this case, however, there must be people present to make the discovery. Patrol officers have excellent opportunities to identify potential fires through smell, sight, and even sound and touch. In some cases, officers observe fires in such an early stage of development that they are able to effectively extinguish them without outside assistance. In addition, by obtaining the cooperation of other people in the environment, the chances of human observation can be increased. Often, these other observers must be given some form of basic training to identify hazards or early stage fire threats so that they can be more effective.

Electronic detection can also be highly effective, especially in areas where chances of observation by people are relatively low due to infrequent travel or visual obstructions. Electronic systems of detection can include sensors that watch for smoke, rapid increases in temperature, temperatures above certain levels (regardless of how quickly that temperature is reached), and even early combustion of airborne particles. Unfortunately, electronic sensors can also trigger alarms as a result of situations other than fires. It is because of this that all alarms must be investigated to determine the actual cause.

The ideal detection program is, of course, a combination of human observation and electronic monitoring. By thoroughly training the protective force and offering basic training to all other people who will be in the area, and utilizing an electronic system as a backup to these components, you greatly increase the likelihood of identifying fire situations. As previously stated, it is essential that fires be identified at the earliest possible moment, so that they have not had a chance to grow too large to be contained and extinguished.

FIRE TYPES

Although based upon the same concept, fires can be divided into four basic types, determined by the nature of the fuel component of their fire triangle. It is important to know these types and the differences in their fuels, as it can make a difference in how the fire is contained and extinguished. The basic classes are:

1. Class A fires generally have common solid, combustible materials as their fuel. This may include such fuels as wood, paper, and cloth. This is a very common form of fire. It is also the most basic.
2. Type B fires are fueled by liquid or gaseous fuels, such as gasoline, kerosene, and compressed gas tanks like propane.
3. Type C fires are initiated by, or contain an element of, electrical involvement. Fires in a breaker box, power strip, frayed extension cord, or item of powered equipment would fall into this category.
4. Type D fires are caused by burning metals, such as magnesium. They are often extremely intense and require special equipment to handle.

Once the nature of a fire is understood, it becomes a determining factor in how to handle a particular situation. For the most part, classes A, B, and C fires of sufficiently small size can be contained and extinguished by a person utilizing an appropriate extinguisher. Class D fires require such specialized equipment that most responders will not be able to effectively handle them, and should be cautioned to maintain a

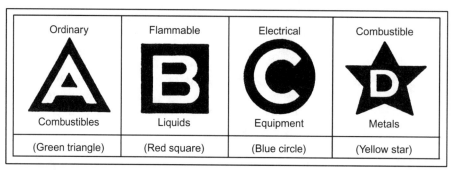

Ordinary	Flammable	Electrical	Combustible
Combustibles	Liquids	Equipment	Metals
(Green triangle)	(Red square)	(Blue circle)	(Yellow star)

FIGURE 18-2   Fire classifications.

safe distance in the process of evacuating the immediate area (Figure 18-2).

EXTINGUISHERS

The most critical aspect of deciding if you are going to attempt to extinguish a fire is determining if you can do so without serious risk to your own safety or the safety of others. Make no mistake: fighting a fire is dangerous. By its very nature, this activity requires that you intentionally remain within, or move within, close proximity to a highly hazardous environment. Care should be taken to ensure that the responding person understands the dangers and the equipment to be used, as well as its limitations. The purpose of fighting a fire is to save lives and property, not to risk them needlessly.

When working in an environment with extinguishers that you may not have used before, it is recommended that a test unit be obtained, even in a group setting, so that the area of effect, limits of range, and duration of use can be explored.

When deciding if it is appropriate to attempt to extinguish a fire, it is important that the equipment you select matches the fire type. Mismatching the extinguisher and fire types may result in a marked increase in the level of personal danger to which the responder is exposed. With this in mind, some of the more

common extinguisher types and the class of fire they are intended to be used on are as follows:

- **Dry chemical**—these utilize a powder that is expelled from the nozzle in a stream of pressurized, nonflammable gas. Dry chemical extinguishers are usually classified as usable on Class A, B, and C fires, as they will be both effective and relatively safe in those applications. Dry chemical extinguishers extinguish the fire by coating the fuel of the fire, making it unavailable for combustion.
- **Carbon dioxide**—these units produce a cloud of snow-like particles that quickly evaporate into a carbon dioxide layer. This layer reduces the available oxygen and cools the area, breaking the fire triangle. They are commonly classified as B and C type extinguishers.
- **Water-based**—water is a good extinguishing agent for Class A fires, but can aggravate other types. If used on burning liquids (Class B), it can spread the fuel, thus enlarging the fire area. If used on electrical fires (Class C), it can cause serious harm to the responder, as it may conduct an electrical charge, causing an electrical shock to be delivered to the holder of the unit or others standing in the runoff from it.
- **Halogenated units**—these are referred to as "clean agent" extinguishers because they

contain a chemical that leaves no residue upon evaporation. They cool and smother fires, making them typically usable on Class A, B, and C fires. These are the ideal type of unit for responding to computer or other delicate electrical equipment fires, as they are far less likely to cause damage to the equipment in the process of extinguishing the fire.

- **Foaming agents**—these units produce a foam layer that blocks the flow of oxygen to the fire area. They are very effective against Class A and B fires. Unfortunately, foaming agent extinguishers often utilize a water-based agent and so should not be used on Class C fires.

In the past, there were extinguishers that had to be inverted to cause a reaction between the main tank contents and a bicarbonate material, resulting in development of pressure. It has been recognized that this motion, the inversion of a heavy extinguisher, may not be within the capabilities of persons with disabilities, and their use has been largely discontinued. In the United States, such extinguishers do not comply with the Americans with Disabilities Act and should not be present in the workplace.

Extinguishers should also be checked and inspected on a regular basis. If there is high traffic in a given area, especially one that is open to the public, checking extinguishers daily, or even on each eight-hour shift, might be in order. It is important to ensure that they have not been discharged or tampered with so that they will be available for use if a fire is discovered.

PERMANENT EXTINGUISHING HARDWARE

In addition to extinguishers, which may be carried by possible responders, there are some more elaborate extinguishing devices that are installed in buildings:

- **Automatic sprinklers**—these operate through a spring-loaded valve that opens when exposed to certain minimum temperatures. These valves, called "sprinkler heads," are located at regular intervals throughout the entire building. Once the valve opens, the feed pipe that is attached to it will continue to supply it with water until the control valve for that area is closed or the sprinkler head is replaced. In most systems, the feed pipe has a sensor added to it to activate the alarm system if the water begins to flow toward an activated sprinkler head.

- **Range-hood systems**—in kitchen areas, there are often specialized systems designed to blanket the entire working area with a special chemical agent. This is designed to be highly effective on grease fires and other common kitchen fires, yet still be relatively easy and sanitary to clean up. These systems are triggered manually by persons who observe a fire.

- **Stand pipes**—based on application of fire codes, most buildings have a stand pipe system that allows for the connection and supply of fire hoses. Like an extension of a fire hydrant, these provide the fire department, or in-house fire brigade, with an available source of water.

It is widely accepted that, even under the best of circumstances, these types of automatic or large-scale systems usually slow or contain a fire, but often do not extinguish it. As a result, it is essential that each activation is investigated and the fire department becomes involved to ensure that the hazard is properly eliminated.

CONTAINMENT

In addition to the actions of responders and the utilization of various systems and equipment, there are usually design limitations that aid in the containment of a fire. In most jurisdictions, and within many companies, there are specific design and construction requirements, with regard to the use of fire-resistant building materials. Such items as fire-resistant doors, designed to resist the spread of a fire for certain periods of time, aid greatly in the containment of a fire. However, to be effective, they must be in their proper position and working in accordance with their original design. As part of every officer's patrol, confirming that fire doors are in proper condition and not propped or wedged open should be a constant component.

FIRE PLANS

Designing a fire plan, prior to an actual event, is the most effective step in any fire prevention, fire detection, and fire response program. It is through this plan that all of these factors should be addressed and given structure and detail.

Developing such a plan must be done in cooperation with those expected to execute the plan, and they should be involved from the beginning. Without this, it is possible that aspects of the final plan may be unrealistic, and could prevent an effective program from being implemented.

The written plan should include the following as a basic guide:

- Emergency contact names and telephone numbers
- A formal chain of command
- Detailed explanations of the responsibilities of each person or department in prevention aspects
- Detailed explanations of the responsibilities of each person or department in response aspects
- An explanation of the equipment available, the frequency of inspection, and the method of documentation
- An explanation of the training that personnel receive, the frequency of retraining, and the specific responsibilities bestowed as a result of this training
- Charts and diagrams of the property, detailing equipment locations, routes of egress, evacuation meeting locations, and similar fixed points

It is essential that senior management review this program and support it. It is also essential, and in some areas required, that the fire marshal have a chance to review the fire plan and approve it prior to implementation.

As part of a formal plan, alarm systems should be regularly inspected and tested to ensure that the components are functioning properly. This should include activation of every sensor through cooperation with a qualified/certified inspector or installer and the presence or approval of the fire marshal.

Above all, the response portion of a fire plan must be realistic in its assignments and expectations. It should be written with the following limitations in mind:

- Assign duties only to people or positions that will always be present. If you work in an area where the patrol officer is the only position that is staffed at all times, the response plan should assume that this will be the only person present for its critical aspects. It is easier to assign an extra person to a new duty than it is to find an extra person for a vacant function.
- Write each phase with the protection of lives as the primary focus, and property concerns as a secondary motivation.
- Write the plan based on existing equipment and supplies only. Do not count on having time to obtain other items before the plan must be put into action.

The most important point about fire plans is that *they must be put into effect!* What good is a plan that is exhaustively researched, designed by a broadly scoped committee, approved by every member of the team, and then put on a shelf and never utilized?

ARSON

Fires are not always accidents or acts of nature. An alarming number of cases are thought to be fires that are intentionally set for any of a vast number of reasons. In some cases, insurance fraud is believed to be the motivator; in others it is due to psychological disorders. Whatever the motive, arson fires are some of the most dangerous. Often, accelerants are utilized to cause the fire to grow rapidly beyond the containment and extinguishing capabilities of the responding fire department. In some tragic cases, this means that those within the structure don't have time to escape before falling victim to smoke inhalation. In even more sinister cases, arsonists have been known to block or lock doors, preventing escape from the flames.

Your best protection against arson is a combination of highly visible patrols to deter the attempt, and effective securing of unused rooms and flammables. These steps will reduce the areas of concealment, which the arsonist often relies on to prepare for the incident, and also cause the arsonist to have to bring their own materials,

which could draw attention to them. Much like other crimes, a motivated and dedicated arsonist will eventually find a way to attempt to carry out their crime, but you can create an environment where the arsonist, looking for a random place to start a fire, will be less likely to feel comfortable.

CONCLUSION

Know the basics and apply them to every patrol. Train each member of the team who is supposed to respond to fire situations so that they are not hesitant when that time comes. Train everyone in how to prevent fires and respond to discovering them, for their own safety. Fire can be a devastating event, especially if the response is uncoordinated or slow. Regularly check and inspect equipment to ensure that it is in usable condition, should the need arise.

SECURITY QUIZ

1. One component of the Fire Triangle is heat.
   a. True
   b. False
2. Class A fires are those involving alcohol as the fuel.
   a. True
   b. False
3. Fighting a fire with an extinguisher is very safe.
   a. True
   b. False
4. Human life and safety should be the primary concerns in fire situations.
   a. True
   b. False
5. Fire plans should include:
   a. Evacuation routes
   b. Defined responsibilities
   c. A chain of command
   d. All of the above
6. The detection of fires can be broken into:
   a. Electronic methods
   b. Human methods

   c. Both of the above
   d. Neither of the above
7. Arson fires are:
   a. Intentionally started
   b. Often made more dangerous through the use of accelerants
   c. Sometimes part of insurance fraud attempts.
   d. All of the above
8. Typical hazard areas include:
   a. Boilers, heaters, and furnaces
   b. Cooking areas
   c. Smoking areas
   d. Vehicle storage areas
   e. All of the above
9. Dry chemical hand extinguishers are usually considered:
   a. Class A
   b. Class B
   c. Class C
   d. All of the above
10. A magnesium fire is an example of a Class B fire.
    a. True
    b. False

Occupational Safety and Health and the Protection Officer

Kevin Palacios

CHAPTER OBJECTIVES

- Definition of work and health
- Consequences of occupational hazards
- Basic elements of an Occupational Safety and Health (OSH) program
- Major causes of occupational accidents and illness
- The role of the protection officer in OSH programs
- Key terminology

INTRODUCTION

Risk can take many different forms. It can affect people, information, tangible assets, reputation, and the environment in all organizations. This list not only describes all the domains a protection officer has to look after, but also highlights the priorities in the job description of the modern professional protection officer.

It is commonly accepted that the protection of people against all types of harm is the top priority of all security and safety efforts.

In many instances the only protective force on duty is the officers patrolling or performing access control duties. Providing a safe and secure physical environment is the major function of all protection officers.

Many organizations combine the disciplines of Occupational Safety and Health (OSH), security, and fire protection into one single department because of their common objectives. This department is usually referred to as the Loss Control Department or the Loss Prevention Department. It is usually directed by a manager or administrator.

The protection officer, by nature of his duties and familiarity with its surrounding, is in the best position to identify and correct unsafe conditions, unsafe acts, and potential hazards. The protection officer can play a significant role in accident prevention, safety awareness, and health promotion in the workplace. As safety and health are broad, diverse, and ever-changing topics of study, the officer must become familiar with the Key Terminology section at the end of this chapter. They must also take continuing education classes on such topics as HAZMAT, fire protection, first aid, and so on.

WORK AND HEALTH

The World Health Organization (WHO) has defined health as "more than just the absence of disease. Rather, it is a state of complete physical, mental and social well-being" (WHO, www.who.int). It is important to highlight this triple dimension of physical, mental, and social well-being, plus the connotation of acquiring this balance in each person.

Work has a direct influence over the worker's health, oftentimes a positive one (i.e., when one develops the physical and intellectual capacities, thus obtaining a better quality of life); but on occasion this influence can negatively impact one's health. Work conditions and workers' acts include many different variables that could be, on some occasions, the most important source of risk to workers.

Contemporary companies develop their activities in an extremely competitive environment. The market demands that production systems achieve social responsibility, profit, growth, and even survival goals. Companies are under pressure to develop "quality" products that are constantly being improved. In many cases, these constant improvements generate changes in work conditions and require modifications in the way work is done. These changes can affect workers' health. When a company's processes, materials, techniques, employees and even organization changes, it is necessary to reassess health and safety conditions. Special attention must be paid to the underlying organizational and psychosocial factors related to change, as their consequences (distractions, physical and mental fatigue, labor stress, dissatisfaction) are not usually as visible as those of accidents and illness, but they can be just as dangerous.

All elements that can negatively influence the work conditions or the health and safety of the workers, are referred to as "occupational hazards."

The consequences of occupational hazards can generate losses such as:

- Temporary/permanent absenteeism of the wounded/ill employee
- Medical treatments/medicine costs
- Temporary/permanent replacement of personnel, equipment, and materials
- Insurance deductible costs and increase of insurance premiums
- Waste of time and resources on the productive process
- Governmental fines, temporary/permanent closure, and even civil and criminal liability
- Diminished motivation and productivity
- Legal fees and investigations costs
- Cost of redesigning processes
- Administrative costs, managerial time
- Increased scrutiny by governmental agencies and insurance carriers

BASIC ELEMENTS OF AN OCCUPATIONAL SAFETY AND HEALTH (OSH) PROGRAM

The protection officer should be familiar with the basic elements of the OSH program at his company because his activities may have an influence on the program. The logic behind all OSH programs follows similar priorities as with any Enterprise Risk Management effort:

1. Plan the prevention, mitigation, and response measures at the inception of the business/design of the workplace.
2. Assess all risks periodically, updating the assessment when circumstances change.
3. Avoid all unnecessary risks by redesigning dangerous tasks or replacing hazardous material, equipment, or surroundings.
4. Treat risks with positive measures to eliminate and/or to control the risks that have been detected.
   - First target must be the source of hazard
   - Second is the medium of transmission

- Third is collective protection
- Fourth is personal protection of the worker
5. Control the effectiveness of the adopted measures.
6. Integrate preventive, mitigation, and response measures in all company programs.
7. Inform each and every worker about the risks their tasks entail.
8. Train the workers in self-protection.
9. Establish control and monitoring of health.
10. Plan for emergency situations.

It is important to note that each country, state, and even city has specific legal requirements that need to be followed. This might include statutory threshold limit values (TLV), task procedures, and even organization and resources that need to be dedicated to OSH efforts. The protection officer must become familiar with the standards of his or her region and industry. In broad terms, an effective OSH program should include at least six requisites:

1. Management Leadership

This is usually documented in a company safety policy. A company safety policy is a guide that outlines the responsibilities of all employees, whether they are hourly workers, supervisors, or managers, in the prevention of accidents, injuries, and illnesses on and off the job site. Without management leadership, the reduction or elimination of accidents is extremely difficult.

2. Assignment of Authority

Documented authority must be assigned to nearly everyone in the company.

- **2.1.** Safety and Health Directors and Managers: These are change makers who can implement all the necessary decisions via company resources (organizational, technical, and people).
- **2.2.** Safety Committees: This is a vital component of a successful OSH

program, as they carry out the following basic functions which enhance the overall safety program:

- Discover unsafe conditions and unsafe practices, identify hazards, and make recommendations to control or eliminate them. Discuss safety policies and procedures with recommendations for management.
- Teach safety to committee members who will in turn teach safety to all employees.
- Review accident reports and recommending appropriate changes.
- **2.3.** Individual Operations: Each employee must look after their own safety and health; protection officers must perform several duties:
  - Preventive—identifying unsafe conditions, practices, and hazards; acting upon and reporting on a continuous basis.
  - Mitigation—by inspecting occupational hazards during patrols and even while performing "standby" duties for the duration of a dangerous activity that is taking place.
  - Response—activating alarms and performing emergency procedures, administering first aid, etc.

3. Maintenance of Safe and Healthful Working Conditions

The protection officer should remember that inspections are one of the best methods to prevent accidents and safeguard employees.

- **3.1.** Inspection of Work Areas: The protection officer should be familiar with safety audits or inspections because these procedures are a principal method of discovering accident causes, unsafe conditions, and unsafe work practices. They also provide the means of promptly correcting these unsafe conditions and work practices.

- A safety program that initiates regular safety inspections or audits demonstrates to employees management's interest and sincerity in accident prevention. Also, inspections enable the individual worker to make contact with loss control personnel on a one-to-one basis.
- The worker can point out unsafe work conditions unique to his work area that would otherwise go undetected. When a worker's suggestions are acted upon, he realizes that he has made a contribution to the safety program and his viewpoints are taken seriously.

3.2. Fire and Specific Inspections: Normally, when specific inspections are conducted, checklists are used. Each company, plant, or department usually develops its own checklist. Items usually included on an inspection report are as follows: housekeeping, material handling, material piling and storage, aisles and walkways, machinery and equipment, electrical and welding equipment, tools, ladders and stairs, floors, platforms and railings, exits, lighting, ventilation, overhead valves, protective clothing and equipment, dust, fumes, gases and vapors, explosion hazards, unsafe practices, hand and power-driven trucks, firefighting equipment, vehicles, guards and safety devices, horseplay, and maintenance.

3.3. Maintenance and Fleet Safety Program: Depending on the nature and type of company, the loss control or loss prevention department may organize a complete program for motor vehicle/fleet accident prevention and operator education.

3.4. Job Safety and Health Analysis: Performed by safety engineers to determine potential hazards and the means to protect employees at their place of work.

3.5. Health Surveys: Performed by industrial hygienists to control and monitor the appearance and development of potential illnesses as detected by the job analysis.

4. Establishment of Safety and Health Training

4.1. Safety Training: An effective company safety program is based on proper job performance. When employees are trained to do their jobs properly, they will do them safely. Supervisors should know how to train an employee in the safe and proper method of doing a job. The immediate task of accident prevention falls upon the supervisor, thus the need for supervisor safety training. Most companies give extensive OSH training to supervisors.

4.2. Awareness and Motivation: OSH requires constant and skillful promotion. Some methods of awareness and motivation that are common in the industry, and the protection officer should be aware of include the following:

- On-the-job safety and health discussions and safety meetings.
- Safety contests with awards are effective in increasing employee safety awareness and motivation, stimulating pride among departmental employees, and improving the safety record.
- Posters and displays.
- Safety campaigns serve to focus the attention of the entire plant on one specific accident problem (e.g., campaign may be undertaken to promote use of safety glasses).

- Educational materials (films, newsletters, booklets, leaflets, etc.).

5. Accident Record/Data Collection System

5.1. Accident Investigation: Accident investigation is essential in the prevention of future accidents. An effective investigation should produce information that will lead to the development of countermeasures which will prevent or reduce the number of accidents.

5.2. Accident Analysis: The near accident or incident should be investigated to determine cause in order to prevent the possibility of a future accident. Near accidents or near misses are much more common than completed accidents. Near accidents usually indicate deficiencies in the system. A thorough investigation can reveal these deficiencies, as well as contributory causes.

- For purposes of accident prevention, investigations should be fact-finding and not fault-finding. The investigation should be concerned only with the facts. The investigating officer, who may be the protection officer, is best kept free from involvement with the discipline aspects of their investigation.

5.3. Records, Rates, and Countermeasures: A comprehensive data management system is mandatory in virtually any safety legislation.

6. Emergency Management, First Aid, and Medical Systems

6.1. EMS: Proper resources must be in place to respond accordingly; protection officers must remember that their security tasks must not be neglected while providing OSH assistance.

6.2. Medical: First aid and professional health care needs to be arranged.

OCCUPATIONAL RISKS

All workplaces have an almost infinite number of potential hazards; it is only because of the presence of risk factors associated with them that negative consequences actually occur. A risk factor is an unsafe/unhealthy condition or action (also referred to as substandard actions or conditions) that enables the hazard to produce harm (accidents, illness, discomfort).

In order to differentiate accidents from illness, we must pay attention to the "hardness" of the aggression and to the "speed" of the production of damage. Occupational illnesses are normally caused by long-term exposure to substandard conditions (physical, chemical, biological, mechanical risk factors); these are physical, psychological, and even ergonomic.

Aggressions that act only once and produce injuries of a temporary, incapacitating, or even mortal nature are called occupational accidents.

Generally speaking, there are four major causes of occupational accidents and illness.

1. Limited managerial understanding of the human consequences and economic losses attached to them.
2. Unsafe/unhealthy conditions—any condition of structures, materials, tools, equipment, machinery, or other conditions of a worker's environment that cause or contribute to an accident or illness. (Examples: inadequate lighting, poor housekeeping, chaotic or badly organized surroundings, or lack of warning systems). Unsafe/unhealthy conditions increase the probability of an accident occurring.
3. Source causes—any unsafe/unhealthy condition has a source cause. A source cause can contribute to or cause an unsafe/unhealthy condition that could lead to

an accident. (Examples: normal wear and tear, pipes corroding from within, ropes becoming rotted creating an unsafe/unhealthy condition, or lack of preventive maintenance). The source cause sets the stage for an accident; it makes the accident possible.

4. Unsafe/unhealthy acts—Human behavior action(s) by the worker that deviate from the accepted safe work procedure that cause or contribute to an accident. (Examples: horseplay or workers not wearing proper personal protective equipment.) Unsafe acts are often what trigger an accident. They may complete the cycle so that the accident event occurs. Personal factor causes often serve as the reason for unsafe/unhealthy behavior. Personal factor causes are any personal characteristic or conditions that may cause or influence a worker to act in an unsafe/unhealthy manner. Examples of personal factor causes include physical or mental conditions, extreme fatigue, intoxication, poor attitude, and tense relationships in the workplace.

THE ROLE OF THE PROTECTION OFFICER IN OSH PROGRAMS

The protection officer is trained to observe and identify potential hazards. The majority of large companies maintain a loss prevention department with protection officers on duty 24 hours a day, 7 days a week. The protection officer is in a position to report and correct unsafe acts, unsafe conditions, and potential hazards while conducting routine patrols.

The protection officer who observes a safety violation by a worker should do the following:

- Record the worker's name.
- Notify the worker's supervisor, advising him or her of the violation.

- Document the safety violation and forward a report to appropriate management.
- The protection officer who observes an unsafe condition, or a safety hazard should do the following:
  - Correct the condition or report it to someone who can correct it.
  - Mark off the condition as a hazard where immediate corrective action is not possible.
  - Document the unsafe hazard or condition and the action taken, forwarding the report for appropriate action.

Unfortunately, most health-related hazards and risk factors can't be easily/directly observed. The officers must be aware of the potential symptoms and consequences associated with their workplace in order to report them for early diagnosis.

Common Safety Hazards

There are numerous safety hazards that the protection officer should be made aware. Some of the frequently encountered safety hazards or conditions include the following:

1. Fire protection
   - violation of no smoking regulations
   - unusual odors, especially smoke
   - obstructed passageways and fire doors
   - inadequate exit signs
   - obstructions in front of hydrants, alarm boxes, extinguishers
   - electrical heaters and coffee pots left turned on
   - improper disposal of waste
   - flammable gases and liquids which are uncontrolled in areas where they may pose a hazard
   - paint or painting areas poorly ventilated and not properly secured
   - gas pumping areas close to operations where an open flame may be used

- use of flame-or spark-producing equipment near flammable substances
- missing fire protection equipment

2. Housekeeping
   - missing handrails on stairways
   - debris on grounds
   - inadequate containers for trash
   - broken glass
   - obstructions on walkways, such as snow and ice
   - oil spills or slippery substances that may cause slipping and tripping
   - cables, pipe, electrical wires across aisles
   - aisle obstructions
   - litter accumulation on shop floors
   - cracks, holes, breaks in parking lots, roadways, and sidewalks

3. Doors and emergency exits
   - burned out or missing emergency lights
   - doors that don't fit properly that would hinder emergency exit
   - improperly fitting door frames
   - equipment or debris blocking emergency doors
   - improper panic hardware for doors

4. Vehicle and fleet safety
   - improper audible warning devices for backing up
   - improper wheel chocking for parked vehicles
   - speeding violations
   - improper preventive maintenance procedures
   - vehicles parked in fire lane or blocking emergency exit
   - vehicles without proper signaling devices or lights
   - improper tires for road conditions

5. Personal protective equipment
   - improper personal protective equipment for the job
   - protective eye goggles not worn
   - safety-toed boots not worn
   - protective gloves not worn
   - hearing protection not utilized

- respiratory protective equipment not maintained
- proper protective clothing not worn

6. Machinery maintenance
   - lack of adequate guarding
   - worn belts, pulleys, gears, and so on
   - frayed electrical wiring that may result in short-circuiting
   - workers operating machinery with loose-fitting clothing
   - dangerous machinery lacking automatic shut-off devices

7. Other hazards
   - first aid supply improperly stored and maintained
   - emergency routes not adequately marked
   - improper labeling of dangerous goods
   - broken or damaged equipment not adequately tagged

These are the more common safety hazards encountered by the protection officer on routine patrol. A good rule of thumb is that the protection officer should devote one complete patrol during his shift to safety. Dedicating one patrol to the observation and reporting of unsafe acts, unsafe conditions, and safety hazards is a good practice.

KEY FACTS IN ACCIDENTS

Definition—an accident is an unexpected event in which physical contact is made between a worker and some object or exposure to a substance that interrupts work.

The protection officer must be knowledgeable of the key facts in accidents. Whether or not all the key facts are present will depend upon the particular case. Key facts are taken from "Accident Prevention Manual for Industrial Operations" (National Safety Council 1980, p. 154):

a. Nature of injury—the type of physical injury
b. Part of body—the part of the injured person's body affected by the injury

c. Source of injury—the object, substance, exposure, or bodily motion that directly produced the injury
d. Accident type—the event which directly resulted in the injury
e. Hazardous condition—the physical condition or circumstance that permitted the occurrence of the accident type
f. Agency of accident—the object, substance, or part of the premises in which the hazardous condition existed
g. Agency of accident part—the specific part of the agency of accident that was hazardous
h. Unsafe act—the violation of a commonly accepted safe procedure that directly permitted the occurrence of the accident event

Other items of information closely related to the key facts that the protection officer should be aware of include age, sex, type of occupation, and type of work.

Remember: The protection officer must be knowledgeable of the eight basic elements of a safety program:

1. Employer or client safety policy
2. Safety rules
3. Safety committees
4. Safety audits or inspections
5. Safety training
6. Safety awareness and motivation
7. Motor vehicle or fleet safety
8. Accident investigation

The protection officer should have some basic knowledge of accident types and accident causes because he may be involved in accident investigation.

These are the three elements to remember about accidents:

a. An accident is an unexpected event.
b. Contact is made.
c. Work is stopped or delayed.

Accident Types

Accidents normally involve physical contact or exposure between the worker and some object or substance. With this in mind, accidents are categorized into the following basic types:

struck by	example: struck by a falling tool
contacted by	example: contacted by hot steam
struck against	example: banging your head against a low beam
contact with	example: touching a hot pipe
trapped in	example: trapped in a tank
caught on	example: pant cuff caught on a board, causing a fall
caught between	example: finger caught in a car door
different level fall	example: falling down stairs
same level fall	example: slipping or tripping
exposure	example: exposure to toxic gasses
overexertion	example: back strain

Key Terminology

Accident—an unplanned event that results in harm to people, damage to property, or loss to process.
Accident causation—The many factors that act together to cause accidents. They include personal factors, job factors, and lack of management control factors.
Personal factors:

• Inadequate capability
• Lack of knowledge/skill
• Improper motivation
• Stress

Job factors:

• Inadequate leadership or supervision
• Inadequate engineering

- Inadequate purchasing
- Inadequate maintenance
- Inadequate work standards/procedures
- Inadequate hazard controls

Lack of management control factors:

- Inadequate program
- Inadequate program standards
- Inadequate compliance with standards
- Inadequate hazard controls

Accident Investigation—The process of systematically gathering and analyzing information about an accident. This is done for the purposes of identifying causes and making recommendations to prevent the accident from happening again.

Accident Prevention—The systematic application of recognized principles to reduce incidents, accidents, or the accident potential of a system or organization.

Administrative Controls—A category of hazard control that uses administrative/management involvement in order to minimize employee exposure to the hazard. Some examples are:

- job enrichment
- job rotation
- work/rest schedules
- work rates
- periods of adjustment

Danger Zone—An area or location where the probability of injury is high (e.g., in the vicinity of saw blades).

Due Diligence—The taking of every reasonable precaution under the circumstances for the protection of the health and safety of workers.

Emergency Plan—Detailed procedures for responding to an emergency, such as a fire or explosion, a chemical spill, or an uncontrolled release of energy. An emergency plan is necessary to keep order and minimize the effects of the disaster.

Engineering Controls—A category of hazard control that uses physical/engineering methods to eliminate or minimize the hazard. Examples of engineering controls include ventilation, isolation, elimination, enclosure, substitution, and design of the workplace or equipment.

Environment—The surrounding conditions, influences, and forces to which an employee is exposed in the workplace.

Ergonomics—An applied science that studies the interaction between people and the work environment. It focuses on matching the job to the worker, incorporating biology and engineering into the process. Ergonomics helps to prevent repetitive motion injuries such as carpal tunnel syndrome.

First Aid—The immediate care given to a person who is injured or who suddenly becomes ill. It can range from disinfecting a cut and applying a bandage to helping someone who is choking or having a heart attack.

Hazard—The potential of any machine, equipment, process, material (including biological and chemical) or physical factor that may cause harm to people, or damage to property or the environment. A hazard is a dangerous condition, behavior, or object that can cause harm or injury.

Hazardous Material—Any substance that may produce adverse health and/or safety effects to people or the environment.

Health and Safety Policy—A policy is a statement of intent, and a commitment to plan for coordinated management action. A policy should provide a clear indication of a company's health and safety objectives. This, in turn, will provide direction for the health and safety program.

Health and Safety Program—A systematic combination of activities, procedures, and facilities designed to ensure and maintain a safe and healthy workplace.

Incident—An unwanted event that, in different circumstances, could have resulted in harm to people, damage to property, or loss to a process. Also known as a near miss.

Incident Investigation—The process of systematically gathering and analyzing information about an incident. This is done for the purposes of identifying causes and making recommendations to prevent the incident from happening again.

Industrial Hygiene—A science that deals with the anticipation, recognition, evaluation, and control of hazards in the workplace. These hazards may cause sickness, harm to employee health, discomfort, and inefficient performance on the job. Also known as occupational hygiene.

Job Design—The planning of a job and the establishment of procedures for performing that job so that the potential for injury and illness is reduced or eliminated.

Job Enrichment—Adding one or more related tasks or functions to an existing job. These may include some managerial functions (e.g., planning, organizing, controlling).

Loss Control—Measures taken to prevent and reduce loss. Loss may occur through injury and illness, property damage, poor work quality, and so on.

Material Safety Data Sheet (MSDS)—A form that contains detailed information about the possible health and safety hazards of a product and how to safely store, use, and handle the product. Under the federal Hazardous Products Act, suppliers are required to provide MSDSs for all hazardous materials as a condition of sale. Organizations that use hazardous products are required to keep an MSDS onsite for each product. This is a provision of the Right to Know Act.

Medical Surveillance—The systematic approach to monitoring health changes in workers to identify and determine which effects may be work-related.

Nature of Injury or Illness—The main physical characteristics of a workplace injury or illness (e.g., burn, cut, sprain, dermatitis, hearing loss).

Occupational Health—The development, promotion, and maintenance of workplace policies and programs that ensure the physical, mental, and emotional well-being of employees. These policies and programs strive to:

- Prevent harmful health effects because of the work environment
- Protect employees from health hazards while on the job
- Place employees in work environments that are suitable to their physical and mental make up
- Address other factors that may affect an employee's health and well-being, such as:
  - Ineffective organization of work
  - Harassment and violence in the workplace
  - The need to balance work and family responsibilities (e.g., elder care, child care)
- Promote healthy lifestyles

Occupational Illness—A harmful condition or sickness that results from exposure in the workplace to a biological, chemical, or physical agent or an ergonomic hazard.

Occupational Safety—The maintenance of a work environment that is relatively free from actual or potential hazards that can injure employees.

Personal Protective Equipment (PPE)—Any device worn by a worker to protect against hazards. Some examples are respirators, gloves, ear plugs, hard hats, safety goggles, and safety shoes.

Physical Agent—A source of energy (e.g., noise, radiation, vibration, heat) that affects the body, a part of the body, or any of its functions. The effects may be beneficial or harmful.

Preventive Maintenance—A system for preventing machinery and equipment failure through:

- Scheduled regular maintenance
- Knowledge of reliability of parts
- Maintenance of service records
- Scheduled replacement of parts
- Maintenance of inventories of the least reliable parts and parts scheduled for replacement

EMERGING TRENDS

Despite the fact that the basic role of most protection officers is currently somewhat limited to physical and logical security, many protection officers already perform several duties in OSH programs. This will be more common in the future as the need for loss control, financial austerity, and competition among organizations grows.

Enterprise Risk Management is the assessment and management of all risks that an organization faces. Business risks such as profit and loss are being managed along with traditional security and safety risks by packaging them together into a single program. Such an approach may be particularly helpful with international operations: going into a foreign country presents a whole new host of risks. Convergence with other risk management functions within the organization (health, environment, safety, and quality) is quickly gaining momentum.

Laws and regulations vary greatly in different regions of the world; nevertheless, major efforts are taking place to standardize procedures, training, and risk management models globally.

Procedure—A step-by-step description of how to properly perform a task, job, or activity.

Risk—The probability of a worker suffering an injury or health problem, or of damage occurring to property or the environment as a result of exposure to or contact with a hazard.

Root Cause—The real or underlying cause(s) of an event. Distinguished from immediate cause(s) which are usually quite apparent.

Task—A set of related steps that make up a discrete part of a job. Every job is made up of a collection of tasks. For example, answering a phone or entering data into a computer are tasks of a secretary.

Task Analysis—A technique used to identify, evaluate, and control health and safety hazards linked to particular tasks. A task analysis systematically breaks tasks down into their basic components. This allows each step of the process to be thoroughly evaluated. Also known as job task analysis.

Threshold Limit Value (TLV)—A threshold limit value refers to the airborne concentration of a substance to which it is believed that nearly all workers may be repeatedly exposed day after day (for 8 hours per day) without harmful effect. Because of individual susceptibility, however, a small percentage of workers may experience discomfort from substances in concentrations at or below the threshold limit. A smaller percentage may be affected more seriously by aggravation of a preexisting condition or by the development of an occupational illness.

Workplace Inspection—A regular and careful check of a workplace or part of a workplace in order to identify health and safety hazards and to recommend corrective action. Workplace factors that have the potential to cause injury or illness to employees include equipment, materials, processes or work activities, and the environment.

SECURITY QUIZ

1. The disciplines of safety and security are dissimilar. They don't share the same common objectives in terms of the overall protection process.
   a. True
   b. False

2. The protection officer must take continuing education in HAZMAT and first aid.
   a. True
   b. False

3. The World Health Organization has defined health as "more than just the absence of disease."
   a. True
   b. False

4. One aspect of a formal safety policy is to prevent accidents and illness on and off the job.
   a. True
   b. False

5. One of the main functions of a safety committee is to administer effective rescue training programs.
   a. True
   b. False

6. The safety committee has the authority to make safety recommendations to management.
   a. True
   b. False

7. The protection officer should carefully inspect the work habits of members of the workforce and report deficiencies detected.
   a. True
   b. False

8. A safety program that initiates regular safety inspections (audits) demonstrates to employees:
   a. Management's concern for improved productivity
   b. Management's interest in accident prevention
   c. Management's concern for the off-duty worker
   d. Management's concern for an unsafe workplace

9. When a safety recommendation made by an employee is acted upon:
   a. Management recognizes the employee's contribution to the safety program
   b. The employee is likely to become a member of the safety committee
   c. The employee is likely to become less safety conscious
   d. Management perceives this kind of action as interfering with the safety committee

10. A safety checklist is useful because (check best answers):
    a. It makes employees aware of safety hazards
    b. It can be used by various departments to audit general safety procedures
    c. It can be incorporated into security patrol procedures
    d. All of the above

20

An All Hazards Approach to Hazardous Materials

Robert D. Jaffin

CHAPTER OBJECTIVES

- To define hazardous materials
- Explore the role of the protection officer in handling hazardous materials
- Explain how to respond to a hazardous materials incident
- Provide response models and templates, as well as tools and resources

The concept of hazardous materials can be a difficult concept to grasp. There are literally millions of materials that could be classified as hazardous. In addition, some materials might not be considered hazardous in their original state, but they become hazardous once they are used or they become "waste." For the purposes of this discussion, a hazardous material is anything that has the potential to cause harm to people or the environment (plants, animals, and waterways) if released in an uncontrolled manner. Beyond that, material that one might never think of as hazardous can become hazardous if released in the wrong place. For example, saline—or saltwater—is ordinarily viewed as a benign substance, one that does not need special attention. However, if an organization is moving saline via tank car and a derailment causes one of the tank cars to rupture, pouring this saltwater into an upstream freshwater fish spawning ground, it can create an environmental disaster. In this case, that saltwater has become an environmentally hazardous material. The same is true for moving milk in bulk using a tank truck or a tank car. Liquids of any sort, including water, when released at the wrong time or the wrong place, can create a life-threatening or facility-threatening situation.

Anything that moves in bulk that could be considered a raw material can meet the definition of a hazardous material if improperly discharged. In 2002, the unofficial estimate was that there are 1.2 million movements of hazardous materials per day in the United States alone. Note the implications—there are hazardous materials moving into and out of almost every industrial operation on a daily basis. Those quantities could be as small as a few ounces or they could be as large as multiple tank cars.

These movement estimates do not even take into account pipelines, which distribute some of the most hazardous, although not necessarily the deadliest, materials in use. From a practical standpoint, it is important to understand the generally accepted concepts and definitions for hazardous materials. The best, but extremely complex, definition is in Federal Standard 313D of the Material Safety Data, Transportation Data and Disposal Data for Hazardous Materials Furnished to Government Activities. That standard takes over two pages to define a hazardous material and references multiple external documents.

On a practical level, hazardous materials have been internationally categorized into one of nine hazard classes. Some of these classes are further divided into divisions. The most widely used and commonly understood classification system includes 23 classes and divisions. Seven of these classes and divisions represent inherently hazardous materials that must be considered immediate and direct threats in any quantity. Those include certain classes and divisions of explosives, mass explosion hazard, projection hazard, fire or incendiary hazard; dangerous when wet materials; toxic inhalation hazards; and high-level radioactive materials.

ROLE OF THE PROTECTION OFFICER

A proactive approach on the part of any business and every individual leads to minimization, if not elimination, of hazardous materials incidents. Education and training that specifically include a full explanation of all the materials that move through or are used within a facility is the first line of defense. Understanding the terminology and federally mandated response framework is a critical part of that training. The fact is, there is nothing heroic or exciting about maintaining good and safe work practices, and proper site security, to eliminate the possibility of an incident

occurring. That is the unglorious but real challenge for the professional protection officer. Yet, in today's world, where the "all hazards approach" has become the standard, weather-related incidents and hazardous materials incidents represent the majority of recurring serious incidents in the workplace.

Awareness of the evolving technologies and the inherent dangers of many new products is an often overlooked part of this job. Today's products, including products carried and used by protection professionals, represent their own set of new and unique hazardous material challenges. Here are some examples of new, and in some cases variations on older, products that represent new and often times overlooked or misunderstood hazards:

1. **Ethanol-enhanced fuels**. It requires a different kind of foam to fight an ethanol- or alcohol-based fire than a gasoline- or petroleum-based fire. Knowing that ethanol is being moved may require a facility, and its protection force, to increase the type and number of both portable firefighting devices and fire suppression systems available.
2. **Lithium ion batteries**. These batteries are one of the most dangerous products that are used in everything from toys to oxygen-generating vests, aircraft black boxes to computers and UPS backup power supplies. These batteries present such a great risk in transportation, as distinct from their individual use in consumer products, that the international community has assigned new identification numbers for them; and in the 2008 Emergency Response Guidebook (ERG), for the first time in over 12 years the U.S. Department of Transportation (U.S. DOT) added a new guide number. That is particularly significant because there are over five million different hazardous materials but there are only 66 guides in the ERG. If lithium ion batteries are short-circuited they will generate a tremendous

amount of power, usually in the form of heat. There are very few satisfactory firefighting techniques for lithium ion battery fires. Realistically, lithium ion batteries, like magnesium, burn at extremely high temperatures and can break down water into oxygen and hydrogen, which is an explosive mixture. While not always practical, the most effective way to fight fires by what are known as "refractory" substances, is to bury them with sand and deny them the oxygen required to support continued combustion.

3. **Compact fluorescent lights (CFLs)**. All fluorescent lighting contains mercury and it is illegal to dispose of such lightbulbs by merely discarding them in the trash. If any quantity of fluorescent lightbulbs are broken, it would generate a surprisingly large release of mercury requiring separate and specific federally mandated cleanup activities. A single broken lightbulb is not a cause for alarm; however, it is still officially an "event" because mercury, which is extremely toxic, has been released into the environment.

4. **Pressurized fire extinguishers**. While fire extinguishers are important to have on hand for safety reasons, the heat generated from a fire can cause those fire extinguishers to explode.

5. **Aerosol lubricants and deicing materials**. These materials are not regulated for private use, so if a private individual has them in a vehicle there are no federal safety "rules" that apply. However, under the U.S. DOT guideline 49 CFR 173.6, if one has those materials in a patrol vehicle, they become "materials of trade" and certain rules do apply. Those rules are based primarily on individual awareness of the inherent hazards of such materials and the need to properly secure them.

The portable radio and the cell phone as well as the "green" vehicle being used for patrol duties all might represent their own unique hazards. Understanding, and therefore minimizing,

the possibility of untoward events involving hazardous materials requires a full awareness of the workplace environment, the products used, and the nature of all materials from janitorial supplies to production processes to power generation and finished products of the business being protected.

HAZARDOUS MATERIAL INCIDENTS

The technological and social changes that occurred at the beginning of the 21st century have forced those in safety and security to reevaluate their roles and better define their responsibilities. Law enforcement, firefighters, emergency medical personnel, and protection officers are not expendable. These personnel form our first line of defense in case of an incident, regardless of that incident's cause. While their overall objective is the protection of life and property, a protection officer's primary objective must always be to survive so that they can continue to provide that protection to the general public. That means the protection officer must understand how to evaluate and take the action that will bring the correct resources to bear for the many different types of incidents that can occur. Rule number one with hazardous materials incidents is to always approach from upwind, uphill, or upstream. Obviously, if one comes upon an incident in the course of normal duties it may not be possible to observe that rule. However, a HAZMAT response team will always observe that rule. It generally would be wrong for a protection officer to take direct action, but for small releases of the more common and less lethal hazardous materials, direct action is sometimes appropriate. Even for the smallest of spills involving the most benign chemicals, no action should be taken until the material has been positively identified and appropriate actions confirmed. Knowing where to find the correct information and/or expertise is much more critical than being a "hero." Nowhere is that more important than when dealing with hazardous materials. Mitigation of danger in a hazardous materials release situation should be left to those with proper training and experience. For protection officers, the first step is to self-protection, the next is material identification, the next is to evacuate as necessary and activate the appropriate contingency or response plans, and the last step in most circumstances is to provide containment. That may be as simple as maintaining a physical security perimeter or as complex as breaking out absorbent materials, turning off entire HVAC plants, and preserving "crime scene" integrity.

TOOLS AND RESOURCES

While protection officers should know some basic firefighting techniques and basic emergency medical techniques including CPR and first aid, most security professionals recognize that they are neither paramedics nor firefighters. The same concept is true for hazardous materials response, containment, and mitigation. Small releases of less deadly materials can be handled by anyone with the right formal training, basic knowledge of hazardous materials response, an understanding of the risks and protocols, and access to the Material Safety Data Sheets (MSDS) to properly identify risks associated with each specific incident or material.

The most universally accepted method to identify and classify hazardous materials comes from the world of transportation. The original work was developed by the United Nations Committee of Experts, who developed the "Orange Book" of recommendations that is the basis for the initial classification and identification of hazardous materials throughout the world; these are not regulations but a set of recommendations. Individual nations, as well as international governing authorities, must recognize those recommendations and codify them into their own regulations. While hazardous materials fall under the Occupational Safety and Health Administration (OSHA), Environmental Protection Agency (EPA), and DOT, the most comprehensive information available on the majority of these hazards comes from the federal DOT guideline 49 CFR parts 100 to 180 which is known as the "Hazardous Materials Regulations" or HMR. The HMR are standardized and harmonized with the rest of the world. Portions of the EPA and OSHA regulations contain language and definitions that are not universally accepted and may be unique to the United States or North America. The HMR is also one of the most difficult federal regulations to read and understand. A good practical tool to use is the most current version of the *Emergency Response Guide*; at the time of this writing that would be the 2008 ERG. This guide is published by the U.S. DOT in conjunction with other North and South American governments, and has been updated on a 4-year cycle since 1996. The next version is likely to be the 2012 ERG, with a new ERG published again in 2016. Copies of the regulations, as well as handy pocket-sized copies of the ERG, are available from a number of sources and the leading providers of this material have been included at the end of this section. The single most valuable site for obtaining additional HAZMAT information (although not emergency response information in the face of a specific incident) is http://www.phmsa.dot.gov/hazmat.

The *Emergency Response Guide* is a tool that should accompany the professional whenever on duty; this author keeps one in the glove compartment of his private vehicle. Learning how to use the ERG is a key to minimizing and mitigating the impact of hazardous materials releases. There are going to be times when the most appropriate action is to turn and run! The ERG is a quick response tool to initiate both protective and response/containment actions. To paraphrase standardized training materials, "it is good for the first 30 seconds." That statement is an oversimplification, but it goes to the heart of the issue. It is better to spend more time reading the ERG in case of a real release than to spend time taking any mediation action. There are cases when the only action might be something as simple as "use a fire extinguisher or cover with sand," but there are other times when the correct action is to "run the other way." Remember that the professional protection officer cannot help anyone or everyone else if that officer has already been harmed.

One of the first things a professional should do in a new job, or for that matter in a new location, is to identify all the hazardous materials that enter, are used in, or leave, the facility. OSHA, under 29 CFR 1910–1200, has defined a "Hazard Communication Standard." The two key pieces that intersect the role of the protection professional are the requirement for the MSDS and the requirement for a workplace Hazard Communication Program that includes easy accessibility to the MSDS in every workspace that hazardous material might pass through. A security professional should review all the MSDS information for each worksite under their protection and know exactly where to find that information in case an incident occurs.

There are a number of other federal guidelines, documents, and consensus standards that impact directly on actions and protocols required in the case of an incident. Any incident that can have an impact outside of the immediate workspace and/or requires response from public safety personnel or might escalate into a larger scale incident requires an appreciation for, and a basic understanding of, the National Incident Management System (NIMS), including the Incident Command System (ICS) structure and function, the National Response Framework, and the NFPA 1600 standard. The protection officer may very well be the "first on scene" and the "first responder" and must be ready and able to communicate effectively with all the outside agencies that quickly become involved in such incidents. One does not need to become an expert, but one does need to understand how municipal, or for that matter private, response is governed and how such incidents are managed.

RESPONSE MODELS AND TEMPLATES

For decades, hazardous materials have been used with little or no training provided to the end users or those individuals charged with responding to a hazardous material release. Traditionally, the common point of view was that "dilution is the solution to pollution." This theory held that no matter how hazardous a substance was, if you were able to dilute it enough (usually with water), it would be rendered harmless. In the event of a hazard release, the common response was to call the local fire department or plant security team, who would then wash the contaminated area down in an effort to decontaminate the area. In the process, the contaminated water was usually washed into the sewer systems and surrounding ground, and ultimately into the environment.

Diamond Designation

A standard, but not legally required, method to broadly identify hazards in facilities is the National Fire Protection Association (NFPA) 704M consensus standard. Driving through industrial areas, one can spot many buildings and sheds with a large "diamond" on them. That diamond is in four colors—blue, yellow, red, and white—and it conveys to emergency responders the nature and severity, in very broad terms, of the materials contained within the structure.

To a limited degree this method worked for a while. The problem is that after diluting so many hazardous materials into the environment for so many years, the environment has become saturated and, as a result, traces of those same substances are appearing in our food and water supplies today—to say nothing of the long-term and short-term health hazards faced by unprotected response personnel, using no or minimal Personal Protective Equipment (PPE).

Today, government and industry agree that just as firefighting requires specialized training, response to hazardous materials requires specialized knowledge, training protocols, and protective equipment to ensure minimal risk to the workplace, the environment, and all individuals. Today there are firms that specialize in enhanced material incident response and cleanup and both public and private safety and security organizations create and train their specialized HAZMAT response teams.

THE INITIAL RESPONSE

Whether or not a facility has a HAZMAT response team in place, there are some basic steps that must be followed.

Identify the Substance Released

There are several ways to safely determine what has been released. But the most important thing to remember is the basic instruction provided in the ERG: always stay upwind, uphill, and/or upstream of any hazardous materials release until able to identify it. One way to identify material at the workplace is to ask the person who was using it. This may not always be possible, since the employee in question may have been injured. However, there are several other safe ways to determine what a released substance is. In the United States, under 29 CFR and 49 CFR, the OSHA and DOT regulations, there is both a requirement for a hazard communication

standard (29 CFR 1910–1200) and Hazardous Communications (49 CFR Part 172, subparts D, E, and F). In addition, the EPA's 40 CFR specifically addresses use of transportation labeling and identifications within workspaces. If material is being used or processed in a workspace those communication standards require easy access to the MSDS. Assuming compliance with those requirements, between the information on an MSDS and the information contained within the ERG, specifically the information provided for each guide number, professional protection officers can identify spilled materials and begin to take mitigating or corrective actions.

Determine the Quantity of the Released Substance

After identifying the substance, it is important to determine how much of it has been released. The uncontrolled release of 8 oz. (1 cup) of acetone, while requiring caution in cleanup, does not necessitate response from a HAZMAT team. The same quantity of cyanide or an explosive would require extraordinary measures to be taken. Quickly determining what substance has been released allows more time for the HAZMAT team to decide what course of action they must take.

If the release is a liquid or solid and has occurred in a more or less open area, it may be possible to see where the substance is leaking from. Never go near the area unless properly trained in the required level of PPE; this prevents the professional from inadvertently becoming another victim of the incident.

It may be possible to read the placard on a transport vehicle or a larger shipment, or the label which should appear on smaller packaging, from a safe distance with or without the use of binoculars. The identifying labels or placards may have a class, such as "Poison Gas," and should have the class or division number or, on placards of large enough quantities, the specific universally recognized "UN number."

That identifier is a four-digit number which can be looked up in the ERG. When reading the guide information in the ERG, be sure to read *all* the information on both pages for that guide number. Labels are the least accurate identifiers and although recognizing the label allows one to enter the emergency response guide to determine what to do in the "first 30 seconds," identifying the four-digit number unique to a spilled material is always the best and most accurate way to determine appropriate response actions. For transportation, that number will appear on the shipping papers. Within the facility, the number should appear in the appropriate section of the MSDS for that material. It takes knowledge of the OSHA requirements and the DOT requirements to most effectively monitor and manage hazardous materials incidents. The more information one can initially provide, the better prepared and equipped the responding organization and personnel will be once they arrive on scene.

Activate the Appropriate Contingency Plan

In many countries, facilities are required by law to have a HAZMAT contingency plan in place that can be activated in the event of an uncontrolled release of a hazardous material. In the United States, this is addressed in part by OSHA's Hazardous Waste Operations and Emergency Response (HAZWOPER) Standard. If there is no legal requirement for a contingency plan or for another reason the facility does not have one, notify the public agency involved in handling HAZMAT incidents for the area. Usually this will be the local fire department. When they arrive on the scene, they will take command and control of the situation. Everyone will then be directed by the incident commander.

Determine the Extent of the Damage

After the material and amount released have been determined, it is necessary to evaluate the extent of any damage that may have been caused. It is necessary to ascertain if there are any fires or fumes being spread by the release.

It is extremely important to keep clear of the area and to keep others clear until this determination has been made. The smoke produced by a fire can carry the contaminating substance a considerable distance, sometimes for miles. A classic example of this was a fuming sulfuric acid release at a General Chemical company facility in Richmond, California. In that case, fumes were carried over 20 miles up the Sacramento River Valley with the effects felt as far away as Antioch in Contra Costa County. It is important to determine what path the fumes or smoke might take, but that must be done from a safe distance. HAZMAT response teams, even if composed of employees, are often not familiar with areas of the facility outside of their normal work area. A protection officer is in the unique position of routinely patrolling all areas of a facility and that knowledge can be invaluable to the HAZMAT team in helping them direct a proper response.

Any injured people should be treated by qualified first aid or medical personnel as soon as they are safely removed from the contaminated area. Once again, the critical issue is proper identification of the hazardous material; the injured person, if contaminated, will need to be decontaminated before treatment can be rendered.

Perform Site Security

In this context, site security simply means keeping onlookers and bystanders out of the contaminated area. This can be a bigger challenge than it sounds. No matter how well the safety and security staff communicate to coworkers or to the general public that there is a hazardous area and that they must keep away for their own good, people seem to have a strong belief that no matter what they do, no harm will come to them. Invariably, people who believe this eventually end up getting hurt. Often they are the ones who get seriously hurt and force rescue workers to jeopardize their own safety to save them. During the initial phases of an incident, the risks of unauthorized personnel interfering with or, worse, distracting response personnel are very high. It is important to remember that initially the first protection professional on scene is the incident commander.

The media will take risks that most normal citizens would never dream of. Reporters have been known to cross barricades and sneak past security to get a close shot of the incident area. This poses several problems: they interfere with the HAZMAT team's operation by attempting to talk to them and generally get in their way; they typically fail to follow safety precautions and risk becoming exposed themselves; and when they do become unintended victims, they must be treated. This last concern increases the workload of response personnel who may be overextended and understaffed initially. Another problem with the media intrusion is that their entry into restricted areas encourages curiosity seekers to follow and go beyond safety barricades.

People like to watch others dealing with problems. On a crowded highway, during rush hour, drivers will always slow down to take a closer look at any incident along their route, even when that incident is on the other side of the roadway. An accident, even on a divided highway, inevitably has the effect of drastically reducing traffic flow in both directions. That same human curiosity draws onlookers to the scene of a hazardous materials incident.

EMERGING TRENDS

Hazardous materials will continue to evolve over time. As new chemicals, medicines, and foodstuffs are manufactured, the potential for dangerous concoctions escalates. Adding to the danger is an increasingly crowded transportation infrastructure. As highways and bridges are more heavily traveled, the potential consequences of a HAZMAT incident increase. A spill or release will affect more people in the future than at present.

Hazardous materials management is a key component of an anti-terrorism campaign. Understanding the scope and nature of danger that surrounds different substances is a necessary first step in protecting against terrorism. Protection officers must appreciate the risks associated with hazardous materials in and near their work environment. Security measures must be enacted so that terrorists cannot divert or detonate existing materials. We have seen with the 9/11 attacks on the World Trade Center what jet fuel can add to the equation.

The Department of Homeland Security, as well as several state agencies, has placed regulations on chemical manufacturing plants. These plants are being required to have security plans and dedicated individuals in charge of the protection function. Such regulation is likely to expand; new jobs and duties will evolve for protection officers at chemical facilities.

Along with a more robust regulatory environment, the current concern with environmental protection will undoubtedly play a role in hazardous materials manufacture and use. Organizations will need to continually assess their risk of hazardous materials incidents in light of potential negative publicity. They will also have to mount comprehensive media campaigns before, during, and after a HAZMAT incident, likely making them more careful in hazardous material precautions.

Resources

ALOHA (Area Locations of Hazardous Atmospheres). http://www.response.restoration.noaa.gov/aloha.

CAMEO (Computer-Aided Management of Emergency Operations). http://www.epa.gov/oem/content/cameo/index.htm.

CHEMTREC. www.chemtrec.com.

CHRIS (Chemical Hazards Response Information System USCG). www.chrismanual.com/.

JJKELLER. A primary provider of publications and training materials. www.JJKeller.com.

LabelMaster. A primary provider of publications and training materials. www.labelmaster.com.

National Response Center (NRC). www.nrc.uscg.mil/.

Pipeline & Hazardous Materials Safety Administration (PHMSA). www.phmsa.dot.gov/hazmat.

SECURITY QUIZ

1. Hazardous material is well defined and easily identifiable.
   a. True
   b. False
2. The emergency response guide is updated and reprinted on a 5-year cycle.
   a. True
   b. False
3. Always approach hazardous material incidents from upwind, uphill, or upstream.
   a. True
   b. False
4. In a crisis involving the release of a hazardous material, the first thing that must be done is to identify what has been released and in what quantity.
   a. True
   b. False
5. The standard response protocol consists of three consecutive steps. The correct order of these steps is:
   a. Identify the material, activate the appropriate contingency plan, perform site security
   b. Activate the appropriate contingency plan, determine the extent of the damage, identify the material
   c. Activate the appropriate contingency plan, identify the material, determine the quantity of released material
   d. Identify the material, activate the appropriate contingency plan, determine the quantity of released material
6. There are several ways to determine what hazardous material has been released in an employee-related spill, but the best way is to:
   a. Ask bystanders and onlookers
   b. Ask the person who was using it
   c. Assemble members of the HAZMAT Response team
   d. Contact the local fire department as quickly and practically as possible
7. There is a standard that should be used for preparing an MSDS.
   a. True
   b. False
8. The media present unique challenges for site security personnel.
   a. True
   b. False
9. The most comprehensive and detailed information concerning a specific hazard would be found in the:
   a. MSDS
   b. 49 CFR
   c. NIOSH handbook
   d. Emergency Response Guide
10. The fumes from hazardous materials release have been known to carry 20 miles or more.
    a. True
    b. False

INFORMATION PROTECTION

21

Information Security and Counterintelligence

Kevin E. Peterson

CHAPTER OBJECTIVES

- Provide important definitions related to information security and counterintelligence
- Explain the difference between "counterintelligence" as used in the private sector versus the federal government sector
- Describe the primary threats to information and intangible assets in both the public and private sectors
- Identify various types of information security vulnerabilities, reasonable risk mitigation, and security measures to counter the threat
- Explore the role of the professional protection officer and security service providers in the protection of sensitive information and intangible assets

KEY TERMINOLOGY

More than any other discipline or aspect of the protection profession, a thorough understanding of terminology and definitions is essential when discussing the topics of information security and counterintelligence. The following discussion of some key terms serves as a solid foundation for the concepts addressed in this chapter.

Information Assets—According to the Protection of Assets Manual (POA), information assets "consist of sensitive and proprietary information, privacy-protected data, intellectual property, intangible assets and information defined under international, federal, and state laws governing trade secrets, patents, and copyrights" (ASIS International, 2008, p. 2-I-1). Although not all inclusive, some examples of information assets are:

- Scientific and technical data
- Formulas
- Knowledge
- Manufacturing and other business processes
- Organizational goodwill and reputation
- Brand
- Personnel data
- Medical records
- Customer information
- Pricing data
- Business and marketing strategies
- Testing procedures and results

- Engineering data and specifications
- Information protected under regulatory requirements (e.g., health care, financial, and grand jury information)

Information assets can exist in a wide variety of forms and formats such as hard copy, computer data (on systems, in transmission, or on media), electromagnetic or electro-optical signals, spoken word, individual knowledge, prototypes, models, and processes. Protection strategies should consider both the content of the information to be protected and the form or format in which it exists.

Information Assets Protection—This is an overarching concept that integrates the subdiscipline of information security along with several emerging disciplines that are focused on protecting information and intangible assets under specific conditions. Figure 21-1 illustrates the concept.

Information security includes traditional information protection measures such as marking, storage, proper transmission, and destruction of information. It also encompasses information technology (or IT) security to protect automated information systems, hardware, software, and the data being stored, processed, or transmitted through them. The third element of information security involves the protection of intellectual property rights (IPR).

FIGURE 21-1 Structure of information asset protection functions.

Similarly, the U.S. Department of Defense defines information security as "the system of policies, procedures, and requirements established … to protect information that, if subjected to unauthorized disclosure, could reasonably be expected to cause damage.…" The same document defines information as "Any knowledge that can be communicated or documentary material, regardless of its physical form or characteristics, that is owned by, produced by or for, or is under the control of [an enterprise]…" (Department of Defense, 1997).

The emerging disciplines complement information security and include the conduct of due diligence investigations as a vetting tool (to establish an appropriate level of trust with potential partners, vendors, contractors, and other third parties). They also include the practice of market entry planning and product security (ASIS International and IAP Council, 2009). These topics will be discussed later in this chapter.

Information assets protection brings these disciplines and elements together in a concerted way and provides a comprehensive approach to maintaining the value of information and intangible assets.

Intangible Assets—These are assets of any organization (including companies and government agencies) that are not physical in nature. Examples of intangible assets are an organization's reputation, brand, relationships, management style, knowledge, and processes. Intangible assets are generally very difficult to measure or quantify—and may often be overlooked when determining where to apply security or protection efforts.

Competitive Intelligence versus Economic Espionage—Although both of these methods involve collecting information for the ultimate purpose of supporting business or government objectives, they represent opposite ends of a spectrum of "ethicalness." Competitive intelligence is a normal business function which can include completely benign activities such as market research. As competitive intelligence measures become more aggressive, they may approach a "gray area" in the center of the spectrum that borders on unethical behavior. This includes activities like making pretext phone calls (or e-mails) to competitors to gather information, or sending individuals to pose as job applicants. Industrial or economic espionage is on the other end of the spectrum and includes illegal activities such as electronic eavesdropping and hiring employees away from competitors for the specific purpose of gaining confidential information (Webster University, 2008).

Compromise—Refers to a situation where sensitive, controlled, or classified information actually falls into the hands of an unauthorized person or organization. This is contrasted with a security violation, for example, in which a policy or procedure was not followed but there is no indication that any information was actually lost.

Counterintelligence—Any measures taken to negate intelligence collection efforts against an organization or its people. In the federal sector, counterintelligence relates to programs designed to counteract foreign intelligence services and recruited agents. In the private sector it is often referred to as "countercompetitive intelligence" and may be focused on protecting against actions ranging from simple market research up to and including industrial espionage. The term is also used in the law enforcement community to refer to actions taken to protect sensitive information from falling into the hands of criminal organizations that may be targeting law enforcement agencies, personnel, or task forces. Counterintelligence activities may be defensive or offensive in nature, and may also be primarily proactive or reactive.

Information Security—(*see paragraph on Information Assets Protection*)

Sensitive Information—Information or knowledge that might result in loss of an advantage or level of security if disclosed to others (ASIS International, Information Asset Protection Guideline, 2007, p. 8).

Technical Security—Measures taken to identify, prevent, or neutralize technical threats including electronic or electro-optic eavesdropping, wiretapping, bugging, signal intercept, covert/illicit surveillance, and attacks on information technology or telecommunications systems (ASIS International, Information Asset Protection Guideline, 2007, p. 8).

Technical Surveillance Countermeasures—Also known as TSCM, they include services, equipment, and techniques designed to locate, identify, and neutralize technical surveillance activities such as covert listening devices.

Trade Secret—Trade secrets are defined by laws, such as the Economic Espionage Act, at the federal level, as well as by state and local laws. Generally, trade secrets are designated by the owner, but must meet certain criteria in order to qualify for applicable legal protections. Although the laws vary, most require that information have demonstrable value to the owner, be specifically identified, and be adequately protected in order to qualify as a trade secret.

THREATS TO INFORMATION AND INTANGIBLE ASSETS

As with any asset protection issue, we must consider three categories of threats: intentional, natural, and inadvertent. Like any tangible asset such as a building or piece of equipment, *information* will be subject to all three categories. Although our primary focus in information asset protection (IAP) is on intentional and inadvertent threats, some attention must also be directed at natural threats. For example, in the wake of Hurricane Katrina (2005), many small businesses failed, not because their facility was destroyed or their people displaced, but because they lost the bulk of their critical business information. It is not uncommon for organizations to prepare their facilities and people for the effects of a natural disaster, while neglecting to take prudent information protection measures.

Preparations such as geographically separated off-site backup or data protection measures for contingency remote computing can mean the difference between successful business recovery and catastrophic failure.

The nature and extent of the threat to information and intangible assets is concisely summarized in the introduction to the economic espionage page on the Federal Bureau of Investigation's (FBI) Web site:

> The Cold War is not over, it has merely moved into a new arena: the global marketplace. The FBI estimates that every year billions of U.S. dollars are lost to foreign competitors who deliberately target economic intelligence in flourishing U.S. industries and technologies …(Federal Bureau of Investigation, 2009).

The methods that comprise the threat to information assets cover the gamut from old, time-tested techniques to new and innovative collection measures. Among the commonly reported collection methods are:

- Open source collection of public information
- Data mining and/or the use of information brokers
- Social engineering and other elicitation techniques
- Co-opting/recruiting a current or former employee (or trusted third party)
- Hiring key employees away from the targeted organization
- Targeting meetings and conferences
- Electronic eavesdropping
- Theft of hardcopy information
- Ttheft of softcopy information/media (e.g., thumb drives, laptop computers, mobile devices, etc.)
- Unauthorized penetration of information systems (e.g., hacking)
- Unauthorized access to information systems by insiders
- Exploitation of joint venture partners or other trusted third parties
- Unauthorized physical access to (or observation of) information

- Misdirected e-mail or other electronic communications
- Deliberate disclosure (e.g., by a disgruntled employee)
- Inadvertent disclosure through errors or by accident
- Inadvertent disclosure through third parties who may not maintain the same security standards that your organization does

(ASIS International/ASIS Foundation, August 2007, p. 28)

One specific threat that is worth mentioning separately is that of laptop computer theft. A recent research report (for the ASIS Foundation) by consultant Glenn Kitteringham, CPP, studied the theft of laptops. The report noted that a 2006 Ponemon Institute survey found that 81% of companies responding reported the loss of one or more laptop computers in the preceding 12 months. Kitteringham's study also mentioned that according to the FBI, 97% of stolen laptops are never recovered (Kitteringham, 2008, p. 5). In a recent interview with the author, Kitteringham mentioned that the original intent of the laptop theft research study was to focus on theft of the hardware, but as he uncovered more information he realized that the real threat in stolen laptops was the loss of the data (or information assets) they contained. This changed the direction of his research and resulted in a conclusion that information protection measures were a more immediate need than hardware theft prevention (Kitteringham, 2009).

There is often a controversy over whether the primary source of the threat to information comes from outside the organization or from insiders (employees and others with a trusted relationship). Several studies, including a report by the U.S. Secret Service and another one by the Defense Department's Personnel Security Research Center (PERSEREC), conclude that a significant portion of the threat is attributable to insiders. Insiders have some level of authorized access, they know "the system," and they know where to look for valuable information. According to the 2007 Trends in Proprietary Information Loss Survey Report: "The largest threats to proprietary information are from those with a trusted relationship with the organization—current and former employees and those partners, outsourced providers, and customers ..." (ASIS International/ASIS Foundation, August 2007, p. 29).

Beyond the question of insider versus outsider, we need to take a look at who our adversaries might be in terms to threats to our information assets. The collectors (or perpetrators) are fairly well defined by the list of methods previously mentioned in this section. However, we should also consider who the "customers" or end users of the information might be. Being able to distinguish between the collector and the end user allows security professionals to develop more effective risk mitigation strategies for information asset protection.

End users may be the same as the collectors, but often are not. Among common end users for compromised information assets are:

- Domestic and foreign competitors
- Foreign governments
- Organized criminal enterprises
- Information brokers
- Activist groups (environmental, animal rights, monetary rights, anticapitalist, etc.)
- Terrorist groups
- Political advisors
- Quasi-government groups
- Financial or business cartels
- Product counterfeiting operations
- Targets of law enforcement activities

HOW TECHNOLOGY IS CHANGING THE THREAT

Today technology is moving and advancing at an amazing pace. This results in wonderful opportunities for information sharing, productivity, and accomplishment, but it also represents a new paradigm for security risks. In some ways the threat remains unchanged, yet in other ways things are very different. David Drab sums it up this way in a white paper on the Economic Espionage Act (EEA):

> The motives and tactics have remained constant over the years—economic gain, competition, career recognition, and vengeance. However, the methods used to collect and transmit information have significantly changed as a result of high technology, the World Wide Web, and worldwide telecommunications (Drab, August 2003, p. 2).

One result of changing technology is that the traditional reaction to an information compromise - containment - essentially becomes obsolete. Previously, when a privileged hardcopy document was inadvertently (or intentionally) disseminated to unauthorized recipients, the immediate reaction was to attempt to retrieve the copies—and hopefully get them all back. This concept no longer works in our 21st-century interconnected world. As the 2007 ASIS report on the Trends in Proprietary Information Loss Survey puts it:

> [We need to recognize the] reality of "speed" at which valuable information-based assets can be acquired and disseminated globally. Once the asset is gone or compromised, containment—in the conventional sense—is seldom a realistic option.
>
> The consequences in terms of lost economic/competitive advantage can be extremely quick and long lasting (ASIS International/ASIS Foundation, 2007, p. 41).

In other words, once information is lost, it is lost permanently *and* globally—and that can happen instantaneously! As security professionals, we need to recognize this fact.

Other technological factors affecting the risk environment for information assets include:

Miniaturization of Media—More and more data is being stored on smaller and smaller devices. Not only can huge amounts of data be stored, but today we can even build an entire computing environment on a flash drive.

Social Networking Media—Sites such as Facebook, MySpace, and Twitter are growing in popularity each day. Although they are extremely popular among almost all demographics, they also have security risk implications. For example, this type of media provides another outlet for instantly sharing information (including possibly sensitive/proprietary information or destructive false rumors) across wide audiences—and in some cases, anonymously. The threat of an unhappy employee posting damaging information in an angry rage (before thinking about the implications or having the opportunity to calm down and regain a rational state) is a growing concern for organizations of all types—and as mentioned: once it's gone … it's gone.

Volume and Dispersal of Data—The enormity of the current volume of data makes it far more difficult in many cases to identify a data breach in real time or to determine if sensitive information has been compromised.

Data Mining and Information Brokers—Emerging threats to sensitive information worldwide. A cottage industry is growing up around the mass collection of data from a multitude of sources and selling it to whoever is willing to pay for it. Modern software tools are available to "mine" (search and collect) information continuously from databases, repositories, archives, Web sites, and other sources. Additional software tools can sort, collate, and analyze data to easily and quickly generate a useful—and very valuable—product on any subject requested. In essence, this is automated intelligence gathering—and it is happening every day and everywhere. It represents a significant threat to information assets in both the public and private sector.

Wireless and Remote Computing Environments—These expose new vulnerabilities as sensitive information can be exchanged through hot spots in public locations, hotel networks, or even home networks. This issue becomes increasingly relevant as more employees participate in telecommuting and/or stay connected while away from the office.

Security of Security Systems—is a growing concern as security systems for surveillance, access control, facility management, intrusion detection, and other functions increasingly ride on the Internet and can be managed remotely (including on mobile devices). The following quote from a research report on this topic is eye-opening to many protection professionals:

> … a general trend to open architectures across TCP/IP-enabled networks, has resulted in new, serious security risks that are often overlooked. Few individuals realize, for example, that closed circuit cameras are misnamed in that they are no longer "closed" from a networking standpoint. When these special systems and devices are connected to organizations' networks, they often introduce a multitude of new, previously unanticipated security risks (Alliance for Enterprise Security Risk Management, 2006, pp. 9–10).

A SUITE OF PROTECTIVE MEASURES

Effectively protecting information and intangible assets presents special challenges, but like any asset protection situation, warrants a well-thought-out strategy that comprises a suite of countermeasures. The measures employed to protect information assets fall into three categories: security, legal, and management.

Security Measures

The following list represents a sampling of security measures that are typically applied to the task of protecting information and intangible assets.

- Assessment (possibly including penetration testing or "red teaming")
- Need-to-know controls
- Information storage and handling

- Physical security (surveillance, access control, intrusion detection)
- Visitor control and escort procedures
- Design and layout of facility (controlled versus open/public areas)
- Security officers/response forces
- Information destruction
- Technical security measures
- TSCM
- Communications, emanations, and signals security measures
- Information systems security (IT security)
- Product security
- Travel security programs
- Training and awareness (for employees, users, contractors, vendors, partners, and trusted third parties)
- Investigation capabilities

Many of these are standard security measures which are in place and protect all types of assets: people, property, and information. Other measures are more specific to information protection. Our challenge is to effectively leverage the standard security measures while identifying and implementing those specific measures that support the information asset protection strategy. While there are a variety of sources (including other chapters of this book) for details on these countermeasures, a few of the items listed above warrant some brief discussion here.

Training and awareness are absolutely essential tools. They must be delivered using a variety of media (classroom programs, computer-based training, computer screen banners, newsletters, intranet resources, and others) on a regular basis in order to keep the subject in the forefront of protection officers' minds. As the Information Asset Protection Guideline mentions:

> ... security awareness and training is one of the most cost effective measures that can be employed to protect corporate and organizational information assets.

> ... where each individual entrusted with sensitive information takes prudent measures and personal responsibility for protecting those assets, a robust security environment should occur naturally (ASIS International, IAP Guideline, 2007, p. 14).

Another strong recommendation for all organizations is that elements of information asset protection be incorporated into due diligence assessments (investigations) for mergers, acquisitions, joint ventures, partnerships, and other key business transactions. This will aid immeasurably in anticipating risks that will or may present themselves after the fact.

Finally, product security technologies including embedded electronic article surveillance, various packaging innovations, RFID, and serialization techniques are, by necessity, becoming commonplace.

Some measures will be reactive rather than proactive. When an information loss is known or suspected, conduct an investigation to support a damage assessment as well as any possible law enforcement, litigation, or asset recovery actions. The results of the investigation should also reveal the root cause of the compromise and be used to implement corrective actions and prevent future occurrences (ASIS International, 2008, p. 2-I-29).

Legal Measures

Beyond their deterrent value, most legal measures are reactive in nature. Nonetheless, they are an important element of the information asset protection strategy. Patents, copyrights, and trademarks are common legal tools in protecting highly valuable information. Another tool is that of a "trade secret," which is generally considered to be the most restrictive or protective measure. Trade secrets have the advantage of not requiring registration but are subject to strict interpretation in court with respect to the need to identify, determine value, and adequately protect the information. The high legal standard of "adequate protection" often supports the use of robust security measures within an organization—which is a welcome situation from a security perspective.

For these legal means to be useful, however, the organization must be willing to enforce the tools in a court of law. This can be a very resource-intensive ordeal, particularly in terms of time, effort, and cost. These are decisions that must be made at the executive level and shared with key players in the organization such as the security and legal departments.

Other legal measures include contract clauses, third party agreements, and possibly even performance incentives for vendors, partners, and joint venture participants. Information and intellectual property protection is a highly specialized discipline and organizations should obtain support from a qualified legal advisor/ firm rather than relying on a generalist or local general counsel.

An important tool in protecting information assets is the 1996 Economic Espionage Act (EEA). This is a very relevant piece of legislation as it makes the theft of intellectual property a federal offense and allows the FBI to investigate such cases even if a foreign intelligence service is not involved.

A Xerox white paper on the EEA reads:

> [Recognizing that] trade secrets are the lifeblood of most process-driven companies ... it naturally follows ... that organizations that fail to safeguard their intellectual assets lose ground.
> The Economic Espionage Act ... [prohibits] misconduct regarding trade secrets ... [including anyone who] steals or obtains [trade secret information] by fraud or deception.

The law includes the following as prohibited activities with respect to trade secrets and related information: anyone who "copies, duplicates, sketches, draws, photographs, downloads, uploads, alters, destroys, photocopies, replicates, transmits, delivers, sends, mails, communicates, or conveys such information." A violator can also be someone who "[knowingly] receives, buys, [or] possesses" information (Drab, August 2003, p. 4).

This is a very forward-thinking law that can and has been applied effectively to resolve trade secret and intellectual property cases in many industry sectors.

Management Measures

An interesting study by the U.S. Secret Service looked at threats to information assets by analyzing a number of specific cases. It focused on "insider" threats and reported some relevant results. In 80% of the cases studied, the perpetrator had come to the attention of management due to inappropriate behaviors before the incident (e.g., tardiness, truancy, arguments with coworkers, or poor job performance) (U.S. Secret Service, 2005, p. 15). This highlights the importance of "management measures" as part of an overall information asset protection strategy.

Other management measures that should be considered, and generally be coordinated with the security program, include effective employee screening (preemployment and periodic), drug screening, establishing relevant policies and procedures, and offering a reporting mechanism that allows employees and others to provide information (and make allegations). When using a reporting mechanism such as an employee hotline, be sure that the organization is responsive to calls and allegations. Otherwise, the hotline will soon lose its effectiveness, and important reports will be missed.

The FBI offers some recommendations on their economic espionage Web page. They present six steps to protect your business from espionage—and all are worth considering. They are:

1. Recognize there is a real threat.
2. Identify and evaluate trade secrets.

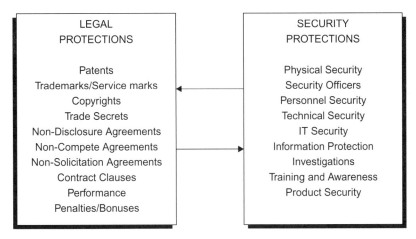

LEGAL PROTECTIONS	SECURITY PROTECTIONS
Patents	Physical Security
Trademarks/Service marks	Security Officers
Copyrights	Personnel Security
Trade Secrets	Technical Security
Non-Disclosure Agreements	IT Security
Non-Compete Agreements	Information Protection
Non-Solicitation Agreements	Investigations
Contract Clauses	Training and Awareness
Performance	Product Security
Penalties/Bonuses	

FIGURE 21-2   Examples of legal protections and security protections.

3. Implement a definable plan for safeguarding trade secrets.
4. Secure physical trade secrets and limit access to trade secrets.
5. Confine intellectual knowledge.
6. Provide ongoing security training to employee

(Federal Bureau of Investigation, 2009).

As indicated, it is important—in any private or public sector setting—to find the proper balance between legal protections and security protections. Figure 21-2 shows some considerations for each.

To achieve protection objectives and ensure they are consistent with the business or organization's strategic goals, these two "communities" of protection measures should work together to develop an integrated risk mitigation approach. Working in a vacuum can result in duplication of effort and significant waste as well as poor results due to internal conflicts.

Finally, according to well-respected consultant and author Ira Winkler, the best approach to addressing risks to information assets is to apply *defense in depth* (layered security) by incorporating both IT and traditional protection measures. Even if one or a few layers fail, other layers will back up the ones that were unsuccessful. As Winkler puts it, when we apply defense in depth, "security [isn't] perfect, but it [is] prepared" (Winkler, 2005, p. 305). Examples of some of those "layers" might be strong password protection, encryption, biometric authentication, physical security measures, personnel screening, attended facility access (security officers), employee training, and password-protected screensavers.

THE ROLE OF THE PROFESSIONAL PROTECTION OFFICER

The most effective protection officers are those who know their customer (the organization they serve) and tailor the way they provide security services to the customer's mission and culture. In many organizations, information assets are absolutely crucial to the survival and success of the enterprise. Officers should recognize this aspect of the organization and factor it into the performance of their protection duties. It should be noted that many contemporary companies are centered on information as their core business function, hence our "information-based society." It is our responsibility to remember that a key objective of information asset protection is

EMERGING TRENDS

Three emerging issues that are relevant to the protection of information and intangible assets are the increasingly interconnected global business environment, the rapid advances in information technology, and the fact that we now have to consider—in a different way—the security of security systems. These issues are discussed in this chapter, but need to be constantly reviewed due to the unprecedented pace of change in today's security environment.

The advances in information technology have a number of implications. One is the new family of risks that are introduced by drastically increased use of information technology in business, organization, government,

and home settings. As such use and popularity increases, systems and the data residing on them become more attractive targets for a variety of adversaries.

These new technology tools can also be exploited by adversaries to support their illicit activities. The best examples at the moment are the new cottage industry of information brokers and the use of sophisticated data-mining tools and techniques to target sensitive information. This trend will expand in the future and newly introduced business tools such as cloud computing and wireless technologies will likely be "abused" by bad actors for nefarious activities.

to enable core business functions, rather than present obstacles. As the past Chairman of the ASIS Information Asset Protection Council puts it, "The ultimate objective is to enable business. Security's role is to help organizations assess and address risk to *enable* 'smart' business transactions" (Heffernan, 2007).

In general, professional protection officers place most of their emphasis on protecting *people* and *property*, but it is important to support the third asset category as well: *information*. Elements of information asset and intellectual property protection should be included in officer and supervisor training, as well as quality assurance standards for security programs.

Security service providers should consider adding information asset protection services to their suite of protective service offerings. This might include conducting information protection assessments, specialized protection services, courier services, or other tools focused on this category of asset.

SUMMARY

Studies have concluded that as much as 75% or more of a company's value may lie in information and intangible assets (Moberly, 2007). Since these assets are the most difficult to identify, measure, and control, they deserve a great deal of attention from a risk management perspective. Following a thorough risk assessment, an orchestrated suite of security, legal, and management solutions should be applied to the identified organizational risks. The mission and culture of the organization (customer) should be factored in to the services provided and the manner in which they are delivered and managed.

Protection officers play a key role in the protection of information and intangible assets. In fact, they can even influence the reputation of an organization by presenting a highly competent and professional image and by acknowledging the nature of the assets (including information assets) they are responsible for protecting.

Through conscientious IAP practices, organizations will be better prepared to deal with today's broad array of threats ranging from competitive intelligence and industrial espionage, to cyber attacks, to counterfeiting and product piracy (ASIS International and IAP Council, 2009).

References

Alliance for Enterprise Security Risk Management (AESRM). (2006). Convergent security risks in physical security systems and IT infrastructures.

ASIS International. (2008). *Protection of assets manual,* Volume III, Chapter 2, Part 1. Alexandria, VA: Information Asset Protection.

ASIS International. (2007). *Information Asset Protection Guideline.*

ASIS International/Information Asset Protection Council, Fact Sheet—"What Is" Series: "What Is Information Asset Protection?" "What Is Information Risk Management?" "What Is Market Entry Planning?" 2009.

ASIS International/ASIS Foundation. (August, 2007). *Trends in proprietary information loss-survey report.*

Drab, D. (August, 2003). *Protection under the law: Understanding the economic espionage act of 1996.* A White Paper by Xerox Global Services.

Federal Bureau of Investigation (FBI). "Focus on Economic Espionage," Investigative Programs-Counterintelligence Website: http://www.fbi.gov/hq/ci/economic, accessed November 10, 2009.

Heffernan, R., President, R. J. Heffernan and Associates, 2007.

Keeney, M., & Kowalski, E. (2005). *Insider threat study: Computer system sabotage in critical infrastructure sectors.* Washington, DC: National Threat Assessment Center, U.S. Secret Service; and Cappelli, D., Moore, A., Shimeall, T., & Rogers, S. (2005). *Insider threat study: Computer system sabotage in critical infrastructure sectors.* Carnegie Mellon University, Pittsburgh, PA: CERT Program, Software Engineering Institute.

Kitteringham, G. (2008). *Lost laptops = lost data: Connection research in security to practice (crisp) report.* Alexandria, VA: ASIS International/ASIS Foundation.

Kitteringham, G. (September 2009). Personal communication.

Kramer, L., Heuer, R. J., Jr., & Crawford, K. S. (May 2005). *Technological, social, and economic trends that are increasing U.S. vulnerability to insider espionage.* Montercy, CA: Defense Personnel Security Research Center.

Moberly, M., President, Knowledge Protection Strategies, 2007.

U.S., Department of Defense, DoD 5200.1-R, "Information Security Program," January 1997.

Webster University, National Capital Region, "Business Intelligence," course materials, 2008.

Winkler, I. (2005). *Spies among US.* Indianapolis, IN: Wiley Publishing.

SECURITY QUIZ

1. Computer security, information security, and information technology (IT) security all mean the same thing and are interchangeable terms.
   a. True
   b. False
2. Counterintelligence is an important function and can be applied in private sector companies as well as in government agencies.
   a. True
   b. False
3. Legal measures are generally "reactive" rather than "proactive" in nature.
   a. True
   b. False
4. According to consultant Michael Moberly, approximately what percentage of a company's value generally lies in information and intangible assets?
   a. 90%
   b. 50%
   c. 10%
   d. 75%
5. The practice of asset protection focuses on which categories of "assets"?
   (Circle all that apply.)
   a. Information
   b. Physical
   c. People
   d. Property
6. Which of the following is NOT a characteristic of the Economic Espionage Act of 1996?
   a. It makes it a federal crime to steal trade secrets
   b. It is a forward-looking piece of legislation
   c. It includes "altering" information as a prohibited act
   d. It must be updated every 5 years
7. According to this chapter, the field of "information security" includes:
   a. Competitive intelligence
   b. IT security
   c. Intellectual property protection
   d. Traditional information security

8. When an information loss is known or suspected, the following actions should be taken:
   a. Corrective actions
   b. Damage assessment
   c. Containment
   d. Determine root cause

9. Information that is lost is not permanently lost
   a. True
   b. False

10. An important tool in protecting information assets is the Economic Espionage Act (EEA) of 1996
    a. True
    b. False

DEVIANCE CRIME AND VIOLENCE

Workplace Crime and Deviance

Norman R. Bottom and
Whitney D. Gunter

CHAPTER OBJECTIVES

- Identify theories of workplace crime
- Provide ways to minimize theft
- Identify the process for responding to theft

In any organization, some employees will steal. The more opportunity allowed for theft, the more theft there will be. Dishonest employees tend to steal what is most available to them. Office personnel steal office supplies, computer users steal technology, cashiers steal cash, and warehouse employees steal merchandise passing through their hands.

Managers, supervisors, and line employees can all steal. Protection officers have been known to steal, too. Many times, dishonest employees use external accomplices, such as family members and friends, to help them steal. An individual employee can steal, or several employees may conspire to commit theft for their mutual benefit.

In addition to theft of products, materials, tools, or information, there may be acts of sabotage committed. Hourly employees who wish to strike at management may damage equipment or interrupt processes. So too may managers who harbor some resentment toward the employer engage in deliberate work interruptions. While not nearly as common as stealing, sabotage is sometimes interwoven with theft. Both may occur together.

This information should not make a protection officer pessimistic, as most people are honest (at least to a degree). The problem is not that everyone steals or does damage; the problem is that everyone has the potential to. As a result, no one is beyond reasonable suspicion.

THEORIES OF WORKPLACE CRIME

Criminology is the study of the causes of crime. There are dozens of mainstream criminological theories that explain theft. However, many of these theories focus on social influences that long precede actual crime (e.g., lack of social bond, poor parenting, lack of legitimate opportunity, etc.). For the purposes of preventing workplace crime, there are a few theories that are particularly relevant to theft prevention.

General Deterrence

Deterrence is perhaps the most well-known theory of criminal behavior. It actually dates back to Cesare Beccaria's *Essay on Crimes and Punishments* (1764). Beccaria lived in a time when crime was typically attributed to evil influence, and punishment was extremely severe. In an attempt to give guidance to the leaders of the time, Beccaria provided a logical rationale for punishment: to decrease crime. He argued that two possible benefits arise from punishing someone caught committing a crime. First, that person might learn his or her lesson and not commit the crime again. This is called *specific deterrence*. Second, others might witness the punishment and learn that committing the crime is not worth the consequences. This more widespread result is called *general deterrence*. Both are important benefits of punishing, although general deterrence is certainly more so.

This, however, only describes why we punish. It is in the specifics of punishment that we learn how to punish properly. Three concepts influence the effectiveness of punishment. First, *punishment certainty* is the likelihood of getting caught. The more often a crime is committed without the perpetrator getting caught, the less punishment certainty there is, and the less of a deterrent there will be. Second, *punishment celerity* refers to the swiftness of the punishment. The quicker a punishment occurs, the more of a deterrent it will create. This aspect of deterrence is less obvious than the others. Think of it like this: if someone is stealing on a regular basis and gets away with it for a year, then gets caught, but does not go to court for another 10 months, the cause and effect of crime and punishment are not as obvious to the public as they would have been if the entire process was quicker. The final element of deterrence is *punishment severity*. The more severe a punishment, the more deterrence it will cause. However, this is only true up to the amount of punishment that outweighs the benefit of the crime

itself. Once the punishment clearly outweighs the crime, additional severity will not further deter.

The overall implication of this theory is probably already the policy of most loss prevention efforts: catch and punish. It is the subtleties of these efforts that can be improved by understanding this theory. Punishment severity is often easiest to increase. As a result, although punishment certainty is not ignored, severity is more of a focus. Beccaria argued that this is backward. As long as the severity of punishment exceeds the benefit of the crime, it is sufficient. Rather, it is punishment certainty that can be improved upon to increase a deterrent effect.

Routine Activity

Although general deterrence is valuable for understanding the importance of detection and punishment, it does not speak very well to specific circumstances. For looking beyond the generalities and probabilities that deterrence theory uses, a more recent theory is appropriate. In an attempt to explain increases in crime several decades ago, Lawrence Cohen and Marcus Felson (1979) developed their theory of routine activity. It should be noted that this theory applies only to "direct-contact predatory violations," which simply means it is a theory of theft.

According to the theory, crime (theft) is a product of three circumstances happening at the same time and in the same place. The first requirement for crime is the presence of a *motivated offender*. For the purposes of this theory, it is assumed that everyone is a motivated offender, or at least that such potential offenders are not scarce. The second requirement for crime to occur is the presence of a *suitable target*. In determining how suitable a target is, four aspects of the potential target should be considered: the financial value, inertia (ease in moving the item), accessibility, and visibility. Because one would not want to decrease the financial value of something, it is the other three aspects of a potential target that should be addressed. Making an item harder to move, limiting access to only those who need access, and keeping it out of sight are all actions that would make a target less suitable.

The third and final requirement for theft to occur is the *absence of capable guardianship*. This concept is the one that ties routine activity theory to deterrence theory. If a guardian is present, punishment certainty is increased to near certainty, and therefore, the crime is less likely to occur. A capable guardian need not necessarily be a protection officer, loss prevention specialist, or other such person. It can be anyone who might report the theft, or even an inanimate object, such as a noticeable security camera, that could result in the perpetrator getting caught. Many standard practices of the security industry already address this theory, including target hardening, CPTED, situational crime prevention, and other such strategies.

Social Learning Theory

Both of the theories discussed so far make a common assumption: that all people are willing to commit a crime if they think they can get away with it. While this is at least partially true, there are other factors involved. Specifically, even in the same situation, different people would be more or less likely to commit a crime than others might be. There are many criminological theories that address this issue. However, most are not particularly useful from a security and loss prevention standpoint. One of the few theories that has potential application to workplace crime is social learning theory.

Generally, social learning theory (Sutherland & Cressey, 1960/2003; Burgess & Akers, 1966) is applied most often to describe how children learn from their parents and peers, and how that influences their decision of whether crime is an acceptable behavior. However, this same model can be applied to the workplace. In its broadest sense, social learning theory describes two categories of learning that can occur. First, one may learn from

peers (or other sources) how to commit crimes. Some crimes, such as pretty theft, require little technical ability to commit. Learning better ways to commit these crimes, however, may improve one's technique, and therefore make it easier to commit the crime, or make it less likely that one will get caught.

The other form of learning, and the one that is more useful to address, is learning to perceive crime, or certain types of crimes in certain situations, as acceptable behavior. If someone notices that other employees are stealing, they are more likely to do it themselves. Not only because it makes it more obvious that it is possible to get away with the crime, but because it makes them feel like it is not taboo. The more often someone is exposed to this message, the more accepted it becomes.

Unfortunately, this theory in and of itself does not contribute policy that might be useful beyond what is already obvious: that employees who steal should be removed to prevent them from tainting other employees (and for other obvious reasons, of course). However, it does imply that efforts could be made to highlight why it is not acceptable to steal or engage in other workplace crimes. Such positive messages can counteract messages that favor crime. To get some specific ideas for what messages to counteract, the techniques of neutralization may be useful.

Techniques of Neutralization

The techniques of neutralization were first described by Sykes and Matza (1957). They listed five categories by which an offender might neutralize his or her behavior to make it seem acceptable, thus preventing guilt (Table 22-1).

In a workplace setting, it's more often denial of injury and denial of victim that are used. For example, if an employee can in some way attribute blame for some personal problem on the employer or even coworkers, whether such blame is deserved or not, that person could convince him- or herself that the company or

TABLE 22-1

Techniques of Neutralization	Sample Usages
Denial of Responsibility	It was an accident. It wasn't my fault.
Denial of Injury	It didn't hurt anyone. I was just borrowing it.
Denial of Victim	He deserved it. His kind deserve it.
Condemnation of the Condemners	The police are corrupt. That teacher plays favorites anyway. He would have done it too.
Appeals to Higher Loyalties	I was just following orders. I was doing God's work.

coworkers deserve whatever the crime costs them. Denial of injury is even easier to apply, as it is not difficult for an individual to fail to recognize that their actions hurt a "faceless" corporation. This is especially true if they realize that an insurance provider will cover losses.

Note that other crimes, in addition to theft may be neutralized by workplace criminals. Condemnation of the condemners and appeals to higher loyalties may be used by those who commit acts of sabotage or espionage. Labor union extremists, terrorists, and spies may focus on the employer, criticizing and blaming them for some perceived wrongdoing. Terrorists involved in religiously based extremism may choose to believe that God has granted them the right to commit acts of sabotage. So, too, may those who steal information and give it to an adversary organization.

Summary for Theories of Workplace Crime

These theories provide some ideas for how criminological theories might be applied to workplace crime and the prevention of such crimes. Moving toward more specific strategies and actions, the next section will provide an in-depth analysis of preventing the most common crime at the workplace: theft.

THEFT PREVENTION

Not all internal (employee) theft is preventable. This section will provide some ways to minimize, moderate, and control this criminal activity, but not stop it entirely. Protection offers can have an impact by preventing, deterring, and displacing theft. When security is tight, thieves look for another place to steal. Making theft so difficult and so much trouble that the would-be thief will decide against it is a reasonable goal for a loss prevention officer. Preventing theft can save many jobs, and that includes one's own.

Opportunities for employee theft come about because of waste, accident, error, crime, and unethical or unprofessional practices. The first letters of these opportunities (which are really threats) come together to form the acronym "WAECUP" (pronounced "wake up"). Below is a list of WAECUP loss threats, with several examples of each.

A. Waste

1. Protection officers who waste time create opportunity for employees to steal.
2. Waste containers are favorite stash places for employees who steal.
3. Discarding usable items causes loss, as does deliberately putting them in trash to be stolen later on.

B. Accident

1. The confusion that surrounds an accident scene may be used to screen employee theft.
2. Arson has been used by employees to cover up theft. (What seems to be an accident can actually be a crime.)
3. Workman's Compensation fraud may occur after an accident where the employee exaggerates the extent of the injury.

C. *Error*

1. Protection officers who err in following procedures, such as failing to make an assigned round, create opportunity for undetected theft.
2. Other (nonsecurity) employees who fail to follow security-related instructions, such as failing to lock up storage areas or exterior doors, create opportunity for theft.

D. *Crime*

1. If protection officers allow employee theft, other employees will get the idea that it is okay to steal and commit other crimes.
2. Failure to recognize valuable merchandise allows more crime (protection staff and management will not be watching the correct items).

E. *Unethical/Unprofessional Practices*

1. A general feeling among employees that it is okay to pilfer (steal) will result in more theft. This is sometimes called the "rolling ball effect." It is similar to the "broken windows" theory.
2. Unprofessional practices by management create resentment among other employees, leading to deviant acts like theft.

Objective

Protection officers *must* reduce employee theft. This section focuses on practical methods to reduce theft. However, it takes more than your presence, standing around in a sharp uniform, or strutting through an area. You must know what to look for, what to report, and what actions to take. You must also know what actions *not* to take.

Thieves can be clever, and new opportunities for employee theft will develop. This chapter is only a beginning. You must continue to study employee theft prevention as long as you are a protection officer. The objective of this section is to whet your appetite on the scope of employee theft prevention and widen your knowledge.

This will give you some tips on observation. For example, employees who bring in empty or almost empty shopping bags and then leave with bags bulging should be viewed with suspicion. Those bulging bags may contain company property. As a general rule, always look for the unusual and out-of-place, and then investigate discreetly. Also, this section will explain some things about reporting, and discuss what to report and to whom. For example, doors propped open (that are normally locked) may be used by thieves as access points to sneak company property outside. Such things should be reported and written up. This will also be a discussion of actions to take and not to take. For example, managers and other executives often work at home during the evening. They are usually permitted to take company property home to do this. Hourly workers (shift workers) seldom have the right to take company property home. Know company rules before you act or accuse.

Definition of Employee Dishonesty

Employee dishonesty is theft. It is cheating customers. It is committing industrial espionage. It is lying on employment applications and falsifying time records. It is claiming sick leave when there is no sickness. Anything that can be moved, or taken apart and the pieces moved, is a candidate for employee theft. Protection officers can reduce the theft of *visible* items of company property. They can catch thieves, of course, but it is better to reduce *opportunity* for theft.

Each organization has its own types of property, including personal (movable property) and fixed (real property). Real property, such as permanent buildings and land, cannot be carried off. In these strategies, only personal property will be addressed. Personal property, in business usage, is not "personal effects." Business tries to protect the machinery or means of production. The materials or equipment used for production (or sale) of goods and services need protection, and those goods, services, products, and so on offered to the public must be guarded.

Business wants to protect and keep its reward: the income received for selling its products, of course. Those categories are what we mean by business personal property. Some business is devoted to manufacturing. Here, the threat of employee theft takes place at several stages. Those stages occur from the time that machines are installed and raw materials purchased through the entire production process—and until the finished goods are delivered.

Other companies specialize in storage and transportation. They warehouse and distribute manufactured products. These companies worry while goods are stored. Each time goods are handled by employees causes theft concern, too. Goods in transit present additional possibilities for theft.

We all shop at malls and other retail stores. Retail is certainly a familiar business to all. There are also wholesale outlets that specialize in selling quantities to the trade. Each retail store, and each wholesaler, worries about losing the property they hope to sell. Employee theft is one way the property can be lost to these owners.

Institutions like hospitals have special employee theft problems. These include the unauthorized use or taking of narcotics, and theft of patients' property. Banking institutions worry about their cash, naturally. The point to remember is that all business needs protection against employee theft, and that necessity demands proper security and loss control effort by protection officers.

First Steps

The first step in employee theft prevention is to learn what can be stolen. A list of property categories is useful for reference. All protection officers can use such a list to help them identify company property.

A similar list of categories can be drawn up for any work environment. Buy a notebook and make your own list, especially if there is no

---

SAMPLE LIST—RETAIL ESTABLISHMENT

Office Area
1. Paper products
2. Typewriters, calculators, computers, telephones
3. Desks, chairs, bookcase, file cabinets
4. Rugs, paintings
5. Petty cash

Stock Room
1. Sales merchandise of various types
2. Shelving
3. Materials, handling equipment
4. Some office supplies

Sales Area
1. Merchandise to be sold
2. Shelving and cabinets
3. Cash registers/computerized sales terminals
4. Product displays
5. Sales receipts (cash, checks, etc.)

Parking Areas and Outbuildings
1. Exterior merchandise displays
2. Equipment stored outside (in the open or in outbuildings)
3. Company vehicles
4. Trash and refuse containers

---

master list available. And if there is no master list, suggest to your supervisor that an official one be created. Test your powers of observation by comparing your list with those of other protection officers. Update your list as new property arrives and old property is replaced. It is good to know as much as possible about all company property, including value. More valuable items, especially if easily moved (portable), deserve a special theft prevention effort.

Markings

Life becomes difficult if company property is not marked to indicate ownership. Learn what marking system, if any, is used to mark all equipment. This includes office typewriters, computer equipment, and so on. Sale merchandise should be marked, too, with special tags. Some marking systems use stick-on labels. Other marking systems involve stamping numbers on metal. Paint and stencil are used by some companies for identification purposes. There are chemical compounds that can be painted (or sprayed) on. These compounds leave markings visible only in certain light.

If valuable items are not marked, you should ask "Why not?" Your supervisor might give you a good explanation. He may commend you for an idea that's time has come. A good protection officer learns how to recognize company property.

A general reminder: Learn, learn, learn—continue to ask good questions. Keep written records of the answers. In that way, you will not have to ask the same question twice. And you will have a ready reference when there is no supervisor available.

Concealment

Hide and seek is a children's game, familiar to most of us. The basic instructions call for someone blindfolded to count while other children hide. The counter then opens his eyes and tries to find the others. It may help to think of employee thieves as the other children who have the time to take and hide your company's property. The protection officer should not, of course, have his eyes closed while this theft and concealment go on.

Trash and garbage containers are time-honored hiding places for employee thieves. Plastic garbage bags are another useful item for thieves. Modern garbage bags are sturdy and unaffected by moisture, and they are opaque—that is, you cannot see through them. The protection officer should look for garbage bags in containers, both inside and outside the building. Garbage bags will be found in corners and adjacent to doorways.

Periodically, check all garbage cans, dumpsters, and sealed garbage bags for stolen merchandise. Be especially alert to those employees who take garbage and trash outside. That activity is a critical junction. It is critical because stolen merchandise can be hidden in the trash. It is a junction because the merchandise is leaving the premises. Normally, only a few trusted employees are allowed to take trash outside. Know who these employees are.

Another trick of the employee thief is to take a particular item and hide it for later pickup. Remember that everything has its place, and everything should be in its place. Be alert to the out-of-place item concealed in a strange or unusual location. This may be an indication of employee theft in progress. Look behind shelved merchandise. Examine storage rooms and broom closets.

Examples

- Valuables, like watches, normally under lock and key, found on open shelves, tucked behind cheap items.
- Office equipment and/or office supplies stashed in an area where there is no desk or clerical work performed.
- Valuable merchandise found in areas set aside for employees to leave their purses and other personal belongings. The same goes for employee locker areas.
- Sheds, lean-tos, truck courts, and other locations outside main buildings, but on company property. Company property found at these locations should be appropriate to the area. For example, office computers do not belong in a garden shed.

Briefcases, lunchboxes, purses, shopping bags, and other containers will be carried to work by employees. Thieves use these containers to remove company property from the site. The officer must realize, of course, that such personal items are entitled to reasonable privacy. Always remember this, or your search will only cause trouble to you. Always check with a supervisor before searching an employee or his property. Many companies have rules about what types of items can be brought onto company property. Know these rules. You may prevent a theft by advising an employee that the gunny sack in his hand cannot be brought in.

Vehicle parking is another factor in concealment. The personal vehicle of an employee should not be parked next to the storeroom door, for example. In fact, employee parking should be at some distance from buildings and doorways. Company policy establishes the parking rules, but you should point out parking hazards that make employee theft easier.

Employee thieves may use their own car or truck. They may also use a company vehicle to haul away the stolen merchandise. For example, a driver may load a few extra cases onto the truck, cases not listed on the manifest. These will be sold for his personal profit and the company's loss.

Some thieves are very bold. They will attempt to walk out with stolen merchandise in their hands. Employees who attempt to remove company property from the premises should have a pass or other authorizing document. Since pass forms may be stolen or counterfeited, it is important to know and recognize authorized signatures. When in doubt, check with your supervisor. And make sure that the pass covers each and every item. If the pass says "six" items, do not let the employee remove seven.

RESPONSE TO THEFT

Reporting

All observed suspicious activity, and especially that involving employees, should be immediately reported. Remember that all observations and concealment findings are a waste of time unless your results are promptly reported. Along with the need for *timely reporting*, there is a second thing to remember. *Get report results to the right individual(s).* The right person or persons will be able to take the necessary action.

So far, there are three main points to remember. First, reporting must follow observation. Observation may involve sighting suspicious activity by employees. Observation includes threat potential, such as open doors. Or the protection officer may discover concealed company property. **First observe; then report.**

The second main point is timely reporting. If you wait too long to report suspicious activity, the theft will take place. If you wait too long to report a suspicious open door, stolen items will exit through that door. If you wait too long to report a concealed item, it will be removed by the thief.

The third main point is reporting to the right person. The right person will react properly to the threat you observed. The right person will authorize or take corrective action in a timely fashion. The right person will see that your work is not wasted. Who is the right person(s)? Your supervisor, if available, is the right person. The nonsecurity supervisor in the hazard area is another. Each company and each business will have a chain of command or leadership tree. Protection officers must know the responsibilities of various managers. They must know how to reach managers in case of an emergency, which can include a serious threat of employee theft.

Reports about employee theft should be both verbal and written. The need for verbal reporting often increases with rapidly unfolding events. The need for written reports is twofold. First is *clarity.* Verbal information often becomes distorted when relayed from one person to another. Second is *record keeping.* Written reports serve as the basis for planning by the security and loss control staff. History tends to repeat itself, and hazards repeat unless records are kept and used.

Written reports from protection officers are sometimes hastily read by management, if read at all. This is especially true of shift reports. It is hard to say why these reports are not properly used. Sometimes, it is the protection officer's fault. Reports are not valuable if poorly written or have illegible handwriting. Other problems relate to forms that are poorly designed. At other times, the boss means well, but just cannot seem to get around to reading activity reports until they are stale.

A protection officer may develop a negative attitude about reporting his observations (to include employee theft hazards). Perhaps nobody asked for an explanation of important observations. No pats on the back or positive feedback. Or nothing seems to have been done to reduce the reported threat. Many protection officers, especially those working the night shift, never see the protection boss or his deputies. That shift, especially, may wonder if their reports are ever read.

What can be done? Verbally report suspicious activity and other employee theft potentials. Discuss your written reports with supervisors whenever you can. Once in a while, take some initiative and call the protection office when you are off-duty and the boss is in. Show your concern for your duties and for your reports. Such dedication is often rewarded. The protection officer bears responsibility for his observations on employee theft or the potential for theft. Your observations must be understood by the top ranks. No excuses or moaning about lack of communication will help the situation.

Preventive Actions

Observation and reporting are crucial in employee theft prevention, as already addressed. Preventive action is also important, but actions can be hazardous. The wrong action can bring unnecessary embarrassment to an employee, the protection manager, and the individual protection officer. Wrongful action can expose you and your company to civil suit. For example, an employee falsely accused of theft can bring suit for monetary damages. Some wrongful actions lead to criminal prosecution and jailing of the protection officer. Be careful when facing accusations. Be especially careful in conducting searches. Search actions are the most troublesome preventive actions.

Preventive actions do not always mean trouble. Many preventive actions are pleasant. They involve heading off employee theft at an early stage. Never forget, the essence of protection is prevention of employee theft. Cultivate a good liaison with as many senior employees as you can. Let these employees be additional eyes and ears.

Search Policy

Occasionally, you may feel it necessary to search a lunch bucket or purse. Or you may decide an employee locker contains stolen merchandise. There may be an excellent reason to suspect company property is in an employee's personal vehicle. However, before you take action, before you search, know your company policy and always follow it.

Do not take actions in conflict with company policy. Policy may state that employee packages or vehicles can be inspected on demand, or policy may instead authorize periodic and random searches of employee parcels, briefcases, and purses. A company without a written and well-communicated policy is buying trouble for itself and the protection staff. When in doubt about search policy, ask your supervisor. Remember that an error on your part could result in your termination or court action.

Searching a company vehicle is less hazardous, but company policy still rules. It may be necessary to break a door seal. A search could delay delivery of overdue merchandise. The union contract may set limitations or requirements. For example, rules may require the presence of a union steward or a supervisor during the search. **Know the rules and follow them.**

Searching other areas, such as storage sheds, or checking trash containers and garbage bags is normally simple, but it is wise to ask your supervisor if such routine checks can be done without giving prior notice to the protection office or some supervisor. Routine searches should be done at different times, of course. If officers always check a trash container at 4:00 P.M., employee thieves will wait until 4:10 P.M. to stash the stolen goods.

Protection officers may not be allowed in some areas unless invited. Such areas often include the research laboratory and executive offices. Barging into a research laboratory could ruin experiments in progress. It is important to remember that company executives do not want protection officers poking around when important business is under way.

Public relations are the key to almost everything the protection officer does. This is never truer than in searching an employee's bag, briefcase, or vehicle. Your attitude during a search must be professional and nonthreatening. Remember that you must work tomorrow with the same employees you search today. An overbearing or nasty attitude will make enemies you cannot afford.

Employee Liaison

No protection officer can be successful without help. Help will come from the protection staff, of course, but you can also get help from nonsecurity employees. It is necessary to cultivate the respect of those employees who can assist you to estimate employee theft threats.

Morale is a good indicator of theft potential. When overall morale is high, there tends to be less employee theft. When moral is low, theft is more likely. The protection officer needs to keep his or her finger on the pulse of employee morale. This can best be done through contacts in the workplace.

Often, nonsecurity employees will witness an employee theft, but fail to report it. This can continue for a long time. A protection officer who has the respect of key employees may receive valuable hints about the deviant activities of employees.

Liaison with nonsecurity employees has other benefits. A roving protection officer will never know an area or the activities taking place as well as employees who work there. Changes in the workplace—for example, getting a shipment of new, valuable items, opening a formerly sealed door, or hiring temporary help—can raise the potential for employee theft. New merchandise represents something additional to observe. Opening a previously sealed door means another access route to remove stolen merchandise. Temporary staff may themselves steal or be blamed as regular employees attempt theft.

SUMMARY

This chapter presented some lessons about controlling employee dishonesty. Employees at all levels may steal from their employers. Most employees steal what is immediately available to them. Opportunities for theft come about because of WAECUP. Protection officers cannot prevent all employee theft, but they can have a positive impact. Theft prevention is a good idea at any time. Today, it is especially important because of the economic climate.

Practical methods to prevent theft have been provided. These include tips on what to look for, what to report, and what actions to take. As a general rule, always look for the unusual and out of place, but be prudent in taking action. An employee may have permission to take company property off premises.

Protection officers can reduce theft of visible items, but it is best to reduce opportunity for theft. Theft reduction requires knowledge of company property, how it is marked, and its value. Make a property list to aid one's memory.

Concealment often comes before removal of company property by the employee thief. Trash, garbage containers, and garbage bags are favorite hiding places. The thief may conceal valuable merchandise behind less valuable items. Everything should be in its place. Look behind shelved merchandise; examine storage rooms and broom closets.

Know the rules about what employees may bring onto company property. You may be able to prevent a theft simply by advising an employee not to bring in a container. Vehicle parking is another factor. Point out parking hazards that make employee theft easier.

Report suspicious activity, both verbally and in writing. Timely observation is critical to the right person or persons. Know who the right person is. Follow up on the reporting in discussions with protection supervisors.

Preventive actions are important to employee theft prevention. Wrongful actions by protection officers can lead to civil and criminal problems. Considerable care is needed in making searches and in making accusations. Some preventive actions are pleasant. Employee liaison is an excellent way to prevent employee theft. Liaison with senior employees means additional eyes and ears.

Company search policy must be understood and applied. Know whether policy allows random searches or searches on demand. A written search policy is essential. Search of company vehicles may be easier, but complications can arise with respect to seals, delays, or contract provisions. Always follow the rules.

Search of trash or storage areas is usually without complication. These searches should be done at staggered times. Some areas, such as research labs and executive offices, need prior permission to enter, even by the protection officer. There are valid reasons for these restrictions.

Public relations are important, especially during any search involving an employee. An officer must work tomorrow with the employee who is being searched today. Cultivate the respect of senior employees. These people can help the officer recognize employee theft potential. As a general rule, morale is a good indicator of theft potential. Low morale is likely to mean more employee theft problems.

Sometimes employees witness theft, but do not report it. If the protection officer develops the respect of key employees, hints to employee deviancy may be given. Liaison with non-security employees has other benefits. Changes in the workplace environment can raise the potential for employee theft. Good liaison will keep you up-to-date on such changes.

The protection officer can do a good job in preventing employee theft, but only if he follows the methods outlined and company policy.

EMERGING TRENDS

Losses caused by employees have been a concern throughout history. At one time, employers in England and the United States forbade employees to talk during working hours. This was to ensure that there was no loss due to wasted time. A more contemporary approach to this issue is the use of temporary employees. Contract service firms provide employees to client organizations on an as-needed basis.

Such an approach cuts waste, but may create the potential for theft, espionage, and other crimes. Obviously, all employees with access to assets must be properly screened and supervised. Employee loyalty and commitment to the employer are also critical if theft, sabotage, espionage, and so on are to be controlled.

Workplace crime is not limited to theft; sabotage by employees can also occur. There are various types of sabotage, from total or near total destruction of equipment and facilities (planting explosives or incendiaries), to damaging equipment, to deliberate work slowdowns. Sabotage may be motivated by a variety of reasons. In construction and other industries, sabotage may be conducted to prolong the work; damage slows completion of the project and keeps hourly workers employed.

Conversely, acts of sabotage may be motivated by labor unrest during contract negotiations or strikes. Sabotage may be committed by those advancing political or social agendas (terrorism), or it may be the work of foreign agents during times of war. Regardless of the motivation, sabotage is a type of workplace crime. The control of sabotage is similar to the control of theft in most cases.

Organized crime has been involved in some workplaces for many years. Infiltration of businesses, with the goal of exploiting their assets, is a common occurrence. Organized crime groups are now becoming involved with identity theft/fraud. Exploitation of an insider who provides confidential customer or employee information is a key concern. As information becomes a more valuable and accessible asset, such scenarios will likely increase.

Intelligence and crime analysis positions are becoming more common. In public sector organizations, there are often crime analysts employed by police departments. Intelligence analysts may be employed within law enforcement or investigative organizations. Major corporations are also using the services of those who can conduct applied research on an organization's loss problems. Crime analysts help pinpoint where crime is occurring by day, time, and location. They aid in more effectively deploying personnel and other resources

to address the crime problem. Intelligence analysts help to spot and track the activity of organized crime groups, terrorists, and embezzlers. The effective use of intelligence analysts helps to detect crime or loss problems that are forming. Intelligence analysts can also direct investigation into crime or loss situations. Exception reporting systems, which spot deviations from the norm, such as an unusual amount of voided sales at a cash register, are part of a theft intelligence system. Simply put, intelligence directs internal theft investigations. It tells us where to start looking.

The individual protection officer plays a key role in reducing workplace crime and deviance. Unfortunately, many organizations do not fully recognize this, relying instead on accountants, auditors, and human resources personnel to manage internal losses. This perspective is most often seen with uniformed security personnel; plainclothes personnel, such as retail loss prevention officers, tend to be more involved in internal loss problems. In retail, loss prevention agents do various forms of auditing, interviewing, and surveillance. In many cases, retail loss prevention officers also are involved in educational programs for employees. Coordinating and delivering awareness programs on internal loss, organized retail crime (ORC), safety, and related topics are functions that are often performed below the managerial level.

References

Beccaria, C. (1764). *Essay on crimes and punishments*. Retrieved August 16, 2007, from <http://www.crimetheory.com/Archive/Beccaria/>.

Burgess, R. L., & Akers, R. L. (1966). A differential association–reinforcement theory of criminal behavior. *Social Problems*, *14*, 128–147.

Cohen, L. E., & Felson, M. (1979). Social change and crime rate trends: A routine activity approach. *American Sociological Review*, *44*, 588–608.

Sutherland, E. H., & Cressey, D. R. (2003). A theory of differential association. In F. T. Cullen & R. Agnew (Eds.), *Criminological theory: Past to present: Essential readings* (2nd ed.) (pp. 131–134). Los Angeles: Roxbury. (Reprinted from *Principles of criminology*, 6th ed., 1960.)

Sykes, G. M., & Matza, D. (1957). Techniques of neutralization: A theory of delinquency. *American Sociological Review*, *22*, 664–670.

Resources

The Association of Certified Fraud Examiners has over 45,000 members. Membership is open to students. There is a series of substantial discounts available to educators who join the Association. The Association sponsors the Certified Fraud Examiner (CFE) designation and has a database of articles on fraud. Visit /www.acfe.com.

Business Controls Inc. offers investigation, consultation, and employee hotline services for employers and educational institutions. In addition, Business Controls provides both online and instructor-led training in fraud investigation, workplace violence, employee handbooks, substance abuse, theft investigation, and related topics at http://www.businesscontrols.com.

Dr. Richard Hollinger's column in *Loss Prevention* magazine is an outstanding discussion on employee theft. *Loss Prevention* also has articles on inventory control, shrinkage reduction, etc. Visit the site at http://www .losspreventionmagazine.com/.

The International Foundation for Protection Officers offers a certificate program in Crime and Loss Investigation. The Crime and Loss Investigation Program consists of texts and a series of online papers. The online papers deal with intelligence, background investigation, and interviewing. They can be located in the Foundation's Article Archives at www.ifpo.org.

The University of Leicester's Department of Criminology conducts a wide range of research on workplace crime, shrinkage control, and related topics. The University is one of the leading research institutions in the United Kingdom and offers a variety of certificate and degree programs online at http://www.le.ac.uk/criminology/ researchmain.html.

SECURITY QUIZ

1. Which of the following is not relevant to general deterrence?
   a. Punishment certainty
   b. Punishment celerity
   c. Punishment carnality
   d. Punishment severity

2. Routine activity theory states that crime will only happen when a motivated offender, a suitable target, and the absence of _____ _____occur at the same place and time.
   a. Suitable guardians
   b. Capable guardians
   c. Protection officers
   d. Probation officers

3. Social learning theory is only about learning how to commit a crime, not why crime might be acceptable.
   a. True
   b. False

4. Which of the following is an example of a technique of neutralization that would be used if the employee believed the company would get insurance money to replace the loss?
   a. Denial of responsibility
   b. Denial of injury
   c. Appeals to higher loyalties
   d. Condemning the condemners

5. Which step must immediately follow observation of suspicious activity?
   a. Marking
   b. Concealment
   c. Reporting
   d. Liaison

6. Liaison with nonsecurity employees has many benefits for the protection officer.
   a. True
   b. False

7. Protection officers may visit any office or activity without notice and at the officer's convenience.
   a. True
   b. False

8. Employee package policies usually include:
   a. Search on demand
   b. Periodic or random search
   c. Neither of the above
   d. Either a or b

9. Suspicious activity should be reported only in writing.
   a. True
   b. False

10. Reporting observations to the right person or persons is vital.
    a. True
    b. False

CHAPTER

23

Substance Abuse

Francis J. Elliott, Glen Kitteringham, and
Terence M. Gibbs

CHAPTER OBJECTIVES

- Provide an overview of the impact of various types of substance abuse
- Elevate the protection officer's awareness about substance abuse in the workplace
- Discuss psychoactive drugs and the behaviors resulting from their use and/ or abuse
- Identify the risks that these behaviors pose for employees and the employer
- Prepare security professionals to deal with substance abuse on the job and effectively communicate observations and information to supervisors
- Identify conditions that may point to a security risk or vulnerability

Today, we live and work in a society in which substance abuse is omnipresent. It is a major problem confronting Canada, the United States, and other countries around the world and is the leading cause of crime, health problems, and child abuse. According to the World Health Organization, the abuse of psychoactive substances is estimated at 2 billion alcohol users, 1.3 billion smokers, and 185 million illicit drug users. It was estimated to be responsible for 12.4% of all annual deaths worldwide (World Health Organization: Substance Abuse Facts). Substance abuse adversely affects our schools and the education of our children; it divides and destroys families, drains the economy of entire communities, and jeopardizes the ability of business and industry to be competitive. Substance abuse is a threat to our society and public safety. It destroys the human will and denies dreams. Substance abuse does not discriminate. It favors no race, age group, intelligence level, social or economic status, or sex. It consumes anyone who dares to embrace its false promises for perpetual self-gratification and well-being.

This chapter is aimed at elevating the protection officer's awareness about substance abuse in the workplace, and about psychoactive drugs and the behaviors resulting from their use and/or abuse. This chapter also identifies the risks these behaviors pose for employees and the employer, and the methods by which to prevent or confront these risks. As a security professional, you must be prepared to deal with substance abuse on the job and effectively communicate your observations and information to your supervisor. Because of your daily interaction with employees and others who visit your workplace, you must be able to recognize conditions that may point to a security risk or vulnerability

For the purposes of this chapter, the phrase "substance abuse" refers to the use, usually self-administered, of any psychoactive drug, in a manner that deviates from the approved legal, medical, or social patterns within a given culture. A drug is defined as any substance that by its chemical nature alters the structure or function of the living organism. A psychoactive drug is one which alters the structure or function of the brain. Psychoactive drugs alter mood, perception, or consciousness. Examples include nicotine, alcohol, marijuana, cocaine, amphetamines, and LSD.

Because our focus is on drugs that directly affect performance and behavior on the job, nicotine will not be a focus of this chapter. However, it is important to note that nicotine consumption produces classic drug dependence characteristics. Along with alcohol, it is considered a gateway drug for those who ultimately use other dependence-producing drugs, such as marijuana and cocaine. Finally, nicotine has been clearly identified as an insidious substance responsible for approximately 5.4 million deaths worldwide and is referred to the biggest "killer in the world" by the World Health Organization (United Nations Press Briefings/Tobacco).

IMPACT ON BUSINESS AND INDUSTRY

In the United States, recent studies reveal that 75% of illicit drug users (Fischer, Halibozek, & Green, 2008) and 90% of alcoholics are employed in the workplace. Many of these employees are poly-drug abusers. That is, they abuse more than one drug in the course of their drug-taking behavior. Employees with alcohol and other drug problems represent 10–20% of any given workforce. Within this workforce, the highest concentration of abusers is within the 18- to 25-year-old age group. A 2007 U.S. Department of Health and Human Services study shows that 20% of workers age 18 to 25 use drugs on the job, while the rate for 27- to 34-year-olds is 10%, 35- to 49-year-olds is 7%, and 50- to 64-year-olds is 2.6% (Larson, Eyerman, Foster, & Gfroerer, 2007). The Canadian Centre for Occupational Health and Safety put the 2002 economic cost of substance abuse to the Canadian workplace at $39.8 billion (www.ccohs.ca/oshanswers/psychosocial/substance.html). U.S. government data suggests that the economic cost of the United States' extensive involvement with mind-altering drugs and alcohol may be close to $400 billion annually to the American business community (U.S. Department of Health and Human Services, 2009). The annual cost for a single employee with a substance abuse problem is reported to be between 5% and 15% of a company's health care budget (Fischer et al., 2008). The European Monitoring Centre for Drugs and Drug Addiction (2009) estimates that at least 100 million Europeans, or 32% of the population, have a lifetime prevalence for using such drugs as cannabis, cocaine, ecstasy, amphetamines, and opioids. It is safe to assume that their workforce is also directly impacted by substance abuse. Aside from the substance abuser population, there exist an unspecified number of employees who are codependent. These employees do not abuse drugs. However, they share a common thread. They are the spouses, children, and significant others who arrive for work each day preoccupied with the physical and emotional condition of their loved ones.

These are some of the tangible costs generated by the substance abuser:

1. **Decreased productivity**—they are 25% less productive.
2. **Accidents**—they are three to four times more likely to have an accident on the job. Fifty percent of all accidents are attributable to substance abusers. Forty percent of industrial accidents resulting in fatality are linked to alcohol consumption and alcoholism.
3. **Absenteeism**—they are absent four times more often. Also, they are more likely to be away from their assigned locations during regular work hours.
4. **Theft**—they are responsible for 50 to 80% of employee thefts.
5. **Worker's compensation**—they are five times more likely to file a worker's compensation claim.
6. **Health care costs**—they use medical benefits five times more often, and the family members of substance abusers generally have higher-than-average health care claims (Protection of Assets Manual, 2007, Vol. I, Ch. 8).

Aside from the tangible costs of substance abuse, many hidden costs exist for which a dollar figure cannot be assigned, such as the following:

- Morale problems
- Intimidation of managers and employees
- Wasted supervisory time
- Overtime costs
- Grievance costs
- Training and replacement costs
- Decreased quality of products and services

To successfully address the adverse consequences of substance abuse in the workplace, we must elevate awareness and change existing attitudes and procedures that enable perpetuation of the problem. There is no single solution. The greatest success will come through the selection of various prevention and remedial components that complement a company's particular philosophy and culture. These components include policy development, training and education, employee assistance programs, the security function, and drug testing measures.

SUBSTANCE ABUSE: WHAT IS THE MOTIVATION?

Time and again the question is asked, "Why do people abuse drugs?" The reasons are usually complex. Early drug use, at any age, may be a result of peer pressure, low self-esteem, insecurity, boredom, or various other social, environmental, psychological, and biological factors that induce stress and anxiety. In all likelihood, some combination of these variables stimulates the initial use and abuse of psychoactive drugs. Initial use is usually reinforced as a result of (1) pleasant effects, (2) a perceived control over the drug, (3) peer acceptance and recognition, and (4) myth and misinformation. What we know is that drugs can quickly relieve unpleasant feelings. Mind-altering drugs quickly affect the pleasure centers of the brain so that the user who is feeling good feels better, and those feeling bad will feel good. The result is nearly immediate self-gratification, but it is only temporary. In reality, sooner or later, the user and others always pay the price.

Continued use of a psychoactive drug will most often result in problematic behavior such as drinking and driving, job jeopardy, or splitting with the family. Ultimately, repeated use can lead to physical and/or psychological dependence. As use continues, there are usually three anticipated outcomes:

1. Return to a drug-free lifestyle.
2. Continue to abuse drugs, avoiding dependence but exhibiting problematic behavior at work, home, or the community.
3. Continue to abuse drugs to the point of dependence and most likely death from his/her disease.

How each substance abuser will land is unpredictable, and is often guided by circumstance beyond anyone's control.

HOW PROBLEMATIC BEHAVIOR AND DEPENDENCE DEVELOP

Today, drug dependency is viewed as a disease with identifiable causes, signs, and symptoms. As such, in many jurisdictions people with addiction issues are protected by human rights councils. Dependency follows a predictable course and outcome, and it is treatable. The disease of drug dependence can be the following:

- **Primary**—it is not simply the symptom of some other problem(s); it is in itself the problem.
- **Contagious**—it attracts others who are vulnerable.
- **A family disease**—it affects entire families, not just the individual abuser.
- **Chronic**—it is difficult to control, is quite often recurring, and although treatable, it is incurable.
- **Fatal**—it takes hundreds of thousands of lives annually.

Drug dependence may be physical or psychological, and it represents an individual's loss of control. Physical dependence occurs when a person cannot function normally without the repeated use of a drug. If drug use is abruptly discontinued, the person experiences severe physical and psychic disturbance, known as withdrawal. Psychological dependence provides a strong psychological desire to continue the self-administration of drugs for a sense of improved well-being.

A great number of programs and treatment approaches exist for the treatment of drug dependencies. What we do know about these various programs is that no single approach or program is effective for every drug dependent person. We also know that there are not enough of these programs to meet the needs of the afflicted. According to the U.S. government, the cost offset is tremendous. For every $1.00 spent on treatment, $7.00 is saved on crime and criminal justice costs. When factoring in health care savings, a total of $12.00 is saved (U.S. Department of Health and Human Services, 2009). In spite of the various programs and models, we know that recidivism rates are high. So, for all that is known, the experts still have much to learn and continue to do so each day. There is, however, a solid body of evidence pertaining to the stages of dependency and associated behaviors which the protection officer should know. An understanding of the process is critical to prevention and rehabilitation efforts.

Drug dependence follows a predictable course of action which, most often, begins with experimentation. This may be the result of curiosity, peer pressure, or a variety of other variables or combination of variables. Everyone is susceptible to the abuse of drugs and some more so than others due to a host of social, environmental, psychological, and biological issues or, in some cases, heredity. What is significant is that each incidence of use makes the user more susceptible to continued use, up to and including dependence. Further, the earlier drug use begins, the more likely it is to progress to abuse and dependence.

Another facet of dependence is recovery. The individual user has a greater opportunity for a full recovery if treatment begins before dependence sets in. The longer one uses a drug(s), the more complex the physical and psychological symptoms become. As a result, recovery for the dependent person, or daily user, is a greater challenge in most instances than recovery from occasional use or experimentation. This is why early intervention is significant.

Whether an intervention occurs at home, work, school, or in the community, it is certain that the earlier the intervention takes place the greater the opportunity is for recovery.

HOW IS SUBSTANCE ABUSE PERPETUATED?

There are essentially five reasons why substance abuse continues to be a problem in the workplace.

1. Denial
2. Mixed messages
3. The "harmless" theory
4. Drug use is controllable by the user
5. The problem is viewed as controllable through attrition

Denial provides the biggest single roadblock to successfully addressing the problem of substance abuse in society or the workplace. Parents, teachers, husbands, wives, managers, and users themselves all tend to deny the problem exists, even in light of hard evidence. Some familiar phrases illustrate the point: "Not *my* kid," "What is wrong with a few drinks?" "Not in *my* company," "Not Joe—he's just a good-natured guy," "It must have been entrapment."

Mixed messages are heard daily, and are confusing to the layperson. Some insist the use of certain drugs for "recreational" purposes is harmless. Others say that the same drugs contribute to many individual, social, and occupational ills. For instance, some marijuana advocates say that this drug is harmless and does not interfere with one's work. Others claim that the drug has a negative impact on education, motivation, and the ability to remember and perform complex or new tasks. Hence, marijuana use may contribute to industrial accidents.

The "harmless" theory contends that the use of drugs such as marijuana, cocaine, and alcohol is considered by many to be an innocuous activity, on or off the job. In fact, some forces are aggressively moving to legalize all psychoactive drugs. In reality, no drug can ever be considered harmless. Any drug is harmful when taken in excess, even aspirin and, of course, alcohol. Some drugs can also be harmful if taken in dangerous combinations, such as barbiturates and alcohol. Some drugs, like over-the-counter (OTC) medications, can be harmful in therapeutic doses if alertness is diminished or drowsiness results. Finally, certain drugs taken by hypersensitive people can be lethal—for example, penicillin. Given the potential harmfulness of some legal, prescription, and OTC drugs, one must realize the increased potential for harm, impairment, and death with illegal street drugs, whose composition is never truly known.

Controllable use is some people's belief that drug use can be "recreational," provided one controls his/her intake of a given psychoactive drug. However, this arrangement is academic because even so-called social, "recreational," or "controlled use" of psychoactive drugs on the job often leads to impairment, which in turn leads to diminished performance, accidents, and other adverse consequences. Everyone pays a price for his/her drug use. Some pay earlier than others, and all too often innocent people suffer first.

Attrition in industry is often seen as a solution to the drug problem. Unfortunately, tomorrow's workforce is intimately involved with drugs today. Consider the following:

> In 1975, 55 percent of high-school-aged children had tried illicit drugs. This increased to 66 percent by 1981. In 2008 the rate of abuse in the United States for 12- to 17-year-olds is 47 percent (D.A.R.E. America Annual Report, 2008, p. 8). Similar statistics from the United Kingdom for 16–24 year olds were reported in the Annual 2002/2003 British Crime Survey. Those who have tried illicit drugs in this age category, at least once were reported at 47 percent. *(Condon & Smith, 2003)*

The data clearly show that tomorrow's workforce is intimately involved with the use and abuse of alcohol and other drugs today. It is evident that business and government will constantly be confronted with a new generation of young people predisposed to tolerating the use and abuse of psychoactive drugs. For this reason, the business community must gather its resources to establish sound drug-free work-place programs that will meet this challenge.

CONDITIONS ADVERSELY AFFECTING THE WORKPLACE

As substance abusers arrive for work each day, they generally fit into one or more of these categories that present threatening conditions for employees and their employer:

1. Appear for work under the influence of drugs and will be openly and obviously impaired, or intoxicated and unfit for duty.
2. Possess and use drugs on the job. Although they are impaired, it will not be evident.
3. Sell or otherwise distribute, or transfer illegal drugs or legal drugs illegally, while on the job.
4. Display impairment due to the residual effects of drugs taken hours or even days prior to coming to work. These effects may include emotional outbursts, personality changes, irritability, combativeness, memory problems, and the inability to complete assignments.
5. Have codependent loved ones working at jobs where they will be less productive.

Keeping in mind that the protection officer is not a diagnostician, recognizing impairment due to sustained low dosages and residual effects, or codependence, will be unlikely unless he/she is informed of this by a third party. If third-party information is received, then the protection officer should bring this intelligence to his/her supervisors immediately. These conditions are best left to supervisors and managers who can evaluate these issues as a matter of job performance and make the necessary referrals, or take disciplinary action when performance is considered to be deteriorating. However, the protection officer should be alert for the outward signs of drug possession, use, and distribution, which are often overlooked

by the layperson. These signs include the following:

1. Observation of drugs and/or drug paraphernalia in the workplace.
2. Observation of suspicious activity, especially in secluded areas of the facility or parking lots. Whenever suspicious activity is observed, you should immediately contact your supervisor and request backup before approaching. However, immediate action may be necessary if a threat to personal safety exists.
3. Scent of chemical odors not commonly present in the workplace.
4. Observation of abnormal behavior, including the signs of intoxication. Keep in mind that not all abnormal behavior is an indication of substance abuse. Some employees may have legitimate medical problems that can result in behavior similar to intoxication. Regardless of the cause, immediate action is required to protect the employee, coworkers, and the company's property and interest.

HOW MUST INDUSTRY RESPOND?

The workplace plays an integral part in the fight against substance abuse. When continued employment is conditional upon being drug-free, then employment becomes a powerful incentive in support of a drug-free workplace. When a company demonstrates commitment to a comprehensive program in support of a drug-free workplace, then the opportunity to affect attitudes, behavior, and the lifestyles of employees is significant. Through the influence of these programs, employees are likely to make healthier choices. Employees who are educated and committed to a drug-free life-style convey this attitude to their families and friends. In effect, the employee not only serves to reduce substance abuse at work, but he/she serves to improve the health of his/her family and community.

Historically, "private enterprise has pioneered most of the programs in drug detection, rehabilitation, and prevention" (Fischer et al., 2008, p. 357). To respond effectively, a multidimensional approach is necessary. A company should consider five components in the development of a comprehensive drug-free workplace program.

1. Policy development
2. Training and education
3. Employee assistance
4. Drug testing
5. Security measures

A company policy is the first step on which to build an effective drug-free workplace program. It must clearly state the company's purpose, what will and will not be tolerated, how the company will respond to violations, and what training and treatment support are available. It should also describe the company's drug testing policy, if they choose to conduct these tests.

Training and education should be provided at all levels of employment, especially supervisors and managers, for they represent a company's first line of defense. Training and education should focus on a review of the company's policy, and provide a clear understanding of the nature and scope of substance abuse and the required response to prevent and properly address the problem.

Employee assistance programs (EAPs) are most often a resource offered by large companies. However, more and more smaller-sized companies are forming consortiums and thereby making the availability of EAP services cost-effective. An EAP may be an in-house function or contracted out through an independent service. These programs assist employees and their families in addressing a wide range of personal problems, including substance abuse. In addition, they offer training programs, consult on matters pertaining to troubled employees, assess employee problems, make referrals for treatment and counseling, and in some instances, oversee drug testing programs. Current data reveals that each dollar invested in an EAP can save a company $5.00–16.00 in the long run. Where an EAP is not available, a company may provide insurance coverage that will allow an employee to seek community resources.

Drug testing programs like those provided by the EAP have traditionally been employed by large companies. One of the restrictive factors for a small company is, of course, cost. As with EAPs, smaller companies are banding together to form consortiums in order to make drug testing more cost-effective. This momentum for testing is being pushed:

- By legislation that all workers in safety-sensitive positions are subject to mandatory testing;
- By insurance companies who threaten to increase rates if drug testing is not carried out; and
- By the resurgence of background checks, partly precipitated by the events of September 11, 2001 (Gips, 2006, p. 54).

The purpose of drug testing is to deter substance abuse, prevent the hiring of substance abusers, and provide for the early identification and referral to treatment of employees with a substance abuse problem.

Several types of testing can be performed by a company, depending on their needs and collective bargaining or legal restrictions. These include preemployment, postaccident, follow-up to treatment or counseling, reasonable suspicion, and random. Urinalysis has been the predominant method used to test for the presence of controlled substances. However, other testing materials being evaluated and/or used include blood, hair, pupillometry, and saliva.

Each of the components discussed above plays an integral part in a drug-free workplace strategy. However, these components cannot address all situations. Sometimes a security response is required. This is true when reckless and wanton behavior places the safety of employees and the interest of the company at great risk. Protection officers should clearly understand why and when the security response is necessary.

There is a small percentage of substance abusing employees, perhaps 4–10%, who will not accept or benefit from an offer of assistance in the way of treatment or counseling. These individuals include drug dealers who may or may not use drugs on the job, and users who are not interested in or ready for recovery because they are in denial. Employees who deal drugs are engaged in criminal activity that cannot be tolerated. They make available the supplies on which troubled employees depend and they establish new opportunities for other types of criminal activity such as gambling, prostitution, and theft. A survey conducted with substance abusing employees revealed that 44% had sold drugs on the job. They sell their drugs in bathrooms, parking lots, vehicles, and secluded areas.

In some cases, major drug trafficking organizations have directed dealers to secure jobs in industry and to develop a clientele. Why? Because (1) there is low police visibility, (2) security forces are well known and predictable, and (3) there is a ready-made clientele. These types of employees create morale and safety problems and, in many cases, create a great deal of intimidation for employees and managers alike.

Theft is a major problem for both employers and employees. Employees who use drugs on or off the job need to support that use. In many cases the cost of drugs is very high, costing thousands of dollars a month. To support this need, employees have been guilty of the theft of valuables such as equipment, money, and trade secrets. By contrast, a person who spends $20.00–40.00 a week for marijuana and/or other drugs can effectively supplement their income by removing valuable equipment or money from the employer or other employees.

To counteract the activities of drug dealers, the company's security department or independent contractor may have to employ certain investigative techniques. For the most part, these techniques include interviews with employees, undercover operations, covert surveillance, or searches conducted by drug-sniffing dogs or chemical process.

Interviews are conducted for the purpose of gathering intelligence that may dictate future action, such as policy changes or the selection of an investigative technique. Employees quite often possess critical information, but may not recognize its significance unless questioned by a trained investigator.

An undercover operation is a specialized investigative technique. It is employed for the purpose of covertly infiltrating a workforce in order to identify violations of company policies or law. These investigations are usually initiated when there is a suspicion or clear knowledge that drug dealing is taking place, but the source and the degree are unknown. Even if a source was identified, in many instances an undercover operation may be necessary to gather the evidence required for disciplinary or legal action.

Covert surveillance or hidden cameras are used when the activity in question is confined to an individual or specific location. When this is the case, a special surveillance camera can be covertly secreted inside a ceiling, wall, fixture, or a variety of other areas restricted only by one's imagination. The greatest advantage to the hidden camera is the undisputed nature of the evidence, a picture of the event, and those responsible.

The act of searching a work area or entire workplace is not a common practice in most industries. When a search is performed it is usually carried out by drug-sniffing dogs or by chemical analysis. Most employers reject searches by dogs, based on the perceived negative impact it would have on employee morale. However, these searches can and do detect the presence of controlled substances. Once detected, a host of questions are raised regarding what legal or disciplinary action may be justified or taken. The action to be taken can only be determined on a case-by-case basis, after analyzing a variety of factors.

The second type of search is less intrusive and much more discrete. The chemical analysis search involves sweeping an area and analyzing the contents for the presence of a controlled substance. The chemical analysis is, however, restricted to the identification of a limited number of drugs. The same legal and disciplinary issues apply, as mentioned above.

DRUGS OF ABUSE, PARAPHERNALIA, AND DEFINITIONS

Although there are many drugs that will fall within the psychoactive classification, it is important that protection officers have an awareness of those that are most prevalent in the workplace. The following are in order of significance:

1. Alcohol
2. Cannabis
3. Stimulants
4. Depressants (other than alcohol)
5. Narcotics
6. Hallucinogens

To facilitate a review of the most popular drugs of abuse within each class, a controlled substance chart is provided that identifies specific drugs, trade or other names, medical uses if any, its potential for producing dependence and tolerance, duration of effects, routes of administration, and possible effects of abuse, overdoses, and withdrawal.

Before continuing, it will be helpful to review the following definitions:

Tolerance: Refers to a state in which the body's tissue cells become accustomed to the presence of a drug at a given dosage and eventually fail to respond to this ordinarily effective dosage. Hence, increasingly larger dosages are necessary to produce the desired effect.

Physical dependence: Often referred to as addiction, this occurs when a person cannot function normally without the repeated use of a drug. If the drug is withdrawn, the person has mild to severe physical and psychic disturbance, known as withdrawal.

Withdrawal: This is characterized by symptoms that occur after drug use is abruptly discontinued. Symptoms may be mild or severe and include seizures, restlessness, irritability, nausea, depression, and more. In some cases, as with alcohol and other depressants, withdrawal can be life-threatening.

Psychological dependence: This is the result of repeated consumption of a drug that produces psychological but not physical dependence. Psychological dependence produces a strong desire to continue taking drugs for the sense of improved well-being, but the body is not physically dependent on the drug. Psychological dependence is the most difficult to treat.

Potentiation: This is concurrent use of two or more depressant drugs with the same action that produce a multiple effect greater than the sum of either drug when taken alone. For example, use of barbiturates and alcohol. Potentiation can result in unexpected lethal overdose.

Lookalike drugs: Drugs (tablets, capsules, and powders) that are manufactured to closely resemble the appearance of well-known, brand name drugs, such as Dexedrine (dexies), and Biphetamine (black beauties). They generally contain drugs found in OTC medications, but usually in larger amounts to provide greater potency.

A word of CAUTION: You should never taste, smell, or directly touch an unknown substance. IT COULD BE HAZARDOUS TO YOUR HEALTH!

INDICATORS AND COMMON SIGNS OF ABUSE

There are various indicators that suggest or positively identify drug involvement in any environment, including the following:

- Presence of a drug and/or drug paraphernalia
- Physical signs (needle marks, dilated pupils)
- Behavioral signs (slurred speech, irritability, personality changes)
- Analytical tests (saliva, urine, blood, hair)

There are many signs of substance abuse that can be identified by the protection officer. However, keep in mind that some people have legitimate reasons for possessing a syringe and needle (diabetics), or having capsules and tablets (valid prescriptions). Having the sniffles and running eyes and nose may be due to a head cold or allergy and not cocaine use. Unusual and odd behavior may not be connected in any way with drug use. For these reasons protection officers cannot and should not view themselves as diagnosticians. The protection officer's role is to observe and report suspicious conduct or behavior to the appropriate supervisory contact within the company, so that they can evaluate each incident and follow through in the appropriate manner.

SIGNS AND SYMPTOMS: CONTROLLED SUBSTANCES

The following are specific characteristics attributable to each drug class:

Cannabis: Marijuana, Hashish, Hashish Oil

1. Initially, the person may appear animated with rapid loud talking and bursts of laughter. In later stages, he/she may be sleepy.
2. Pupils may be dilated and the eyes bloodshot.
3. Use results in distortion of depth and time perception, making driving or the operation of machinery hazardous.
4. Smokers may be impaired for as long as 24 hours following intoxication, which may last 1–2 hours.
5. Short-term memory is impaired.
6. Long-term use of marijuana is associated with mental deterioration in some users and presents a significant health risk to adolescents, the unborn, diabetics, the emotionally disturbed, and those with respiratory problems.

Marijuana is the most commonly used illicit drug in the workplace, because it is easily concealed and use can be accomplished quickly.

This drug is often a brown, herbaceous substance, but may be shades of brown, red, green, or yellow depending on its origins. Marijuana is smoked as a "joint" (cigarette) or through various types of pipes. When the joint is reduced to a butt and can no longer be held with the fingers, it is referred to as a "roach" and held with a "roach clip" for continued smoking. Another method used to smoke marijuana is to hollow out a cigar and fill it with the marijuana. This preparation is referred to as a "blunt."

Marijuana may also be taken orally when used in the preparation of food or drink. However, smoking is the preferred route of administration.

Cost is based in large degree on availability and/or its potency, which is determined by the percentage content of the psychoactive chemical called THC (Delta 9 Tetrahydrocannabinol). It is often packaged in clear plastic baggies, but any type of container may be used.

Marijuana users attempt to avoid detection on the job by smoking small amounts of marijuana, called "sustained low dosages," throughout the workday. This enables the user to avoid intoxication and therefore detection, because the euphoria or impairment is not outwardly obvious. The user experiences mild effects along with a level of impairment that can adversely affect one's fitness for duty and safety on the job.

Hashish and hashish oil contain concentrated levels of THC, which result in increased potency over marijuana. These forms of cannabis are generally not consumed at work because of the preparation required, but they are readily distributed.

Stimulants: Cocaine, Amphetamines, Crystal Meth, Lookalikes

1. The user may be excessively active, irritable, argumentative, nervous, or restless.
2. The user generally shows signs of excitation, euphoria, talkativeness, and hyperactivity.
3. May perform the same tasks repeatedly.
4. Dilated pupils and dry mouth are common.
5. Regular users can go long periods without sleeping or eating. This can result in fatigue, depression, and weight loss.
6. Long-term heavy use can produce delusions, psychosis, paranoia, or death.
7. Specific to cocaine—the user may exhibit runny nose, sniffles, watery eyes (symptoms similar to the common cold), and ulcerations of the nasal passage.
8. Paraphernalia consists of razor blades and mirrors for chopping cocaine into fine particles. Straws and small spoons are then used for snorting.

Cocaine is a drug produced by chemically processing the leaves of the coca bush, which is indigenous to South America.

Cocaine is usually a white, crystalline substance that looks like snow. When sold and used as "crack," it takes the form of solid matter and resembles small rocks or pebbles. Various containers are used to conceal or store the drug, such as tin foil, paper, and small glass vials.

Cocaine is taken by various routes of administration, including snorting (the most popular route), injection, and smoked as crack. On-the-job use is usually confined to snorting, which can be accomplished quickly and surreptitiously.

Cocaine can be snorted with the use of a coke spoon, a straw, the corner of a matchbook cover, or the tip of a long fingernail. When using a straw, which might be a rolled-up piece of currency, the user refers to this as "snorting a line" of cocaine. In addition, there is paraphernalia available today that is disguised as common sinus inhalers but is used to dupe unsuspecting employers into believing the user is treating a cold. In some cases employees have been dismissed on sick leave to address their symptoms!

Although traces of cocaine remain in the body for up to a week, its mind-altering effects, which users seek, last only 15–30 minutes. This is important because following this brief drugged state, the user experiences varying degrees of depression, exhaustion, and dullness, due to chemical disturbances in the brain that reinforce readministration of the drug. This may lead to continued or compulsive use and quite often to new routes of administration to achieve a more potent effect. The high cost is a powerful force that can lead to theft, drug dealing, and other criminal activity in the workplace.

Amphetamines are produced by both legitimate pharmaceutical companies for medical purposes and by clandestine laboratory operators (drug traffickers) in makeshift laboratories located in bathrooms or garages, or in elaborate facilities including workplace laboratories. Their effects are similar to cocaine with one important exception: They last for hours rather than minutes. When these drugs are used for nonmedical reasons, they are commonly obtained through (1) pharmacy theft, (2) clandestine manufacturers, or (3) unscrupulous doctors who write illegal prescriptions for monetary gain.

Some of the more popular amphetamines are methamphetamine (Speed), Biphetamine

(Black Beauties), Dexedrine (Dexies), and Ben-zedrine (Pink Hearts). Ritalin and Preludin are amphetamine-like substances that are also popular.

Amphetamines are taken orally as tablets or capsules that vary in color, shape, and size. Some, like methamphetamine or methcathinone (CAT), are available in powder form and are injected, snorted, or taken orally.

In addition to the drugs listed above, a whole new class of substances referred to as "looka-like" drugs have become problematic. Initially utilized by truck drivers and students, these substances have now infiltrated the workplace and are taking their toll. These substances can be distributed legally. They consist of capsules, tablets, and powders that contain legal, OTC stimulants such as caffeine and ephedrine. They are marketed as "stay awake" and "stay alert" drugs. However, their use can cause irritabil-ity and fatigue that in turn has contributed to morale problems within the workforce.

The use of stimulants, often referred to as "uppers" or "speed," on the job poses three serious problems. First, being under the influ-ence of these drugs gives one a false sense that they are capable of achieving any task or conquering any challenge. In this condition, employees may use poor judgment or attempt tasks that are beyond their training and knowl-edge, resulting in wasted time, property or per-sonal damage, safety infractions, and accidents. Second, in a stimulated, talkative, and hyperac-tive condition, users often disrupt coworkers, thereby creating employee morale problems. Finally, stimulant users tend to repeat tasks. This reduces productivity and quality control, and can affect morale in an environment depen-dent upon a team effort.

Note: Many precursor chemicals necessary to manufacture illegal drugs are legitimately used in private industry. To avoid theft of these chemicals by drug traffickers, a company should establish safeguards. Also, the work-place has been used to manufacture illegal drugs. This not only creates an image problem, but also a safety problem, because many of the necessary precursor chemicals are highly flam-mable and/or explosive.

Depressants: Alcohol, Barbiturates, Tranquilizers, Rohypnol

1. Behavior like that of alcohol intoxication, but without the odor of alcohol on the breath
2. Staggering, stumbling, or decreased reaction time
3. Falling asleep while at work
4. Slurred speech
5. Constricted pupils
6. Difficulty concentrating and impaired thinking
7. Limited attention span

These drugs, with the exception of alcohol, are produced and obtained in the same manner as amphetamines.

The most commonly abused drugs in this group, aside from alcohol, are the barbiturates, such as Secondal (Red Devils), Tuinal (Rainbows), and Nembutal (Yellow Jackets), and the benzodi-azepines, such as Valium and Librium. Another popular drug in this classification is Rohypnol.

The depressants possess two important char-acteristics that bear mentioning. First, as stated in the definitions at the beginning of this sec-tion, they are potentiating when combined with other depressant drugs. Second, withdrawal from alcohol and other depressants is life-threatening, and should always be done under medically supervised conditions.

Valium and Librium are the most widely pre-scribed and abused tranquilizers. They are also potentiating when combined with alcohol, bar-biturates, or other tranquilizers.

"Lookalike" substances containing antihis-tamines and analgesics like acetaminophen are also available as described for the stimulants.

Rohypnol is one of the latest fad drugs of the 1990s, and is becoming increasingly popular with young people. It has Valium-like effects and is referred to as "Roofies."

Depressants are taken orally and no specific form of packaging is outstanding.

The use of depressants diminishes alertness and impairs judgment, making the operation of machinery difficult. Manipulative skills and coordination are also affected. This type of impairment can lead to accidents and poor quality control, as well as diminished work performance.

Depressants are frequently referred to as dry alcohol, and alcoholics routinely substitute these drugs for alcohol during the workday in order to avoid detection from alcohol's odor.

Narcotics: Heroin, Dilaudid, Percodan

1. Scars (tracks) on the arms or on the backs of the hands, caused by repeated injections
2. Pupils constricted and fixed
3. Scratches oneself frequently
4. Loss of appetite
5. May have sniffles, red watering eyes, and a cough that disappears when the user gets a "fix" (injection)
6. User often leaves paraphernalia such as syringes, bent spoons, cotton balls, needles, metal bottle caps, eye droppers, and glassine bags in lockers or desk drawers. They may also be discarded in stairwells, remote areas of a parking lot, or a secluded location within the workplace.
7. Users, when under the influence, may appear lethargic, drowsy, and may go on the "nod" (i.e., an alternating cycle of dosing and awakening).

Natural narcotics (opium, morphine, codeine) are a product of the opium poppy, which is cultivated for the purpose of extracting these powerful drugs for medical use. Major growing areas include Southeast Asia, Southwest Asia, the Middle East, South America, and Mexico. In addition, semisynthetics like heroin and Dilaudid, and synthetics like Demerol, Percodan, and Fentanyl, are popular.

Narcotics are usually available in tablet, capsule, or powder form, and can be injected, smoked, snorted, or taken orally. In addition, capsules may be used to conceal heroin in powder form to produce a legitimate appearance. Heroin is generally packaged much like cocaine in tin foil, paper, balloons, baggies, and vials. Heroin is usually white, brown, or black ("black tar"), or in shades of these colors. Synthetic and semisynthetic tablets and capsules appear in various colors, shapes, and sizes.

The narcotics are not popular drugs of abuse in the workplace, because their use suggests a long history of abuse, which contributes to unemployment and criminal careers. The time required to prepare an injection is another factor discouraging heroin use on the job. However, the administration of heroin via snorting is becoming more popular. If this trend continues, then heroin may become as popular as cocaine. Aside from the issue of use, narcotics are quite often encountered for sale and distribution on the job.

Hallucinogens: LSD, PCP, DMT

1. Behavior and mood vary widely. The user may sit or recline quietly in a trancelike state or may appear fearful or even terrified.
2. Rapid eye movement, drooling, flushed and sweaty appearance, trembling hands, and dizziness.
3. There may be changes in sense of light, hearing, touch, smell, and time.

Hallucinogens are rarely utilized by employees on the job because of their long duration of effects (2–12 hours) and their unpredictable nature. Also, impairment is total, therefore obviating any degree of productivity. Hallucinogenic drugs are especially popular with 18- to 25-year-olds, and are frequently available at the workplace for distribution in their various forms. The most popular hallucinogens include LSD and PCP.

Hallucinogens, often called "psychedelics," are a group of drugs that alter perception and awareness. Their effects are generally unpredictable and in some cases, bizarre. The nature and intensity of the drug experience are determined by the potency and amount taken, the user's personality, mood expectation, and the social and environmental setting.

The LSD experience is labeled a "trip" that is characterized as "good" or "bad." The nature of the trip can only be determined after ingestion, and can last as long as 10–12 hours. The "good trip" is characterized by a passive trancelike state with pleasant hallucinations, perhaps a kaleidoscope of colors and altered sensations. Senses sometimes cross so that the user sees sounds and hears colors. These characteristics result in the hallucinations being touted as mind-expanding drugs. The "bad trip" is characterized by unpleasant experiences including terrifying hallucinations, panic, and irrational acts, which have resulted in injury and death.

LSD is sold on the street in tablet and blotter form. As tablets, they are commonly referred to as "microdot acid," and are sold in variety of colors, shapes, and sizes. When liquid LSD is dabbed on blotter paper, it is called "blotter acid." Because of LSD's negative reputation as an unpredictable and bizarre drug, it is commonly sold to unsuspecting buyers as THC or Mescaline.

Mescaline (Mesc), PCP, Psilocybin (mushrooms), and DMT (Dimethyltryptamine) are other commonly used hallucinogens.

5. Presence of plastic or paper bags or rags containing saturated quantities of the inhalant
6. Slurred speech

Inhalants represent a diverse group of psychoactive chemicals composed of organic solvents and volatile substances. These chemicals like glues, paint products, gasoline, and white erasing fluid, can be readily found in the home and workplace. Their easy accessibility, low cost, and ease of concealment make inhalants, for many, one of the first substances abused.

Inhalants are usually sniffed directly from an open container or from a rag soaked in the substance and held to the face. This is usually referred to as "huffing." Some users have been known to place open containers or soaked rags inside a bag, where the vapors can concentrate, before being inhaled. These substances are rapidly transported to the brain, and can result in unconsciousness or death.

These substances are not widely abused in the workplace. However, incidents of workplace inhalant abuse have been reported. Many of the chemicals used by some businesses can and are diverted for the purpose of inhalation. In some cases, the diversion and subsequent use have resulted in death on company property (Figure 23-1).

For further information on drugs of abuse, a comprehensive description and photographic collection of drugs and paraphernalia can be found in "Drugs of Abuse," published by the U.S. Department of Justice, Drug Enforcement Administration (2005 Edition).

INHALANTS: GLUE, GASOLINE, ERASING FLUID

1. Odor of substance inhaled on breath and clothes
2. Excessive nasal secretions and watering of the eyes
3. Poor muscular control
4. Drowsiness or unconsciousness

PROTECTING PEOPLE AND ASSETS

The role of any protection officer is that of protecting people and assets. The protection officer accomplishes this responsibility by observing and reporting incidents or situations which present a threat to the people and assets he or she has a duty to protect. Substance abuse is one such

Drugs	Trade or Other Names	Medical Use	Dependence Potential		Tolerance	Duration of Effects (in hours)	Usual Method of Administration	Possible Effects of Abuse	Effects of Overdose	Withdrawal Symptoms
			Physical	Psychological						
Narcotics										
Fentanyl	Innovar, Sublimaze	Analgesic, anesthetic	High	High	Yes	10 to 72	Injected	Euphoria, drowsiness, respiratory depression, constricted pupils, nausea	Slow and shallow breathing, clammy skin, convulsions, coma, possible death	Watery eyes, runny noses, yawning, loss of appetite, irritability, tremors, panic, chills, and sweating, cramps, nausea
Morphine	Morphine	Analgesic	High	High	Yes	3 to 6	Oral, Smoked, Injected			
Codeine	Codeine	Analgesic, antitussive	Moderate	Moderate	Yes	3 to 6	Oral, Injected			
Heroin	Diacetylmorphine, Horse, Smack	None in U.S.	High	High	Yes	3 to 6	Injected, Snorted			
Methadone	Dolophine, Methadone, Methadose	Analgesic, Heroin substitute, analgesic, antidiarrheal, antitussive	High	High	Yes	12 to 24	Oral, Injected			
Other Narcotics	Dilaudid, Darvon, Demerol, Percodan		High	High	Yes	3 to 6	Oral, Injected			
Depressants										
Chloral Hydrate	Noctec, Somnos	Hypnotic	Moderate	Moderate	Yes	5 to 8	Oral	Slurred speech, disorientation, drunken behavior, stumbling	Shallow respiration, cold and clammy skin, dilated pupils, weak and rapid pulse, coma, possible death	Anxiety, insomnia, tremors, delirium, convulsions, possible death
Barbiturates	Amytal, Nembutal, Phenobarbital, Seconal, Tuinal	anesthetic, anti-convulsant, sedation, sleep	High-Moderate	High-Moderate	Yes	1 to 16	Oral, Injected			
Glutethimide	Doriden	Sedation, sleep	High	Moderate	Yes	4 to 8	Oral			
Alcohol	Ethyl Alcohol, Ethanol	Ingredient in some medicines	Moderate	Moderate	Yes	2 to 8	Oral			
Benzodiazepines	Ativan, Halcion, Equanil, Librium, Miltown, Serax, Tranxene, Valium, Verstran	Anti-anxiety, sedation, sleep	Moderate	Moderate	Yes	4 to 8	Oral, Injected			
Other Depressants	Equanil, Dormate, Noludar, Placidyl, Falmid	Anti-anxiety, sedation, sleep	Moderate	Moderate	Yes	4 to 8	Oral			
Stimulants										
Cocaine	Coke, Snow, Flake, Crack	Local anesthetic	Possible	High	Yes	1 to 2	Injected, Snorted, Smoked	Increased alertness, excitation, euphoria, dilated pupils, increased pulse rate and blood pressure, insomnia, loss of appetite	Agitation, Increase in body temperature, hallucinations, convulsions, possible death	Apathy, long periods of sleep, irritability, depression, disorientation
Amphetamines	Biphetamine, Ice, Desoxyn, Dexedrine	Narcolepsy, weight control	Possible	High	Yes	2 to 4	Oral, Injected, Smoked			
Phenmetrazine	Preludin	Weight control	Possible	High	Yes	2 to 4	Oral			
Methylphenidate	Ritalin	Hyperkinesis, narcolepsy	Possible	High	Yes	2 to 4	Oral, Injected			
Other Stimulants	Plegine, Sadorex, Adipex	Weight control	Possible	High	Yes	2 to 4	Oral, Injected			
Hallucinogens										
LSD	Acid, Microdot	None	None	Degree Unknown	Yes	8 to 12	Oral	Illusions and hallucinations (with exception of MDA); poor perception of time and distance	Longer and more intense "trip" episodes, psychosis, possible death	Withdrawal symptoms not reported
Mescaline and Peyote	Mescal, Buttons, Mesc	None	None	Degree Unknown	Yes	8 to 12	Oral			
Amphetamine Variants	MDA STP, Ecstasy, COM, MDMA	None	Degree Unknown	Degree Unknown	Yes	Variable	Oral, Injected			
Phencyclidine	PCP, Hog, Angel Dust	None	Degree Unknown	High	Yes	Days	Oral, Smoked, Injected			
Other Hallucinogens	DMT, DET, Psilocybin	None	None	Degree Unknown	Possible	Variable	Oral, Injected, Smoked, Snorted			
Cannabis										
Marijuana, THC	Pot, Grass, Sinsemilla, Thai Sticks, Marinol (Synthetic THC)	Marijuana - None, THC - Antiemetic	Degree Unknown	Moderate	Yes	2 to 4	Oral, Smoked	Euphoria, relaxed inhibitions, increased appetite, depth and time perception distorted	Fatigue, paranoia, possible psychosis	Insomnia, nervousness, and decreased appetite
Hashish and Hashish Oil	Hash, Hash Oil	Hashish - None	Degree Unknown	Moderate	Yes	2 to 4	Oral, Smoked			
Steroids										
Testosterone	Depo-Testosterone, Delatestryl	Hypogonadism	Degree Unknown	Degree Unknown	Degree Unknown	14 to 28 days	Injected	Virilization, acne, edema, aggressive behavior, testicular atrophy, gynecomastia	Unknown	Possible depression
Nandrolone	Nortestosterone, DECA	Anemia, Breast Cancer	Degree Unknown	Degree Unknown	Degree Unknown	14 to 21 days	Injected			
Oxymetholone	Adadrol - 50	Anemia	Degree Unknown	Degree Unknown	Degree Unknown	24	Oral			

FIGURE 23-1 Controlled substances: Uses and effects. (*Source: National Drug Institute.*)

threat, and the protection officer represents a critical component in a company's effort to combat this threat and maintain a drug-free workplace. By understanding the scope and nature of this problem, along with the specific security-related concerns, the protection officer will be prepared to recognize and report substance abuse situations that undermine safety and security.

Finally, every protection officer should communicate his/her knowledge about the causes and effects of substance abuse beyond the confines of the workplace. By sharing this vital information about the perils of abuse, the protection officer can influence his/her family and community in a most positive way.

EMERGING TRENDS

As we have seen in this chapter, substance abuse is nothing new in our society. In recent years, however, a new face of this menace emerged on the scene, presenting an immediate and future threat to our well-being. It is the face of prescription drug abuse. Even children are abusing prescription drugs.

Prescription drug diversion and abuse are rapidly growing phenomena in our population. The U.S. Drug Enforcement Administration's "Fact Sheet: Prescription Drug Abuse—a DEA Focus," presents sobering data regarding this emerging trend, including:

- The number of Americans abusing prescription drugs increased from 3.8 million in 2000 to nearly 7 million in 2006, a startling increase of 80%, more than the number who are abusing cocaine, heroin, hallucinogens, Ecstasy, and inhalants combined.
- Prescription pain relievers are new drug users' drug of choice, vs. marijuana or cocaine, with hydrocodone being the most commonly diverted and abused controlled pharmaceutical in the United States.
- Opioid painkillers now cause more drug overdose deaths than cocaine and heroin combined.
- Nearly 1 in 10 high school seniors admits to abusing powerful prescription painkillers. A shocking 40% of teens and an almost equal number of their parents think abusing

prescription painkillers is safer than abusing "street" drugs (www.usdoj.gov/dea/concern/prescription_drug_fact_sheet.html. Retrieved on October 5, 2009).

The ready accessibility of prescription drugs subject to abuse and the misperception that they are safer than street drugs must be addressed and corrected. The Substance Abuse and Mental Health Services Administration (SAMHSA), in its 2006 National Survey on Drug Use and Health (September 2007), reports that 70% of pain relievers, both prescription and OTC drugs, are obtained from friends or relatives (www.usdoj.gov/dea/concern/prescription_drug_fact_sheet.html. Retrieved on October 5, 2009).

The implications of this growing trend are of great concern to security professionals. The teenagers of today who are abusing prescription drugs are the adults of tomorrow who may very well continue that abuse. Entering the workplace, they will bring with them the yoke of drug abuse and addiction that can lead to numerous security threats, including employee theft and workplace injury and violence.

To rise up and effectively defeat this challenging trend, we must develop and deliver to all stakeholders in our society a competent training program that will raise their awareness level and enable them to promptly and adequately identify the telltale signs of prescription drug abuse. This training must include the requisite steps to be taken to restrict teen access to these drugs and encourage them in their lawful, proper, and responsible use, thereby enabling our children to grow and develop into healthy adults who will contribute to communal safety and security rather than threaten and undermine it.

References

Condon, J., & Smith, N. (2003). *Prevalence of drug use: Key findings from the 2002/2003 British Crime Survey*. London: Home Office.

Fischer, R. J., Halibozek, E., & Green, G. (2008). *Introduction to security* (8th ed.). Boston, MA: Butterworth Heinemann.

Gips, M. A. (February 2006). High on the job. *Security Management, 50*(2), 50–58.

Joseph, D. E. (Ed.). (2005). *Drugs of abuse*. Washington, DC: Government Printing Office. U.S. Department of Justice, Drug Enforcement Administration.

Larson, S. L., Eyerman, J., Foster, M. S., & Gfroerer, J. C. (2007). *Worker substance use and workplace policies and programs*. Department of Health and Human Services: Substance Abuse and Mental Health Services Administration Office of Applied Studies. Rockview, MD: SAMHSA Office of Applied Studies.

Protection of Assets Manual Vol. I, Chapter 8, Part II. (2007). *Workplace substance abuse: Prevention and intervention*. Alexandria: ASIS International.

25 Years "D.A.R.E. America" Annual Report. (2008). Inglewood, CA: D.A.R.E. America U.S. Department of Health and Human Services (June 2009). Cost offset of treatment services, Substance Abuse and Mental Health Services Administration, Center for Substance Abuse Treatment. Rockview, MD: SAMHSA Office of Applied Studies.

SECURITY QUIZ

1. Drug dependence is a primary disease.
   a. True
   b. False

2. Which of the following applies to drug dependence?
   a. It is fatal
   b. It is a family disease
   c. It is contagious
   d. All of the above

3. The biggest single roadblock to addressing a person's substance abuse problem is their drug of choice.
   a. True
   b. False

4. A company can effectively fight substance abuse by just starting a drug testing program.
   a. True
   b. False

5. A person who does not use drugs, but is preoccupied with a loved one who does, is said to be codependent.
   a. True
   b. False

6. The first step in developing a Drug-Free Workplace Program is to:
   a. Provide education
   b. Start an employee assistance program
   c. Write a policy
   d. Start drug testing

7. The most widely used drug testing material in use today is:
   a. Blood
   b. Saliva
   c. Urine
   d. Hair

8. Psychoactive drugs affect which of the following:
   a. Brain
   b. Blood
   c. Lungs
   d. None of above

9. Nicotine and marijuana are referred to as which of the following:
   a. Equal in terms of habit forming drugs
   b. A harmless recreational drug
   c. The most dangerous drug
   d. Gateway drugs

10. The protection officer is to take which of the following actions in reference to substance abuse behavior in the workplace:
    a. Set up an undercover operation
    b. Arrest the perpetrators
    c. Observe and report to your up line
    d. None of the above

24

Workplace Violence

Timothy A. Pritchard and Roger Maslen

CHAPTER OBJECTIVES

- Define the parameters of workplace violence
- List levels of workplace violence
- List violent actions in each level of workplace violence
- Explain the basic role of a security officer in a workplace violence situation
- List the components of a workplace violence prevention plan

Violence is pervasive in our world and has been part of human society since its earliest recorded time. Violence in society, in one form or another, is unfortunate and is simply unavoidable. Workplace violence is a specialized problem, one that security professionals must deal with in their day-to-day work lives. Whether it is at a large governmental facility, a retail store, or a small, privately owned professional business, there is no industry, profession, or organization that is immune from the threat of workplace violence. There are many definitions of workplace violence. The U.S. Department of Labor, Occupational Safety and Health Administration (OSHA), states,

"Workplace violence is violence or the threat of violence against workers. Violence can occur at the physical workplace or outside the workplace (such as a taxi cab driver) and can range from threats and verbal abuse to physical assaults and homicide, one of the leading causes of job-related deaths [in the United States]" (OSHA, http://www.osha.gov/OshDoc/data_General_Facts/factsheet-workplace-violence.pdf).

Categorizing the types of incidents can be helpful in understanding the scope of workplace violence. There are three levels of workplace violence. These incidents may be subtle, and a situation can move from one level to another very quickly or slowly.

Level 1—Least Injurious

- Refusal to cooperate with immediate supervisor
- Spreads rumors and gossip to harm others
- Argues with coworkers
- Belligerent toward customers/clients
- Swears at others
- Makes unwanted sexual comments
- Minor violations of company policy
- Pranks

Level 2—Moderately Injurious

- Argues increasingly with customers, vendors, coworkers, and management
- Refuses to obey company policy and procedures

- Sabotages equipment and steals property for revenge
- Verbalizes wishes to hurt coworkers and/or management
- Sends sexual or violent notes to coworkers and/or management
- Sees self as victimized by management (me against them)

Level 3—Highly Injurious

- Physical attacks and assaults
- Psychological trauma
- Anger-related accidents
- Rape, arson, murder

Once you understand the types of workplace violence, you must also understand their sources. There are generally four sources of workplace violence:

Criminal acts. A perpetrator has no relationship to the business and commits a violent act at a worksite in the course of committing another crime. For instance, a homicide or assault occurring in the course of a robbery.

Customer/client/patient violence. The perpetrator is not an employee, but has a relationship with the business as a customer, client, or patient, and becomes violent while receiving services, or for reasons engendered by the business relationship. For instance, when a psychiatric patient assaults a physician, or a disgruntled client or customer threatens a company or one of its employees.

Worker-on-worker violence. Stems from an employment relationship; this includes incidents in which a current or former employee (or independent contractor) harms or threatens to harm another employee.

Violence stemming from a personal relationship. They occur in the workplace, but arise from a personal, or intimate, relationship between the perpetrator and victim. Someone may be harassed, threatened, or harmed at their workplace by an abusive partner. This may occur in instances where the abused partner, the abuser, or both are employed at the workplace in question.

However it manifests itself, "workplace violence is a growing concern for employers and employees nationwide" (OSHA, 2002). While we intuitively know that workplace violence has occurred in organizations for as long as organizations have existed, only in recent decades has the U.S. government measured and statistically reported on the topic. One of the first workshops held on the topic was on occupational homicide prevention in 1990 in Washington, DC. This workshop, which was sponsored by the National Institute for Occupational Safety and Health (NIOSH), concluded, in part, that "it is clear from the available data that workplace violence is a public health problem of significant proportion" (Bell & Jenkins, 1992). In that report, which covered the years 1980–1985, it was reported that homicide was the third largest cause of occupational injury death in the workplace. The statistics gathered in this study speak specifically to homicides. Today's workplace violence analysis has a much better view of the problem.

In a 2006 survey conducted by the Bureau of Labor Statistics, U.S. Department of Labor, for the National Institute for Occupational Safety and Health, Centers for Disease Control, for the period from September 2004 to June 2006, shows a broader and more detailed outlook of the pervasiveness of workplace violence. From that survey, we learn that nearly 5% of the 7.1 million private industry businesses in the United States had a workplace violence incident in the 12 months prior to the survey. The survey found for employers with over 1000 employees:

Workplace Violence Experience	
Have Had an Incident	49.9%
Criminal	17.2%
Customer/Client	28.3%
Co-worker	34.1%
Domestic Violence	24.1%

Some practical conclusions can be deduced from these statistics. First, a workplace violence incident can be perpetrated by either an internal or external source, as evidenced by the "criminal" and "coworker" numbers. An "external source" typically refers to those individuals who are not employed with an organization, whereas "internal source" is most often used to identify an employee of a particular organization. We have seen a shift in the statistics, whereas in the past, most workplace violence incidents were committed by individuals who are external to the organization (nonemployees). The most recent statistics show the threats are from internal sources. An example of an external source would be an armed robbery of a convenience store clerk and an example of a workplace violence incident committed by an internal source would be one employee physically assaulting another employee while at work. Second, most workplace violence incidents occur in occupations that are *somewhat* predictable, such as taxi driving and retail work. This means that if a security officer works in any of the known "high probability of violence occurring" professions, then he or she knows that there is an inherently greater probability of an incident occurring than in a profession with reduced exposure to workplace violence incidents. Third, when we have an idea of what workplace violence threats our workers are likely to encounter, we can implement precautions that reduce the probability of incidents occurring. Finally, just because most workplace violence incidents occur in occupations that are somewhat predictable, this does not mean that a workplace violence incident cannot occur in any business or organization at any time. It is imperative that both security managers and security officers understand this and are prepared for such an incident, should one occur. The other key stakeholders in addressing workplace violence are the human resources and legal departments.

The generally recognized primary objective of a security program, and the priority hierarchy, is the protection of people, property, and information. Of this protection hierarchy, people always come first, and a workplace violence incident always affects the people in the organization, including friends and family, in one way or another. The cost of a workplace violence incident is, at minimum, exorbitant. In the survey conducted by NIOSH, the effects of a workplace violence incident are reported by the respondents. In this survey, for employers with over 1000 employees, the effects were reported as:

Effects of Workplace Violence	
No Effect	51.4%
Absenteeism	12.2%
Turn Over	6.3%
Fear Levels	29.7%
Productivity	14.2%
Morale	22

These impacts can have a profound effect on the overall business success. Should an organization ignore this phenomenon within their environment, they could be placing themselves in a very precarious position. Workplace violence affects many aspects of the business:

Interruption of business. This can happen in many forms within all three levels of violence. An employee may be effected by another's actions as stated in Level One, and may be required to take sick leave or seek counseling, affecting their performance. Customers may develop a negative feeling toward the organization.

Increased legal and medical fees. Should a traumatic event occur within the workplace, the additional costs incurred by an increase in counseling services would be borne by the company or their insurance carriers. There could also be additional, significant costs for legal services, as the potential for lawsuits would be very real. Costs for losses could also be incurred over and above any insurance the organization may have.

Loss of productivity. Employees placed in stressful situations and faced with traumatic events of varying levels will quite probably experience a reduction in productivity. For companies already doing more with less, as a result of current financial realities, this could have significant impact on projects and core business.

Repair or replacement of equipment and facilities. Vandalism, theft, damages caused by an event of any level, could incur unnecessary costs to the corporation.

Therefore, it is incumbent on the organizational leadership to do all they can, at all levels, to prevent a workplace violence incident from occurring. All individuals in the security department, including all security officers, must be an integral part of this prevention process to achieve the maximum level of success.

A successful workplace violence prevention program requires participation of several departments inside an organization, including security, human resources, risk management, and trade unions. This list is only an example; each organization may include or exclude certain departments as makes sense for their business. The key is that the plan requires active participation by many. The plan consists of several components, including:

- A general workplace violence policy which is supported by the highest level of the organization and clearly supports a zero-tolerance position
- Identification of organizational risks
- A prevention plan
- A response plan to workplace violence incidents (including testing of the plan)
- An employee communication and awareness program, which includes training for all levels of staff and plan-active participants

The security department is a key component of the workplace violence plan, and security officers will likely be among the first on the scene if an incident occurs. Thus, it is essential that security officers possess the personal demeanor and professional skills necessary to respond to and successfully manage a workplace violence incident. Security personnel can provide valuable assistance to law enforcement officers who respond to a threat or violent incident. A good, positive relationship with local police agencies should expedite police response to an incident. Each sector of our workforce requires different skills from the security officer (i.e., a security officer working at an industrial site requires different skills from one working at a mall or hospital). However, the following skills and attributes can considerably add to the individual's ability to have a positive impact on the workplace violence prevention plan:

- Sound powers of observation
- Vigilance of the activities in the workplace
- Ability to identify signs of potential violence and effectively communicate them
- Strong skills in dealing with difficult people
- Ability to respond in a crisis
- Verbal communication skills
- Clear understanding of the policies, procedures, and plans

Preparation for a likely incident, especially one involving an external threat, is much easier than preparing for any eventuality involving an internal incident. Of all the workplace violence threats, there is little question that internal workplace violence threats cause organizational leaders the most significant level of anxiety. This is due to the uncertainty of when and how a threat can emerge within the organization.

Upon investigation of incidents after they occurred, it became apparent that people who perpetrated workplace violence displayed warning signs prior to the incident. The good news is that only a very small percentage of employees who have violent propensities will actually perform a violent crime. Employees who committed workplace violence often started out at the very first levels of workplace violence, being rude to coworkers. There was an escalation that then occurred, culminating in homicide.

It is crucial for security professionals to know the warning signs of a person who is a potential workplace violence threat. These are some general warning signs and clues:

- Has little tolerance of others
- Intimidates others around them, including through verbal threats
- Gets away with overinflated and unearned performance evaluations
- Has a history of family problems
- Has a history of alcohol and/or drug abuse
- Frequently talks about or is obsessed with violence or killings
- Is fond of violent films and television shows
- Has a fascination with weapons
- Has a history of job losses
- Is depressed, feels desperate; has mood swings
- Displays feelings of job dissatisfaction
- Frequently complains and appeals—always seems to be the victim
- Has a history of violent episodes or criminal acts
- Does not have a communicative personality
- Has a chemical imbalance
- Known as "crazy," "wound tightly," "strange," or "a time bomb"
- Has extreme reactions to new policies or procedures
- Has a hard time with persons of authority and may challenge authority
- Is very neat or very sloppy
- Has a history of lying or exaggerating
- Is self-centered
- Seems aloof, distant, and detached
- Lacks little or no social skills
- Overreacts to small changes on a regular basis
- Tolerates attitudes of violence
- Has a history of continuous stressors in life
- Ties their self-esteem and self-worth to their job

Even though they may appear normal or somewhat normal, security officers should remember that individuals who commit a workplace violence incident are not mentally stable. The reality is that there is not one distinguishing warning sign or clue that indicates mental instability. Thus, it is important to "read the big picture" and not focus on specific actions, drawing broad-based conclusions from those actions. The list of warning signs above provides a very large scope for assessing an individual's potential for workplace violence, some of which would not necessarily be known by the security staff. For this reason, cooperation between departments is imperative. When security, human resources, and operations can share information, the pieces of a puzzle come together to create a picture that leads to an intervention with the employee or the implementation of protective measures. The security officer's contribution to this is most likely the proper and timely reporting of incidents that seem out of the "ordinary."

It is also essential that every organization provide meaningful training on the topic of workplace violence to all employees. If employees are not educated about workplace violence warning signs, then the probability is greater that management will find out about a workplace violence incident as it is occurring or after it occurs. According to the U.S. Office of Personnel Management's Office of Workforce Relations, "[Employee] training is a critical component of any prevention strategy. Training is necessary for employees, supervisors, and the staff members of each office that may be involved in responding to an incident of workplace violence" (United States Office of Personnel Management, 1998, February). Employee training is one of the best and least expensive measures organizations can take to help combat workplace violence. All organizations should have a zero-tolerance policy for violence and threats of violence.

The purpose of this chapter has been to identify what workplace violence is, to identify steps

EMERGING TRENDS

In recent years, the Internet has had an effect on workplace violence. There is much information on the Internet about weapons, bomb making, and other strategies, and yet, there is also a lot of information on workplace violence and how to prevent it. Naturally, this has lead to more public awareness of the issue.

There is also more legislation, both in place and being written, to reduce the risk of workplace violence. In some jurisdictions, Working Alone Legislation either prevents employees from working alone, or ensures that if they are working alone, they must be checked on at regular intervals.

that an organization can take to prevent a workplace violence incident from occurring, and to better prepare the security officer to recognize a potential threat and take appropriate preventive action, or properly react to an incident as it occurs. There is not one response plan or program that fits the needs of all organizations. In fact, the opposite is true. Every organization has its inherent risks, and those risks must be identified and mitigated by the organization's leadership. The security team should be a significant part of this planning and mitigation effort. If an organization fails to plan, then it is planning to fail.

References

Bell, C. A., & Jenkins, E. L. (1992). *Homicide in U.S. workplaces: A strategy for prevention and research*. Morgantown, WV: United States Department of Health and Human Services.

Duhart, D. T. (2001). *Violence in the workplace 1993–99*. NCJ Publication No. 190076. Washington, DC: United States Department of Justice.

Occupational Safety and Health Administration. (2002). *Workplace violence fact sheet*. United States Department of Labor.

United States Office of Personnel Management. (1998). *Dealing with workplace violence* (OWR-09).

Sygnatur, E. F., & Toscano, G. A. (2000). *Work-related homicides: The facts*. United States Bureau of Justice Statistics.

Bureau of Labor Statistics, U.S. Department of Labor, for the National Institute for Occupational Safety and Health, Centers for Disease Control. (2006). *Survey of workplace violence prevention, 2005*. <http://www.bls.gov/iif/oshwc/osnr0026.txt>.

ASIS International. (2005). *Workplace violence prevention and response guideline*. ASIS International.

SECURITY QUIZ

1. Workplace violence is broadly defined as the use of violence against workers.
   a. True
   b. False

2. Workplace violence can be categorized into three levels. Fill in the blank for each level, and cross reference with the examples of each level.

   _____ Injurious (A)_____ Argues with customers
   _____ Swears at others
   _____ Injurious (B)_____ Physical attacks
   _____ Pranks
   _____ Injurious (C)_____ Verbalizes desire to hurt coworkers
   _____ Causes psychological trauma

3. Workplace violence can occur in almost every workplace: small businesses, large companies, government facilities.
   a. True
   b. False

4. An employee who exhibits rude manners toward his or her fellow workers is a definite workplace violence threat.
   a. True
   b. False

5. In a 2006 survey conducted by the Bureau of Labor Statistics, U.S. Department of Labor, for the National Institute for Occupational Safety and Health, Centers for Disease Control, what percentage of workplace violence events were perpetrated by coworkers?
   a. 22.7%
   b. 34.1%
   c. 24.1%
   d. 12.5%

6. There are many effects of workplace violence on an organization. Find the most correct group of effects below.
   a. Interruption to sales, Increased wages, Loss of management, Repair/replacement of equipment/facilities
   b. Interruption to business, Increased legal/wages, Loss of machines, Repair/replacement of equipment/facilities
   c. Interruption to business, Increased legal/medical fees, Loss of productivity, Repair/replacement of equipment/facilities
   d. Complete organizational failure

7. Although the 2006 survey discussed in this section indicated that 51.4% of respondents reported that workplace violence events had no effect on their workplace, 29.7% reported that this effect was observed:
   a. Absenteeism
   b. Turnover
   c. Fear levels
   d. Productivity
   e. Morale

8. Examples of workplace violence situations are
   a. One worker's aggression toward his or her fellow employees in the workplace
   b. An armed robbery of a taxicab driver
   c. Criminal activity involving personal injury to a worker
   d. All of the above

9. According to this chapter, the generally recognized primary objective of a security program is the protection of:
   a. Property and the organization's employees
   b. People, property, and information
   c. Fire, property, and information
   d. People, property, and money

10. According to this chapter, a very small percentage of employees who have violent propensities will actually perform a violent crime.
    a. True
    b. False

25

Crisis Intervention

Michael A. Hannigan and Christopher A. Hertig

CHAPTER OBJECTIVES

- Discuss causes of disruptive behavior
- Review stages of management of disruptive behavior
- Explore crisis development behavior models
- Develop protection officer guidelines
- Emphasize the importance of empathic listening and nonverbal communications
- Discuss team intervention approach
- Review safety considerations in crisis management

INTRODUCTION

Over 100 years ago, Walter Bagehot, a British journalist wrote, "Violence heads the list of inherent fears that are experienced by mankind." It is safe to say that the risk that violence may be perpetrated against individuals in our modern workplaces has to be a major security/loss control concern.

The protection officer, by the nature of his/her job function, must deal with individuals who present the threat of violent behavior. This can stem from factors such as involvement with alcohol or drugs, being a victim of a crime, suffering from an accident, illness, an argument with their spouse, or even the loss of a loved one. These individuals not only pose a serious threat to themselves, but most certainly to employees, the public, and of course, protection personnel.

There is a method of behavior management that can be used to allow more control of the outcome of a situation that involves a person who is behaving in a violent manner. A positive outcome can be achieved by suggesting certain proactive behaviors to these individuals through staff actions. It can also occur by what protection officers say and how the message is verbally or nonverbally communicated. This technique is *behavioral management*, or perhaps better known as *crisis intervention*. Crisis intervention is a relatively safe collection of techniques designed to aid in maintaining the best possible care and welfare of agitated or out of control individuals while lending maximum safety to protection personnel.

CAUSES OF DISRUPTIVE BEHAVIOR

The reasons people become violent or disruptive vary greatly but most frequently fall into at least one of the following categories:

1. Illness or Injury

People who are suffering from insulin shock, have severe breathing problems, or are in need of a particular medication can become physically violent until they receive medical attention. Sustaining a head injury, for example, could cause a person to become aggravated. In all of these situations, the affected individual may not have control over their actions or even remember what they have done.

2. Emotional Problems or Mental Illness

People with these types of problems may become verbally abusive or physically assaultive. They could be suffering from severe depression, psychosis, or schizophrenia. These individuals require prompt professional attention. The psychiatric or medical professional may order new medication or a change in existing medication.

3. Substance/Alcohol Abuse or Medication Reaction

Those who abuse alcohol or other substances such as PCP (animal tranquilizers), cocaine, LSD, heroin, and so on are prime candidates for violence. It is not possible to predict behavior patterns without having some indication of the kind of substance involved.

4. Stress

Stress is often referred to as the "silent killer." Everyone suffers from various levels of stress from time to time. Stress that more frequently leads to depression, remains a personal matter. However, individuals who are not able to manage personal stress may be susceptible to severe aggravation, which can precede violence directed against others.

5. Anger/Frustration

These conditions are often exhibited by individuals who lack the common decency to behave in a manner that is socially acceptable. Often the level of individual maturity will dictate the extent of objectionable conduct. But in some cases, the anger and lack of emotional control can lead to any number of violent reactions on the part of the subject.

STAGES OF MANAGEMENT OF DISRUPTIVE BEHAVIOR

The management of disruptive or violent behavior consists of five states or stages. These stages are based upon conditions that a protection officer must learn to recognize.

1. Evaluation

What is going on? Why? Who is involved? Is the protection officer, disruptive person, or others in immediate danger? Is support needed from fellow officers or resource personnel such as supervisory staff, social workers, medical personnel, or police?

2. Planning

Now that I know what is going on, what do I need to do? How do I do it? Do I have the resources available, such as people or equipment? Remember that situations usually start out one-on-one, but should never be permitted to stay that way for long—no longer than it takes to get back-up personnel. Once the plan of action has been determined, whether it be to continue talking, containment, restraint, removal of the person(s), referral or arrest, communicate the decision to team members. When planning, seek input from others when possible.

3. Implement

Put the plan into action. At this stage, things may not go as anticipated, but regardless, remain calm. A contingency plan can be activated that may be more fitting for the circumstances. In all crisis situations, the officer's personal safety is of prime importance. Protection officer actions should be dictated accordingly. Do not attempt to resolve a volatile situation alone. Observe exactly what is happening, position yourself with personal safety in mind, and await support staff.

4. Document

Effective documentation of a crisis incident is vital for future reference and guidance. A well-documented report will also serve to provide litigation protection should legal actions result from actions or inactions on the part of crisis respondents. The final report should include the standard who, what, where, when, how, and why. Address each of these questions carefully so that the report can be read and understood by all individuals and organizations involved.

5. Review

This is the final stage of the crisis management phase, but by no means any less important. This is when staff critique the entire crisis event. Carefully examine all documentation. It is imperative to openly discuss exactly what happened. It gives all protection personnel involved the opportunity to vent feelings and frustrations and gain the needed confidence to deal with future similar situations. Talk openly about what happened, why it happened, and if it could have been prevented. Could it have been handled more effectively? If so, how? This is the reconstruction state that must be managed in a positive manner. It is not a "fault finding mission" but, rather, a time to reflect positively on the actions taken and develop safeguards for future occurrences.

CRISIS DEVELOPMENT BEHAVIOR MODULES

During a crisis development situation, there are four distinct and identifiable behavior levels.

1. Anxiety
2. Defensiveness
3. Anger/frustration
4. Tension reduction

For each level there is a demand for a specific response to provide the maximum chance of defusing the crisis (see also Table 25-1).

1. Supportive
2. Directive
3. Nonviolent physical crisis intervention
4. Therapeutic rapport

It is important to relate each behavior level to a specific response.

Behavior Level

1. Anxiety: A notable state of dismay/torment
2. Defensive: Beginning stage of loss of rationality. Unreasonable and challenging
3. Anger/frustration: Loss of control, physically acting out
4. Tension reduction: Regaining of rationality after physically acting out

Staff Response

1. Supportive: Active, friendly, empathic attempts to alleviate observed behavior

TABLE 25-1   Behavior levels and protection officer responses

Behavior Level	Response
Anxiety	Supportive—attempt to help the person by eliminating the cause of the anxiety.
Defensive	Directive—setting *reasonable* and *enforceable* limits. Repeat limits if necessary.
Anger/frustration	Nonviolent restraint—prevent movement without causing pain or injury.
Tension reduction	Therapeutic rapport—communicate, debrief, and reassure the person.

2. Directive: Set limits, suggest expected outcomes

3. Nonviolent crisis intervention: Safe, prudent control and restraint techniques

4. Therapeutic rapport: Communication with individual during reduction

PROTECTION OFFICER GUIDELINES

Written policy and procedures will vary from one organization to another, but there are three basic guidelines that are applicable for any situation.

- Remain calm—move a little slower and speak a little lower. Remember that *"calmness is contagious,"* and lead by example.
- Act appropriately—be serious but human.
- Be objective.

Do not allow the subject to anger the officer(s) or to make him or her act inappropriately. Losing one's composure will most certainly intensify the situation. Remember that *"when you lose your temper; someone else has control over you."* Don't become complacent and take anything for granted. Always be alert. In terms of personal protection, never stand directly in front of the individual; this could make them feel threatened. Stand just off to the side, at an angle; this is considered a non-threatening position. Use the person's name, treating him or her with respect. Keep a minimum of 3 feet distance between officer and subject. This serves two purposes: first, it will preserve the individual's personal space; and second, it will provide time to react if the individual begins to physically act out. Remember, the amount of personal space may vary according to the individual and the situation. For example, if the person is highly agitated, he or she may need more room and coming closer may intensify the crisis. By contrast, a troubled person may want to have other people closer; their presence may feel reassuring. Identify the amount of space needed to develop a calming effect.

How to react, and how quickly to react, will depend on the nature of the disturbance and whether there is an immediate threat constituting a safety hazard. If you do not perceive such a threat, use the time to calm the subject and to continue your evaluation of the situation. If you have an audience, move them or move the situation. Only people who could provide probable support should be allowed to remain in the area—not spectators.

It is important to know how and why the situation started and always make sure help is available.

VERBAL AND PHYSICAL DISRUPTIVE BEHAVIOR

When a person is verbally acting out, they may or may not be fully aware of what they are saying or doing. They may express anxiety or defensiveness, make demands or threats, or use abusive language. This is especially true when the subject is in insulin shock, having severe breathing difficulties (lack of oxygen to the brain), or has suffered a head injury. These individuals are not usually able to control their actions and may suffer memory loss.

Subjects who are physically violent and require preventive measures can be easily detected by the protection officer. Typically, they throw objects or use them as weapons, kick, or attempt to grab or strike other individuals. These physically out-of-control people may even try to barricade themselves in a room or a particular area.

Protection officers need to be aware of the indistinct signs of physical acting out (violence). Certain signs are likely to precede more combative behavior. Watch for indicators such as gritting teeth, closing and opening hands, and tensing. These are strong indicators of a possible outbreak of physical aggression.

EMPATHIC LISTENING

Empathic listening is an active process which enables the interviewer to more fully understand what a person in crisis is trying to say. There are five measures that will enhance the listening and understanding process.

1. Never be judgmental. Never come on with the attitude that the other person "caused his or her own problem." Don't adopt the position that the subject's actions have been carefully thought out with a view to inflict pain or injury to others. This is sometimes difficult not to do, but it must be done in order to professionally deal with others.
2. Don't fake attention or ignore. If the officer ignores the individual, this will not only make them upset, but staff will experience difficulty in learning what is really happening. Encourage free-flowing communications.
3. Carefully listen to what the subject is really saying. This presents the opportunity to gain accurate insight into what is actually happening and what may have caused the crisis to develop. Listen for verbal clues that may be used to help defuse the situation. Look for repeated and underlying themes in the message.
4. Use silence and listen carefully to clarify the message. This technique serves two useful purposes. First, it provides the opportunity to better understand what the subject is actually trying to say, and second, it indicates that the officer is genuinely concerned.
5. Reflection or reflective listening can be used to reinforce. When the individual completes his or her statement, state to them what message is being received. An example might be *"You are very concerned about this, aren't you?"* or *"You're feeling frightened by this."* The subject will agree with the reflective statement or clarify it in some manner.

NONVERBAL COMMUNICATIONS

Nonverbal communication deals with body language—a message that is conveyed to someone without words. Subtle or obvious body movements or gestures can provide clear indications as to what another person might be thinking. Only a small percentage—perhaps 7–10%—of what is said is conveyed by the words that are spoken, whereas at least 85% of interpersonal communications are paraverbal or nonverbal. Individuals who are functioning under a stressful or emotional state of mind will often communicate even more useful information in a paraverbal or nonverbal manner. Practice identifying what people are saying without words. Here are some useful points to consider.

Proxemics or personal space—Respect the subject's personal space, which is considered to be 1.5 to 3 feet in front of them. Note that upset or violent persons may require much more space; sometimes as much as 12 feet. Avoid crowding or "getting in their face." Note also that different age groups and cultures have varying amounts of personal space.

Kinesics—Body posture and movement are critical in a crisis situation. Avoid toe-to-toe or eye-to-eye gestures that can be considered challenging.

Supportive stance—Approximately one leg length away, on an angle, and slightly to the side of the individual. This is sometimes referred to as a 1.5 or "interview" position. This avoids any feelings of encroachment or invasion of personal space. It provides the person being interviewed with enough room to escape, as well as the officer doing the interviewing. It also enhances officer safety as the subject must step forward in order to assault the officer.

CONTROLLING DISRUPTIVE OR VIOLENT BEHAVIOR

There are a number of useful methods that can be applied to control violent or aggressive behavior, such as verbal communications, use of chemicals, physical force, or a combination of all three.

Verbally—Assume a neutral body stance, let the individual talk and listen to what they are saying. Do not argue or threaten. Acknowledge feelings and thoughts. This can be achieved without agreeing or disagreeing. Consider voice tone, volume, and rate when communicating verbally (paraverbals). Use the person's name and maintain eye contact. It may be necessary to make the subject aware that his/her actions are inappropriate, and he/she will be held accountable for his/her actions and responsible for the outcome of the situation.

Chemically—In most crisis situations that occur, the protection officer seldom has the use of chemicals as a viable option. The decision to chemically control an individual can only be made by qualified medical or psychiatric personnel. Medications that could be used in these instances are generally depressants, such as Valium, Thorazine, or Haldol. There are other medications to choose from and the qualified medical professional will use what is felt to be most effective after evaluating the behavior of the individual.

Physically—Physical control techniques are used to prevent harm or injury to the individual or others in the immediate vicinity of the incident. Application of physical force should be considered only if no other feasible options are possible. If an individual has to be restrained, nonviolent techniques are the logical choice. These techniques are intended for personal safety and self-defense and must be taught by a qualified instructor. The primary focus is to protect employees and clients from injury.

Other—Whether or not to use pepper spray, electronic defense units, tasers, and so on is a question to be addressed by local laws, ordinances, and organizational policy. Intensive training is a must before any consideration can be given to the use of these kinds of protective equipment.

TEAM INTERVENTION

Team intervention is considered to be the best approach to be used during crisis development. Personnel should use the least restrictive method to control aggressive/disruptive individual(s). The objective, as in almost all volatile conditions that require security intervention, is to defuse the situation in a manner that reduces the risk of guilt, pain, or injury.

POSITIVE FACTORS RESULTING FROM TEAM APPROACH

The team should consist of no more than five people, all of whom must be capable of dealing with a crisis situation. More than five members tends to lead to confusion and a lack of unit cohesiveness. When team action seems inevitable, reserve/resource members should remain out of sight, nearby, and ready. These are some of the advantages of the team approach:

1. Team members enjoy more personal safety and a feeling of security resulting from the presence of fellow officers or other support staff.
2. Team members are able to maintain a professional profile because of the support and reliance that result from team member interactions.
3. Team members do not feel that the violence or unruly behavior is directed against them personally; rather it is directed at the team as a whole.
4. Team members can provide verification of actions and inactions. The verification can support a legal position in the event of complaints or litigation being initiated by affected individual(s).

The manner in which the team gets to the scene is vitally important. A mass convergence of staff will be perceived as a show of force and have an unsettling effect on the disruptive individual(s). Try to avoid the attraction of a crowd. Protection officers should carry two-way radios that facilitate effective communication with other team members.

Resource staff that is involved in deployment to the scene must receive preincident training and instruction in all facets of the intervention process, particularly methods of communications.

LEADERSHIP IN THE TEAM APPROACH

As in any kind of teamwork approach, there has to be a leader. The team leader can be anyone who has special skills, training, or expertise that will lend strength and unity to the team. When the leader arrives at the scene, he/she must be prepared to "take over." Here are some additional points to consider when selecting a team leader.

1. The leader will likely be the first person on the scene. Accessibility to the scene is an important consideration.
2. The leader must be confident.
3. The leader must be familiar with personnel who occupy the facility or facilities who may be a target for a crisis.
4. The leader must be familiar with the physical layout of the facility.
5. The leader should, ideally, be familiar with the acting out person or persons.

When the event occurs and team action is called for, the team leader must take charge and ensure that the following measures/steps are taken as quickly and prudently as possible:

1. Assess the situation, and then determine what action will be taken.
2. Formulate the action plan and put it into play as quickly and effectively as conditions allow.
3. Apprise the team of what is happening. Each team member must know his/her

responsibilities. In the event practice/drills have not been conducted, the leader must improvise.
4. Begin the communication process. Assess the situation. Take whatever remedial actions are warranted. Activate contingency plan(s) as required. Keep team members appraised.

SAFETY CONSIDERATIONS IN CRISIS INTERVENTION

The goal in any crisis situation is to neutralize the threat/risk while maintaining the safety and welfare of everyone involved. Mentally deranged or violent individuals will often resort to throwing objects or try to grab or strike the person they envision as a threat. Usually this is the person in charge, most often the protection officer. In these instances, being resourceful is important. Protection can be obtained through the effective and safe use of a pillow, chair back cushions, or any object that is readily available. A blanket or coat can be used to help restrain an individual while distracting their attention.

Note the location of windows, doors, and furniture in the area. Normally you would not want to block a door with your body, nor would you want the disruptive person between you and the door that may be your only escape route. Stay away from windows. Try to keep the subject away from things that can be used as weapons: chairs, water pitcher, phone, glass, desk accessories, or any kind of blunt or sharp object.

CONCLUSION

Disruptive individuals can have a serious adverse effect on organizational operations. If such incidents are perceived as a threat by employees, it will reduce productivity, lower morale, and instill a sense of fear. The presence of a capable, confident protection officer, willing and able to effectively communicate with

EMERGING TRENDS

Crisis intervention is becoming increasingly important as we deal with an aging population and the widespread abuse of prescription medicine. There are also greater expectations for safe, efficient, and effective management of aggressive behavior. Protection staff at health care facilities, schools, treatment centers, and special events need to be particularly adept at handling a crisis.

This requires practice, experience, and hands-on instruction. But such instruction can be preceded by and reinforced by distance education. Reading and observing video reenactments of crisis management situations, as well as taking exams, is part of distance learning. Distance delivery is playing a key role in crisis intervention training.

One means of managing crisis and workplace violence is to emphasize customer service. Organizations that do this can reduce the number of angry people in their environment. They can blend customer service skills with crisis intervention. Such an approach is certainly cost-effective. It is also in keeping with an organization's mission and values. If each and every employee is thoroughly indoctrinated with customer service skills and attitudes, they will have gone a long way toward managing crisis.

Another trend is a greater recognition of the adverse effects that crisis may have on people. Victims, witnesses, and protection staff are all impacted emotionally by crisis. Post-traumatic stress disorder is a concern. So too are staff depression and burnout due to continual exposure to crisis. Critical incident stress debriefing may be appropriate for the aftermath of a crisis. Rotation of personnel away from constant exposure to violent people may be necessary.

employees, will have a stabilizing effect on the workplace.

In a post-crisis intervention situation, the protection officer may experience anger, fear, or frustration; this is a natural reaction that must be controlled. It is not uncommon for the officer to feel that he/she has been the victim. This can result from a real or perceived lack of management support during and after the crisis or being exposed to the crisis for a prolonged period of time. Do everything possible to resolve the crisis in an expeditious manner. Getting it over as quickly as possible will reduce team frustration and apprehension.

The officer must waste no time in committing thoughts to paper. By promptly composing a well-written report, the writer can vividly recall what exactly has happened. Documenting the report will provide a vehicle to vent frustration. Discussing the matter with other team members will help. Above all, avoid being discouraged and maintain a positive attitude.

Remember, when crisis intervention is required, stay calm, be objective, and act appropriately. Let common sense prevail. Remember the plan for success: EVALUATE, IMPLEMENT, DOCUMENT, and REVIEW.

Resource

For more information, visit the Crisis Prevention Institute (CPI) at <www.crisisprevention.com>. CPI is an international training organization that specializes in the safe management of disruptive and assaultive behavior. CPI has been in existence since 1980 and has trained over 5.5 million persons. The Institute offers a variety of courses and instructor certifications. These programs are offered around the world. The Institute also has various forms of instructional materials such as videos and posters.

SECURITY QUIZ

1. This is often referred to as "the silent killer."
   a. Insulin shock
   b. Diabetes
   c. Stress
   d. Mental illness

2. "When you lose your ___, someone else has control over you."
   a. Cool
   b. Temper
   c. Money
   d. Job

3. Some rules for setting limits are to:
   a. Set reasonable limits
   b. Set only limits that can be enforced
   c. Repeat the limits if necessary
   d. All of the above

4. Being complacent during a crisis situation is good; it allows the individual not to know what you are thinking.
   a. True
   b. False

5. The best stance during a crisis situation is just off to the side at an angle.
   a. True
   b. False

6. Indistinct signs of possible physical acting out, such as gritting teeth, closing and opening of hands, and tensing, may precede more combative behavior.
   a. True
   b. False

7. Experts say that 7–15% of the messages we convey are nonverbal.
   a. True
   b. False

8. Paraverbal communications—how we deliver our words or verbal intervention—includes which of the following?
   a. Tone
   b. Volume
   c. Rate
   d. All of the above

9. Persons who are behaving in a physically violent manner may be controlled in all of the following ways except:
   a. Verbally
   b. Challenged
   c. Physically
   d. Chemically

10. When involved in a one-on-one situation, the first action taken should be:
    a. Make a plan of action
    b. Do not block the doorway
    c. Communicate with the individual
    d. Be sure assistance is en route

26

Strikes, Lockouts, and Labor Relations

David J. DeLong

CHAPTER OBJECTIVES

- List three types of strikes
- List thirteen security procedures before or during a strike
- Provide advice on what to document during a strike
- Define employee misconduct and related disciplinary techniques

The protection officer should have a thorough knowledge of the security practices and procedures in existence at his/her place of employment, and their role in the labor relations process. Labor relations are a subsection of industrial relations in existence at any company, particularly those with unionized employees. Labor relations include employers and employees dealing with matters such as collective bargaining and associated activities.

The role of the protection officer and his/her activities can have a major influence on labor relations at any given company. Security's role in the following activities can have a major influence on labor relations: strikes, searches, employee discipline, employee misconduct and dishonesty, arbitrations, and interviews.

STRIKES

Strikes are an almost inevitable occurrence for many unionized companies. Indeed, it may be argued that for such companies, strike costs are an integral part of the *labor* costs to maintain the operation.

Work stoppages as a result of labor relation activities and difficulties will arise primarily in three instances.

1. **Wildcat strike or illegal walkout**—this type of strike is an unauthorized work stoppage that is in violation of the law and/or a collective agreement in existence. The most common reason for a wildcat strike is the result of the union considering some action to be unjust.
2. **Lawful strike**—this type of strike takes place in accordance with applicable laws and the collective agreement in existence. The lawful strike usually occurs as a result of terms and conditions of employment. For example, at the expiration of an existing collective

agreement, a strike may commence after a strike vote has been taken. Wages or certain aspects of the collective agreement, such as health and safety, may not be satisfactory to members of the union, resulting in a strike.

3. **Lockout**—this type of work stoppage takes place in accordance with applicable laws and the collective agreement in existence. Lockout refers to management's refusal to allow members of the bargaining union onto company property. The purpose of a lockout by management is to put economic pressure on members of the union to cause a behavior change that members of the union are not willing to accept.

The protection officer should be familiar with the company strike plan and manual in place. The strike plan will highlight and provide guidelines for the protection officer to follow. Normally, the strike plan is designed and updated to eliminate problems that occur during a strike and provide guidance for security and management.

The protection officer should be aware of the following security procedures during or prior to a strike, whether they are covered in a strike manual or not:

1. Access Control

Will locks be changed on all gates surrounding the property? How will premise access be handled? Normally, the majority of company vehicles are left within the plant main gate. The fewer the number of company vehicles crossing the picket line, the better. Nonunion employees who travel to work should travel in a fleet and cross the picket line at the same time. Other than those nonunion people working, who else may desire access to the property?

2. Escorts

Any union member desiring access to the property should be escorted by a protection officer

at all times. An employee may want access to the property for a variety of reasons (e.g., employee has quit and wants to remove tools). Any visitors who have authorization to access the property should be escorted by a protection officer from the property line to their contact on the property, and escorted off the property once business has been conducted.

3. Chain of Command

The protection officer should be fully conversant with the chain of command in existence during a strike. Normally, the site security supervisor or the security chief will be responsible for all security and fire watch responsibilities.

4. Police Assistance

The security department should notify the police of the labor situation ahead of time, should a strike appear inevitable. Arrangements should be made for the police to be present at the picket line during shift changes to avoid problems.

5. Communications

The main security gatehouse is normally designated as the command post because of its rapid response capabilities. This command post is occupied 24 hours a day by a protection officer.

6. Prestrike Vandalism

Employees may attempt to sabotage operations just prior to the strike commencing, especially if they know the company intends to continue production. The protection officer must be especially alert on patrol rounds for any indications of sabotage.

7. Fire Safety

The protection officer may have fire responsibilities in the absence of a fire crew or maintenance crew during a strike. These responsibilities may include inspecting extinguishers, testing sprinkler systems, and inspecting fire alarms, hoses, and fire equipment.

8. Building Security

The security department recovers keys from all but essential persons prior to the strike commencing. If there is any reason to believe that strikers have keys for exterior doors, then the locks should be changed. It is common for strikers to make locks nonfunctional by driving spikes into keyholes or filling the lock with glue. Plenty of spare locks should be available.

9. Security Lighting

All security lighting should be checked prior to a strike. All perimeter and yard lighting should be available.

10. Purchasing

The purchasing department ensures that there is an adequate supply of raw materials available for any work that is to be continued during a strike. Constant communications exist between purchasing and security in the event that special shipments may need access to the property.

11. Threatening Phone Calls

Frequently, strikers or their sympathizers will telephone threats to the company or to officials' homes. The protection officer should record such phone calls and be prepared to be part of a security investigation.

12. Crossing the Picket Line

The protection officer may be required to cross the picket line for a variety of reasons. The protection officer should keep in mind the following points when crossing a picket line:

- Cross the line only if necessary.
- Do not cross on foot.
- Try not to cross the line alone. Two witnesses to an incident are better than one.
- Move slowly and steadily in your vehicle, trying not to stop.
- Only stop when directly confronted by picketers who are in front of your vehicle.
- Don't leave the vehicle if stopped.
- Keep vehicle windows up and doors locked.
- Be cautious about verbal exchange with picketers. Be aware of the mood of the picketers.
- Observe and report any picket line infractions.

13. Picket Line Surveillance and Documentary Coverage

Surveillance of picket line activity is crucial during a strike to monitor and gather appropriate evidence that may be used in supporting company discipline imposed on an employee, supporting criminal charges, supporting or defending complaints about unfair labor practices, and supporting obtaining an injunction, which is a court order requiring a party to do or refrain from doing a particular act. For example, a company may obtain an injunction to try and limit the number of pickets on a picket line.

One of the primary functions of the protection officer during a strike is picket line surveillance. This surveillance should continue 24 hours a day for all or part of the strike. The protection officer should be trained in the use of both still and movie cameras with telescopic lenses to capture activity. The protection officer should also have a tape recorder to keep a running verbal account of picket line activity. If a tape recorder is not available, then a detailed written diary of events should be kept on at least an hour-by-hour basis. The following should be documented:

- Location of pickets (attach plan showing pickets by company property lines and gates) and whether pickets are on company property.
- Number of pickets, location (i.e., whether spread out or in a group) and description of their conduct.
- Time and place that picketing commenced and ended.
- Identity of pickets and union affiliation. License numbers of any vehicles at or near the picket line.
- Number, size, wording of placards, and general description.
- Conversations with pickets: Caution should be used. It is quite proper to ask the pickets their names, who sent them, how long the picket line will last, and its purpose. Relate conversations overheard between pickets or between pickets and other persons. Make notes of all conversations.
- Behavior of picket lines: Provide details of whether pickets are stationary or walking, whether talking to employees or other persons. Note any threats, threatening behavior, damage to property, acts of violence, and so on, and make notes. Provide details if any vehicles have been unable to enter or leave company property.
- Photographs: It is recommended that color photographs be taken with a Polaroid camera. Each should be marked on the reverse side with the name of the photographer and the date and time, with a brief explanation.
- Witnesses: Full names, addresses, and occupations of other people who have witnessed any illegal activity on the picket line should be recorded.

The role of the protection officer is essential prior to and during a strike. His/her role can be vital to the protection of company assets, especially during a strike.

SEARCHES

There is not much literature available on searches and labor relations for the protection officer. The protection officer should only conduct searches under the following conditions:

1. If an employee consents, a search can be conducted of his/her effects.
2. The employer or his/her representative, who is usually the protection officer, can conduct a search of an employee or his effects if there is an expressed term in the collective agreement. Also, a search can be conducted of an employee or his effects if there is an implied agreement or implied term. An implied term can be derived by the company developing a formal search policy that is practiced regularly, consistently, and in a nondiscriminatory manner.
3. If no expressed or implied term exists on employee searches in a collective agreement, the protection officer should have reasonable and probable grounds before conducting a search.

There may be some question as to why searches are conducted at every shift change at a plant or facility, but **remember, every company has a right to protect its assets.** A protection officer conducting searches of employees and their effects on a regular basis can help a company protect its assets in the following manner:

1. May reduce accident rates (alcohol- and drug-related).
2. May reduce company material loss through theft and through employees hoarding materials in their lockers.

3. May reduce the use or possession of contraband on company property.
4. May increase employee morale because employees will feel that the company is concerned about maintaining a safe and secure physical environment.
5. May develop employee awareness about theft. Regular searches conducted by protection officers deter employees from taking material off a property. Remember, the key to a good security is prevention, not apprehension.

EMPLOYEE MISCONDUCT AND DISHONESTY

There are many types of dishonesty and employee misconduct at the workplace that the protection officer should be involved in. The protection officer should be aware of these types of dishonesty and employee misconduct:

1. Employee theft
2. Employee fraud—falsification of employment records, falsification of time cards and employee rebates, or falsification of worker's compensation insurance claims
3. Sabotage
4. Conflict of interest—kickbacks, selling information
5. Fighting, assault
6. Alcohol and drug use
7. Insubordination
8. Sleeping on the job
9. Safety violations
10. Leaving work early
11. Horseplay

All of the above may merit some form of discipline. The protection officer should be aware of the variety of disciplinary actions available to his/her employer.

EMPLOYEE DISCIPLINE

The protection officer should be aware of the types of discipline available to his employer for these reasons:

- The type and severity of discipline imposed may depend on how thorough the protection officer's investigation is.
- The protection officer may be in a position to recommend the type of discipline to be imposed.
- Discipline is an effective deterrent in the asset protection program.

TYPES OF DISCIPLINE

1. **Verbal**. This type of discipline is given by an immediate supervisor where normally there is no documentation of the conversation.
2. **Written warning**. A formal warning is given by the immediate supervisor and placed in the employee's file as a record of discipline.
3. **Suspension**. This type of discipline is normally the first step toward discharge. The time off provides the employee an opportunity to think about the infraction(s) committed and whether the employee wishes to pursue employment with the company.
4. **Demotion**. This type of discipline is used infrequently. An employee may be removed from the job for discipline reasons or because of physical or emotional difficulties in performing the job.
5. **Termination or discharge**. This type of discipline is the most severe. Before terminating an employee, a company must consider the following factors:

   - Age of the employee
   - Company seniority
   - Marital status of the employee
   - Previous work record of the employee with the company

- Severity of the offense (e.g., extent of damage to equipment in case of negligence)
- Willingness of the employee to cooperate with the company investigators
- Whether or not the employee shows remorse
- Whether or not the offense was premeditated or a spur of the moment act
- Whether the discipline is in accordance with past practice (i.e., do all employees receive the same discipline for the same act?)

ARBITRATION

The protection officer may find himself involved in an arbitration case as a witness of a breach of company policy where discipline has been given. The union representing the penalized employee may feel that the discipline is too severe or unjust, thus taking the case to arbitration. An arbitrator acts as an impartial third party to determine whether the discipline was just. Both the company and the union reach agreement in choosing an arbitrator.

The arbitrator is not bound by formal rules of evidence, so the arbitration is less formal than courtroom proceedings. In an arbitration hearing, the onus is on the company to establish the existence of just cause. In other words, the company has to show good reason why an employee may have received the type and nature of discipline.

Remember: The protection officer could find himself going both to court and to arbitration over the same employee offense.

Interviews

The protection officer should keep in mind that a union representative should be provided if a witness or a suspect makes such a request. The protection officer may face accusations of harassment or unfair labor practices should a union representative not be provided.

SUMMARY

The protection officer must be aware of the union in existence at his/her plant or facility and the influence it may have on the following security functions: strikes, searches, employee misconduct and dishonesty, employee discipline, arbitration, and interviews.

SECURITY QUIZ

1. Labor relations include the employee/employer relations dealing with matters pertaining to which of the following activities:
   a. Strike parameters
   b. Lock out regulations
   c. Collective bargaining and associated activities
   d. None of the above
2. The role of the protection officer has an influence on the labor relations climate at any given company. Which of the following activities does the protection officer influence:
   a. Wildcat strikes
   b. Lawful strikes
   c. Lockouts
   d. All of the above
3. Which of the following is a legal move by management to put pressure on the unions:
   a. Lockout
   b. Legal strike
   c. Locked gate process
   d. A and C only
4. A wildcat strike is a legal strike.
   a. True
   b. False
5. Work stoppages as a result of labor relations difficulties will arise when union officials order production limitations.
   a. True
   b. False

6. The protection officer should be aware of the types of discipline available to his employer because:
   a. The protection officer may hand out discipline
   b. The protection officer will be disciplined if he doesn't know the types of discipline
   c. Discipline is an effective deterrent
   d. The protection officer should know what is going on
7. Which of the following is not illegal during a legal strike?
   a. Picketing of residences
   b. Obstructing highways
   c. Carrying placards
   d. Picketing within the premises
8. An incident of theft whereby an employee is discharged can become an issue in:
   a. Civil court
   b. Criminal court
   c. An arbitration hearing
   d. All of the above
9. The strike plan is designed and updated to eliminate problems that occur during a strike and provide guidelines for security and management.
   a. True
   b. False
10. When stopped at a picket line in your vehicle, you should:
    a. Cross the picket line on foot
    b. Roll down the window and demand that you be let through
    c. Remain in the vehicle and proceed with caution
    d. Unlock the windows and doors

UNIT VIII

RISK AND THREAT MANAGEMENT

CHAPTER

27

Security Risk Management

Kevin E. Peterson

CHAPTER OBJECTIVES

- Explain the basis for all protection functions, regardless of environment in which they are practiced

- Identify and define two key elements of security risk management

- Explain the risk management cycle/ process

- Reinforce the idea that the practice of risk management requires both a thorough risk assessment and an ongoing program of risk monitoring

- Provide the tools to apply security risk management strategies to assess a situation, develop a menu of feasible options, and recommend a realistic solution set to meet defined asset protection objectives

THE HISTORICAL BASIS FOR RISK MANAGEMENT

The idea of "risk" and "risk management" is not unique to the security field—in fact, it is relatively new to us. The idea probably originated in the financial industry, where risks can result in significant loss of money or missed opportunities to grow financial assets. In recent years, financial risk has been highlighted by major losses in worldwide financial markets and public scandals such as the Enron collapse (2001) and the Bernie Madoff fraud case (2008). In fact, Madoff's scheme has been described as "the biggest financial swindle in history" (Frank & Efrati, 2009).

Concern for managing risk is also critical in other fields such as business, science and technology, politics, and insurance. In reality, some degree of risk is inherent in almost any business decision. Should we develop a new product line? Establish a joint venture or partnership with a particular company? Manufacture or distribute our products in a different country or region of the world? Expand the business? Build a new facility? The answer to any one of these questions can result in tremendous growth for a company and its revenues—or it can mean disaster (in business terms).

If we think about these questions from our perspective, however, we can see that the answers usually have *security* risk implications as well. Because of this, it is extremely important that security professionals be included in discussions over important business or organizational decisions.

The same can be said of fields such as scientific research and development and the application of new technologies. Almost any program or project decision in these areas can have significant implications for the future— including security and asset protection issues. As an example, consider the selection among various ballistic missile defense technologies for the United States. This is clearly an issue of technology risk when comparing such diverse options as ground-based interceptors, space-based interceptors, the airborne laser and seaborne platforms. Besides the obvious factors of cost, schedule, and performance, each of these approaches also has security implications. Think of how to go about developing a security approach to protect the people, equipment, communications, and information associated with each of these options. This will probably show quite different security challenges and recommendations for each platform.

Finally, the insurance industry is almost entirely focused on the concept of "risk." In fact, one of the earliest uses of the term "risk manager" is attributed to companies that recognized the increasingly clear relationship between business practices and insurance costs in the 1950s (Thompson, 2003). The role of risk management in the insurance industry is further illustrated by the fact that in 1975, the American Society of Insurance Management changed its name to the Risk & Insurance Management Society (RIMS) (Hampton, 2007). Essentially, the insurance providers are taking on (or accepting) a portion of their policy holders' risk for a fee (their premiums). As we will discuss later, insurance is the most common example of "risk transfer," one of the five avenues of addressing security/asset protection risks.

WHAT IS SECURITY RISK MANAGEMENT?

So how do we (protection professionals) fit into the picture of risk management? As

mentioned in an article by Diana Thompson, a well-respected consultant in organizational risk management based in Australia:

> To most businesses, the concept of risk management is confined to financial aspects … but the risk game is fast changing … [now] covering everything from a computer meltdown to a terrorist attack.… (Thompson, 2003)

Today, risk management is a central concept in the fields of security, asset protection, and crime/loss prevention. Risk management principles are used to help us conserve our limited resources (in terms of time, effort, manpower, and money), apply the right solutions in the right places, and keep up with changes in our operational environment. Plus, as shown in the quote above, it keeps us attuned to the broad array of threats that we face in any type of organization.

TWO KEY ELEMENTS: ASSESSMENT AND MITIGATION

The practice of security risk management (SRM) begins with a thorough and well-thought-out risk assessment. Why? Because we cannot begin to answer questions until we know what the questions are—or solve problems until we know what the problems are. A good assessment process naturally leads directly into a risk mitigation strategy. These two key elements will be discussed further in this chapter and are mentioned at various points throughout this book with respect to specific protection applications.

Note: The following material is extracted from "Primer on Security Risk Management" and is used with permission.

Whether in the public or private sector, and whether dealing with traditional or cyber security (or both), asset protection practice is increasingly based on the principle of *risk management*. The concept is a perfect fit for the field of *asset protection*, since our primary objective is to *manage* risks by balancing the cost of protection measures with their benefit.

TAKING A STRATEGIC RISK MANAGEMENT APPROACH

Too often, organization leaders look for the "quick fix" to satisfy their security needs. They buy a popular security system or are convinced by a sales representative that a particular product or service is the all-encompassing answer to their protection needs. They are convinced that their critical assets are then completely safe without even asking what those assets are or what types of threats they face. This is a particular problem for small and medium-sized businesses, but it certainly could apply to any size enterprise.

Taking a "strategic approach" means basing the enterprise's asset protection practice on sound *planning, management, and evaluation*, and taking into consideration both the organization's mission and the environment in which it operates. A "strategy" should articulate—to the security professional and executive decision makers—*what* is being protected, *why* it's being protected and *how* it's being protected.

The National Infrastructure Protection Center (NIPC)[1] defines *risk management* as "a systematic and analytical process by which an organization identifies, reduces and controls its potential risks and losses." They further state that *risk management*:

- Identifies weaknesses in an organization or system
- Offers a rational and defendable method for making decisions about the expenditure of scarce resources and the selection of

cost-effective countermeasures to protect valuable assets
- Improves the success rate of an organization's security efforts by emphasizing the communication of risks and recommendations to the final decision-making authority
- Helps security professionals and key decision makers answer the question, "How much security is enough?"

(National Infrastructure Protection Center, 2002)

THE RISK MANAGEMENT PROCESS

The five components of the risk management process—which lead to a comprehensive asset protection strategy—are depicted in the accompanying diagram (Figure 27-1). The process begins by identifying realistic asset protection *objectives* and then conducting a comprehensive risk assessment (described below). This can be done at the enterprise-wide level and/or at the specific process or project level. Depending upon the nature of the business, it may be appropriate to do it at multiple levels.

Risk Management Process

FIGURE 27-1 The risk management cycle.

[1]With the establishment of the Department of Homeland Security (DHS) within the U.S. government, the responsibilities of the NIPC were redistributed between the DHS Information Analysis and Infrastructure Protection (IAIP) Directorate and the FBI's Cyber Division.

Assets. The first step in risk assessment is identification and valuation of assets. As Gardner asserts, "the first step in establishing [any] effective [asset protection] program involves identifying the businesses' assets" (Gardner, 1995). Although this is a step that is frequently overlooked, no effective security program can be implemented without a thorough understanding (on the part of both the asset owner *and* the security professional) of what is being protected—or *should* be protected. All three types of assets—tangible, intangible, and mixed—should be considered and incorporated into the risk assessment process. Too often, asset owners and security professionals focus exclusively on tangible assets or those which appear on the accountant's balance sheet.

Each component of the risk management process must be evaluated (gauged or rated) and this can be done either qualitatively or quantitatively. The value of assets is often expressed in dollar amounts, but assigning such a number is not always possible, particularly in the case of intangible and mixed assets.

This provides a natural lead into the debate over *qualitative* versus *quantitative* assessment approaches. Each approach has inherent pros and cons.

> *Qualitative analysis* is any approach which does not use numbers or numeric values to describe the risk components. Generally, comparative terms such as "critical," "high," "medium," "low," and "negligible" may be used to gauge the asset value and levels of risk components and risk itself.

> *Quantitative analysis* is any approach which uses numeric measures to describe the value of assets or the level (severity or probability) of threats, vulnerabilities, impact, or loss events. It can vary from simple scale ratings (e.g., 1 to 5) to sophisticated statistical methods and mathematical formulas.

Many executive decision makers prefer information to be summarized in charts and graphs which can display a great deal of data in a concise manner. (One example is shown in Figure 27-2.) This is the strongest argument for using a quantitative approach. The other major advantage is the ability to automatically manipulate the data using computer programs and algorithms. Qualitative methods, by contrast, are generally simpler and quicker to use, and often provide results that are just as meaningful as numeric calculations.

Among the factors to consider in determining asset value are immediate response and

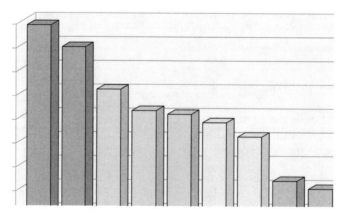

FIGURE 27-2   Most prevalent risks by severity level.

recovery costs, investigation costs and replacement costs, and indirect costs (which are often overlooked in the overall assessment). Indirect costs may include things such as:

✓ temporary leased facilities	✓ recruiting/staffing costs for permanent workforce
✓ equipment rental/ purchase	✓ increased security costs (temporary or permanent)
✓ alternative suppliers/ vendors	✓ increased communications capabilities
✓ alternative shippers/ logistics support	✓ data recovery/IT system (Information Technology)
✓ temporary warehousing facilities	✓ administrative support
✓ special employee benefits	✓ increased travel
✓ counseling/employee assistance	✓ marketing/public relations efforts
✓ loss of market share (temporary or permanent)	✓ emergency/continuity plan revamps
✓ decreased employee productivity	
✓ increased insurance premiums	
✓ temporary workforce/ staffing	

In addition, intangible and mixed assets must be considered even though they are generally very difficult to value. Executive decision makers need to be educated with respect to intangible and mixed assets. Although it is often difficult or impossible to place a specific dollar value on intangible assets, they are certainly subject to loss events and can have a significant impact on the organization's vitality and mission performance.

Threat. Enterprises—regardless of size, location or mission—face a wide variety of threats that fall into three categories: *intentional, natural,* and *inadvertent*. A comprehensive—and hence more meaningful—threat assessment will consider all three categories of threats.

Since September 11, 2001, it is common to focus heavily (sometimes almost exclusively) on the terrorist threat when conducting corporate or organizational risk analyses. However, terrorism is only one aspect of one category of threats that should be considered. This tendency is not unique. In the mid-1980's, for example, there was an overemphasis on the theft of advanced technology. At other times, the security community has focused too heavily on white collar crime, cyberattacks, natural disasters, or other calamities.

A balanced approach to threat assessment is necessary. Of course, some types of threats will be more prevalent at certain times and in certain places. Long-term asset protection strategies, however, must be based on a realistic, full scope, and balanced threat assessment. According to security expert and author Ira Winkler, "accurate assessment of the level of threat against your organization is critical to the success of your ... security plan." "Threat is an essential factor in your risk reduction formula, and you must consider it carefully. If you don't, you'll simply be flying blind when it comes to prioritizing countermeasures ..." (Winkler, 1997, p. 37).

In terms of evaluating levels of threat consider the following three primary categories:

Intentional Threats—Evaluation of intentional threats is based on identification and study of potential adversaries. Assessors should think "outside the box" when listing potential adversaries. For example, the most obvious adversaries in a particular case may be international terrorist organizations, organized crime, or aggressive business competitors. Other important potential adversaries, however, may be activist groups (such as environmental rights activists or other special interest groups)—and their threats could be easily overlooked. The identification and assessment of adversaries are growing challenges today based on the post—Cold War environment, the global nature of our economy, worldwide demographic shifts, and the emergence of a far more asymmetric (less conventional and more difficult to define) nature of modern-day threats.

In most cases, adversaries can be judged according to their *capabilities* to cause a loss event (or attack) and their *intentions* to do so. Among the sources of information on adversary capabilities and intentions are past history, organization rhetoric, public pronouncements, other open sources, internal communications (newsletters, websites, etc.), law enforcement reports, automated databases, and threat assessment professionals.

Natural Threats—Rather than adversary capabilities and intentions, natural threats are typically evaluated using historical trends and statistics. Long-term data is generally collected on weather and other natural hazards for specific geographical areas, terrains, and environments. In some cases, data has been assembled on natural hazard effects for particular industry sectors or facility types. Although this data provides extremely useful planning information, assessors must recognize that the unexpected can, and usually does, occur. Therefore, comprehensive contingency planning and at least some degree of all-hazard preparedness are strongly recommended by most professionals.

Inadvertent Threats—Perhaps the most overlooked or neglected threats are inadvertent threats. These include accidents, errors, and omissions. Security expert and author Ira Winkler put it best when he wrote that "… the biggest threat to U.S. corporations is human error" and "People make mistakes, and those mistakes are the most likely things to hurt you" (Winkler, 1997, p. 39).

Another key consideration—which is a subset of the inadvertent threat—is that of peripheral threats—for example, a threat that is targeted at a neighboring facility but that may have a major impact on the post operation. The effects of peripheral threats can include utility interruptions, required evacuations, closure of access routes to the facility, unwanted attention or traffic at the facility, full or partial operation

shutdowns, productivity disruptions, and environmental effects (e.g., smoke, debris, water, or chemical runoff, etc.).

Inadvertent threats are the most difficult to predict and prepare for. Although, to some degree, the nature of the workforce, operations, or other environmental factors can influence the level of the inadvertent threat, there is usually little or no historical data to use for planning purposes. The best defenses are preparation, education and awareness, and realization that the threat exists.

Vulnerability. The most common view of "vulnerability" is a security *weakness* or *problem*. Although this can be the case, we must also recognize that some vulnerabilities are simply existing conditions or business practices which support mission accomplishment. For example, engaging in sales by e-commerce can be viewed as a vulnerability, but it may also be an essential way of conducting business for a particular company. One concise definition of "vulnerability" is "a weakness or organizational practice that may facilitate or allow a threat to be implemented or increase the magnitude of a loss event" (ASIS International, 2007, p. 8).

One important difference between a *threat* and a *vulnerability* is that a vulnerability is a characteristic of the organization or facility. As such, it is generally something over which the organization can exercise at least some degree of control. Threats, by contrast, are usually outside the control of the organization.

Vulnerabilities can be evaluated in different ways, but one common approach is to measure them in terms of *observability* and *exploitability*.

- *Observability* is the ability of an adversary to see and identify a vulnerability. For example, a hole in a chain-link perimeter fence is likely observable by a potential adversary, whereas an inoperable CCTV (Closed-Circuit Television) camera is not.
- *Exploitability* is the ability of the adversary to take advantage of the vulnerability once they become aware of it.

In assessing natural threats, we can still use the concepts of observability and exploitability, although from a slightly different perspective. The observability factor would essentially be reversed and refer to *our* ability to observe—or become aware of, track, etc.—the oncoming threat (e.g., storm). This involves mechanisms for early warning and notification of the impending threat. By contrast, exploitability would be expressed in terms of the capability of a particular threat to cause damage specific to the facility, mission, or organization.

Using this observability/exploitability approach, AP (Asset Protection) professionals can assess and develop plans to mitigate vulnerabilities both in the long-term (strategic) and immediate (tactical) time frames.

For inadvertent threats, the observability/exploitability approach is again slightly different. In this case, we measure our vulnerabilities via two questions:

- Are we aware of the vulnerabilities?
- Are the particular vulnerabilities subject to relevant inadvertent threats?

Again, both the inadvertent threats and associated vulnerabilities are generally the most difficult for any organization to identify and measure. This should not, however, be used as an excuse for neglecting this aspect of the overall risk posture.

Risk Analysis. In this step, the assessor puts all of the information on assets, threats, and vulnerabilities together, and then considers the potential impact or consequences of a loss event. In all risk analyses, but particularly in quantitative ones, it is advisable to determine the evaluation levels (for threat, vulnerability, and impact) by committee. In other words, assessments should be performed by a multidisciplinary team of subject matter experts[2] in order to reach credible and justifiable numbers as input to the analysis. Justifying the numbers is the area that assessors are most often challenged when reporting their risk-analysis results to clients, executives, and decision makers.

There are many effective and time-tested approaches to calculating risk results once the numbers (evaluation levels) have been identified.

Risk analysis results should be presented to the client or decision maker in a manner which assists them in understanding the data and making decisions. This includes placing the identified risks in a priority order or into priority categories to help show, from the assessor's perspective, which risks should be addressed first.

A final note about risk analysis, as discussed in a 2000 *Security Management* article entitled "Truth & Consequences," we need to consider low-probability/high-consequence risks as well as those that are most likely to occur in our workplace (Garcia, 2000). Many corporate executives and decision makers only want to hear about the risks that represent the highest probability of occurrence—that's where they want to expend their resources. We must also, however, give serious consideration to potential losses that, although they are not highly likely to occur, will result in very significant consequences (mission impact) if they do occur. Examples of such risks are terrorist attacks and catastrophic workplace violence incidents. Again, the objective of a comprehensive asset protection strategy is a rational balance between the focus on high-probability-of-occurrence risks and low-probability/high-consequence risks.

LIKELIHOOD VERSUS CONSEQUENCE SCATTER CHARTING

Another method for considering organizational risk is the use of a "Likelihood versus Consequence" matrix, sometimes referred to as

---

[2]Team members and the required expertise must be tailored to individual assessment. Examples of team member expertise may include Physical Security, IT Security, Information Protection, Personnel Security, Technical Security, Operations, Audit, and Safety.

a "scatter chart." Conceptually, any organization must consider the question of *likelihood versus consequence* (impact) for their relevant risk or potential loss events. Figure 27-3 illustrates this issue by way of four quadrants.

Logically, a risk (potential loss event) located in Quadrant 1 would require the most urgent **attention and resource allocation. These risks have a high likelihood of** occurring and, if they do, will have significant consequences or impact on the organization. The consequences may be in the form of increased operating costs, damage to reputation/public trust, decreased safety or efficiency, loss of personnel resources, loss of, or damage to, facilities/equipment, or loss of critical information.

The priority of addressing risks will generally decrease with each successive quadrant. Many organizations, however, neglect the fact that Quadrant 2 warrants significant attention. Risks which lie in this quadrant have a low-to-moderate likelihood of occurrence, but a high consequence of impact if they do occur. Examples of risks that typically fall into Quadrant 2 are dramatic workplace violence incidents and terrorist attacks.

Risks that fall into Quadrants 3 and 4 should not be automatically discounted. Various events (reorganization, expansion, adding new missions, change in neighbors, change in threat level, etc.) can easily move some risks from one quadrant to another. For this reason, security and management officials must periodically review the risk posture as well as operational and administrative changes that may influence the "likelihood versus consequence" equation.

The likelihood versus consequence scatter chart technique may be used in combination with a traditional risk analysis method. This often provides a more comprehensive and accurate picture of the risk environment (and contributing factors) than the use of one method alone.

Risk management is a cyclical process—one that must regularly evaluate changes in assets, threats, vulnerabilities, and loss event impact. These factors are in constant flux and must be deliberately and carefully monitored to ensure that the asset protection strategy and its components remain both effective and efficient.

Following a thorough risk analysis, the next step is to recommend a suite of solutions or "mitigation measures" to address the risks that have been identified and prioritized. By "suite," we mean a series of measures that work together and comprise elements of a deliberate plan—or a "mitigation strategy."

THE FOUNDATION OF A MITIGATION STRATEGY

Taking a truly *strategic* approach helps avoid major mistakes such as knee-jerk reactions to incidents/events, introducing inefficiencies, over-relying on vendors or salespeople for solutions, and serious resource misallocations. Any risk mitigation strategy should consider three underlying or foundational concepts: the five avenues to address risk, the "Four D's," and layered security (defense in depth). The best and most effective protection programs are based on strategies that integrate the philosophies embodied in all three of these foundational concepts.

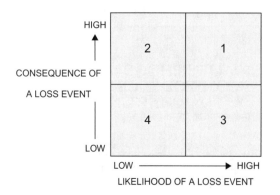

FIGURE 27-3 Likelihood versus consequence considerations.

THE FIVE AVENUES TO ADDRESS RISK

The concept of the five avenues to address risk is directly related to the comprehensive risk management approach. It contends that there are five distinct avenues we can follow to address identified risks to assets. Generally, a comprehensive asset protection strategy incorporates a well-thought-out combination of all or most of these avenues. The five avenues are risk avoidance, risk transfer, risk spreading, risk reduction, and risk acceptance (Figure 27-4).

The following diagram illustrates the application of "the five avenues to address risk." It begins with an initial consideration of risk avoidance then proceeds to three additional avenues of addressing risk (transfer, spreading and reduction). Ideally, these three avenues are employed in concert with one another as part of a comprehensive strategy. Finally, Figure 27-5 shows that any residual risk must be acknowledged and accepted.

Risk avoidance—this is the most direct avenue for dealing with risk. It simply involves removing any opportunity for the risk to cause a loss event. Many security professionals consider *risk avoidance* impractical—and therefore, essentially irrelevant—since the measures required to completely avoid risk will essentially negate the enterprise's ability to perform its mission or accomplish its objectives.

Risk spreading—this very effective practice avoids putting "all your eggs in the same basket." The best example of this is geographically distributing an organization's assets. If a company maintains an inventory of high-value merchandise, for example, and stored all of it in a single warehouse, the potential loss could be 100% of the merchandise if that warehouse experienced a major loss event (e.g., theft, flood, fire, etc.). If, however, this merchandise were distributed among three geographically separated warehouse facilities, the loss event would result in a potential loss of only about one-third of their total inventory. This simplified example provides an excellent illustration of the concept of *risk spreading*. Another good example of risk spreading is the practice of off-site backups for computer data. By storing a copy of this highly valuable "asset" in another location, a relatively quick recovery from the loss of original data can be effected. Risk spreading can increase the cost of an operation, but the generally modest costs are usually offset by the decrease in risk to critical assets.

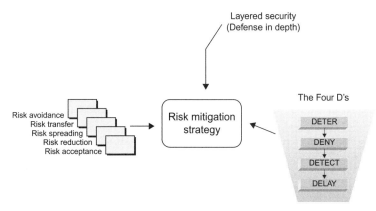

FIGURE 27-4 Five avenues to address risk.

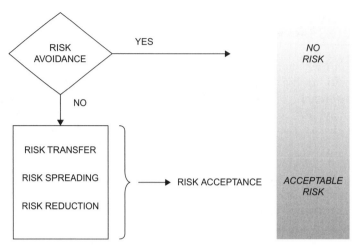

FIGURE 27-5   Five avenues to address risk. (© 2006 *Innovative Protection Solutions LLC*)

Risk transfer—the typical example of risk transfer is the purchase of insurance. Although not commonly viewed as a part of the traditional "security" function, insurance is generally a key element of an organization's (or individual's) risk management strategy. Another form of risk transfer is the act of making oneself a less attractive target than other potential targets (such as neighboring facilities). Although it may not be considered "polite," this is a way of "transferring" a portion of the risk to a neighbor. In some cases, a portion of risk can be transferred to suppliers, vendors, or others through contract clauses or other types of formal agreements.

Risk reduction—essentially, risk reduction involves any security measures or other actions that would reduce the risk to assets. The most common and direct means of reducing risk, in this sense, are actions that decrease the *vulnerability* in the risk equation (whereas risk spreading and risk transfer primarily decrease the *impact* of a loss event).

Common risk reduction mechanisms are security measures, policy enforcement, and employee education and awareness, as well as financial and legal positioning.

Risk acceptance—after all risk spreading, risk transfer, and risk reduction measures have been implemented, some risk will remain since it is virtually impossible to eliminate all risk (except as discussed under risk avoidance). This risk is termed "residual risk." One example of risk acceptance is the setting of shrinkage tolerance levels in the retail industry. In addition, some organizations established a formal process for risk acceptance. For example, the U.S. Department of Defense requires a "Designated Approval Authority" to sign a document indicating that they accept the residual risk in IT (Information Technology) systems under their jurisdiction after they have reviewed the threat and the protective measures in place. In fact, this recommendation is part of the IT System Accreditation Process across all U.S. government agencies.[3]

---

[3]"Accreditation is a process whereby a Designated Approval Authority (DAA) or other authorizing management official authorizes an IT system to operate for a specific purpose using a defined set of safeguards at an acceptable level of risk" (National Institute of Standards and Technology, 2002, p. D-1).

Carefully considering the five avenues to address risk is an excellent exercise and can be very effective at helping (protection) professionals and management to think outside the box in terms of multiple approaches to protecting assets.

"THE FOUR D'S"

The "Four D's" is a classic principle in the crime prevention community and applies equally well to almost any aspect of asset protection or security risk management. It nicely complements its "cousin" concepts: the five avenues to address risk and layered security (defense in depth) (see Figure 27-6). The "Four D's" are *deter*, *deny*, *detect*, and *delay*. Under this concept, the first objective in protecting assets is to *deter* any type of attack or attempt by a potential adversary.

The second objective is to *deny* the potential adversary access to the target (or asset). This is typically achieved through traditional access controls and other physical, personnel, or technical security measures.

The next objective—should deterrence and denial fail in whole or part—is to *detect* the attack or situation. This can be done in a variety of ways, traditionally using surveillance and intrusion detection systems, human observation, or even a management system that will immediately identify or flag shortages or inconsistencies (e.g., an inventory tracking system which reports out-of-tolerance conditions).

Finally, once an attack or attempt is in progress, the intention should be to *delay* the perpetrators enough to either convince them to give up/terminate the attempt or to allow an appropriate security/law enforcement response to the scene.

Like the other foundational concepts, the "Four D's" can be applied in a traditional security environment or in the logical security sense with respect to IT systems. Such tools as access control, authentication, encryption, intrusion detection systems, anomaly reporting, firewalls,

FIGURE 27-6 The Four D's of crime prevention.

port management, and content filtering work together to support the concept of the "Four D's" in the world of cybersecurity.

LAYERED SECURITY (DEFENSE IN DEPTH)

A closely related concept is that of layered security, which is also known as *defense in depth*. Again, this principle applies across the board to physical, logical, and converged environments. Defense in depth recognizes that a single protection measure is not adequate, and that a series of well-planned and complementary levels of security measures comprise an effective asset protection scheme.

The ASIS International Glossary of Security defines "layered security" as:

> A physical security approach that requires a criminal to penetrate or overcome a series of security layers before reaching the target. The layers might be perimeter barriers; building or area protection with locks, CCTV, and guards; and point and trap protection using safes, vaults, and sensors. (*ASIS International, August 2006*)

In a more comprehensive sense, however, the concept can include personnel security, technical security, policies and procedures, security education, facility layout, traffic patterns, and even—in the case of shopping centers, for example—Neighborhood Watch programs.

In short, asset protection should involve a comprehensive strategy, not a combination of piecemeal elements (officers, CCTV, access control systems, etc.). Developing such strategies, particularly in today's complex global environment, requires both broad expertise and a very thorough thought process based on underlying concepts such as those described above.

MITIGATION MEASURES

A comprehensive strategy incorporates all aspects of protective measures that are appropriate to the environment based on its mission, nature, physical attributes, and risk assessment results. As mentioned, these should be viewed as part of a *suite* of solutions. Among the families of measures to be considered are:

- Physical security (barriers, locks, access control, etc.)
- Electronic security systems
- Security officers
- Policy and procedure/business practices
- Employee training and awareness
- Layout, design, and architecture
- CPTED (Crime prevention through environmental design)
- Contracts and clauses
- Legal and financial posturing
- Insurance
- Personnel security
- Technical security (IT and non-IT)
- Travel security
- Liaison and relationships
- Business continuity and crisis preparedness

(end of extract from "Primer on Security Risk Management")

TAILORING A PROGRAM TO THE SETTING AND ENVIRONMENT

Any risk-mitigation strategy should be tailored to the specific industry setting, location, and organization being protected. There are important factors that affect how protection measures will be implemented, how well they will be accepted, and how effective they will be. Even within subsets of industry sectors, fine distinctions exist that can significantly impact the effectiveness of protection strategies and individual protection measures. For example, there are very significant differences between a worldwide intermodal cargo shipping firm and an urban subway system, even though both are components of the transportation industry.

Different industry sectors and subsectors are subject to different risks in terms of the type, extent, and nature and may view the risks themselves, as well as recommended mitigation strategies, very differently. In addition, factors such as the type of people who are employed, the nature of the work, working hours, type of facility, location, and even management style may affect the way protection measures work—or even if they will work.

In today's global environment, we also need to consider how the components of our mitigation strategy will operate in countries around the world where our organization may have facilities, people, joint ventures, or partner firms. Laws, language, culture, treaties, and international agreements all impact relevant aspects of the threat as well as the applicability of security measures and other risk management tools.

THE ROLE OF THE PROFESSIONAL PROTECTION OFFICER

According to Karim Vellani, a well-respected professional security consultant and author, "risk is the most significant factor that drives the deployment and redeployment of security forces" (Vellani, 2007, p. 234). This statement seems simple, but is very profound. It attests to the extremely significant role of security risk management as well as its direct application to professional security services and security officers. Risk management principles can and should be applied at three levels related to modern-day professional protection officers. Each level is briefly described below.

Individual Officer

Every security officer makes decisions on a wide variety of levels during their shift. They range from mundane to life-and-death. Some of these decisions include:

- Whether to report an incident/information, or note it and hold it
- How to respond to a call for service
- How to deal with an aggressive individual
- How to word a report
- How in-depth to investigate a situation
- Who to call in a particular nonroutine situation that is not specifically outlined in post orders
- Whether or not to grant access to a particular individual or to allow entry of a package
- Whether or not to draw a weapon
- Whether to use nonlethal force
- Whether or not to call for backup
- Whether or not to overlook an ethical lapse

In every case, the best decisions are based on a sound risk management process. Whether this is a formal, documented process laid out in a neat flowchart, or an instantaneous thought process that yields a split-second decision, risk management *should* be at play.

By integrating risk management into each security professional's mind-set and normal business practices, it will become completely natural—a part of the way they think and act. More effective decision making will result in both strategic and tactical situations, and asset protection—people, property, and information—will be enhanced.

Customer or Client

As implied in Vellani's statement, risk management should be used to make decisions regarding the deployment of security resources—including officers and staff. Decisions such as the best mix of proprietary and contract officers, appropriate officer functions, patrol procedures, the contents and format of post orders, arming, standard procedures, and security systems will be better informed. Risk management can be applied in every aspect of an organization's asset protection program planning, management, and evaluation. It can also be used as the basis for interaction between the client and security service providers to support planning, training, evaluation, reporting, and liaison.

Risk management helps avoid imprudent security. An example of this was revealed during a series of security risk assessments shortly after the September 11 terrorist attacks. Consultants visited numerous locations of a large news organization with sites nationwide. The sites ranged from large news bureaus in major cities to small communications/server sites manned by only a few people.

After September 11, the corporate executives ordered that *every* site be staffed with a security officer—and they immediately (and massively) expanded the scope of their existing security services contract. During the assessment, consultants asked each of these new security officers about their role and function in support of the client. Without exception, the officers had no idea why they were there or what they were supposed to do. A number of officers stated, "They just told me to stand here." Now that IS imprudent security! However, it is not that uncommon and is exactly the type of dangerous and wasteful situation that can be prevented by applying sound risk management principles and having those discussions between the client and the security professionals.

Another important decision-making process which can be formed by effective risk management thinking, regards the proper mix of security technology, security forces, and other solutions. Efficiency and effectiveness of security services in typical threat environments can not only save resources but also save lives.

Security Services Provider (Security Company)

Service providers can base their core business model on risk management principles. This will assist in determining the types of services to offer, staff composition, market objectives, industry sectors to emphasize, and many other corporate functions. It should also be incorporated in business processes such as the quality assurance program and training program (for corporate staff, officers, and others). For example, Vellani recommends using benchmarking as a key quality control function to help set baseline performance measures for officer assessment (Vellani, 2007, p. 247). The practical applications for risk management in the security field are almost limitless. Be creative. It will help distinguish the security company as a forward-looking and high-performance provider.

In terms of client interaction, use risk management as a foundation for discussions regarding customer requirements, staffing, and services. Not only will it result in more effective security services for the client but also may lead to an expanded role for the security provider.

EMERGING TRENDS

The practice of security risk management is being increasingly formalized here and around the world. Examples of this include various protocols established by the U.S. Department of Homeland Security (DHS) in the wake of the September 11, 2001, terrorist attacks, and additional work performed by the Department of Energy. These protocols have been expanded and adapted to specific elements of our critical infrastructure such as chemical plants and water supplies.

On a global scale, international standards are focusing more and more on security practices and taking a risk management approach. One example is ISO 27005 (2008), an international standard for Information Security Risk Management. This standard is based largely on previous work done primarily in Australia and Great Britain.

Other standards being developed include an All Hazards Risk Management Standard and a first-ever ANSI (American National Standards Institute) Standard on Organizational Resilience.

Although there is a lot of work going on around the world—and being applied to many different environments, all of the guidelines, protocols and standards are closely aligned with the basic security risk management model presented in this chapter. Risk management principles will become even more important in the future as the threats we face are increasingly ambiguous, while at the same time security resources (such as budgets and manpower) continue to be tight.

SUMMARY

Risk management is a critical process that touches every aspect of organizational asset protection as well as the activities of the professional protection officer. There are many specific and formalized models—even some sophisticated computer models—for risk management, but all are based on a basic "asset-threat-vulnerability-impact" model. The simple objective is "smart security decisions," whether it is how to structure a huge multi-national corporation's security function or how to word an incident report.

Every protection professional should become intimately familiar with the concepts of security risk management—and incorporate them into their mind-set and business practices at all levels.

References

ASIS International. (August 2006). *International Glossary of security terms.* <http://www.asisonline.org/library/glossary/index.xml>.

ASIS International. (2007). *Information asset protection guideline*, ASIS GDL IAP 05 2007.

Frank, R., & Efrati, A. (2009). "Evil" Madoff gets 150 years in epic fraud. *Wall Street Journal*, June 30.

Garcia, M. L. (2000, June). Truth & consequences. *Security Management*, 44–48.

Gardner, R. A. (1995). CPP, "Small business: Reducing the risk." <www.crimewise.com/>.

Hampton, J. J. (2007, October 8). 40 Years of risk management highlights start with the birth of the profession. *Business Insurance*, *41*(41), 26.

National Infrastructure Protection Center. (2002, November). *Risk management: An essential guide to protecting critical assets.*

Peterson, K. (March 2009). *Primer on security risk management, a white paper* (draft). Washington, DC.

Thompson, D. (2003, June/July). Risk management—a brief history. *Business and financial S*, pp. 30–32.

Vellani, K. (2007). *Strategic security management.* Burlington, MA: Butterworth-Heinemann.

Vesper, J. (2006). An incomplete history of risk management. www.pda.org/bookstore in *Risk assessment and risk management in the pharmaceutical industry: Clear and simple.*

Winkler, I. (1997). *Corporate espionage.* Roseville, CA: Prima Publishing.

SECURITY QUIZ

1. The terms "threat" and "risk" can be used interchangeably; for example, a "threat assessment" is the same as a "risk assessment."
   a. True
   b. False

2. The concept of "risk management" originated within the security profession.
   a. True
   b. False

3. Because vulnerabilities are actually a characteristic of the organization or facility, they are:
   a. The risk factor over which the organization has the most control
   b. Impossible to accurately assess by an outside consultant
   c. The risk factor that is most expensive to correct
   d. The only risk factor that can be influenced by the organization

4. According to "Primer on Security Risk Management," the primary categories of threats are (circle all correct answers):
   a. Criminal
   b. Intentional
   c. Inadvertent
   d. Terrorist
   e. Natural

5. In a scatter chart used for risk analysis, which quadrant represents a "high-likelihood/high-consequence" risk?
   a. Quadrant 1
   b. Quadrant 2
   c. Quadrant 3
   d. Quadrant 4

6. In order to effectively mitigate risks, a security professional should:
   a. Limit their strategy to using proven security measures only
   b. Assess all possible threats to the organization
   c. Apply a protection strategy that employs a suite of solutions
   d. Ensure that management is aware of existing vulnerabilities

7. Buying insurance is one example of:
   a. Risk spreading
   b. Risk transfer
   c. Risk avoidance
   d. Risk reduction

8. Which one of the following is not one of the underlying concepts on which a

risk mitigation strategy should be
based?

   a. The five avenues to address risk
   b. The "Four D's"
   c. Layered security
   d. Quantitative analysis

9. Risk management is a critical process that
   touches every aspect of organizational
   asset protection—and the activities of the
   professional protection officer.

   a. True
   b. False

10. Service providers should not base their
    core business model on risk management
    principles.

    a. True
    b. False

28

Emergency Planning

Ernest G. Vendrell and Scott A. Watson

CHAPTER OBJECTIVES

- Explore the scope of emergency management in the United States
- Look at the potential impact that emergencies can have on people and organizations
- Explain emergency management as a critical organizational function
- Describe how applying effective emergency management principles can help to stabilize a serious incident
- Emphasize the importance of hazard identification, vulnerability analysis, and risk assessment
- List the many internal and external stakeholders that will be involved in times of crisis
- Explore how effective communication leads to coordination and collaboration among emergency responders

INTRODUCTION

The word "emergency" may conjure up images of epic but rare events such as the

September 11, 2001, terrorist attacks on New York City and the Pentagon, Hurricane Katrina's landfall in the Gulf Coast, or the seasonal wildfires that sweep through California and other western states. While all of the aforementioned events are correctly classified as emergency situations, in a broader sense an event does not need to be on such a large scale to be classified as an emergency. The fact is that emergencies happen every day and in all types of environments. While not all emergency situations are of the same scale, they have a number of things in common.

1. **An emergency situation impacts people:** Emergency situations increase the risk of death or injury and may result in the need for long-term counseling for those impacted by the event. Proactive organizations engage in extensive pre-planning to mitigate injury and loss of life, as well as to effectively respond to the psychological needs of those directly touched by the event.
2. **An emergency situation disrupts normal operations:** Normal organizational activities are impacted by emergencies. Injured people can't perform their normal duties, damaged

equipment cannot properly function, and evacuated facilities do not produce goods or services. Proactive organizations build redundancies into their response and recovery plans. These redundancies mitigate disruptions and serve to speed an organization's recovery.

3. **An emergency situation impacts the local community:** Those in the local community who rely on goods or services produced by the affected organization, are personally impacted when the normal operations are disrupted. Proactive organizations have plans in place to mitigate the impact of these disruptions on communities.

4. **An emergency situation stretches resources:** In an emergency, additional resources will be needed to handle immediate response needs, the needs of those served by the organization, and initial preparations for long-term recovery. The need to address all of these issues stretches resources. Proactive organizations will make arrangements to obtain needed equipment, supplies, and additional response personnel in advance.

5. **An emergency situation will receive a postmortem analysis:** In this era of instant global communications, the response to an emergency is likely to draw both internal and external scrutiny. This scrutiny is often manifested as a sort of referendum on the quality of the organization's leadership (Knight & Pretty, 1996). As a result, the quality of the response to an emergency impacts long-term organizational recovery. Proactive organizations engage in a regimen of continual planning and exercising of their response plans; they also train key personnel on how to respond to media, governmental, and public inquiries (Figure 28-1).

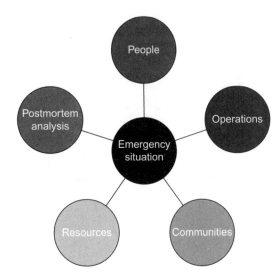

FIGURE 28-1 The wide impact that emergencies can have on people, organizations, and communities.

TYPES OF POTENTIAL EMERGENCIES

Given the importance of planning for and responding to emergency situations, the professional protection officer must be prepared to deal with a multitude of emergency situations. These situations include, but are not limited to, the following (Figure 28-2):

1. **Medical Events and Accidents:** Medical events and accidents resulting in injury are common emergencies at all organizations. All professional protection officers should be trained in at least basic first aid and CPR. Depending on the specific requirements of the organization, additional training may include the use of automatic external defibrillators (AED), or training as a first responder or emergency medical technician (EMT).

2. **Fires and Evacuations:** Fire and smoke can quickly sweep through a building, resulting in injury or death of people and significant damage to property. The professional protection officer must be confident in his or her ability to facilitate an orderly evacuation

Natural Hazards
Floods
Earthquakes
Hurricanes
Tornadoes
Wildfires
Tsunamis/Tidal waves
Blizzards
Droughts
Avalanches
Technological Hazards
Fires
Hazardous materials incidents
Nuclear accidents
Terrorism
Weapons of mass destruction
Civil unrest

FIGURE 28-2 List of various natural hazards and technological hazards. *(Haddow, Bullock, & Coppola, 2008)*

of the facility according to the organization's response plans. In addition, basic familiarity with local fire regulations, as well as any equipment that is on site and that the officer has been trained to use (such as fire extinguishers and self-contained breathing apparatus [SCBA]), is critical.

3. **Shelter in Place and Lockdown Incidents:** Hazardous material (HAZMAT) events, such as a chemical spill, or acts of armed violence, may result in the need to shelter or lock down personnel inside a facility for their own protection. The professional protection officer must be familiar with his or her organization's shelter in place procedures, and lockdown/active shooter protocols. In addition, familiarity with electronic access control systems, and a working knowledge

of facilities, systems, is helpful in such situations.

4. **Bomb Threats and Suspicious Packages:** Bomb threats and suspicious packages occur at many facilities. While most of these incidents turn out to be harmless, they all must be taken with the utmost seriousness. In the aftermath of the September 11, 2001, terrorist attacks, a series of highly publicized incidents took place in which media representatives and public officials received packages containing anthrax (Shane, 2008). In the case of the Unabomber, package bombs were sent to university researchers (FBI, 2008). In other instances, judges and corporate executives have been targeted (Carlson, Shannon, & Winbush, 1990; Elliot, 1994). Bombs and suspicious packages have even been sent as a result of ongoing domestic disputes. In order to be effective at responding to such issues, the professional protection officer must have detailed knowledge of their organization's response plan, as well as training on how to recognize suspicious packages and utilize a bomb threat checklist.

5. **Civil Disobedience:** Civil disobedience can take place as a result of labor disputes, political unrest, environmental protests, racial tensions, and a host of other controversial issues. Given the complex and interdependent nature of modern society, an organization should not be directly involved in controversial activities to avoid becoming a target. Financial firms have been targeted due to investments they made in companies that perform controversial activities. Biotechnology companies, that do not perform tests on animals, have been targeted by animal rights groups because of a perception that they engage in such activities. The professional protection officer must be familiar with the many types of threats that may arise out of actual or perceived controversial activities in which the organization they serve may be involved.

6. **Power Outages:** All organizations have power necessities and all organizations eventually experience a power outage. When the power goes out, lights, machinery, and HVAC systems all come to a halt. The professional protection officer must be prepared to deal with safety issues that arise as a result of a power outage. Many organizations have emergency batteries and generator back-ups. The professional protection officer should be familiar with how these systems operate.

7. **Disasters:** Disasters, whether natural or technological, pose a threat to all organizations. Natural disasters include such events such as a tornado, or hurricane, blizzard, wildfire, earthquake, flood, tidal wave, and a host of other naturally occurring phenomena. Technological disasters include such events as explosions, collapses, HAZMAT incidents, and industrial fires. The professional protection officer should be familiar with the potential impacts of natural and technological disasters and how those disasters may impact the organization they serve.

8. **Terrorist Actions:** Terrorist acts can include bombings, armed assaults, kidnapping, sabotage, hostage-taking, and a host of other serious incidents. While the probability that an act of terrorism will occur at a given site on any given day is low, the impact of such actions can have serious and long-lasting consequences on people, organizations, and communities. The professional protection officer should take the time to become familiar with terrorism and terrorist groups, their tactics, goals, and, most important, preincident indicators (red flags) of potential terrorist actions.

Case Studies

The professional protection officer is in a unique position to respond to emergency situations. Since the protection officer is usually stationed at the facility where the emergency is taking place, they are typically the first personnel to arrive on the scene. These first several minutes constitute a critically important window of opportunity. Professional, quick, and decisive action on the part of the protection officer can contain the situation, ensure that people are safe, and mitigate damage to organizational assets by taking required initial steps. Although often unnoticed by the public, the actions of professional protection officers save lives and property on a regular basis. Here are just a few examples

1. **Active Shooter:** On June 10, 2009, an 88-year-old white supremacist entered the Holocaust Memorial Museum, in Washington, DC, with a .22-caliber rifle and immediately began firing. One of the gunman's rounds killed Security Officer Stephen T. Johns. Johns's fellow officers engaged and killed the gunman, thus preventing a mass shooting in a crowded museum. Such readiness can only be achieved by thorough planning and a continual commitment to training (Stout, 2009).

2. **Natural Disaster:** Hurricane Katrina's high winds and storm surge made landfall on August 29, 2005, overwhelming New Orleans and much of the rest of the Gulf Coast. Homes and businesses were destroyed by the high winds and flooding, and power outages became widespread, leaving much of the area in darkness. In this chaotic environment, order broke down in many places as the public authorities were stretched thin. Protection officers from a wide variety of organizations helped people impacted by the storm and its aftermath, protected property, and assisted public authorities. The provision for additional protective personnel is a key element in planning for emergencies. In the case of Hurricane Katrina, the supply of these additional resources was outpaced by the demand (*Washington Times*, 2005).

3. **Civil Disobedience:** A financial firm was targeted for a large-scale protest by an environmental group. The environmental group objected to investments the firm made in a company that was engaged in construction projects in an ecologically pristine area. The financial firm became aware of the date and time of the planned protests and quickly deployed additional protective personnel. On the day of the protests, members of the environmental group attempted to enter one of the firm's buildings and handcuff themselves to a stationary object located just inside the main entrance. Protection officers successfully kept the protesters from entering the building. Additional preplanning also allowed the firm's public relations personnel to have statements already prepared for the media. Had the protesters succeeded in handcuffing themselves inside the building, operations could have been impacted and the media attention to the event would certainly have been greater.

4. **Medical Emergency:** Protection officers in a large high-rise building were called to the scene of a collapsed individual. Upon arrival, the protection officers, who were trained as emergency medical technicians, checked the scene to ensure that it was safe to enter and then began to assess the situation. The patient was found to have stopped breathing and had no pulse. Utilizing an automatic external defibrillator (AED), the protection officers were able to revive and stabilize the patient until emergency medical services personnel arrived on scene and transported the patient to a nearby hospital.

5. **Flood:** A protection officer on routine patrol at his facility discovered a major water leakage that was spilling into a hallway located just outside of a critical computer room. The protection officer immediately called for assistance over his radio and then proceeded to follow the emergency procedures outlined in the organization's response protocols. The protection officer took highly absorbent material from a nearby crash cart and began to divert the water away from the computer room. In the interim, the command center officer dispatched additional help to the scene, sent out an emergency notice, set up a conference bridge for the crisis team, and contacted a preselected vendor to respond to assist with the cleanup. As a result of these quick actions, the computer room suffered minimal damage and the organization was able to maintain its operations without disruption.

These and many other types of emergency situations can happen to any organization, at any time. The professional protection officer must be prepared to respond to such events in accordance with his or her organizational protocols, training, and, most important, good judgment.

SCOPE OF THE PROBLEM

Over the years, limited research has been conducted with respect to emergency preparedness in the private sector (Tierney, Lindell, & Perry, 2001). The research that does exist indicates that many private sector organizations have not been proactive in this critical arena (Tierney et al., 2001). This is unfortunate, since not having an effective plan in place can ultimately lead to a variety of negative consequences ranging from adverse publicity to significant operating losses, as well as loss of life. Viewed from a homeland security perspective, this is troubling, considering that approximately 85% of the critical infrastructure in the U.S. is owned by the private sector (Bennett, 2007; Bullock et al., 2006; Purpura, 2007). Fortunately, the private

> **Some key terms and acronyms in emergency management:**
>
> **Hazard:** A sure of danger that may or may not lead to an emergency or disaster
>
> **Risk:** The probability or frequency of an event occurring
>
> **Vulnerability:** A weak point
>
> **Impact:** The consequences an event has on people, property, operations, and communities
>
> **Disaster:** An event that demands substantial response capability beyond the scope of normal operations
>
> **ICS:** Incident Command System
>
> **NIMS:** National Incident Management System

FIGURE 28-3   Key terms and acronyms in emergency management. *(Adapted from Haddow et al., 2008)*

sector has made additional investments in security and emergency preparedness since the tragic events of 9/11 (Bullock et al., 2006). However, relevant research indicates that additional public-private sector partnerships, as well as public police-private security cooperation, are needed (Purpura, 2007).

In contrast, some organizations that have come to realize that emergency response planning is vital, have created elaborate policies and procedures designed to deal with a variety of emergency situations. Moreover, these organizations usually feel confident that they are prepared to deal with any contingency. Their emergency response plans detail specific actions to take in the event of a catastrophic event and outline the steps that should be employed during the ensuing recovery effort. However, far too often this is where the planning process ends. Typically, the planning document is filed away and forgotten until a critical incident occurs (Joyce & Hurth, 1997; Phelps, 2007; Reid, 1996). Furthermore, as Canton (2007) points out, a plan is merely a snapshot of an organization's intention at that particular point in time, and many are out of date as soon as they are published.

EMERGENCY PLANNING CONSIDERATIONS

No one emergency response plan can be applied to every potential crisis situation. However, a comprehensive plan that takes into consideration potential, natural, technological, and man-made threats, and involves key personnel in the planning process, can help organizations to systematically manage emergencies in an effective and efficient manner. Consequently, the planning process is a key element that enables protection officers to explore viable options that can be employed in the event of a critical incident. In essence, it helps to ensure that an organization is prepared for various emergencies and can take steps to reduce losses to both people and property (Perry & Lindell, 2007). It also serves as internal documentation concerning the direction and control of the response, as well as the basis for periodic drills and exercises (Tierney et al., 2001). Additionally, the planning process can facilitate effective problem solving and communication among various stakeholders, thereby creating a flexible and adaptable environment for managing critical incidents (Canton, 2007).

Being prepared for emergencies involves four important components: planning, reviewing, training, and testing. These are the cornerstones of any emergency response plan and it should be noted that it is a circular rather than linear process. Perhaps Nudell and Antokol (1988) explain this concept best when they describe the above components, when implemented, as an umbrella of preparation against the thunderstorms of a potential crisis.

Regardless of the type of crisis, Nudell and Antokol (1988) point out that there is a series of common requirements that must be taken into account for an organization to be successful when a critical incident occurs. These include:

- Deciding policy
- Assessing threat
- Identifying resources
- Selecting crisis team personnel
- Locating the crisis management center
- Equipping the crisis center
- Training crisis team personnel
- Testing contingency plans and emergency procedures
- Dealing with the media
- Dealing with victims and their families
- Dealing with other affected persons (such as employees)
- Getting the organization's usual work done during the crisis
- Returning to normal operations after the crisis (both operationally and in human terms)

Lindell and Prater (2007) contend that an established planning process does not necessarily guarantee that an organization or community will be prepared. Instead, the planning process should be viewed in terms of milestones in combination with the environment. This interaction leads to eight planning guidelines that are based on relevant research as well as observations of local emergency planning processes. Complying with the following guidelines increases the chance that emergency plans will be more effective and efficient:

- Manage resistance to the planning process
- Adopt an all-hazards approach (consider all potential disasters)
- Promote multi-organization response
- Rely on accurate assumptions
- Identify appropriate actions while encouraging improvisation
- Link emergency response to disaster recovery and hazard mitigation
- Train and evaluate
- Adopt a continuous planning process

There are a number of established standards for emergency planning. One highly regarded standard was developed by the National Fire Protection Association (NFPA). NFPA Standard 1600, "Recommended Practice for Disaster/ Emergency Management and Business Continuity Programs" was created with the participation of the Federal Emergency Management Agency (FEMA), the International Association of Emergency Managers, and the National Emergency Management Association. It sets criteria for both developing and evaluating existing emergency management programs, including private sector business programs (Lindell & Prater, 2007). NFPA 1600 "Standard on Disaster/ Emergency Management and Business Continuity Programs", which is widely recognized by professionals in government and industry, defines 14 criteria for programs (Lindell & Prater, 2007):

- Laws and Authorities
- Resource Management
- Direction, Control, and Coordination
- Communications and Warning
- Operations and Procedures
- Finance and Administration
- Exercises, Evaluations, and Corrective Actions
- Crisis Communications and Public Information

- Hazard Identification, Risk Assessment, and Impact Analysis
- Hazard Mitigation
- Mutual Aid
- Planning
- Training
- Logistics and Facilities

VULNERABILITY ANALYSIS

Hazard identification, risk assessment, and impact analysis are important steps in the planning process, since many of the key decisions made relative to the emergency plan are based on this information. Many times this procedure can be accomplished by using a simple numerical rating system (scale of 1 to 5, with 1 as the lowest and 5 as highest) to list potential emergencies (such as fire, flood, terrorist attack, etc.), estimate the probability of each emergency occurring, assess the potential human impact (death and injury), property impact (losses and damages), potential business impact (loss of market share), and, finally, the strength of the internal and external resources that may be available (1 being weak

resources and 5 indicating strong resources). Next, you would total the score for each potential emergency, taking into consideration that the lower the score, the better. Although somewhat subjective, the comparison will be of significant assistance in determining planning priorities. The following example helps to illustrate the process (Table 28-1) (FEMA, 2007):

The Incident Command System

Molino (2006) identified five common concepts relative to the control and management of emergencies. According to Molino, these concepts (referred to as the Five Cs of Command) form the basis of the Incident Command System (ICS):

- Command
- Control
- Communications
- Coordination
- Cooperation

ICS was developed in the early 1970s after a series of major wildfires in southern California. The fires affected all levels of government

TABLE 28-1 Vulnerability Analysis Chart

Type of Emergency	Probability		Human Impact	Property Impact	Business Impact	Internal Resources	External Resources	Total
	High Low		High Impact		Low Impact	Strong Resources	Weak Resources	
	5↔1			5↔1			5↔1	

Note: The lower the score, the better.
Source: Adapted from FEMA's Emergency Management Guide for Business and Industry (2007).

(federal, state, and local), and highlighted various recurring problems that prevented responding agencies from working together. In particular, determining who was in charge of the overall response effort, duplication of efforts, poor coordination due to no joint planning, lack of a common organization, and ineffective intra-agency communications, hindered the overall emergency response to the fires. ICS established an on-scene management system that would help responding agencies work together using a coordinated and systematic approach that can be used for all types of incidents regardless of size (Bullock et al., 2008; Canton, 2007; McEntire, 2007):

- **Common Terminology:** Common vocabulary is used instead of signal codes. Functional assignments are standardized and easily understood.
- **Integrated Communications:** To accommodate various agencies, a common communications plan is used with assigned frequencies.
- **Unified Command Structure:** The command structure expands when there is more than one responding agency, and all organizations share a common set of incident objectives and strategies.
- **Unit Integrity:** Typically, responding units are not broken up before being deployed.

Most responders receive orders through their existing chain of command.
- **Unity of Command:** To avoid organizational confusion, every individual has a designated supervisor.
- **Effective Span of Control:** One supervisor for every 3–7 subordinates, with 5 being the optimum number.
- **Modular Structure:** Can expand or shrink based on needs.
- **Comprehensive Resource Management:** Human, material, and equipment resources are always checked in, and their status maintained at all times.
- **Consolidated Action Plans:** A single planning process, leading to one incident action plan.

The ICS structure is built around five major management activities or functions (McEntire, 2007) (Figure 28-4):

- **Command:** The incident commander (IC) determines strategy and objectives and is responsible for overall command of the incident. Three positions/functions work closely with the IC:
  - **Information Officer:** Works with the media and releases information to the public as appropriate.

FIGURE 28-4 Basic incident command system organizational chart. (*Adapted from U.S. Department of Homeland Security, 2008*)

- **Safety Officer:** Monitors operations and advises the IC on all matters related to safety.
  - **Liaison Officer:** Is the IC's point of contact with representatives of other organizations.
- **Operations:** Responsible for directing and coordinating all tactical operations to meet incident objectives.
- **Planning:** Responsible for all incident-related data (gathering and analyzing) as well as the status of all available resources.
- **Logistics:** Responsible for providing the necessary support (facilities, services, and materials) to meet all needs for the incident or situation.
- **Finance:** Responsible for on-site financial and administrative management, including monitoring and documenting all costs related to the incident. This is especially important for reimbursement by the federal government when there is a Presidential Disaster Declaration.

It is important for protection officers to understand how ICS works for several reasons. First, it is a relatively simple on-scene management tool that has proven effective in a variety of settings over the years, including the private sector. Second, any time there is a serious incident that requires public safety personnel from any level of government to respond, they will likely be using ICS. Consequently, understanding ICS, and being able to seamlessly fit into this management system in an effort to solving problems, would be advantageous for all of the entities involved in the incident.

The National Incident Management System (NIMS)

In recent years, the United States has been impacted by a number of devastating disasters. In particular, the terrorist attacks of September 11, 2001, and Hurricane Katrina in 2005, highlighted the need for a comprehensive national approach to incident management. The National Incident Management System (NIMS) provides a systematic, proactive, all-hazards approach that guides all levels of government, nongovernment organizations, and the private sector to work together to respond to, and manage, incidents of all sizes and complexity. NIMS is a template that works well with the National Response Framework (NRF), which provides the structure for national-level policy for incident management (FEMA, 2005).

Clearly, as we have seen over the years, the private sector plays a vital role in incident response. For this reason, the private sector should be incorporated into all facets of NIMS, and should prepare for all-hazards incidents that may affect their ability to operate. This is particularly important for private sector organizations that are part of the critical infrastructure, or those that have a role in emergency response. Moreover, those private sector organizations that play a role in emergency response are encouraged to become NIMS-compliant through various training programs offered by FEMA (2005).

It should also be noted that ICS is an integral part of NIMS. This is another reason why private sector organizations and protection officers may wish to have a thorough understanding of ICS and be able to apply the concepts readily in the event of a serious incident that will require a multi-agency response.

Emergency Operations Centers

An Emergency Operations Center (EOC) serves as a centralized area for the management of emergency operations. The EOC is where decisions are made by the emergency management team based on information provided by emergency responders and other personnel (FEMA, 2007).

The EOC can range from a dedicated, well-equipped center (comprehensive emergency communications capability including radio, telephone, fax, Internet access, computer, and television; self-sustaining power sources; bathroom, eating, and sleeping facilities for staff, etc.) to an ad hoc room that is used as circumstances dictate. Of particular importance is that an organization identifies its requirements ahead of time and establishes the type of arrangement that best suits its needs (FEMA, 2007; Nudell & Antokol, 1988).

Although the EOC should be near senior management, it should not interfere with everyday operations. In addition, an alternate site should always be selected ahead of time. Hawkes and Neal (1998) state that "an effective command center ready to respond to any emergency is a critical component of a headquarters security plan" (p. 54). They further contend that "a successful command center is the result of careful planning, clearly defined structure and job descriptions, and comprehensive training" (p. 54).

Media Relations

Procedures for dealing with the media are another important area that cannot be overlooked. When a critical incident occurs, the security manager will undoubtedly be pulled in many different directions. Faced with a considerable number of important tasks, the security manager may not view media relations as a primary concern. However, being prepared ahead of time to deal with the media can help an organization to get through the incident without the additional damage that can be caused by misinformation and speculation. In addition, the negative publicity that an organization receives as a result of a critical incident can have far-reaching effects. An organization's image and business can be adversely impacted. Litigation is bound to result as victims, the families of victims, employees, customers, and perhaps various interested outside parties will be seeking to lay blame and recover damages. Attorneys are bound to examine every newspaper account and TV report of the incident. They will, of course, be looking for statements from representatives of the organization for any admission or confirmation that the organization was in some way negligent (Gardner, 1997).

Nuss (1997) defines a crisis as "… an event requiring rapid decisions involving the media, that, if handled incorrectly, could damage the organization's credibility and reputation" (p. 1). He further provides a number of effective crisis communication steps that organizations should consider:

- Have a media plan
- Build a relationship with the media before a crisis strikes
- Train employees in crisis communications
- Maintain a good relationship with the media after [a] crisis

Cooperating with the media provides an organization with a number of important benefits that far outweigh the benefits of denying them access. In particular, it provides the organization with an opportunity to provide its side of the story. This is important since oftentimes the spokesman for the organization can release background information that may provide a different perspective on the situation. Furthermore, working with the media may prevent reporters from seeking out secondary sources that are typically less informed and more likely to misrepresent the organization. Consequently, it is far better to have the organization give an accurate statement of the situation as opposed to leaving it up to the reporter to locate an "informed" source, which can lead to speculation and misinformation. Saying "nothing" also has its own risks. Ignoring bad news will not make the incident go away and usually this tactic raises additional questions (Gardner, 1997).

FEMA (2007, p. 41) provides a number of important considerations for dealing with the media in an emergency:

- Designate a trained spokesperson and an alternate spokesperson
- Set up a media briefing area
- Establish security procedures
- Establish procedures for ensuring that information is complete, accurate, and approved for public release
- Determine an appropriate and useful way of communicating technical information
- Prepare background information about the facility

FEMA (2007, p. 41) also provides the following guidelines when providing information to the media during an emergency:

Dos

- Give all media access to the information
- When appropriate, conduct press briefings and interviews. Give local and national media equal time
- Try to observe media deadlines
- Escort media representative to ensure safety
- Keep records of information released
- Provide press releases when possible

Don'ts

- Do not speculate about the incident
- Do not permit unauthorized personnel to release information
- Do not cover up facts or mislead the media
- Do not put blame on the incident

It is quite evident that, although safety issues are always a top consideration, an organization cannot overlook the importance of having an effective crisis media relations plan in place and training protection officers with respect to their roles. This is critical, since the plan must be implemented quickly during a critical incident

in order to provide accurate and timely information while safeguarding the reputation and interests of the organization.

DEVELOPING THE EMERGENCY RESPONSE PLAN

The development of a comprehensive emergency management plan requires considerable time and effort, and sufficient time should be provided for its completion. Representatives from key organizational units must be involved from its inception, and upper management support is essential throughout the entire process. Typically, this can be readily accomplished by having the chief executive officer or facility manager issue a mission statement that introduces the emergency management plan, its purpose and importance to the organization, and defines the structure and authority of the planning team. Additionally, it is important, in the initial planning stages, to select an individual within the organization to assume responsibility for the plan and act as the planning team leader or coordinator.

Ultimately, capabilities and hazards should be analyzed, specific roles and responsibilities should be carefully outlined, and critical company products and services should be identified in order to ensure a coordinated and effective response when a critical incident does occur. This will typically involve meeting with outside groups, and establishing mutual aid agreements where appropriate. According to Canton (2007), resource management under NFPA 1600 is broad in scope, enabling organizations to establish a baseline and determine where they are deficient. Organizations can then make plans to meet these shortfalls through procurement or establishing mutual aid agreements with outside groups or agencies.

Some outside groups or agencies could include (per FEMA, 2007):

- Local police department
- Local fire department

- Emergency medical services
- City or county office of emergency management
- Local emergency planning committee (LEPC)
- Public works department
- Electric utilities
- Telephone companies
- Volunteer agencies such as the American Red Cross, the Salvation Army, and so on
- Essential contractors
- Suppliers of emergency equipment
- Company insurance carriers
- Neighboring businesses
- Trade associations
- National Weather Service (NWS)

In crisis situations, organizations respond differently based on variations in tasks and level of preparedness, as well as political considerations. Conferring with outside groups or agencies ahead of time will undoubtedly decrease confusion and delays during the response phase of an emergency, improve communication and coordination during the management phase of the incident, and help organizations transition to the recovery phase much faster. However, it is important to note that these agreements should clearly define the type of assistance as well as the procedures for activating the agreement in order to avoid unnecessary conflict.

REVIEWING AND INTEGRATING THE EMERGENCY RESPONSE PLAN

Once the initial plan is complete, it is essential that its various components be reviewed in depth by planning team personnel and revised as necessary. The draft plan could then be presented to key management personnel as well as any individuals who may be required to perform or provide support services. Many times, a tabletop exercise provides an excellent opportunity to review potential critical incidents with key personnel since problem areas can be readily identified and discussed. The plan can then be modified accordingly and later presented to the chief executive officer for final approval. Upon approval, the plan can be distributed to all affected personnel who should be required to sign that they have received the document. It is then important that the plan be quickly and clearly communicated to all affected personnel (Gigliotti & Jason, 1991).

It is imperative at this point that the plan be fully integrated into the organization's standard operating procedures (SOPs). According to FEMA (Guide for All-Hazard Emergency Operations Planning, 1996), "… SOPs and checklists provide the detailed instructions that an organization or individual needs to fulfill responsibilities and perform tasks, assigned in the EOP [emergency operations plan] …" (p. 3-3). Clearly, a comprehensive checklist that includes major planning, implementation, training/testing, response, and recovery components would be an invaluable asset to any organization's emergency response plan.

Training and Testing

After the plan has been finalized, communicated to all affected personnel, and integrated into the organization's standard operating procedures, it must be thoroughly tested. An emergency response plan will not work properly unless realistic training is provided and it is thoroughly tested prior to implementation in an actual emergency. Testing the plan helps to identify problem areas, as well as inherent weaknesses, that must be corrected in order to ensure that the plan will work as designed. Training and testing thus serve to identify areas in need of improvement, thereby enhancing coordination and communication among emergency response personnel.

The first step in the training process is to assign a staff member responsible for developing an overall training plan and the requisite goals and objectives for each component. Additionally, a determination must be made as to the following:

- Who will actually perform the training?
- Who will be trained?
- What types of training activities will be employed?
- What materials and equipment are needed?
- When will the training take place?
- Where will the training take place?
- How long will the training last?
- How will the training be evaluated and by whom?
- How will the training activities be documented?
- How will special circumstances be handled?
- How will training costs and expenses be budgeted?

It should be noted that critiques, or evaluations, are an important component of the training process and must be conducted after each training activity. Sufficient time should be allotted for the critique and any resulting recommendations should be forwarded to the emergency planning team for further review and action. Additionally, organizations should consider how to involve outside groups and agencies in the training and evaluation process. As previously mentioned, this could certainly help to avoid conflict and increase coordination and communication when a critical incident does occur. Emergency response training can take a variety of forms. FEMA (Emergency Management Guide for Business and Industry, 2007) describes six types of training activities that can be considered:

- **Orientation and Education Sessions**—Sessions designed to provide information, answer questions, and identify needs and concerns.
- **Tabletop Exercise**—This is a cost-efficient and effective way to have members of the emergency planning team, as well as key management personnel, meet in a conference room setting to discuss roles and responsibilities and identify areas of concern.

- **Walk-Through Drill**—The emergency planning team and response teams actually perform their emergency response functions.
- **Functional Drills**—Designed to test specific functions such as medical response, emergency notifications, and communications procedures, although not necessarily at the same time. The drill is then evaluated by the various participants and problem areas identified.
- **Evacuation Drill**—Participants walk the evacuation route to a predesignated area where procedures for accounting for all personnel are tested. Participants are asked to make note of potential hazards along the way and the emergency response plan is modified accordingly.
- **Full-Scale Exercise**—An emergency is simulated as close to reality as possible. Involves management, emergency response personnel, and employees, as well as outside groups and agencies that would also be involved in the response (p. 22).

Practical "hands-on" training always provides personnel with excellent opportunities to use skills that are taught and to learn new techniques and procedures. For emergency response training, simulations such as tabletop exercises, drills, and full-scale exercises are particularly valuable for practicing decision-making skills, tactical techniques, and communications. Moreover, simulations serve to determine deficiencies in planning and procedures that can lead to modifications to the emergency response plan (ASIS, 1994; FEMA, 2007; Nudell & Antokol, 1988).

Evaluating the Emergency Response Plan

Phelps (2007) advocates that training should occur every 3 months, and that eight major areas should be tested. These include:

- Internal communications
- External communications

- Resources
- Systems
- Safety
- Coordination
- Record-keeping
- Legal issues

With respect to communications, this is a critical area that has posed many problems for emergency responders over the years. In particular, during multi-agency responses to critical incidents, responding personnel have not been able to communicate and coordinate their responses because their radio equipment has not been compatible (interoperable). The World Trade Center response on September 11, 2001, certainly highlighted the extent of this problem, which had disastrous consequences for emergency responders. Unfortunately, according to Straw (2009), "… nearly eight years after 9-11, the national goal of ensuring that commanders from different public safety agencies and jurisdictions have interoperable communications remains elusive …" (p. 68).

Regardless of the training schedule selected, a formal audit of the entire emergency response plan should be conducted at least once a year. Furthermore, in addition to the yearly audit, the emergency response plan should be evaluated, and modified if necessary, as follows (FEMA, 2007):

- After each drill or exercise
- After each critical incident
- When there has been a change in personnel or responsibilities
- When the layout or design of a facility changes
- When there is a change in policies or procedures

Of course, any modifications or changes to an emergency response plan should be communicated to affected personnel as soon as possible. Similarly, changes to the planning document should be incorporated and distributed in a timely manner.

EMERGING TRENDS

Conducting Exercises in Difficult Economic Times or with the Reluctant Organization

The only way to truly tell if a plan is effective is to either experience an actual incident or to conduct an exercise. While most organizations understand the need to exercise plans, too few actually take the time and money necessary to accomplish this task. This tendency not to conduct exercises is even more pronounced during difficult economic periods and with organizations that haven't completely adopted resiliency concepts into their corporate culture.

In these challenging economic times, some organizations have taken to developing board games or other simple means of conducting a table-top exercise. When designing an exercise, it is important to keep in mind that adult learners are generally focused on how they can readily apply the information to their organizations. Therefore, interactivity and application should be the touchstones of any such exercise plan. The use of board games and other low-cost simulations can help organizations that would normally not engage in an exercise to start thinking seriously about the risk their organizations face and whether their plans are up to the task.

CONCLUSION

Since emergency situations take on many forms and have significant impacts for organizations, individuals, and communities, it is imperative that professional protection officers and the organizations they serve maintain a 24/7 (24-hour-a-day, 7-day-a-week) state of readiness. Readiness involves a thoughtful approach and continual planning, training, and testing in all four phases of the emergency planning cycle: Mitigation, Response, Recovery, and Preparedness. Professional development is also an important part of this process, and organizations and officers should take advantage of various professional development activities designed to increase knowledge and skills. By making continuous, incremental improvements to incident response plans and the teams that carry them out, the professional protection officer can work as part of an interdisciplinary team to save lives, prevent property damage, and maintain order.

References

ASIS International. (2003). *Emergency planning handbook* (2nd ed.). Alexandria, VA: ASIS International.

Bennett, B. T. (2007). *Understanding, assessing, and responding to terrorism: Protecting critical infrastructure and personnel.* Hoboken, NJ: John Wiley & Sons, Inc.

Bullock, J. A., Haddow, G. D., Coppola, D., Ergin, E., Westerman, L., & Yeletaysi, S. (2006). *Introduction to homeland security* (2nd ed.). Burlington, MA: Butterworth-Heinemann.

Canton, L. C. (2007). *Emergency management: Concepts and strategies for effective programs.* Hoboken, NJ: John Wiley & Sons, Inc.

Carlson, M., Shannon, E., & Winbush, D. (1990, January 1). *Murder by mail.* Retrieved August 18, 2009, from <http://www.time.com/time/magazine/article/0,9171,969089,00.html>.

Elliot, S. (1994, December 12). *Bombing in New Jersey: The victim; executive had vaulted to no. 2 post at agency.* Retrieved August 18, 2009, from <http://www.nytimes.com/1994/12/12/nyregion/bombing-in-new-jersey-the-victim-executive-had-vaulted-to-no-2-post-at-agency.html>.

Federal Bureau of Investigation. (2008, April 24). *Headline archives FBI 100 the Unabomer.* Retrieved August 18, 2009, from <http://www.fbi.gov/page2/april08/unabomber_042408.html>.

Federal Emergency Management Agency. (2007). *Emergency management guide for business and industry.* Retrieved August 18, 2009, from <http://www.fema.gov/library/viewRecord.do?id=1689>.

Federal Emergency Management Agency. (1996). *Guide for all-hazard emergency operations planning.* Washington, DC: U.S. Government Printing Office.

Gardner, R. (1997). Getting ahead of the headlines. *Security Management, 41*(7), 115–119.

Gigliotti, R., & Jason, R. (1991). *Emergency planning for maximum protection.* Boston, MA: Butterworth-Heinemann.

Haddow, G. D., Bullock, J. A., & Coppola, D. P. (2008). *Introduction to emergency management* (3rd ed.). Burlington, MA: Butterworth-Heinemann.

Hawkes, K., & Neal, J. (1998). Command performance. *Security Management, 42*(11), 77–83.

Joyce, E., & Hurth, L. (1997). Booking your next disaster. *Security Management, 41*(11), 47–50.

Knight, R. F., & Pretty, D. J. (1996). *The impact of catastrophes on shareholder value.* Oxford, England: The Oxford Executive Research Briefings; a Research Report sponsored by the Sedgwick Group.

McEntire, D. A. (2007). *Disaster response and recovery.* Hoboken, NJ: John Wiley & Sons, Inc.

Molino, L. N., Sr. (2006). *Emergency incident management systems: Fundamentals and applications.* Hoboken, NJ: John Wiley & Sons, Inc.

Nudell, M., & Antokol, N. (1988). *The handbook for effective emergency management.* Lexington, MA: Lexington Books.

Nuss, R. (1997). *Effective media crisis communication during a critical incident.* Winter Springs, FL: Nuss and Associates, Inc.

Perry, R. W., & Lindell, M. K. (2007). *Emergency planning.* Hoboken, NJ: John Wiley & Sons, Inc.

Purpura, P. P. (2007). *Terrorism and homeland security.* Burlington, MA: Butterworth-Heinemann.

Phelps, E. F. (2007). No lights, no camera, just action. *Security Management, 51*(11), 55–61.

Shane, S. (2008, August 4). *Anthrax evidence called mostly circumstantial.* Retrieved August 18, 2009, from <http://www.nytimes.com/2008/08/04/us/04anthrax.html>.

Stout, D. (2009, June 10). *Museum gunman a longtime foe of government.* Retrieved August 18, 2009, from <http://www.nytimes.com/2009/06/11/us/11shoot.html>.

Straw, J. (2009). Communicating to save lives. *Security Management, 53*(5), 63–69.

Tierney, K. J., Lindell, M. J., & Perry, R. W. (2001). *Facing the unexpected: Disaster preparedness and response in the United States.* Washington, DC: Joseph Henry Press.

U.S. Department of Homeland Security. (2008). *National incident management system.* Retrieved August 18, 2009, from <http://www.fema.gov/pdf/emergency/nims/NIMS_core.pdf>.

Washington Times. (2005, September 5). *Katrina-hit states turn to security firms.* Retrieved August 18, 2009, from <http://www.washingtontimes.com/news/2005/sep/09/20050909-104738-8181r/>.

Resource

Broder, J. F. (2006). *Risk analysis and the security survey* (3rd ed.). Burlington, MA: Butterworth-Heinemann.

SECURITY QUIZ

1. Regardless of the type of crisis, there is a series of common requirements that must be taken into account for an organization to be successful when a critical incident occurs. These include all the following except:
   a. Assessing threat
   b. Selecting crisis team personnel
   c. Training crisis team personnel
   d. Being willing to spend lots of money on a solution

2. Observing which of the following guidelines increases the chances that emergency plans will be more effective and efficient:
   a. Promote multi-organization response
   b. Allow resistance to the planning process
   c. Separate emergency response from disaster recovery
   d. None of the above

3. The National Fire Protection Association (NFPA) standard 1600 sets criteria for both developing and evaluating existing emergency management programs.
   a. True
   b. False

4. The Incident Command System (ICS) identified common concepts that form the basis for the control and management of emergencies. Which of the following is not one of those concepts:
   a. Control
   b. Communications
   c. Concentricity
   d. Cooperation

5. The National Response Framework (NRF) established an on-scene management system that would help responding agencies work together using a coordinated and systematic approach that can be used for all types of incidents regardless of size.
   a. True
   b. False

6. The ICS structure is built around five major management activities of functions. Which of the following is not one of these functions:
   a. Operations
   b. Planning
   c. Safety
   d. Logistics

7. The National Incident Management System (NIMS) provides a systematic, proactive, all-hazards approach that guides all levels of government, non-governmental organizations, and the private sector to work together to respond to and manage incidents of all sizes.
   a. True
   b. False

8. Effective crisis media communications steps that organizations should consider include all the following except:
   a. Have a media plan
   b. Build a relationship with media before a crisis
   c. Develop strict restrictions on what media can do on your property
   d. Train employees on communications with the media

9. An emergency response plan will work regardless of any realistic training prior to the implementation in an actual emergency.
   a. True
   b. False

10. In addition to a yearly audit of the emergency plan, that plan should be evaluated and modified, if necessary, at all of the following times except:
    a. When there has been a change in personnel
    b. When the layout or design of a facility changes
    c. When there is a change in policies and procedures
    d. None of the above

29

Terrorism

Robert Metscher

CHAPTER OBJECTIVES

- Define terrorism
- Discuss why terror tactics may be employed
- Differentiate between international and domestic terrorism
- Explain "lone wolf" terrorism and "leaderless resistance"
- Explore selection and attack planning concepts

The world is experiencing a new era of terrorism. We will likely hear similar words in the decades to come as well. Terrorism is certainly not new, and even the techniques are not especially different. What has changed is the publicity, awareness, and the realization that terrorism, international and domestic, affects everyone. A determined foe, given sufficient resources, will find the weakness in any defense. The terrorist attacks of September 11, 2001, opened an otherwise unaware population's eyes to the fallibility of their nation's armor. This cycle has been repeated throughout history, as terrorists have sought to employ tactics that offer success against established political power structures. While life may have reached equilibrium since 9/11, there are noticeable differences to our society. Today's security professional must be aware of the fundamental aspects of terrorism as it exists today, how it came to be, what it may look like in the future, and how that affects their role as an organizational guardian.

WHAT IS TERRORISM? A DEFINITION DILEMMA

Defining any term is essential to reach an objective understanding. Without a common definition, the term is defined by individual bias and opinion. Consider that there is no one common definition of terrorism today. This creates considerable difficulty in developing policies to manage a very real problem. Merriam-Webster defines "terror" as a state of intense fear. In turn, "fear" is defined by Merriam-Webster as an unpleasant, often strong emotion caused by anticipation or awareness of danger. It might appear that terrorism is the cause of an unpleasant emotion anticipating danger. Clearly this is too broad and vague to be useful. Historically, the term "terrorist" can be traced to 1795 and the treatment by the French revolutionary government of its own citizens (Williams & Head, 2006). Operational tactics, that we might consider terrorism today, can be found much farther back with the Zealots as early as 30 BC. Zealots used violence and intimidation to forward their agenda of resisting the Roman occupation of Israel.

The term "terrorism", however, has been defined in many ways over the decades. The mere mention of the word terrorism today has the ability to affect the perception of nearly any issue. The use, and overuse, of any term also tends to obscure its definition. The end result is a term that everyone believes they understand but no one agrees upon one definition. To paraphrase Associate Justice Stewart of the U.S. Supreme Court in his discussion of pornography, "I'll know it when I see it," may also be the most accurate way to describe terrorism today. Unfortunately, such a subjective method of defining any issue allows for misinterpretations, distortions, confusion, and finally a term with little value beyond emotional appeal. Recognizing the disparate definitions that exist, as well as popular public application of the term, permits the security professional to avoid potential pitfalls while advising organizational management.

The dilemma of finding a common definition is conveniently illustrated by the U.S. government. The United Nations has had tremendous difficulty in producing a definition of terrorism for fear of inadvertently excluding legitimate efforts at self-determination within nations. Multiple agencies have each presented their own definitions within their literature:

U.S. Department of Defense (2001)
The calculated use of unlawful violence to inculcate fear, intended to coerce or to intimidate governments or societies in the pursuit of goals that are generally political, religious, or ideological.

Federal Bureau of Investigation (1999, p. i)
[T]he unlawful use of force and violence against persons or property to intimidate or coerce a government, the civilian population, or any segment thereof, in furtherance of political or social objectives.

U.S. State Department (2003, p. xii)
[P]remeditated, politically motivated violence perpetrated against noncombatant targets by subnational groups or clandestine agents, usually intended to influence an audience.

Each of these definitions revolves around the use of unlawful violence to forward an agenda. As the term has gained more popular use, additional terms have been introduced. Other, newer, activities that have been included under the umbrella of terrorism do not require violence in the traditional sense of the term (that is, a definition of violence requiring the use of physical force). Agro-terrorism attacks on the agricultural capabilities of a society could either poison a population or significantly disrupt their ability to provide sufficient foodstuffs to the population. Cyber-terrorism attacks disrupt the information technology infrastructure of a society causing essential services to fail. Bio-terrorism attacks introduce viruses or bacterial agents into an unprepared population causing a widespread health crisis. None of these attacks necessarily requires an overtly violent act to initiate them. There can be little doubt that an action using these "non-violent" techniques still inflict, and are intended to inflict, significant harm on the target population.

In his 2002 article, "Terrorism: Notes Toward a Definition," published in *Slate Magazine*, Christopher Hitchens simplified the definition of terrorism to "the tactic of demanding the impossible, and demanding it at gunpoint." And in

C. Maria (Marijke) Keet's paper titled "Towards a Resolution of Terrorism using Game Theory," she simply identifies, terrorism parenthetically as "the use of physical and psychological violence as a means to achieve a political goal" (2003).

Occasionally, in an effort to define something, it is helpful to identify what it is not. For example, the terms activist, extremist, and terrorist are occasionally used almost interchangeably in the media. Yet definitions of "activist" or "extremist" do not mention violence or harm. Remember that the earliest modern use of terrorist came from the French revolution and the "Reign of Terror" in which political opponents were beheaded. In foregoing definitions that indicate a terrorist is one who advocates terrorism, the term terror means "a state of intense fear" (Merriam-Webster, 2009). Thus, a terrorist would advocate creating a state of intense fear. It is unlikely that such fear would come from anything short of a threat of violence or severe harm. From this, it is safe to argue that neither an activist nor an extremist necessarily advocates using a state of intense fear in their efforts. An activist is extremely active in their cause; an extremist advocates extreme views or measures; however, neither is automatically violent nor accepts violence as a way to usher in change. Placing these terms onto a continuum using the First Amendment to the U.S. Constitution for protected speech as a reference point, both the activist and the extremist might engage in illegal activity, such as acts of civil disobedience, outside of protected expression. These actions, however, would not likely be far enough along the continuum to create a state of intense fear. An example might be animal rights advocates standing naked with signs protesting the use of animals for clothing material. While the protestors could certainly be considered activists and even extremists, they do not necessarily create a state of intense fear, advocate violence, or attempt to harm those nearby. Moving farther along the continuum is the use of arson by the Animal Liberation Front and Earth Liberation Front to destroy property, but not harm people or animals. They insist that they have not harmed a person; however, the use of such a destructive force—fire—often creates an intense state of fear. And it is a rational fear that those targeted, or their family, friends, and co-workers, could be injured or killed in a subsequent event. Even farther along the continuum, then, would be those actions involving direct physical harm such as during the well-publicized attacks over the past decade. While a terrorist may be an activist or extremist, the same does not hold true in reverse. Terrorism then requires the threat of or actual harm.

In some instances, terrorists are called mass murderers. But not all mass murderers are terrorists. Because they have different motives for committing violence, most mass murderers are not considered terrorists. However, Eric Rudolph, who was convicted of four bombings, wrote about the reason for his attacks, "even though the purpose of the Olympics is to promote these despicable ideals, the purpose of the attack on July 27th was to confound, anger and embarrass the Washington government in the eyes of the world for its abominable sanctioning of abortion on demand" (Rudolph, 2005). The Olympic Park bombing killed one person and injured 111. It was not mass murder, but certainly an act meant to instill an intense state of fear. A similar theme may be found in far too many other instances world wide, where the total loss of life does not accurately reflect the level of fear driven through a wider population.

For simplicity's sake consider terrorism in this light: How the few affect the many, by affecting the few through significant harm, or threaten significant harm, to forward a political or social agenda.

As a security professional, it is often less important to classify a potential threat as terrorism or crime than to identify and address the threat itself. By recognizing some of the difficulties created by not having one accepted definition, the security professional can focus on the threat and risk created by these various acts. In the end it may be of little importance whether an attack comes from a determined and skilled criminal or a terrorist organization. With the exception of any press coverage, identical attacks will cause comparable losses. This is not to say that understanding terrorism is of no small significance. A lack of understanding could result in failing to accurately identify and address all potential threats against an organization.

Furthermore, the definition of a terrorist and of what constitutes terrorism will likely change through time.

WHY VIOLENCE? WHY THEY DO WHAT THEY DO

Why threats and acts of violence? What causes an individual or group to embrace these tactics? More than one reason exists to explain why any specific act of terrorism or a series of actions may be undertaken. An individual act may be expected to bring about a specific change, such as meeting a demand or making a particular change in public behavior. This act may be in concert with other acts that have slightly different goals. Some goals of specific terrorist actions within terrorism campaigns, or for entire campaigns, include:

- Bringing publicity to a plight or cause.
- Inciting retaliation to justify further actions or encourage popular support.
- Moving the middle of acceptable behaviors.
- Changing public perception of acceptable activities.
- Creating a gradual change in public view of a cause.
- Injuring the opponent (Keet, 2003).

The value of terrorism comes from the fear generated by the realization that nearly any member of the target population could have been a victim—and could be a victim in a subsequent attack. Terrorism is a form of asymmetric warfare, of guerilla warfare, in that it pits a smaller group against a much larger group that is often entrenched in legitimacy, as a society or a subset of a society. For instance, the Weather Underground in the United States focused on driving a socialist revolution and targeting institutions of perceived oppression (FBI, 1976) – American society as everyone knew it. In contrast, the Animal Liberation Front targets only those they perceive as exploiting animals (ALF, 2009) – a subset of society. Instead of open warfare against the military forces of a nation, a terrorist uses their ability to move among the target population to create a situation in which confusion and uncertainty will drive fearful action. It is this fearful action that ultimately accomplishes the terrorist's goal. This goal is distrust in the security apparatus of their government and a corresponding willingness to acquiesce to the terrorist's demands.

In its modern sense, terrorism has been argued to have such root causes as poverty, social injustice, political exclusion, and violent oppression. Amy Zalman, PhD, a Middle East advisor and consultant, sums up two causes for terrorism:

- Social and political injustice: People choose terrorism when they are trying to right what they perceive to be a social, political, or historical wrong – when they have been stripped of their land or rights, or denied these.
- The belief that violence or its threat will be effective, and usher in change. Another way of saying this is the belief that violent means justifies the ends. Many terrorists in history said sincerely that they chose violence after long deliberation, because they felt they had no choice.

In his paper "Understanding and Combating Terrorism," Major S. M. Grass of the U.S. Marine Corp refers to Ernest Evans, a research associate at the Brookings Institution, who suggests that there are five specific goals of terrorism. These goals are:

1. To publicize a cause on a regional and international level.

2. The harassment and intimidation of authorities to force them to make concessions.
3. Polarization of society to bring down the regime.
4. To aggravate relations between states or nations.
5. To free political prisoners and secure monetary ransoms to finance their cause.

THE REASON FOR THE ACTION

The various reasons that terrorist acts are committed include the central component of forwarding an agenda or cause and the general perception that non-violent acts will be ineffective in achieving their agenda. In his book, "The Logic of Political Violence," Craig Rosebraugh discusses the lack of value of non-violent movements seeking political change. He refers to Mikhail Bakunin:

> Was there ever, at any period, or in any country, a single example of a privileged and dominant class which granted concessions freely, spontaneously, and without being driven to it by force or fear? *(Maximoff, 1953)*

There are many causes and agendas that represent political discontent around the world. It is typical for any particular cause to have a range of supporters from those that passively agree, to those with extreme views and a willingness to take direct, even violent, action to forward their beliefs. Between these two elements are those that actively engage in open, or aboveground, dissent; organizing and fundraising for activities that are within the legal framework of dissent or marginally outside of it. Once again, an example of a non-violent extremist might be an animal rights supporter who uses no animal products at all. They may or may not be active in spreading this belief and still be extreme in their views. It is those few, who embrace a belief and use violent action in

an attempt to change the behavior of those who do not agree, that fall under the definition of terrorist. There are certainly examples of causes without supporters that progress to such levels of extreme action.

In many instances, the mass media will classify a terrorist organization or cause as left-wing or right-wing. The origin of these classifications also comes from the French. In the National Assembly in the 1780s, the physical seating layout had the revolutionary estate seated to the left and the nobles seated to the right. As a result, the left is often associated with liberal political themes and the right with more conservative themes. To characterize the inaccuracy of these terms, the domestic terrorist organizations of the United States offer a convenient data set. The Weather Underground from the 1970's sought to overthrow of the government and replace the capitalist economic system with communism. They were considered a left-wing organization. The various white supremacist groups, such as the KKK, skinheads, and others, were considered right-wing groups. However, understanding the underlying beliefs of any organization or movement, and their potential for destruction, is of greater importance than a simple classification. As a security officer, recognizing the beliefs, and the significant personas involved, is essential to determining the nature and extent of the threat posed to our charges. Effective evaluation and communication of the threat allow a client, employer, or principal to manage protective efforts at an optimum level.

International

The phenomenon of international terrorism became a familiar concept as airline hijackings began in the 1970's. International terrorism can be considered those organizations and acts that go beyond domestic issues. They may target foreign nations, their citizens, corporations, or other resources. The evolution of the phenomenon of international terrorism is more a function of international relations and commerce, convenient travel, and most importantly, worldwide almost instantaneous media coverage. Remember that the theatrical importance of the larger population witnessing the action is to create a state of fear, but this is only permitted by the improvement in communications and the ability of the media to operate and broadcast images worldwide. Imagine the anti-climatic effect of a terrorist attack when news traveled by horseback. Reading about a terrible event a continent away that occurred days, weeks, or even months earlier, in a newspaper without images, would have little effect. Now, when the citizens of an entire nation (and the world) can witness the body of a murdered sailor being thrown out of an aircraft, there is an immediate and real effect on the population. This was the case when Petty Officer Robert Stetham was murdered during the hijacking of TWA flight 847 in 1985. The same can be said for the incidents of September 11, 2001, in New York, March 11, 2004, in Madrid, and July 7, 2005, in London when the whole world witnessed the destruction of these attacks.

Domestic

If international terrorism reaches across international boundaries, then domestic terrorism is contained within a nation's interest. For instance, the second worst terrorist act on U.S. soil was the bombing of the Murrah Federal Building in Oklahoma City on April 19, 1995. This attack claimed 168 lives and injured nearly 700. One stated reason for this attack was the federal government's handling of the Branch Davidians in Waco, Texas, and Randy Weaver in Idaho. There was no international issue being addressed by the attack. Similarly, the Irish terrorist groups maintained their conflict in the United Kingdom with the various attacks in Great Britain over control of Northern Ireland. In Spain, the Basque ETA (in English: Basque Homeland and Freedom) seeking independence

is also an example of domestic terrorism. Domestic terrorism can be found in nearly every country, much of it unheard of by those outside that particular nation. It can be just as dangerous as international terrorism, although possibly just a bit less newsworthy on the international stage.

WHAT THEY LOOK LIKE: FROM INDIVIDUALS TO ORGANIZATIONS

To support an ongoing campaign against a foe, an individual, or antagonist, generally needs allies or companions, due to the resources it takes to carry out multiple operations. While the Unabomber stands out as an exception, the tempo of his attacks was most certainly tempered by his own limited resources. As a terrorist organization grows to include financial and logistical support capabilities, the severity and tempo of the operations can increase. The extent of available support varies from one organization to the next. Furthermore, the larger an organization grows, the more likely its infrastructure will be discovered and destroyed. The necessity for secrecy and compartmentalization of information makes larger organizations considerably more difficult to effectively maintain.

Popular media routinely refers to terrorist cells. A cell is a small group of individuals operating with a common purpose. There are operations or tactical cells, which are the cells that carry out actions against others. These consist of the individuals who trained for the mission. Although they have a common purpose – the mission – they may not all be aware of all the details of the mission. There has been debate concerning whether all the 9/11 hijackers, specifically the "muscle" team members, were aware of the intended outcome or were intentionally kept in the dark.

To support the cells conducting the operations, logistics cells exist to provide assistance. These may be multi disciplinary in staffing to provide a wide range of skills, or they may be focused on a specific task. Each action requires accurate intelligence about the target, its defenses, weaknesses, and expected responses. They may funnel financial resources or make arrangements for lodging, transportation, food, weapons, explosives, or other materials needed for a successful mission. Furthermore, separate support cells may provide specific components, again to avoid drawing suspicion to the operations cell.

And there are sleeper cells. These may get the most attention if for no other reason than their unique name. A sleeper cell is a cluster of individuals who are sent to infiltrate a population. They will typically exist in their day-to-day lives separate from each other. This lack of contact works to avoid creating a connection or causing suspicion. In some instances the members of a sleeper cell will be unaware of each other. Instead, they may be given some type of an authentication method to identify another cell member making contact, or an activation code that directs them to take some predetermined action. Since 2001, each release of a video or audio message from Al-Qaeda drives concern that they contain hidden activation messages.

While the cell is the basic unit of an operation, they vary in size. The smallest is an individual. Although individuals are capable of carrying out acts, most often they will have a support structure to assist them. The Unabomber is one example of an individual who operated entirely alone in his endeavor. There has been much discussion of the "lone wolf" terrorist, especially in the United States concerning Timothy McVeigh and the Oklahoma City bombing. However, McVeigh did not operate entirely alone. His support chain included, at a minimum, a few friends who provided some logistical support.

In his 2005 *Washington Post* article, "Behind the Lone Terrorist, a Pack Mentality," Mike German, a retired FBI agent, stated:

"Lone extremism" is not a phenomenon; it's a technique, a ruse designed to subvert the criminal justice system. McVeigh did act as a lone extremist, as the FBI says. He was trained to do it this way. But his act of lone extremism was part of an ongoing conspiracy that continues to inspire violent attacks to this day, and to close our eyes to this conspiracy is to deny reality. It's a matter of connecting the dots. *(German, 2005)*

The idea of "leaderless resistance," or a movement with no formal organization to support its cause, has proven to make capture of those involved difficult at best. Possibly one of the best descriptions of the model of leaderless resistance comes from Edward Abbey's novel, *The Monkeywrench Gang*. This book describes a small group of friends engaging in prank-like property destruction to prevent the construction of roads through undeveloped wild land in the American west. One conversation describes it well:

"I'll bet – listen, I'll bet right this very minute there's guys out in the dark doing the same kind of work we're doing. All over the country, little bunches of guys in twos and threes, fighting back."

"You're talking about a well-organized national movement."

"No I'm not. No organization at all. None of us knowing anything about any other little bunch. That's why they can't stop us." *(Abbey, 1975, p. 182)*

This non-structure has been embraced by both the Animal Liberation Front (ALF) and the Earth Liberation Front (ELF). They have each published a set of guidelines for those wishing to support their cause with direct action. Adhering to these principles provides some continuity of effort without compromising the core values, and makes it very difficult to identify persons involved in specific incidents.

While leaderless resistance offers some advantages, it is not the model for all causes. Those with formal structures gain advantages from greater logistical resources. These resources may then be used in a wider variety of strategies. They may be concentrated on a particular target or used across many targets. Greater resources also enable the organizations to provide training, conduct complex mass communication and marketing efforts, and coordinate the activities of multiple cells. Terrorist groups may be organized in many different ways, much like any organization. Some may have a clear pyramid with a strong centralized authority and multiple layers over a large base of supporters. Within such a structure the central leadership would exercise strict authority over giving orders and confirming logistical resources. Others, may be structured as an umbrella with several self-contained, and somewhat autonomous, groups under an overarching organization. Each of these larger organizations is able to effectively employ tactics that have planned losses, without bringing an end to their cause. For instance, a "suicide bomber," where the individual carries or wears the bomb to the target and detonates it intentionally, would bring a premature end to the cause of a lone wolf. Such tactics involving the sacrifice of individuals necessitate a larger organization to carry on the efforts after the attackers die.

With the easy communications offered by the Internet, it is possible to form virtual groups with members who never meet each other in the physical world. Such groups would most likely be found involved in cyberspace attacks, but could certainly use cyberspace to coordinate attacks in the physical world. A demonstration of how such a cell might operate was offered by Dr. Dwight Toavs at the 2008 Director of National Intelligence Open Source Conference in Washington, DC (Shachtman, 2008). In the presentation, he demonstrated a fictitious online conversation to coordinate an attack on the White House using a World of Warcraft map as an overlay to the Washington, DC map. These cyber worlds offer a convenient medium for discussing, in "game code" no less, an upcoming operation. Consequently, it is now possible to coordinate an operation with complex logistical needs and multiple cells with little fear of detection.

Understanding the organizational structure of a terrorist organization provides guidance on tactics for disrupting their operations. At the tactical level, such organizational aspects have less importance when attempting to identify or disrupt an attack. However, understanding the wide range of organizational structures offers the security officer possible insight into the funding of a potential foe and ultimately their ability to engage in complex and resource-intensive activities.

TARGET SELECTION AND ATTACKS

With the knowledge that terrorism is a largely theatrical activity to affect a wider audience, it is less difficult to recognize why specific targets are selected. Returning to the five goals of terrorism: publicity, harassment and intimidation, societal polarization, aggravating political relations, and freeing political prisoners/securing monetary ransoms, it is possible to ask important questions of potential targets. Consider whether an attack on the target, such as a person, place, event, or object, could further one or more of these goals. Further criteria and tools should also be used in this evaluation process.

The CARVER model of target selection offers a useful tool for considering a target. While CARVER methodology is just one tool, it offers value because the factors may be considered from both an offensive and a defensive point of view. The components (presented from an aggressor's point of view) include:

Criticality – How critical is this target to the operations of the opponent?
Accessibility – How easy or difficult is it to gain access to and egress from the target?
Recuperability (recovery of operations and response) – How quickly can the opponent recover from the attack? How quickly can they mount an effective response?

Vulnerability – How vulnerable is the target itself? What training and tools will be needed to carry out the attack?

Effect or Effectiveness – What will the attack accomplish? Is this the best target for that effect?

Risk – What are the chances of the attack being unsuccessful? What factors affect success?

An additional component of SHOCK has since been added to CARVER. The SHOCK factor represents the wider psychological impact of the attack. This is the true theatrical value discussed earlier; the widespread fear throughout the target population caused by the impressiveness of the attack.

Another useful model for understanding the attack process involves twelve steps. Carrying out a successful attack requires planning and preparation. In many instances individuals must be trained, resources obtained, and then moved into position to facilitate the attack. It is highly unlikely that all the elements for an attack would be in position and ready by sheer chance.

1. Choose multiple targets
2. Perform initial surveillance
3. Identify softest target
4. Categorize
5. Perform secondary surveillance
6. Plan operation
7. Rehearse
8. Move to target
9. Conduct operation
10. Escape
11. Exploit the incident
12. Debrief

Consider this process through the lens of two attacks: the 9/11 attacks on the U.S. by Al-Qaeda and the Oklahoma City bombing at the Murrah Federal Building. According to the 9/11 Commission Report, "… KSM describes a grandiose original plan: a total of ten aircraft to be hijacked" (9/11 Commission, 2004, p. 154).

Planes were to be crashed into buildings on both coasts of the United States with one plane landing and being turned into a media platform from which Khalid Sheikh Mohammed would murder the male passengers and disseminate propaganda. In *American Terrorist: Timothy McVeigh & the Oklahoma City Bombing*, the authors state that McVeigh used a list with specific criteria for the target of his attack. Reconnaissance of facilities in Arkansas, Missouri, Arizona, and Texas was conducted. An additional comment on McVeigh's selection process reinforces the theatrical aspect and the desire to exploit the incident (as in number 11 above). "He wanted a big federal building, with plenty of open space around it, to allow for the best possible news photos and television footage" (Michel & Herbeck, 2001, p. 169). He further sought "to deliver a quantity of casualties the federal government would never forget." When asked why he did not bomb the building at night, McVeigh's response was, "That would not have gotten the point across to the government. We needed a body count to make our point." (Michel & Herbeck, 2001, p. 300). McVeigh was also reported to have used soup cans in a friend's kitchen while planning the arrangement of the barrels containing the explosives in the truck.

With an understanding of the motivations driving our foe, it is possible to identify potential targets deemed valuable to them. Knowing a few of the tools and methods available for planning an attack is then helpful to us in preparing our defenses to protect those targets of value. Each of these methods shows weaknesses in the selection and preparation process that can be exploited in our defensive planning.

SECURITY PREPARATIONS AND DEFENSIVE MEASURES

In addition to using prudent physical and network security precautions, the security professional must think beyond their own facilities when coping with terrorism. It is a somewhat dated concept to consider the property line as the first line of defense. While it is most likely the first place for which a security professional is able to establish protective tools, there is certainly more that can be done. As noted above, there are at least two instances prior to an attack when surveillance is conducted. This typically involves being within relatively close proximity to a facility and likely accessing it as well. The purpose for the reconnaissance is to determine suitability of the target—this offers yet another opportunity for discouraging the attack. Furthermore, significant attacks often cause damage to property surrounding the target. Being located next to a government office, pharmaceutical company, or religious organization may seem harmless from one day to the next. This close proximity could be the only reason for damage from an attack. Consequently, on many levels we share the same threats as our neighbors. The daily role of a security professional managing the threat of terrorism requires awareness of the nature of the threat; vigilance toward the known threats, the desire to

identify new threats early, keep constituents and organizational leaders informed, as well as recommend and implement sound countermeasures to mitigate an attack.

The security professional must consider the threat environment surrounding their organization. Who or what is likely to cause harm, interrupt operations, or damage the organization's reputation? Monitoring known threats, and seeking to identify new ones early, offers an advantage. Formal threat assessments are certainly important; however, regular monitoring of the environment offers the opportunity to identify potential problems earlier. Whether this involves automated online searches, active monitoring of Web sites and discussion groups, or walking around and speaking with the organization's neighbors, early detection is valuable. It is often after a successful attack that individuals come forward to report their observation of "odd behavior." Security professionals frequently argue the importance and value of awareness programs. This is an example of the professional heeding their own advice.

EMERGING TRENDS

"Emerging Trends—Terrorism"

Throughout history, terrorism has been an evolving concept. Some tactics are tried and true and will likely be used well into the future. Newer tactics are evolving today using our improved communications networks and easier access to other technologies. The deplorable events committed by Al-Qaeda in the past decade show a desire to capitalize on greater casualties and more dramatic events. With the increased availability of nuclear, biological, and chemical substances it is likely that these will be part of future attack plans. The increase in networked

infrastructure also creates vulnerabilities to electric grids, power generation stations, water sanitation systems, bridge operations, and such. The largest difference between a physical and virtual attack is the necessary location of the attacker. A physical attack requires the attacker to be present, but a virtual attack can be conducted from potentially anywhere on a network. If that network is connected to the Internet, then the attacker can literally be anywhere in the world.

Attacks by nuclear means and radiological materials have the potential for casualties far beyond the immediate attack location and to deprive the opponent of the use of considerable land area. Even if the unusable land area is small, it is significant when that small area is a vital transportation mode, commercial area, water source, or infrastructure feature. Dirty bombs are radiological devices that, rather than initiating a nuclear explosion, use conventional explosives to scatter fine particles of radioactive material. Small amounts of this material can prove fatal over time, which makes areas uninhabitable for long periods of time. There are other delivery methods besides explosives that permit the release of these materials. Biological agents have the ability to cause severe illness. The anthrax attacks in the United States proved the validity of this concept. Mailroom processes throughout the country were affected by merely a few attacks. Bio-agents released into the water supplies or sprayed over areas can have enormous effect. However, a highly infectious agent could be distributed simply by infecting just a handful of individuals. The same holds true for chemical weapons. The attack on the Tokyo subway proved this concept as well. Chemical agents operate to affect the body's nervous system. Nerve agents prevent nerve impulses from traveling through the body, causing the heart and breathing to slow and possibly stop. Other chemical agents have nasty effects such as causing mucous membranes to bleed or significant blisters to form. Currently, chemical agents delivered are usually not spread too much after that delivery. However, persistent agents, much like some pesticides, are able to remain in an area making it unusable for a considerable time.

Network, or virtual, attacks are the newest among emerging methods. Given the ability of the attacker to reach around the world and the difficulty in capturing the perpetrator makes it an attractive tool. Network attacks offer a double punch. First, the effects of the actual attack could be incredible. Second, the trust that the target population loses in networked systems may not be quickly repaired. Consider all the activities that require these networks: traffic lights, air traffic control systems, power generation, and in some instances, water sanitation, to name a few. It would not be difficult to lose faith in many of these essential services. The use of the Internet for coordinating terrorist activities may increase as new, less detectable methods are developed. These will then be countered and newer ones developed over time.

Knowing that in many ways terrorism functions as a theatrical event indicates that the methods will change. Changes will be necessary to fit new audiences with different beliefs. Identifying what these are in advance will be difficult, but not impossible. Continuously scanning the environment and monitoring changes offers us a tool to prepare for these changes. Using gathered information to stay aware of the changing threat has proven elusive in the past. It is necessary to learn from our mistakes and develop methods to adapt to new threats and effectively deploy countermeasures.

References

Abbey, E. (1975). *The monkey wrench gang*. New York: Harper-Collins.

Animal Liberation Front (ALF). (Unknown). Animal liberation front primer. <http://www.animalliberationfront.com/ALFront/ALFPrime.htm>. Retrieved October 30, 2009.

Activist. (2009). In Merriam-Webster Online Dictionary. <http://www.merriam-webster.com/dictionary/activist>. Retrieved October 30, 2009.

Activist. (2009). In Dictionary.com. <http://dictionary.reference.com/browse/activist>. Retrieved October 30, 2009.

Boudreau, A., & Zamost, S. (2008, February 18). *University shooter's girlfriend: "I couldn't believe it."* <http://www

.cnn.com/2008/US/02/17/shooter.girlfriend/index .html#cnnSTCText>. Retrieved October 30, 2009.

Extremist. (2009). In Merriam-Webster Online Dictionary. <http://www.merriam-webster.com/dictionary/ extremist>. Retrieved October 30, 2009.

Extremist. (2009). In Dictionary.com <http://dictionary .reference.com/browse/extremist>. Retrieved October 30, 2009.

Fear. (2009). In Merriam-Webster Online Dictionary. <http://www.merriam-webster.com/dictionary/fear>. Retrieved October 30, 2009.

Federal Bureau of Investigation. (1976, August 20). Weatherman Underground Freedom of Information Act file.

Federal Bureau of Investigation. *Serial murder – Multi-disciplinary perspectives for investigators*. (2005). <http:// www.fbi.gov/publications/serial_murder.htm>. Retrieved October 30, 2009.

Federal Bureau of Investigation. *Terrorism in the United States*. (1999). <http://www.fbi.gov/publications/terror/terror99 .pdf>. Retrieved October 30, 2009.

Foreman, D., & Haywood, B. (1987). *Ecodefense: A field guide to monkeywrenching* (2nd ed.). Tuscon, AZ: Ned Ludd.

German, M. (2005, June 5). Behind the long terrorist, a pack mentality. *The Washington Post*. <http://www.washing-tonpost.com/wp-dyn/content/article/2005/06/04/ AR2005060400147.html>. Retrieved October 30, 2009.

Grass, S. M. (1989). Understanding and combating terrorism. <http://www.globalsecurity.org/military/library/ report/1989/GSM.htm>. Retrieved October 30, 2009.

Hitchens, C. (2002, November 18). Terrorism: Notes toward a definition. Slate Magazine. <http://www.slate.com/ ?id = 2074129>. Retrieved October 30, 2009.

Keet, C. Maria (Marijke). (2003, December). Towards a reso-lution of terrorism using game theory. <http://www .meteck.org/TERRORISM_WP.pdf>. Retrieved October 30, 2009.

Keet, C. Maria (Marijke). (2003). Causes of terrorism. <http://www.meteck.org/causesTerrorism.html>. Retrieved October 30, 2009.

Maximoff, *The political philosophy of Bakunin: Scientific anar-chism*. edited by G. P. Maximoff. 1953

Michel, L., & Herbeck, D. (2001). *American terrorist: Timothy McVeigh & the Oklahoma City bombing*. New York: Harper-Collins.

Morgan, D. (2008, February 16). *NIU shooter described as "gentle, quiet."* < http://www.cbsnews.com/stories/ 2008/02/16/national/main3840072.shtml>. Retrieved October 30, 2009.

National Commission on Terrorist Attacks upon the United States. (2004). The 9/11 commission report. New York: W. W. Norton.

Rudolph, E. (2005, April 14). *Full text of Eric Rudolph's confes-sion*. <http://www.npr.org/templates/story/story.php? storyId = 4600480>. Retrieved October 30, 2009.

Shachtman, N. (2008, September 15). Pentagon researcher conjures warcraft terror plot. *Wired*. <http://www .wired.com/dangerroom/2008/09/world-of-warcra/>. Retrieved October 30, 2009.

Terror. (2009). In Merriam-Webster Online Dictionary. <http://www.merriam-webster.com/dictionary/ terror>. Retrieved October 30, 2009.

U.S. State Department. (2003). *Patterns of global terrorism*. <http://www.state.gov/documents/organization/ 31932.pdf>. Retrieved October 30, 2009.

U.S. Department of Defense. (2001). *Department of defense dictionary of military and associated terms*. <http://www .dict.mil/doctrine/jel/new_pubs/jp1_02.pdf>. Retrieved October 30, 2009.

Williams, A., & Head, V. (2006). *Terror attacks*. London: Futura.

Zalman, A. (Unknown). The causes of terrorism. <http:// terrorism.about.com/od/causes/a/causes_terror.htm>. Retrieved October 30, 2009.

SECURITY QUIZ

1. Historically, the term "terrorist" can be traced to 1795.
   a. True
   b. False

2. As a security professional it is often less important to classify a potential threat as terrorism or crime than to identify and address the threat itself.
   a. True
   b. False

3. The worst terrorist act on U.S. soil was the bombing of the Murrah Federal Building in Oklahoma City on April 19, 1995.
   a. True
   b. False

4. The acroynom ELF refers to:
   a. Equal Liberation Front
   b. Earth Liberation Front
   c. Earth Liaison Front
   d. Earth Liberal Front

5. The smallest sized cell is:
   a. 3—5
   b. 5—10
   c. 10—15
   d. Individual

6. The CARVER model of target selection offers a useful tool for considering a target.
   a. True
   b. False

7. A security professional need only concentrate on their own facility when coping with terrorism.
   a. True
   b. False

8. Formal threat assessments are certainly important; however, regularly monitoring of the environment offers the opportunity to identify potential problems earlier.
   a. True
   b. False

9. An example of a non-violent extremist might be an animal rights supporter that uses no animal products at all.
   a. True
   b. False

10. It is impossible to identify potential targets.
    a. True
    b. False

30

Antiterrorism and VIP Protection

Christopher A. Hertig and
Ted Wade

CHAPTER OBJECTIVES

- Define terrorist actions and activities
- Explain steps for creating an antiterrorist strategy
- List four antiterrorist techniques
- List twenty specific techniques used for antiterrorist security
- Define personal protection specialists
- Explain the concept of protecting the principal
- Explore what to do in hostage situations
- Explore what to do if taken hostage
- Define the Stockholm Syndrome
- Suicide Attacks

Concerns with terrorism and workplace violence have been growing over the past several decades. We have seen spectacular terrorist acts, such as the airline attack on the World Trade Center, the Madrid train bombings, and the attacks on Mumbai. We have also seen disgruntled current or former employees open fire in their workplaces. We have seen assaults on staff at abortion centers and acts of violence perpetrated in our courthouses.

Protection officers play an important role as they are often the ones who control access to facilities, guard payrolls and armored trucks, drive executives to the airport, escort VIPs through crowds at public affairs, and maintain the physical security at airports, courthouses, power plants, corporate headquarters, and military bases. In order to play this role safely and professionally, they must have a basic understanding of the threat(s) confronting their work environments. They also need to be competent in crucial job tasks such as operating detection technology, searching personnel and vehicles, driving vehicles, and so on.

TERRORIST ACTIONS AND ACTIVITIES

Terrorist activities are contingent upon the capabilities of the terrorist organization, the philosophy of that organization, and the area in which the action takes place. Whereas Middle Eastern terrorists drive car bombs into target areas, European groups may attack police stations, airports, and so on, and North American terrorists may plant bombs, murder members of certain ethnic or professional groups (police, doctors at abortion clinics), and rob banks or armored cars.

One cannot assume what terrorists will or will not do, but antiterrorist security personnel should be familiar with the groups in their particular area and those that may target their industry. This will provide them with sufficient indication from which a more accurate assessment of terrorist activities can be made.

Task b, Element D in "Nuclear Security Personnel for Power Plants: Content and Review Procedures for a Security Training and Qualification Program" (NUREG 0219) lists the following characteristics involved in the planning and execution phases of a terrorist attack.

1. Terrorists will learn as much as possible beforehand about the engineering details of a facility.
2. They will assess power plant security ahead of time by observing the plant, talking to plant personnel, talking to an insider, and intercepting radio transmissions.
3. They will attempt to recruit an accomplice into the security force.
4. Terrorists will also try to recruit nonsecurity employees as accomplices.
5. They will consider kidnapping an employee, or an employee's family member, prior to an attack.
6. They may take hostages during the attack to force cooperation.
7. Terrorists will isolate the target site by cutting off communications and power supplies.
8. The group will assemble the necessary weapons and equipment to use in the attack (this can include firearms, military issue shoulder weapons, SMG's or Sub-Machine Guns, antitank rockets, high explosives, radio jamming or monitoring devices, power tools, construction equipment, and incapacitating agents).

9. The terrorists may use diversionary tactics such as sniping or detonating explosives.
10. They will try to intercept, delay, or destroy responding police forces so that security personnel cannot rely on local law enforcement assistance.
11. They may use unaware personnel as part of an attack plan, such as duping truck drivers into carrying explosives.
12. Terrorists will take advantage of periods when security performance is lowered such as adverse weather (rain, snow, fog) or when there are workers on site.
13. The terrorists will plan and rehearse the attack.
14. The attack will be planned to take the fire objective in less than 3 minutes.
15. Terrorists will not attack unless they are 100% confident that they will be successful.

While the foregoing was written with nuclear power plants in mind, the concepts are applicable to virtually any fixed site facility such as a bank, airport, or residence. Attacks against vehicles for the purpose of securing hostages also utilize the elements of surprise, speed, diversion, and, ultimately, violence. What can be gleaned from this is as follows:

1. **Communications and computer security is paramount.** Communications security protects against the compromise of information to terrorist/adversary groups. It also plays a key role in maintaining an effective physical security posture. Disgruntled employees/customers/terrorists will undoubtedly target computer systems more in the coming decade than they have previously.
2. **Confidentiality of information is essential!** The less a terrorist or other adversary can learn about an organization and its defenses, the less likely that an attack will be planned. An organization's information protection program can be the cornerstone of a terrorism defense strategy.

3. **Personnel security**—the protection of the workforce from infiltration by terrorists, foreign agents, criminals, and competitors who wish to steal proprietary business information is important. Much of the workplace violence issue revolves around the screening and management of employees.

4. **Access control**—over both personnel and vehicles—must be designed into the physical security system and maintained through the efforts of protection officers. Terrorists can be deterred from selecting a facility as a potential target if they perceive that target as being too well protected.

Personnel security, physical security, and information security all work cohesively to protect against terrorist threats:

Personnel Security
Physical Security
Information Security +
TERRORISM PROTECTION

ANTITERRORIST STRATEGY

In essence, defending against terrorism is no different from defending against other types of threats. Even though terrorism is complex insofar as assessing the threat is concerned, the physical security planning process is the same as it would be with any other threat or situation. Physical security must always be planned in several stages.

1. **Assets are identified.** What has value to the organization? What has value that is *strategic, monetary,* or *symbolic* to terrorist groups/individuals? What assets can be used to attack other targets, such as aircraft, weapons, chemicals, flammable materials, tampered foodstuffs?

2. **Loss events are exposed.** These are easily employed tactics that can be performed by a single individual and have a substantial impact on the organization. They include bombings or arson, assassination, kidnapping for "fund-raising" or publicity, sabotage of machinery, implanting computer viruses, or product tampering.

3. **Occurrence probability factors are assigned,** such as *certain, highly probable, moderately probable,* and *improbable.*

4. **Impact of occurrence is assessed.** Direct (replacement), indirect (loss of business), and extra expense (added fees, such as advertising and room rentals) costs are identified.

5. **Countermeasures are selected.** This can include the following risk management approaches:

Risk avoidance, such as not operating in a hostile country or having a business operation that is prone to attack.

Risk reduction includes target hardening by patrols via locks, lights, barriers, and so on. *It is usually the most expensive means of risk management. It is also inconvenient to employees, customers, and so forth.* As such it should not be employed without first considering alternative approaches to addressing the risk. CPTED (Crime Prevention Through Environmental Design) principles can be used to harden a facility without making it resemble a fortress. For example, unsightly bollards and barriers can be replaced by raising landscaping above the road or parking surface and using retaining walls as an attractive yet effective barrier.

Risk spreading involves having several facilities in different areas so that if one facility—or key executive—is annihilated, the entire organization is not crippled.

Risk transfer means transferring the financial risk of the loss event to another entity. Generally, this is via insurance coverage. Kidnap insurance policies have been used for the past two decades by major corporations. All organizations must assess the potential costs of extended business interruption, civil litigation, and negative publicity in the event of a death. Once this is done,

TABLE 30-1   Terrorism Protection Strategies by Countries and Corporations

National	Corporate/Organizational
Diplomacy/projecting a positive image to the world community	Public and media relations/ projecting a positive image in the operating environment
Intelligence efforts	Intelligence efforts
Investigation of suspect activities	Investigation of suspect activities
Target hardening/physical security	Target hardening/physical security
Tactical/emergency planning	Tactical/emergency planning

various modifications to existing insurance coverage can be made.

TERRORISM DEFENSIVE STRATEGIES

Obviously *liaison* with various organizations is important to strategies designed for defense against terrorism. This is important for both nations and corporations (Table 30-1). Liaison is important when planning for public events (Olympics, concerts, speeches, etc.), responding to incidents (fires, floods, bombings, power outages, etc.), and planning for terrorist attacks. There are some specific things that can be done by both public and private entities regarding counterterrorism (Table 30-2):

ANTITERRORIST TECHNIQUES BY ORGANIZATIONS/FACILITIES

Using the physical security concepts of deter, delay, deny, and detect in regard to terrorist attacks, include:

1. Techniques used to **deter** terrorist activity include target-hardening so that the terrorists have a lesser chance of success. Checking IDs, packages, and vehicles before they enter a secured area; making patrols or routes of travel

TABLE 30-2   Governmental and Corporate Partnership Activities

Government Agencies	Private Organizations
Provide and share intelligence to the macro environment: the city, state, or nation	Provide and share intelligence to the micro environment: the facility, other branches
Offer available seats in training classes to security personnel	Offer general employees available seats in corporate training programs
Provide consultation on terrorism, threat response, HAZMAT, etc.	Provide facilities for conducting training such as performing drills in buildings that are closed
Provide instruction on terrorism, hostage negotiation, WMD (Weapons of Mass Destruction) response	Locate facilities for incident command when a crisis arises
Share equipment obtained through government grant monies or military giveaways	Provide funds for equipment purchase such as robots, bomb suits, dogs, vehicles, etc.

unpredictable; and maintaining confidentiality are all target-hardening approaches.
2. Terrorists can be **delayed** by the use of barriers, locks, and response forces. Vehicular access to potential targets should also be controlled as much as is practical under the circumstances. This can be via barriers as well as access/parking arrangements that prevent quick and easy access to the target.
3. **Denial** of terrorist objectives can be accomplished through the use of contingency plans for dealing with the media and negotiating for hostages. These deny the terrorists the ploy of widespread panic and media leverage which they attempt to exploit.
4. **Detection** of terrorist activity can be accomplished through the analysis of threat intelligence. It can also occur by conducting entry searches, using detection technology (X-ray, metal, explosive), CCTV (Closed Circuit Television), alarm systems, lights, patrols, and access control systems.

Detection equipment must be paired with protection personnel who can evaluate what is detected and assess if the situation poses a threat. Detection equipment deserves special consideration. The use of this equipment was limited to metal detectors in nuclear power plants, airports, and prisons a decade or so ago. The events of 9/11 ushered in a wave of new technologies for explosive detection and the detection of WMD's manufactured with biological, chemical, and radioactive agents. The use of dogs for explosive detection has increased. Obviously there will be additional uses of detection equipment in the future.

These are a few key points to consider when purchasing and using the equipment:

- Initial cost
- Volume of traffic to be screened
- Single or progressively higher levels of screening, such as with layered access control
- The time needed to scan—delays, man-hours of searches and operators
- Aesthetic interface with the environment
- Response to alarm/detection—there should be a systematic process in place for investigation, isolation of the person being screened who emits an alarm and the area, communication with the cover officer/access controller/floor detective, etc., and control over the person who made the detector give warning
- Ease of use ("idiot proof") and amount of training required (note that hand searches are often necessary with metal detectors and X-rays). Vendors should provide training materials (manuals, videos, or e-learning modules) specific to the equipment to ensure operators understand how to use and how and when to service the equipment
- Cultural fit with the environment—it must be accepted by management and users such as employees, students, visitors, and so on

- Durability—how long the equipment will last is key
- Reliability/pick rate/false alarm rate—consideration should be given to independent testing or endorsement by a regulatory agency (TSA – Transportation Security Administration, NRC – Nuclear Regulatory Commission). Purchase of equipment and services certified and designated as effective by the U.S. Department of Homeland Security under the SAFETY Act provides liability protection to users of the equipment under U.S. law
- Routine maintenance needed—cleaning, start of shift tests, and so on
- Service contracts to maintain the equipment, possibly conduct in-depth performance tests, and repair of the equipment
- Education of those being searched so they cooperate with the search effort
- Training of users such as preemployment training, in-service instruction, and audits/inspections or drills/scenarios to ensure competency on the job

SPECIFIC TECHNIQUES FOR ANTITERRORIST SECURITY

Some specific techniques that antiterrorist security personnel (personal protection specialists, airport, power plant, military security officers) may utilize include the following:

1. **Become thoroughly familiar with any and all security equipment.** While this sounds overly simple, routine audits at airports and nuclear facilities commonly reveal that equipment is not being properly used for any one of a number of reasons.
2. **Check and test equipment frequently.** Develop overlapping auditing systems for the equipment, such as having technicians, officers, and supervisors all

performing their own tests. Protection officers must be familiar with equipment manuals for equipment and perform tests of the equipment at the start of their shift. Operational tests using standard test components must also be conducted at prescribed intervals.

3. **Rotate personnel assignments** as often as practical, take notes, and perform communication checks to maintain and insure personnel alertness.

4. **Check all areas** that the person, or materials being protected, are about to enter before they enter.

5. **Maintain weapons and other emergency equipment in position** so that they can be employed instantaneously. If it can't be, something is seriously deficient.

6. **Ascertain the legal implications of carrying or using weapons** before they are carried. Never assume something is legal; check it out first.

7. **Be familiar with what belongs in an area and what doesn't**, so that explosives, weapons, and surveillance devices can be detected.

8. **Use cover and concealment to their utmost**. Stand behind objects which can shield you from bullets (cover) and have the protectee do the same whenever possible. Hide movements via darkness, tinted glass, or drawn blinds (concealment). Maintain light and noise discipline at appropriate times such as on patrol. *"See others before they see you; hear others before they hear you."*

9. **Select positions that provide the greatest visual vantage point.** This may be a corner of a room or an elevated position.

10. **Stay close enough to persons who are being protected** so that effective defensive actions can always be taken, yet not so close as to intrude on the principal's personal space.

11. **Plan for communication failures** and develop alternate means of communications. There should always be at least two means of communication available to the PPS.

12. **Practice duress codes** (verbal and nonverbal) so that secret, emergency messages can be transmitted at all times.

13. **Take appropriate action in a tactful manner** to ensure that antiterrorist security personnel (airport or nuclear plant protection officers; personal protection specialists) do not become occupied and burdened with nonsecurity duties. Auxiliary duties are important; *they are nice to do* but security duties are the most important; *they must be done*.

14. **Vehicles should be driven so that there is always room to maneuver** in case escape is necessary. Drive on the left side of the road to prevent the vehicle from being forced off the shoulder. Protective services personnel who drive should have specialized training!

15. **Always keep parked vehicles locked and secured** as much as possible with alarms, guards, or other techniques.

16. **Check out the vehicle prior to departure** for basic mechanical soundness (gas in the tank, fan belts, and tires in good condition). Have a detailed check done regularly by a mechanic.

17. **Before departure, check in and around the vehicles for the presence of unauthorized personnel**, or any attempts at tampering with the engine, gas tank, doors, tires, or undercarriage.

18. **Assess the security of the route and location being traveled** prior to departure.

19. **Establish and maintain positive working relationships** with agencies or departments that can provide support services. Be friendly, polite, and tactfully inquisitive enough to find out how much and what type of assistance they can and will provide.

20. As searching is almost always part of the security function, **keep in mind and practice the *principles* of searching** which can be applied to any type of search.

a. **Identify the search object; know what is being looked for**. The more known, the better! Protection officers must know what weapons or explosives look like. Recognize that the ability to conceal a device is only limited by the imagination and resources of the adversary. Look for indicators that might reveal an explosive device; improvised wiring and switches, overweight vehicles, odors of chemicals, fertilizer, or fuels, and recent "repairs" that might hide a concealed compartment. Ongoing professional education is valuable.

b. **Establish parameters for the search; know boundaries for the search**. Determine how *thorough* and *intrusive* the search effort must be.

c. **Assess the environment to be searched for obvious items, as well as the development of a search system.** A general scan of the area (visual, audio, olfactory or smell) should always be used.

d. **Devise a systematic method for conducting the search such as top to bottom, front to rear** (with bomb searches, go bottom to top) after analyzing the search environment. Each pattern or system must be based upon the complexity and time necessary to conduct the search. How large an area/person; how complex—how much stuff to search—and how much time available will determine the type of pattern used. In many cases, a priority search is used. This means that the most obvious or accessible areas are searched first. Lobbies and restrooms of buildings searched for explosives would be an example. Another would be searching the hand, ankle, and waist areas of a person for weapons—the weapons are most likely to be hidden there and are most accessible to the person carrying them. Alternatively, priority searches can be of areas that are most vulnerable, such as the computer center, or power or heat center of a building. An explosive placed in these locations would do the most damage. Radiological, biological, or chemical WMD's would be most damaging near air intake systems. In the event of a threat, these areas might be searched first. Other than priority searches, search patterns should incorporate *overlap* so that no area is missed during the search.

e. **Search thoroughly using *visual assessment*, touch, hearing, and aids such as detection equipment, dogs, flashlights, and mirrors.** "Look before touching" is always good advice! One technique is to use visual angles. Walk around the object, vehicle, or person to be searched in both directions. Look at them from various angles to see if there is anything hidden. Do this before actually moving in to conduct a search.

f. **Spread out or open up the person, package, or vehicle to be searched.** If a vehicle is searched with all the doors, etc., open it is easier to see items that don't belong. The same is true with baggage or persons. Have the baggage opened up with the contents carefully removed and stacked. Have the person assume a posture with his/her arms outstretched and feet a shoulder width or more apart.

g. **Continue searching until the entire area has been searched**—don't stop after finding one item (or person, if it is a building search). Terrorists may have planted secondary explosives. Don't become a secondary victim! And don't call in a bomb squad until the entire area has been searched and the technicians know precisely what the extent of the problem is. They do not like surprises!

h. **Disturb the environment as little as possible during the search; try to observe before you touch something.** Look before touching. This is important for safety as well as human relations concerns—nobody wants their person, personal effects, vehicle, or office to be rummaged through.

i. **Be as polite, considerate, and courteous as possible**. Professional conversations with those being searched make the search more efficient. *Interview the individual being searched* to learn more about what may be found. This is part of the assessment of the search environment.

j. **Search with appropriate personnel** such as a searcher and a cover officer/access controller. The searcher conducts the search while the cover officer or access controller oversees it so that it is done properly. The cover officer also acts to insure that everything is done safely. He/she intervenes appropriately if there is an imminent threat against the search officer.

k. **Evaluate the search effort.** This is done with an observer such as a cover officer/access controller. The search must be done properly and completely. The final part of evaluation is to determine when the search is finished.

PROFESSIONAL DEVELOPMENT FOR PERSONAL PROTECTION SPECIALISTS

Antiterrorist security personnel must have highly developed professional knowledge and skills in order to be effective. They must think in terms of the various areas of competency required. By focusing on these competencies, the protection officer can better chart a course for continuous professional development. In general, counterterrorist security personnel operating in any environment (i.e., personal protection specialists, nuclear security officers, airport security officers, etc.) must be proficient in the following areas:

1. **Knowledge of physical security concepts and techniques.** A personal protection specialist or other counterterrorist security person should be a physical security specialist first and foremost. An understanding of the theory of physical security and risk management, including various responses to risk and the physical security planning process are crucial to the success of his/her mission.

2. **Knowledge of terrorism,** especially of terrorists operating in the immediate work area and those who have targeted similar facilities. Reading various newspapers is essential. So, too, is keeping in contact with professional groups such as a local chapter of ASIS (American Society for Industrial Security) International or state crime prevention officer associations.

3. **Public relations skills,** so that security can be maintained unobtrusively. Manners, etiquette, and public speaking are all essential.

4. **Education (college),** sufficient to communicate, understand, and record information that is learned during training or on the job.

5. **Physical fitness,** so as to be able to perform strenuous tasks during emergencies and so that martial skills can be learned (one must be fit to fight).

6. **Martial skills,** such as the *practical* use of weapons and defensive tactics. Training for the "five-second fight" where the adversary is neutralized as quickly as possible, or as a means of low-key, almost invisible control over a disruptive person who is approaching a principal, is important.

7. **Familiarity with explosives and the weapons of terrorists,** so as to be able to identify dangerous items. This means knowing standard military and commercial explosives as a start. It also means being able to recognize improvised explosives and keeping abreast of the latest means of employing them.

8. **Knowledge of security equipment**. The application of technology can be a great asset, but only when done correctly. Attending professional meetings and trade shows can help a great deal. This is a key area of competency in counterterrorist security. Unfortunately, it is often ignored. Antiterrorist security personnel should read a lot of equipment manuals!

9. **Searching skills used for bomb, personnel, building, package, and vehicle searches.** This is usually a sorely neglected area; oftentimes officers conduct searches just for the sake of following procedures. Keep in mind that the purpose of a search is to find something.

10. **Professional dedication** to enable one to put up with boredom, long hours, and uncooperative persons.

PERSONAL PROTECTION SPECIALISTS (PPS)

Many people still think of a "bodyguard" as being a physically tough individual who has an imposing appearance and/or highly developed martial skills (martial arts, firearms, other weapons). While there may be a need for such an individual, and the martial skills have practical application, there is much more to the makeup of a personal protection specialist (PPS). Like other counterterrorist security personnel, the PPS must be a security practitioner first and a "trained killer" second. Of even greater importance to the PPS is to have highly developed communication and human relation abilities. Etiquette and the ability to blend in with the protectee are more important than being able to destroy all opposition.

Few people perform PPS duties on a regular full-time basis. Those who do generally have proven themselves through a series of assignments. They usually obtain their positions through networking. Organizations such as Nine Lives Associates are invaluable in this regard.

Generally, a protection professional is called upon to protect a principal for a short period of time. It may be during a speech, a concert, a meeting, and so on. A typical example would be a police department that deploys a few officers to VIP duty while a celebrity is in the city. For this reason, PPS functions are probably important in the repertoire of professional competency for virtually all protection officers.

Knowledge of the protectee's business and personal habits is very important. PPS's must be able to plan out security measures in accordance with the principal's business and personal lifestyle. He or she must be able to devise protective strategies that are reasonable and unobtrusive. Embarrassment to the principal is a major threat; the PPS should not do anything to cause this!

Driving skills and knowledge of vehicles are especially important to the PPS. Much of the time spent guarding executives and other VIP's is while those persons are traveling. Specialized driving classes should be attended. Knowledge of airline customs and regulations should be acquired and kept up to date. In effect, personal protection specialists should be "travel consultants"!

Study and master personal security systems to prevent crime. In many areas, attacks from local criminals are the most probable threat. A PPS should be adept at performing home security surveys. They should be able to set up security systems at residences, hotel rooms, and apartments.

Develop emergency medical skills. Every PPS should be certified in first aid and CPR (cardiopulmonary resuscitation). They should be aware of, and plan for, any medical problems that the protectee might have. Advanced emergency medical training is a real plus for personal protection specialists as medical emergencies can arise at any time.

Martial skills are important. These skills must be practiced and refined. In order to learn them adequately and safely, and employ them in an emergency, security personnel must be in excellent physical condition. Here are some tips on physical training:

- Develop endurance and stamina through running, swimming, or sports activities.
- Develop explosive power by sprinting, lifting light weights rapidly, lifting heavy weights, and maintaining flexibility. Plyometrics are often used by athletes and can certainly be adapted to emergency skill development.
- Static strength, or the ability to apply force for an extended period of time, can be developed by practicing holding weights up or remaining in push-up or pull-up position for a period of time.
- Hand strength—which is important for grabbing and using any type of weapon—can be developed in any one of a number of ways. Squeezing a rubber ball is the most effective. Crumpling up newspaper pages with one hand, doing fingertip push-ups, pull-ups, and virtually any type of weightlifting involving a pulling type of motion are other approaches.
- Flexibility is important not only because speed is increased, but because injuries are prevented and body tension caused by stress may be reduced. Stretch first thing in the morning! This "sets" your body's range of motion for the rest of the day. Stretching should be done after a warm-up that gets blood flowing to the muscles. During all workouts, stretch and contract muscles. Once the muscles have been contracted, stretch them. Rhythmic stretching is a fast, effective method of stretching. It involves ten repetitions of a stretch. Taking care to stretch a little farther each time develops flexibility. At night to relax, *static-passive stretching* can be employed. Try holding in a stretched position for at least 30 seconds. This will make the muscles grow longer and help you relax. Ensure that the muscles are moved around after the static stretch or one will lose speed of movement.

Manners, deportment, and decorum will "make or break" a PPS more quickly than anything else. Proper dining etiquette and the ability to understand such aspects of corporate protocol, such as the conduct of meetings, are everyday issues that confront a PPS. In many cases, persons with a criminal justice background have great difficulty adjusting to upper-class society. Anyone wishing to become involved in executive protection must become adept at manners and dress. A trip to the library or research over the Internet for information on this might be the most important career investment that an aspiring PPS can make.

PROTECTING THE PRINCIPAL

The operational aspects of guarding executives, celebrities, political leaders—or witnesses—encompass a wide range of tasks and duties. Personal protection is a specialty that requires immense dedication. Here are a few things to bear in mind when acting as a security escort:

1. Never leave the protectee unguarded.
2. Always be alert and ready to respond to emergencies.
3. Position yourself between the protectee and possible threats.
4. Enter rooms first to make sure they are safe. Completely scan the room. Consider closing the blinds to avoid being visible from outside adversaries.
5. When trouble starts, move the protectee to safety immediately. He or she is your first and only responsibility.
6. Carry items, such as briefcases, in the nongun or nonweapon hand.
7. Always watch the hands of potential assailants.
8. Review the itinerary and prepare for the day's activities well beforehand. Know it! At the same time be able to make necessary changes and adjustments.

9. Become acquainted with a wide range of sports and hobbies in which the protectee may engage so that you may accompany him/her.
10. Conceal your position as a personal protection specialist from everyone except those who need to know. Blend in and be part of the principal's team, not an unwanted appendage! *Bear in mind that one of the biggest detriments to executives and celebrities is embarrassment.* Out-of-place dress, language or behavior must be avoided.

HOSTAGE SITUATIONS

Hostage-taking has become a serious problem. The criticality of these incidents (when a life or lives are threatened), coupled with the myriad of emotional, legal, and public relations problems that accompany them, make hostage incidents a concern for all security practitioners. In short, the *direct* and *indirect costs* of these incidents make them a serious problem. Security personnel must be prepared to deal with these situations; they are simply too dangerous not to worry about.

Hostage situations can occur with organized politically motivated terrorists. They may also take place with criminals who use hostages as shields in order to escape. Domestic incidents and the actions of the mentally deranged comprise additional threat scenarios. Hostage scenarios end when the hostage taker/s give up, attempt to flee, or are overtaken by tactical units. In the overwhelming majority of hostage incidents, negotiation is the key to resolving them. Protection officers need to contain, control, and calm the situation. They need to set the stage for negotiation or tactical assault if that is necessary.

1. **Isolate the area of the incident (crisis point).** Keep the perpetrators contained and don't allow anyone except negotiators or tactical personnel near the area.
2. **Obtain as much information as possible.** Use a predesigned threat form when

receiving a hostage/extortion call. Question available witnesses. Find out as much as possible about the hostages, hostage takers, and the immediate physical environment. This includes their prior life history, medical condition, and emotional condition. Building layout with access/egress points, structural strength, and utilities must be collected as well. *Intelligence data is crucial to the successful handling of a hostage incident. Security forces play a key role here in having this information available to hostage negotiators and special response teams!*
3. **Notify the central alarm station or dispatcher of the incident** and keep the information flowing.
4. **Maintain perimeters, supply information, keep a low uniformed officer profile, and await further instruction.**

Don't try to make a play or be a hero, simply *contain the problem* and *report* any and all relevant information. Isolation of the problem and information regarding it are the key concerns of protection officers during a hostage situation.

HOSTAGE THREAT RECEIPT

According to the U.S. Nuclear Regulatory Commission (NUREG 0219 Task 57), the following procedures should be followed whenever a hostage threat call is received:

1. Stay calm.
2. Attempt to verify that the caller actually has a hostage by asking for information about the hostage and asking to speak to the hostage.
3. Record precise details of the call.
4. Notify the central alarm station or the security shift supervisor.

Obviously there should be a hostage threat contingency plan that is operational and updated periodically. A hostage threat report form should be readily available to security officers and telephone operators.

IF TAKEN HOSTAGE

If a security officer is taken hostage *or* is in close proximity to the hostage taker, there are several key points to bear in mind.

1. **Do not do anything to excite or aggravate the hostage taker**. Accept your fate, speak little, and lower your voice. Speak a little slower (*"slower and lower"*). Assume a passive/*supportive* body posture. Display palms, keeping hands at your sides or folded in your lap. Shoulders should be rolled slightly forward and your head a bit forward and down. This must be comfortable and natural; it needs to be only a very slight change in posture to be effective.
2. **Identify yourself by your first name and use the hostage-taker's first name**. This will aid in having him or her view you as a *person* rather than an *object* with which to bargain.
3. **Don't speak unless spoken to and weigh your words carefully**. As with any emotionally charged individual, avoid the words "you," "should," and "why." These are too direct/pointed and tend to place the person's reasoning process on trial.
4. **Be patient, remain calm, and try to rest**. Conserve your energy! This helps to prevent becoming stressed out, preserves your ability to think objectively, and prepares you for what will probably be a long ordeal.
5. **Analyze the hostage taker(s) as much as possible.** Try to see things through his eyes. Empathic listening is key.
6. **Analyze the physical environment as much as possible.** Look for cover, escape routes, means of communication, and obvious hazards.

MANAGING THE HOSTAGE INCIDENT

Management of a hostage situation—or other crisis event—consists of several key elements.

These are control, coordination, communication, and information. By employing each of these concepts, the incident can be successfully negotiated without anyone getting hurt.

1. **Control access to the area.** Set up an **inner perimeter** around the crisis point where only negotiation and tactical personnel are authorized to go. An outside perimeter excludes members of the public and any other unauthorized personnel. Within the outside perimeter is the command post. All communications and agency liaison emanate from the command post. Media personnel should be restricted to a secured location within the outer perimeter that is not too close to the command post. The media's needs should be facilitated as much as possible in terms of access to power supplies, office/work rooms, and telephones. Their comfort and work needs should be met as much as possible by a public information officer. They need to do their job, yet they cannot be allowed to roam around unescorted.
2. **Coordination is also handled through the command post.** Persons who have a "need to know" should be supplied with information; actions of the negotiator(s) are not to be divulged to tactical personnel.
3. **Communication is centered in the command post.** Communications with the hostage taker should be set up immediately, preferably by telephone. The communications monitoring capabilities of the hostage taker and the media must be carefully assessed and restricted.
4. **Information is the key to successful resolution be it through negotiation or assault**. Everything possible concerning the psychological, physical, and background characteristics of all those involved in the incident should be collected at the command post. Details regarding the physical layout of the crisis point, such as the location of utility

lines, room layout, and building structure, should be obtained.

NEGOTIATION

While hostage negotiation is a complex professional skill demanding education in psychology and years of interviewing experience capped off by specialized training, it is important for security personnel to understand something about it. Security personnel must be able to render first aid. They must be able to provide immediate, necessary actions to reduce the level of violence. Hostage negotiators may not be immediately available.

Hostage takers may initiate the negotiation process with someone close at hand and simply not want to talk with negotiators when they arrive. These are the basic concepts of negotiations:

1. Stall for time as much as possible. Say that you have to check with your boss.
2. Don't give the hostage taker something without getting something in return.
3. Make the hostage taker think. Wear him out mentally by forcing him to constantly decide things. *Slow it down.*
4. Never give hostage takers weapons or intoxicants.
5. Don't make promises or threats that you cannot keep.

THE STOCKHOLM SYNDROME

Hostages who are in captivity for extended periods of time may begin to empathize with and later sympathize with the hostage takers. This phenomenon is called the Stockholm syndrome and is named after a 131-hour standoff with police in Stockholm, Sweden, in 1973. After the siege went on for a while, the hostages began to think that they knew better than

the police what was needed to gain their release and save their lives. They then sided with the hostage takers.

This syndrome is important to understand. After the hostages begin to sympathize with the hostage takers they may deny that any abuse or aggression took place. They may also make statements to the media that are supportive of the hostage takers and any cause which they have. The syndrome can also be used by hostage negotiators who can use the rapport built between hostages and hostage takers in order to resolve the situation (Becker, 2009).

SUICIDE ATTACKS

Suicide attacks have been used throughout history by extremist groups and soldiers during war. What has changed is the use of suicide bombings as a tactic. Beginning with the Beirut bombing of 1983, there have been numerous other incidents of suicide bombers. Suicide bombing has spread to many countries. It continues to evolve as a terrorist technique.

Defense against suicide bombings includes proactive intelligence. Finding out who is ready to launch a suicide attack and intervening are obviously the best defense. In some cases protection officers can identify terrorist attempts to conduct surveillance and reconnaissance. Obviously anyone taking photos or notes should be reported and investigated. Also, persons walking around a facility moving against the flow of traffic may indicate surveillance in progress. As Maggio (2009) points out: if the terrorists can see the target, then the target can see the terrorists.

In terms of physical security planning, extending facility perimeters outward helps to limit the effect of a suicide bomber. So, too, does limiting access that a bomber may have to a group of people—large groups of people are the preferred targets of suicide bombers. Another consideration is blast effect. Within the confines of a bus or train car, explosive force is compressed and increased, and casualties are higher.

Suicide bombers are thwarted by security officers. Officers notice the bombers or their handlers and take action. Basic indications of a suicide bomber are bulky clothing in which to conceal the explosives, a briefcase, or knapsack. Behavior includes disorientation, mumbling, profuse sweating, and nervousness. The handler will be nearby and will have a cell phone. There may also be a vehicle, perhaps a van, which is used to drop the bomber off near the target. *Note:* stopping a suicide bomber may involve moving people out of the area—quickly! It may also involve getting control of the bomber's hands so that they cannot detonate the device. Some devices, however, are detonated by the handler.

Obviously, protection officers in areas where suicide bombings are a credible threat need specialized training and procedures for dealing with this threat. Employer and client policy must be adhered to. Grabbing someone without just cause constitutes the tort of battery. Suicide bombing attacks must be managed as any other risk. Suicide attacks must be carefully weighed against the threat of civil and perhaps criminal charges filed against the protection officer.

EMERGING TRENDS

In the late 1970s a branch manager for Burns International Security Services, Inc. was interviewed by a local newspaper. In the interview the manager stated that executive protection would be the future of the contract security industry. This did not happen right away, but it is largely becoming a reality.

Antiterrorism and VIP protection will continue to evolve with the threats that confront protection officers. In order to meet the challenges of the future—*and be a part of that future*—there must be a greater emphasis on the following:

1. The study of various types of threat groups and individuals by individual protection officers. There must also be published research on this in the professional literature. It cannot be the exclusive domain of political science or the general news media. Security magazines and journals must feature recent, relevant articles on threat groups and individuals. This is occurring but only within the past few years. The professional literature must be on top of developments regarding terrorism and related threats.

2. The development of theoretical and practical aspects of conducting searches is imperative so that training programs can produce graduates who are truly proficient and professional at the searching function. This must be studied and protocols developed.

3. An emphasis on manners and deportment by protection officers so that they can join the management team and have a voice in the organization. As PPS develops as a more common job function—whether on a regular or occasional basis—there is a greater awareness of upper management manners by protection staff.

4. More academic programs in security and loss control at colleges and universities are needed so that both theory and technology can be studied. This will also aid in making

security a more visible career option to students who are the future of the industry. At present security programs are a hard sell to criminal justice students. Courses in security, however, do fit in nicely with emergency management or homeland security curricula.

5. Embracing of the principles of risk management by protection officers. This assists in more creative solutions to threat problems. It also helps to marry security to insurance and accepted business practices. The current emphasis on enterprise risk management helps to support risk management utilization by protection officers.

6. Elevation and professionalization of the protection officer is occurring. Responsibilities and wages are rising. Government agencies are seeing the role that they play in antiterrorism. So must the general public and the legislators who mandate training and licensing. In particular, the role of the protection officer in collecting intelligence and assisting in emergency response must be appreciated. It might be said that "The biggest asset in *public* safety is *private* security."

References

Becker, R. F. (2009). *Criminal investigation*. Sudbury, MA: Jones & Bartlett.

Maggio, E. J. (2009). *Private security in the 21st century: Concepts and applications*. Sudbury, MA: Jones & Bartlett.

U.S. Nuclear Regulatory Commission. (1978). *Nuclear security personnel for power plants: Content and review procedures for a security training and qualification program*. Washington, DC: U.S. Nuclear Regulatory Commission.

Resources

ASIS International has an Information Resource Center on their Web site, which is available to members. There are also a variety of books and videos in the ASIS bookstore. ASIS hosts seminars relating to Terrorism and has a Council on Global Terrorism. Visit www.asisonline.org.

AST Corporation (hits@astcorp.com) has numerous CD-ROMs and online programs within the HITS Program on Executive Protection and Homeland Security. Note that members of the International Foundation for Protection Officers receive discounts on AST Corporation programs.

BSR (Bill Scott Racing School) (http://www.bsr-inc .dreamhosters.com/ or 304/725-9281) provides training in evasive driving and executive security training.

CRC Press (www.crcpress.com) offers a variety of books on terrorism and related topics.

Butterworth-Heinemann offers a wide variety of titles relating to terrorism and emergency management. Please visit http://stbooks.elsevier.com/security or call (800) 545-2522.

Executive Protection Institute (http://www.personal protection.com/ or (800) 947-5827) offers numerous programs relating to executive protection, corporate aircraft security, and so on. They also publish *Providing Executive Protection* and *Providing Executive Protection Volume II*. In addition, the Institute administers Nine Lives Associates, a professional organization of personal protection specialists.

Executive Security International (http://www.esi-lifeforce .com/ or (888) 718-3105) provides training courses in executive protection and counterintelligence. They also offer an outstanding book, *The Executive Protection Bible*, and distance education courses.

The **International Foundation for Protection Officers** (www.IFPO.org) maintains an Article Archives on their Web site, which contains articles on detection equipment, terrorism, and related topics.

The **Professional Security Training Network (PSTN)** offers programs on bomb search, vehicle search, and executive protection. Visit www.pstn.com.

Tony Scotti Associates (http://www.securitydriver. com/vdi.html) offers courses in evasive driving and other aspects of executive protection. There is also an article bank, blog, e-mail newsletter, and books for purchase.

SECURITY QUIZ

1. Personal protection specialists should attempt to stand out as obvious security personnel in the principal's entourage so people know whom to rely on in an emergency.
   a. True
   b. False

2. Personal protection specialists should only worry about assassins and kidnappers, since common criminals are unlikely to attack a VIP.
   a. True
   b. False

3. A principal is about to enter a room; a protection specialist should enter the room before the protectee to make sure it is safe and consider closing the blinds to prevent outside adversaries from observing activity in the room.
   a. True
   b. False

4. When in the presence of a hostage taker or other violence-prone individual you should attempt to take what actions?
   a. Assert your authority so they know you are in charge, not the hostage takers
   b. Let them know you are skilled in martial arts and it would be dangerous to confront you
   c. Remain calm, use your first name, and cooperate with the hostage takers
   d. Use your time with the hostage takers to convince them their cause is wrong so they are more likely to release the hostages
   e. All of the above

5. There has been a hostage-taking in a building on your employer's property. What items of information would be valuable to hostage response teams?
   a. The physical layout of the facility
   b. The numbers and descriptions of hostage takers
   c. Psychological and background information on all those involved in the incident
   d. Numbers, identities, and descriptions of the hostages
   e. All of the above

6. A polite respectful approach will make those being searched more cooperative with a search officer and make the search more effective.
   a. True
   b. False

7. Searches should be conducted randomly without a pattern that can be detected by adversaries.
   a. True
   b. False

8. Counterterrorist security personnel should read and become intimately familiar with detection equipment manuals, calibration techniques, and capabilities.
   a. True
   b. False

9. Terrorist groups frequently attempt to infiltrate a facility's workforce, including the security department, prior to conducting an attack.
   a. True
   b. False

10. Which of the following is the least agreeable time to detect a terrorist plot?
    a. While the terrorists are conducting surveillance to learn about the facility
    b. When a terrorist operative applies for a job at the site and undergoes a background check
    c. When a terrorist attempts a rehearsal by attempting to penetrate the facility
    d. When the terrorists arrive at the site to conduct the attack

INVESTIGATIONS

31

Investigation: Concepts and Practices for Security Professionals

Christopher A. Hertig

CHAPTER OBJECTIVES

- Define investigation and protection
- Explore the scope of investigative activity
- Provide a brief history of investigation
- Explain the need for preliminary and follow-up investigation
- Identify the relevance of intelligence, liaison, writing reports, auditing, and interviews to the investigatory process.
- Explain undercover investigations and surveillance
- Define behavior/condition analysis
- Identify 10 points to keep in mind when testifying in legal and quasi-legal proceedings

Investigation comes from the Latin word *investigere*, which means to track or trace (Bennett & Hess, 2001). Investigation can take many forms—from the simple asking of a few questions and noting it in a report to a full-scale forensic examination. An unfortunate reality is that many people greatly underestimate the importance of investigation within the security field. Few texts on criminal investigation even mention private investigation or security investigation. Save for the obligatory treatment of Pinkerton, the texts are mute on the topic.

There seems to be a feeling that investigation is a highly specialized process that is performed only by police or supervisors. The popular image of private detectives who wear trench coats with their collars turned up and have cigarettes dangling from their lips has been created and reinforced by the entertainment media. However, there needs to be a readjustment of attitudes by the public, managers, academics who write texts, and officers themselves. With the threat of terrorism and the proliferation of organized criminal groups, security personnel must become involved in the investigative process. And they need to be recognized for their contributions.

The fact of the matter is that investigation is performed each and every day by entry level protection officers as well as specialized investigators. The work of these persons rarely makes it onto the evening news, but it aids the asset protection process in innumerable ways. The contemporary protection officer acts as a management representative, a consultant, an enforcement agent, and an intelligence agent.

The roles of intelligence agent and consultant are perhaps most closely related to investigative activity. In the former role, the protection officer reports the presence of actual and *potential* loss-causing situations to management. In the consultant role, the officer must be knowledgeable of the legal ramifications involved in searching persons, vehicles, and so on. They must appreciate the privacy considerations related to surveillance.

Investigating suspicious changes in the environment they are protecting is "part and parcel" of what protection officers do. It is essential to acquiring information that may be useful in taking legal actions after a loss. It is also critical toward obtaining intelligence on organized criminal activity so that preventive actions can be taken.

Perhaps a start toward a better understanding is to see the scope of investigative activity that is performed by various entities (see Table 31-1).

Investigations are performed by police, lawyers, government agencies at the federal (FBI), state (attorney general's office), or local levels (municipal police). They are also performed by corporate staff—either investigators or supervisors—as well as private investigative firms. Most investigative activity is conducted "in-house" on a proprietary basis by and for the investigator's employer. Some activity is contracted out to private investigative agencies that are licensed to perform investigative services to another for a fee.

Private investigators can be useful if the client entity (corporation or government agency) does not have the expertise or manpower resources to conduct the inquiry. Some cases of complex financial inquiries or computer crime require the hiring of specialists. Undercover investigation is almost always outsourced. Insurance companies may use private investigators to conduct surveillance in areas where travel by a proprietary investigator would be impractical. Surveillance also requires some equipment; specialists in this field have the expensive equipment necessary for conducting difficult inquiries. Background screening firms are often used as they rely on local personnel to conduct records searches at courthouses. While some data can be obtained via computer, in many cases there is a real need for an old-fashioned hand search of records.

Private investigators generally must be licensed. They and their employees must meet regulatory standards often set by state agencies, which also regulate security officers. There may be restrictions on offering investigative or security services on a contractual basis without a license to do so. There may also be a requirement to work

TABLE 31-1   Investigative Activity by Type and Entity

Investigation Type	Investigating Entity
Criminal—felonies, misdemeanors, summary offenses, or ordinance violations	Police officers, protection officers, corporate investigators, state or federal agents, private investigative firms
Accident—work stoppage mishaps involved in production; slips and falls, vehicle accidents	Police officers, security officers, private investigators, insurance investigators, regulatory agency investigators (OSHA)
Personnel—violations of employer policy; may or may not be a crime or tort (civil offense)	Supervisory or managerial personnel, private investigators (undercover), corporate investigators, protection officers
Background—prior employment checks, criminal or credit checks done for hiring or promotion to sensitive positions or for bonding	Private investigative firms, human resources departments, corporate investigators, federal or state agency investigators

for only a single licensed firm at a time, or to carry an identification card, pay an annual registration fee, recertify by periodically taking training, and so on. The Fair Credit Reporting Act in the United States also places extensive requirements on third parties who conduct background investigations. It is important that persons working with investigative firms as employees or clients fully understand the legal requirements of such arrangements. In North America, the International Association of Security and Investigative Regulators lists state and provincial regulations on their Web site at http://www.iasir.org.

Investigation and Asset Protection Go Hand-in-Hand

Uniformed protection officers on patrol or plainclothes loss prevention agents must be intimately familiar with their patrol environments. They must be able to discern when something isn't right. In many cases, unusual or unexplained situations indicate criminal activity. The investigating officer on patrol must be able to first recognize things that aren't quite right. This could be a vehicle parked in an unusual place, persons taking photographs, unusual trash disposal procedures, graffiti, hand gestures, clothing or "colors" worn around the area, persons conversing with others in an unusual way, etc. The list goes on and on. Each indicator could mean a variety of different things; terrorists or criminals conducting surveillance on a target, theft of materials, gang activity, or drug dealing.

One lesson to be learned regarding investigations is that major cases are solved via minor incidents. Murderers get caught parking illegally or shoplifting. While detectives and other investigative specialists may piece incidents together, it is the patrol officer who takes note of something and acts upon it that supplies the key information. Small observations often yield big results: "Minor Is Major."

Along a similar vein, a review of accidents, terrorist attacks, or acts of workplace violence all have indicators that they are about to take place. After the unfortunate event has happened, it is often noted what all the indicators were present that should have been seen earlier. Perhaps better playing of the intelligence agent role is one means of taking corrective action before tragedy strikes.

In order to fulfill the intelligence agent role effectively, protection personnel must also be able to report what they observe in an articulate manner. They must "get it right" on paper. And they should always reinforce the written report with a verbal report to the appropriate personnel.

Investigation has nothing to do with stylish clothes, gunfights, or flashy cars. It is not glamorous. Rather, it is tedious and exacting. It has to do with *fact-finding* and *research*. Investigation is simply an objective process used to discover facts about a situation, person, or behavior. Once those facts are discovered, they are recorded in an appropriate manner. Investigation has a great deal to do with research; those who like to do Web or library research may acclimate themselves to investigative activity better than those who disdain research. Investigation requires precision and attention to detail. It culminates in writing reports about the known facts. These reports are the product of the investigation.

Investigation is important because without facts, management cannot make the correct decisions. As the security officer is a member of the security management team, it may be his/her responsibility to provide management with information. Usually the security officer will give investigative information to his or her supervisor and they will provide it to management. He/she reports this information after conducting some type of investigative activity (searching for something, talking with people, observing something, etc.).

INVESTIGATIVE LOGIC

Investigation is a logical, systematic process. Investigators use two types of logic: *inductive reasoning* and *deductive reasoning*. With inductive and deductive reasoning, a hypothesis is constructed about what has occurred. Facts are then gathered that either support it or reject it. There may be only a few pieces of the puzzle available so that the investigator must try and search for other pieces. The investigator must look at what is most likely to have occurred so that investigative efforts are not wasted. Note that investigation often seeks to *narrow the focus of the inquiry*: instead of pursuing a vast array of possibilities, the investigator seeks to reduce them logically to a more manageable number. Inductive and deductive reasoning may aid in doing this. Inductive and deductive reasoning is also more likely to be used in intelligence analysis. When assessing intelligence information, it may be necessary to construct a theory of the case.

In inductive and deductive reasoning, facts are collected. Next, a theory about what occurred is formulated. The pieces of the puzzle are obtained and put into place. The fictionalized Sherlock Holmes and the real-life Allan Pinkerton used deduction. Investigation of crimes, accidents, or work rule violations require the use of inductive and deductive reasoning.

Each form of reasoning has its place. An investigative inquiry may begin with inductive reasoning and then become deductive. Investigators must always make sure that they are logical and objective. Investigators must never let their prejudices or preconceived notions interfere with their work. If exculpatory evidence—evidence that tends to disprove that the suspect committed the offense—is discovered, it cannot be ignored!

HISTORY OF INVESTIGATION

History teaches some important lessons regarding investigation, including the following:

1. **Writing and investigation go hand-in-hand.**
   Investigation has been popularized through works by Henry and John Fielding and Allan Pinkerton, among others. Henry and John Fielding published the *Covent Garden Journal*, which described wanted persons. Based on the ideas of Patrick Colquhoun, the *Covent Garden Journal* was similar to many loss prevention department newsletters, *America's Most Wanted* television show, and the FBI's tip line on the Internet. Pinkerton wrote about his detectives and in retirement wrote dime-store novels (these were popular forms of entertainment, comparable to contemporary videos or DVDs). Pinkerton is credited with coining the terms *sleuth* and *private eye,* which were popularized through his true life accounts of detective work as well as the fictionalized dime-store novels that he wrote.

2. **Advertising and media relations are essential for continued investigative success.**
   This seems to be true for public entities as well as private investigative firms that depend on direct customers for fees. The Fieldings published *the Covent Garden Journal*. Pinkerton used posters to advertise, featuring a large eye and the saying "We Never Sleep." J. Edgar Hoover, who ran the FBI from 1924 until 1972, had a weekly radio show and hired a publicist. It would appear that what the Fieldings started in terms of marketing/public relations was taken to new levels by Allan Pinkerton and J. Edgar Hoover.

3. **Reward systems tend to breed corruption.**
   Jonathan Wild, a sort of prototype for contemporary private investigators, worked under the Parliamentary Reward System. This system paid government rewards to those who captured felons. Under the Parliamentary Reward System, the thief taker could keep the felon's property; including his horse if he had one. Wild also retrieved stolen property for his clients and received a percentage of the value of the property. He used the Parliamentary Reward System to great effect: he would have an associate steal the property, collect the fee from the client for its return, and perhaps turn in the associate and get

the Parliamentary Reward. In America, private detectives used criminal informants extensively and collected rewards. They were the predecessors of municipal police detectives, who also collected rewards. Allan Pinkerton forbade his agents from obtaining rewards, even though in the mid- to latter 19th century, municipal police detectives in the United States commonly did so. Present-day civil demand in retailing can be thought of as a type of reward system. A civil demand letter is sent by a third party to apprehended shoplifters requiring them to pay a fee under fear of civil suit. This may create ethics issues: is the loss prevention department in existence to prevent loss or gain profit from the fees collected from shoplifters?

4. **Ethics is crucial to success.** Individuals and organizations that don't have good ethics may profit initially, but in the long run they fail. The same is true of investigators and investigative organizations. Allan Pinkerton's firm (which emphasized good ethics) became the largest investigative and security firm in the world and is still around after 150+ years.

5. **New markets and new investigative services must be explored.** Whether the customer is internal, as with a proprietary security department, or external, as with a private investigative agency, it is essential to envision the needs of end users. Currently, background investigations are being used by more and more organizations. Certainly computer and Internet crime are growing concerns; some firms are moving into that market. The key question is: *"What investigative services could our organization offer that it currently does not?"*

PRELIMINARY INVESTIGATION

This is the most important aspect of the investigative process. It is also the investigative stage that security personnel (or uniformed police officers) generally get involved with. The

preliminary investigation is the initial fact-finding component of the investigative process. It is performed when the crime or incident is first discovered and is crucial to the success of the follow-up investigative effort. Preliminary investigation consists of several key steps:

1. **Attending to injured persons.** This must be the first priority! First aid followed by care and concern are the order of the day when dealing with victims.
2. **Detaining those who may have committed the crime.** If possible, engage in conversation with any subjects who may be in or near the scene. Some simple inquiry can go a long way toward solving an investigative issue. This must be done carefully and professionally.
3. **Finding and questioning witnesses.** A neighborhood canvass of the area to seek out witnesses should be performed as soon as possible. Systematically find and interview those who may have seen or heard something.
4. **Preserving the crime/incident scene for evidentiary purposes.** *Protect, preserve, make notes!* Control access to the scene, take photographs, and note observations. The scene must be in pristine condition.
5. **Forwarding information about the incident to the dispatcher, central alarm station (CAS), or the shift supervisor.** Officers should always keep the command post apprised of their current situation. The command post must know where officers are, what they are doing, and what the situation is at the officer's location.
6. **Completing a preliminary report so that follow-up investigators have *adequate information* with which to proceed.** Ideally, a follow-up investigator should have the case handed to them "on a silver platter."

FOLLOW-UP INVESTIGATION

This step in the process begins where the preliminary investigation ends. It is a process of examining the information provided by the preliminary report and proceeding to uncover additional data until the case is solved and a complete understanding of the event is attained.

Obviously, the success of the follow-up investigation is heavily dependent upon the preliminary investigative effort. Without adequate records, evidence, or witnesses, little or nothing can be determined, even if the follow-up investigator is extraordinarily proficient.

Follow-up investigations may be completed by the officer who performed the preliminary investigation, but in most cases they are handled by investigative specialists, police detectives, or supervisory personnel. For this reason, close liaison must exist between those conducting the preliminary investigation and those with follow-up investigative duties.

INTELLIGENCE

Intelligence is information. It is data or facts regarding current, past, or future events or associations. Intelligence collection can be thought of as a part of the follow-up phase of investigation. However, in many cases, intelligence is collected as an ongoing process, not after a specific event. One reason for collecting intelligence is to be proactive, to be able to see problems developing rather than investigating them after they have occurred. Protection officers play several key roles. One of them is the "intelligence agent" role. In order to perform this role effectively, officers must do the following:

1. Be observant.
2. Know what to observe.
3. Report the information in an effective manner.

Being observant is self-explanatory. Alert, attentive patrol officers will gather information. Inattentive ones will not.

Knowing what to observe comes from being properly trained and socialized by management.

It also includes ongoing professional development such as knowing the signs and colors of local gangs, the types of drugs that are being distributed, and the indications that extremist groups who may resort to acts of terror are in the area. These may include handbills, graffiti, and the observation of extremists congregating. Educational sessions sponsored by local police are a good way of keeping up-to-date on these topics. So, too, is reading professional literature.

Proper reporting is essential. Good writing skills are part of this. Proper management of the information within an intelligence system is another key component.

A structured, highly developed intelligence process consists of the following steps:

1. **A need to collect the information is identified.** No information should ever be collected until a demonstrated need for it exists. There must be a clear connection between collecting the information and the protection of assets. There must also be a management decision to begin the collection; there must be a policy regarding it. In very simple terms, management will instruct protection officers on what type of information they are to collect as part of the intelligence agent role that they play.
2. **The actual collection process.** This is where observations of protection officers and investigators come in. It is also where data searches are performed and information from other agencies is obtained. In order to be effective, the collection process cannot be impeded by having protection officers involved in too many tasks. If they have too much to do, they won't take the time to notice things or the care to report them. Officers must also receive positive feedback from managers regarding their observations. An additional concern here is the liaison that is conducted with other organizations. It must be positive and productive.

3. **The information is evaluated and collated or organized.** The information is evaluated to determine if it is worthwhile and correct. It must be timely. It should be verified. It is filed in an organized manner and collated so that it can be compared with other information. The establishment of files for cross referencing is important. Without this step, information is not referenced with other bits of data and "the pieces of the puzzle" don't get matched together. The use of computerized data systems such as the PPM2000 report writing software aids this effort.
4. **The information is analyzed and interpreted.** The meaning of the information is determined. After collation of the data, a professional intelligence officer will make a hypothesis on what the data means.
5. **The information is disseminated.** The information is given to authorized users within the organization or to external agencies. This must be done in accordance with policy and based on a need-to-know.
6. **The information is reevaluated.** Intelligence and the process used to collect and analyze it are reviewed. This is the "feedback loop" of the intelligence cycle. This enables the process to be reviewed and improved upon.

LIAISON

In many—if not most—cases, investigative efforts are undertaken in cooperation with other organizations. A simple example is counterfeiting. The problem is discovered by a teller or cashier who notices a suspect bill. The teller or cashier contacts a manager and/or the security department. Next, the local police and U.S. Secret Service are brought in. Each plays a role; counterfeit currency is not simply the domain of the U.S. Secret Service. Another example would be an accident in a parking lot. Security and maintenance would be involved. If there are injuries, local emergency medical services and police are called. In the wake of the accident, there may be an investigation by an insurance company. Many investigations involve more than one organization.

In order to be effective, liaison with other organizations must be developed and maintained. During the development phase of liaison, it is important to note the following:

1. Understand the role and purpose of each organization. This begins with the employing organization. Protection officers or investigators who do not know their employer's mission statements or philosophies are in trouble to begin with! Once this is done, the external organization is studied. Employer, client firm, and external agency must all be studied.
2. Examine the capabilities of each organization. With the flow of funding, these are in a constant state of flux. Determine what specific services each is capable of offering to the other, such as surveillance equipment, surveillance locations, vehicles, and software.
3. Meet with and get to know the key persons in other organizations. For a protection officer, this may be the local police officers and their sergeant. For an investigator, it may be his or her counterparts with different organizations. For a manager, it would be the agency heads. The point is to develop a comfort level in working with people from different organizations.
4. Consider meetings or joint training exercises. Also consider hosting seminars that various organizations can attend. In many cases, corporations have conference rooms and other resources that can be used by external entities. Informally "talking shop" is fostered at these face-to-face get-togethers. Informal intelligence exchange occurs.

Once a liaison is developed, it must be maintained. The need for a positive working relationship with an outside agency cannot be overstated. Such a relationship requires continuous care to maintain.

1. **Be respectful.** Ask how you can help. Oftentimes protection officers can perform simple tasks for outside investigators such as holding the end of a tape measure at an accident scene.
2. **Get to know people individually.** Introducing oneself with local police and other investigators is a start toward building a trusting relationship.
3. **Know the law!** One way of doing this is to ask police and government investigators questions. An investigator who works a specific area of investigation (identity theft, auto theft, check fraud, etc.) becomes intimately familiar with the legal aspects of the offense.
4. **Know policy!** Complying with employer policy is necessary. Appreciating another organization's rules and values is also important.
5. **Protect incident scenes effectively.** Providing another agency with a safe, secure, sterile scene from which to carry on their inquiry is critical.
6. **Be proficient at preliminary investigation.** If calling on local police detectives to initiate a follow-up investigation, providing them with a quality, *professional*, starting point is a necessity.
7. **Be proficient at case presentation and testifying effectively.** Being able to present a case effectively is important as it is the culmination of an investigation. Deficiencies at this juncture can sour relations between cooperating agencies.
8. **Keep the other agency informed.** Keep them "in the loop." Remember that when you are working with government agencies in all likelihood you are acting under "color of law." The Constitution of the United States may be involved here and always be in a support services mode when working under "color of law."
9. **Provide external agencies with resources as appropriate.** Accommodate their needs for working space, phone lines, and so on. A police department doing an interview or interrogation may need to use a conference room. They may also need to review surveillance tapes or disks. There are also equipment needs that can be met such as loaning vehicles, surveillance equipment, and so on, to police agencies.
10. **Consider joining investigative organizations.** Membership in a professional or social organization that local police also belong to may be an effective way of forming a bond with them.

NOTES AND REPORTS

Notes are the *foundation* of a report. It is sometimes said that testifying—the *last* step in the investigative process—*begins* with note-taking. Without adequate notes on the crucial details, there can be no effective report, follow-up investigation, or testimony. Reports are what make or break investigators. They are the summation of the investigator's or protection officer's work. Here are some key points on note taking and report writing.

- Think of notes as aids in remembering key details. Don't think of them as another chore to do.
- Headings should be placed at the beginning so that the notes are organized. The type of incident, date, time, and place can be recorded first at the top of the notes. This same principle applies to notes taken during classes.
- Start each set of notes on a new page. Also make sure to skip a few lines after each entry so that additional information can be added. This also applies to notes taken in classes!
- Always have a notebook available, even if tape recorders or computers are being used; old-fashioned paper and pencil are needed as backup note-taking aids.
- Periodically check notes. Summarize what is written to witnesses giving statements

so that you are sure to get the information correctly recorded. This should always be done at the conclusion of an interview; it can also be done at various junctures throughout the interview process.

- Use abbreviations judiciously. If they are commonly known abbreviations, use them. Make certain that the abbreviation used is correct and that anyone reading the notes would understand it. "If there is any doubt, spell it out."
- Use rough sketches in notes to pictorially represent incident scenes. Simple hand-drawn figures can aid in making the notes useful later on.
- Treat notes as the part of the official record that they are. Start each set of notes on a new page. Number each page. Write in ink and cross out and initial each correction that must be made. The best evidence rule requires that the original, best, and highest quality of proof must be used in legal proceedings. For this reason, original notes should be maintained. However, check with your company policy on notes. Many security departments insist that all notes be destroyed immediately after the incident report is completed and signed off by your supervisor or manager.

AUDITING

Auditing is something in which loss control personnel should be involved. An audit is simply a check (or investigation) as to whether or not operations are proceeding as expected. There are operations audits which determine if procedures are being followed as well as financial audits to see if there are any fiscal irregularities. Audits can take many forms, depending upon the organization's present need.

- Security officers audit locks and alarms to maintain the integrity of the physical security system. They may also do audits of the fire

protection system or of safety procedures on a weekly/monthly/quarterly basis.
- Security supervisors audit reports, procedures, personnel performance, and training/certification records of protection officers to ensure that things are being done the way they are supposed to be.
- Both contract and proprietary security managers audit policies, procedures, and training records to see that services are being properly given to client firms.
- Increasingly, we will see managers and supervisors auditing for compliance with standard-setting organizations, such as government agencies and insurance carriers. Also, professional organizations, such as the Joint Commission on the Accreditation of Healthcare Organizations (JCAHO), International Association of Campus Law Enforcement Administrators, and others, will establish sets of standards. As the security industry professionalizes, such developments are inevitable.
- Accountants and/or fraud examiners perform financial audits of records such as payroll, accounts receivable, purchasing, or petty cash.
- Forensic accountants may review individual points of sale in retail facilities, parking garages, restaurants, or bars.

Audits enable the auditor to spot irregularities. This can mean a lack of commitment to proper work procedures caused by inadequate training, poor supervision, or demoralized job holders. It may mean that the level of service being given by the organization is not up to standard and changes are necessary! It can also signal attempts at thefts, completed thefts, or simply the presence of the opportunity to commit thefts. Audits are often the starting point of an investigation, the basic leads being uncovered during routine audits. In other cases, they are part of the follow-up investigation. In these instances, the investigator needs to either expand or narrow the focus of the inquiry. Conducting an audit can help to make this determination. Additionally, they can be part of a corrective approach taken to remedy any problems that have been uncovered.

When conducting an audit, there are several important points to remember.

1. Compare what is being audited (job behavior, procedures, or conditions, etc.) with clearly defined, measurable standards. These can be written instructions, procedures, post orders, and so on. The analysis of the job behavior (e.g., not signing in visitors), procedure (price checks on merchandise), or condition (e.g., faulty alarms) must be *objective*. It cannot simply be the auditor's professional opinion.
2. Communicate the purpose of audits to all employees. Obtain the positive cooperation of those who have input into the audit process.
3. Conduct audits in a fair and uniform manner with a set standard that relates to everyone and is used to evaluate everyone.
4. Utilize a variety of techniques. Each technique gives the investigator a specific type of information. Each provides the auditor with a different view. Each shows a different "angle" or perspective. Use a combination of techniques to see the whole picture.
5. Document the results of audits. Professional reports are essential.
6. Evaluate and review audits with relevant personnel. An exit briefing is one means of doing this. In an exit briefing, the auditor briefly discusses his or her findings with management prior to the submission of a complete report. This gives management rapid feedback upon which to make necessary modifications.
7. Follow the chain of command, be tactful, and make sure the information gets to the right people, and only those people.

As with any type of investigation, there are a variety of approaches to auditing. Each approach has its strengths and weaknesses; each has its time and place. Some that may be of use include:

1. Document review by either systematic (every document in a set) or random selection (a sample of documents in a set).
2. Deliberate error technique in which an error is deliberately made to see if it is detected. An example would be a mispriced item at a point of sale (POS) terminal.
3. Drills are good ways to evaluate the performance of both systems and personnel. These must be done safely and in such a manner that they are not overly disruptive. In most cases, drills can be "compartmentalized" so that someone only needs to describe (orally or in writing) the procedures to be followed. Another method is to have the scenario limited to a single department or unit. Full-scale scenarios are often not feasible—even though exercises involving the entire protection operation and outside agencies are the best "final examination" possible for a security system.
4. Observation of job behavior or systems is a simple technique that can still provide useful information. This can be with the unaided eye or by reviewing videotape (openly taken) of someone performing job tasks.
5. Interviewing personnel is a method that may be used to investigate practices. In addition to one-on-one interviews, survey forms can be used.
6. A conference held with supervisors is a technique often used by managers to investigate workplace problems, practices, and procedures. This can be scheduled with regular supervisor meetings or as a separate meeting prior to an external audit by a government agency or accrediting body.

INTERVIEWS

The conducting of interviews is something that security officers do all the time. In many cases, these interviews are conducted informally. Whether formal or informal, *an interview is a conversation with the objective of obtaining information.* Loss control practitioners who are adept at their jobs can collect information from every conversation. Here are some basic rules of interviewing.

1. Be pleasant, friendly, and helpful to the interviewee. They are taking their time out to help you!
2. Thank people for their help and always end an interview on a positive note. Providing them with a business card for future contact is a good policy. In some cases witnesses contact investigators later on about the same case. Sometimes they contact them about other cases. Leaving the door open for future communications is part of being an effective interviewer.
3. Ask open-ended questions that require an explanation rather than a simple yes or no answer. "Can you tell me what you saw?" "Can you tell me what happened?" or "Could you describe that?" are examples of open-ended questions.
4. Use silence ("the long pause") after the person has answered a question. Don't say anything; let the interviewee continue the conversation. Most people will feel obligated to keep the conversation flowing and add more detail.
5. Interview in private—to the greatest extent practical; a quiet, relaxed, private setting will yield more information. The interviewee must feel comfortable. They cannot be distracted by noise or activity.
6. Be approachable and friendly. Pleasant people are easy to talk to. Astute protection professionals are approachable and can gain the trust of people. Put the person at ease with a smile, joke, or off-the-subject questions (sports, family, current events). Also make the person comfortable; offer them a seat and sit next to them (picture the seating arrangements that TV talk show hosts use). This helps to establish rapport.
7. Take notes in a manner that records the key data but does not impede the interview. Don't take notes if it makes the interviewee uncomfortable. Oftentimes, note taking should take place after the incident has been related by the witness. Going over the information again and taking notes on it often does not upset the interviewee's comfort level.
8. Summarizing and then taking notes may help. The interviewee may add information that was previously overlooked. It is also a good way to make sure that all the information is correct. It is, in effect, an audit of the interview.

INVESTIGATIVE OR FOCUSED INTERVIEWS

Investigative or focused interviews are different from interviews with witnesses or victims in that the focus upon the person is as a suspect. A focused interview is only conducted after a substantial amount of information from other sources indicates guilt of an individual. Focused interviews are conversations with the purpose of acquiring information, but with obtaining admission of guilt or a full confession from the subject as the final objective. They should not be conducted by inexperienced and untrained individuals! Investigative specialists should perform them. Unfortunately, there are instances where a protection officer without extensive information may come upon someone committing a crime or policy violation. In these cases, a brief focused interview is appropriate.

These are some interrogation techniques:

1. **Be nonaccusatory.** Do not blame or accuse the subject. If the facts are wrong and they are not guilty, there is an obvious problem. Additionally, setting up a hostile relationship does no good. The investigator must "sell" the subject on telling the truth.

2. **Discuss the seriousness of the incident with the person being interrogated.** This is helpful in those cases where the individual falsely believes that they can act with impunity, that it is "no big deal."

3. **Request that the subject tell the story several tines.** Inconsistencies can be better noted in this way.

4. **Appeal to the emotions of the subject.** Let him/her know that everybody makes mistakes. Allow the subject to *rationalize* what they have done. Allow them to *minimize* the harm that has occurred. Allow them to *project* blame onto someone or something else.

5. **Point out inconsistencies in the story to the subject.** This is better done later in the interview. Anything done to make the interviewee defensive should be used as a last resort.

6. **Confront the subject with part of the evidence.** Be careful!

There are various legal restrictions active during interrogation. Basically, these standards do not allow any use of force, threats, or intimidation. The *Miranda* decision required all law enforcement personnel in the United States to advise suspects of their rights before asking them any questions which focus upon them as the suspect and which are asked in a custodial setting. Failure to follow these procedures will result in all evidence obtained via illegal questioning to be excluded from criminal proceedings (the Exclusionary Rule).

While in most states, private security personnel are not bound to the *Miranda* decision, a few courts have placed this obligation upon them. All U.S. courts place *Miranda* standards on private individuals who are acting at the direction, request of, or in close cooperation with public law enforcement personnel. Obviously, the Miranda rule applies if the security officer has any type of police powers. Such officers are, in fact, agents of the government, and acting under "color of law."

Another standard that the U.S. Supreme Court imposed upon employers is the Weingarten Rule.

Under Weingarten, any time that an interview is held with an employee that could *reasonably be expected* to result in disciplinary action, the employee is entitled to representation by a union steward or another individual. **This rule is limited to those employees who are represented by a collective bargaining unit (members of a labor union).** Failure to comply will result in an unfair labor practice charge being filed through the National Labor Relations Board. Discipline imposed as a result of the illegal interview may be set aside in an arbitration hearing. Employees who have been terminated may be reinstated and given back pay for the time that they were off work!

While unlike *Miranda* in that management is not obligated to advise employees of this right, once an employee asks for a union representative (union steward or co-worker) the interview must cease until the union representative arrives—provided the representative is reasonably available. Employees cannot ask for a specific representative who is on vacation simply to avoid being interviewed. In these cases, the interview may proceed without the representative present. Alternatively, the interview may cease. Employees can be told that management will take action with the facts that they have (Table 31-2). As a general rule, it is best not to force an interview with anyone!

TABLE 31-2

Miranda	Weingarten
Police interrogation of suspects in a custodial setting.	Employer questioning of employees concerning violations of employer rules.
Warnings are required before questioning.	Warning is not required—the employee must make the request for the representative.
An attorney is the representative of the accused.	A union steward or interested co-worker is the representative, not an attorney.
The Exclusionary Rule prohibits statements made in violation of the law from being used in a criminal proceeding.	An unfair labor practice charge may be filed; this may result in the setting aside of discipline.

There are legal obligations to caution persons being interrogated. There are also other considerations to be addressed within the legal arena. Knowing the laws of your state regarding interrogation is important. In Minnesota there is something called the "Tennessen Warning" given during administrative hearings. This law states that the subject of the interview may not remain silent, must give the information requested, and anything they say can be and will be used against them in any future criminal or civil investigation or trial. This is just the opposite of the Miranda Warning. We believe this is a Minnesota State Law only. As a general rule, the following procedures can save security practitioners a considerable amount of trouble in court:

1. **Review the case thoroughly before starting the interrogation.** The more that is known about the incident or scheme, the better. This is where good preliminary investigation comes into play.
2. **Interrogate in private,** but remove all possible suggestions of duress, such as weapons, locked doors, and intimidating individuals from the environment. If the subject is not being arrested or under arrest during the interrogation they must be told and they must understand they are free to leave at any time. The subject must understand that they are volunteering to remain and are not restricted from leaving at any time in the process.
3. **Avoid making threats or promises.**
4. **Never physically touch a subject!**
5. **If the subject is of the opposite sex, do not question alone.** Have a member of the same sex present. In fact, regardless of sex of the subject, it is always a good idea to have a witness present in every interrogation.
6. **Advise the suspect of his/her rights,** if there is any chance of an obligation to do so.

7. **Have the subject sign each page of the statement and initial all corrections.** (There should be some corrections so that the integrity of the document can be clearly demonstrated in court.)
8. **Have someone witness the statement.**
9. **Use the statement as supporting evidence,** not the entire case! Corroborate the statement with other evidence. Back it up as much as possible.
10. **Make sure the statement is in the subject's own words and that it is dated and signed.**

INFORMANTS

Informants are a key tool in many types of investigations. Often informants provide basic leads that alert loss control personnel to the presence of a problem. They are of particular importance when investigating the activities of a social network such as substance abuse, sabotage, gambling, and internal theft investigations. There are several kinds of informants operating under different types of motivations:

1. A desire to assist the investigator, either through public spiritedness or a feeling of indebtedness to the investigator.
2. A need to "play cop" and act like the police.
3. Revenge against a criminal competitor such as a rival drug dealer.
4. Manipulation of the investigator. This is common with criminal informants; they are called "cons" for a reason!
5. Financial gain such as the collecting of rewards from the investigator.
6. The investigator "having them over a barrel" and the informant wants leniency from charges.

Investigators using informants should try to understand the informant's motivation. They should investigate their background and fully comprehend any and all relationships that they have had with the subject. One can never be too careful with informants. These are some tips for dealing with informants:

1. **Treat all informants with dignity and respect.** While most informants are good people, the occasional criminal informant will also be used for leads/information. Avoid using demeaning terms to describe informants; they perform a valuable service. Also, the use of such terms is hardly professional.

2. **Keep informants "at arm's length."** Avoid close personal involvement with them. Many informants are master manipulators who attempt to obtain confidential information from the investigator.

3. **Closely evaluate the value of the information that has been given.** Be vigilant against attempts to mislead the investigator or exaggerate the importance of the information they have provided.

4. **Attempt to verify the accuracy of the information through independent sources.** Don't rely solely on the information that an informant provides to build a case. Corroborate with other evidence.

5. **Keep a "tight rein" on the informant; don't let them represent themselves as members of the security or police organization.** Don't allow them to do anything that is unauthorized or illegal. Some informants perceive that they have a license to commit crimes. Never allow that situation to develop.

6. **Take care of the legitimate needs of the informant.** Assist them when possible in finding work, transportation, child care, and so forth. Be helpful but don't be duped. Restrict the help to legitimate needs.

7. **"Telephone tipsters" should be kept on the line as long as possible.** They should be *interviewed*. They should not be given any confidential information. They should be thanked and asked to call back in the future if they have any additional information.

UNDERCOVER INVESTIGATIONS

Occasionally, there arises the need for an undercover investigator. Generally there is no need for them except when other techniques (surveillance, informants, etc.) have failed to yield information or when the special perspective available to an undercover operative is needed.

Undercover (UC) investigation is a very expensive and risky method to use, and there are numerous problems that can occur during an undercover investigation. For these reasons, it should not be used unless it is absolutely necessary.

Ferraro (2007) maintains that the following conditions lend themselves to undercover investigation:

1. Cases where consistent, reliable information suggests employee misconduct and/or criminal activity without sufficient detail to prevent the behavior or identify those involved in it.

2. Known losses occur in a specific area but no information exists as to how they occur or who is responsible.

3. A strong suspicion (or actual indicators) exists of on-the-job substance abuse and/or drug dealing within the workplace.

4. When strong suspicion or actual indicators of on-the-job impairment or substance abuse exist and supervision is not responsive to the problem or is incapable of managing it.

5. When there is an absolute need to compare actual practices with required or specified practices and routine auditing is not possible.

6. When a high probability exists that the use of undercover investigation will yield significant results and all other methods of inquiry have been ruled out.

Undercover investigation should only be performed by competent professionals who specialize in this type of work. Proper training, education, and experience are necessary to prepare the agent for the role they will be playing. Proper supervision and control over the agent is essential to ensure that the overall operation is effective. Controls need to be in place to reduce the risk of danger and legal problems from arising.

In order to use undercover investigation to the greatest advantage, the following considerations must be weighed:

1. **The objectives of the investigation must be clearly defined.** Management must know exactly what information is required and for what purpose the investigative effort will be initiated.
2. **The entire situation must be carefully weighed from all perspectives (legal, labor relations, economic, operational).** UC investigations can easily cause more serious problems than they rectify. Aside from civil liability issues, there can be the threat of an irritated workforce. Obviously, that situation has potential for serious loss. And the losses can last a long time.
3. **Strict confidentiality on a need-to-know basis must be maintained.** Many operations are compromised when the persons being investigated find out about it.
4. **The proper agent must be selected.** They must have the necessary job skills to fit in with the work environment. They must be sociable and dedicated enough to see things through when difficult decisions (turning in friends, accompanying suspects during illegal activities, staying on the job when illegal activities are not occurring) must be made. Simply "looking the part" is not enough.
5. **Liaison with law enforcement agencies for the purpose of gathering information or prosecuting suspects must be done.** This can compromise the agent. It can also create numerous other problems if not done properly. Always assess the goals and objectives of the organization a liaison is being affiliated with so that conflicts are kept to a minimum.
6. **Corroborate the agent's testimony with other evidence.** Agents may not be credible with arbitrators, judges, or juries. While they should be credible, it is always best to back up one's case.

SHOPPING SERVICES

Shopping services are a type of "short-term undercover" inquiry where the investigator poses as a shopper. They are designed to achieve the following purposes:

1. **Uncover criminal or unauthorized activity.** Sometimes called "honesty shopping," this may involve making purchases and observing what the cashier/waitress/ bartender does with the money. Attempts to under-ring a point-of-sale terminal, pocket money, and so on are noted. Other investigations may audit how items are priced, how return merchandise is handled, or items without price tags are processed.
2. **Assess customer service and employee efficiency.** This involves "shopping" a location and seeing how attentive the sales personnel are to customers.

Shopping can be done by specialized investigative firms or in some cases on a proprietary basis. In the latter instance, a manager from another store or branch of the business may be used. This provides an expert view on how things are supposed to be done. It also aids in organizational development as the managers participate in an audit process.

SURVEILLANCE

Surveillance is an essential investigative activity to loss control practitioners. It can be stationary (hidden cameras, "plant" or "stakeout"), mobile, or contact (rolling surveillance or invisible dyes). Surveillance can accomplish various objectives:

1. Identify suspects in a crime.
2. Record the movements and associations of suspects.

3. Identify patterns of criminal or unauthorized activity.
4. Collect information for prosecution.
5. Locate and apprehend suspects.
6. Prevent crimes from being committed. This can be done via overt or covert surveillance.

Once objectives have been identified, the planning process can begin. The entire planning process consists of the following steps:

1. **Establish the objective of the surveillance.** Write a clear, concise sentence as to why the investigator is doing the surveillance. What is the purpose behind the investigation?
2. **Reconnaissance of the area where the surveillance will be conducted.** Examine it for avenues of entry and exit as well as vantage points from which to observe. There should be several of these!
3. **Collect as much information as possible on the background(s) of subject(s).** The more known about the person being observed, the better. Having a firm idea of the person's appearance is essential to ensuring that the right person is being surveilled. Knowing the person's habits or potential for danger is also critical.
4. **Calculate the personnel requirements.** A minimum of two people will be needed if the surveillance lasts for any appreciable period of time or if there is danger present.
5. **Establish communication.** Cell phones, radios, and phone booths as a backup method can all be used. Security and continuity of communication are essential.
6. **Calculate equipment needs.** Equipment may consist of binoculars, videotape units, log or report forms, possibly weapons, and disguises such as hats, coats, and glasses.

If surveillance operations are planned properly, the chances for success are much higher. As the costs of initiating surveillance activities are high, it certainly behooves the loss control investigator to carefully scrutinize all aspects of the operation before wasting precious time and money. Special attention must be devoted to communications and the response to incidents. Investigators must decide what may occur and how they will react to it. With this in mind, personnel and equipment needs can be addressed logically.

Recording of activity observed during surveillance must be done with care. The following is a sample outline for a surveillance log:

Location/objective (an introductory paragraph should be written)
Date
Time (all activity occurring at a specific point in time is detailed)
Attachments (photographs, sketches, etc.)
Summary (brief concluding comments on observations)

BEHAVIOR/CONDITION ANALYSIS

Another tool that investigators can use is behavior/condition analysis. Whenever there is a crime or accident, the behavior of the perpetrator and/or victim can be examined and analyzed, as can the conditions present. The behavior and conditions can be divided into three segments:

1. **The behavior/conditions that existed before the incident.** This view can provide valuable insight into the criminal method of operation and can also be used for analyzing vulnerabilities. One can gain a better understanding of what took place and develop more effective prevention efforts. An example might be the approach/entry used by a robber at the target. What protection was given to the target? Who would know what the target was? Who would be attracted to that type of target ("score")? What kind of insurance coverage was held by the victim? When applied to crimes or accidents, contributing factors to the event can be identified. What was the physical, mental, and emotional condition of the accident victim? What was the lighting and noise level

at the time of the accident? Would anyone gain by making a false report? What was the victim doing at the crime or accident scene?

2. **The actual incident itself.** What actually took place during the robbery? What did the robber say and do? What did the burglar do when inside the premises (the burglar's "prowl")? What happened during the accident? What was the sequence of events in the accident (struck by, caught on, falling, etc.)?

3. **The behavior immediately after the incident should be identified and examined.** How did the robber make his escape? Where did the burglar exit from? How was the stolen merchandise disposed of? How was the accident handled? What did the victim or perpetrator say? Who reported it? When and to whom was it reported? Who responded to the crime, fire or accident?

Once all the behaviors and conditions of an incident are identified, it becomes much easier to analyze and understand that incident. Developing a list of questions for each phase of the event also helps to unfold lines of inquiry and perform a more complete investigation. While this technique is commonly used to investigate robbery, burglary, and homicide, there is no reason to limit its application to these types of cases. Embezzlement, passing bad checks, credit card fraud, accidents, bombings, fires, and chemical spills can all be dissected in this manner. Behavioral/condition analysis aids in understanding the human factors in a loss event.

Key point: Keep the initial questions general rather than specific. Focus the inquiry by going from general questions to more specific ones. Never start with highly specific lines of inquiry or the behavioral/condition analysis will fail.

TESTIFYING IN LEGAL AND QUASI-LEGAL PROCEEDINGS

Once a case has been investigated, it may become necessary to present it in a court,

disciplinary hearing, or labor arbitration. Officers are also called upon to give depositions in civil suits. In many cases, the officer will testify in several different legal arenas; one never knows precisely where an incident will be decided! Each of these proceedings has a different format and takes place in a different environment, but all require providing factual information in a professional manner. Each of these proceedings places the officer on the opposing side of the defendant or plaintiff. During these proceedings, the successful investigator does everything possible to appear credible and convincing.

Here are some things to bear in mind when testifying in court:

1. **Always be positive.** Project a positive, affirmative image. Sell yourself to the judge, magistrate, jury, etc.

2. **Be neat, clean, and conservatively dressed, as if you were going on a job interview.** Project a businesslike, professional image. Avoid dressing or talking like a cop or a soldier.

3. **Sit and stand erect with shoulders squared.** Face and look at the jury and judge. Be serious! This is a serious issue that must be handled in a thoroughly professional manner.

4. **Project your voice to the jury or judge.** Maintain eye contact with them. Address them when you're talking to them. Project your voice to the person farthest from you. This will ensure that you are heard by everyone who needs to hear you.

5. **Answer "yes" or "no" to questions posed by counsel or the judge.** Don't clarify or elaborate on your answers unless it is necessary to do so. If you must clarify a point, choose your words carefully and know what you're going to say before you open your mouth. Prior to the proceeding, consider what questions may be asked.

6. **Have the case prepared before trial.** Any reports or evidence presented must be carefully prepared. Consult counsel about the case beforehand to ensure that

preparation is adequate. Go over the case, review evidence. Plan a strategy with the guidance of counsel. Review all notes and reports before the proceeding starts.

7. **Any notes or reports taken to the stand may be examined by the opposing attorney.** Be critical of and careful with notes for this reason. Don't simply read from notes; consult them only if necessary. Don't take something that could cause embarrassment and a loss of credibility. Only professional information should be in an officer's notebook.

8. **Avoid any show of sarcasm, conceit, or disgust with the defendant.** Be objective and unemotional. A professional is objective. Don't be afraid to say something positive about the defendant.

9. **Never try to argue with the judge or attorney.** Be polite and professional, addressing them appropriately as "Sir," "Ma'am," or "Your Honor." Find out how to properly address them beforehand.

10. **If unsure as to what occurred, say so.** Don't be afraid to admit you don't know something or aren't sure. If you are sure, state so in a positive, affirmative manner. Try to avoid saying "I think" or any other expression which displays uncertainty.

11. **If you don't understand a question, ask that it be repeated or say that you simply don't understand it.**

12. **Don't be afraid to admit that you're wrong and be honest in all matters.**

13. **Critique your performance in order to improve future testimony.** Experience is a good "teacher" for giving testimony. Look at every occasion as a learning experience. Don't be afraid to watch others testify or to ask for critiques from others on your testimony.

MANAGING INVESTIGATIONS

Just as investigation is an integral part of management, so, too, is management an essential element within the investigative process. If the investigative effort is not carefully controlled, man-hours will be wasted, confidentiality may be compromised, and objectives will not be met.

To begin with, the individual investigator must have personal management skills. He or she must set objectives, make daily priorities, and manage time effectively. Proper filing and administration of records is important. Critically evaluating one's work is crucial.

In an organizational sense, investigations must be managed by a series of procedures and controls. These are some techniques to consider when supervising an investigation:

1. Selecting and assigning investigators properly. Only the most qualified and efficient personnel should be entrusted with investigative duties. Individual cases should be assigned in accordance with the individual expertise of the investigator. Note that this does not necessarily mean the investigator with the most seniority.

2. Investigators must be properly trained in the basics of investigation (interviewing, report writing, surveillance, interrogations, etc.) before assuming investigative responsibilities. They must also be trained in specialized areas (narcotics, fraud, espionage, undercover, computer forensics, etc.) should they be assigned these investigative duties. Training needs must be analyzed carefully. Periodic upgrading must be done in regard to legal and technological development.

3. All investigations should have clearly defined objectives. These objectives should be observable and measurable. The effectiveness of the investigative effort can be gauged by assessing whether or not the objective was met, how quickly it was met, and what the total cost was. This can be calculated in man-hours expended and other expenses.

4. Case worksheets should be designed to meet the needs of individual organizations. These

forms list dates, investigator's names, case numbers, persons contacted, time invested, expenses, and results of contacts. Their efficient design and utilization are musts for the investigative effort to be properly administered in a cost-effective manner.

5. Forms for efficiently reviewing reports can also be used to great effect. These forms enable supervisors to objectively audit reports submitted by security officers or investigators. Their use helps to streamline the investigative process while at the same time ensuring that errors are caught early enough to prevent disaster.

6. Coordination of the investigation with persons who have a "need to know" is important. Law enforcement agencies and victims should be kept informed of the progress of the investigation. (Keep in mind your status with respect to "color of law" discussed above. You don't want to jeopardize the evidence in any way.) This is important for maintaining supportive relationships and receiving additional information. Special concern must be given to the victim. Victims need emotional support and a clear explanation of judicial procedure if they are to feel comfortable following through with the prosecution process.

Investigations can be supervised and evaluated through a number of techniques. As with auditing, no single technique is adequate to provide a complete assessment. Using several methods in concert with each other provides the best results.

1. Statistical analysis of numbers of apprehensions, conviction rates, amounts of stolen property recovered, and numbers of complaints against the investigator can also be used as an indicator of job performance.

2. On-the-job visits can always be used as a technique. Good supervisors are "coaches" to their subordinates. However, as an assessment method it is limited in effectiveness and lacks

objectivity; it *must* be used in conjunction with other evaluative methods.

3. Review of investigative reports. This gives the supervisor a "quick feel" for how the investigator is performing.

CONCLUSION

Investigation and asset protection are interrelated functions. Neither can exist in any real sense without the other. The contemporary protection officer serves as an intelligence agent for security management. As such, he or she is tasked with collecting and reporting all manner of information on potential loss-causing conditions. Information relating to crimes, accidents, and unethical/unprofessional practices has traditionally been collected by protection officers. Contemporary concerns with terrorism mandate that intelligence relating to potential terrorist activities be collected. Future officers will probably perform more auditing functions designed to catch errors and minimize waste.

In most cases, protection officers are involved in performing preliminary investigations. As the preliminary investigation is the most important phase of the investigative process, it is essential that it be conducted properly. This ensures that both security management and public police agencies can uncover facts necessary for the completion of their respective missions.

Proficiency and future growth and development in investigation depend on a mastery of the basic skills. Protective service professionals must master interviews (*every conversation is an interview*), note taking (edit and review notes at various stages of the investigation), and report writing. Efforts must also extend to testifying in legal and quasi-legal proceedings. Effective oral communication skills are a necessity if cases are to be presented effectively. They are also integral to the development of a professional image and more productive relations with management, police, clients, and the public at large.

EMERGING TRENDS

As we deal with large scale disasters, arsons, or terrorist bombings, our ability to move from the emergency response phase of the event to the investigative phase is improving. Fire and EMS personnel are being taught crime scene preservation. Crime scenes must be more carefully processed than ever before. New scientific advances are enabling the collection of physical evidence such as DNA.

General loss interviewing is being done more frequently. This is a general conversational interview performed after an inventory has been conducted. It may also be performed after an "Orientation to Loss Prevention" session. It is somewhat open and informal; interviewers do this to uncover possible loss issues. Patrol officers also do this, as a general conversation with people encountered on patrol may lead to some indication of a problem. This initial information is then studied and further investigation conducted. The key is to make every conversation an interview, albeit in a subtle, easy, conversational manner.

Interviewing is becoming a more structured, methodological undertaking. There is more planning before going into an investigative interview and more time spent in building rapport. In law enforcement, videotaping is being used more often, whereas corporate interviews are using a two-person team approach. At the conclusion of the interview, the interviewer is debriefed by another investigator. This debriefing session is done for both operational reasons (making the interview better) and as part of Critical Incident Stress Debriefing (CISD). CISD is designed to help the interviewer deal with stressful situations. The latter may occur after a focused interview where the interviewee gets very emotional and/or discusses a traumatic event.

Background investigations are becoming more commonplace. Increasingly, there is a legal requirement to conduct a preemployment check such as with schoolteachers, child care workers, nurses, etc. Background checks are the fastest growing area of investigative activity. Most of these investigations are being conducted by specialized firms such as USIS. There has been an explosive growth in the number of private investigative firms specializing in employee background investigations. There are hundreds of such companies in the United States alone.

Not all background investigations are performed by investigative firms. Some are conducted by governmental agencies such as the U.S. Office of Personnel Management. In-house security departments may also conduct backgrounds; in other cases human resource departments do them. HR departments may also conduct part of the inquiry and contract out portions of it such as criminal records or credit checks.

With increasing privatization, it is likely that a greater proportion of investigative tasks will be performed by private investigative agencies and proprietary security departments. Driving forces for privatization are decreased budgets for public agencies and the need for specialized expertise. Public police agencies will probably contract out for various types of investigative services in the future more than at present. Investigative functions not currently envisioned will be carried out by both proprietary and contract security organizations.

In many corporate settings investigative plans are developed by investigative teams. These consist of human resources, legal, security, IT, and so on. The results of the investigation are reviewed by top management. Obviously, thoroughness and precise documentation are required in these situations.

There is a greater need for investigators to have computer skills. MS Office software is used extensively. Research and intelligence functions are performed online. Access control and surveillance logs are reviewed; the latter is becoming more important as video surveillance increases. Analytic video is becoming more common in both work environments and public streets. Once the information is collected, there is a need for some manner of human review. The information may also be moved into separate files for reporting purposes.

Liaison between different investigative entities is increasing and is taking place earlier in the investigative process. Obviously it is unfair for a retail loss prevention agent to suddenly give a police detective 30 bad check cases all at once. Managing the investigative workload must be given some thought. We cannot "dump on" our investigative partners.

References

Bennett, W., & Hess, K. (2001). *Criminal investigation*. Belmont, CA: Wadsworth.

Ferraro, E. (2007). Undercover investigations in the workplace. In J. Fay (Ed.), *Encyclopedia of security management*. Burlington, MA: Butterworth-Heinemann.

Resources

ASIS International (703/522-5800 or www.asisonline.org) has a Council on Investigations. ASIS also has an extensive library of books and videos for members to borrow (Information Resource Center) or purchase (ASIS Bookstore). There is also the Professional Certified Investigator (PCI) designation for investigators who have case management experience.

Association of Certified Fraud Examiners (800/245-3321 or http://www.acfe.com/). The Association sponsors the Certified Fraud Examiner (CFE) designation and produces a number of computer-based home study programs. There are also local chapter meetings and seminars in various locations. Student membership is available to ACFE. So, too, are a series of faculty discounts.

AST Corporation (http://hits.astcorp.com/) provides an array of CD-ROM and online programs for investigative and security personnel. People who complete these programs may receive certificates from the International Foundation for Protection Officers.

Butterworth-Heinemann, an imprint of Elsevier Science, offers numerous investigative texts such as *Legal Guidelines for Covert Surveillance in the Private Sector, Corporate Crime Investigation, The Art of Investigative Interviewing, The Process of Investigation,* and many others. Visit http://stbooks.elsevier.com/security or call 800/545-2522.

CRC Press Inc. (800/272-7737 or www.crcpress.com) offers several investigative texts.

The International Foundation for Protection Officers (877/247-5984 or www.ifpo.org) offers a certificate program in Crime and Loss Investigation. This program is designed to aid students in learning about key investigative topics so that they may better perform investigative functions. It also helps prepare the learner for future professional certification. There are two texts (this being one of them) and a series of online papers. The papers cover Surveillance, Intelligence, Background Investigation, and Interviewing. The Foundation also has membership opportunities available to protection officers and investigators.

The **Loss Prevention Foundation** offers a variety of courses and certification programs in Retail Loss Prevention. Visit http://www.losspreventionfoundation.org/

LPJOBS.COM features jobs, educational programs, and articles about retail loss prevention in the magazine *Loss Prevention*. The magazine has articles on interviewing and other aspects of investigation.

The National Association of Investigative Specialists offers books and membership to private investigators. Visit http://www.pimall.com/NAIS/dir.menu.html.

The Professional Security Training Network (www.pstn .com or 800/624-2272) has an extensive array of instructional programs dealing with investigation, interviewing, and testifying.

John E. Reid and Associates specializes in interviewing and the detection of deception. Reid offers videos and training courses on interrogation. See www.reid.com or call 800/255-5747. Members of the International Foundation for Protection Officers receive a discount on Reid programs.

Security Supervision and Management: Theory and Practice of Asset Protection has chapters on Investigation, Report Writing, and Testifying. The Investigation chapter details how investigations can be managed and provides useful information on intelligence. The book is the text for the IFPO Security Supervision and Management Program and is available from Elsevier (http://www .elsevierdirect.com/index.jsp). Completion of the Security Supervision and Management Program is the first step toward designation as Certified in Security Supervision and Management (CSSM).

Wicklander and Zulewski (www.w-z.com) offers a variety of investigative services. They specialize in interview training and are highly regarded within the investigative industry.

SECURITY QUIZ

1. Accident investigations can be investigated by any of the following except:
   a. Private investigators
   b. Insurance investigators
   c. Federal or state agency investigators
   d. Security officers

2. The foundation of a good report lies in and begins with:
   a. Intelligence
   b. Notes and reports
   c. Interviews
   d. Investigative logic

3. Weingarten established the Exclusionary Rule, which prohibits statements made in violation of the law from being used in a criminal court:
   a. True
   b. False

4. A case effort undertaken in cooperation with other organizations is called:
   a. Auditing
   b. Intraintelligence
   c. Undercover investigation
   d. Liaison

5. Which of the following is a good investigative interviewing technique?
   a. Request that the subject tell the story multiple times
   b. Thank people for their help
   c. Summarize
   d. Don't allow the subject to sleep

6. All except which of the following is a key step in preliminary investigation?
   a. Attending to injured persons
   b. Preserving the crime scene
   c. Interviewing the suspect
   d. Detaining those who have committed the crime

7. Informants are a very expensive and risky method to use:
   a. True
   b. False

8. An officer can testify in several different legal arenas for a single case:
   a. True
   b. False

9. On-the-job visits can be used to evaluate investigations:
   a. True
   b. False

10. The single overarching goal of all investigations is:
    a. To discover facts about a situation, person, or behavior
    b. To continue an ongoing process of collection
    c. To win the "credibility battle"
    d. To analyze the behavior of the perpetrator and/or victim

32

Crime and Incident Scene Procedures

Dennis Shepp

CHAPTER OBJECTIVES

- Define an incident that requires the protection officer's attention
- Clarify the protection officer's role at an incident scene
- Define incident scene boundaries and explain how to maintain them
- Define evidence and explain how to preserve it
- Emphasize the importance of the protection officer's role in maintaining the integrity of the incident scene
- Provide guidelines on how to interact and work with responding and investigating law enforcement

It is the protection officer's objective to protect assets through the prevention of loss. To do this, they will use the knowledge and skills they have gained toward preventing incidents or crimes that cause losses. Nonetheless, incidents will occur and some of them will result in losses.

Some incidents might merely require the recording of information in an incident report for investigation or statistical tracking. When an incident occurs, it is important that the scene is protected so that evidence is not damaged or lost. This chapter will relate valuable information and skills the protection officer will require to manage a scene until expert and professional assistance arrives.

WHAT IS AN INCIDENT?

An incident is a loss-event occurrence of some type that in some way impacts an organization. This may be a loss (like stolen property) or something that happened that the organization wants tracked through reporting (like false alarms). Most organizations want to track the number of incidents that happen for various reasons, mainly:

- To track the cost of a loss event (example: cost of lost property)
- To analyze trends of loss costs (example: "How much the organization loses to computer thefts in a year." This is also referred to as statistical tracking.)

To track loss event information, the organization needs to know:

- What was lost?
- Who lost the property?
- Who owns the property?
- Where was it lost?
- When was it lost?
- Why was it lost?
- How did it happen?

The importance of effectively collecting the information needed to report and investigate incidents cannot be emphasized enough. This is why protecting the area where an incident has occurred is important. This enables a more effective investigative process.

Some incidents involve criminal activities. Here are some examples of typical criminal activities likely to occur:

- Theft
- Vandalism
- Fraud
- Assault
- Homicide
- Burglary

As previously noted, many incidents, probably in most cases actually, an incident will not involve a criminal situation. Some examples of noncriminal incidents could be:

- Alarms (fire, HVAC)
- Responding to an accident (vehicle, workplace, recreational)
- Service requests such as responding to calls for assistance to an employee or visitor as a security escort
- Complaints of lost and/or found property
- Insecure doors
- Fires
- Harassments
- Administrative breaches with organizational policy and procedures

THE SCENE

An incident scene can be found in a variety of locations. An incident scene can be an area of land or property, such as a room where a burglary has occurred and computers were stolen. An example on an even larger scale could be an entire property where an explosion and fire have occurred. In this case, the boundaries can be quite large and include a huge area within them. When the protection officer responds to the scene they must determine what the boundaries are and what exactly needs to be protected and why. For example, the scene could involve an area as small as a notebook computer. In this example, the scene that requires protection could have narrow boundaries, for example, the computer room and immediate area around where the computer was stored.

The important consideration is that when responding to a call, or as part of a patrol, a protection officer may discover an incident scene that will require security. In most cases, the expectation from management for the protection officer will be to protect the scene until someone with more expertise arrives to conduct an investigation. This is normally the case; the responding officer will have an investigative role, however minor that may be. In almost all situations a successful conclusion of an incident will begin with protection of the incident scene.

HAZARDS TO AN INCIDENT SCENE

To protect the scene, the protection officer should understand what they are protecting the scene from.

The reason an incident scene needs boundaries and protection is from contamination, either deliberate or from accidental external influences. Here is a partial list of common examples:

- Weather conditions contaminating evidence
- Bystanders or witnesses inadvertently walking on, touching, or taking evidence
- Suspects tampering with evidence
- Vehicles passing through the scene
- Hazards associated with the incident that may contaminate or damage the scene (fire, electricity, chemical leaks, debris, water, sewage, etc.)
- Assisting responders (security officers, EMS, fire, and often police officers who are merely bystanders and not investigators or connected to the incident)

DETERMINING BOUNDARIES

Essentially, and as indicated by Martin A. Fawcett, CPO in the 7th edition of *The Protection Officer Training Manual*, the protection officer's objective when responding to a crime or incident scene is to:

1. Establish the boundary (perimeter)
2. Protect the scene
3. Preserve evidence and scene integrity
4. Maintain detailed and accurate notes of everything (Fawcett, 2003)

These are similar rules established for law enforcement personnel.

When establishing boundaries for a scene, the protection officer will need to consider how spread out the evidence seems to be around the scene. Although establishing a larger protected or secured area is best, it may not be possible. Determining the boundaries of a crime or incident scene may depend on already established naturally existing barriers. For example, the protection officer needs to protect the office where the notebook computer is located. Locking the

office door, posting a security officer, and posting notices may be sufficient.

In other situations where the scene needs a larger area protected, establishing a perimeter is more difficult and requires more resources. The officer may need to obtain assistance from other security personnel to protect the area by posting officers at strategic locations to deter access and deploying temporary barricades (crime scene barrier tape, temporary fencing, and Jersey barriers). Imagine the resources needed to protect an entire city block from passing bystanders and traffic.

PROTECT AND PRESERVE THE SCENE

The protection officer is likely to be the first responder to the scene, assigning him the responsibility to protect the scene immediately. As soon as possible, establish the boundary or perimeter and use whatever resources you have immediately available to protect the area. Some other recommendations are to:

1. Call your supervisor for assistance.
2. Request assistance from other officers to protect the scene.
3. Keep bystanders away from the protected area. Consider that some bystanders may be potential witnesses; therefore do not immediately dismiss them from the area but keep them waiting a safe distance from the perimeter.

To best protect the scene and preserve evidence, the protection officer should consider how they would investigate the incident. This will give them a better perspective on how best to protect the area.

Unauthorized personnel do not need to access the protected area. This includes other security personnel and even emergency responders, such as the police. Unless the scene has officially been taken over by the investigating authority, keeping people away from evidence and inside the perimeter is a paramount responsibility of the protection officer in charge of the scene. Unless a supervisor has taken responsibility for the scene, the person responsible is typically the initial responding officer. Ensure instructions are clear when someone takes responsibility for the scene and make detailed notation of:

1. The time and date
2. The name, rank, and authority of the person who has taken responsibility

Bystanders will need to be contained outside the perimeter while the protection officer is protecting the scene. Although there is a tendency to have bystanders leave the area and carry on with their own business, the protection officer does not want to dismiss potential witnesses to the incident. There is a delicate balance between having bystanders keep their distance from the perimeter yet remain in the area so they are accessible to the investigators for an interview. Here are some recommendations:

1. To identify potential witnesses, ask if anyone saw what happened.
2. Ask potential witnesses to remain in the area to be interviewed by investigators.
3. Make notes of contact details, including name, date of birth, address and phone numbers of potential witnesses before allowing them to leave the scene.

The protection officer needs to be considerate with potential witnesses. People are typically busy and will not want to remain at the scene and wait for investigators. It is a responsibility of the protection officer to try to politely convince these people to wait. The protection officer has no authority to detain a potential witness; therefore, they may need to exercise discretion and be very polite while attempting to convince a potential witness to wait until the investigators arrive. If the circumstances permit, the officer may request the witness provide a written statement while they wait. At the very least, the officer must obtain the name and contact details of the potential witness.

Protecting the scene means the area must be preserved exactly as it was at the time of the incident. Nothing should be moved, removed, or altered in any way. Nothing should be introduced to the scene either (example: cigarette butts, garbage, foot- and fingerprints, or people). This includes touching anything at the scene (which introduces fingerprints). In fact, the protection officer must not touch or walk in any area where evidence may be disturbed or inadvertently introduced to the scene. There are times, though, when the officer or a responder may need to move a person or object; here are some examples:

1. Remove a victim from a potential danger or hazard at the scene.
2. Introduce a foreign substance (such as chemicals) to a scene to extinguish a fire or prevent an explosion from a fuel spill. For example, water or chemicals from a fire extinguisher.
3. Allow temporary access to the site to evacuate bystanders or other victims because it is the only path for an exit.

When something like this happens, the protection officer needs to make detailed notes of what was changed at the scene and how it was contaminated. The protection officer must remember that although protecting the scene is important, the protection of life is paramount and takes priority. Victims may need to be removed from the scene so that no further harm comes upon them or the responding protection officer.

Eating, drinking, or smoking should never be allowed at an incident scene (Schiro, n.d.), as these activities provide other opportunities to contaminate the scene.

EVIDENCE

It is important to understand what could be considered evidence. There are several types of evidence, but for the purposes of protecting the scene, the type of evidence most relevant is known as real evidence. This is evidence that is directly involved in the incident (DiCarlo, 2001). It is the physical evidence present at a scene that connects a suspect (person of interest) or helps explain what exactly happened. Physical evidence can have numerous forms, such as:

- Blood (including blood spatter patterns)
- DNA samples (blood, bodily fluids, skin, hair, bone, etc.)
- Fiber samples (clothing, carpet)
- Markings or impressions from tools, tires, footprints, handprints, etc.)
- Fingerprints
- A person (a body or evidence of an assault such as injuries, marks, or contact with an object or another person)
- Documents (electronic and paper)
- Computers and accessories (peripherals such as hard drives, disks, memory sticks, CD/DVDs, MP3 devices, storage mediums, etc.)
- Pieces from a suspect vehicle (damage left behind, paint samples, glass, parts)
- Tools or items related to the incident, victim, or suspect
- Chemicals
- Digital or analog images (video, CCTV, photos, audio recordings, etc.)
- Vehicles (automobiles, motorcycles, bicycles, etc.)
- Furniture
- Anything that is associated to an incident or crime that may be necessary for the investigation, prosecution, or litigation

The previous list is only a sampling, as the types of physical evidence that can be relevant to an incident are varied and can include almost anything. For example, most of the evidence listed above is quite visible, yet the protection officer needs to understand that many forms of evidence are invisible to the human eye. Fingerprints, for example, which are latent or impossible to see without investigative aids such as ultraviolet lights and detection powders. Another example is electronic and digital evidence that is contained on a hard drive. You may not know it is even there without expert assistance. This is extremely important to consider when protecting a scene because it will be difficult to protect something you cannot see.

Collecting and protecting evidence can be a huge responsibility, considering the vast list of potential items that could qualify as physical evidence. The collection of evidence should only be conducted by a qualified person, but if somehow the protection officer is required to take custody of a piece of evidence, it must be done so with extreme care. Often the officer has no choice but to accept evidence if provided to them by a victim or suspect. If evidence is found while on patrol it may be necessary to collect and preserve it so that it is not contaminated. If it is imperative that the evidence be collected by the Protection Officer, then here are some general recommended procedures to follow:

- Consider a piece of evidence as FRAGILE and handle it accordingly.
- Do not alter or adjust the evidence in any fashion—keep it as you find it.
- Only one person should handle evidence. Assign one person to take responsibility for the evidence and only allow that officer to collect or handle the evidence.
- Minimize the amount it is touched or handled and use proper hand protection (gloves) appropriate for the type of evidence. (Other pieces of personal protective equipment may be required, such as eye protection, full body suit, breathing apparatus, hard hat, etc.)
- Keep individual items separate so they do not contaminate each other.
- If the item was brought to you in a container or package—keep the container and package as evidence.
- If the item needs to be repackaged (moist items should never be kept in plastic containers), use the appropriate package and keep the original as evidence.

- The new container or evidence should be marked with:
  - Protection officer's name
  - Date and time of possession
  - Reference number to incident
- Prepare detailed notes outlining:
  - How you came in possession of the evidence
  - When you came in possession of the evidence
  - Where you came in possession of the evidence and where exactly it came from at the scene
  - Indicate who provided the evidence to you
  - Describe what the evidence is in detail
  - Photograph the evidence
- Continuity of possession of the evidence (chain of custody) is very important. Evidence needs to be stored in a proper manner and secured so that no one but the protection officer who accepted the evidence can access it. If the evidence needs to be moved or changes possession, the change and chain of custody must be documented and continuity maintained.
- Maintain a detailed log of what happens to the evidence while it is in your possession.
- If possession changes, document in the log and your notes:
  - Time and date of change
  - Who took possession of the evidence
  - The purpose of the change of custody (transfer to police, laboratory for testing, taken from evidence locker to court, etc.)

The proper collection and preservation of evidence is a topic that should be further researched. Additional resources can be found online at *Crime and Clues: The Art and Science of Criminal Investigation:* http://www.crimeandclues.com/crimescene.htm.

It should be rather clear at this point that the collection of evidence at a scene needs to be handled by professionals who are specially trained. The improper handling of a piece of evidence could impact the outcome of a criminal or civil trial, jeopardizing the appropriate course of justice and/or costing the organization additional losses or damages. The best advice is to protect the scene and allow the investigators to collect and handle the evidence.

MAKING DETAILED AND ACCURATE NOTES

The importance of detailed, neat, and complete note taking and reporting cannot be emphasized enough. As already mentioned, the protection officer must keep detailed and accurate notes of everything that happens or that is observed at the scene. The notes may take different forms, too. For example, drawing a sketch of the room or property layout can help in a later description and report. Sketches also are a terrific way to refresh your memory if you need to testify at a later time. Notes are often also recorded using an audio recorder. The portability of such devices has made the technology more convenient to use. Some cell phones have a feature to record digitally using dictation. These notes can be saved and later transcribed into written form to be included in a report. The purpose of good notes is also to facilitate a good report. Reports are intended to inform the reader of the following essentials:

- Who
- What
- Where
- When

A reader should be able to read a report and develop a clear picture in their mind of exactly what the protection officer saw when at the scene. Recreating the scene in written form will assist the investigators and make the protection officer a better witness. It is important to be a good "story teller," but more important to remember is that it is all about the facts. Reports should not contain predictions, opinions, or concepts—just the facts of what was seen, heard, and experienced.

It is also important to realize that a protection officer's notes are not confidential. There is a high probability the notes may be presented to an open tribunal as evidence. Additionally, a protection officer's notes could be copied and presented to the criminal defense or litigation plaintiff team and form part of their case. Because of the potential of full disclosure, whatever the Protection Officer writes in their notes should be in a very professional manner. Here are some suggestions:

- Only write about factual information and avoid opinions.
- Do not write anything derogatory about anyone.
- Write your notes neatly and if something is written in error, stroke a single line through the notation and write the correction clearly. Someone should be able to decipher the crossed-out mistake.
- Never tear out a page with notes—if it is necessary to tear an empty page from the book—make a note in the remaining margin of the time, date, and why the page was removed.

A good rule to follow when you maintain your notebook is to consider the following rule: *Whatever you write in your notes, you should be comfortable seeing someday written in a major newspaper like the New York Times*.

WORKING WITH LAW ENFORCEMENT AND INVESTIGATORS

It may seem as though the role a protection officer has at a crime or incident scene may not be as critical as that of investigators or police, but that is not the case. It is highly likely the protection officer will be the first responder who arrives or discovers the scene. This places a tremendous responsibility on the individual to:

1. Preserve life
2. Protect property

When the protection officer arrives at the scene, they will be responsible to provide first aid, call for assistance, be alert for hazards, protect the scene, handle witnesses and bystanders, watch for evidence, handle hectic communications, and coordinate other responders and officers who arrive. The stress level will probably be significant.

When the investigators and/or police arrive, the protection officer will be a valuable resource, as the investigators will want to interview and collect as much information about the incident as possible. This is in addition to the continued support that will be expected from the protection officer to protect the scene and assist in other ways (rescue, traffic control, etc.) while investigators collect evidence.

The protection officer is a member of the incident team and should act in a manner that will impress and instill confidence in the other members of the team. This also includes performing in a professional manner when interacting with the victim, suspect, and witnesses.

When law enforcement or internal investigators arrive, they will likely take charge of the incident. There is a well-planned incident command structure practiced in most communities and organizations around the world that will outline who takes command at an incident scene. The incident commander could be a member of law enforcement, EMS, or fire service. In some cases, it could be a representative from the organization responsible for the site.

As a member of the incident response team, the protection officer will be required to take instructions and direction from someone from a public agency (police, fire, EMS) or someone from the organization where the protection officer provides their service.

EMERGING TRENDS

Societies subjected to tougher economic times and reduced public spending will expose the security industry to increased responsibilities that were traditionally reserved for public law enforcement. Governmental budgets will undergo closer scrutiny by taxpayers, resulting in reduced funding for police and government agencies. This reduction in available funds will impact all resources, including personnel. Reduced manpower will mean security personnel and protection officers will be required to undertake more responsibilities at crime and incident scenes. In particular, the private sector will be expected to manage more of the investigation and reporting for incidents that could be considered minor.

The result of these trends will be the need for additional specific training for protection officers to prepare them to better fulfill the nontraditional roles and new responsibilities. These new quasi-governmental responsibilities will subject protection officers to more regulation and scrutiny, holding them to a higher standard.

CONCLUSION

The protection officer is an important resource when it is necessary to respond and protect a crime or incident scene. Often the outcome of a crime or incident will not be immediately apparent when the officer arrives as the initial responder. This means they have to act in a professional manner and practice the knowledge and skills gained in this chapter while protecting a scene and preserving evidence. The final outcome of a criminal or civil court case could depend on how well the evidence was protected, collected and managed.

References

Dicarlo, V. (2001). *Summary of the rules of evidence*, FindLaw; retrieved September 9, 2009, from <http://library.findlaw.com/2001/Jan/1/241488.html/>.

Fawcett (2003)

Schiro, G. (n.d.). *Protecting the crime scene*, retrieved September 9, 2009, from <http://www.crime-scene-investigator.net/evidenc1.html/>.

SECURITY QUIZ

1. The security officer's responsibilities when arriving at a crime scene is which of the following:
   a. Establish a boundary
   b. Protect the incident scene
   c. Maintain detailed notes
   d. All the above
2. To track loss-event-occurrences, the organization needs to know all of the following except?
   a. What was lost
   b. How long was it lost
   c. When was it lost
   d. Who lost it
3. Physical evidence found at the crime scene may explain what exactly happened and/or provide a list of suspects. Which of the following is not an item of physical evidence found at a crime scene?
   a. Blood
   b. Fiber samples
   c. Low levels of CO_2 in the soil samples
   d. Fingerprints

4. If it is imperative that evidence at a crime scene is recovered and protected by the security officer, which of the following is a recommended procedure?
   a. Keep individual items separate so they do not contaminate each other
   b. Gloving up before touching evidence is not necessary
   c. Wrapping evidence in sheets of newspaper is a good way to keep the evidence from being contaminated
   d. None of the above

5. When writing a report from your notes, which of the following will not be included:
   a. The names, dates of birth, addresses and phone numbers of witnesses and suspects identified at the crime scene
   b. A description of what happened
   c. Your best interpretation of why the incident happened
   d. A description of the crime scene where the incident took lace

6. Which of the following is the first responding officer responsible for at the crime scene:
   a. Take emergency actions necessary to preserve life and protect property
   b. Do nothing until the security supervisor arrives
   c. Start picking up items that look like they may be evidence
   d. Start taking pictures of the crime scene to create a record

7. Once the protection officer arrives on the scene, the first priority is to:
   a. Get the names of all those present
   b. Lock all the doors and wait for the police
   c. Preserve evidence found at the scene
   d. Provide first aid and call for assistance

8. The scene of a crime or incident will always require a boundary using police tape.
   a. True
   b. False

9. The boundaries of a crime scene will be immediately evident once the protection officer arrives on the scene.
   a. True
   b. False

10. It is necessary to establish the boundaries of a crime scene before an investigation can begin.
    a. True
    b. False

IX. INVESTIGATIONS

33

Interviewing and Statements

Dennis Shepp

CHAPTER OBJECTIVES

- Explain the process of interviewing witnesses, victims, and suspects
- Provide examples of verbal and nonverbal behavior
- List six recommendations for establishing rapport as a listener
- List five steps for conducting a successful interview

INTRODUCTION

When an incident or crime occurs, the responding protection officer is expected to protect the scene until investigators arrive to take over the investigation. The investigator can be from law enforcement or from the organization interested in the incident.

It is the investigator's duty to conduct interviews and obtain statements. However, the protection officer will often be in a situation where persons will speak to them and reveal information that is important to the incident or crime. While performing duties to protect the scene, the officer will interact with the victim, suspect, and potential witnesses. It is therefore important that a protection officer understands the importance of statements, whether written or verbal, and how to properly conduct oneself when engaged in an interview while obtaining information or a statement.

WHAT IS INTERVIEWING?

Interviews are part of the investigative process. An investigation is a systematic and thorough examination or inquiry into something or someone that involves the collection of facts and information and the recording of that examination in a report (ASIS International, 2006). Investigations can involve the police or private security regarding administrative incidents (policy and/or procedural infractions) and/or criminal matters. (Investigations are examined in more detail in Chapter 31.)

Interviews will review information that will often be vital to the investigation of an incident or crime. The most effective tool for gathering information about an incident is interviewing people (ASIS International, 2006). Therefore, any information gained from an interview, typically in the form of statements, will be considered evidence. This may form a type of evidence known as testimonial evidence or if involving a written statement, documented evidence. The detailed explanation of types of evidence is not important at this stage, what is important for the protection officer is to understand that when interviewing someone, even if it appears casual and unofficial, will produce a statement, either verbal or written, and this statement could become important evidence. That is why it is important to understand the procedures that should be followed when interviewing someone and obtaining their statement.

What is the difference between an interview and an interrogation? Typically, interviews involve witnesses or victims and an interrogation is an interview of a suspect. The goal of an interrogation is not only to seek the facts of what happened but also obtain a confession. It is not likely that a protection officer will be required to conduct an interrogation as part of their duties and only trained investigators skilled in the techniques of interviewing should conduct interrogations. Trained interviewers and interrogators spend years learning and practicing to become skilled in this art and science.

Understanding people is another important aspect of interviews and statements. Many studies have been conducted on human behavior and crime. Investigators have learned from the research about how to effectively interact with individuals to facilitate useful communications which in turn can produce valuable information for the investigation. The protection officer can also benefit from understanding human behavior.

THE POWER OF COMMUNICATION

Interviewing someone involves communication in two ways:

1. Verbally
2. Nonverbally

Verbal communication is the most commonly understood form of interview and statement. The interviewer speaks and the interviewee responds, or vice versa. This seems simple; however, in many situations the interviewer seeks to obtain information from people who are reluctant to speak or cooperate. This is where some insight into human behavior and psychology helps the interviewer.

Research has shown that people form their basic impressions of one another during the first few minutes of an interview (Quinn and Zunin, 1972). Therefore, it is very important for the interviewer to always think about how they are presenting themselves to the other person. If the officer does not initially conduct himself or herself in a professional manner, this may create a negative relationship with the interviewee. A negative mood will be counterproductive in an interview. The interviewer needs to be an active listener or someone who the interviewee would want to talk with. To do this, the interviewer needs to develop *rapport or a relationship* with the interviewee. This means the interviewer will attempt to establish a bond between them that is a connection where the interviewee perceives the interviewer to be a caring, impartial, and concerned individual. Here are some recommendations:

1. **Be empathetic**—show the person you understand and care about how they feel. This helps the interviewee accept and feel comfortable with the interviewer and will facilitate open and honest communication.
2. **Eliminate your prejudices**—try to detach yourself from any personal prejudices or bias you may have against the interviewees:
   - **Actions**—detach yourself from what the accused may have done, no matter how bad it was.
   - **Race**—do not discriminate against the person based on race or ancestry.
   - **History**—show the person that you are not prejudging based on past history.

Try to be nonjudgmental and do not place immediate blame.

3. **Be patient**—show the person you can wait to listen and understand their story of what happened and why. This is a sign of a very good listener when they can show they are patient. This is a sign to the interviewee of tolerance, acceptance, and understanding.

4. **Reflect feedback**—repeat back to the interviewee statements, facts, and comments they have related. The interviewer acts like a "mirror," reflecting back to the interviewee their words, feelings, and attitudes, showing to them you are listening and care about what they say (Nirenberg, 1988).

5. **Do not interrupt**—it is rude to interrupt, just like in any communication or conversation, so do not interrupt the interviewee when they are relating their story to you. Allow them to finish what they are saying.

6. **Concentrate**—interviewing someone requires complete concentration on what they are saying and how they are saying it. Concentration can best be equated to playing a game of chess—the interviewer needs to concentrate on what is currently being said, but also must think ahead to expect what the interviewee might (or should) say.

Why would concentration be important and matter when the interviewee is telling the story and relating the facts as they know it? This is because the interviewee will sometimes not tell the truth and attempt to deceive the interviewer, for a variety of reasons. This is why the interviewer needs to concentrate on what is said and follow the story and attempt to detect deception. Detecting deception is explained in more detail later.

"Nonverbal communication" is a type of communication between persons that involves written statements (discussed later) and bodily movements which are considered a form of communication. This is important for an interviewer to understand because how a person (this includes the interviewer, too) projects themselves can relate significant information about their state of mind. For example, someone who shows by their nervous voice tone, shaking hands, and darting eyes that they are anxious and afraid should be recognized by the interviewer so that they can try to calm the interviewee and make them feel more relaxed. This helps toward developing rapport between the interviewer and interviewee. Additionally, changes in behavior and body movements can indicate stress. Stress is an important indicator for an interviewer. This can be the stress of the interview itself or from a specific and directed question such as: *"Did you take the money?"* A guilty person may show signs of "flight or fight syndrome." Fight or flight is an instinctual phenomenon, based on when humans relied on this instinct to help them either run from danger (flight) or face it (fight). It actually is a manifestation of bodily reactions to stress that humans will experience even nowadays when confronted with stress. Asking a question that may compel the interviewee to lie will often cause this type of stress. A well-trained interviewer can act as a human polygraph (lie detector) when someone attempts to deceive by telling a lie or not revealing information. Many of these telltale signals come from nonverbal and verbal responses to stress and are evident in clusters of observed body movements and reactions. As mentioned, it can take many years of training and experience for a skilled interviewer to recognize these signals of deception and further specialized training is recommended before anyone attempts to seek or analyze verbal and nonverbal behavior in an interview. Nonetheless, here are some examples of verbal and nonverbal behavior when subjected to stress:

• Changes in voice and speech patterns, such as changes in the types of words used.
• Changes in the rate and volume of speech (louder, softer, faster, or slower). Tension will often cause speech to become more rapid and stammered, sometimes two to three times the normal speed.

- Burst of anger (threats to sue you, complaints of how the interviewee has been handled, comments about your incompetence).
- Pausing, stalling, or delaying tactics (the interviewee suddenly needs to leave for an appointment, long pauses to try to think of an answer, changing the topic in an attempt to delay the interview, suddenly wants a lawyer).
- Nervous or false laughter (this is a form of energy release when someone is under stress).
- Sudden shifts in body movement not normally displayed by the interviewee during the interview (some examples: shifting body position, pacing, jumping out of chair, waving hands and arms, shaking, kicking legs and feet, coughing, yawning). These are also forms of energy release when someone is feeling stressed.

It is vital for the protection officer to understand that nonverbal indicators need to be analyzed by a trained investigator and interviewer. It is important to understand as a protection officer (interviewer) you will outwardly display your feelings by how you present yourself. Therefore, be careful and aware about how you may appear to the interviewee.

THE INTERVIEW PROCESS

When interviewing anyone, the interviewer needs to consider the following:

"Do to others as you would have them do upon you" (Yeske, 2002).

Here are some steps to consider when preparing to conduct an interview:

1. **Prepare yourself, physically and mentally.**
   - Examine your appearance—how do you look to the interviewee? Are you professional in appearance? Are you

showing the right attitude to conduct the interview?
   - Are you mentally prepared? Can you focus on the interview? Do you appear confident and prepared?

2. **If possible, try to use a suitable location for the interview.**
   - There can be many distractions to interviewing someone, especially if the interview occurs at the scene of the incident.
   - Try to find a quiet and private place to conduct the interview, away from potential distractions.
   - Avoid interviewing anyone in the presence of other witnesses—their testimony or account of observations can be tainted if they listen to another witness's account.

3. **Ask open-ended questions.**
   - Avoid closed-ended questions that will typically require a simple "yes" or "no" response.
   - Open-ended questions are the type that prompt longer answers and compel the interviewee to provide a narrative response. For example:
     - *"Please tell me everything that happened."*
     - *"In detail, can you please explain what occurred here today?"*
     - *"Please describe everything you saw regarding what happened here."*

4. **Record the interview.**
   - The most common method is to write detailed notes of what the person says.
   - If possible and the local legal system permits, audio- or videotape the interview—this is the best method of maintaining an accurate account of what exactly is stated.
   - When taking a statement, the best method is to obtain a "pure version" statement.
   - Pure version statements allow the interviewee to provide their version of

an account in a narrative format without any prompting from the interviewer other than a request, similar to: *"Please write in detail everything that happened from the time you left your house to the time the police arrived at the scene."*

- If the person responds with: *"What exactly do you want me to say?"* the protection officer's response should be: *"Please explain in as much detail as possible everything that happened from the time you left your house to the time the police arrived at the scene."*

- The pure version statement remains the best method to obtain the interviewee's account of what happened. This statement becomes the basis for further questions that can be asked by the investigator to complete a detailed account of what occurred.

- Be careful what questions you ask. It is part of the psychology of interviewing that an interviewer needs to consider the questions they ask an interviewee— the famed investigator, Avinoam Sapir, who discovered through his extensive research the process known as "Statement Analysis," has aptly said: *"Specific questions are not designed to obtain information. Specific questions are designed to detect deception. The most serious disadvantage of questions is that one can ask only about what is already known. What is not known would not be explored and therefore would remain unknown."* It is also from an interviewer's questions that an interviewee can learn how much the interviewer already knows (or doesn't know) about the incident.

5. **Remember the elements for useful statements** (Sennewald and Tsukayama, 2006):
   - Identify who wrote the statement (interviewee's name and identification information)

- Date, time, and location of the interview
- Indicate if the statement is voluntary
- Signed by the interviewee

Other guidelines for written statements (Sennewald and Tsukayama, 2006):

1. Use lined paper and write margin to margin.
2. The text should flow into additional pages (if necessary).
3. If corrections are required, draw a line through the sentence or word and sign your initials on the change.
4. Sign your initials next to the last word on a page and where the page number is written: (Example: "Page 1 of 3" INITIALS).
5. Ensure the interviewee understands what is written (if the statement is written for them)—have the interviewee read back what is written.
6. Include a sentence acknowledging the statement is voluntary, without the influence of drugs or alcohol, and is the account of the interviewee.

DECEPTION

There may be times where the interviewee may provide inaccurate information or may try to deceive the interviewer. Deception can take additional forms other than what some may immediately think is a lie or untruthful statement. Sometimes deception is avoiding facts that are known by the interviewee or changing the account of how something happened. It is not only a suspect that may try to deceive; witnesses and victims may often avoid facts for various reasons.

Detecting deception from an interviewee and knowing how to react properly while continuing the interview requires an investigator's skill. These skills will have developed from training and experience. This is where the interviewer becomes a "human polygraph" and is able to react in an appropriate manner. The best practice for the protection officer facing a deceptive interviewee is to make detailed notes of the statements made by the person and have them commit to the statement in writing and under their signature. This written statement can be used quite effectively by a skilled investigator during a subsequent interview.

CONCLUDING THE INTERVIEW

When the protection officer concludes the interview he or she should make detailed notes of the following:

1. Name of the interviewee.
2. Contact details (residence and employment):
   - Telephone numbers (mobile, work, residence, other)
   - E-mail addresses (work, residence, other)
   - Addresses (work, residence, other)
3. Identification (date of birth, ID number, passport, etc.)
4. A brief account of the interviewee's involvement in the incident (witness, victim, suspect, or person of interest)

The protection officer should continue with a professional demeanor when dealing with witnesses, victims, and persons of interest. Notwithstanding the fact that an interviewee may have confessed to a crime or committing a breach of organizational policy, they should still be treated with respect and dignity. This behavior will benefit the officer in the long term.

CONCLUSION

The protection officer will undoubtedly become involved in an incident where he or she will be required to conduct an interview. It is highly recommended that further training be obtained from recognized training organizations such as John E. Reid and Associates Inc., Laboratory for Scientific Investigation, and other internationally recognized groups. Proper training in the knowledge and skills needed to manage effective interviews is essential. Any time the protection officer is faced with a situation in which the interview may require these skills, the officer should seek assistance from a professional investigator qualified to conduct interviews.

EMERGING TRENDS

Although the process of interviewing has been around for centuries, the methods have and will continue to evolve considerably. Statement analysis is a relatively new science as applied to investigations, but it illustrates that the process of investigative interviews will constantly evolve and improve.

What seems most interesting is the improvements mainly involve learning more about linguistics and human psychology and applying refined or new techniques to better interpret communications. Humankind has not been investing new gadgets or technology to do this, it has been improving traditional methods such as verbal interviews, nonverbal kinetics, and written statements.

We will continue to learn more about human behavior and how to apply our understanding toward seeking truth from communications. Technology will also improve and will likely provide more tools to investigators in their pursuit of the facts.

References

ASIS International. (2006). *Protection of assets manual,* Chapter 1, Part 1, p. 8.

Quinn, L., & Zunin, N. (1972). *Contact: The first four minutes.* New York, NY: Ballantine Books, Inc.

Nirenberg, J. (1988). *Getting through to people.* Prentice Hall.

Yeske, C. (2002). *The art of investigative interviewing* (2nd ed.). Butterworth-Heinemann.

Sennewald, C., & Tsukayama, J. (2006). *The process of investigation: Concepts and strategies for investigations in the workplace* (3rd ed.). Elsevier/Butterworth-Heinemann.

Resources

Gordon, N. J., & Fleisher, W. L. (2006). *Effective interviewing: Interrogation techniques* (2nd ed.). Academic Press.

Reid technique: Interviewing and interrogation. (2005). 2-CD-ROM Training Collection, <http://www.reid.com/store2/detail.html?sku=cd-rtiivs/>.

Yeschke, C. (2002). *The art of investigative interviewing* (2nd ed.). Butterworth-Heinemann.

Zulawski, D. E., & Wicklander, D. E. (2002). *Practical aspects of interviewing and interrogation* (2nd ed.). CRC Press.

SECURITY QUIZ

1. When an incident or crime occurs, the responding protection officer is expected to protect the scene until investigators arrive.
   a. True
   b. False

2. It is important that a protection officer understands the importance of statements, whether written or verbal.
   a. True
   b. False

3. Interviewing people is NOT the best way to gather information as there are many other more effective methods and resources.
   a. True
   b. False

4. Nonverbal communication is the most commonly understood form of interviewing.
   a. True
   b. False

5. Tension will often cause speech to become more rapid and stammered sometimes _____ times the normal speed.
   a. 1—2 times
   b. 2—3 times
   c. 5—6 times
   d. 10 times

6. Avoid close-ended questions that will typically require a simple "yes" or "no" response.
   a. True
   b. False

7. Guidelines for written statements may include:
   a. Use lined paper and write margin to margin
   b. Text should flow into additional pages (if necessary)
   c. If corrections are required, draw a line
   d. All of the above

8. Deception can take additional forms other than what some may immediately think is a lie or untruthful statement.
   a. True
   b. False

9. When the protection officer concludes the interview they should make detailed notes of the following:
   a. Name of the interviewee
   b. Contact details
   c. Identification
   d. All of the above

10. The protection officer should continue with a professional demeanor when dealing with:
    a. Witnesses
    b. Victims
    c. Persons of interest
    d. All the above

34

Foundations for Surveillance

Michael Stroberger

CHAPTER OBJECTIVES

- Define and describe the four types of surveillance: covert, overt, personal, and electronic
- Explore the scope of equipment requirements for surveillance
- Discuss legal ramifications of privacy and retention issues

In most popular media, the concept of surveillance is either portrayed as a man in a wrinkled, coffee-stained suit or an extremely large, sophisticated, and complex electronic array that requires three or more people to monitor. In reality, the typical surveillance operation falls between these.

The basic goal of surveillance is to obtain information that might not be immediately available without a concerted effort and a focused attention. In most cases, it is the watchful, knowledgeable, and sometimes lucky selection of points of focus that yield the best results. In other cases, it is the act of watching that produces results.

Of utmost importance in all surveillance operations is a proper understanding of privacy and the limits to which one can surveil another

without violating legal restrictions, company policy, or common sense.

GENERAL TYPES

Surveillance operations can be broken down into a matrix of sorts with the headers being *covert* and *overt* on one side, and *personal* and *electronic* on the cross-referenced edge. As such, it is only appropriate that the bulk of this discussion be framed within the four possible combinations of these types.

- Covert operations are those done in secret without the knowledge of those being observed. Blending with the surroundings is critical to the success of these operations.
- Overt operations are out in the open, and can usually be easily identified as what they are.
- Personal operations are those carried out in person by individuals or teams of operatives. Although the initial setup of such an operation may not be overly expensive, the continued use of manpower quickly increases the amount of required funding and quickly outweighs the cost of electronic alternatives.
- Electronic operations can range from CCTV (Closed-Circuit Television) systems to transmission interception and receipt of

other electronic information. Usually, the operators are well out of sight, even if the equipment is clearly visible.

COVERT PERSONAL SURVEILLANCE

Covert personal surveillance is the act of watching another from a location of concealment, or in a manner in which this act is not obviously being carried out. This is the main focus of the services of some investigators dealing with cases such as marital strife, insurance fraud, and even law enforcement investigations. While this surveillance is personal rather than electronic, it should be noted that some electronics are usually involved, but this is often limited to a camera, a voice recorder for the retention of comments on the observations, and similar low-end electronics. The primary advantage of this method is that it provides for a human decision-making option as the situation evolves. By being on the scene, the operative(s) can determine how to refocus the operation to obtain better results. The major drawback is that this is extremely manpower intensive. In order to not attract too much attention, it is best to randomly exchange operatives so that the same person is not in the area for an extended period of time, drawing potential interest through being conspicuous. When performing vehicle surveillance, this is even more of an issue, as specific vehicles are easily recognized if they continuously pass into and out of view.

These operations can yield interesting results stemming from the fact that, when properly executed, those observed are not aware that others are paying attention to them.

OVERT PERSONAL SURVEILLANCE

This type of operation ranges widely in its application. Most people in the field of protection engage in this type of operation on a regular basis without realizing that it falls within this category. Overt personal surveillance is the execution of visible and open inspection, such as when on patrol. The act of gathering information is shared in importance with the deterrent value of such an operation. The person executing these duties may be looking for specific types of incidents or situations. Through their presence, and the fact that they are paying attention to their surroundings and the persons in those surroundings, this may cause those in the area to reconsider intentions of violating company policy or legal restrictions.

The performance of this type of operation is most likely to alter the behaviors and responses of persons in the observed environment due to the fact that there is clearly a person paying attention to those present.

COVERT ELECTRONIC SURVEILLANCE

The use of hidden cameras, voice and electronic recording equipment, and similar devices falls within this category. It is within this type of operation that the surveillance agent must pay the closest attention to privacy issues, as the unwelcome observation of persons, under certain circumstances, may violate state or federal restrictions on such actions. Care must be taken and counsel sought when designing such operations, so that violation of such restrictions does not occur.

Some equipment options might include pinhole cameras; cameras concealed in sprinkler heads, clocks, books, and other nondescript items; scanners tuned to permissible frequencies; and even long-range audio amplifiers as permitted. The equipment selection, given the right budget, can look very much like the property of a movie spy. The actual selection is often limited only by the budget of the operation.

Much like personal covert operations, this method often yields very interesting results. If the operation is properly executed, those being watched are not aware that they are being observed. As a result, they will act in a manner that is completely natural to them in the given environment.

OVERT ELECTRONIC SURVEILLANCE

The classic example of overt electronic surveillance would be the pan/tilt/zoom camera domes found in most department stores. These provide a significant amount of information to a trained operator and are also a very visible deterrent to certain types of crimes. Often, if the recordings of such a system are replayed, persons can be seen behaving in one manner, looking up to find that a camera is in the area, and immediately altering the previous behavior to bring it more in line with the expectations of that environment. It is not that the devices themselves have any potential to bring harm to the individual. It is the concept that, absent of a clear view of the operator of the system, there is no way to know if the camera watching that specific area is being paid attention to at the given moment. It is the fear of possibly being observed that provides the deterrent factor in this case. It is because of this that CCTV systems, in such setting as industrial locations and employee-only areas of other types of businesses, should be placed in such a manner as to make it plainly obvious that CCTV is in use, but without providing a view of the monitors themselves. Those in the area should know that observation occurs but not be able to determine which area at any given time is being observed.

EQUIPMENT REQUIREMENTS

As previously stated, the equipment may vary widely. In the case of personal surveillance, either covert or overt, it may be as simple as binoculars, a camera, a mini-recorder, and a notepad. The initial outlay might be as low as a few hundred dollars, and the equipment retained over a period of many operations. In electronic operations, the initial outlay may be thousands, or tens or hundreds of thousands, of dollars. This is based upon the scope and sophistication of the intended operation. As an example, moderate grade pan/tilt/zoom camera operations require not only the camera dome itself but also a control unit, video cabling, power sources and cable, and a method of recording the input. A single PTZ (Pan/Tilt/Zoom) camera, in a stand-alone system, could be thousands of dollars and would still have to be manned at least occasionally.

The equipment must be appropriate to the nature and scope of the operation if it is to be of optimal effectiveness. Experience and common sense will dictate the exact requirements.

Regardless of the nature and method of the operation, the underlying goal of obtaining information must also be addressed in the equipment. If this information is to be used in a truly effective manner, it must be recorded in some way. Certainly, in cases of criminal and civil actions, the best possible method of recording the information should be sought. To appear in court without physical evidence would be of almost no use at all. In many cases, simple still photographs can make a significant impact. Videotape, made through camcorders or more complex systems, can often solve certain cases, such as insurance fraud.

PRIVACY ISSUES

Although the pursuit of justice and the protection of personal or company property is highly important, it is also critical that the laws protecting privacy be honored and protected. As such, it is essential to understand the basic concepts and research laws that could have bearing on the specific operation to be undertaken. Do not ever assume that the privacy laws of one area apply wholly to another area.

As an example, in some states, recording a telephone conversation may not be done without the prior knowledge and consent of both parties on that call. In other states, only one person must be aware that a recording is being made. In some cases, an employer may listen in to employee telephone conversations, based on legal permissions, specific content in the employee hiring agreement or employee handbook, or simply because the telephones are owned by the employer and provided only for the execution of work-related duties. Without a clear understanding of the laws and restrictions that apply to the location in which you intend to perform a surveillance operation, it could be very easy to violate those laws.

Although there are many "rules of thumb" on this issue, the fact is that local laws vary so widely that the best guideline to follow is to research those that apply to your target area.

RECORDING AND RETENTION

As already noted, it is best to make some durable record of the surveillance operation's results. In some cases, this can prove a suspicion; in others, it could be used to defend the execution of practices of those involved in the operation. The materials produced by such activities should be retained for a period of time that is appropriate for the material and actions identified through that investigation,

or for the locally defined period of time that those involved might be allowed to enter into a civil action, whichever is longer. In short, be prepared to prove your case for however long it might be an issue, and be prepared to defend your operation against civil accusations. Some companies have a policy that directs all closed case materials to be destroyed after a certain period of time, such as a 2-year retention policy. Research these directives before executing them. In some states, those involved are permitted up to 4 years to file civil suits. It would be in the best interest of those involved that they have supporting evidence should this occur within the allowed period of time. Again, research the laws and restrictions that apply to not only your location, but also the specific location where the operation takes place.

Save everything if possible, especially in retaining video and imagery evidence, as you never know what might be seen in the secondary areas of the image. Some cases have begun and been proven based on the background scene in video recordings. Even when the primary action, the focus of the video, did not prove to be a violation as previously thought. Pay attention to your background, and review all materials with this in mind. If storage space becomes an issue, it might be that noncritical materials have to be discarded. Review these materials prior to removal to ensure that there is nothing of value in them.

SECURITY QUIZ

1. Covert operations are intended not to be known or recognized.
   a. True
   b. False
2. Personal operations are the least expensive in the long run.
   a. True
   b. False
3. Equipment requirements vary depending on the location, nature, and goal of the operation.
   a. True
   b. False
4. A proper understanding of privacy issues is only important if the case goes to court.
   a. True
   b. False

5. Electronic surveillance could include:
   a. CCTV
   b. Interception of radio transmissions
   c. Interception of other electronic information
   d. All of the above
6. Considerations for the retention of records could include:
   a. Company policy
   b. Statutes of limitation
   c. Storage space
   d. All of the above
7. Overt personal surveillance:
   a. Relies on being properly concealed
   b. Could deter some incidents
   c. Both of the above
   d. Neither a nor b
8. A simple camera surveillance system will often include:
   a. A camera
   b. A recorder
   c. A cable and connections
   d. All of the above
9. In some states/provinces/countries, recording a telephone conversation may not be done without the prior knowledge and consent of both parties on that call.
   a. True
   b. False
10. If storage space becomes an issue, it might be that noncritical materials have to be discarded.
   a. True
   b. False

Report Writing and Field Notes

Rav-Zuridan Yisrael

CHAPTER OBJECTIVES

- Explain the basics of report writing
- Emphasize the usefulness of report writing
- Explain the purpose of field notes
- Identify the essentials of good report writing

INTRODUCTION

As in many other professions, reports are essential to the security industry. In fact, report writing is one of the most essential functions for security officers. Some security professionals list the primary directives of a security officer as detecting, deterring, and reporting. Other professionals state that the main duties of security officers are observing and reporting. However, in any instance, it is widely accepted that report writing is of the utmost importance in the security industry. Many reasons exist that explain the importance of report writing within the security industry.

IMPORTANCE OF REPORT WRITING

One of the most important issues of report writing has to do with liability. Proper report writing may significantly reduce the potential liability faced by security officers or their employers. Reports can aid in documenting potential loss that an organization may face and the response that the organization takes to mitigate the risk of loss. Additionally, reports may aid in determining who is accountable for an incident.

For example, if a security officer is working for a contract security company and he/she notices a torn carpet that presents a trip hazard, that security officer has a duty to report the hazard. If the hazard is not repaired and someone is injured, the fact that the officer reported it reduces the liability of both the officer and the officer's company. Once the officer submits the written report, it is now primarily the responsibility of the property owner or property manager to develop an adequate safety or security measure to remedy the situation (i.e., repairing the carpet). However, if no measures are taken to remedy the hazard and someone is injured, the owner of the property can likely be held liable and accountable for their inaction. Therefore, it is evident that reports are important in determining liability as well as accountability.

FIELD NOTES

It is imperative that reports be accurate and factual. To ensure that reports meet this requirement, field notes should be written while conducting one's duty as a security officer. Field notes should be written in an easy-to-carry pocket-sized notebook. While on patrol or responding to incidents, field notes are taken as the initial step in reporting incidents, unsafe conditions, and breaches in security, violations of policy, or any unusual events.

Field notes are useful in many situations. For example, if an incident arises that requires the police department, fire department, or ambulance to arrive at a work location, it is much simpler to write down the necessary facts while handling the incident. Handling certain events can be stressful; however, it will be more stressful to have to search for a piece of paper to write down important details. Additionally, recording the information as soon as possible after the occurrence of the incident helps to ensure the accuracy of the incident report. For example, if an officer observes a vehicle crash into a parked vehicle and then drive off rapidly, it is easier to write down the make and model of the car and its license plate number in the field notebook than it is to remember the information 20 minutes later while writing an incident report. Field notes provide a means of recording the intricate and specific details of an event or unusual or unsafe circumstance. Information to record in field notes may include:

- Descriptions of suspects
- Names and badge numbers of emergency services personnel
- Vehicle numbers of emergency service vehicles

- Names of witnesses
- Notes from interviews of witnesses
- Descriptions of vehicles
- List of items stolen
- List of items broken
- Names and contact information of victims
- Time of incident
- Arrival times for emergency service personnel
- Nonworking lights (security hazard)
- Torn carpets (trip hazard)
- Leaking pipes (trip hazard or damaged fire suppression system) or any other detail or event that will be needed for a report at another time

REPORTS SHOULD BE WRITTEN

Considering that reports are critical to adequately perform one's duties as a security officer, it is necessary to discuss reports in better detail. Security officers should write all reports; even if a verbal report of an incident is given, written reports are necessary. Written reports are more dependable than verbal communication. For example, do you remember what you were wearing on the 13th day of last month? What did you have for lunch that day? What was the description of the first person that you saw that day at work? The average individual does not remember such specific details of past events. Additionally, even with the best of intentions, either party can forget a verbal report. If there is a conflict regarding whether a verbal report was *submitted*, the issue becomes a matter of hearsay or a case of "he-said/she-said." A written report is a means to recall the intricate details of an event and to verify submission of the report. Verification of submission of a document can be via a signature on a traditional report or by printing a copy of a report that has been inputted into a database. Not only should the report be in written format, it should be written as soon as possible after an incident and notes should be taken during the incident if possible. This will ensure the most accurate record of the details that took place.

WHAT SHOULD BE REPORTED

Determining which incidents require reporting may seem complicated to novice security practitioners. A good rule to follow is: if it is an uncommon event, then report it. It is far better to have an incident report that is not needed than to need a report and not have it. When there is doubt on whether a report should be written, it is better to err on the side of writing the report. Some examples of events to report include broken equipment or property, illegal activities, trespass, activities against company policies, accidents, injuries, hazardous situations, fires, breaches in security, and vandalism.

QUALITIES OF GOOD REPORTS

There are certain qualities that all effective reports should have. A good way to remember the qualities of a well-written report is the "Three (3) C's of report writing." The 3 C's of report writing are a guideline to the characteristics of a good report. Reports are to be clear, concise, and complete. Each of the 3 C's will be discussed in further detail.

Clear—Refers to the readability and understandability of the report. A report should be written legibly or typed to ensure that others can read it, as it has little value if not understood. Clear also relates to the words used and the sentence structure. It is best to write a report in the simplest and clearest terms, again, to ensure it is easily understood. Reread the report, or have others read it, to make certain the correct message is being conveyed. Additionally, word

usage is important to create a clear and precise report that is useful to others. An example of a statement that demonstrates poor word usage is "the subject is a short, white male." That sentence is very vague and leaves the height of the suspect to the interpretation of the reader. Better reporting of the suspect's description is that "the subject is approximately 5 feet and 5 inches tall." This makes the description more concrete, as opposed to a subjective description, such as *short*, which may vary from person to person. Finally, punctuation, grammar, and spelling are important to report writing. If you are unsure how to spell a word, refer to a pocket dictionary. Remember that a report is a reflection of your professionalism.

Concise—A good acronym to remember when it comes to writing reports is K.I.S.S. (Keep It Short and Simple). Conciseness has to do with the brevity of the report. It is not necessary to expound extensively on an incident. However, it is necessary to include all relevant information and to ensure that this information is factual and accurate. Additionally, reports are to be objective and impartial; *never add your opinions or assumptions to a report*. Your opinions can be shared with necessary parties as needed; however, they have no place in a report. If your opinion is a likely truth, an objective party is probably going to reach the same conclusion or consider your conclusion by an objective review of your report. However, it is important to ensure that the conciseness of a report does not affect its completeness.

Complete—This means ensure that all of the details are included in the report. One method to accomplish this is to consider the "5 W's and 1 H of report writing," which is a guide to ensuring that a report is complete. It requires that you answer the following questions as they relate to the incident: Who, What, Where, When, Why, and How? Obviously, each question is not applicable to every incident; however, this is a very thorough starting point.

Examples of questions that should be answered in the report are listed below:

Who:

- Who is the victim/complainant?
- Who is the culprit/accused?
- Who responded?
- Who was notified?
- Who witnessed the incident?

What:

- What happened?
- What was the consequence?
- What was the response?
- What was the badge number of the police who arrived?
- What was the truck number of the ambulance that arrived?

Where (be exact: include address, floor, room number, etc.):

- Where did the incident occur?
- Where was the victim taken?
- Where was the suspect taken?
- Where in the building?

When (this includes the date and time):

- When did the incident occur?
- When did the police or ambulance arrive?
- When was the incident reported?

Why:

- Why did the incident occur?
- Why were the police called?
- Why did security respond?
- Why did the alarm sound?

How:

- How was the incident reported?
- How was the incident discovered?
- How was the suspect apprehended?
- How was the issue resolved?

Writing a quality report is one of the most important duties of a security professional. It is essential to remember to remain truthful and honest in your reports. Security professionals are entrusted with the responsibility of protecting the assets of others; are given access to areas, items, and information only because of the responsibility of their position; and, therefore, should act in an ethical and moral manner. One's ability to communicate effectively through written reports may directly affect career advancement. Reports are a reflection of the author and in many ways reflect their competency at performing their job functions. Additionally, reports may be used for legal matters, recalling the details of incidents, and determining which security or safety issues must be addressed more thoroughly.

EMERGING TRENDS

Many organizations are moving toward having their incident reports compiled and stored in a database. The database allows various managers to view incident reports without having to hand-deliver a hard copy. Additionally, the database allows users to sort incidents based on the nature of the incident. The ability to sort a year's worth of incidents with the click of a button is of great benefit to managers conducting risk assessments on the facility as well as determining trends with certain types of incidents.

References

Hess, M. E., & Wrobleski, H. M. (1996). *Introduction to private security* (4th ed.). New York, NY: West Publishing Company.

International Foundation of Protection Officers. (2003). *Protection officer training manual* (7th ed.). New York, NY: Butterworth and Heinemann.

Security Guard Management. (2004). *Report writing* [Motion Picture]. <http://www.sgmnow.com/pages/videos.htm>.

State of New York Division of Criminal Justice Services. (1995). Eight hour pre-assignment training course for security guards.

SECURITY QUIZ

1. Incidents must always be written in a way that shows the organization in a favorable manner.
   a. True
   b. False

2. Verbal reports are equally as reliable as written reports.
   a. True
   b. False

3. There are six (6) questions that every report must attempt to answer and they include: Who, What, Where, When, Why. What is the additional question?
   a. If
   b. Could
   c. How
   d. Summary

4. The three (3) Cs of report writing are:
   a. Clear, Complete and Concise
   b. Complete, Competent, Clear
   c. Clear, Concise, Compartmentalized
   d. Concise, Clear, Clever

5. It is important to state your opinion in incident reports to ensure that management can figure out what really occurred.
   a. True
   b. False

6. Incident reports must be treated as legal documents.
   a. True
   b. False

7. Field notes are equivalent to incident reports.
   a. True
   b. False

8. Writing a report is one of the most important duties of a security professional.
   a. True
   b. False

9. A good rule to follow is: If it is an uncommon event, then report it.
   a. True
   b. False

10. A good acronym to remember when it comes to writing reports is H.U.G.
    a. True
    b. False

UNIT X

LEGAL ASPECTS OF SECURITY

36

Legal Aspects of Security

David L. Ray

CHAPTER OBJECTIVES

- To provide an overview of the development of our current legal system
- To reduce the liability of the security officer and the employer
- To explain how to avoid the costs of litigation and damages for false arrest, illegal search, or failure to provide an appropriate level of security
- To describe to the security officer what opportunities are available to minimize risk of exposure to various actions by acting within the law

INTRODUCTION

From the earliest times we have created laws to ensure that others will keep their promises, not cause us harm, and act in the best interests of society. Laws may be written, verbal, or implied (e.g., when a customer walks into a restaurant and orders a meal the establishment can assume that the customer intends to pay for that meal). Laws may be based on religious requirements such as the Ten Commandments, the Code of Hammurabi, Buddhist Dharma teachings, the Koran, or other religious codes, and they may also be based on other societal concerns such as business and economics. For our purposes we will define laws as the rules governing society. These rules not only set down our obligations to each other but establish penalties in the form of fines, judgments, or incarceration to punish the perpetrator who breached the obligation or to compensate the victim for the breach. These rules would be ineffective if there were not also established procedures for enforcing the obligations, whether a ruling by a tribal chieftain or more modern procedures that provide for search warrants, arrest, incarceration, probation, and so on.

Protection officers often provide a role similar to law enforcement, wear a uniform, and are viewed by the public as authority figures who are there to look after their safety and the protection of their property. The protection officer is also involved in activities that are inherently dangerous, which may include protection from criminal activity and life-safety programs such as bomb threats, fire, and evacuation procedures. Trespassers and criminals will view the protection officer as someone who is there to intervene if they commit a criminal act. Protective duties may require the officer to make decisions that raise questions of liability against the officer, the property owner, or the employer. In conducting enforcement duties, the protection officer may be required to arrest, detain, use force, seize property, and testify in court when charges are laid. For all of these reasons, it is important that the protection officer understand his or her duties and responsibilities and the potential liabilities which could arise from them. Their role is complicated by the fact that in some cases protection officers do not have the same authority that law enforcement has, while in other cases they have more.

Protection officers may also be required, in the course of their duties, to ensure that a person's rights are protected under the U.S. Bill of Rights or the Canadian Charter of Rights and Freedoms. For further information on authority in these areas refer to the chapters on Arrest and Detention and Use of Force.

THE DEVELOPMENT OF OUR LAWS

We tend to think of laws as being words written in books and passed by a government authority, but that is only one source of our laws. There are actually three:

1. Common law and the civil code of France
2. Case law
3. Statutes

The Common Law

The Common Law was developed in feudal England. At that time most people could not read or write and, therefore, written statutes would not be of much benefit. In order to resolve issues between citizens they would go to the feudal lord with their disputes. There was an expectation that the feudal lord would be consistent (or common) in resolving these disputes from one issue to another. Citizens therefore believed that "laws" were common throughout the land, even though they were not written down as statutes and even though

there was no written record of the decision. In fact, the decisions were far from consistent and the feudal lords would often have difficulty resolving an issue and would order that the dispute be settled by combat between the parties (trial by combat). In other cases the feudal lord would order that there be a trial by ordeal such as drowning, under the assumption that the decision would be made by a "higher power."

Case Law

After the establishment of the royal courts in England, judges would travel out to rural districts to sit at trials and would return to meet at the Inns of Court in London. They would discuss their recent decisions, which led to a greater degree of consistency among them. Law students would sit with the judges and would write reports of the judges' decisions and these became the first instances of case law that are still used today. Once cases were reported in books, it became much easier to refer to those decisions and follow universal principles. This "case law" is also referred to as "precedent" or "the doctrine of stare decisis." The principle of case law is fairly simply stated: A court must stand by previous decisions.

This case law provides influence in our present day courts and helps judges to interpret statutes and arrive at decisions which are fair, equitable, and consistent with previous court decisions. Case law also provides defenses at criminal trials (e.g., self-defense) and procedures that govern the police handling of search and seizure processes.

The principle may sound fairly straightforward but the common law is still evolving to adapt to changes within our society and, in application, the doctrine can become extremely complex. The weight given to any previous decision of another court will depend on a number of factors including whether the court was within the same legal jurisdiction, the level of the court where the decision was made, or the similarity in the facts of the case.

Statutes

Statutes are the law in black and white. As education became more commonplace in feudal England, the government authorities began to pass statutes that would guide everyday life. Today statutes may be passed by any one of several levels of government from municipal right up to federal. Statutes are also continually being amended, new statutes are passed, and old ones are repealed. Our society is constantly changing, and so it is necessary that statutes change as well to meet new requirements or to fill a need in our society. Sometimes the need is economic (e.g., an amendment to income tax laws, to "plug a loophole") and sometimes the need arises as a result of changes in society (e.g., new computer crime legislation).

Regulations on the private security industry have been passed in most jurisdictions. The regulations may address areas of the industry including uniformed staff, private investigators, locksmiths, security guard dog handlers, or armored car services. The regulations may cover training requirements, age restrictions, education, licensing, or criminal background checks. The authority of the protection officer may come from these regulations and from other statutory authority such as extended rights of arrest when acting on behalf of a property owner.

The Effect of the European Civil Code on Our Legal System

Prior to feudal times, laws developed differently in continental Europe. The Roman empire's early dominance in this part of the world brought a higher degree of literacy, and written Roman Law was codified by the Emperor Justinian in A.D. 533. After the fall of the Roman empire, the legal system was entrenched in European society. This Roman codified law differed from the English Common Law because it had been reduced to written statutes whereas the English law comprised the verbal decisions and the particular customs of the landowners and nobles who adjudicated cases. The Justinian Code was similar to our present legal system and included differentiation between public law, which is related to the relationship between the individual and the state (e.g., constitutional law or criminal law) and private law, which is concerned with the relationship between individuals (e.g., commercial law, family law, and torts). The dominance of Roman Law declined in continental Europe but by the 11th century, with the development of international trade and more complex business arrangements, the Justinian Code returned as a standard. This system of laws is referred to as civil law.

When William the Conqueror occupied England in 1066, he was astute enough to realize that the English Common law system should not be replaced entirely by the civil code. He established royal courts which allowed the system of precedent to continue, but developed consistency in the application of laws and introduced written statutes based on the Roman law or civil code principles which could clarify the common law. Our legal system today is a marriage of those two traditions.

In 1804 the Napoleonic Code was created in France; it addressed issues of equality of the classes and was the predecessor of modern human rights legislation. The civil law system and the Napoleonic Code still have an effect today on many of the states that were originally settled by the Spanish and on the Canadian Province of Quebec. Today, the term "civil law" not only refers to the system of laws found in Europe and other noncommon law jurisdictions, but also to our system of private law that allows one citizen to recover damages from another.

TYPES OF LAWS—CRIMINAL AND CIVIL

Protection officers may be involved in the enforcement of laws or as a witness in both civil and criminal proceedings and should understand the fundamental difference between the two.

Criminal Law

Criminal laws appear to be established to protect people, but they are actually passed to ensure peace and good order in society. For example, it is an offense to assault someone but criminal law treats assault as an offense against society and it is the state which will initiate prosecution against the offender and will impose the punishment. If a fine is imposed it will be paid to the state or the offender may be imprisoned in a state institution. The prosecutor will act on behalf of the state, not on behalf of the victim (although in some cases, there are provisions for private prosecutions or compensation for victims of crime).

Types of criminal offenses vary from jurisdiction to jurisdiction but they are generally divided into those that are more serious (felonies in the United States and indictable offenses in Canada) and those that are less serious (misdemeanors in the United States and summary conviction offenses in Canada). Table 36-1 details examples of criminal offenses and Table 36-2 lists the different powers of police, security and prosecutors.

TABLE 36-1 Examples of Some Types of Criminal Offenses[*]

Crime	Description
Murder	Intentional and unlawful taking of the life of another and may include a death resulting from the commission of another crime (felony murder)
Manslaughter	Causing the death of another as a result of negligence or a reduced level of intent
Assault	Deliberately causing menace or bodily harm to another
Kidnapping	Unlawful confinement of another and may include false imprisonment
Sexual offenses	Sexual interference with another without their consent
Arson	Unlawful and deliberate destruction of property by fire
Burglary	Breaking into a premises with the intent to commit a criminal offense
Robbery	Unlawfully obtaining the property of another through threats or infliction of bodily harm
Theft	Unlawful taking of the property of another. There are also offenses for possession of property obtained by crime
Forgery	Creating a false document for the purposes of depriving another
Disorderly conduct	Causing a public disturbance
Willful damage	Unlawfully causing damage to the property of another
Computer crime	There are a number of computer crimes related to the unlawful altering or deletion of data or the unauthorized use or misuse of a computer
Bribery	Providing or receiving an unlawful benefit in return for doing or forbearing to do something in relation to employment or office

Police, security, and prosecutors have different powers under the criminal code. Table 36-2 details some of those powers.

[*]Note that some criminal offenses may be called by different names; e.g., burglary may be called breaking and entry.

Civil Law

Unlike criminal laws, the purpose of civil law is to protect private rights and not public rights. In civil cases, it is the individual who has been wronged who will undertake the civil action. The public prosecutor will not be involved and the individual must pay for his own attorney and hire an investigator if one is required. Any award that the court orders the defendant to pay will go to the victim (plaintiff) and not to the state, as it would in the case of a fine.

Any particular cause of action may be both civil and criminal. If someone is assaulted, the police may investigate the matter as a criminal assault and the person responsible may be charged with that criminal offense. At the same time, however, the person assaulted may decide to sue civilly for damages for the assault and battery. Both cases may proceed at the same time, although through a different court system (see Table 36-3). The person responsible may be fined or sentenced to jail in the criminal court but also ordered to pay damages in a civil court. Some areas of the civil law include:

Contracts—The law covering binding agreements between two or more parties. For example, a contract to provide security personnel to protect a property.

Warranties—A special type of promise or statement. For example, a guarantee that a fire extinguisher is effective on a certain type of fire.

Agency—An important concept in the security industry. Agency raises a question of whether one person is acting on behalf of another. For example, a protection officer uses excessive force in subduing a suspected shoplifter. Is the protection officer an agent of the retail establishment and is the establishment therefore responsible for damages (vicarious liability) that may have been inflicted in the course of the arrest?

The authority of the protection officer comes from the agency relationship with the property owner, occupier, or employer that they are assigned to assist. That authority may be addressed in the contracts issued or by internal policies set up by the customer or employer. There may also be a number of written procedures, manuals, or post orders that provide instructions on the completion of duties whether the protection officer is contracted or in-house. These written instructions give the officer authority as directed by the property owner or employer but can also make them vicariously liable for the actions of the protection officer.

Torts—A tort is a civil action that may be an intentional wrong (e.g., assault, battery, wrongful imprisonment, or defamation) or it may be

TABLE 36-2   Criminal Law Powers

	Private Security	Public Police	Prosecutor
Investigate	Investigate on behalf of private party	Investigate on behalf of public	May have investigative authority
Seize	Some seizure authority on behalf of private party	Criminal powers to seize or obtain search warrants	May have some power to obtain search warrants
Arrest	Citizen's power of arrest	Criminal law powers	May have some powers of arrest
Indict	Only when by private prosecution	May lay charges	May authorize or lay charges
Prosecute	Only when by private prosecution	Usually turned over to prosecutor	Yes

negligence (e.g., the failure to provide an appropriate level of security in an employee parking lot).

Many intentional torts are closely aligned to criminal offenses but Table 36-4 shows some others.

Civil liability has caused increasing concern for the business community, and damages in court actions have increased insurance premiums; hence, some types of liability insurance have become prohibitive to organizations. Executives and property owners have found it necessary to defend against these crippling costs by increasing security measures and through stringent screening and training. The protection officer has a strong role to play in protecting businesses against civil liabilities.

TABLE 36-3   Crime and Civil Law Comparisons

Crime	Civil Wrong
Theft	Conversion
Assault	Assault or battery
Trespass	Nuisance

TABLE 36-4   Examples of Some Types of Torts

Tort	Description
Intentional infliction of mental suffering	Often initiated in conjunction with torts of assault, battery, or false imprisonment. Causing fear, shame, embarrassment, or other emotional distress
Malicious prosecution	Knowingly initiating a legal proceeding that does not have cause
Defamation	Making or publishing a statement that is untrue and causes damage to another
Invasion of privacy	Unreasonable and offensive intrusion on the private affairs of another. Note that this may also be regulated by privacy statutes

Negligence may result in liability during the performance of or failure to provide security duties. Negligence is an actionable cause under common law so that someone who suffers damages as a result of the negligence of another may sue to recover their losses. Negligence may be due to failure to provide an appropriate level of security, failure to have a contingency or evacuation plans in place, or failure to warn someone who is at risk as a result of a security exposure. Negligence can also be established through statutes such as occupiers' liability or occupational health and safety legislation. Those statutes require that the occupiers of premises provide a safe work environment not only for employees, but also visitors to the property and sometimes even trespassers. It is the security officer's duty to assist the property owner in reducing risks on the property and to recommend appropriate methods of handling those risks. It is also the security officer's duty to ensure that emergency procedures are properly followed, that training takes place to ensure those procedures work, and that everyone is familiar with them.

Administrative Law and Other Standards

The security industry is also regulated by a number of other rules and these, together with quasi-governmental standards, may create liability if not properly followed. In the United States, these regulations include those passed by the Offices of Homeland Security and the Inspector General or any one of a number of federal, state, or local authorities. Both Canada and the United States have federal regulatory requirements such as defense, air and commercial transport, port security, and government operational security regulations. There are also a number of other standards that are not regulated, such as those from the International Organization of Standardization or Canada Standards Association, that have recommended standards for the security industry. Many trade associations such as ASIS International have published security standards, as have industry groups (e.g., the chemical industry's security code). Despite these standards not being regulated by law, organizations should be aware of them as they may be used in a civil or criminal action to suggest that the organization did not meet a generally accepted industry norm. Insurers may also publish standards (e.g., terrorism security requirements) that affect premium rates or the insurer may assess whether the organization is meeting some of the standards indicated above to assess premiums, risk, and liability.

Labor Laws

Labor laws are established to set parameters for employers and employees or their counsel, associations, and unions to develop and enforce employment contracts. Table 36-5 delineates differences among criminal, civil, and labor laws.

Interaction of Criminal, Civil, and Labor Laws

It is a common misconception that initiation of procedures in one sphere of the law will preclude or forestall action in another. For example, if one employee assaults another at the work site the police may be called in to initiate a criminal investigation, but this does not preclude the assaulted employee from initiating a civil action for recovery of damages or the employer from terminating the offending employee for the workplace infraction. In fact, there may be other parallel regulatory actions such as an occupational health inquiry or an arbitration hearing to assess the grounds for termination.

Young Offenders

Legislation exists requiring special treatment of juveniles (they may also be referred to in legislation as minors or young offenders) in the course of interviews, detention, or arrest and the protection officer should be familiar with legislation for their local jurisdiction. Legislation will vary in terms of the age prerequisite, may require the presence or notification of a parent or guardian, or may include liability for failure to properly protect the confidentiality of the young offender's personal information.

Search and Seizure

What are the rights of the protection officer to conduct searches and seize property at the work site? Many employers have policies that establish procedures for searches of vehicles, lockers, or personal effects in order to deter theft, misuse of company property, or the possession of illicit drugs or alcohol on site. When these policies are challenged by labor unions or through the courts, the company may be required to establish that the search was reasonable, that

TABLE 36-5 Criminal, Civil, and Labor Law

	Criminal Laws	Civil Laws	Labor Laws
Purpose	Protect the public good	Compensate for damages	Imposition and enforcement of employment contracts
Applies to	Whole community	Private parties	Employers and employees
Responsibility for handling	Public prosecutor	Attorneys for the parties	Management and union
Potential outcome	Fine or incarceration	Damages or court order	Court or arbitration award

there was some evidence to believe an employment offense had taken place, and that the search would result in the discovery of further evidence. The company may also be required to show that the policy is applied consistently within the workforce or facility and that it does not target specific individuals or groups. Courts and arbitrators will try to strike a balance between the rights of the employer or visitor and the right to privacy of the individual. They may also look at whether the company considered all other reasonable investigative means before embarking on search procedures. This is especially true in cases where searches are conducted on employees or their personal effects, as the company will be required to show that they established procedures to protect the privacy of its employees.

The Private Security Advisory Council* advises that the following are instances where there may be legitimate grounds for a search:

1. Where there is consent by the person being searched
2. Where there is implied consent as a condition of employment
3. Where it is incidental to a valid arrest (although some jurisdictions require probable grounds for the conduct of the personal search)
4. Where it is incidental to valid conditions (e.g., as a condition of boarding a commercial aircraft)

Many companies also have policies requiring people to submit their vehicles or personal effects to search on leaving the property. These are usually in conjunction with a notice at the entrance indicating that these items may be subject to search. Even though an employee or visitor may imply that they will allow their vehicle or personal effects to be searched by entering the property, they have the right to change their mind

while on the property and may refuse to comply with the search when leaving. The protection officer should not force the issue and should simply report the matter. Management then has the opportunity to treat it as a disciplinary infraction if it is an employee, or has the right to refuse further entry if it is a contractor or visitor.

During the course of a consented search, the protection officer has the right to seize items found, such as the following:

1. Property of the employer or property owner that the officer is required to protect and for which the subject has no obvious permission to possess
2. Evidence of the commission of a crime (i.e., company property, burglar tools, controlled substances, etc.)
3. Weapons that could be used to injure the officer, an innocent third party, or the subject
4. Items that could help the subject escape detention

If no consent exists, the protection officer has no right to conduct a search. Any items found as the result of an illegal search cannot be seized and may not be accepted in judicial proceedings. However, any of the previously listed items that are in plain view may be seized because the seizure is not the result of a search. All authorized searches and seizures must strictly comply with established procedures developed by the employer or property owner. Additionally, protection officers should be familiar with statutes for their jurisdiction concerning search and seizure by private persons. This will minimize the possibility of criminal or civil actions against the officer and the employer or property owner. Familiarity with the local laws will also help assure that the employer's or property owner's policies and procedures concerning search and seizure are in compliance with the statutes. Searches are

---

*Private Security Advisory Council, *Scope of Legal Authority of Private Security Personnel*, Law Enforcement Assistance Administration, U.S. Department of Justice, 3 (1979).

very personal and can cause great embarrassment, especially if the subject has committed no crime. Searches should be conducted discreetly to minimize public embarrassment for the subject and adverse public/employee reaction to the officer conducting the search.

Evidence

Evidence is the proof that is required to establish the guilt or innocence of the accused. Evidence may be one of the following:

1. Real—a physical object, a gun, a piece of stolen property
2. Documentary—a contract, a photograph
3. Testimony—the oral statement of a witness while under oath

Evidence must meet certain requirements in order to be admissible in court. For example, a protection officer seizes a stolen computer from an accused, but fails to secure the evidence before it is turned over to the police. Several months later, the officer is called to testify in court. He is presented with the computer and asked if it is the same one that was taken from the accused. He is forced to admit that he cannot be certain. The judge refuses to admit the evidence and the accused goes free. Chain of custody requires that real evidence remain basically unchanged since time of acquisition and this is best achieved with chronological tracking of custody and transfer of anything that may be required for court purposes.

Any real or documentary evidence must be protected from the time that it is obtained. If possible, an identifying mark (e.g., initials and the date) should be put on it so that the officer can later identify it in court. Extensive notes should also be taken during the inquiry, or immediately after, while it is still fresh in the mind of the investigator. The judge will place a great deal more weight on testimony where a witness's memory can be refreshed from notes made at the time of the inquiry. The time that passes from the event to the trial can be several months or even years and the importance of notes cannot be overemphasized. The protection officer should also ensure that reports are accurate and detailed. The report itself may be entered into evidence and the officer may be required to explain discrepancies. Likewise, statements taken from witnesses should be accurate and detailed. The officer should properly prepare for any trial or discovery hearing and questions should be answered as clearly and directly as possible. Many witnesses lose credibility because they are afraid to answer a question by saying "I don't know" or by trying to answer a question that has not been properly clarified.

Any one of the forms of evidence indicated above may be direct or circumstantial. Direct evidence proves the facts in issue directly. Circumstantial evidence proves the facts in issue indirectly. A smoking gun does not prove that the person holding it pulled the trigger, but the inference may be drawn and it is therefore circumstantial evidence that may be admissible in court. It is a common misconception that a person cannot be convicted on circumstantial evidence alone. If the evidence is admissible and the case is strong enough, then it does not matter whether it is circumstantial or direct.

The common law developed a rule making hearsay evidence (assertions of someone other than the witness who is testifying) inadmissible in court, but exceptions to the hearsay rule are as important as the rule itself. The rule was developed so that the court would hear from the person who uttered the words rather than having those words repeated by someone else. One important exception to the hearsay rule is testimony from expert witnesses. Normally a witness is only allowed to testify about matters that they saw or heard but, where a court accepts a witness as an expert on a certain matter, that witness can testify based on their education and professional experience. Another exception is business and banking documents that, depending on evidentiary statutes for the jurisdiction, may be accepted as proof of their content.

Another important exception to the hearsay rule is the admissibility of confessions in court. A protection officer would not normally be allowed to repeat (in court) a statement made by a suspect, but if the statement is accepted as a confession, it may be admitted as long as it was voluntary. A confession cannot be admitted in court as evidence if there were threats, intimidation, or promises that induced the accused to make the statement. A threat does not necessarily have to be a threat of violence. A threat to terminate someone's employment if they don't tell the employer what happened may be enough to question whether the accused confessed because he really did it or whether he confessed because he wanted to keep his job. Similarly, a simple promise that "things will go better for you if you tell us what happened" may be sufficient to question the reliability and admissibility of a confession.

Usually the police will be involved in interviewing an accused to receive a confession, but there may be occasions where a statement made to a protection officer will amount to a confession and may later be used as evidence in court. A confession is simply a written or oral statement made by an accused. Even a denial by the accused may amount to a confession if the prosecutor is able to prove that the accused lied in making the denial (e.g., an attempt to set up an alibi). The protection officer should keep detailed notes of anything that an accused says because it may later contradict a statement made to the police. For example, an accused may tell the protection officer that he wasn't in the area when the offense was committed and he may later tell the police that he was in the area but he didn't do it. The two statements constitute a lie and may be admissible in court as proof of guilt.

Interviewing witnesses and suspects requires techniques that not everyone can master to the same degree. Generally, the protection officer will interview witnesses, victims, and/or suspects during a preliminary investigation. More thorough interviews may be done later by investigators or law enforcement personnel during the follow-up investigation. A bad interview during the preliminary investigation can cause information obtained during later interviews to be unusable. The protection officer should know what he or she legally can and cannot do during interviews.

Under the *Miranda* rule in the United States and Charter of Rights requirements in Canada, the police are required to advise an accused of their right to counsel, that they are not required to make a statement, and that the statement may be used at trial. There is no duty to "Mirandize" or Charter Caution the private individual who gives a confession. There have been some attempts to argue that private security may be in a "position of authority" in conducting investigations and interviews and therefore the U.S. Fifth Amendment or Canadian Charter rights apply. These challenges have been largely unsuccessful, although in Canada it has been held that an employer in a governmental function (e.g., federal, provincial, or municipal government bodies) must follow Charter provisions in conducting investigations. Generally, the protection officer need only ensure that the confession was willingly given. A confession need not be a lengthy written statement; it may be a simple oral statement such as "I shouldn't have taken it." The officer should accurately note any statements by the accused so that there will be no confusion later in court as to exactly what was said.

If the officer has occasion to interview a suspect, the following steps will help ensure the admissibility of a confession:

1. The suspect must be offered a chance to contact counsel and should be given the opportunity to carry on a private conversation with counsel.
2. The object of the interview is to learn the truth, not to induce a pattern of deceit or obtain answers that the questioner wants to hear.
3. There should be no actual or implied threats or promises.
4. The accused should be given the opportunity to give a full explanation.

5. The accused should be questioned in a language and phraseology that they understand—"legalese" or technical terms not known to the accused should be avoided.
6. The interviewer should not ask ambiguous questions.
7. The interviewer should not be aggressive or abusive to the person being interviewed.
8. Where possible, a signed statement should be obtained and a second witness should be present.

The Burden of Proof

The burden of proof is different in a civil action than it is in a criminal matter. In a civil action the plaintiff need only prove their case on a balance of probabilities, while in a criminal trial the prosecutor is required to prove guilt beyond a reasonable doubt. This is why a plaintiff may be successful in a civil matter while the same defendant may be found not guilty in criminal court for the same set of circumstances. As an example, O.J. Simpson was found not guilty in criminal court, but the families of his victims were successful in a civil action for wrongful death. Some jurisdictions apply a burden of proof somewhere between the two in labor arbitration cases involving moral turpitude (e.g., workplace theft). They may use terms such as "clear and convincing evidence" or "a preponderance of evidence."

In a criminal trial in common law jurisdictions, the burden is always on the prosecutor to prove that the accused is guilty beyond a reasonable doubt. The onus is not on the accused to show that he is innocent. This has been referred to as the "golden thread" that runs through our judicial system. Because of this rule, the security officer must take steps to protect the admissibility of any evidence that is collected.

Trespass

Both the common law and statutes recognize the property owner's right to control access to, use of, activity on, and protection of their property. The employer or property owner designates the protection officer as their agent to protect the property and enforce their guidelines concerning it. Many protection officers are responsible for property with public access for business or recreation purposes and, as a result, it may seem difficult to determine when a trespass occurs. Generally, one or more of the following must be present for a trespass to occur:

1. The subject does not own or have other legal rights to access the property.
2. The subject must know this.
3. The subject does not have the permission of the property owner or agent (i.e., the protection officer, tenant, etc.) to enter upon or remain on the property.
4. The property is posted in accordance with local ordinances with signs prohibiting trespass or fences and/or other barriers present that would cause a reasonable person to believe they are not to enter the property.
5. The property owner or agent has lawfully requested the subject to leave the property.
6. The subject enters the property, or refuses to leave, after seeing posted notices or physical barriers, or after receiving a lawful request to leave.

The protection officer should be familiar with the statutes and local regulations concerning trespass to assure that he or she is acting within the law when dealing with a possible trespass. Generally, the protection officer will not have to arrest a trespasser unless the subject is suspected of or known to have committed, other crimes on the property or unless the suspect had been previously evicted from the property and has returned when instructed not to do so. In most cases, the subject will leave when advised that they are trespassing. In others, the subject may not leave unless the protection officer tells them the local police will be contacted to arrest the individual for trespass. However, if the protection officer must make an arrest, he or she must know the statutes and regulations for that jurisdiction concerning arrests by private citizens, property owners, or agents.

CONCLUSION

A review of the development and current status of our legal system reveals two important trends. The first is the ever-increasing number of laws, regulations, and standards being imposed on industry. These include legal requirements directly related to protective services or requiring adaptations to the way we undertake business because of legislation such as human rights, privacy requirements, or occupational health and safety regulations. This increased complexity has necessitated protection officers to undergo constant training, updating, and research to stay abreast of the legal requirements to undertake protection work.

The second trend is the shrinking world and increased globalization of business. One of the consequences of this trend is the accessibility of terrorists to businesses in North America and abroad and the resulting increase in the number of regulatory requirements to properly protect organizations and people. The second consequence is the requirement that organizations and the security industry be cognizant of the requirements of foreign governments in order to do business abroad and to engage in international trade. These sometimes result in a conflict of laws or cultures that ultimately produce more regulations, such as foreign corrupt practices laws.

SECURITY QUIZ

1. A protection officer may force a search of an employee where there is a company policy.
   a. True
   b. False
2. A store can be liable for the actions of its protection officer if it can be proven that the officer was:
   a. Their contractor
   b. Their agent
   c. Licensed
   d. Acting in the best interests of the store
   e. Did not use excessive force
3. A person can be convicted on circumstantial evidence alone.
   a. True
   b. False
4. If a law is not written down and passed by government it is not law.
   a. True
   b. False
5. The purpose of our legal system is to:
   a. Set down our obligations to each other
   b. Set penalties for breaching those obligations
   c. Establish procedures to enforce those obligations
   d. All of the above
6. The common law is not used in North America today.
   a. True
   b. False
7. You cannot sue someone and press criminal charges. It is double jeopardy.
   a. True
   b. False
8. At criminal trials, the prosecutor must prove the accused guilty:
   a. On a balance of probabilities
   b. Beyond a reasonable doubt
   c. By a preponderance of evidence
   d. Without a shadow of doubt
9. The police will investigate:
   a. Civil matters
   b. Criminal matters
   c. Whatever the prosecutor asks them to investigate
   d. All of the above
10. A confession may not be admissible in court unless it can be shown that (check all that apply)
    a. There was no threats
    b. It was made to the police
    c. There was no promises
    d. There was a witness present
    e. A signed statement was provided

OFFICER SAFETY AND USE OF FORCE

37

Use of Force

Charles T. Thibodeau and
Christopher A. Hertig

CHAPTER OBJECTIVES

- List general concepts for use of force
- Explain when force is justified
- Indicate when to retreat
- Define excessive force liability
- Reinforce importance of officer safety while using force
- Reinforce importance of maintaining self-control
- Describe use of force alternatives
- Explain the escalation/deescalation continuum
- Define verbal deescalation
- Lethal and less-than-lethal weapons management

USE OF FORCE

The legally and socially acceptable use of force by protection officers is a key issue in our contemporary—and future—society. As security personnel, we enforce rules and ensure compliance with them. We are the *"preservers of the corporate culture,"* management's representative, charged with keeping an orderly, safe, and productive environment in accordance with the organizational philosophy of our employer. We are the ambassadors of the organization and serve a substantial public relations role. We enforce rules, extend ourselves to help others, and assist in making the organization run more smoothly. We touch all parts of the organization and help it to function.

Unfortunately, though, there are times when protection officers must use force. We have a right to protect ourselves from physical assault and we have a duty to protect others from harm as well.

Obviously, the use of force is something that is unpalatable, yet at times very necessary. As much as possible, we need to decrease the frequency and degree of force used, without creating a personal safety hazard. As a general rule, the more proficient the officer is at their duties, the less that force is needed. Professional protection officers understand how to manage the behavior of others with firmness and diplomacy. They know that the ideal security person is "the iron fist in the velvet glove."

If we find ourselves resorting more and more to the use of force, it is indicative of a systemic failure. It could be that we are not following instructions, we are a little shortsighted in our planning, or we have failed to be alert enough to observe imminent danger. When this happens in private security settings, the potential exists for extensive damage, injury to people, and loss of expensive assets. The potential also exists for increased legal liability and expensive court litigation. Simply put: "If you have to force it, you're doing something wrong."—*H. H. Thibodeau*

"Security," at least ideally, implies a stable, relatively predictable environment in which an individual, group, or community may pursue its ends without disruption or harm and without fear of disturbance or injury. This definition necessarily includes personnel safety, fire safety, and emergency medical response, as well as safe and secure streets, homes, commercial businesses, parking areas, and work sites.

To accomplish our society's need to maintain order, we have formed governments based on laws, which express the desires of its citizens. In addition, we rely on physical security, which consists of those countermeasures required to promote a state of well-being, to protect life and property, and to avoid or minimize the risks of natural or man-made disasters and crimes. Unfortunately, from time to time, we have no other alternative than to use force to accomplish a legal goal. This may occur when we have no ability to retreat. Or we have tried verbal persuasion, set limits, used loud-verbal commands, and all attempts have failed. We can only accomplish the required goal by using force.

The information in this unit of study will deal with this important aspect of the security officer's responsibilities. It is presented as a general educational guideline; specific procedures must be developed and adopted by the officer's employer. This chapter is a starting point on a lengthy journey. Each officer is strongly recommended to obtain additional education and training in this important area of a protection officer's professional development.

USE OF FORCE IN GENERAL

A definition that attempts to describe the reasonable use of force as "an amount of force equal to or just slightly greater than the force used by the aggressor" is sometimes misleading. Use of force is much better defined with respect to the concepts of *belief, reasonableness*, and *necessity*. For instance, an officer may choose to use pepper spray to disarm a person with a knife. In that case, the officer actually uses *less* force than the aggressor does. At the same time, the choice of a less-than-lethal defensive weapon supports the assertion that the officer's use of force was reasonable.

Use of force is any tactic used to control, disarm, capture, restrain, or otherwise physically manage an aggressive or uncooperative subject. Force is *any touching* of a person. Force is predicated on the security officer's reasonable belief that the choice of weapon(s) and the amount of force used were necessary, reasonable, and the only alternative.

Each use of force must accomplish a legitimate and lawful purpose. At the same time, each use of force must appear, to a prudent and judicious person under identical circumstances, to be reasonable and necessary. Reduced to its lowest common denominator in a court of law, the appropriateness of each use of force will be measured by an "objective reasonableness and necessity standard" versus whether the use of force was a "deliberate and wanton infliction of pain."

In use of force litigation, the following motives will most likely not help acquit the security officer: fear, retaliation, punishment, accident, or loss of control. If the officer claims that the subject was inadvertently injured while in custody, that admission may be viewed in court as an indication of negligence. All force used by security personnel must be based on the officer's *belief* that the assaulter was showing a manifest intent to cause the officer or a third party severe bodily harm or death, or that the subject of an arrest would escape if force was not used. Even under these conditions, that use of force must be a *reasonable* and *necessary* solution, and the execution of force was *calculated, measured, deliberate,* and at all times *controlled.* Failure in any one of these tests could lead to discipline by the employer, a civil suit, and possible criminal prosecution. The protection officer can lose their job, get tied up in an expensive lawsuit, or potentially go to prison.

The above rules apply to any use of force. This can include restraining an overzealous fan at a concert, holding down a mental patient in a hospital, or apprehending a shoplifter. Use of force may also occur during the removal of a person who is trespassing or causing other kinds of disturbances (i.e., in bars, taverns, and clubs).

The reasonableness of any force used by a security officer is largely dependent upon the totality of the circumstances of the incident. In simple terms this means that every aspect of the situation must be examined. Where the subject presents no threat to the officer, no attempt to escape an arrest, and no resistance to ejection from a building, no use of force is permitted. For example, several cases have held that the use of force during interrogation of a suspect is not justified in the absence of evidence that the suspect attacked the officer. *Note:* Interrogation (or focused interviewing) should never involve touching the suspect or witness being interviewed. A simple rule is: "When touching starts—interviewing ends!"

JUSTIFYING THE USE OF FORCE

The primary defense in a charge of excessive use of force will have to do with the question of *assault.* That is, did the subject trigger a use of force due to their assault of the officer or the assault of others? It is therefore helpful to know that the claim of assault consists of five parts: *ability, manifest intent, imminent jeopardy, ability*

to retreat, and *preclusion.* These questions should be asked after the officer's use of force:

1. Did the aggressor have the *ability* to cause harm or injury? Were they able to hurt the officer or others?
2. Did the aggressor exhibit a *manifest intent* to cause harm or injury? Did the aggressor display intent to injure?
3. Was the officer or others in *imminent* (immediate) *jeopardy* of harm or injury?
4. Did the officer or others have the ability to *retreat* and avoid harm or injury?
5. Was the officer in *preclusion*? In other words, were they precluded or prevented from taking actions other than using force? Was there no other alternative than the use of force?

If the officer cannot answer all of these questions in the affirmative, that officer may have serious trouble justifying his or her use of force.

There are five primary justifications for using force. These justifications consist of the officer's reasonable belief:

1. That harm would come to the officer or to someone else if force was not used
2. That the actions taken were necessary
3. That the actions taken were reasonable
4. That the actions taken conformed to employer policy and training
5. That the officer was precluded from escaping or taking other defensive/control actions and as a result had to use force

It is always better, of course, if force is used under the definition of an assault described above. Using force to defend property may be legally permissible, but it is generally frowned upon by the courts. Courts prefer that property owners utilize legal options, such as civil recovery "replevin" actions and injunctions to retrieve property. When using force to protect property it is wise to remember the following: *Property can be replaced; people cannot.*

If a security officer is arrested or sued for use of force, there are several additional factors that will have an impact on the outcome of that case. Courts will consider the following issues:

1. Did the officer act under a reasonable belief?
2. Did the officer have a duty to retreat?
3. Did the officer give the aggressor a request or command to desist?
4. Did the officer follow department policy and procedure?
5. Did the officer follow department training?
6. Did the force used produce the desired results?
7. Did the officer place any third party in jeopardy?
8. Will the truth be relevant?
9. Will the witnesses tell the truth?
10. What or who will the jury believe?
11. What or who will the judge believe?
12. What or who will the public believe?

RETREAT

The basic rule is: *"If you can retreat without injury to yourself or others, you must retreat."* The word "retreat" does not mean to run away and go hide somewhere. It means to move to a safe place, remaining in view of the conflict zone, but at a safe distance. It includes being behind cover (objects or materials that protect the officer) and calling for backup.

If, while under attack, the officer sees an opportunity to retreat, that officer must terminate the use of force and retreat, but only if he/she is not placing him/herself, or others, in jeopardy. In deadly force confrontations, the officer has no alternative but to retreat if that option is available.

FORCE ALTERNATIVES DEFINED

Alternatives to the use of force amount to any method or tactic that can be used to deescalate incidents without the use of defensive weapons, threats, or aggressive action. This definition necessarily connotes the use of verbal deescalation, removing persons from the "conflict zone," negotiating conflict resolution, maintaining a noncombative atmosphere, and calling in public law enforcement. These are some of the many alternatives that should be attempted before using force.

1. Take time—slow down the action. Haste gets people hurt! Haste makes casualties.
2. Awareness—recognize potential threats. Being alert is a key issue.
3. Evaluate—get all the facts and pieces of evidence that are available. Understand the problem before acting to solve it.
4. Never respond in anger! Take a step back. Take a few deep breaths. Take your time.
5. Be an actor—preclude (prevent) the problem from escalating and erupting—not a reactor.
6. Maintain a safe distance.
7. Smile. Be as pleasant as appropriate under the circumstances.
8. Be polite—show respect to everyone, including the aggressor.
9. Really care about people! Caring is projected in an officer's demeanor.
10. Apply active listening techniques to show interest in what another is saying.
11. Call for backup before acting, using force including the police when necessary.
12. Recruit assistance from nearby persons if necessary.
13. Ask the perpetrator's friends and relatives to speak to the perpetrator.
14. Be slow to speak, slow to anger, quick to listen.
15. If all else fails, expect to be hit or grabbed.
16. Expect any hit to hurt, but brush it off. *It is not the end of the world.*
17. Engage in tactical retreat; when things get hot, back off and get behind cover.
18. Use loud assertive commands: "STOP!" and "NO!" Hit him with your voice.
19. Use repeated commands: "DROP THE KNIFE!" "DROP IT." "DROP IT." "DROP IT!"

"DO IT NOW!" "DO IT NOW!" "DO IT NOW!" Hard verbals are effective in certain circumstances.

20. Continue verbal deescalation. Be patient for as long as it takes. Remember: *Managing human behavior is lot like fishing. It takes time.*

EXCESSIVE FORCE LIABILITY

An examination of use of force cases, that resulted in injury and/or liability, shows that these cases commonly involve the following:

1. Use (or threat) of any force where the subject offers no resistance.
2. Negligent use of normally nonlethal force, resulting in death or serious injury.
3. Excessive force as an overreaction to subject's resistance to officer commands (force continued past the point of no resistance).
4. Intentional infliction of pain (excessive force) considered summary punishment.
5. Use of deadly force in a situation in which it is not permitted.
6. Failure to provide medical treatment for injuries from an officer's use of force.
7. An officer deliberately strikes or inflicts pain upon a subject after the subject is placed in restraint—using force to punish. Obviously any force used after a person has been restrained will be looked at very critically.
8. An officer entices or provokes a subject into reacting aggressively, so as to create cause for using force. Poor interpersonal skills create crises!
9. Death of a subject under the officer's control due to positional asphyxia (also known as "restraint asphyxia"). Use of proper restraint techniques, which do not impede breathing, is critical! All persons restrained must be continuously monitored for health problems and escape attempts.
10. Officer mistakenly reacts to a subject with a severe medical problem, such as confusing

diabetic shock with alcoholic disorientation (both can include staggering and slurred speech). First aid training and constant monitoring of the subject are necessary for his or her safety.

INJURIES TO OFFICERS ARE AVOIDABLE

If we were to analyze the last 100 injuries to security officers, we would probably find that the officer was not the victim, he or she was a participant. Most injuries occur due to the officer's own failure to follow their training and common sense. The following are some examples of how security officers become participants in their own injuries:

1. The officer is injured by taking a bad position, such as standing directly in front of the subject, too close to the subject, or not using cover.
2. The officer is injured by having the wrong attitude. Carelessness, overconfidence, demeaning tone of voice, cockiness, and so on all cause problems with others.
3. The officer is injured by relaxing too soon. "It's not over till it's over." Do not turn your back on a subject too soon.
4. The officer is injured by failing to search a suspect—always do a visual search at a minimum!
5. The officer is injured by failing to watch the suspect's hands—look at the palms of each hand. The palms will be where a weapon is held.

ARREST AND DETENTION SEARCH AND SEIZURE

An arrest is completed whenever the security officer detains a subject and refuses to let that person leave, over the subject's objections. The hold may technically be a "detention" according to state or provincial law. The civil tort that will be filed, however, is for false arrest. All stops where the subject is not allowed to leave are by definition an arrest in a civil suit.

In addition, there is no room in the law on arrest for cuffing someone for officer safety like the police do, with the intent of uncuffing them and letting them go after the danger has passed. Putting the cuffs on, no matter the reason, implies the subject is under arrest. Taking the cuffs off later and "unarresting" the person will require a lot of explaining! In most cases a citizen, who is not a sworn peace or police officer, has no qualified immunity (protection from suit under certain circumstances, such as having "reasonable suspicion" or "probable cause") and is subject to suit.

If you do not intend to follow through with calling the police and having the subject taken to jail, never put cuffs on him or her in the first place. The only reason to cuff a subject is to prevent them from escaping during your citizen's arrest, and for the protection of the officer and others while waiting for the police to come. Remember, *only* the police can remove those handcuffs! If the security officer removes the handcuffs for any reason, other than a medical emergency, they are becoming a "liability initiator."

During the arrest process, searches are allowed, but only weapons searches. These are searches of the outer clothing for hard items which could reasonably be expected to be a weapon. Generally speaking, security officers should not be searching purses, backpacks, pockets, fanny packs, or any other part of the person or property of the person during a citizen's arrest. It is probably best to secure these out of the reach of the arrestee and have the police search them when they arrive.

A FORMULA FOR SELF-CONTROL

Use of force is all about control. Sometimes pro-active preventive security plans break down, and force is required to maintain control. The question is: "Who is the person we most earnestly want to control?" Is it the drunk, the jealous spouse, the angry employee? No, it is **us**! In order to maintain control of others, we first must find a way to control ourselves when under pressure. Remembering the formula set out below might help keep everything in perspective when faced with high-stress, potentially aggressive situations.

The Control Formula

$C = I/E$

1. **CONTROL = INTELLECT over EMOTIONS**
2. **Add a Problem: I/E + P = E/I**
3. **Add Training: E/I + T = I/E**
4. **I/E = CONTROL**

Key:

C = Control/I = Intellect
E = Emotion/P = Problem
T = Training

The above formula means that control is equal to "I" (intellect) over "E" (emotions). Thus, we are in control when our intellect rules our emotions. When we introduce "P" (problem) to the equation, it may have the effect of turning the equation upside down. Thus, $I/E + P = E/I$. Emotions then are in control of our intellect! When running on raw emotions, we can get hurt or we lose control and hurt someone else. Without realizing it, we might use excessive force, which might lead to getting sued.

However, adding "T" (training) to the equation tends to reverse the negative effects of "P." At this point the equation is $E/I + T = I/E$. In addition, as is pointed out above, $I/E = Control$.

What all of this means is that by developing a trained response to perceived use of force situations, emotions can be held in check. With the intellect in charge, officers can more effectively maintain control. That is why verbal deescalation, if practiced regularly, has proven to be an excellent nonlethal defensive weapon to use in aggressive situations. Verbal deescalation can eliminate the use of physical force in the vast majority of situations and can also help the officer to get along better with those in the work environment. Resolving conflict amiably is the essence of a protection officer's job and those who excel at it have long and rewarding careers, absent of all sorts of trouble, including lawsuits. *Conflict resolution is the cornerstone of officer survival.*

CONFLICT RESOLUTION FORMATS

Most contract and proprietary security departments adhere to a form of security called "hands-off" security. That means that we must do the job outlined for us without touching anyone. Generally speaking, after an unsuccessful attempt at resolving a conflict by use of verbal deescalation, we just call the police and let them handle it.

In other security groups the use of hands-on security tactics is not only allowed but expected. For instance, an officer assigned to secure a bar, tavern, or nightclub where drinking of alcoholic beverages is taking place can expect that from time to time the use of force will be necessary. Working in any hostile environment such as hospital emergency rooms, some concerts, and sporting events will require a hands-on approach. So, too, will some retail stores where arrest of shoplifters is a common experience. Gang-infested apartment projects will also call for a hands-on security contingent.

Thus, keep in mind that these two types of security, hands-off and hands-on, exist for a reason and the officer must follow the standard operating procedures of the one they are assigned to.

RESPONSE TO AGGRESSIVE BEHAVIOR

The Escalation/De-escalation Continuum

To help guide the security officer's use of force we turn to a process called the escalation/deescalation continuum. There are many forms

of this continuum in use today. These exist in corporate and contract security as well as in the ranks of public law enforcement. The following outline is only a basic model. It represents a continuum that the security officer might want to follow.

Realize when reading the following steps that individual circumstances will necessitate modifying them. The steps used in the application of force change when the aggressor skips some of the lower level steps. Keep in mind that each step does not have to be taken in every situation. The escalation/deescalation continuum outlined can best be thought of as a general guide that changes with the circumstances of each situation. In the final analysis, security officers must always follow the use of force policy established by their employers!

The Escalation/Deescalation Continuum Content

The word "continuum" as used here means to follow a set path or series of steps in a particular order. These steps can be flexible, as mentioned above, but Steps 1 and 2 must be present in every use of force, no matter what. In addition, notice there is no step for sneaking up on a subject and taking advantage of the element of surprise. The tactic of surprise may work well for sworn law enforcement officers but it will probably create lawsuits for security personnel.

Step 1. Officer presence or "uniform presence" is the first step in the continuum. The mere presence of an authority figure establishes a degree of psychological deterrence. In some cases that is all it takes to terminate a potential conflict. The hostile atmosphere may break down and the participating parties may walk away if they realize the potential for the police being called and going to jail if they continue.

Step 2. The second step in the escalation/deescalation continuum is verbal deescalation. Offering help and asking questions of the subject, as the initial communication approach, will give the officer an edge. By asking questions, the officer is increasing his/her psychological control over the situation. The first sign of this working is when the action slows down and the participants direct their communication to the officer. Persuasion and limit setting can be part of this step. Informing the aggressors that the officer will call the police if the aggression does not stop can be a great tool only if the officer is actually willing to follow through and call the police. Bear in mind that any limits set must be realistic. The officer must be ready, willing, and able to enforce them.

Many times, commands are necessary. "Heavy control talk" or "hard verbals" used to direct the subject, such as "Stop," "Back off," "Drop it," "Do it now," and so on, provide a psychological control factor. Note that there should be short, simple, emphatic, loud verbal commands given to a subject who is physically resisting or aggressive. Doing so ensures that the use of force follows a logical, and justifiable, continuum. It also dramatically increases the effectiveness of any physical force exerted. Additionally, witnesses to the event will hear the command and will be better able to place the use of force in its proper perspective.

Once the verbal deescalation effort starts, it must continue throughout all continuing escalation of physical efforts, all the way up to deadly force. Protection officers should not stop verbalizing until the aggressive behavior and participants are gone.

Step 3. Hands-off security: In hands-off security departments (which most security departments are), the department does not allow the officer to touch anyone unless they are attacked by the subject. In these departments, this third stage necessitates a 911 call to the local police. Since soft, empty-hand physical escort is not allowed, calling the police if verbal deescalation fails is the logical step. By contrast, if a nonphysical hands-off escort is working, keep it going until the subject leaves the area.

Hands-on security: Soft, empty-hand control, such as grasping the subject's elbow and wrist, and leading them away (or any other escort hold) may be required to remove the subject from the conflict zone and out of the public eye. This maneuver is done for two purposes. First it will add incentive for the subject to cooperate and leave the area. Second, it will give the security officer an immediate response, and indicate if the aggression is truly over or if the subject needs more coaxing. That is, at the first point of touching the subject, the subject may react aggressively and engage in a fight. If the subject complies and does not complain about the physical contact, then it is a pretty good indication the aggression is over. It must always be borne in mind, however, that *"it is not over until it is over."* Be on alert the entire time for a reversal in the subject's behavior.

WARNING: With the first touch of the subject in a soft empty-handed escort, it is reasonable to expect to be hit and anticipate it to hurt. Officers should not allow themselves to be surprised by a "sucker punch." Additionally, emotional responses are counterproductive. No revenge response is allowed. Force must always be used to prevent harm or injury, not to "get even" with an aggressor. Whenever touching any subject, expect an immediate response and an escalation of aggression. Being punched, kicked, stabbed, hit with an object, or shot are possibilities. It is best to evaluate the situation carefully before attempting to intervene at this stage in the continuum. The officer MUST BE 95% CERTAIN that the aggression is over and the control tactics being used are working.

A rule-of-thumb practice in the protective services industry is that the officer should never approach the aggressor alone. Having one more officer than the number of persons being approached is a good rule of thumb. Generally speaking, the more bodies the officer brings to an intervention, the less likely hostility will be directed at the officer.

Step 4. In some cases, officers will be forced to use a less-than-lethal incapacitation device, such as an oleoresin capsicum aerosol (pepper spray), on the subject to protect themselves or others, or to obtain compliance with restraint techniques. Weapon retention and spray-back are key concerns, however, bringing a weapon to a confrontation that can be used creates problems for protection officers. It complicates the situation in that officers must protect themselves and others. Regular practice of weapon retention techniques is a wise course of action.

After spraying the individual, it will be necessary to arrest the aggressor for a specific crime, handcuff the aggressor, and call the police. The crime the aggressor was arrested for should have a lot to do with "self-defense" or "defense of others." There should be a very clear observation of this aggressor making a threat of assault. Be aware, it is required that the officer administer first aid to the subject immediately after they have been restrained.

The aggressor must display the ability to perform the threatened assault by showing a manifest intent to carry through on it. There must be a clear and obvious presence of imminent jeopardy. Retreat must not be an option and there must be a clear and obvious preclusion of the officer or others. If all these conditions are present, then the officer should use the weapon level needed to accomplish a legal purpose. The officer must always restrict the amount of force necessary to reach the goal of "just enough force, no more."

Step 5. The next level of defensive escalation is hard, empty-hand control, such as joint manipulation, restraint, and/or pain

compliance. As set out in number 4, it will be necessary to arrest the aggressor for some specific crime, handcuff the aggressor, and call the police. Keep the subject restrained until the police arrive. Monitor and assess the subject for medical problems, escape attempts, or violent behavior. The crime the aggressor was arrested for should have a lot to do with self-defense or defense of others. There should be a very clear observation of the aggressor being assaultive.

WARNING: The above should not be attempted without documented, professional training. Get lots of help; never approach alone.

Step 6. The next level of escalation is the empty-hand impact. Delivery of stunning techniques to motor points and other soft tissue targets.

As with Step 5, cautions from Step 4 are applicable: arresting the aggressor for a specific crime related to officer self-defense or defense of others; handcuffing the aggressor; calling police; observing the aggressor make a threatening assault.

This step can be bad choice based on a mismatch with the aggressor and the officer's ability to effectively use unarmed defense. Also, the more punches and kicks that are used by the officer, the more difficult it will be for the witnesses to decide who the aggressor is in the incident. It may be much better to move on to Step 7 at this point.

WARNING: The above should not be attempted without well-documented, professional training. In addition to training, there must be continuous practice in order to do this effectively. The best advice is to for the officer to get lots of help, never approach alone, continue verbal deescalation, and keep retreat as an option.

Step 7. The next level of escalation is the use of intermediate weapons such as batons and other impact weapons, stun guns, and tasers.

WARNING: Weapons should not be carried or used without documented, professional training.

Step 8. The next level of escalation is the use of deadly force such as firearms, impact weapon strikes to the head or neck, or empty-hand blows to the head, neck, throat, and so forth. This level of force must be the absolute last resort. There is only one acceptable justification for the use of deadly force, and that is the protection of human life. Use of deadly force to protect property will open the officer and their employer up to both civil and potential criminal prosecution.

WARNING: Taking a human life or causing serious injury carries a heavy cost. It is an act the officer will remember for the rest of his/her life and will most likely result in a civil suit. These drag on for years and cost massive amounts of money. Additionally, there may be criminal charges filed. Obviously, avoiding this is advisable. Retreat if at all possible, always verbalize, and know where cover is and get behind it.

Escalation/Deescalation Continuum Applications

To better understand the applications of the Escalation/Deescalation Continuum, the following scenarios have been prepared:

1. **Uniform presence.** The officer arrives on the scene, observes the situation, and makes his or her presence known to all those involved. This is known as "uniform presence" and it is a very powerful tactic, correcting 25% to 50% of aggressive situations.

The officer radios for help if needed, identifies escape routes, identifies items to use to block aggression if needed, identifies weapons of opportunity that could be used against the officer, and evaluates each person in the immediate vicinity of the aggressor. The communication stage will commence as soon as the officer has reported the incident and taken a safe position.

2. **Verbal de-escalation.** After getting the attention of the subjects involved in the aggression, the officer commences a communication with them. This verbal communication can be anything from a friendly greeting to a loud verbal command. The officer should never be alone; one to three others should be with the officer for safety when possible. *Always bring one more backup person than the number of people that must be confronted.* This may not be possible in all cases but it does offer a safer approach to a dangerous situation.

If the officer is within the grasp of the aggressor, the officer should use force to break away, give space, put something between the officer and the aggressor, and then continue the dialogue at a safer distance.

The officer must ensure that the aggressor is not forcing him or her into a state of preclusion, where maximum force will be necessary to escape. At the same time, the officer must ensure that the aggressor has a back door or escape route, and is not being backed into a corner. If the aggressor escapes from the area, the security officer should not give chase but should secure the area and the individuals in that area. *Note:* Chasing suspects may be appropriate but it is filled with risks, including injuries to the officer, the suspect, and most importantly, innocent bystanders. Employer policy must be followed regarding pursuit.

3. **Soft empty-hand tactics.** After the initial introduction of uniform presence, the aggression may suddenly stall out for a short while. During verbal de-escalation communications the officer should offer to help the subjects, ask questions, and give advice. If the truce holds longer, the officer and support personnel attempts to remove the aggressors one at a time by use of a

soft empty-hand tactic. The officers must be extremely careful when first touching a subject. At this point, officer safety becomes job number one! The officer depends on backup assistance for his personal safety. If the officer is successful and the subject starts to move out of the area, the officer will escort the subject out, keeping a constant vigil on the subject's behavior. The subject's apparent cooperation could change at any time into a second round of aggressive behavior but this time it may be directed at the officer.

4. **Control and compliance.** When the aggressor escalates aggression, the officer backs off and takes cover, keeping a safe distance. The officer combines verbal deescalation techniques with his move to safety. The only justification for an officer's escalation of aggression at this point would be to break the aggressor's physical hold on the officer. The officer must break the hold and get to safety. Restraining a subject until help arrives may be the best course of action, but officers should not engage in a situation where they will lose. Breaking away and creating distance is the best option if losing the encounter.

5. In these situations, the armed security officer will escalate choice of defensive weapons in response to the aggressor's choice of offensive weapons. If the aggressor uses hands and feet, the officer will want to use pepper spray, a taser, or an impact weapon. If the aggressor threatens with a club or weapon of opportunity, the officer may use a weapon of opportunity, a shield of opportunity, or just retreat from the conflict zone to a place of safety. An escalation and

deescalation back-and-forth will continue until the aggressor succumbs to the force of the officer or retreats from the area.

The officer must win every round of aggression and call for police assistance. The officer must also call for medical assistance and administer first aid immediately after the subject has been restrained. The officer must provide security for the aggressor, assuring the aggressor is safe from injury by third parties. These can be persons who the aggressor was fighting with, angry onlookers, or the aggressor's spouse or family members.

6. **Deadly force:** The two main weapons to watch out for are guns and knives. When confronted by one of these two types of weapons, it is important to retreat; get away from the attacker; move away from the attacker on the attacker's weapon side (this makes it harder for the attacker to adjust their attack); or get behind cover! It is always good policy to continually look for cover, as cover may eliminate the need for deadly force. In those cases where it is necessary to employ it, the cover may provide a little more time to assess the situation before using deadly force. Always verbalize using loud, forceful, and repeated commands while moving out of harm's way and creating distance. Use a weapon if no other alternative is viable. Use the weapon to *stop* the assailant and stop using the weapon once the assault has ended. Warning: make sure that the aggressor is not armed before approaching them. It may well be better to stay behind cover and/or at a distance rather than approach someone who may start the fight all over again.

SAFETY TIP

Remember that when applying a soft, empty-hand tactic there is no pain compliance applied. The touching is merely a gesture to get movement started in the direction the officer wants the subject to take.

In most cases, protection officers are not armed with firearms. There is not a lot of advice that can be given beyond verbal deescalation. Sometimes, using logic works when nothing else will. If talking buys a few seconds of time and seems to be working, keep it going. Hopefully, the aggressor will see the error of his or her ways and drop the weapon or flee from the conflict zone.

Summary: Obviously, officer safety is job number one. Retreat tactics are essential when experiencing imminent jeopardy. Avoiding physical confrontations at all costs is as essential as avoiding preclusion. In addition, the best nonlethal defensive weapon an officer carries (and they all carry this one) is their communications skills. Verbal deescalation skills are of paramount importance. *This is the essence of defensive tactics.* Assignments with a lot of violent, aggressive incidents should be manned by officers who are devoted students of hostile communications mitigation. In this way, most uses of force can be averted.

OFFICER SAFETY ISSUES

There are four individuals or groups who the security officer is concerned with protecting. They are the security officer him-/herself, the apparent victim, the general public, and the perpetrator. It is critical to understand that the order of importance is as listed; officer safety is primary, because if the officer is taken out, there may be no hope for the victim or anyone else.

As pointed out above, self-control is the most important factor when engaging in the use of force. It is not unusual, when faced with an aggressor, for the officer to become extremely nervous, tense, and shaky. These signs are the body's warnings that it is approaching a fearful situation. Left unabated, this shaking and fear may escalate into something called tachypsychia. "Tachy" means rapid or accelerated and "psyche" means the mind, functioning as the

center of thought, feeling, and behavior, which is consciously or unconsciously adjusting and relating the body to its social and physical environment. Some identifying characteristics of this phenomenon are the following:

- Rapid heartbeat
- Rapid mental processing
- Sweating
- Dilated pupils
- Tunnel vision
- Auditory occlusion blocking out sound
- Numbness and heaviness felt in extremities
- Loss of dexterity in fingers, arms, legs
- Shortness of breath
- Everything perceived in slow motion
- Loss of bodily functions—stopping breathing, bladder release, passing out, or paralysis

If this happens to the officer as he/she approaches an aggressive person, there is no telling what might result. Either the officer will be rendered defenseless or he/she may respond with excessive force. Those who feel this happening should make a tactical retreat until they can regain their composure. Only deep relaxation can counter this condition and alleviate the symptoms. Unfortunately, in most critical incident situations, there is not enough time to retreat. The only way to prevent this condition is through training. An officer who is trained to handle critical incident situations and aggressive persons is not as prone to these symptoms. One other helpful option is to call the police for assistance if the officer is alone and/or the symptoms of tachypsychia appear. The symptoms could be a warning sign that the officer is overwhelmed by the incident and needs to retreat.

OPTIMAL DISTANCE

While approaching an aggressive subject, an officer can inadvertently set off an act of aggression simply by getting too close to the aggressor. Entering the aggressor's private space can make the aggressor so uncomfortable that he/she strikes out in anger.

Optimal distance is a term that defines that area which extends out in all directions from an individual, within which the person feels safe and secure. Invasion of this personal space will result in a reflex reaction. This space is also known as a person's "comfort zone" or "epheric zone." Unwelcome invasion of a person's optimal distance will result in escalation of tension. Most people don't like others to "get in their face." It is important that security officers respect this optimal distance. Our job is to be part of the solution at all times and never part of the problem.

One reason, other than for officer safety, that we recommend communication at 10 feet or more from the subject, is to respect the subject's personal space. While this is a great distance, violent persons often have an extended personal zone. They need lots of space—in some cases it is as much as 15 feet.

As for additional safety, the officer must be aware of the different distances that the officer must honor to keep safe, called the "reactionary gap." This gap is the distance between the subject and the officer, within which, if the subject decides to punch, stab, or hit the officer, the officer may, or may not, be able to defend against the attack. The officer should be aware that a reactionary gap of 8-10 feet away from the subject would provide some added reaction time for the officer to defend against the punch, kick, or lunging attack. However, the reactionary gap for defense against the knife is approximately 22 feet. This is the distance that an officer armed with a firearm must be, in order to draw and accurately fire two shots into the attacker's torso.

The reactionary gap, to defend against the gun, works in just the opposite way. In fact, the closer to the gun the better, to allow for disarming techniques that may be necessary, but ideally officers should only try them if they are trained in those techniques. Other than in a disarming attempt, reactionary gaps are fairly irrelevant when it comes to guns: it is very difficult to outrun a bullet! However, every increase in distance away from the gun increases the chance of a miss. Running in a zigzag path will also increase the chance of the shooter missing. *The more movement of the target, the less accuracy the shooter has with the weapon.* Taking shelter and running might work, depending on a number of variables. Let the circumstances guide the approach.

Never rush in and attempt to touch the aggressive subject. To escort the subject, approach from the side, not the front or the rear. These are the most sensitive areas of someone's personal space zone. Even then, unless the aggressor is handcuffed, try to control the subject without bodily contact. Verbal communications, commands and gestures should be employed.

DEFANGING THE SNAKE

"Defanging the snake" is a term that refers to eliminating the means of aggression from an aggressive person. It could include the removal of weapons; the rendering of arms and/or legs useless, by pain, paralysis, or breakage, or the use of restraints. The fangs of the snake are where the poison that can hurt us is located. In our case, the knife blade, the bullet, the club, the feet, the knee, the elbow, and the fists are the fangs that can cause us harm.

Another way to defang the snake is to eliminate the fuel of the aggression. Separating warring parties, or removing the combatants from the conflict zone, could have the same effect as pouring water on a fire. Take away the fuel and the fire goes out. Thus, in many cases, removing the less aggressive of the two combatants can achieve the same effect as taking the weapon away from the aggressor. *A word of caution here, though:* Only do this with backup present. Always keep officer safety in mind. Remember the rule *one more officer than the number of aggressors* being considered. A lone officer should never intervene in a fight. He or she should yell, use hard verbals, clear bystanders, and remove dangerous items, but they should never attempt to separate people who are fighting.

ELEMENTS OF AGGRESSION

An aggressive situation is usually more complex than a simple case of one person being upset with another. There are usually highly charged emotions driving the aggression. The trick is to attend to the business of assisting, without getting dragged into one side or the other of the controversy. It is important to recognize that aggression has two parts: the fuel of aggression and the means of aggression. The fuel of aggression consists basically of the emotional side of the confrontation and may include any number of the following:

- Perceptions/attitudes
- Belief systems
- Rebellion
- Mental/medical conditions
- Chemical abuse problems
- Revenge, jealousy, passion
- Feelings of inadequacy

The means of aggression consists basically of the weapons of the confrontation and may include any number of the following:

- Hands, feet, elbows, and head
- Nonlethal weapons (aerosol or chemical sprays)
- Lethal weapons (knife, gun)
- Vehicles
- Weapons of opportunity (things lying around)

DEALING WITH AGGRESSION

Violence-prone situations can easily lead to injury of the officer or others. In addition, a lawsuit could result. What can be done in violence-prone situations to reduce the risk of using excessive force? The following are a few ideas on safely managing violence-prone encounters:

1. **Recognize your own emotions.** In itself, this causes the professional to calm down. In most people, violence is reached in stages—from anxiety, to defensive behavior, to physically acting out violent behavior. Cooling off the escalating violence-prone situation is best done by remaining calm and professional.

2. **Remember that when a person is in a rage, options cannot be seen.** As people grow angrier, they fail to realize that they have several options. They usually only see their options of **fleeing** or **fighting**. Other options, such as discussing the problem and seeking a solution, may not be considered. Rage takes over cognition. The formula for rage is clearly $C = E/I$ (Control = Emotion/Intellect).

3. **Avoid humiliating subjects.** Some officers create problems when speaking to a subject in a sensitive situation. When this happens, the subject will shut down communication, a condition that could become explosive. The best policy is to play it low key. Say as little as possible. Protect your space and be ready to execute self-defense plans at the first indication of aggression. Remember that **everybody**—even the serene, little old lady—is potentially violent under the proper circumstances.
Slowing down the action, respecting the subject's personal space, and using empathic listening skills help to deescalate the situation.

4. **If the encounter becomes tough, get or give space.** As the aggression level escalates, the best relaxant is space. **Clear the conflict zone!** If two people are exchanging heated words, both should take a walk—in opposite directions. Immediate separation of antagonists can prevent a confrontation; they both should be *"out of sight"* and *"out of sound"* of each other. Get them turned around and as far away from each other as is practical. If possible, use walls to separate the subjects.

5. **Proactive prevention works better than reaction.** Officers must be receptive to warning signs of violence, rather than reactionary. Understand that people who are antagonized by others may go from calm to rage in seconds.
6. **Sharpen observation skills.** Observing alcohol use and levels of intoxication can provide obvious warning signs, as can playful pushing and shoving and loud "in-your-face" types of communications. Boyfriend/girlfriend jealousy situations and domestic problems can sometimes develop into a volatile level.

Some instigators will try to provoke a hostile, angry response from protection personnel. This is often done with an ethnic or racial slur or other derogatory statement. It is essential to recognize that the "button pusher" is trying to cause the officer to lose control, thus creating an escalation of violence. Many hostile persons will try to push one "button" after another. Protection officers who are wise and wish to have a lengthy career realize that: *When you lose your temper, someone else has control over you.*

Remember the formula for control: $C = I/E$. Remember, **whoever loses control—loses**! Therefore, it is in one's best interest to identify the indicators of aggression, which we call "red flags" of aggression:

Weapons of opportunity
Disguised weapons
Weapons in plain sight
All edged weapons
All piercing weapons
Perpetrator's hands
Relatives, friends, others in close proximity
Subject's red face
Subject's direct prolonged eye contact
Subject's quick and deep breathing
Subject's head and shoulders back
Subject standing as tall as possible
Subject's hands pumping
Subject's finger pointing
Subject moving in and out of other people's personal space
Subject's belligerence, yelling, cursing
Subject's pounding fist on walls and tables
Subject's verbal threats

VERBAL DEESCALATION

Verbal deescalation is just about anything an officer can say that fits the situation at the incident scene. The successful deescalation will be more a product of officer attitude and level of professionalism than that of the actions taken.

At some point, a protection officer may be surprised by an aggressor or overwhelmed by more than one aggressor. They will be in a fight/flee/flow situation. That is, if fighting and fleeing are not options, flowing is. "Flow" means verbal de-escalation. The officer will have to talk their way out of the predicament. *Note:* There cannot be a prepared list of canned verbal communication that will fit every situation. The officer will be more successful drawing on their own words, customized for the particular circumstance. The key to a successful verbal deescalation is in the level of professionalism. There must be an appropriate amount of care, empathy, command of the language, personal sincerity, and candor.

> **WARNING:** When practicing verbal de-escalation it is imperative to keep alert. Always keep in mind officer safety. Remember: "Safety first"!

APPLYING VERBAL DE-ESCALATION TO AGGRESSIVE SITUATIONS

If called to a routine confrontation where the participants appear to be reasonable and the likelihood of injury is low, then the officer may wish to follow some of these deescalation suggestions:

- Respect the subject's dignity. Be as polite as possible and never demean people.
- Do not shout commands.
- Be careful not to become part of the problem.
- Assume officer safety distance (10 to 15 feet).
- Provide a pleasant greeting such as "May I help you?" or "How can I help you?"
- Assume a noncombative attitude.
- Use nonthreatening questions, and avoid "Why?" These tend to put someone's reasoning process "on trial."
- Slow everything down. Speak a little slower and move a little slower. Just a little.
- Be calm, as "calmness is contagious."
- Keep hands chest-high and ready to react.
- Attempt to move subject away from conflict zone.
- Listen intently to subject's words.
- Project empathy with subject's cause.
- Observe subject's hands and body language.
- Conduct a visual frisk; and check for observable weapons.
- Look for weapons of opportunity.
- Listen to peripheral persons. They can be witnesses, "cheerleaders," or assailants.
- Keep talking and negotiating a solution.
- Practice officer safety at all times.
- Make the decision to arrest or release.

Procedures for dealing with a violence-prone individual differ somewhat from dealing with the average aggressive situation. If the likelihood of injury is certain or extremely high, the officer may wish to follow some of these suggestions.

- Subject's dignity is not the main priority. "Defanging the snake" is the priority!
- Try to respect the subject's dignity even though this is not the main priority.
- Respect officer safety distance.
- Assume a self-defense attitude.
- Use loud, clear, directive commands for officer safety.

- Keep hands on the preferred weapon, or have weapons drawn.
- Call for backup before entering the conflict.
- Give subject directives to reach a solution.
- Keep talking and negotiating a solution.
- Listen intently to subject's words.
- Project empathy with subject's cause.
- Observe his hands and body language.
- When backup arrives conduct a search for weapons.
- Cuff and search for officer safety.
- Continue dialogue with subject.
- Listen to witnesses; take names, addresses, and phone numbers.
- Take notes of what witnesses say. Use quotes from the witnesses.
- Make the decision to detain, arrest, or release.
- Use deadly force only when a life is threatened or serious bodily injury is imminent.

LETHAL AND LESS-THAN-LETHAL WEAPONS MANAGEMENT

The employment of weapons is often grasped at by protection officers in the wake of a frightening experience. Fear is usually the primary motivator for protection officers asking management if they can be armed. Unfortunately, weapons do not solve the threat problem all by themselves. They are tools that are necessary in certain circumstances. They require increased responsibility and skill to be employed in an acceptable manner. Handcuffing a resistant subject is difficult, and must be done tactfully and tactically. Spraying an assailant does not negate the threat; it merely helps to control the person. The officer must still step out of the way of the aggressor and take appropriate follow-up measures. The same is true with impact weapons and even firearms. Protective movement out of the danger zone, employment of the weapon, and proper follow-up must be done for any weapon.

Regarding weapons in general, it is important to remember that:

Weapons are only useful when in the hand of someone proficient at using them, in the correct situation where they are the appropriate tools to use.

Weapons offer added protection—if properly selected and employed—but they also dramatically increase the professional obligations of the protection officer. Their use involves substantial judgment and skill on the part of the officer. Such judgment and skill only come after extensive instruction and practice in interpersonal communication, deescalation, interviewing, unarmed defensive tactics, legal considerations, and so on. These are some of the proficiency areas that must be mastered *prior* to the effective use of weapons. The following saying helps to put this into perspective:

You can't use a weapon if you can't use your hands. You can't use your hands if you can't use your voice. In addition, you can't use your voice if you can't use your brain.

Whatever weapons are being employed, be they handcuffs, pepper spray, firearms, or impact weapons, the following guidelines will help to maintain that they are handled in a professional manner:

1. Weapons should only be handled by persons who have been trained in how to use them. Training must be refreshed periodically. In some states and provinces, certification and/or licensing must be attained before any weapons, including handcuffs, can be carried by a security officer. All weapons training must be thoroughly documented.
2. Weapons should remain holstered or locked up unless they are to be employed in an actual confrontation, cleaned, or used during formal, supervised training. There must be no showing of weapons to curious persons and absolutely no playing with weapons.

3. All weapons should be thoroughly checked by the officer carrying them prior to starting duty.
4. The supervisor should check weapons on a regular basis.
5. A maintenance system should be in place for all weapons to include routine maintenance, as per the manufacturer's instructions, as well as work by armories or manufacturers when needed.
6. Weapons should be supplied by the employer. The employer must exercise and retain control over the weapons.
7. Weapons, ammunition, holsters, and so on should not be modified except by a manufacturer's representative or certified gunsmith.
8. All laws, property owners' wishes, and insurance carrier regulations on the carrying and use of weapons must be respected.

Unfortunately, weapons are occasionally "sold" by someone to management without management completing a full assessment of the product. A seemingly impressive demonstration of a weapon's capability, put on by an expert who stages the demonstration, is not the reason to select a weapon for a protective force. Neither is following a fad or the securing of a "bargain"!

Weapons selection is a serious decision, which must be made only after extensive research. On the other extreme, vacillating on a weapons decision—and not arming security officers when this is needed—raises unacceptable levels of risk to protection forces and to those they are employed to protect. The following is a list of considerations, which managers should review when selecting a weapon/weapons system:

1. For what specific need is the weapon required?
2. How is the weapon most likely to be used (tactical research)?
3. What selection process will be used for adopting the weapon?
   a. Why is the specific weapon being chosen over other weapons?

b. Who made the decision?

c. What is the decision-making process based on?
- Independent research studies?
- Medical research?
- Comparative bids?

4. What type of initial training is required?

5. Who can provide this training?

6. What type of refresher training is given?

7. Who can provide this training?

8. Can instructor qualifications be clearly demonstrated to the satisfaction of a court?

9. Is training adequately documented?

10. Is a continuous tactical review of the weapon's use in place, which shows how it is actually being used? This must be as detailed as possible so that it is possible to create effective procedures on the use of the weapon.

11. What training have supervisors had in the use of the weapons?

a. Initial training?

b. Periodic training?

c. Training or education above and beyond what line officers receive?

12. Are reasonable and enforceable policies governing the use of the weapons in effect?

13. Are weapons carried by, or accessible to, officers who are off-duty?

14. Is weapon retention addressed?

15. What is the skill level required for the use of the weapon?

16. Does the weapon fit in with other weapons used by the organization or other agencies that the organization may interact with during an emergency?

REPORT WRITING IN USE-OF-FORCE CASES

What is involved in writing the report of an incident where use of force was reasonable and necessary? It should be enough to just sit down and write, in chronological order, the truthful facts of the case. Unfortunately, in our litigious society, where cash-hungry lawyers and an aggressive media lie in waiting for the next abuse of force case, the officer cannot be carefree. The report must be written, taking into consideration the technical requirements of criminal and civil liability, in both state and federal court.

Know the audience! Assume that the paper about to be written will be in the hands of an opposing attorney, and that you, the officer, will be in front of a judge in the near future. If the use of force required a firearm, drawdown, or shooting, a pain compliance tactic, a chemical or electronic incapacitation device deployment, use of a baton, fists or feet confrontation, the report must be timely, thorough, concise, and accurate. Above all, the report must be true. The facts are what is important to record.

While writing the report, the officer must cover the following:

1. NECESSITY (What the subject did)
   a. Self-defense.
   b. Defense of others.
   c. Incident to arrest and escape prevention.
   d. Incident to ejection from the property.
   e. Protection of property.

2. REASONABLENESS (What the officer did)
   a. Followed department policy.
   b. Followed department training.
   c. Followed supervisor's instructions.
   d. Deployed each tactic with restrained, measured, intentional and minimal force.
   e. Assured no offensive moves were made and that all tactics were defensive as applied.
   f. Provided medical follow-up (first aid, 911 call, etc., as needed).

3. THE REPORT MUST BE BALANCED AND COORDINATED
   a. The report is clear, concise, and complete.
   b. The report follows a chronology of events.

c. The report has synergy, meaning that all parts of the report connect to make the whole greater than any individual part.

d. The report has no contradictions.

e. Times stated are close to other reports and other records.

f. Facts stated are reasonably supported by other reports and records.

Any one of the above components that are lacking in the report will provide an opportunity for the opposing attorney to attack the integrity of the report and ultimately the officer's testimony could fall apart. The officer may have performed perfectly, followed all the rules, provided a truthful report, and still lose the case over the fact that there was failure to provide one or more of the above items.

In reviewing the report, it is useful to play "devil's advocate." The writer should try to anticipate what the lawyers or media might try to make out of what is about to be written.

Astute report writers review their employer's policy before writing. Leave no gaps in the report to be filled in later. Don't assume anything. Never leave out a fact because it seems obvious that everyone would understand it. Being specific and detailed is critical. What may seem to be common sense or common knowledge may not be to the reader. And an omission or careless statement may be distorted by the opposing attorney to appear as if it is a careless mistake or a deliberate attempt at deception.

Keep in mind that the main thrust of the defense lawyer, or the plaintiff's lawyer, is to present their client as the victim in the case, not the perpetrator. They will work hard to accuse the officer of being the perpetrator and using the "but for" test; they will say, "but for the illegal or negligent acts or omissions of the officer, this plaintiff would not have sustained the injuries that he did." It is wise to be sure that nothing in the report supports the false assertion that officer's actions were illegal or negligent.

The officer's report should pass the "reasonable person" test. That is, either the jury or the judge should be able to read the report and form a mental picture of what actually took place. From that picture, he or she should be able to determine what their own actions would have been under exactly the same circumstances. If the report follows the above guidelines, it should lead that person to the logical conclusion that the officer acted in a reasonable and necessary fashion.

EMERGING TRENDS

Protection officers are increasing in number and society expects more of them. Where public police were once the principal protective force, privately employed security officers are now stepping in. With the constriction of government budgets coupled with the extensive cost for police, security forces will continue to grow. Many of these forces have some type of police authority. They also are carrying more and different types of weapons.

Society also has a lower tolerance for acts of violence, coupled with a greater fear of crime and terrorism. The expectation of employees, shoppers, students, and guests is that they will be protected. As a result, security forces must be more reactive than in the past. Security officers are expected to step in and help those facing the threat of violence more than in the past.

Post-traumatic stress disorder (PTSD) is recognized as a hazard today. PTSD affects not only those directly involved in a traumatic event, such as use of force, but it impacts those who witness it. Protective services personnel need be aware of this and seek help. Employers of protection officers have an obligation to address this issue. Officers who are adversely affected by major use of force incidents need help. And their employers need a system to deliver that assistance.

Training in communication skills is becoming more critical to manage aggression and deal with violent persons. Enhanced communication ability also aids in dealing with public events and persons higher in the organizational food chain than the officer (top management, clients, VIPs). Enhanced communication skills are also necessary so officers can relate to and manage diverse populations. As a result, more officer survival and defensive tactics instructors are emphasizing communications in their classes. This trend will likely continue.

The employment of weapons has also grown. There are more weapon options available than in the past and this trend will continue. Less-than-lethal weapons provide protection officers a wider range of options. At the same time, they require additional training and practice. More initial and refresher training is required for officers who are armed than for those who are not. Armed officers are also more likely to be subject to governmental regulation. Armed security officers and those employed by security service firms are the most likely industrial sector to be licensed.

The merits of force continuums are also being debated. They are one-dimensional and perhaps a bit simplistic. There is also a danger that persons reviewing a use-of-force event mistakenly believe that all steps in the continuum must be followed in sequential order. As a result, new models that depict the exercise of force are being developed.

References

Fisher, R. J., & Green, G. (1992). *Introduction to security*. Stoneham, MA: Butterworth-Heinemann.

The American Heritage Dictionary, 2nd ed.

Ouellette, R. (1993). *Management of aggressive behavior*. Powers Lake, WI: Performance Dimensions Publishing.

Resources

Butterworth-Heinemann, an imprint of Elsevier Science, is the largest publisher of Security texts. There are numerous titles available; many of these relate to the use of Force and Defensive Tactics. Visit **www.elsevierdirect.com** or call (800) 545-2522, ext. 200.

Calibre Press (calibrepress.com or (800)323-0037) is the leading officer survival concern. They provide seminars, books, and videos covering a vast array of officer survival topics.

The Crisis Prevention Institute (800)558-8976 **(www.crisisprevention.com)** is a leader in violence management instruction. CPI provides certification in Nonviolent Crisis Intervention for both officers and instructors.

The International Law Enforcement Educators and Trainers Association (www.ileeta.org). ILEETA offers membership to those who instruct police, security, and corrections professionals. There are extensive membership benefits, including an online journal, discounts on instructional materials, and an outstanding annual conference.

MOAB® Training International offers Management of Aggressive Behavior (MOAB) instructional programs. MOAB Training also offers Oleoresin Capsicum Aerosol Training ("pepper spray"), and Practical and Tactical Handcuffing (PATH). **www.moabtraining.com** (215) 723-2533.

The Military Book Club (www.militarybookclub.com) offers books at a discount on a variety of military-related topics. Some titles, such as Loren Christensen's excellent work *far beyond defensive tactics*, are of use for protective services personnel.

SECURITY QUIZ

1. Force is any touching of another person.
   a. True
   b. False

2. Using force is generally the first option that an officer chooses when managing the behavior of others.
   a. True
   b. False

3. Persons that force is used against must demonstrate that they have the _____ to cause injury, that they manifest intent to do so, and that they are placing the officer in imminent jeopardy.
   a. Means
   b. Ability
   c. Plans
   d. Weapons

4. _____ means that officers must show that they had no other alternative than to use force.
   a. Jeopardy
   b. Retreat
   c. Preclusion
   d. Manifest intent
5. Objects or materials that protect one from bullets or other projectiles such as rocks that are thrown is:
   a. Concealment
   b. Cover
6. Control = _____ /emotions.
   a. Training
   b. Experience
   c. Problems
   d. Intellect
7. The security officer must use alternative use of force whenever possible. Which of the following is an alternative to the use of force:
   a. Take time, be patient, and slow down the action
   b. Evaluate the situation, gather facts
   c. Call for backup before approaching
   d. All of the above
8. There are five primary justifications for using force. Which of the following is not one of them?
   a. That the aggressor was known to be a troublemaker
   b. That harm would come to the officer or a third party if force was not used
   c. That the actions taken were necessary

d. That the actions taken conformed to employer policy and training
9. The following are three recommendations on how to safely manage violence-prone encounters. There is also one recommendation that you should never try. Which one is the recommendation you should never do?
   a. Recognize your own emotions
   b. Remember that when a person is in a rage, options cannot be seen by the aggressor
   c. Do not waste time evaluating the situation; react immediately before anyone gets hurt
   d. If the encounter becomes tough, get or give space
10. Report writing after a use of force is very important. What the officer writes or fails to write can get that officer in trouble if the subject decides to bring a lawsuit. Therefore, remember that you may be writing to the lawyers, a judge, or a jury in a civil lawsuit. While writing the incident report, the officer must include all the following, except:
    a. Be sure to describe the facts in such a way as to support a case for NECESSITY
    b. If the subject was injured, be sure to state that you accidentally injured the subject; it was not intended
    c. Be sure to explain how the officer followed training, policy, procedure, and supervision
    d. Be sure to describe the facts in such a way you can prove REASONABLENESS

38

Defensive Tactics and Officer Safety

Inge Sebyan Black

CHAPTER OBJECTIVES

- Explain why safety is the security officer's responsibility
- Indicate the appropriate times/situations when defensive tactics should be used
- Emphasize why training is so critical
- Discuss the importance of one's own limitations
- Explore the role of weapons in defensive tactics

THE PROFESSIONAL SECURITY OFFICER'S ROLE

A critical review of the subject of defensive tactics is necessary in the litigious world in which we live, where the actions taken will have others quick to be the "Monday morning quarterback" (to criticizes with hindsight). In addition, those actions will indeed have numerous, if not serious, consequences, including criminal charges in addition to lawsuits for actions not justified.

It is important to stress the use of good judgment and common sense. Real life is not at all like a Hollywood movie. Getting punched, or for that matter, punching someone, can result in serious injury or even death. Size, the size of an opponent, and the physical condition of both parties will determine the extent of harm done. Avoiding physical contact is ALWAYS preferable.

Defensive tactics are subject to individual state, federal, or provincial laws. They are also defined by the organization one works for. Furthermore, use of certain defensive tactics should be strictly subject to the level of training received and competency in that area. Training and continual retraining are what will determine the confidence and skill being used.

This chapter will look at officer safety, what situations warrant using defensive tactics, various options of defense tactics, training, weapons, alternatives to weapons, and current trends.

Protection officers, are trained to observe, report, and, in certain circumstances, resolve conflicts. Officers are taught that their job is to protect people, property and assets. Most importantly, however, is the officer's personal safety. This is each officer's responsibility. To do this, each officer must understand that they are in the best position to provide for their own safety.

Every person's primary goal is to avoid being injured. Secondary to that would be the protection of others, and then protection of property or assets. Officers need to be aware of basic conflict resolution concepts and must be prepared to use them if the situation calls. While it is impossible to train for every given scenario, it is important to emphasize the necessity of training. Training is the single most important factor in preventing an officer from being injured or killed.

AVOIDING POTENTIAL SITUATIONS

In most cases, avoiding direct conflict is the ideal tactic. Officers are often told to "observe and report," yet they rush into conflict despite this. The execution of duties can be achieved, in most cases, without being directly in harm's way. Observing an intruder, while calling the incident in to dispatch or local law enforcement, is the ideal response, and provides the relative safety of distance from the subject. Trying to apprehend an intruder can quickly escalate the situation.

Words are the most effective tool for overcoming resistance and hostility; however, there are clearly situations when force appears to be the only remedy. At those times, officers must be prepared to use some type of force, within appropriate limits.

While at a post, officers often encounter situations where circumstances require use of a defensive tactic. Surprisingly, one of best defensive tactics is the avoidance of unnecessary conflicts. When performing protective duties, one should do the following:

1. Use caution at all times. Do not rush into areas that provide concealment for potential aggressors.
2. Call for assistance.
3. Use lighting to the best advantage. When patrolling an area at night, a security officer should walk behind any ground-mounted

lights, so that they illuminate the area of observation and not highlight the officer.
4. The security officer should use all senses. Often, the sense of smell or hearing will give away a potential threat long before it is seen.

Of course, the underlying theme is that potential threats should be watched for and responded to accordingly. Do not rush into potential conflicts, as this does not allow time for consideration of additional threats, or a full understanding of the incident itself. There are times that training will help in choosing the appropriate response if the officer or others are in imminent danger.

KNOW YOUR LIMITATIONS

A thorough understanding of what can be done, and what is permitted to be done, is absolutely essential. Without this, any combat situation can result in extreme physical injury, followed by emotionally painful litigation.

The security officer should become familiar with his or her own physical conditioning. Most people do not know how quickly they tire when faced with a prolonged combat encounter. Certainly a fight which ends up on the ground in a grappling situation is extremely tiring. Regular cardiovascular conditioning, within a physician-approved program, will not only benefit one's ability to endure such stressors, but will give a far better understanding of what the officer is physically capable of sustaining.

On the legal side, it is imperative to study local laws and determine what is permitted in the area with regard to responses to aggression, observed crimes, and similar situations. One must act within these guidelines to reduce the likelihood of litigation. If a person is injured as a result of one's actions, or an incident in which the security officer participated, chances are good that litigation will follow. If the officer has acted within the guidelines of that jurisdiction, the charge will be easier to defend. In many cases, a lesser level of force, applied with more thought and preparation, will effectively defend against an aggressor. The security officer should find out his or her limits and prepare accordingly.

FOCUS ON PREVENTION

Being properly equipped will greatly enhance defensive abilities and lessen the ways in which an aggressor can do harm.

The following items are suggested as equipment worthy of serious consideration. The applications of some are self-explanatory, while other items will be discussed in a future section:

- Flashlight
- Two-way radio/cell phone (with fully charged batteries)
- Bulletproof vest
- Kevlar gloves
- Helmet
- Proper footwear with nonslip tread
- Binoculars
- Night vision equipment

Using the environment to the best advantage is another effective defensive tactic. It is not inappropriate to consider retreating from a dangerous situation while awaiting response from law enforcement or others. It is imperative to know at all times what options are available for a safe place to avoid attack or other danger. Some suggestions for safety are:

- Guard hut
- Secure building
- Fenced and locked compound
- Vehicle

Each of the above may be a place of safety to avoid aggressors. Be aware of all options and escape routes at all times. It is also important that the officer you knows his or her location at all times and does not become complacent. Calling for help on a radio or cell phone is of no use if the direct responders cannot find the location.

There will be times when security officers are faced with dangerous situations where there is no retreat or possibility of safe haven. In these situations, surviving an attack may come down to some very basic and commonsense tactics. Analyzing these possibilities ahead of time may enable one to react more quickly and appropriately.

Something as simple as the way the body is positioned may prevent injury. Be aware of the threat being faced when unavoidably out in the open. When face-to-face with a potentially violent person, do not stand facing them; instead stand at a 90% angle. This protects more of the body and gives the attacker less of a target. If facing gunfire with no place to retreat, the officer should crouch or lie down, with the head away from the shooter as much as possible, and make the body drawn-up into as small a target as possible.

Improvisation for defensive tactics is also a protection that may help. A garbage can lid, for example, can act as a shield to fend off projectiles. A fire extinguisher, or anything close at hand, can be considered an appropriate defensive weapon in extreme circumstances.

Certain weapons, such as an axe or a bat, are simply not as effective when used at extremely close quarters, so when faced with this type of armed attacker, the officer may actually want to position within inches of the assailant. This is something that needs to be assessed at the time, giving consideration to the attacker's size and condition in comparison with with the officer's size and abilities.

THREAT ASSESSMENTS

A threat assessment is a tool used by law enforcement, government, industry, and most security professionals. These can be very detailed and comprehensive written documents, or simply an awareness of the potential threats faced in various situations. Security guards can utilize this information at the beginning of their duty.

When a threat assessment is done, it may be shared with the security force or the security guard may have to mentally perform his or her own assessment. Some of the threats that may be faced are listed below. To repeat, knowing what is being protected will help determine which of the threats are most likely to be encountered. The next step in a formal threat assessment is to examine the risks. This chapter will not go into great detail about this, but it needs to be understood that once the threat has been identified, it is imperative that a security officer understand the risks associated with that particular threat.

Simply put, a threat assessment is likely something every security officer does daily without realizing exactly what they are doing. It means knowing in detail what it is that is being protected and what the value of that asset is to others. This will help in identifying where threats may come from and the type of attack that may be encountered. Each post that is assigned will have its own unique challenges. For example, one might reasonably assume that an attack from organized crime might involve firearms, while the threat from a radical group might be bomb-related. Potential threats include:

- Terrorists
- Organized crime
- Common criminals
- Disgruntled employees
- Radical groups (i.e., animal rights, anti-abortion extremists)
- Vandals

DEFENSIVE TACTICS AND WEAPONS

Some of the weapons that might be faced in today's world are guns and bombs. It is important to be vigilant about other weapons that may

kill or injure to fully understand defensive tactics. Some of these are broken bottles, Molotov cocktails, rocks, and miscellaneous projectiles. Also, an unplanned attack may result in the use of weapons of opportunity, such as a pipe or board. If a security officer has at least some of the equipment listed earlier in this chapter and has learned to conduct a threat assessment, he or she has a much improved likelihood of a long and safe career in the security profession.

The possession and use of a weapon are typically controlled by the employer, client, and local law enforcement. In many cases, possession of a weapon is prohibited; in others, required. In any case, a thorough understanding of the policies and laws that apply to a specific situation is critical.

One of the greatest liabilities an organization can face involves issuing deadly weapons to security officers. This is true for both proprietary and contract officers. Obtain and review all legal, company- or client-imposed regulations prior to carrying any form of weapon. The expectations of all involved parties must be clearly understood, if one is to follow them. Once this is achieved, the regulations must be followed at all times. They are typically designed to protect the weapon carrier from increased liability related to improper usage. If any questions arise related to those regulations, it is essential that proper explanation and clarification are sought.

Once the security officer understands the regulations in which a weapon will be carried and used, one must then be properly trained to do so. Just as training for unarmed techniques, the level of realism in weapons training must be high, with numerous repetitions. Continued training, to retain a skill level, is also critical. Having been considered an expert at one time does not guarantee that the skill will remain high over time. Constant review and practice are required if one is to retain an achieved level of proficiency.

It is also essential to know and understand the specific functions and abilities of any weapon that may be carried. For example, officers issued a firearm should be aware of their own level of accuracy at various ranges, as well as the penetration abilities of the ammunition they will carry. This knowledge will help an officer, when deciding whether to shoot or not, be aware of potential penetration risks in the areas behind the target or even over-penetration of the target itself.

When dealing with firearms, learn what can be used for cover in the environment and what might just provide simple concealment. Objects that provide refuge are those that will block or significantly reduce the level of threat from an attack, such as brick and cement walls that make great cover. Concealment simply reduces one's ability to be seen. Shrubs are an example of concealment. It is difficult to see a person through a shrub, but a firearm will still be effective if fired through the bush. Some things might seem to be cover when dealing with a certain level of force but may become less effective if the level of force escalates. A car door, for example, might provide reasonable cover against an assailant with a .22 but might barely slow a shot from an assault rifle. Familiarity with the environment is essential when identifying these areas. It is essential to constantly look around; identify where to go for cover and which of the areas will only provide concealment.

Carrying a weapon is a great responsibility. The proper and effective use of that weapon is an even greater one. Ensure that all restrictions are known and followed, that all properties of the weapon and its use are understood, and that sufficient training is obtained and maintained.

POST ORDERS

Another valuable tool at an officer's post is post orders. Again, this chapter will not examine all the particulars about post orders; however, it is important to know that these orders, written by management, may give some insight

as to their policies regarding confrontations, tools that will be at the officer's disposal, possible threat risks (such as disgruntled employees), and updated management lists. Be sure to be familiar with these orders.

SPECIAL CIRCUMSTANCES

Some security officers will be assigned to posts where they face daily challenges, while others will have relatively safe and mundane duties. However, anyone in the security field is potentially going to encounter situations that are beyond the norm and may pose much greater threat to the safety of the security officer and those they are assigned to protect. Labor disputes can be one of the most stressful and dangerous situations to be encountered. Removing a person's ability to earn a living can turn the most peaceful and law-abiding citizens into unruly and unpredictable crowds. The "mob mentality" can affect labor disputes and violence can erupt without notice. The same is true of sporting events, political demonstrations, and concerts. Be proactive and analyze the potential threats and the best way to respond if they become reality. Hospitals, inner-city posts, and various other assignments can put security officers in proximity to substance abusers and mentally unstable individuals. It is highly recommended that officers have special training for dealing with this segment of the population. The skills discussed here and in Chapters 23, 26, and 37 should give some guidance as to the proper response needed in these situations.

USE OF FORCE

By definition, the purpose of force is to persuade, to seek compliance, to impede actions, or to stop actions. When the purpose is any of these, the force to be used should be determined by the perceived threat. Critical to the understanding of how one responds to a threat is the concept of a relative level of force. Levels of resistance can be summarized as:

- Psychological intimidation
- Verbal threat and/or resistive dialogue
- Passive resistance
- Defensive resistance
- Active aggression
- Aggravated active aggression

The actions of the persons that is not complying will determine the level of force used.

It is critical that company policies regarding use of force are adhered to. Some companies require that before officers can physically restrain an individual, the subject must first be placed under arrest by either the security officer or a certified peace officer. The only exception to this is when an officer defensively uses physical force to create space between him-/herself and the subject, or when separating individuals who are engaged in a verbal altercation.

Other policies may limit the use of force, to the least amount reasonably necessary to accomplish the intended objective, to overcome any resistance encountered, and for protecting the safety of others. In determining the amount of force reasonably necessary, the following guidelines should be considered:

- Officers do not attempt to use types and degrees of force which appear to be inadequate to accomplish the officer's intended objective.
- Officers do not become involved in protracted struggles or protracted hand-to-hand combat, which can frequently result in an increased risk of injury to the person being arrested. The officer is encouraged to use a type and degree of non-deadly force which appears reasonably necessary to bring the person under control quickly.

In Table 38-1, the various types of defensive responses are ranked, based upon the relative level of force for which they represent. When following this progressive chart, one should note that the responses appearing at the top are generally perceived to be less forceful than those that appear near the bottom. With this in mind, it is essential that any response to a situation falls as close to the top of this chart as possible, while still allowing those responding to protect themselves or others from great bodily harm. In most cases, any response should start at the top of this progressive flow, and then move toward more forceful responses. If the current level of force is insufficient, this will show that as the responder, there was no intent to cause great harm and the less forceful options were first applied. Often, it is the attempt to do less harm initially that convinces a court that an officer responded to an existing threat with only due care and required force. It is the officer that immediately jumps to the bottom of the chart when responding to a threat who more often find himself/herself on the losing end of a civil suit or facing criminal charges.

In Table 38-1, you will note that the situation and perceived level of force are indicated in the following ways:

Control of Cooperative Persons— Individuals who do not carry out a lawful order but are not threatening or resistive in their actions. They may require some convincing to do as they are ordered.
Control of Passive-Resistive Persons— People who refuse a lawful order and attempt to pull away from being led in the right direction. These persons do not attempt to harm or manipulate the officer but refuse to cooperate.
Control of Active-Resistive Persons— A situation in which the subject is not only refusing a lawful order, but is intentionally pushing the officer away, trying to manipulate the officer's hands or arms in such a manner as to make low force options ineffective. These persons may make

TABLE 38-1   Use of Force Continuum

Situation	Perceived Level of Force	Officer Response or Actions
Control of Cooperative Persons	No Force	Verbal Persuasion
Control of Cooperative Persons	No Force	Body Language and Positioning
Control of Cooperative Persons	Low Force	Physical Contact Controls
Control of Passive-Resistive Persons	Low Force	Joint Control Techniques
Control of Passive-Resistive Persons	Low Force	Pressure Point and Pain Controls
Control of Passive-Resistive Persons	Medium Force	Chemical Controls
Control of Active-Resistive Persons	Medium Force	Weapon-Assisted Controls
Control of Active-Resistive Persons	Medium Force	Weapon-Assisted Pressure Point and Pain Controls
Control of Active-Aggressive Persons	High Force	Striking Techniques
Control of Active-Aggressive Persons	High Force	Weapon-Striking Techniques
Control of Active-Combative Persons	Deadly Force	Striking Techniques to Critical Targets
Control of Active-Combative Persons	Deadly Force	Firearms

occasional aggressive movements or lash out in a disorganized and relatively ineffective manner.

Control of Active-Aggressive Persons—Subjects who, through their verbally or physically expressed intentions, intend to inflict harm upon those attempting to impose a lawful order upon them or others who are nearby.

Control of Active-Combative Persons—Subjects who, through verbal or physical intentions, intend to inflict great harm, including an attempt to kill, on those attempting to impose a lawful order upon them, or to others who are nearby.

The perceived level of force would be an indication of how the average reasonable person, upon witnessing the techniques performed, might assess the aggressiveness of the officer's response. In general, it is better to respond with as low a level of force as possible, while still acting to preserve the health and safety of all persons involved.

The specific responses can be explained as follows:

Verbal Persuasion—Describing the lawful order to the subject without placing the officer's body in their intended line of movement, or in any manner intimidating or directing them through physical motion or presence. In most cases, this is the first moment of contact with a subject. Often, if handled properly, the level of force does not need to progress beyond this point!

Body Language and Positioning—Placing an officer in a doorway that the subject is attempting to enter. Position an outstretched hand, palm forward, to indicate that entry would be resisted if attempted. There is absolutely no physical contact at this level of response!

Physical Contact Controls—By making contact with the body of the subject, the officer is now utilizing perceived force. This level of contact would include actions as simple as a hand on the arm to guide the subject to the proper exit door. Any contact made with the subject will fall into this, or a higher level, of force.

ALL FORCE BEYOND THIS POINT REQUIRES TRAINING BEYOND THE INTRODUCTORY OFFICER LEVEL

Joint Control Techniques—These techniques rely on manipulation of limbs to entice the subject to move in a desired direction, cease or initiate a desired action, or comply with the wishes of the person executing the technique. An example would be grasping the arm at the wrist and elbow and turning the arm in such a manner that the subject is inclined to walk forward.

Pressure Point/Pain Controls—Applying pressure to key parts of the body with the intent to cause pain. These are usually nerve bundles or muscle and connective tissue locations, which cause an inordinate amount of pain if manipulated properly. In contrast to the previous level, where joints are manipulated to produce the *expectation* of pain, if the desired order is not complied with in this phase, the actual sensation of pain is the motivator.

Chemical Controls—Use of such tools as chemical sprays or OC sprays, commonly referred to as "pepper spray," which cause a great deal of pain and limit vision and the ability to resist in a coordinated manner.

These are the limit of what most observers would call "low force" responses. In fact, some observers might rank the chemical controls response higher in the use of force continuum when noting the extreme level of pain that the subject suffers. In most cases, these tools do not result in permanent harm, although any officer utilizing them should have some form of decontaminating wash or spray available in

case the subject has an unusual reaction to the chemicals.

Weapon-Assisted Controls—Use of an expandable baton, nightstick, or even a radio to physically manipulate the subject falls into this level of force or a higher level. Through the introduction of a weapon or tool, the officer has increased the overall level of force in the situation. This phase would include not only directing a person with the use of a tool or weapon, but also the use of these to increase the effectiveness of joint manipulation techniques.

Weapon-Assisted Pressure Point and Pain Controls—Use of a weapon to increase the level of pain that a subject experiences, as a result of applying it to critical points such as nerve bundles. In many cases, observers could perceive this type of response to be excessive, unless the subject has clearly made a reasonable attempt to cause physical harm.

Striking Techniques—Use of techniques, without the assistance of any weapon or tool, to strike the subject on areas of the body that are not critical in nature. It is essential that these areas of the body are well understood. A strike to the head or neck will usually be considered "deadly force" and would thus be a higher level of force.

Weapon-Striking Techniques—Use of weapon- or tool-assisted striking techniques to strike the subject in areas of the body which are not critical in nature. As with the "striking techniques" phase, targeting areas which could have life-threatening effects will be considered a higher level of force. As weapon-striking techniques tend to produce more impact energy, critical areas of the body are expanded to include the torso of the body. For example, a strike to the lower area of the ribcage with an expandable baton is likely to cause fragmentation of the floating ribs, and punctures to the internal organs as those fragments travel inward. Weapon, striking techniques, in this phase, should be limited to the long bones of the limbs in an attempt to limit the subject's ability to inflict injury upon others.

Striking Techniques to Critical Targets— Intentional targeting of critical areas of the subject's body in response to a reasonable perception that they intend to inflict great bodily harm or death upon the officer or others. These techniques should only be employed when no other, lesser force options exist.

Firearms—Use of firearms, in any form, is the final phase of the continuum. In the eyes of most courts, firearms are designed and used simply to kill the intended target. They should *only* be deployed in response to situations where it is believed the subject's intent is to kill or cause great bodily harm to others, that the perpetrator has the ability to do this, and is in a position to do so imminently. This is the "last chance" response.

In all interactions with subjects, it must be the officers' goal to utilize the least amount of force possible while continuing to protect the lives and safety of themselves and others. When officers find they are engaged at a level of force greater than the "no force" levels, options to reduce the level of force and deescalate the conflict should be sought. Officers facing a potentially dangerous subject should consider disengaging from the conflict as an alternative to escalating the level of response, but only if by doing so they do not increase the danger to others in the area.

As a general rule, the subject will not typically attempt to deescalate the level of force. It is up to the responding officer to try to reduce the level of threat reasonably.

TRAINING FOR SUCCESS

When designing an effective training program, the most critical factors should be realism and repetition. Without these, the officer will either be working toward a goal that will prove ineffective, or unable to execute the techniques due to lack of effective experience.

Design the training around the types of threats that are perceived to be likely within the working environment. It does no good to practice handgun skills if the client does not allow firearms. Likewise, when designing a program for a location that will be staffed with armed officers that have a history of exchanges with firearms, but rarely involves physical contact with subjects, the training program should be divided between armed and unarmed response techniques.

It is essential that this training be conducted with a strong sense of reality. Training should be in the actual environment when possible and under less-than-ideal conditions. Does it make sense to train in loose clothing on a floor with good traction when instead the security officer wears a bulky uniform and patrols an area that frequently ices over? The training program must mimic the actual environment if it is to be effective. Again, different environments may require handling irate persons or persons with behavioral issues and the skills for these requires special training.

Training programs should stress how important it is to avoid becoming careless and complacent. Oftentimes, officers will work for long hours with great stress, causing them to tire, which in turn can cause carelessness or apathy. Remaining constantly alert is necessary for safety reasons.

When dealing with physical techniques, the ideal training program will provide repetition sufficient that the specific techniques will be a reflexive response. Without a reflexive response, the decision making may be delayed enough to be fatal. Developing the necessary level of response requires extensive repetition. As many as 7,000 repetitions may be required before the technique begins to be performed reflexively. It is also essential that these repetitions be technically sound. It is highly counterproductive to do the first thousand repetitions with incorrect technique. Vast amounts of time and energy will be wasted, not to mention the time necessary to retrain the reflexes. Once a specific level of skill is achieved, regular review and practice will be required for retention.

A training program should include a component that focuses on an understanding of the flow and dynamics of combat. The more realistic the training, the better the trainee will be able to handle the actual situations if they occur. This is why it is essential that some training time be spent learning to confront multiple opponents. This type of encounter is common and can prove to be far more dangerous than a single aggressor. Effective training in confronting multiple opponents will allow one to understand how to use movement and speed to shift position effectively. Despite the presence of multiple aggressors, a combatant with a superior understanding of movement and a good use of the environment can find ways of interacting with only one person at a time.

Documentation of all training is extremely important to track dates of training, progression, frequency, and skill level, along with the instructor's credentials. In the event of scrutiny or any legal consequence, the documentation is even more important.

State regulations and security guidelines should be studied, frequently revisited, and understood, allowing the security officer to make better informed decisions when faced with aggression.

FOCUS ON PREVENTION

There are prevention steps that each protection officer should know and understand. Although ideally we want to solve any matter with words, at some point, greater force may be required. This is when the officer must rely on training and judgment. Whatever actions are taken, be prepared to justify them.

The focus should be on preventing confrontations by encouraging:

- Continuous training
- Good communication skills
- Maintaining a safe distance
- Physical conditioning
- Site-specific (industry-specific) training
- Post-incident training

CONCLUSION

Safety is paramount, and training, along with good judgment and common sense, will help in taking the appropriate actions in any given situation. The use of force, whether for self-defense or to make an arrest, should always be the last resort. It is hoped that the material in this chapter will provide the reader with some insight into the alternatives that should be considered first.

EMERGING TRENDS

Society is becoming more complex and as it changes the role of the security officer will also have to change. This will mean an increased need for additional staffing and training. The demand for increased professionalism, along with the need to better trained officers in weaponry, report writing, communications, and legal issues, will grow in importance. The future will include focus on site-specific training, such as terrorism training for all nuclear sites and other utility locations. Security officers will surely need to increase their human interaction skills, as current economic limitations on public police forces are causing security personnel to take on more traditional policing roles.

The world is changing rapidly and security officers must maintain professionalism and keep abreast of new technology, legal precedents, and training. Failure to do so, allows for vulnerability to litigation, criminal prosecution, or public scrutiny. Thus, education and training are keys to a long and safe career, attaining retirement without encountering the need to justify actions to superiors, clients, the public, or the courts.

SECURITY QUIZ

1. Caution should be used at all times.
   a. True
   b. False
2. Additional support will never be required if you are cautious.
   a. True
   b. False
3. It is always wrong to withdraw from a situation.
   a. True
   b. False
4. Firearms are the final phase (highest level) of the range of response.
   a. True
   b. False
5. The critical factors when designing a training program are:
   a. Realism
   b. Repetition

   c. Neither a nor b
   d. Both a and b
6. The possession and use of weapons are dependent upon which policies?
   a. The employer
   b. The client
   c. Applicable law
   d. All of the above
7. The three basic factors of combat include:
   a. Weapon selection
   b. Control over space
   c. Body armor
   d. None of the above
8. Points of consideration when entering into physical confrontation include:
   a. Limits of physical ability
   b. Number of potential opponents faced
   c. Legal restrictions
   d. All of the above
9. Never get close to an aggressor, no matter what the weapon.
   a. True
   b. False
10. Training that is going to help every day in a security job is:
    a. Communication skills
    b. Maintaining physical fitness
    c. Written documentation
    d. Knowing the company policies and law
    e. All of the above

39

Industrial Hazards, Safety, and the Security Patrol Officer

Brian D. Baker

CHAPTER OBJECTIVES

- Define potential hazards and risks associated with working in an industrial or manufacturing setting

- Outline the various forms of workplace violence and motives that influence the risk of criminal violence in the workplace

- Show how the security officer can conduct security risk assessments and self-assessments to identify hazards in the industrial workplace

- Suggest methods to minimize workplace hazards and threats

- Explain basic fitness, health, and wellness issues relating to an officer's duties in an industrial setting

Much attention is placed on the role of the security officer as a member of a facility safety team. Indeed, this role is critical for prevention, reporting, and investigation of workplace accidents and the overall maintenance of a secure workplace. As other chapters in this book emphasize,

the role of security personnel should also be focused on identifying those risks that may evolve into a critical safety condition.

While the security officer is tasked with the mission of facility safety, there are often significant circumstances where the officer's patrol duties expose him or her to direct and serious hazards. These can be industrial hazards that are taken for granted by those workers who function in a facility for many hours during a routine work week, such as maintenance, production, supervisors, or quality control personnel. However, the risk posed by these hazards multiplies for the security officer who may only patrol certain areas occasionally or for a limited number of hours per week, often alone and outside of normal facility operating hours. Statistics from the U.S. Bureau of Labor Statistics reinforce that potential injuries to security officers are more likely to result from falls, exposure to unhealthy materials, and industrial accidents than from violence or assault.

The security officer, by virtue of his or her position, assumes certain risks in the workplace where he or she patrols. Foot patrol of an industrial facility is a common responsibility for many professional security officers. This duty post is not often seen as challenging, technologically engaging, or even social or exciting. In fact, it is not too bold to refer to this duty post as less than glamorous. Yet, the need for an industrial security patrol will always be present. Whether an industrial facility is in full operation, vacant, or transitioning, the employment of a skilled security patrol person remains a necessity. The following chapter is aimed at providing the industrial security officer with information to perform industrial security duties safely while recognizing, and avoiding potentially life-threatening hazards.

DEFINITION OF INDUSTRIAL HAZARDS

The topic of security officer safety in the workplace generally calls to mind the use of self-protection and defensive tactics. Any act of violence or aggression against a security officer falls into the category of workplace violence. The FBI Critical Incident Response Group (2004) categorized workplace violence into four typologies:

1. Violent acts by criminals with no connection to the workplace (such as robbery or other crimes)
2. Violence directed at employees or others committed by clients or service consumers
3. Violence between employees, including against supervisors or executives
4. Violent acts against an employee by a nonemployee, particular to domestic or relationship issues

While the threat and danger of criminal attack (human threat) is present in every workplace, the industrial security officer will likely also encounter hazards—*those conditions existing because of the physical and natural environment of the facility that may pose risk to the personal health and safety of those who come into contact with them.* Industrial hazards are a form of risk that must be managed by the security force. These hazards create unique considerations for officers who must complete their patrol and duties while preventing personal injury, avoiding short-term and long-term health problems, and reducing potential risks to the facility and other officers. By observing certain practices, security officers can safely enhance their performance and enjoyment of their duties at industrial hazard posts.

To further expand on the distinction between threats and hazards, a threat definition should focus on the term "criminal," as in criminal attack or criminal event. Workplace violence as defined above is a significant and common type of threat, although the theme and emphasis of this chapter are that this is an overall rare occurrence.

Some common examples of workplace violence threats include:

- Domestic violence/ex-spouse or lover violating a protection order
- Terminated employee enacting revenge on a supervisor or manager
- Drug dealing or gambling debts being collected
- Disgruntled worker sabotaging equipment to injure workers

Other types of criminal threats include:

- Burglary of office areas
- Theft of copper or other valuable metals
- Car theft
- Vandalism, trespassing, drug use, or underage drinking

These events are termed "threats" because they involve individuals on the facility property committing acts that a security officer is most likely to detect, encounter, and provide response to. The threat of violence toward the officer is present should the criminal decide to fight instead of flee the scene or surrender cooperatively to the lawful interventions of the officer. The professional security officer should observe the event, position him- or herself safely, and make an immediate notification to police or to a supervisor according to the post orders.

Unfortunately, some criminals will respond to any form of detection with violence. Among the many theories for aggression include cognitive links between authority figures and equipment (such as a security officer with radio or handcuffs) and discomfort caused by blockage of goals (such as escape or monetary gains of a burglary). This linkage may cause certain people to act quickly on the basis of emotions and without deliberation or forethought; such actions may result in violence (Bartol & Anne, 2008). Again, the Bureau of Labor Statistics reinforces that this is often a low probability for industrial security officers yet it is a threat that officers assume and must be trained to handle.

Threats may exist in remote oil fields, urban parking garages, retail stores, or logistic centers. One can't automatically assume that a warehouse in Guatemala or an electric sub-station in Montana is less vulnerable to crime than a pipeline in Nigeria or a hospital in Washington, DC. The volume of human contact and the value of assets are possible factors that raise or lower the likelihood of criminal violence upon a security officer; however, no site must be assumed to be without threat. Certain crimes require certain settings and the officer must recognize the possibilities for his or her specific location.

In the industrial setting, however, the risk of serious personal injury to a security officer lies in the conditions existing by virtue of the industrial and natural environment.

Table 39-1 outlines how the threats mentioned above and other common types of security posts can translate into industrial hazard examples.

Indeed, these nonspecific examples cover only a few areas of industrial hazards. The hazards exist in the environment of the site—either manmade conditions or natural conditions—but do not directly involve criminal or violent actions of humans upon the security officer. These environmental risks, known as hazards, may be managed through commonsense awareness, training, and officer self-evaluation. The professional security officer must concentrate on being

TABLE 39-1   Industrial Hazards

Oil Field	Vehicle accidents caused by poor roads
	Attack from wild animals
	Slippery walking conditions from rain or oil spills
Urban Parking Garage	Speeding cars
	Loose handrails
	Greasy or oil-coated surfaces
Ski Resort	Severe weather
	Fire in lodges, cabins, or villas
	Avalanche or ice storms
Logistic Center	Heat exhaustion
	Deteriorating building construction
	Falling boxes
Hospital	Radiological waste
	Wet floors
	Poor lighting

vigilant but not fearful of these hazards. The officer must be respectful of the hazard and not take further actions that increase his or her risk of injury. This respect not only applies to the immediate steps taken on every foot patrol but also to exposures and hazards that may affect the officer's long-term health. To achieve this, one must rely on the components that make an excellent security officer in the first place: five senses, personal instinct, and understanding one's own health and fitness.

INDUSTRIAL HAZARDS, ACCIDENTS, INJURY, AND ILLNESS

While factories, foundries, and heavy equipment manufacturing are a few examples we consider with the term "industrial," the types of hazards present are not specific to only the typical assembly, production, or raw material processing activities of these sites. Schools, hospitals, logistic/distribution centers, high rises, shopping malls, chemical storage, energy facilities, parking garages, office/commercial, and high-tech research facilities are all examples of potentially hazardous environments.

Hazards can result in obvious slips and falls, poisoning, blunt force trauma, burns, heat stroke, hypothermia, frostbite, and broken limbs. Aside from potentially fatal injuries, especially when an officer is working alone, industrial hazards can result in long-term health problems such as hypertension and cancer. Disruption to an officer's natural sleep habits and exhaustion are common problems with officers working night shift or a second job. Abuse of caffeine, stimulants, and tobacco to cope with fatigue, will further detract from an officer's health. Abuse of alcohol to counteract stimulants, or to help with sleep problems, can lead to even further physical deterioration. The officer should always strive to achieve the right amount of sleep, relaxation, and exercise necessary to perform his or her duties comfortably and safely. This is challenging to manage in our busy world, but it is possible to establish a sleep schedule that can be coupled with exercise and a healthy diet in order to reduce blood pressure and other unhealthy effects. In the event that an officer cannot effectively achieve the sleep necessary to perform the duties at an industrial facility, he or she should seek a change of assignment before being injured or possibly disciplined for poor performance.

Consider some of the following scenarios of actual hazards and how the security officers could have prevented or mitigated the resulting injuries. With many facilities employing multiple officers per post, the teamwork and supervision roles should not be ignored when also protecting fellow security officers.

1. A healthy 30-year-old officer started on a new night shift post at a 35-acre office complex. Without adequate sleep, he drank several caffeine energy drinks to cope with his exhaustion. Following a strenuous foot patrol of a parking lot area he returned to the command center and suddenly collapsed. His head struck the floor, causing a severe concussion that immediately resulted in a seizure. His body convulsed and his head again struck the floor, causing lacerations and significant blood loss. He was rescued by a fellow patrol officer and rushed to a trauma center by ambulance.

2. An experienced 60-year-old officer was working a mobile patrol post at a retail complex in the late evening. He exited his patrol truck briefly to check on an illegally parked car. Upon returning to his vehicle, he slipped on grease leaked from a tractor-trailer that had been parked in the same spot for several days. The officer fell hard on his right side and then managed to crawl back into his patrol vehicle and return to the security station. He was working alone at the time and the management of the site had not provided the officer with a cell phone or radio. The officer was in severe pain and went into shock from a fractured hip. His relief officer arrived an hour later and summoned an ambulance. In addition to the officer working without any communications, it was later determined that he did not have a flashlight and was wearing a hard-sole dress shoe with no tread.

3. A healthy 40-year-old officer suffered lung injuries while patrolling through an area containing ammonia gas storage tanks. The tanks had recently vented, and a warning alarm in the area had been disconnected for repair. She was working alone inside the facility and was away from her command center, where a working alarm indicator would have alerted her to the hazardous condition. The security officer on the prior shift had also failed to document the verbal instructions from the maintenance director that patrols in that area should be avoided

due to safety issues. She was quickly rescued by cleaning personnel who recognized her distressed breathing. Her injuries terminated her ability to work.

4. An overweight and diabetic young contract security officer returned to the reception post after completing a walking patrol and lockdown of three warehouse and production buildings. It was a hot summer day and the officer began to experience chest pains. He was relatively new to the post and had difficulty locating the phone number for the command center that he was required to call if there were any emergencies. He instead phoned his branch office, located an hour away, and reported that he felt ill. He was unable to transmit further information and it took the office personnel nearly twenty minutes until they could confirm his location and dispatch a patrol officer/EMT to assist him. It took the patrol officer nearly 40 minutes to reach the site, and he soon determined that neither the officer in distress nor the receptionist at the branch office had summoned an ambulance. Fortunately, a fire station was less than half a mile away and within 1 minute of calling 911, the patrol officer and firefighters managed to stabilize the patient. His condition was directly attributed to his health and the exertion of the post.

The above examples are only a few situations of hazards that could impact a security officer. Additionally, all of these situations could have been prevented by a combination of proper training, equipment, and personal vigilance by the officer and his or her peers. While none of these incidents involved gruesome injury or horrific death, the events all had a significant life-changing impact on the officer. Again, these incidents were preventable.

The officer in the first example should have prepared for the new shift by adjusting his sleep cycle and reducing his caffeine intake. His peer officers should have recognized that he was not rested and alert and assigned another officer to that patrol. The officer in the second example was not provided with the necessary basic communication tools and flashlight, and was not wearing the proper footwear. In the third example, the officer entered an area that should have had a warning sign posted and her prior officer did not properly document and pass down the safety instructions. She was working alone inside a facility and was without proper communications or monitoring. In the fourth example, the officer was unfit for duty at this post and by not taking steps to pace himself or drink enough water, he further exaggerated his health situation. The fact that he was poorly trained and also in distress, further hampered his ability to obtain assistance quickly.

The cost to each officer was significant but there was also a latent cost to the facility or contract security company through worker's compensation payments and overtime to fill the shifts left vacant from the injured officers. Consider these additional hazards that were clearly recognized by the security officer and therefore should have been avoided:

- Officer bitten by ticks on two occasions while patrolling a perimeter fence line with heavy grass and vegetation
- Officer injured her back while holding open a heavy steel door at a bank
- Officer slipped on a tiled floor in an elevator because he had snow packed into the tread on his boots
- Officer suffered carbon monoxide poisoning while using a kerosene heater inside a guard shack with poor ventilation
- Officer stepped on a loose metal floor plate that tipped, causing the officer's leg to plunge into a drainage channel, resulting in ankle, knee, and back muscle injuries

An officer should not assume that the employer or supervisor would clearly recognize all hazards. Events that result in injury will not always result in corrective action. Unfortunately this is the nature of business and industry. However, the officer should utilize all legitimate means to report new and potentially unrecognized hazards to his or her supervisor through the proper chain of command. While some facilities do not allow security officers to take corrective action on safety or maintenance matters, the security officer must recognize his or her responsibility to the protection of others, including fellow security officers. If a loose floor plate can be safely repositioned, for example, the officer should take action. The officer should also provide for his or her own safety and comfort through a minimal investment in comfort or safety supplies. A good insect repellent could prevent tick bites. A small pocket flashlight could have helped the officer recognize the loose metal floor plate. The self-protection section of this chapter will further discuss personal equipment for the security officer.

RISK ASSESSMENT

Risk assessment is a thorough, comprehensive, and ongoing evaluation of the key assets, threats, hazards, vulnerabilities, and procedures in place to protect a facility from loss. While risk assessment sounds like a huge task that should be undertaken by a security supervisor or director, it is actually an important skill that should be developed and practiced by the industrial security patrol officer as well. Security managers and consultants utilize customized checklists and formulate formal reports when conducting a facility risk assessment. The patrol officer, by direction of post orders and patrol duties, is an extension of the risk assessment, particularly in the ongoing evaluation stages (known as auditing).

Much of what is written about risk assessment actually pertains to threat assessment and the determination of crime probability, or likelihood of criminal attack or events. The more accurate definition of risk assessment takes on what is known as a whole hazards approach, incorporating crime along with the numerous other possible events and risks beyond crime that can impact a facility. Risk assessment should address any event or condition that could create a loss to the facility.

Human life should always be considered the most important asset at a facility. Secondary to human life, risk assessment should identify those assets that are critical to the operation of the facility. Certain employees within the facility, such as executives or plant engineers, may be particularly valuable assets as well.

The whole hazards approach seeks to identify the negative things that can occur to the key assets as well as the likelihood that specific events will occur to those assets. For example, the assets listed above are all obviously critical to the facility and post duties and instructions in many ways refer to crime prevention and crime detection priority for the patrol officer. But assuming that industrial environmental hazards are more likely than crime, consider some potential events that could cause a loss aside from crime:

- Smoke and fire.
- Water leaks and flooding.
- Vehicle accidents and vehicle fires.
- Medical emergencies.
- Structural failure and building collapse.
- Fuel leaks.
- Dangerous debris, vegetation, tree limb hazards.
- Weather-related conditions.
- Smells from chemicals, solvents, malfunctions.
- Asbestos and airborne contaminants.
- Hydraulic leaks.
- Appliance failures such as office, refrigeration, or cooking equipment.

SELF-ASSESSMENT

The professional security officer should recognize the value and process of the risk assessment and practice this daily while patrolling the facility. When viewing the facility from a crime prevention angle, security officers should ask themselves, "What are some things a thief might want to steal inside this facility? Where are some places that I would hide if I were a burglar? If I wanted to bomb or sabotage this operation, what target would I choose?"

But when viewing the facility from the broader whole hazards vantage point, the questions an officer should ask are elemental:

- Where are the fire alarms and emergency exits?
- Do I have a flashlight and is there emergency lighting if the power goes off?
- Where is the safest place for me in a tornado?
- Do I know how to shut off the water supply if a pipe bursts?
- Can I get locked inside any rooms?
- Who do I call if this machine malfunctions?
- What labs should I avoid because of the chemicals?
- Where is it dangerous for me to walk?
- Is it necessary to check the outside perimeter at night if there are video cameras?

This self-assessment process assumes a higher order of thought and should be undertaken regularly once the officer is oriented to his or her site and knows the patrol routes and procedures. Much of this becomes common sense and second nature to the officer and within a few months it may become subconscious. An important aspect of the self-assessment must be for the officer to recognize what hazards exist by virtue of the officer's presence in the facility.

- Rooftop patrols.
- Climbing scaffolding.
- Improper monitoring by command center.
- Lack of training regarding weak spots on walkways or paths.
- Traversing through active production areas or maintenance activity.
- Vulnerabilities from torches, demolition, or vehicles.

- Overhead hazards such as ventilating gases or falling pipes.
- Unnecessary patrol through active areas not requiring security presence.

There is also a distinction between officer-created hazards—being in the wrong place at the wrong time or just being in the wrong place—and the officer's hazardous behavior. While the former assumes that the officer is attempting to do his or her job thoroughly, and may become inadvertently entangled or exposed to a hazard, the latter engages in risky or consciously unsafe or foolish behavior.

A significant number of workplace injuries result from unsafe acts, showing off, or otherwise blatant disregard for personal safety. Among these is the hazard of driving a vehicle on patrol. Mechanical failures, accidents caused by the other driver, and that aside, we all have a tendency to sometimes push the abilities of a vehicle. The definition of vehicle can vary from a Segway to bicycle, to pickup truck to motorboat. It is easy to forget, or ignore, basic safety equipment such as a helmet or seatbelt. The use of cell phones and text messaging devices is also another factor that contributes to accidents. Speeding, choosing impractical routes, and laziness are major causes of preventable accidents.

Other hazardous behavior includes operating forklifts, cranes, or equipment without proper training or authorization. Officers must overcome their curiosity about such equipment in order to avoid injury. In a complex industrial setting, many machines may be linked through one electrical system. The key or switch that is used to start or activate a particular piece of equipment may not be the same key or switch that turns the equipment off or shuts down the process.

Exploring electrical switching rooms or confined and underground spaces is extremely hazardous, as is climbing or descending ladders. Another bad practice, with good intentions, is exercising while on patrol. Officers who jog,

Smoking while on patrol is extremely unwise because it interferes with one's ability to smell smoke, gas, or other olfactory hazards.

use raw materials as free weights, or hang from scaffolding to do pull-ups are at significant risk of injury.

Just as the risk assessment process prepares the officer for knowledge of key assets and potential hazards, the officer should also understand what could happen to the facility and others if he or she is injured or killed as the result of a hazard. More important, the officer should recognize the impact if he or she is unable to perform the duties as a result of a hazard they created or from hazardous behavior.

The following are generic suggestions for minimizing hazards and threats (this list is not specific to any particular environment):

- Use caution when approaching partly open doors or overhead loading doors.
- Do not eat or drink except in approved areas to avoid risk of food poisoning.
- Turn off coffee pots and appliances when empty or not in use.
- Always use a handrail when ascending or descending stairs.
- Move slowly and carry a flashlight.
- Watch out for open areas that may not be marked and areas that were closed or sealed yesterday that could be open today. Avoid falling into pits and drainage tunnels.
- Avoid the curiosity of patrolling in restricted or marked danger areas.
- Stand clear of high-speed roll-up doors and forklift traffic.
- Avoid greasy areas that are slip hazards. Also, avoid wearing greasy shoes into your home or vehicle.
- Be aware that some work areas are abandoned when the shift ends as workers will leave tools and parts lying on the floor, posing a trip hazard.

- Never enter or tamper with vehicles, storage areas or tool cribs.
- Be careful of stairs, catwalks, and scaffolding.
- Padlock controls are important tools for loss prevention but also to control access and preserve housekeeping. Report all padlock issues immediately.
- Avoid confined spaces.
- Avoid walking on uneven floor plate steel decking or areas where the floor is concealed by wood or cardboard.
- Always know the work area and location of emergency exits.
- Avoid dusty areas or enclosures where known pollution cleanup work is being performed.
- Avoid forklift traffic areas such as ramps and blind corners. Give the forklift the right of way unless the operator stops, makes eye contact, and motions you by.
- Observe foreign object debris (FOD) and make sure that the walkway is clean before making access or others approach.
- Avoid treacherous walkways, bridges, or paths with no railings or over deep holes.
- Never cross or walk on bent or bowed flooring.
- Know what hazards exist to the exit doors. There may be machinery, FOD, and protruding raw materials. Attempt to keep exit pathways clear.
- Avoid overhead cranes, tilting loading docks, or walking under elevated lift trucks and boom lifts.
- Don't approach trenches and other areas where work is in progress.
- Be aware of doors that are welded closed, bolted shut, or temporarily barricaded with 2×4 boards.

- Be cautious of steep ramps and pitted or uneven walkways.
- Unexplained water may not be a concern, but running water/flooding areas and water running onto electrical panels could be treacherous.
- Be familiar with HAZMAT areas and also with HAZMAT signs that no longer apply. This may be needed in case of an emergency to guide the fire department.
- Avoid entering work areas from narrow hidden walkways.
- Never walk through any liquid if it can be avoided.
- Choose to walk over concrete flooring rather than temporary flooring or wood or metal grates.
- Be aware that diamond plate steel flooring is designed for traction but when it is wet, or coated with grease, it becomes very slick and dangerous.
- Be careful of patches in flooring, cracks in concrete, and areas of new construction where walkways may be unfinished.

SELF-PROTECTION

In addition to awareness of site hazards and the ongoing evaluation as described in the risk assessment section above, there are two areas where the professional industrial security officer must take personal responsibility: fitness for duty and personal safety equipment.

Fitness for duty refers to an officer's personal physical and mental ability to perform the duties of the post. As mentioned in the beginning of this chapter, much of the patrol duties involve walking. In fact, a patrol can involve significant amounts of walking at a slow and steady pace. In large industrial facilities, the officer may use a combination of foot patrols inside buildings and vehicle patrols between buildings. Some sites may require an officer to walk as many as 6 or 7 miles per shift. This requires some stamina, especially if the patrols require ascending stairs or hills.

The walking patrol is not an efficient method to cover a large amount of territory if there are numerous duties such as meeting visitors or contractors, or repetitively unlocking gates or storage areas. However, during off-production hours a walking patrol has fewer random demands and by walking through a facility, the security officer can check for unlocked doors, listen and smell for unusual conditions, and become comfortable in the environment. This allows a thorough and careful evaluation of the many types of industrial hazards previously discussed.

When walking at a moderate pace for several hours, it is possible to cover many miles and for the body to burn hundreds of calories. You should eat wisely to avoid food that is filling to the point of discomfort. Carbohydrates such as bread and grains are a good source of energy. Fruit and plenty of water or electrolyte drinks are important in both hot and cold weather. Getting in shape for a walking post is not always possible but once walking becomes part of your job, you should consider walking and exercising during your days off as well. If you have medical issues that impact your ability to walk or your fitness for duty, discuss these with your supervisor to see if accommodations are possible. Some industrial sites have an electric cart available to save the officer from fatigue. At other sites it is not possible to use a cart or other conveyance and walking is required.

Remember that when on a foot patrol your primary responsibility is to protect the facility from all types of losses. When encountering workers, be pleasant and professional but not overly social. It is best not to develop close relationships with people outside of the security department as this will allow you to act objectively and appear fair and impartial. The relationship that employees have with security officers varies by the culture of the facility and the size of the workforce. You will want to appear approachable should someone need your assistance but do not treat the workplace as your social network.

As the first line of defense between the facility and the public, you should appear alert, well groomed, and physically capable. You are not a police officer, however, and if you wear a uniform and a shield or ID badge, the purpose is to make you recognizable but not to intimidate or project law enforcement authority. If there are individuals on the property that do not appear to belong, your confident presence and polite request for identification according to the post orders, should go a long way in preventing loss. If you appear to be out of shape or intimidated, you will negate the effectiveness of the entire security department and may also lead yourself into a dangerous situation.

In addition to the physical demands of foot patrol, the industrial facility has significant differences from other, more open, posts. These include the presence of equipment, running air compressors that start and stop depending on pressure or demand from other parts of the plant, humming electrical transformers, random buzzers signaling break times, dead silence, pigeons and rodents, and loud clanks and bangs as metal buildings expand and contract. Several excellent and free health tips may be found on the Internet or via your local YMCA or private fitness center, but fitness for duty is a commitment that can be achieved through a daily 20-minute workout and a low-fat, vitamin-charged diet.

Perhaps one of the most heavily broadcast industrial health hazards has been asbestos exposure. Asbestos cancer, known as mesothelioma, is caused by a scarring of the deep lungs or stomach due to asbestos exposure. According to the Mesothelioma Center (http:www.mesotheliomacenter.org), not all exposures will result in illness or cancer; nonetheless, once a person believes they have been exposed to asbestos, they should report this to their physician for further monitoring. Asbestos is a mineral product that has been used in mining, milling, foundry operations, and other manufacturing. The Mesothelioma Center's website

contains details on exposure risks, health effects, legal updates, and products and locations where asbestos can be located. It is the employer's responsibility to protect workers from exposure health risks, so the industrial security officer should pay attention to such information. It is the officer's duty, to himself or herself, to be vigilant and self-protective. If an environment becomes harmful or the officer notices significant unhealthy symptoms, they should consult their supervisor as well as a physician.

The final piece of advice for the comfort and safety of every security patrol officer is regarding footwear. As previously mentioned, an officer is far more likely to be injured from a fall than from a violent assault. Boots and shoes can be an expensive investment for many officers. Discounts and copayments for footwear by the employer or contractor should be considered, along with recommendations and on-site safety policies regarding foot protection. Steel toe and safety shoes can be heavy and uncomfortable if not properly fitted and broken in. In many cases, the ideal style may not be available in a color that matches the officer's uniform or in a style that is personally preferable. Consider that in an industrial setting, most boots will become severely worn and blemished and that fashionable appearance must be sacrificed for safety.

Law enforcement and military-style boots can cost over $100 but may not be durable in some industrial settings. These boots should fit comfortably and provide a flexible tread with reinforced shank protection. Most of these boots are waterproof, insulated and enhanced with special vapor barriers and breathing membranes. With proper care and careful walking, the officer may be pleased with the investment if he or she understands that exposure to grease, oil, dust, and metal will challenge the upkeep and appearance.

Sneakers and dress shoes should be avoided in an industrial setting. This includes the popular black tennis shoes often acceptable in uniformed professions, including security posts in less hazardous settings. Tennis shoes typically are comfortable for walking moderate distances but do not afford the protection or support necessary for industrial settings. Uniform dress shoes may also be comfortable, but the soles of these shoes are far less safe for industrial patrols. If a patrol officer spends over 7 hours behind a console, but must be prepared to leave that post for 1 hour to cover a patrol, escort, or inspection elsewhere, the minimum choice for footwear should be for the most hazardous possibility. If the officer's duties involve significant walking, the boot or footwear selection must provide sturdy comfort or the result will be severe knee and back pain.

Layering or doubling socks can help add comfort and absorb perspiration. A frugal option that many officers choose involves purchasing a low- to mid-cost black leather boot with either a 6- or 8-inch ankle, typically found in discount retail stores. These boots are usually waterproof and insulated with 200 grams of Thinsulate. To compensate for the low-cost comfort, the boot can be greatly improved with a full insole and arch insert, as well as a heavy-duty appropriate length bootlace. Effectively, this inexpensive boot can be transformed into the comfort, safety, and performance necessary for the officer's duties. When the boot is blemished or damaged with oil or solvents, the insoles and bootlaces can be transferred to replacement boots. If footwear damage and expense are concerns, the security officer may find this option to be a minimum of three times more economical than investing in a law enforcement or military-style boot.

EMERGING TRENDS

Security in the industrial and manufacturing setting relies on the same protection concepts as other locations, namely, deter, deny, delay, and detect. Technology continues to help us with these objectives and if properly implemented, technology can accomplish these goals while decreasing the risk of harm to the security patrol officer. Digital video analytics, computerized guard tour matrixes, and unmanned or robotic patrols are just a few examples of future security technology that could be used to save lives and increase efficiency.

Among these, digital video analytics holds the greatest potential to improve the detection capabilities of the weakest link in the security program—the human security officer. Instead of a security officer walking through a hazardous industrial setting, the computer can detect changes or predesignated conditions within the video camera field of view, interpret those conditions, and begin a preprogrammed response plan such as notifying a security officer or sounding an alarm. For example, video analytics can detect motion along a remote fence line, but instead of simply recording the activity, the software monitors the activity and can detect if the subject is moving parallel to the fence or crossing the fence as an intruder. Video analytics holds the potential for detecting industrial accidents, for instance, workers who may be unmoving and injured on the floor, or detecting changes in the number of persons in a specific area, as in a fight or disturbance in a cafeteria. Video analytics may even be programmed to detect the absence of required personal protection equipment such as hard hats or safety lines, not only indicating a risk to workers but also the potential presence of an intruder.

Digital video analytics allows the security officer to detect activity around high value assets while also providing clear real-time images of the activity that can be later retrieved for use in an investigation. The need for a security officer to sit for long hours and view monitors with no activity is also eliminated, therefore freeing the officer for other patrol functions, such as a visible perimeter patrol that may serve as a deterrent. In the event of an incident or alarm, the system can transmit information to a remote security officer for his or her attention. Digital video analytics has the potential to monitor movement of people and materials in specific directions, as well as in predetermined zones that are off-limits. Physical

locks, signage, fences, and lighting will remain important for facility protection, but the potential of technology will help improve detection abilities for the industrial security officer while reducing his or her risk of harm or exposure to dangerous circumstances. More information on video analytics is available on the Internet or at http://www.pelco.com/software/videoanalytics/ (offering no particular affiliation or bias regarding Pelco).

References

Bartol, C. R., & Anne, M. (2008). *Criminal behavior: A psychosocial approach* (8th ed.). Upper Saddle River, NJ: Pearson Education Inc.

The Mesothelioma Center. <http:www.mesotheliomacenter.org>.

U.S. Bureau of Labor Statistics. <http://stats.bls.gov>.

SECURITY QUIZ

1. The definition of a hazard specifies those conditions in the physical or natural environment which can harm the security officer.
   a. True
   b. False
2. An example of workplace violence may include when a security officer is surprised and attacked by a burglar in a warehouse.
   a. True
   b. False
3. Environmental risks are unavoidable regardless of the officer's training and self awareness.
   a. True
   b. False
4. Most injuries to security officers are a result of falls.
   a. True
   b. False
5. The security officer must make personal choices in health and fitness to help them adjust to a hazardous environment.
   a. True
   b. False
6. A security officer's supervisor or a member of facility management should be relied upon to identify and communicate all hazardous conditions.
   a. True
   b. False
7. Risk Assessment is a thorough, comprehensive, and ongoing evaluation of the key assets, threats, hazards, vulnerabilities, and procedures in place to protect a facility from loss.
   a. True
   b. False
8. Risky behavior or improper operation of equipment by the security officer are a few examples of environmental hazards.
   a. True
   b. False

9. The most important asset that should be protected within a facility is the security command post.
   a. True
   b. False

10. Durable, safe, comfortable footwear is a key piece of personal safety equipment for the industrial security officer.
    a. True
    b. False

40

Apprehension and Detention Procedures

Richard P. Fiems

CHAPTER OBJECTIVES

- Explore definitions of arrest and implications for security professionals
- Emphasize importance of authority and jurisdiction
- Explore perception of arrest and submission to authority
- Explain importance of reasonableness
- List civil and criminal laws that can get officers in trouble
- Provide a methodology for approaching apprehension and detention

There is probably no topic in the security profession that generates as much discussion and misunderstanding as apprehension and detention. It is not only the source of many complaints by the clients we serve, it can also be the beginning of a very lengthy and costly legal action. For these two reasons alone, it is worth a long look by people in the business. But there are other, more critical reasons: we also have to look at the possibility of injury, and

even death, that could result from a misunderstanding of just how much authority a security officer really has to control the movements of another person. For that reason we have to start from the beginning. We need to look at a few basic definitions.

Black's Law Dictionary defines an arrest as: "To deprive a person of his liberty by legal authority." Note the use of the word "authority." That implies that the person making the arrest has the legal ability to do what they are attempting to do. *Black's* goes on to define an arrest by saying, "Taking, under real or assumed authority, custody of another for the purpose of holding or detaining him to answer to a criminal charge or civil demand."

The second portion of that definition has two big components. First, assuming the authority to do something does not necessarily mean that the authority really exists. The person could be basing the assumption on bad information or they could just be mistaken about the level of authority they have been given. Either way, the end result could be problematic for the officer. Second, all arrests have to be made with the intention of bringing the arrested person before a judge of some type. An arrest of any kind is never made to inconvenience someone, delay their departure, or as a way to get even for some perceived wrong. If there was no intent to take them before a judge, the arrest is unlawful. *Black's* goes on to further define an arrest by saying, "Arrest involves the authority to arrest, the assertion of that authority with the intent to effect an arrest, and the restraint of the person to be arrested."

What this means is that in order for an arrest to be legal and binding, the person making the arrest and the person being arrested both must know the following:

1. The authority to arrest is real.
2. That authority is being intentionally used.
3. The person being arrested must be restrained in some way.

So what does it mean to be restrained? *Black's* definition of an arrest goes on to say: "All that is required for an 'arrest' is some act by an officer indicating his intention to detain or take a person into custody and thereby subject that person to the actual control and will of the officer; no formal declaration of arrest is required." In other words, if someone who assumes the authority to make an arrest indicates by words or by actions that they are taking another person into custody, and that other person believes that they are being taken into custody, an arrest has happened.

This is why police officers are told to make their intention to take someone into custody as clear as possible to the person being arrested. They are trained to tell the person that they are under arrest and then give them clear orders and commands about what they want them to do in order to submit to the custody.

Since citizens are legally required to submit to an arrest by a police officer, this places the citizen in the position of facing charges for resisting if they don't comply. But security officers are not police officers. Security officers have the same authority to make an arrest as a citizen, unless some special circumstances exist.

A "citizen's arrest" is defined by *Black's Law Dictionary* as follows: "A private person as contrasted with a police officer may, under certain circumstances, make an arrest, generally for a felony or a misdemeanor amounting to a breach of the peace."

Security officers generally fall into the category of private citizen. There may be certain instances, such as a local ordinance, that grants certain police and/or arrest authority to a security officer. Your obligation as a professional is to find out what laws and ordinances apply in the place where you are working.

DEVELOPING A WORKING MODEL

The law in most jurisdictions allows for a security officer to detain people when such a detention is for a reason that falls within the security officer's authorized duties. Authorization can come from one or more of three basic places.

1. The law can outline the statutory authority of a security officer within the arena that they are working. That can be a federal, state, or local law. Look for phrases in the law like "special officer," "auxiliary officer," "special police," or "special deputy." Be sure to be very clear of the definition as stated in the law. They can be very specific.
2. The security company that the officer works for can have a contractual agreement with the client for the officers to exercise a certain level or degree of authority on their property. The source of this authority then is the contract that exists between the client and the security company.
3. Authority can also come from a job description for security personnel in a proprietary department. The contract of a particular company or the handbook from a human resources department might contain language that establishes the authority of the officer, too.

The bottom line is simple. It is, and always will be, the responsibility of the individual security officer to get totally familiar with the basis for the authority that they carry with them onto the job. Ask questions, check around, and, by all means, get the verification in writing. This is one area of the job where it will pay huge dividends to do your homework.

WHAT CONSTITUTES AN ARREST?

Being arrested is one of those situations where the perceptions of the arrested person are what really matter. In short, an arrest does not really happen unless the person being arrested submits to the authority of the person making the arrest. A few examples might help make this point.

Let's assume that you are working as a security officer in an area that gives you limited authority to detain trespassers. While you are on walking patrol you meet an elderly lady who has gotten separated from a group that was taking an escorted tour of the facility. You question her about how she came to end up in a restricted area and she is cooperative, but very nervous. While you are trying to sort out the problem so you can locate the rest of the group, you get an emergency call to respond to an accident where someone has been injured. You take off running to the accident after telling the woman to "Wait here!" Forty-five minutes later, you are just finishing up the accident call and you remember the elderly lady. You go back to the restricted area and find her still standing there. She stayed there because she thought she had been arrested. Her background and experiences in life have taught her to respect authority figures and do what they told her to do. The determining factor here is that she *reasonably believed* that she was *not free to leave*. She submitted to your authority. You may not have intended to give the impression that she couldn't leave, but it was reasonable under the circumstances for her to feel the way she did.

Contrast that with a small change in location and subjects. You are on motor patrol in the same facility and you happen across three young boys who are riding skateboards in a clearly posted restricted parking lot. You are on the opposite side of a chain link fence. You stop the boys and tell them to stay where they are. You then drive down the road and through the gate to get into the lot and by the time you get there the three boys are long gone. They took off as soon as you drove away from them to get to the gate. If you did happen to locate them later, you would have a very difficult time getting them charged with trespassing or resisting your authority in any way. They took off like jackrabbits because they did not believe for one second that they were under arrest. There was no arrest because there was no submission to authority.

THE IMPORTANCE OF REASONABLENESS

As with most things legal we find the word *reasonable* popping up in any discussion about apprehension and detention. It is the common-sense standard that you are going to be held to in almost everything that you do as an officer. It has particular application here because we are talking about taking an action that essentially deprives another person of their liberty, even if only for a short time. That is something that has never been taken lightly in a free society. While it may be true that the security profession does not have the same restrictions placed on it as our counterparts on the police department, the standards are still the same.

When we take an action that limits the freedom of another person, we have to make sure that we are acting in a manner that would seem logical and obvious to a reasonable and cautious person.

WHAT GETS SECURITY OFFICERS IN TROUBLE?

When a security officer is placed in the position of having to take control of another person, a world of opportunity for trouble begins to open up. It has to be stressed that the security officer who acts in a reckless or indefensible way will be in for a rough ride. This fact stresses the importance of documentation. Whenever physical contact is made with a citizen, for any reason, the security officer should sit down as soon as possible after the event and write a detailed report about what happened and why they felt that they had to do what they did. Basically, the laws that can cause the problems come from two directions: criminal and civil.

Criminal laws that can get a security officer in trouble

Assault

Contrary to popular belief, at least in most jurisdictions, you do not have to touch someone to be charged with criminal assault. You only have to place another person in a reasonable fear of being battered. Attempting to lay hands on someone and failing to do so can still be classified as an assault. In many cases, all you have to do is have the means at your disposal to commit a battery and communicate to the other person that you intend to do just that. For example, if you yell across a football field that you are going to put someone on the ground and handcuff them, the court would probably not consider that an assault. You were too far away to actually take control of the person and it would not be reasonable for them to think that you could reach all the way across the field and grab them. However, if you were standing right in front of the person, with the handcuffs in your hand, and you made the same statement, it would

be reasonable for them to think that you were going to do what you said. You have the means and the proximity. If you do not have cause to take them into custody, you could be looking at an assault charge.

Battery

Battery is the actual physical touching of a person that is either hurtful or insulting in nature. A reasonable person would think that being taken into custody, which involves being stopped, searched, secured in some way, and not permitted to leave, would be a hurtful or insulting set of circumstances. Once again, this stresses the importance of being right in your assessment of the situation and reasonable in taking the actions that you take.

False Arrest

This involves taking someone into custody without the legal authority to detain. Most jurisdictions, and it is your responsibility to find out the law in the one where you work, will allow for a citizen to take another citizen into custody for an offense, other than a misdemeanor or an ordinance violation, that is committed in the arresting person's presence. In other words, the violation must be a serious one and the person who makes the arrest must have direct knowledge of the commission of the violations. You cannot rely on hearsay or rumors. You can only act on firsthand knowledge.

Civil law violations that can get a security officer in trouble

(*Note:* A civil violation, also known as a tort, does not carry with it the same burden or amount of proof necessary to establish responsibility in court. In criminal court, the State must prove its case "beyond a reasonable doubt." In civil court, the plaintiff must prove their case by a "preponderance of the evidence." Stated another way, guilt in criminal court requires 99% proof. Guilt in civil court requires 50.1% proof. Torts are somewhat easier to prove than crimes.)

1. **Assault.** Once again, the act of placing someone in reasonable fear of being battered. The belief of the victim must be reasonable.
2. **Battery.** This is the intentional touching of someone in a non-consensual, non-privileged manner. Consensual touching means that you have the other person's permission. Privileged touching would be the act of giving someone first aid if they were unconscious.
3. **False imprisonment.** This is the unlawful detention of someone else for no reason, within fixed boundaries.
4. **Malicious prosecution.** This happens when a security officer detains someone with no intention of bringing criminal charges against them, or filing criminal charges without probable cause.
5. **Invasion of privacy.** This is an unjustified intrusion into the privacy or personal business of another person.

What are the keys to avoiding criminal and civil liability? Good human relations and communication skills are a crucial part of the process. But, basically, you can go a long way toward avoiding problems by following these simple guidelines:

1. Do your job in a reasonable manner. Know your responsibilities and know your limitations. Get familiar with the laws and regulations in your area and stick to the rules.
2. Conduct yourself in a reasonable manner. You are doing a job in an arena full of spectators. It is your responsibility to behave as if someone is watching every move that you make. If the time ever comes that you do have to take control of a person, it would be a great benefit to have the witness testify that

you did what you had to do in a tactful and professional manner.
3. Keep detailed notes and records about what happened. It is no secret that memories fade over time. Complaints are seldom filed about an officer's actions right after the incident occurs. It is not unusual for a period of several months to lapse between an incident and a complaint. There is no such thing as too much information in a report describing an apprehension or detention. Be specific and be thorough.
4. Keep your supervisor informed. Any contact between you and a citizen or employee that could be looked upon as confrontational or potentially explosive needs to be reported to the people in your up line (the sooner, the better). Supervisors are not particularly fond of surprises in the first place and late information about what a security officer did or said in a confrontation with someone else will not help your cause at all.

DETENTION AND APPREHENSION METHODOLOGY

What follows is a discussion that centers on tactics. As you know, there is no way that a trainer or teacher can outline a set of tactics that will work in every situation you will encounter as a security officer. So, these are going to be presented to you as tactical guidelines and are intended to get you to think about the situation before things get to the point of having to take physical control of another person. A good team never goes to the competition without a game plan. A good security officer never goes to a situation without a tactical response in hand.

Let's assume that the situation you are dealing with has developed, or degenerated, to the point that you have made the determination, based on the totality of the circumstances, that you have to take physical control of another person. As with most things on the job, the first rule of security work comes into play: Go home healthy at the end of your shift!

1. Get some backup headed your way. The Latin term *non solis* (never alone) should be the first thing that comes to your mind. Often the presence of another security officer will deter someone from resisting or causing further problems. Some departments like to use what is called a "swarming technique" that involves getting as many officers there as they can to aid in the situation. At the very least you should be communicating with your department and should also contact the local police as soon as possible. Remember, *non solis*.

2. Maintain a safe distance and good positioning. You should know what your reactionary gap is. That is the minimum amount of distance that you need to respond to a threatening move made by someone else. Blade your body so that you are balanced and ready and hold your hands up in front of you with your palms facing the person you are dealing with, about shoulder high. This will allow you to protect yourself and deflect an object or a blow if you need to. Leave yourself a way out of the area if you can and try to avoid cornering the other person. You could be injured if they feel that the only way out is through you.

3. Communicate your intentions. Tell the person that they are under arrest or apprehension, whichever is appropriate for your jurisdiction. In many states, the intention to arrest or detain someone must be communicated clearly to the person being detained. It is also possible that they could be held responsible for resisting the arrest if it is made clear to them exactly what the situation is. If the person demands to know why you are detaining them, tell them in as few words as possible. It is not generally necessary for you to be able to quote the law they have violated to them chapter and verse. Just be clear about what you saw them do and your intention to hold them there until the arrival of the police or a supervisor.

4. Give the person simple, direct commands. Do not yell or threaten. Use a calm and clear tone of voice and tell the person what you expect them to do. If you want them in a chair, ask them to "Sit down, please." If you want them to move to another spot in the room, point to the location and simply say, "Over here, please." If they start to shout or become loud say, "Lower your voice, please." You have to maintain a cool and professional demeanor throughout the entire process. The people who are watching should be able to testify that you were not the problem, the other person was. In the interest of your safety, you should not hesitate to say, "Keep your hands where I can see them, please." if they start to reach inside a coat or a pocket. There is not a requirement that I have ever seen that stipulates or even encourages you to do anything that would compromise your safety. So don't.

5. Move in with extreme caution. If you make the determination that the person needs to be placed in handcuffs, you must proceed with a great deal of caution. The closer you get to them, the more vulnerable you are. Handcuffs should only be used when you are convinced that not using them poses a greater threat to your safety or someone else's than letting them stand there until the police arrive. In any event, you must remember that handcuffs are *temporary* restraining devices. They in no way guarantee your safety once they are put on another person. Caution is still the rule. Have the person turn around and face away from you. Tell them to place their hands behind their back with the backs of their hands touching. Grasp their right hand with your right hand and place the handcuff on their right wrist with your left hand. Then

grasp the loose cuff in your right hand and grab their left hand with your left hand. Using your right hand, place the remaining cuff on their left wrist. DO NOT strike their wrist with the handcuff. It looks cool in the movies but it really seldom works without causing harm to the subject you are cuffing. Tighten the cuffs until they are snug, but not so tight as to reduce the person's circulation. ALWAYS lock the cuffs in place! Always!

Handcuffing techniques should be practiced under the watchful eye of a trained instructor. Your goal is to restrain the person as quickly as possible. This is one of those situations where you will most definitely play the way you practice.

THE USE OF FORCE

The most critical time of your professional life will come when you or someone you are protecting is in imminent danger from the actions of another and you have to use force of some kind to protect yourself or them. It is never an easy situation to be in or an easy decision to make. Common sense tells you that the only time you can use force against another person is when there is absolutely no other choice. Security professionals are trained to use the escalating scale, starting with voice commands and moving upward in the scale to physical force if nothing else will work, or clearly would not have worked under the circumstances. Remember, too, that security officers are not authorized to use overpowering force like police officers are. We can use the same kind of force that a citizen can—neutralizing force, and nothing more. When the person we are dealing with stops using force, we have to stop, too. Neutralize; don't overpower.

Prior to the development of that kind of a circumstance, you need to be comfortable with the decision-making process that you have used.

In other words, you have to ask yourself some questions:

1. Was I in imminent (immediate) jeopardy? This has to be clearly established by the circumstances known to you at that point in time.
2. Was someone whom I have a duty to protect in imminent physical jeopardy? What, exactly, is your duty under your orders and rules and regulations?
3. Was my mission as a security officer in imminent jeopardy? Was the action taken to protect property in proportion to the value or criticality of the property itself? In other words, did you behave in a reasonable way given what you were protecting?
4. Did I have any alternatives to using the force that I did? Force can only be used if there is no other way to respond and solving the problem is something that must be done immediately.
5. Is the harm I am trying to prevent greater than the harm I might cause? Property is replaceable, people are not. Deadly force is NEVER permitted to protect property.
6. How will the actions that I took be viewed by others? Was I reasonable? Did I do what needed to be done and nothing more?

These are hard questions. That is why they need to be thought about and mulled over before you find yourself in a situation where force may be required. Your head will need to be clear if the situations call for you to go tactical.

DEALING WITH THE AFTERMATH

If you are careful and reasonable in your apprehension and detention procedures, you are going to be able to justify what you do. But if a complaint is made or a lawsuit is filed, you need to know that you are not going to go into litigation defenseless. The law does provide some rationale for you in building your case. This is called "affirmative defense."

1. **Self-defense.** There is no requirement under law that you have to allow yourself to be attacked. Under law everyone has the right to defend themselves. Just be sure that when you defend yourself, you don't go too far and become the aggressor.

2. **Necessity.** If you shove someone out of the path of a speeding car you have committed a battery. You had to in order to protect them from great harm or death. No court in the world would hear a charge against you for that.

3. **Mistake of fact.** If you are acting in good faith and believe that you are doing something legal and aboveboard, and it turns out that you were misinformed, you have made a mistake of fact. Ignorance of the law has never been an excuse for violating the law, but a good faith mistake defense can still protect you if the circumstances are believable.

The defenses listed above have the effect of taking "intent" out of the equation. If you did not do something in a criminal state of mind you can defend yourself from a claim that you violated a law or committed a tort. The concept of reasonableness still applies.

CONCLUSION

No one really likes the thought of having to take someone else into custody. Hopefully, we can be proactive enough in the way that we do our jobs and we will avoid having to deal with this kind of situation. However, it is your job to be prepared. Keep up with the changes in the law and be very conversant in the rules, regulations, guidelines, and policies of your department when it comes to this subject. You cannot go into one of these situations half prepared and expect that everything is going to be

all right. Murphy's Law has been around since before laws were written. Be ready.

SECURITY QUIZ

1. *Black's Law Dictionary* defines an arrest as: "To deprive a person of his liberty by legal authority."
   a. True
   b. False
2. In order for an arrest to be legal and binding, the person making the arrest and the person being arrested have to know:
   a. The authority to arrest is real
   b. Specifically why the person is being arrested
   c. The person being arrested is not allowed to leave
   d. All of the above
3. Security officers do not have the same authority to make an arrest as a citizen unless some special circumstances exist.
   a. True
   b. False
4. Based on the circumstances a private person may make an arrest for which of the following offenses:
   a. Felonies
   b. Misdemeanors
   c. Breech of the peace
   d. All the above
5. Authorization to make an arrest will come from all the following places except:
   a. Statutory authority
   b. The local Police Department
   c. The contract between the client and the guard company
   d. The security officer's job description
6. Contrary to popular belief, at least in most jurisdictions, you do not have to touch someone to be looking at a criminal assault

charge. You only have to place another person in a reasonable fear of being battered.
a. True
b. False

7. Assault is the intentional touching of someone in a non-consensual, non-privileged manner.
a. True
b. False

8. Guilt in civil court requires what percentage of proof?
a. 99%
b. 75%
c. More than 51%
d. 100%

9. Malicious prosecution happens when a security officer detains someone with the full intention of bringing criminal charges against them, or filing criminal charges without probable cause.
a. True
b. False

10. Under law everyone has the right to defend themselves.
a. True
b. False

RELATIONS WITH OTHERS

CHAPTER

41

Human Relations in a Global Environment

Christopher A. Hertig and
Darrien Davenport

CHAPTER OBJECTIVES

- Define human relations as it relates to the security industry
- Provide relevant advice from Dale Carnegie
- Explain the importance of understanding and respecting diversity
- Outline important practices regarding women in protection and sexual harassment
- Provide tips for effective communication and ethical behavior

HUMAN RELATIONS

Human relations is the study of how humans interact with one another and the residual effect of those interactions. It is based on the continual evolution of human relationships and the ability to extract value from those relationships, whether good or bad. We must understand that we can always grow from human relations, as long as the participants can be open about the experience.

In a practical sense, human relations is the application of knowledge about human behavior to enhance one's job performance. Human relations also aids in one's personal relationships. Within the broad spectrum of human service (teaching, social work, corrections, law enforcement, and security) human relations is a core competency. Protection officers who master it are more effective on the job, as they have an easier time dealing with people.

To be effective investigators, to fulfill the intelligence agent role, protection officers must have excellent human relations skills. They must be approachable. People must feel comfortable talking with them. Maintaining honest and open relations with others is one key to this. There must be trust in the relationships officers have with others. *Trust is the glue that holds civilization together.*

Being optimistic and positive is very important. The old saying "no one buys anything that is negative" is very true. In a crisis, protection officers must be the ones inspiring others. Overall, having a positive attitude and making positive remarks will aid an officer.

Greeting employees and others in the workplace is generally a good policy. The slightest acknowledgment of others helps to form a bond with them and these are the people that officers must convince to follow the rules, obey commands in emergencies, and provide information when something is amiss.

Part of good human relations involves thinking before speaking. Know what to say before saying anything. This is especially important when dealing with others who are in crisis, when addressing a group of people (a crowd of some sort), or when enforcing rules. Also, avoid flaunting your background. Some people in the protection business have a tendency to boast or brag about their job qualifications. It is not uncommon to hear people mentioning their prior job experience in the military or law enforcement while they are employed within the security industry.

ADVICE FROM THE MASTER

Dale Carnegie could easily be called the "Master of Human Relations." His time-tested principles have been taught to untold numbers of people. Salesmen, managers, coaches, and many others who must work with people have taken his advice and benefited from it. His principles are as follows:

Principle 1. Become genuinely interested in other people.
Principle 2. Smile.
Principle 3. Remember that a person's name is to that person the sweetest and most important sound in any language.
Principle 4. Be a good listener. Encourage others to talk about themselves.
Principle 5. Talk in terms of the other person's interests.

Principle 6. Make the other person feel important—and do it sincerely.

Carnegie's principles may be applied to virtually any human interaction. Certainly interviewers will want to employ them to develop rapport with the interviewee.

Additionally, developing a relationship with people in one's work environment, where the people will feel comfortable talking to the officer, is very important. Such a relationship facilitates the employee, student, or guest informing the officer about unusual conditions or situations. Protection officers may find that when employees talk about their job functions, they provide valuable information. Principles 4, 5, and 6 may all relate to discussion about job functions. By understanding what occurs on the job for employees, the officer is better able to see if something is out of the ordinary.

DIVERSITY

The concept of diversity refers to recognizing differences in others and embracing the ways these differences can enrich us as individuals. People who experience other cultures gain a tremendous amount of understanding. They see "the other side" of things. They can begin to appreciate the different perspectives that other cultures bring.

Too often, society focuses on the negative aspect of diversity and the differences that drive us apart, instead of focusing on those differences which complement us and bring value to the overall community. Diverse experiences aid in seeing situations from various perspectives. A fuller, more complete view of things is achieved. Diverse perspectives aid in creative problem solving.

Successful leaders value diversity. They use it to their advantage, channeling the creativity that comes with it to aid in planning and problem solving. Strong, successful leaders thrive on diverse input from subordinates. They realize the value it holds and are not intimidated or alienated by it. One example of a leader who valued diverse opinion was the American World War II General George Patton, Jr. General Patton sought diverse perspectives from among his staff. A quote that has been attributed to him is: "If everyone is thinking alike, someone isn't thinking."

As good leaders value diversity, so, too, do many employers. Organizations in the public, private, and nonprofit sectors are attempting to hire a diverse segment of people. Many organizations now have a Director of Diversity or Multiculturalism who develops diversity within the workplace.

Unfortunately, we all inherently have prejudices. We tend to feel most comfortable with people who are most like us. We usually associate with those who look, talk, and dress like we do. Those who share our physical and cultural characteristics are those we understand. Those who are different from us are those we do not understand. Those things that we have not seen before, or which we do not understand, can frighten us. The more unfamiliar the culture is to us, the more we are likely to misunderstand it.

Farivar (2009) discusses his exposure to American society, a culture that was in stark contrast to his native Afghanistan. He grew up in a tribal society where there were close family relationships. His cousins were his best friends. Outsiders were viewed with suspicion. Religion was a very large part of life, with prayers said several times per day. Men wore beards. Women's arms and legs were covered; there was no exposed skin.

Once he became a college student in America, the culture clash was quite extensive. In Afghanistan, men would hold each other's hand. In America, this was not done, and such behavior was considered a sign of homosexuality. People wore shorts in warm weather with their arms and legs exposed. Few men had beards, and at his college, the wearing of his flat

woolen pakol hat was not allowed in the classroom. He saw his roommates, naked bodies in the shower, something that would not occur in Afghanistan.

Farivar's experience illustrates the adjustments necessary in dealing with two very different cultures. He learned from the experience of studying and working in the United States. From this experience, he was able to launch a career as a successful journalist, weaving together his Afghan and American experiences.

Name-calling is significantly negative and represents a substantial step toward the development of extensive prejudice. Derogatory names represent the prejudice that is behind their use. Using them also tends to shape our views of the people we use them about. Obviously, there is no place in a professional setting for name-calling. Doing so can set the stage for further negative behavior.

Be careful to avoid the "us versus them" syndrome. This can develop when dealing with distinctly different cultures, as well as the cultural differences between various groups in the work environment. It can also develop when enforcing rules upon a specific cultural group. Members of the group might not obey the rules, or may give the protection officer a hard time, leading to conflict that can be deemed cultural conflict. If there is the slightest inclination of prejudice present, it gets magnified through daily interactions. Continuously experiencing problems, such as noncompliance from a particular group, builds upon the existing prejudice.

Protection personnel in a shopping center may encounter elderly persons on a regular basis. Conflict may result when the elderly persons have different expectations than the younger security personnel. Security personnel at that same shopping center may also deal with youths who are members of particular ethnic groups. When the youths are of another ethnicity, it is quite easy to attribute any adolescent misbehavior as a product of that ethnic background, rather than a general conflict due to age and immaturity.

Other groups within the work environment may be those established not due to race, ethnicity, age, or gender, but, rather, their job status or function. Students, guests, contractor employees, visitors, and so on are all categories of facility/environment users that may be the subject of prejudice by security personnel.

There are many negative behaviors that may occur due to discrimination. A concern for American police and security forces is racial profiling. This is the targeting of an individual because of their race, skin color, religion, or appearance. Police officers have been accused of stopping a disproportionate number of African American men for traffic violations, which has come to be known as the offense of "driving while Black." Retail loss prevention agents have also been known to focus on African American shoplifters. An old scheme used by some professional shoplifters was the "salt and pepper" team. This consisted of a white and a black shoplifter. The African American shoplifter was watched by the retail security personnel. This served as a diversion and allowed the white team member to steal.

Magill (2003) found that racial profiling by retail loss prevention staff was counterproductive for several reasons. One was that, if customers from a certain demographic group felt as though they were discriminated against, they would avoid shopping in that store. Many good customers would be lost. Additionally, there is the threat of a civil suit due to discrimination claims. This can be a substantial loss, as the attendant legal costs and negative publicity may be quite extensive. Perhaps more importantly, focusing on a particular ethnic group deprives the investigator of professional objectivity. The reality is that people from all cultures steal. Focusing on only one group takes the agent's attention away from those who are actually stealing.

Obviously, prejudice against one group of people is due to the convergence of many factors. Reinforcement of prejudice by coworkers and

supervisors can play a role. So, too, can working long hours where one becomes tired and irritable. Intense exposure to uncooperative persons is another. An obvious example of this would be a protection officer working at a demonstration or strike.

Another concern regarding the development of an "us versus them" workplace subculture is the abuse of force. When one does not understand another and is frustrated, there may be a temptation to use more force than is necessary. When one dislikes someone due to their membership in a particular group, there is a tendency to use force. And when one is afraid of someone because of what they do not understand, applied force may be driven by fear of the unknown—not for any legitimate reason.

All of these factors may magnify prejudice the officer has. Without the presence of prejudice in the first place, the factors may not be as significant. Quite simply, the presence of prejudice is where the problem begins.

An individual must recognize that they have prejudice concerning different groups of people. Once they recognize their preconceived notions, they can take the time to educate themselves to break that mental barrier. We live in an age where knowledge and education are readily available to us, and for free! There is no excuse for not knowing or understanding those who may be different than we are, be they of different races, religions, ages, or cultures.

An individual can prepare for encountering another culture by doing homework on that culture. This will help the individual to become comfortable with it and know what is or is not offensive. Cultural awareness is the key to good human relations. Studying the history of other cultures is a good start. History helps to explain why a group of people think as they do, and why they have the customs they do. Holidays and celebrations generally mark an event of historical significance. Knowing about the holidays and what they represent offers a clue to understanding a culture.

GLOBALIZATION

Globalization is the inevitable intertwining of cultural expansion and economic development. It is also the generational relative of industrialism and colonialism, which preceded it and had a similar impact on the world. Globalization, then, is not entirely new, but it is taking a new form.

The search for global markets has meant that business has moved into different countries. This was initiated to a large degree by the development of standard-size shipping containers. These containers became increasingly common in the decades after the 1950s. Their use revolutionized commercial shipping. Before the advent of containers, shipping was expensive in terms of man-hours and time in rail terminals, trucking facilities, and ports. Once all of the cargo was handled in a container, moving it from truck to rail car, or ship to truck, was much simpler. Note that the use of the containers also reduced the incidence of pilferage. Loss due to both waste (time) and crime (theft) was reduced.

Once the use of standard-size containers became a universal practice, the cost of shipping dropped dramatically (Krepinevich, 2009). Just-in-time manufacturing also took hold. This method works by only manufacturing items when they are needed. Waste in warehousing costs was reduced. Combined with the just-in-time manufacturing, reduced shipping costs also increased the efficiency of supply and manufacture. Inventory levels and costs were reduced. Manufacturers began to shop around to see where they could obtain parts more cheaply.

As a result, global supply chains developed. This pushed the world toward a global economy. The Internet pushed it even further, with electronic commerce occurring almost instantaneously throughout the world at a very low cost.

A global economy creates a series of interdependencies. One aspect of asset protection is a focus on supply chains. Supply chains are increasingly complex. The finished product consumed by an end user is manufactured in different places around the globe. Raw materials may come from one country. They are then shipped to another, where they are processed or refined and even assembled. They may then go to a third country, where the distribution chain begins. Obviously, there are innumerable opportunities for interruptions in the global supply chain. Cargo theft, hijacking, piracy, major storms, civil unrest, labor disputes, and so on are all concerns. They move the focus of business—and security—to an international level.

Corporations have sought out partnerships with foreign entities. There are varied reasons for doing this besides reduced shipping costs. Better service of a local market may be one factor. Cheaper manufacturing costs may be another. The presence of large markets and economic growth also propels global trade. Economies in some countries are expanding quite rapidly. Some Asian countries offer a steadily increasing number of customers for various goods and services. Businesses see the future customers and reach out to them. Partnerships, contracts, and the opening of overseas facilities are the natural consequence.

Globalization is not limited to the commercial arena. Politically and militarily, there is a globalization trend taking place. The need for energy sources, such as oil and natural gas, fuels an international interest by foreign countries that depend on those commodities. Precious minerals also create a need for stable relations between the countries that have the minerals and those who use them in manufacturing. As one country develops an interest in what is occurring in another country, it may station troops there, train the host country's armed forces, and so on. The fight against terrorism requires some degree of military presence in other countries so that the local situation can at least be monitored.

Failed states that are rife with poverty, large numbers of unemployed young men, and the right motivation (religious, political, charismatic leadership, etc.) may become breeding grounds for terrorism. The upsurge in piracy on the seas is also caused, in large part, by high unemployment;

indeed, pirates have historically been out-of-work mariners. With globalization, there will be economic growing pains underwritten by cultural differences. There are also the wounds inflicted by industrialism and colonialism. Some developing countries have a bad taste in their mouths from the days when they were exploited by another power. We must study their history and appreciate their perspective.

WOMEN IN PROTECTION

Women have played some significant roles in policing and security over the years. They have also, however, faced a tremendous amount of prejudice. In policing, women were often given jobs dealing with female prisoners or juveniles. In some security applications, they were used as receptionists. They have experienced "the glass ceiling" in terms of promotion: failing to rise in the ranks due to discrimination and lack of access to male colleagues in personal social settings (the men's room, the locker room, etc.). Child care responsibilities have also impeded their progress, in some instances.

Fortunately, women have made tremendous strides within society as a whole, assuming leadership positions in both government and corporate organizations. Nonprofit organizations often have women at the helm. The International Association of Chiefs of Police has had a female president. Over the years, ASIS International has had several female presidents.

Allan Pinkerton, founder of the Pinkerton National Detective Agency, employed the first female investigator in the Western world. Kate Warne worked for the agency beginning in the late 1850s. She was instrumental in solving many cases and was Pinkerton's "right-hand man," so to speak. Pinkerton saw that women could play roles that men could not. He used women in surveillance and undercover operations. A woman can pose as a secretary or administrative assistant in a protective service

detail. Females can also assume planning roles in executive/VIP protection. They can coordinate trips, do advance work, and so on.

Women have faced discrimination, but are increasingly taking on leadership positions in protective service. There have been recent movements to utilize women in protective roles. One of these is as door supervisors in nightclubs. While the traditional brawny male is what most people expect, a woman can easily check identification, greet customers, and control access. In a similar vein, women can relate to females better than men. The U.S. Army has developed a female unit in Afghanistan for this very purpose. The female unit can obtain better intelligence than a male unit would if they attempted to converse with women. In 2009, the International Foundation for Protection Officers trained the first female security officers in the Kingdom of Saudi Arabia.

SEXUAL HARASSMENT

One type of discrimination that females face is sexual harassment. Sexual harassment in the workplace is nothing new. In years past, the classic type of harassment, known as quid pro quo, occurred quite often. It was where sexual favors were requested in exchange for a promotion, pay raise, better assignment, improved work resources, and so on.

Obviously, this was and is wrong. What has transpired is that another, more common type of sexual harassment, known as "hostile environment" has emerged. This occurs when someone is subjected to offensive language, drawings, and so on. They may get offensive e-mails or see pornographic Web sites being viewed by others in the workplace. Sometimes, a hostile environment takes the form of jokes and banter around the workplace. In traditionally male-dominated workplaces, this is a common problem. People say things that are offensive, sometimes with the knowledge that they are doing so, and sometimes unintentionally. In some cases, the creation of a hostile environment is unintentional, and in other cases, it is deliberate.

A simple test of whether or not behavior or language is offensive is to ask these four questions:

1. Would I feel comfortable if my behavior was on the six o'clock news?
2. Would I want my wife, sister, or mother to hear what I am about to say?
3. Would I want the joke or remark I am about to say to be written down or videotaped?
4. Would I be embarrassed to discuss my language or behavior with my supervisor or someone else in management?

It is sound practice to become familiar with your organization's sexual harassment policy and complaint procedure. This helps to prevent violating the policy, as well as being able to play the proper role with the policy. Someone may tell a security officer about an incident of sexual harassment. It may also occur that someone will mention a suspected sexual harassment that they think has happened to someone else. Knowing the policy is essential. Following proper procedure is the next step.

Sexual harassment is a civil wrong under federal and state laws. It is a form of discrimination, but may also be pursued as a tort action (assault and/or battery) in some extreme cases. While, in general, the liability attaches to the employer as a form of discrimination, in some instances, the person doing the harassing can also be charged with one of the above-named tort actions.

Note that in cases in which the harassment has been ongoing and the employer did not take adequate steps to resolve it, the amount of monetary damages can be quite extensive. Judgments in the millions of dollars have been awarded in cases in which there has been a long-standing or widespread pattern of harassment going on. The negative publicity surrounding such large awards drives employee recruitment costs higher. It also negatively impacts attracting new customers to the organization.

EFFECTIVE COMMUNICATION

Effective communication is a useful tool for any protection officer who wants to further their professional development. Effective communication can serve to resolve a conflict, provide personal direction, or educate others. Educating personnel in the work environment becomes increasingly important as new concerns and threats emerge. Security and safety awareness is a dynamic, ongoing process that calls on officers to send the right messages.

When communication is used correctly, an officer can gain the trust and respect of their audience, while delivering a message that may be detrimental to the receiver. This is what makes the communication "effective." Officers do not have to be the most articulate, charismatic individuals in order to communicate effectively, but must exhibit confidence while communicating their message. In a multicultural environment, it is important that the officer also use inclusive language, which means using language or speech that is comprehensive and makes the audience feel comfortable with the communicator. This will build a level of comfort with the audience. The officer also must use a filter when communicating with one or multiple individuals. In other words, communicate with a sense of impartiality and use terminology that is not offensive or discriminatory. The protection officer's ability to effectively communicate will also be enhanced by active listening. It is imperative that an officer is able to listen to their audience attentively in order to communicate properly. If not, either the officer or the audience might misunderstand what is being communicated, which can lead to distrust of parties on either side.

ETHICAL BEHAVIOR

The concept of ethics is valuable in the security industry, and displaying ethical behavior in the workplace will provide a protection officer with a reputation of being respected, both internally and externally. This does not mean that any given outcome will always be positive in nature, but it does imply that the officer will take the appropriate ethical steps to determine the outcome.

Ethical behavior is also important to be successful in a multicultural workforce. A protection officer will benefit by following the ethical code of their organization, or cultivating their own beliefs, so long as they are in line with the value system of their employer or client. They should be discouraged from using a personal ethical code if those "ethics" will result in discrimination against a class of people. Ethical behavior takes professional courage, self-accountability, and the ability to manage relationships on all levels. Ethical behavior does not only mean self-governance; a protection officer may find him or herself in a situation where he or she has to account for a colleague's ethical (or unethical) actions. The ability to provide ethical sustenance to coworkers may also be a measurement of an officer's own ethical behavior.

One particular aspect of ethics and diversity revolves around the "war on terror." Persons suspected of terrorist activity, or of simply sympathizing with terrorists, may be mistreated. Police and security personnel believe that they are involved in helping society at large, and generally, they are. Unfortunately, they may use this concept of the greater good to justify discriminatory, unethical, or illegal actions. At times, a dose of empathy can be applied to gain perspective. Putting oneself in the other person's shoes may help provide some perspective of fairness.

CUSTOMER SERVICE LEADERSHIP

Countless individuals will rely on a protection officer to provide them with some form of protection. The greatest asset is the customer, as they are the sole reason for an officer's professional existence. In a multicultural world, leadership ability can determine if the officer has the aptitude and capacity to protect that asset.

The customer does not always have to be right, but the customer *must always* be protected. There is a vast difference between an officer who *manages* situations and an officer who *leads* through situations. Often, an officer who manages attempts to apply the same systematic approach to each customer's issue; an officer who leads is able to assess a situation, explore various options, and then come to a solution to fit that particular issue.

The officer must listen well, assess the issue, and then find a path toward resolving it. They must lead the customer to a solution. Leadership, particularly when applied to customer service, is partnership. True leadership is for the benefit of the followers, not that of the leaders (Ortmeier, 1999).

Solving a problem for some protection officers can be an issue in itself. If you find yourself in a situation where your experience and/or training still do not provide you with the solution to an issue, find someone who can help lead you to the solution. Part of being a leader means locating resources to make up for one's own deficiencies. By no means does this negate who the officer is, as a leader or protection officer, but it demonstrates that they have the wherewithal to provide their customer with the service that they committed to.

Another key to customer service leadership is availability. Due to silos, it can be difficult for a protection officer to meet the needs of his or her customer. A silo is an intangible barrier created by an individual that prohibits them from being exposed to new ideas or experiences. Silos can create barriers in communication between individuals or departments, which can lead to impotent and ineffective relationships. Often, silos are created to protect traditional processes, procedures, or beliefs, but unbeknownst to the silo builder(s), they are stymieing their own development. It is important to remember that silos can lead to individuals or departments becoming obsolete as they willingly reject what is necessary for personal or professional preservation.

Security is the "grease in the machine"—it touches all parts of the organization and helps it to run more smoothly. When assets are protected, investigations are initiated, or emergencies are responded to, security personnel work across department lines. Obviously, there is no room for a silo.

SUMMARY

Security personnel are obligated to help and protect all persons in their work setting. They cannot prejudge people or discriminate against them. A customer is a customer, an employee is an employee, and a victim is a victim. A person needing assistance is just that; they need help. It must be given promptly and professionally. That is what professional protection officers do: they help.

Discriminatory behavior toward others is unprofessional and unproductive. It is therefore unacceptable. The bottom line of human relations is: *Treat people the way that you would want to be treated.*

EMERGING TRENDS

More employers want a diverse workforce. This is evidenced by recruitment efforts, the establishment of positions such as Diversity Director, and so on. At the end of the day, most of us will work in or with organizations that are more diverse than at present.

Protection officers, particularly those employed by security service firms, are expected to be better at customer service. There is a greater appreciation of the role that protection officers play in dealing with the public, specifically diverse groups of people. Immigration trends demand that officers be able to work with groups from other countries. Demographic trends mandate that protection officers be able to relate to the elderly and the disabled.

Legal protection for members of certain groups is expanding, and will likely continue to do so. This protection may take various forms, such as recognizing a new minority as a protected group. It may occur at the municipal or state level, as well as the national or federal level. A city may add gay persons as a protected group. A state human relations commission may begin to recognize discrimination against those with disabilities. Hate crime legislation is but one example of expanded legal consequences for discriminatory behavior. After the assassination of Martin Luther King Jr. in 1968, laws were enacted in almost all states that increased penalties for crimes committed as a result of hatred against people based on ethnicity or religion.

U.S. President Barack Obama signed hate crime legislation that extended coverage to people based on sexual orientation in October 2009. This legislation expands federal hate crimes to include those committed against people due to their gender, sexual orientation, gender identity, or disability.

With the increasing demand for professional officers in metropolitan settings, it is necessary for today's protection officer to be well educated and astute to the issues surrounding the audience that they protect. To maximize their skills, officers will have to acknowledge that "future policing in large part will depend on the type of society being policed—the social, economic, and political realities and, in more-developed countries, the technological sophistication of the populace" (Stephens, 2005, p. 51). Awareness of this will help professional officers to better oversee populations that they protect, especially those that are culturally diverse. Education is the key and is an emerging trend in today's security society. The educational standard for professional officers is increasing, and more training is being provided to professional officers to prepare them for their roles in the community. This includes diversity training.

When it comes to emerging trends, some experts focus specifically on growing technologies. The use of technology in a multicultural world will impact many areas, whether used for protecting the public, educating officers, or preventing crime. According to law enforcement professional Tom Cowper, "Technology will create a rapidly changing social environment to which police will have to adapt. At the same time, technology will permit radical new policing methods, systems, and processes that police will have to envision, create, incorporate, and learn" (Stephens, 2005, p. 51). This will be of importance as protection officers identify trends and cultural similarities in order to protect the innocent. This should, by no means, provide a protection officer with a "license" to culturally profile individuals; technology should be used as a tool to secure those investing in the services of professional officers. The new tools must be used ethically.

Supply chain security is a rapidly growing area for both corporations and governments. In a global economy, supply chains become longer and more complex. Security personnel working in some aspect of supply chain protection are likely to increase in number due to the effects of terrorism, organized crime, piracy, political upheaval, and natural disasters.

References

Carnegie, D. (1936). *How to win friends and influence people*. New York, NY: Simon & Schuster.

Farivar, M. (2009). *Confessions of a mullah warrior*. New York, NY: Atlantic Monthly Press.

Feller, B. (2009, October 29). New law a victory for gay community. *York Daily Record* 2A (October 29).

Kaplan, R. D. (2005). *Imperial grunts: The American military on the ground*. New York, NY: Random House.

Krepinevich, A. F. (2009). *7 Deadly scenarios: A military futurist explores war in the 21st century*. New York, NY: Bantam Dell.

Magill, M. (2003). *Racial profiling in retail—Myth or reality*. New Orleans, LA: ASIS International (September 15).

Ortmeier, P. J. (1999). *Public safety and security administration*. Woburn, MA: Butterworth-Heinemann.

Purpura, P. P. (2002). *Security and loss prevention: An introduction*. Woburn, MA: Butterworth-Heinemann.

Stephens, G. (2005). Policing the future: Law enforcement's new challenges. *The Futurist*, 39(2), 51.

Resources

The Human Resources Department in most organizations will have information related to diversity and multicultural relations. The Society of Human Relations Management (www.shrm.org) may also be able to assist in the research effort.

There are a number of books that may aid in studying diversity and multiculturalism. A few of them are:

The World's Religions (Huston Smith)

The Diversity Toolkit (William Sonneschein)

Kiss, Bow, or Shake Hands (Terri Morrison and Wayne A. Conaway)

Diversity Consciousness: Opening our Minds to People, Cultures and Opportunities (Richard Bucher and Patricia Bucher)

Understanding and Managing Diversity (Carol Harvey and M. June Allard)

The Web site (www.DiversityInc.com) has various resources relating to diversity issues.

AST Corporation (www.hits@astcorp.com) has online instructional programs for law enforcement and security personnel. Some of these programs discuss diversity and multicultural issues.

360 Training (www.360training.com) offers programs for security personnel dealing with diversity and related issues.

The Professional Security Training network provides programs on sexual harassment, diversity, etc. Visit www.pstn.com.

SECURITY QUIZ

1. In a multicultural world, what type of language must a protection officer use to gain the trust of their audience?
   a. Invasive
   b. Inclusive
   c. Inquisitive
   d. Terse

2. The protection officer's ability to effectively communicate will also be enhanced by _____ listening.
   a. Active
   b. Effective
   c. Selective
   d. All of the above

3. In a multicultural world, leadership ability can determine if a protection officer has the aptitude and capacity to protect their customer.
   a. True
   b. False

4. Future policing will depend in large part on the type of society being policed—the _____, _____, _____ realities and, in more developed countries, the technological sophistication of the populace.
   a. Situational, intellectual, and familial
   b. Ethical, political, and multicultural
   c. Legal, societal, and personal
   d. Social, economic, and political

5. Globalization has grown largely due to the lowering of shipping costs.
   a. True
   b. False

6. Sexual harassment has traditionally taken the form of a hostile environment.
   a. True
   b. False

7. Women in protection are taking on more leadership roles than ever before. There is, however, a _____ ceiling that prevents them from being promoted beyond a certain level.
   a. Raised
   b. Glass
   c. Plastic
   d. Acoustic

8. The first female investigator was Kate Warne.
   a. True
   b. False

9. Racial profiling in retail is counterproductive as it:
   a. May alienate customers who belong to the group being watched
   b. Take the loss prevention agent's attention away from actual thieves
   c. May result in civil litigation
   d. All of the above

10. Supply chain security is a rapidly growing area for both corporations and government.
    a. True
    b. False

42

Public Relations

Charles T. Thibodeau, Christopher A. Hertig, and
George A. Barnett

CHAPTER OBJECTIVES

- Definition of public relations
- Importance of projecting a positive image
- List ten qualities of public relations officers
- Promoting effective customer relations in the department
- Being other-people-centered, not self-centered
- Having a "can-do" attitude
- Positive media relations
- Risk analysis and public relations

PUBLIC RELATIONS DEFINED

Public relations consists of a mutual understanding between an organization and its constituent publics (*Encyclopedia Americana*, 1995). The term *"publics"* is defined as the general community, the people as a whole, or a group of people sharing a common interest (*American Heritage Dictionary*, 1973). With respect to security, we define the term "public" as a group of people sharing a common interest relative to our work environment, plus the general public. The actual people we come in contact with changes from work site to work site, with the exception of one constant—the general public.

If we are working in entertainment security, where crowd management is the main responsibility, we have a very broad and diverse constituency. If we are working in executive protection, we deal with a much more restricted group of people. However, no matter what the primary responsibility is, and no matter who our primary constituency is, the general public has an interest in how we perform our duties.

For the sake of example, assume we are security at a factory. Our primary constituency would be the employees who work for the company, and any number of vendors, repair persons, and other visitors. However, we cannot forget the general public. The factory is located in a community, and is an integral part of that community. The community has a number of interests, including health interests, financial interests, image interests, and so on.

Health interests can be in the form of working conditions within the factory that may make employees from the community sick or injured.

There may be toxic smoke belching from the factory, reducing air quality in the community. Either of these conditions would be of great concern to those affected by the factory, and would result in very poor public relations.

The financial interest might be in form of a paycheck for employees who live in the community, resale of the products made in the factory to members of the community, or sales of raw materials to the factory by other businesses in the community. This would have a positive impact on the community, and therefore, would result in very good public relations.

As for image, if a factory is making bombs for the military, it projects a different image in a community than a factory that is making baby formula or toys for children. The community may become quite disturbed having a bomb factory in their backyard, and they may revolt. Thus, the venture of the business will have either a positive or negative image in the community that reflects directly on public relations.

No matter what the business is involved in, the security officer is many times the "out front" person for that company, frequently the first contact that anyone will have with the company, and therefore must pay particular attention to the topic of public relations. Based on the wide variety of responses the general public may have to your company, first contact could be anything from very friendly to very unfriendly. Therefore, a sincere "How can I help you?" must be permanently at the ready when making first contact. Being a helper, a pleaser, and a "can-do" problem solver are the traits of a successful public relations-minded security professional.

PUBLIC RELATIONS PLANNING

In maintaining a good public image, the security officer must not only look professional and perform in a reasonable and necessary manner, but must also appear truly concerned, speak with a pleasant and polite voice inflection, and show respect. The officer must make the person being served feel like his or her needs are very important, and that they are about to receive superior service. Most importantly, the officer must come to the job equipped with the skills to deliver what is promised. All of these things are part of a well-planned public relations program.

Alone, the security department cannot carry out a successful public relations program. The entire parent or client organization must be involved. However, the security contingent has no control over the entire company, and is not responsible for what other departments in the company do. Security officers can only be responsible for their own conduct. In the area of public relations, the security contingent must conduct themselves in a planned and organized fashion, sometimes with blinders on. It would be most unfortunate if the security contingent followed bad examples set by those in other departments.

To accomplish the goal of projecting a positive image, the security contingent must first have a quality program in place. Image is meaningless if it is a false veneer. Once this is done, the Ten Rules of Public Relations in Private Security can be applied.

1. "The customer is not always right or wrong."

While you may disagree with this from a security perspective, the most important thing to remember is to never tell the person with whom you are dealing that they are wrong. It is to the benefit of all concerned that the security officer work toward a position of mutual cooperation and prevent all situations from escalating into a win-lose proposition. The person you are dealing with must be skillfully redirected into appropriate behavior, not bullied. This person must, as often as possible, leave a situation feeling that they were well served by the advice and assistance they received from the attending officer. This is not to say that self-defense and defense of others will never be the case for the officer. We mean to say here that you will probably go in the "direction your nose is pointed," so keep things upbeat and positive. The officer must be a part of the solution, not a part of the problem!

2. Know your department's capabilities, as well as other departments' capabilities.

Successful salespeople always know their product inside and out. They are then in the position to continuously fit the product and service to the needs of the purchaser. A good security officer should be able to do the same. However, it is not good enough for the security officer to only know his or her products and services; the truly successful protection officer will know every other departments' products and services as well. This will be a valuable asset in situations where a referral to another department is required. Thus, the successful public relations-minded security officer will spend many hours studying the inner workings of the organization he or she is assigned to protect.

3. Always accentuate the positive.

People do not want to hear negative things; in many cases, the negative is obvious and needs no introduction. If you emphasize the positive aspects of your service or the situation, you will seldom go wrong. If you emphasize the negative, you will be treated accordingly.

4. Image is a valuable asset.

Organizations spend considerable amounts of time and money developing and maintaining a certain image. Single negative events can destroy that image. Chronic unprofessional job behaviors can erode it. The image you project as a representative of the company you work for can, and will, help to mold the company's image. Included in the image-building perspective of a security officer are the following 10 behavioral goals (PSTN, nd):

1. Be dependable.
2. Be courteous.
3. Show interest and concern.
4. Use tact.
5. Be discreet.
6. Respect confidences.
7. Be impartial.
8. Be calm.
9. Be patient.
10. Be helpful.

5. Remember that the most powerful advertising is negative customer service.

People who are dissatisfied with an organization's service tell their friends and associates—lots of them! This interpersonal message sending is very powerful. You can achieve 10 great tasks of service in a day, but one cross word or failure to satisfy someone will be the service task remembered far into the future. You cannot afford to fail in the arena of public relations. You may not be successful in every attempt to help, but the person you were trying to serve must be convinced that you did everything possible. If you can achieve this level of success, you have not failed that person.

6. Be attentive to the other person's needs.

Each person has his or her own individual needs. Find out what they are, and do what you can to address them. You may feel that this is a bit like soliciting work and you have enough to do already without asking people to give you more. However, with a little gentle coaxing, you can get a reluctant person to express what it is they are really after. Serving their needs will be very well received and a great boost to the public relations record of the department.

7. Never "cut someone off cold."

When someone asks for assistance or information, and you are not able to help that person immediately, ask the person to let you get back to him or her after you have researched the problem. Then do so. Ask others for assistance, do the research, and solve the problem. Help that person. Remove the following phrases from your vocabulary:

- "No, we do not do that."
- "No, we cannot help you with that."
- "It is not security's job."

8. When you can help someone, seize the opportunity and do it.

Whenever possible, help others. If necessary, volunteer to help them. This can make a lasting impression. It can also be a deterrent to crime, as it puts would-be criminals on notice that someone is aware of their presence and behavior. Be friendly; do not be afraid to speak with those who seem to be in need. If helping someone will not create other problems, then there is no acceptable reason for not doing so.

9. Have something tangible to give the person.

People like to receive things. Even if the tangible item is of little consequence, people seem to be pleased whenever you put something in their hands. Just as the salesman is able to respond to requests for literature on the product he is selling, so must the security officer have brochures, maps, phone books, or even handwritten instructions. No good salesman would do any less, and neither should you.

10. Have a "can-do" attitude.

The U.S. Navy Seabees have a motto: "Can-do." They say they can do anything if given enough time, and the impossible takes just a little longer. What a great motto for your department to follow. Eliminate the words "can't do", and replace them with the words "can do." Whenever a person comes to you with a request, just say "Yes!" Then figure out how you will serve that person's needs. Pride yourself in being able to do the impossible when it comes to serving others. This does not eliminate the need for referral of some requests to other departments. However, always try to check back to see if the person received adequate service from your referral.

PROMOTING EFFECTIVE CUSTOMER RELATIONS WITHIN THE SECURITY FORCE

There are a number of steps that security supervisors can take to enhance the customer relations capabilities of their subordinates.

1. To start with, the supervisor's basic personnel management skills should be effective enough to minimize the "malcontent syndrome." Security officers should not be forced to work long hours without relief, miss out on vacations or days off, or be constantly given less-than-desirable assignments.
2. Security supervisors should conduct an inspection and briefing of each shift prior to that shift going on duty and "on stage." Security supervisors should take this opportunity, whether it is done formally in groups or informally with individual officers. This inspection should include a physical inspection of equipment, officer appearance, and officer demeanor. It should also include an evaluation which shows that each officer knows what has happened during previous shifts and what is happening that day on the work site.
3. Brief each department member on current events within the work site, as well as on current problems and changes in procedures. This helps to make the protection force members function as ambassadors for the organization.
4. In addition to this daily refresher training, supervisors should make certain that the following work behaviors are adopted by all security force members during periodic staff meetings or other methods of professional development:
   a. Have necessary references at the ready. These may include staff directories, maps, telephone books, procedures, and anything else that the person you serve is likely to inquire about.

b. Be ready and capable of responding to security problems, such as fires, bomb threats, disorderly persons, and other critical incidents, in a prompt and professional manner. **Developing proficiency in dealing with people in crisis is a good investment for anyone in security.**

c. Present a professional appearance at all times. Neatness and precision should be obvious attributes of all security officers, easily seen by even the most casual observer. Alertness, openness, and concern must be radiated by posture and behavior.

d. Be prepared to do the job by having the necessary tools for the job. Always have a pen—or better yet, two pens—and a small notepad to write down important notes or to give someone directions. Never come to work without a watch, a small pocket knife, and a pocket flashlight. If your job calls for other hardware, such as keys, handcuffs, mace, or defensive weapons, be sure they are all in place on the utility belt and in top operating condition.

e. Two additional pieces of equipment that project the image of security are the officer's ID card and two-way radio. The ID card should be worn in an obvious location on the front of the uniform. Avoid using a strap around the neck to hold the card, for this would place the officer in jeopardy during physical confrontations. Likewise, the two-way radio should be worn in a holster or fastened to the belt by a belt clip. This leaves the officer's hands free.

f. The officers should be instructed to make personal introductions properly. A smile, a look in the eye, and a firm handshake are all important aspects of human relations that security personnel must master. Security personnel must be salespeople. As representatives of management, they must sell themselves, the department, and the work site to everyone who enters the site.

g. Be especially attentive to the security officer's breath. They should be instructed to never ingest alcohol, garlic, tobacco, onions, or other items that might leave an offensive odor when speaking to someone. Breath mints are a necessary tool for the public relations-minded security officer. Making it a rule that no one on the security team be allowed to drink alcoholic beverages 8 hours prior to a shift, and no smoking or tobacco chewing be allowed during the hours of work, will go far in ensuring that the officer's breath will be pleasant.

h. Encourage the officers to be "professionally connected." This means that officers should complete certification programs that clearly demonstrate to other members of the parent organization, and customers alike, the officer's professional achievement. Seniority alone is not the answer to this; neither is experience from previous employment.

i. Aside from certification programs, the officers should belong to professional organizations for *security* and *safety* professionals. There should be professional literature available for officers to read: something which generally comes automatically with membership in professional organizations.

j. In addition to the above suggestions, the officers must be introspective regarding their own worldviews, beliefs, fears, suspicions, biases, prejudices, and insecurities toward dealing with certain categories of individuals (Hess & Wrobleski, 1996).

k. The International Chiefs of Police Training Key 94 contains suggestions for improving one-on-one communications, which would be greatly helpful during attempts to serve the needs of others. The following recommendations are adaptations taken from those suggestions (Fay, 1993):

- Officers should always remain polite, respectful, and sensitive to the needs of the person being served. Use empathy, not sympathy, in dealing with people. Remember that you have no more power than that of any other citizen; you are not a police officer (even sworn officers must realize that *power struggles* are unproductive). Remain detached, and ignore personal insults. You are only enforcing your employer's policies and procedures; they are not your policies and procedures. The insults are actually directed at your employer or the situation, not at you.
- Be businesslike at all times. Treat the person you are interacting with the way you would want to be treated under similar circumstances. Anger, impatience, contempt, dislike, sarcasm, and similar attitudes have no place in public relations.
- Treat each contact as a *process*, consisting of several phases, instead of a happening. Slow everything down, and take time to evaluate the environment you are about to enter. Size things up as accurately as possible before making contact.
- Remember that although you intend to deliver customer satisfaction with each contact, be it conflict resolution, or simple assistance, it must be resolved within the guidelines of civil law, criminal law, administrative law, policy, procedure, and ethics. Be sure not to stray outside these parameters.
- Avoid arguing at all times. Never back the person you are dealing with into a corner. If the situation becomes heated, give or get space, and continue to use verbal deescalation to defuse the situation.

- Avoid giving the impression that your presence should be interpreted as a threat. Your demeanor should project your concern and care for the needs of the person you are interacting with. A great opening statement is "How can I help you?"
- Even if the person you come in contact with is being aggressive, avoid physical contact if at all possible. Use verbal deescalation whenever possible. If physical contact is necessary, be sure that your physical response is in self-defense, reasonable, and necessary. Most of all, remember that your physical response may be witnessed by the general public, and therefore, must look *professional*. It must appear that you are in *control*.
- You are under no obligation to disarm an assailant with a knife or a gun, or to chase down an assailant. Officer safety comes first. Instead of disarming or capturing the bad guy, evacuate the area, create a safety zone, and keep your distance until assistance can arrive. This will look a lot more professional to the media and will keep everyone safe.

HANDLING CUSTOMER COMPLAINTS

While constant practice of the principles of customer relations will preclude most complaints from occurring, there are still times when security officers must play the role of ambassador or diplomat. In some cases, they must even act as "referees." A few points to remember about handling complaints are:

1. Treat all complainants with respect.

Every complaint or objection should be handled with respect for the complainant, no matter how absurd it is. Always treat the person with dignity. Never argue. There are no winners in an argument.

2. Allow the complainant an opportunity to save face.

Do not embarrass a person who has been abusive or mistaken. Say, "I can understand why you misunderstood. This policy is very confusing!" This rule is integral to conflict resolution, as well as situations where actual physical restraint may be necessary.

3. Build the ego of the complainant.

Give them credit for their contribution. "You have a good point there. Not many people would have thought of that," is a technique that can be applied.

4. Show genuine courtesy and respect to the complainant.

Be respectful and considerate to the complainant. Interview the person and allow for venting of frustrations. Use active listening techniques to demonstrate your concern about the person's irritation and the problem.

SERVICE THAT CAN MAKE THE DIFFERENCE

Protective service departments must be just that: service departments. Persons who wish to survive in contemporary security/safety environments must be willing and able to take on new responsibilities. In essence:

Security Only Exists for the Services It Can Provide

Some service options that may be feasible within a security/safety department include those listed here.

Communication

- Administration of a central operator/voice-mail system

- Whole facility intercom communication systems
- Two-way intercom access controls at each perimeter door
- Use of tape dialers, with sensitive equipment to enunciate system failures
- Utilization of computerized remote dial-up networking for critical system diagnosis
- Emergency call stations in remote parts of the facility tied to the CCTV system
- Two-way intercoms installed near all overhead CCTV cameras

Transportation

- Employee transport within the work site complex
- Visitor transport within the work site complex
- Administering the parking garage

Risk Analysis

A risk analysis is a detailed evaluation of identified threats, probability and criticality hypotheses, vulnerability studies, and security surveys of facilities and systems (man-made and natural crises, critical incident responses, sensitive information losses, and so on). By performing a risk analysis, the security department is placing itself in a consulting relationship with the parent organization. Risk analyses also help in the *loss control* effort, and pay for themselves many times over. A risk analysis can be performed for the following:

- Executive/employee homes
- Work site offices
- Satellite facilities
- New construction/renovation
- Proposed property acquisitions

TRAINING

Training and educational services help to integrate the security department within the organization and make it more visible. Here are some options for providing training services:

- New employee orientation
- Periodic safety/security training
- Nonviolent crisis intervention
- Employee college tuition reimbursement programs for security officers
- Security officer cost reimbursement programs for attainment of certifications
- Employee tuition reimbursement for security officer CEU attainment

THE MEDIA: GOOD DREAM/BAD DREAM

With respect to the media, it can be the thing you have been dreaming of, there to promote the good work the security department is doing, or to send the message that your security department is not soft on crime, or to help at budget time to make your department look good, or to send any number of helpful messages. **In today's society, no organization can survive without positive media relations.**

If you save someone's life, intervene in an assault and arrest the bad guy, or drag someone from a burning vehicle at a crash scene just moments before the vehicle blows up, the media wants to know. They will break their necks to get to the scene and start looking for heroes to interview. They will usually arrive with the first responders because they are out there listening to the emergency scanner frequencies.

On the other side of the ledger, if you mess up, the media can be your worst nightmare. That negative story will hit the media with bigger headlines, more repeat stories and sidebars, than anything positive you can do. The negative story will seem to last forever. From that day on, your security department will be known by the negative story line. Unfortunately, bad news sells better than good news.

Regardless of the story the media finds when they arrive at the scene, if it is too bland, unexciting, or lacks titillation, the media will fill the gap. They are more than willing to create filler to make their stories more appealing to the general public.

If you have ever been quoted by the media, you probably found that the words you said during the interview and the words that were attributed to what you said, do not match exactly. Something has been deleted. Something has been added, and sometimes, the entire quote is a fabrication. You wonder how that can be since you spoke into a tape recorder during the interview!

Now imagine that you have an incident at your place of employment. The media shows up, and they stop at the first person they see. Who would that be on most occasions? You! The security officer. They want to interview you regarding the incident. Do you give them an interview or direct them to the public information officer for the client company? The answer is that you have no choice; you cannot give them an interview. However, you must refuse the interview in the right (professional, courteous) way. Here are some ideas of what to do:

- Use your very best public relations skills, as pointed out previously.
- Be polite, and give the media the number to reach the public information officer (PIO).
- If they press you for a statement, be polite, and continue to refer them to the PIO.
- If the PIO is on site, direct them or take them to the PIO.
- If they press you further, call in your supervisor, who will repeat the above.
- NEVER, NEVER, NEVER give an interview!
- NEVER say, "No comment!"
- NEVER be discourteous.

Other problems with the media that are of a security nature can be anticipated at the scene of a critical incident. These include:

a. Access control
b. Disruption of business operations

ACCESS CONTROL AT THE SCENE OF A CRITICAL INCIDENT

Access control is an absolute priority at the scene of a critical incident. However, access control can set up a power struggle between security and the media. Under most circumstances and for any number of reasons, mainly safety and legal reasons, security must deny access to anyone who is not a public assistance professional: police, medical, or fire professionals. This includes the media.

The media will sometimes utilize devious means to attain a story. They may try to sneak in a back door or simply walk in when you are not looking. They may even be involved with diverting your attention to allow a reporter to scoot in the front door. They may overwhelm you with numerous reporters attempting to gain access at the same time, on the theory that some will get through the lines. Fortunately, in most cases, after meeting a modicum of resistance, the media will back off and revert to other ways of getting the story. Once they have made contact with the PIO, the pressure is usually off the security department.

The "feeding frenzy" of reporters at the critical incident scene relates back to what we pointed out in the beginning of this unit. We told you that the public has a "right to know" because they have an interest in what businesses are doing in their community. The media are the keepers of that public right to know, and they doggedly go after the facts to get the story. The key for security is to know where to draw the line. However, you cannot reduce perimeter access control to appease the media. That is why it is so important that the public relations department of your company appoints a public information officer to take the pressure off security during critical incidents.

DISRUPTION OF BUSINESS

Disruption of business operations is another area of concern for security. If the critical incident is of such a nature, like a murder or rape or other crime, that the place of business is intact and continues to operate, the valuable security processes must also remain intact. Patrols must be maintained, property must be protected, alarms must be responded to, restricted traffic control within the business must be maintained, and so on. This is true even if the business is shut down due to a fire, explosion, or accident. What this means is that there must be a contingency plan to meet the needs of all types of incidents. For this purpose, the company has two alternatives:

- Create a plant emergency organization (PEO).
- Call in a contract security contingent.

PLANT EMERGENCY ORGANIZATION CONTROL

The plant emergency organization (PEO) is a group of people who work in other departments and are trained to respond to emergencies. Usually, a group of a dozen to two dozen individuals, scattered over all shifts, will make up the PEO. During critical incidents, this group stops what they are doing and reports immediately to a predetermined assignment or location. This immediately expands the private security capabilities so that both the critical incident and the critical security procedures continue to be serviced at the same time.

These trained PEO members are under the direction of the security director, regardless of who they work for in the company. The best candidates for this detail are usually the maintenance and facilities workers. However, anyone can be used in the PEO, and they sometimes take volunteers from all departments.

CONTRACT SECURITY CONTINGENT ACCESS CONTROL

Your security department will want to identify a local contract security company to be called in during certain emergency situations. The contract security company will commit to a certain number of emergency staff, each hour, until the required number of personnel can be assembled. Special pricing will be established to ensure immediate response. For instance, during the first hour of the emergency, the contract security company will ensure that at least six security officers will respond. Another six officers will arrive within the next 2 hours, and the remainder of individuals required will arrive within the next 3 hours. At that point, three shift contingents will be set up until the emergency is over. Flexibility will be built into the plan, so that the security director can control the number of individuals sent by the contract security company.

With these PEO and/or contract security people available, they can block all the perimeter doors and set up emergency access control to help control the media. In addition, the security department will have large, special, color-coded tags for everyone to wear during the emergency. If the employees are sent home, everyone who enters the building will have to enter through one door and receive their special tag at that door. These tags will signify times and levels of access, and whether or not escort is required. Large, brightly colored tags with the word "MEDIA" printed on them are reserved for use by the media, and these tags should always require escort.

Anyone found without a tag, except public service personnel, should be required to report to the main door and log in or leave the property. If the employees are not sent home, then they should be required to show a badge for access, and should be asked to remain in the building and avoid talking with the media. All employees who are also witnesses to the events surrounding the incident should be asked to go to a debriefing room set up by security, and they should be asked to give statements of what they have witnessed. Public law enforcement may want to be in that room under certain circumstances. These witnesses should be given special instructions to keep out of the public eye until the issues are resolved. Public disclosure of information vital to the prosecution may destroy the prosecutor's case.

The preceding security measures are not exclusively set up to control the media. Relatives of injured parties, children, and other innocent parties may be placing themselves in danger by gaining access to an emergency scene under certain circumstances. Your job is to prevent that from happening. However, your primary responsibility is to do your job while maintaining good public relations, and that means maintaining good relations with the media. The media must be accommodated—they need to do their job. They must also be managed so that they do not jeopardize that asset which is valuable to every organization's image.

CONCLUSION

The overwhelming majority of the rule-keeping practices of security officers consists of public relations. We are not bossy, disrespectful, or discourteous. We are the "goodwill ambassadors" of the clients we serve. We are mostly hands-off practitioners. Verbal deescalation is our first and most successful tool. At the same time, when necessary, we can become the defender of people and assets, capable of mitigating threats. Hopefully, this chapter will help the reader understand how important public relations is to security.

Performing public relations involves being other-person-centered. We do not spend our day finding ways to make our jobs easier for ourselves at the expense of others. It is our duty to spend our time designing ways of helping others, even if the only way to accomplish that goal causes us to work harder, longer hours, or to exert more energy. Providing superior customer service is the best way to greatly improve public relations because the public truly values good customer service.

EMERGING TRENDS

With respect to public relations as a major part of a security officer's job description, the main emerging trend is to expect that standard operating procedures will, in the future, place a very high emphasis on public relations through effective customer service. It has been our experience that where we find good public relations and good customer service, those two attributes are followed by a high level of safety and security. That is, proactive prevention is operating through all that contact with the people the security officers meet and serve every day. The security officer's presence announces to all who see it that this facility is a hard target. Criminal activities should not be practiced in this hard target area, less the perpetrators are willing to experience harsh consequences.

There is also a trend in the security industry to emphasize public relations and customer service in mandatory training curriculums set up by state licensing boards. In as much as there exists a current trend in the United States toward mandatory pre-assignment and continuing training for security guards, a trend is developing for additional learning and practice in numerous prime topic areas. One of these prime topic areas of study is public relations through providing top-notch customer service. In the future, an even stronger bond between these two concepts will continue; public relations through customer service will continue to be a primary, critical, proactive, preventive safety and security strategy.

References

American Heritage Dictionary of the English Language, 1973 edition, p. 1057.

Encyclopedia Americana, 1995 edition, Vol. 22, p. 760.

Fay, J. J. (1993). *Encyclopedia of security management: Techniques & technology.* Stoneham, MA: Butterworth-Heinemann p. 592.

Hess, K. M., & Wrobleski, H. M. (1996). *Introduction to private security* (4th ed.). St. Paul, MN: West Publishing Co. p. 328.

PSTN (Professional Security Television Network). "Basic Security Officer Training Series, Public Relations."

See Media section, this unit, below.

SECURITY QUIZ

1. No matter what the security officer's primary duties and responsibilities are, and no matter who the security officer's primary constituency is, which of the following people groups have a legitimate interest in how those duties and responsibilities are carried out?

    a. The local public law enforcement department
    b. The general public
    c. The licensing board that licenses security officers
    d. All of the above

2. There is more to department of the security officer than looking professional, and performing in a reasonable and necessary manner. The security officer must have all the following characteristics but one. Which one of the following is not mentioned in the text?

    a. The security officer must appear to have real concern for others
    b. The security officer must also keep the patrol vehicle clean to make a good impression
    c. The security officer must speak with pleasant and polite voice inflection
    d. The security officer must show respect for anyone he or she comes in contact with

3. To accomplish the goal of projecting a positive image, the security department must first have a quality program in place. Once this is done, the Ten Rules of Public Relations in Private Security can be applied. Which of the following is not one of these rules?
   a. The Security Officer must select the persons he or she will serve
   b. The Security Officer must be attentive to the other person's needs
   c. The Security Officer must believe that image is a valuable asset
   d. The Security Officer must have a "Can-Do" attitude

4. In addition, the Ten Rules of Public Relations in Private Security instruct the security officers in the following ways. Which one of the following rules is incorrect?
   a. When you see someone looking around like they are lost, approach them and ask if you can help them
   b. Realize that public relations is not about being right all the time; the customer is sometimes wrong. However, being right or wrong is not what is important. Service is.
   c. When the person you are serving only wants to be argumentative, you *must* cut them off cold and take over the conversation
   d. When approached by someone for help, say "yes" even before they tell you what they want. You work in the "Yes" department. YOU have a "Go-to attitude."

5. There are many actions that a security supervisor can take to motivate their subordinates to do a better job at public relations. Which of the following is not one of those actions?
   a. Brief each security officer on current events within the work site daily
   b. Give each officer extended smoke breaks as a reward for a job well done
   c. Conduct a personal inspection of each officer before the shift starts
   d. Assure that security officers are not "shafted" out of vacations and days off

6. In addition to daily refresher training, supervisors should make certain that the security officers in his or her command adopt favorable work behaviors. Of the following work behaviors, which is not included in the text?
   a. The security officer should be schooled in money management so they will be able to live very comfortably on the wages they receive from being a guard
   b. The security officer should be encouraged to belong to professional organizations that serve safety and security practitioners
   c. The security officer should wear the picture ID in a conspicuous location on the front of the uniform
   d. The security officer should be instructed to watch his or her breath, excluding garlic or onions before work to prevent offensive smelling breath when talking to those being served on the job

7. Handling customer complaints is not always fun. In some cases, the security officer may wind up acting like a referee. Of the following, which is a good recommendation for how to handle complaints?
   a. Treat all complainants with respect, and never allow yourself to be dragged into an argument
   b. Allow the complainant an opportunity to save face. Do not embarrass them in front of others
   c. Give the complainant credit for their contribution, with a compliment like, "You have a good point there. I can see how others have made this same mistake."
   d. All of the above

8. Security departments are service departments. The personnel in security departments can be found doing all kinds of jobs to help their companies. Of the following activities that security officers might be asked

to do, which is *not* likely a task they will follow?

a. Lining up catering services for the CEO's annual vice presidents' meeting and golf outing

b. Administering of a central operator/voice-mail system

c. Employee transport within the confines of the facility

d. Training new recruits and providing orientations for new hires

9. By performing a risk analysis, the security department is placing itself in a security consulting relationship with the company. Risk analysis can also help with loss control efforts. Which of the following is *not* a setting where a risk analysis would be very helpful?

a. New construction/renovation

b. Executive/employee homes

c. Work site offices

d. None of the above

10. Whenever a facility has a critical fire, explosion, or other cataclysmic event, the media is sure to be there. When they arrive, they will attempt to interview the first person they see so they can get the story on the evening news. Many times, that person is the security officer. Which of the following is a good idea of how the security officer should respond?

a. Be very, very polite and direct the media to the designated media liaison person

b. If media presses you for a statement, contact your supervisor, and let the supervisor deal with the media in that case

c. Just put your hand over the camera lens and say: "No comment; you have to leave now."

d. Never, never, never, under any circumstances, give an interview.

43

Community Relations: Making the Strategy Come Alive

Mark E. Puetz and K.C. Poulin

CHAPTER OBJECTIVES

- Discuss the concept of an experience economy as it applies to private security
- Give a list of options and identify the five areas necessary in creating a positive experience
- Discuss the concept of costs of quality as it applies to private security
- Discuss branding and how it is an important part of a security operation's business strategy
- List the three phases of relationship building within a community
- Convey the importance of contact protocols in managing the relationship with the client or users of security services

INTRODUCTION

When you arrive for work, you know what is expected of you. The skills of your profession are learned through education or training programs, on-the-job training, or even through certification programs like this one. It is not enough, though, to focus solely on those "hard skills." In order to be truly effective, you must understand and appreciate how your efforts fit into and support the overall strategy of your security operation, whether a contract agency or an in-house department. You must also be able to employ the "soft skills" of interacting with people to create positive outcomes. Being able to work with others in a manner consistent with your operation's strategy is the mark of a true professional.

In this chapter we will explore some ideas about how what you do fits into the business success of your security operation. We will consider the experience you provide to those who use or benefit from your services, followed by a look at how what you do impacts the costs to the operation. How all of this is important to, or supports, the strategy and branding of the security operation, and your role in that, makes up the third section. The last section examines the idea of engaging the community itself as part of the security effort. When all of these are aligned, the effects can be powerful.

Before we get started, consider …

Two teenagers stand before a gumball machine at the mall. They insert a coin and watch one of many colored gumballs fall through a dizzying array of chutes and slots on its way to being dispensed at the bottom. The machine lights up and plays music as the gumball makes its journey. Neither teenager takes any of the gumballs they purchased. Instead, they just laugh and giggle. They seem simply to enjoy the show.

You purchase a new gadget from the local electronics store. When you get home, you find out it does not work. You call the store and they ask that you return it. When you do, your defective gadget is exchanged for a brand new one, no questions asked.

In July 1969, Neil Armstrong became the first man to set foot on the moon. NASA folklore says President Kennedy visited NASA sometime months before the launch. He spoke with a number of people on his tour. At one stop he asked a janitor what his role was in the space program. "Mr. President," the janitor responded proudly, "I am helping to put a man on the moon."

What do these short stories have in common? How do they relate to what you do? If you are the suspicious type, you may think to watch the teenagers more closely, or wonder if you are being watched for making a bad return as part of a larger scam, or maybe you wonder if the janitor was a plant. Indeed, a certain amount of suspicion is necessary to be successful in our business. However, we are going to consider these anecdotes a bit differently. We are going to look at them from a larger, business perspective, one of how you fit into ensuring business success. As suggested above, how these tales are interpreted is the difference between a security officer and a practitioner, between one who merely punches a clock and a true professional.

SECURITY AND THE EXPERIENCE ECONOMY

In the 1990s, B. Joseph Pine II and James H. Gilmore took a close look at how businesses and economies have evolved through human history and suggested we were then moving into what

they called an "experience economy" (Pine & Gilmore, 1999). From the earliest days until fairly recently, most of our economic activity was designed to get the things we need directly from the earth through hunting and gathering or farming. Ours was an agrarian economy. In the 19th century, we moved into an industrial economy where most of our effort was dedicated to making things. We used raw materials pulled from the earth and mass-produced all manner of goods. As recently as the 1980s and 1990s we started to see more businesses geared not toward making things, but in doing things for others. In this service economy we saw companies built around personal assistants, dog walkers, international shipping corporations, and so on. According to Pine and Gilmore, the experience economy is evolving as the next step. To be sure, there is still a significant amount of agrarian economic activity going on, and service businesses of one sort or another have existed for a very long time. However, overall, the notion that our economies have evolved or can be broken into categories is interesting and informative.

The notion of the experience economy suggests that people are buying not only because they need this or that, or they need something done, but because they want a particular thrill. The teens putting money into the flashy gumball machine wanted the "experience" of watching the gumballs fall through the maze and listening to the music. We go to concerts or the theater because we want the "experience" of the music or the show, something we cannot get with just a CD or video. We go bungee jumping or hang gliding or even skydiving because we want the thrill of our stomachs in our throats, the adrenaline rush. Business leaders have learned the lessons here. Look at advertising today. How many car commercial messages, for example, are based on the qualities of the car itself and how many are based on a "feeling" you will get when you drive that particular car: the "experience"?

In an environment where the basic good or service is rather common, not all that different from any other, or is more or less a commodity, we have to stand out from the crowd somehow if we are to be competitive. Think about what this means for the business of security. Almost anyone can check a door to ensure it is locked, or read a gauge to ensure it is within certain parameters. It does not take specialized training to read an ID badge or check a name against a list at an access control point. The ultimate "buyers" of our services (where security is part of a service economy) know this and they pressure our agencies or departments for more services, higher standards, or lower prices or costs. If security is provided by a contract agency, they may threaten to buy from a competitor. If security is provided in-house, they may threaten to decrease our budgets or outsource the security function. Whether contract or in-house, this can cause downward pressure on our wages. Sure, we may require licensing or certification, personal discipline, and even some expertise in identifying security risks before they become security threats. Sure, the costs to our users if we do not do our jobs can be extensive, suggesting we should be compensated accordingly. But the end user may not dwell on all of this when he makes his buying decision, when he chooses our agency over any other, or sets our department's budget. We will consider these perceptions below. For now, though, how can a security operation, whether a contract agency, in-house department, or some other differentiate itself from every other option and offer an "experience"? How can the experience be built into the relationship we have with the community or setting in which we operate and be employed as part of the overall security effort?

Creating a positive experience involves being effective in five areas. Any security operation seeking to do so should make it a part of its strategy and management infrastructure to develop processes that address each area. Any security officer, committed to professionalism, the success of the operation for which he works, and ensuring the security of those he protects, will make every effort to do his part as well.

Create a Consistent Theme: Have you ever taken a road trip and stopped at your favorite fast food chain for a quick bite to eat? Did you notice that it looked almost like every other you have seen? Maybe the physical layout of the building was a bit different, but the signage, the menu, the uniforms, the countertops, and tables all looked and "felt" essentially the same, right? What makes that fast food chain different from all others, and competitive against all others, is just that. Every one you enter reminds you where you are, that you are in their place and no other. This builds a sense of familiarity, comfort, and trust. Every interaction any user of your services has with your operation or you should "feel" the same. If your operation's strategy involves providing highly competent antiterrorism officers at critical areas such as nuclear or power plants, then every time the client or overseeing authority calls, meets in your office, sees your duty vehicles, or talks with you or one of your fellow officers, he should "sense" that he is dealing with highly competent antiterrorism officers. If your operation's strategy is to provide professional security officers for access control in high-end office buildings, then every interaction should have that feel to it as well.

An effective security operation will likely develop a focused strategy, one that allows it to dedicate its resources to maintaining that consistency. If there is no such strategy, and the operation falls into the trap of taking on any business it can, the consistent theme will not be there. Security officers working different sites will "look" different. Where an established operation identifies different strategies that are complementary, a slightly different look may be acceptable here and there, but the overall theme should remain the same. This also means the operation should create a powerful and consistent brand in the marketplace. Whenever anyone sees that operation's logo or one of its officers or vehicles, there should be no doubt as to who they are. The brand follows the strategy. A well-armed security officer wearing a distinctive uniform with a clear logo on his truck or utility vehicle fits well as an antiterrorism officer, less so as the access control officer in the professional building. Conversely, a security officer wearing a blazer and tie or a crisp uniform does fit well in the professional environment, and maybe not so much so in an antiterrorism deployment.

You are part of that strategy and branding. You should wear your uniform, whatever it may be, correctly. You should endeavor to look sharp, according to your operation's rules for uniform wear. The uniform is not an exercise in self-expression. It is designed, by definition, to make everyone wearing it appear "uniform." It is designed as part of a consistent theme. Part of this, too, is your demeanor and how you present yourself to your superiors, those you protect, and other users. You should maintain an even temperament, be well reasoned, and think clearly and critically. Your reports should be thorough, yet concise. You should be an image of competence at being an antiterrorism officer, an access control officer, or whatever sort of security officer fits your operation's strategy and brand. When others in the community or environment see you, you are your operation's brand!

Layer the Theme with Positive Cues: When you visit an amusement park you are teased almost as soon as you enter the parking lots. Signs with images of the park's characters direct you through traffic. As you get closer to the front gate, you may hear the screams of guests already inside as they fly by on one of the twists and turns of a rollercoaster. Once at the gate, you hear theme music, you see costumed characters walking around, and park employees are all "on stage" doing everything they can to make you feel welcome and wanting more. Everywhere you turn you see or hear another "something" sending you the message that this is a fun place to be. These cues are not accidental. They are designed to send those messages to you. More often than not, they work! Your operation should develop a series of cues that send positive messages, and reinforce the strategy and brand. Sticking with our antiterrorism versus access control officer example, what cues can be seen between the two? The antiterrorism officer, protecting critical infrastructure, may carry an assault rifle, a very powerful cue. He might be dressed in a manner that appears militaristic and combat ready, with helmet, tactical vest, heavy boots, and so on. To the potential attacker, he sends a very powerful message of "Do not come here!" which translates to a positive set of cues for those in the community or environment he protects, "This security officer is very well equipped to protect us." The security officer working in the high-end professional building might be dressed in pressed trousers and shirt, with a conservative tie, a classy looking blazer with a distinctive patch on the pocket. Or maybe he will wear a uniform shirt and trousers reminiscent of law enforcement or military dress. The message he sends is that he is a professional and fully capable of interacting in this environment. If he wears a uniform, an added duty belt may send an additional message that, while professional, he has tools available to support him when he needs to be stern (as in when denying access to those not authorized to enter). Even the security officer at that amusement park can send those positive cues. He may interact proactively and personably with guests. While he is making the guests feel welcome, he is also letting them know he is there and that he is watching out for them. This sort of "preventive interaction" can be very powerful, as we will see later.

Positive cues sent by the security operation may consist not only of the deliverable of regular reporting, but also of having a key manager or account representative contact the client or supervising executive and reinforcing whenever a positive security event occurs. This point of contact may or may not read all of the operation's reporting as often or in as timely a manner as he may like. He may have other work or issues he needs to address. When the account representative makes a proactive call and informs him that the operation's officers coordinated with law enforcement the previous night to have arrests made of subjects attempting a burglary, or that they found an important area unsecured and were able to secure it, what is the cue sent? He may see all of this in the operation's report when he gets to it, but the message sent is that the security operation understands and cares about his security concerns and wants to be sure he is aware of key issues. A proactive reporting process may also offer commentary on the rhythms of the environment, beyond simply noting events. For example, imagine how useful it may be for a factory to learn the night shift employees seem to be suffering from low morale or that a particular employee recently suffered a loss in her family. Factory management could investigate further the cause of the low morale, a leadership issue, and resolve it in order to inspire more efficient production, a management issue. Or they could reach out to the distraught employee with compassion, sometimes an incredibly powerful leadership technique in and of itself. The security operation should communicate not only when there is an issue, but also when there is not. If things seem to be quiet and running smoothly, regular contact should continue. Positive cues build strong relationships, which allow for presenting more positive cues. The process can feed on itself and grow.

As the security officer working at a given site, you must interact professionally and personably with everyone. Interacting professionally sets in the minds of others that you are competent and fully capable. Being personable, or friendly, lets them know you are approachable. You end up conveying that they can come to you with their concerns, that you are available to assist them in their worries about safety or security in the environment, whether it be a workplace or some other area. When you become aware of a potential issue, address it. You may or may not have the authority to address it directly, but you should at least have the ability to pass it on to the correct person. When people recognize you as a professional, personable, and proactive security officer, imagine the comfort level, the "experience," you create for them. Imagine the sense of community you can build. That is the goal.

Eliminate/Manage Negative Cues: Nothing ever goes right all the time. When it seems like it does, we likely have been grossly misinformed. Although it is always important to address things that go wrong, our concern is to eliminate or manage the negative message others may get from us. When a security officer is found to be dressed or behaving inappropriately, it sends a negative message to all who interact with him. A dirty patrol car or messy work area sends a similar message. One of the largest amusement parks in the world does a full inspection of its property, inspecting every single ride, replacing any burned-out lightbulbs, cleaning the park thoroughly, … every night. They invest a great deal into an entire secondary workforce that never sees a guest. Their only purpose is to ensure the negative cues of a malfunctioning or closed-for-service ride or even the silly small things like a burned-out lightbulb are never sent.

Communicating openly about the bad news with a client contact or supervising executive is important. The security operation should make the first notification wherever possible to ensure he hears it from the source. He should never get such information secondhand, and be left wondering about what the security operation may or may not have done. When a breach occurs or a threat becomes an incident, an informative call lets the contact know security personnel are addressing the issue directly. The damage may be done, a negative cue. But the account representative called, informed, and has taken direct action to address the matter. This can be a very powerful positive cue. The agency has negated, or managed, the negative cue in doing so. The security operation should be ahead of the point of contact wherever possible, too, in developing solutions for any security worry he may have. When the business plans an expansion, for example, he may have myriad other things on his mind, only to find out later that he missed something important. If the security operation knows about the expansion and makes suggestions as to potential security risks that can be addressed, the contact can see them as an operation interested in solving his problems before they become headaches.

On the ground, day or night, you should adopt a similar approach. When issues or worries are identified, address them. Act within your scope of authority and do whatever you can to solve the problem. When the solution is outside your scope of authority, refer it to the appropriate party, whether your supervisor or a point of contact, depending on your own operation's rules for such things. Never let an issue fester unattended, though. They have a surprising knack for growing well beyond mere headaches then, and tend to become cancers that can seriously infect your operation and those you protect. Your challenge, as a security officer, is to educate yourself so you can identify what is or is not an issue. Some things are easy; an unsecured external door after hours is likely a concern. Some things are not so easy; what do you do when a day shift employee wants to get into the building on a weekend to get something from his desk so he can work on a project at home? Policies and procedures can offer valuable guidance, but they cannot predict every possible circumstance. At some point, you must make a decision. When you address such issues fairly and responsibly, your supervisors and the client contact or supervising executive see them being addressed—a positive cue—before those issues become real concerns for them—a negative cue.

Offer Memorabilia: Have you ever gone to a concert or event and come home with a tour t-shirt? Have you ever eaten at a restaurant and left with a toy for the kids, a commemorative glass, or some other such gift? Have you ever gone anywhere and come back with a souvenir? These items are designed to trigger your memory every time you see them, to serve as "mementos" of the "experience" you had when you first got them. They act as "positive cues" long after the experience is over.

Many companies send birthday or holiday cards to clients. When personally signed, these show a "human touch" and often are displayed on the recipient's desk or wall for a few days or through the season. A lot of companies also offer pens or pads or mugs or any manner of things with their logo emblazoned on them. Military or law enforcement organizations may give certificates, special plaques, or even challenge coins. Offering a memento that is unique to the agency can go a long way in reminding clients of the security operation even when its personnel are not in front of them or reaching out to them to follow up on an issue or maintain the relationship of the account.

Where you, as the security officer, may be authorized by your operation to do so, pass out mementos as appropriate. While some security operations create related literature, brochures with security tips, for example, many of us on the front lines do not have this available to us. If these are available, pass them out freely. If you have nothing like this available to you, you can offer compliments or affirmations, recognizing or encouraging those you contact in their efforts. What stays in the person's mind is when you greet everyone with something like a simple, "Good morning, Mr. Jones, good to see you again," versus, "Good morning, Mr. Jones. I certainly appreciate having alert people like you around. It makes the whole place a lot safer when everyone is paying attention." If possible and appropriate in your environment, engage Mr. Jones in simple conversation when you see him. It may sound trite, but Mr. Jones now feels welcomed as part of the security effort and appreciated for who he is (something all people secretly want). Over time, that relationship will grow, as will the relationship you have with all others you greet or with whom you talk. The message will eventually get back to your supervisors and maybe even your client contact or the supervising executive himself.

Consider All Five Senses: As humans, we take in everything we know about the world around us through use of our five senses. If we want to send, or reinforce, the message of creating a positive experience for others, we should try to do so through every sense we can. While there may not be many messages we want to send through smell, for example, we can at least consider these in the abstract. Look at Table 43-1 below. We have summarized the suggestions made in this section so far and offer some bullets as to how you might think about the five senses. None of this is set in stone. It is limited only by the security operation's strategy, branding, and the imagination of those who make it happen … you, the security officer.

Creating a positive experience involves being effective in five areas. The security operation will likely make it a part of its strategy and management infrastructure to develop processes that address each area. Any security officer, committed to professionalism, the success of the operation for which he works, and ensuring the security of his customers and end users, will make every effort to do his part as well.

COST OF QUALITY

As security officers, we are aware of what might happen if things go wrong. We know breaches in security are not acceptable; compromises of our client's or business's interests are to be avoided. Aside from the damages of the loss itself resulting from the breach, we lose the goodwill of those who benefit from our work. We can easily imagine that our client, or the larger business of which our department is a part, will lose faith in our operation and us should such things occur. Those who work, live, or play in the areas we protect will suffer a similar loss of confidence where they are affected. Our fellow officers are embarrassed and may become disheartened to work alongside us. Indeed, our operation may even lose some of its competitive position in the marketplace. What client wants to contract with a security agency that cannot keep things secure, after all? What executive wants to keep an in-house team that cannot do so?

Back in the 1950s, engineers and managers in industry, particularly in manufacturing, began looking at what has since become known as the "cost of quality" or "quality costs." They noticed, for example, that when making a particular item, a widget, there was a certain amount of raw material that went into the production of that widget. That raw material was purchased at a price. The wages paid to the workers who made the widget were paid at a given rate. The cost of running the machines was calculated as well. Should there be a defect in a widget, it would have to be fixed or perhaps even scrapped. If fixed, additional costs would be incurred: materials, wages, use of machines. If scrapped, the costs already incurred would now have been effectively wasted. These additional or lost costs, separate from what it actually costs to make the widget in the first place, are the costs of poor quality.

Mistakes happen, though. So these same engineers and managers started to put fail-safes into their processes. They used inspections at multiple phases to catch defects early. They wrote manufacturing guidelines for frontline personnel to minimize human error. They even spent more time trying to design the manufacturing process itself to be more efficient and have fewer opportunities for error. The inspectors had to be paid, of course, so their wages represented a cost. The time it took to write out

TABLE 43-1   Creating a Positive Experience

	Security Agency	Security Officer
Create a Consistent Theme	• Focus the strategy and all following actions. • Create a powerful and consistent brand.	• Wear the agency uniform correctly and look sharp. • Maintain an even temperament. • Write all reports and communiqués professionally.
Layer the Theme with Positive Cues	• Provide regular reporting. • Talk about the successes. • Reach out often. • Be accessible.	• Interact professionally and personably with everyone. • Be proactive when faced with problems or challenges.
Eliminate/Manage Negative Cues	• Communicate openly about the bad (bad news must travel fast). • Develop solutions for worries the client or oversight authority may have.	• Do not let issues fester. Address them. • Be liability conscious.
Offer Memorabilia	• Remember key events (birthdays, holidays, etc.). • Offer agency mementos.	• Use affirmations and positive reinforcement in all interactions. • Distribute agency-approved literature.
Consider All Five Senses	• **Sight:** Ensure everything (uniforms, materials and literature, vehicles, etc.) is visually appealing. • **Sound:** Keep all conversations professional, yet friendly. • **Smell:** Pass the "smell test" with all actions (contacts, reporting, investigations, etc.). • **Touch:** Make every "touch point" a positive experience. • **Taste:** Never leave a "bad taste in the mouth" of the client or oversight authority.	• **Sight:** Ensure your uniforms, grooming, and bearing always appear professional and inspire confidence. • **Sound:** Speak clearly and authoritatively. • **Smell:** Keep yourself clean and well groomed, with no offensive body or perfume odors. • **Touch:** Use firm handshakes. Take excellent care of client equipment. • **Taste:** Never leave a "bad taste in the mouth" of anyone.

more detailed procedures represented a cost. Even redesigning processes represented costs.

It does not stop there. Remember that electronic gadget you purchased in the second example at the very beginning of the chapter? Imagine that as the widget. Now you have a defective widget. You took time out of your day to complain. That is time you could have been doing something else, a cost to you. The person who took your call probably had to be paid either way, but he could have been doing something else, too, another cost. You took more time out of your day to return the widget,

a cost. It was returned and sent back to be fixed or scrapped, costs. The only saving grace in this example is that they made the exchange with no questions asked which, hopefully, meant for a positive experience and well-managed negative cues for you.

All of these costs are known as the "total quality costs." Whole disciplines and countless consultants have sprung up to help companies reduce these costs. Keep in mind that the money spent in these areas is money that cannot be spent elsewhere, such as in business expansion or on wages and benefits for you and your fellow security officers. So you, the security officer, have a significant interest in ensuring the quality of your services is the highest possible. This is not just a question of ensuring there are no breaches or compromises. For the true professional and practitioner, it is also a matter of ensuring the "experience" is always a positive one. Every complaint, similar to your return of the widget, must be addressed somehow and that means costs will be incurred. Minimizing the need for those complaints also minimizes costs.

Consider Table 43-2 (Campanella, 1999, p. 5). Imagine how you, as the security officer, can do your part to reduce these costs by creating a positive experience. All of these costs, considered together, are known as the "total quality costs." The money spent in these areas is money that cannot be spent elsewhere, such as in business expansion or on wages and benefits. In a service-related business, such as security, these costs can be significantly reduced by providing a positive experience for the customer.

Remember the old adage from Ben Franklin, "An ounce of prevention is worth a pound of cure"? The same concept certainly applies here. The costs incurred to ensure a high-quality security effort before the service is ever delivered are often much less than the costs incurred after a breach, compromise, complaint, or other loss.

Prevention Costs: Prevention costs, the costs incurred up front to create a high-quality experience or ensure an error or failure does not occur, ideally are accepted or even encouraged

TABLE 43-2 Total Quality Costs

Prevention Costs	**Failure Costs**
The costs of all activities specifically designed to prevent poor quality in products or services. Examples are the costs of new product review, quality planning, supplier capability surveys, process capability evaluations, quality improvement team meetings, quality improvement projects, quality education and training.	The costs resulting from products or services not conforming to requirements or customer/user needs. Failure costs are divided into internal and external failure cost categories.
Appraisal Costs	**Internal Failure Costs**
The costs associated with measuring, evaluating, or auditing products or services to assure conformance to quality standards and performance requirements. These include the costs of incoming and source inspection/test of purchased material; in-process and final inspection/test; product, process, or service audits; calibration of measuring and test equipment; and the costs of associated supplies and materials.	Failure costs occurring prior to delivery or shipment of the product, or the furnishing of a service, to the customer. Examples are the costs of scrap, rework, re-inspection, retesting, material review, and downgrading.
	External Failure Costs
	Failure costs occurring after the delivery or shipment of the product, and during or after the furnishing of a service, to the customer. Examples are the costs of processing customer complaints, customer returns, warranty claims, and product recalls.

Total Quality Costs
The sum of the above costs. It represents the difference between the actual cost of a product or service and what the reduced cost would be if there were no possibility of substandard service, failure of products, or defects in their manufacture.

as part of doing business. A security operation often incurs the additional cost of conducting a threat assessment or other security review prior to taking on a new account or new responsibility for just this reason. Similarly, they hold managers' or supervisors' meetings to ensure the regular flow of information and early identification of issues. Licensure, certification, and training may also be counted as prevention costs. As the security officer, you can ensure you are aware of the layout and security issues of the facility or property you are assigned to protect. You should also communicate regularly with your supervisors just as they do with theirs. Most important, you should be proactive in your patrols and duties, especially in building relationships, thus creating a positive experience for those who live and work in the environment you protect.

Appraisal Costs: Appraisal costs, the costs associated with checking up on ourselves, are an important part of anything our agency does, or we do if we are serious about ensuring a positive experience for those who use our services. Reporting and statistics allow the security operation to identify concerns or trends and address them proactively. Inspections of security officers and sites do the same. Even security drills and performance tests may be appraised. You should always be conscious of the quality of your patrols and inspections, to ensure you have covered and considered everything for which you are responsible.

Internal Failure Costs: Failure costs, those incurred as a result of some shortcoming on our part, are to be avoided or minimized wherever possible. Not doing a thorough threat assessment, and thus failing to consider a material security risk or a security officer not making complete rounds and missing an unsecured door, are incidents representing failure costs. Even not connecting with the members of the community you patrol and missing something they could have told you about could be considered a failure cost. Can you see where a

checklist, an appraisal cost, may be useful in avoiding this, for example?

External Failure Costs: Some failures occur after our services have already been delivered. Just as with all the costs incurred when you returned your defective widget in the opening example above, complaints from any party and all that must be done to address their concerns represent failure costs. Even though some cannot be avoided, since mistakes do happen or because some people seem simply to enjoy complaining, our efforts to create a positive experience at the point of service delivery, when we are on our rounds and interacting with others, can go a long way to minimize them.

FROM STRATEGY TO BRAND TO OFFICER

At its most basic, business strategy is about who, what, when, where, why, and how. Who are the buyers or primary users of our services and who are the other users? What product or service do we provide for them? When do we get it to them? Where do we compete, either geographically or in the marketplace? Why do we provide that product or service? What problem are we trying to solve? How does our product or service solve that problem? Another question that may be added is one of how we prepare for or deal with change (Davidson, 1996). Although far beyond the scope of this work, answering these questions in detail and exploring them fully can lead a business into developing a powerfully competitive strategy. With some tweaking, even an in-house operation will probably address these questions, considering everyone to whom it is accountable and what their concerns may be.

For our purposes, though, let us consider these questions briefly, in a different order, in terms of three different hypothetical security operations: one contract agency that provides electronic access control and camera monitoring systems (see Table 43-3); an in-house operation that provides security personnel at high-end vacation resorts (see Table 43-4); and the last, another contract agency that patrols factories and industrial complexes (see Table 43-5).

It is easy to see that each of these security operations provides a very different type of service to different primary users with different needs. All provide security solutions, but are distinctly different from one another. At some point, the first agency decided it would provide technological solutions and not officers. The second operation works in resorts only and has to be responsive as a department of the entire business. The last agency made a decision to serve industrial facilities. Because where and

how they do what they do are so different, how they present themselves is also very different. How they present themselves is "branding."

The operation's brand is a function of all of the "experiences," as we explored above, perceived by the various users of its services with whom the operation comes in contact. It is a lot more than just a logo on a letterhead. It is the uniform, the way its officers present themselves and the security operation. It is the make, model, and livery on its vehicles. Branding is about the image of the operation at every touch point, at every single place anyone has any contact whatsoever with the operation, even down to how the phones are answered, e-mails are written, or the timeliness

TABLE 43-3 Strategy Summary for E-Security

Strategy Question	Answer (Example)
Who: Who are our customers?	Our customers are private businesses or commercial interests who need to provide controlled access to restricted areas, and document who enters or exits those areas.
Where: Where do we compete, or find our customers, either in terms of geography or the marketplace?	We service customers in the greater metro area and up to 25 miles outside the city limits. We service customers who have office buildings or gate access to outside areas. We do not service private homes or government facilities.
Why: Why do we provide a product or service to them? What problem do we solve for them?	We allow our customers to keep unauthorized people out of restricted areas, and to track who does enter and when.
What: What product or service do we offer?	We offer electronic key card, biometric scans, and video surveillance with internal monitoring. As an additional offering, we provide external monitoring.
When: When do we provide this product or service to the customer?	Our products provide real-time monitoring and customizable reports with frequency and distribution determined by the customer.
Change: How do we prepare for and deal with change?	Executives attend trade shows. Executives, account representatives, and senior supervisors subscribe to trade magazines. Our board and executives consider trends in our industry and threats at least annually. Key clients are invited to participate in our strategy board meeting.

TABLE 43-4   Strategy Summary for Resort Security

Strategy Question	Answer (Example)
Who: Who are our customers?	Our customers are the owners and executives of the resort chain.
Where: Where do we compete, or find our customers, either in terms of geography or the marketplace?	We service the entire range of resort properties in our company throughout the southeastern United States, particularly along the coastlines. Our resorts serve exclusive, high-profile clientele and boast five-star facilities.
Why: Why do we provide a product or service to them? What problem do we solve for them?	Our resorts want their clientele to enjoy their vacations without the hassle of outsiders, whether paparazzi or news media.
What: What product or service do we offer?	We offer highly professional, concierge-type security officers who dress in casual resort attire so as not to offend guests, but with distinctive uniforms to make their roles clear. We also partner with a provider of CCTV and other technological solutions to monitor perimeters and gates.
When: When do we provide this product or service to the customer?	Our security personnel are present 24/7 on all of our sites.
Change: How do we prepare for and deal with change?	We coordinate closely with our executives and operating managers and attend resort conventions to fully understand our business and its many issues.

TABLE 43-5   Strategy Summary for Industrial Security

Strategy Question	Answer (Example)
Who: Who are our customers?	Our customers are factories, industrial complexes, and similar businesses.
Where: Where do we compete, or find our customers, either in terms of geography or the marketplace?	We service customers in the midwestern United States. Our customers are manufacturers or raw material extractors.
Why: Why do we provide a product or service to them? What problem do we solve for them?	Our customers are worried about safety conditions for their onsite employees and monitoring of gauges and readouts after hours.
What: What product or service do we offer?	Our security officers are highly trained in government regulations about workplace safety, particularly in industrial or factory settings. We check key readouts or indicators to ensure critical equipment is operating within acceptable parameters. We also assist in developing safety training programs.
When: When do we provide this product or service to the customer?	Our security personnel are available day and night for our clients.
Change: How do we prepare for and deal with change?	Our senior staff regularly watches legislative changes and keeps abreast of regulations about workplace safety issues that affect the business of our clients.

of when invoices or budgets are sent. One bad experience in the mind of anyone we meet can affect the brand negatively. Most businesses work very hard to ensure the integrity of their brands and guard them jealously. The security operation's brand should lend itself to supporting the cues it wants to send. The brand of an in-house security operation is often considered and designed, too, to be consistent with the overall brand of the business within which it operates.

When President Kennedy spoke with the janitor at NASA, we do not know if the janitor was wearing a fancy uniform or not. The story that has been handed down does not include that tidbit. But his response indicated, without doubt, that he knew he had a place in the larger scheme of things. He knew he was incredibly important to a most honorable effort. He knew that without his efforts, others would be hindered. He was part of an amazing team leading up to one of the greatest achievements in human history. As the security officer on the front lines, or even as a supervisor, you are part of the more important effort of keeping people and physical assets safe. While you may not always know the finer points of your agency's or department's strategy, you probably do know that your operation provides technological solutions, works in-house in resorts, services industrial clients, or competes in some other strategic niche. Whatever the case, your role is an essential part of ensuring those very important things are protected. You also know that you have a uniform, a work area, and certain equipment to maintain. You have rules or policies about how to interact with those around you. If strategy leads to branding, which is a composite of the experience presented, and you are at the front line of providing some of the most important elements of that experience and being the brand, you are also integral to making the strategy come to life.

If deciding where and how to compete, as questions of strategy, allows the business to remain focused on what it does best and not become watered down trying to do too many different things for too many people, then developing a strong brand allows the business to solidify its position in the minds of others. The stronger the brand, the greater the value perceived by the clients or the parent business. The greater the value perceived by the client or parent business, the more they are willing to pay or allocate to the budget. It may even be argued that a stronger brand reduces complaints (i.e., negative experiences) because it engenders trust. The more the client or parent business is willing to pay or allocate to the budget and the fewer costs incurred as a result of poor quality, the more your operation has available for reinvestment or wages.

Notice that a large part of the burden falls on you! A security operation can brag all it wants about how good it is. They can dress everyone in excellent uniforms and buy the newest and most advanced equipment. These sorts of cues lend themselves to strong perceptions of professionalism and competence in the mind of the various users. But if the external perception is greater than the internal reality, it will not take long before the difference is noted and the complaints start coming in. You have a responsibility to meet those standards, to ensure the internal reality meets the external perception. You are the face of your operation to the customer and others most of the time. You are the brand.

BUILDING A COMMUNITY OF SUBSTANCE

Business leaders have long recognized the competitive edge to be gained in doing more than merely meeting a customer's needs but in going beyond them and surprising the customer with additional thrills. Marketing professionals refer to this as offering "satisficers" versus "delighters." Anything we do that merely meets the customer's needs at any touch point is a "satisficer." Whereas, anything we do that goes above and beyond the customer's needs and makes his "experience" that much more interesting and positive is a "delighter."

Most of the other chapters in this book are about the various technical aspects of security: how to patrol, current technologies available, risk or threat assessments, and so on. Mastery of these is absolutely essential to success and cannot be shortchanged if the operation or the officer is to be taken seriously. Without these, everything else is little more than illusion, smoke and mirrors. That being said, the challenge of a security operation, or its officers, is to find ways to make these satisficers into delighters. By now it should be abundantly clear that the key to this in our business likely lies in the "experience" perceived by those who benefit most from our services. In developing a focused strategy, maintaining a strong brand, and in creating positive experiences we move away from simply checking doors and rattling windows and into developing relationships with our various users that serve to delight them. We want them to become part of the security effort, active participants.

Aside from all of the examples we have already given about building an experience, how many other successful businesses use similar tactics in building a strong sense of community among those who use their products or services? High-end car dealers offer rallies or car shows. Motorcycle manufacturers merchandise jackets, hats, t-shirts, and so on. Theme parks and museums offer memberships and special events for members only, so their clientele feel part of the "club." If you think about it, you can probably come up with even more examples. All of these create the "experience" and serve as delighters, inviting the client or parent business into a relationship that goes well beyond that of simply being a buyer or user of our services.

How can we build relationships with our primary users and others that go beyond the traditional client/contractor or business/department satisficer and into a partnership/community delighter? If all we want to do is sell hamburgers or cars or museum tickets, we can probably get away with rather superficial efforts like those already noted. But if we want to get people involved in making their community safer, whether they are in an apartment complex, a factory, a resort, or almost any other place where people gather, we need to be able to offer something much more substantive than commemorative t-shirts and special club patches. How can we build an "experience" that leads to "community" and really goes to the heart of security and making people feel safe? A deeper question might be, "How can we build a community with substance?"

Primary User Relations: We have already hinted at some of the things we can do to bring our primary user, the one who contracted with us or is responsible for allocating budget dollars or issuing directives to our department, into the fold; a dedicated key manager or account representative, proactive communication, or memorabilia, as examples. Ideally, the primary user always feels as though he has easy access to key personnel with the security operation for any issues or concerns he may have. But how can we really bring him in and make him more than just a "user"? How can we develop the client relationship into more of a partnership? Or, in the case of in-house operations, how can we "manage" the primary user so he sees us as valuable contributors rather than another non-revenue-generating cost center?

The partnership concept often begins at the very beginning. That is, we must impress upon the primary user, before he even becomes one, that we are not merely to be contractors or just another cost center, but partners in the security effort. The language of our contracts and any related literature should express the responsibilities of both parties in this partnership. Our conversations from then on should be held on equal footing. While we strive to meet the needs of our primary user, just like any relationship, he has his part to play, too. We are his partner, not his servant, as contractors or in-house departments are sometimes viewed or treated. Our account representative, our executives, even our officers should interact with him as though "we are in this together." In-house operations may have key managers or directors, possibly even executives, who are able to interact at the highest levels of the business. Policies and directives, all communication, is written in language that recognizes the importance of the security operation in the overall business success. The security operation should develop protocols, management infrastructure, policies, and training that support these ideas. The officer should be very aware of his role in making this partnership work. It may be greater with some operations than others, depending on the strategy.

Community Relations: This is it. This is where the rubber meets the road. If you come away with nothing else from this work, focus on this section. No matter what type of strategy your operation has chosen, no matter what type of business you are in, it is a people business. That is, at some point, somewhere along the line, with everything you do, there are other people involved. You may or may not ever see all of them, or any of them. But they are there. They are the ones who benefit from your efforts, either directly or indirectly. They are the community in which you operate, whether they are part of a business, a housing development, a construction site, a government complex, or wherever. They need you.

Consider, as an example, how you might work to build a sense of community in a residential property, an apartment complex. You are part of a strategy that services living communities, with many different people. Remember, your goal is to provide positive experiences for all those who belong on the property, to minimize or manage any negative cues they may receive and keep costs of poor quality at a minimum. The key to your success lies in your ability to build positive, meaningful relationships with the communities in which you serve.

You must adopt a holistic approach. That is, you must consider the community as a whole, not just as a random collection of individual parts or even as a sum of parts. All of those various parts of the community interact to give the community its particular "personality." Together, the property management (very likely the person who is your primary point of contact), the employees of the property, every resident and guest, law enforcement and other public and social services in the area, the businesses in the neighborhood, and even the surrounding properties, all interact to shape the community. To build the partnership, you must network with and coordinate the positive efforts of these various elements wherever possible. This is done through a combination of "proactive intervention" and "preventive interaction," and can usually be seen working in different ways depending on how positively organized the particular community may be.

"Proactive intervention" involves tactics whereby the external sources of crime and community predation are removed from the equation. Overt criminal acts, such as gang activity and open drug sales or prostitution, are discouraged from the property. Nuisance issues, such as noise complaints, loitering in parking lots and stairwells, people who have no legitimate business on the property, are managed and minimized wherever possible. The physical assets of the property, such as perimeter walls, exterior lighting, landscaping, and facilities, are improved. "Preventive interaction" then sows the seeds for long-term growth. Relationships are built, networking is encouraged, and the community takes a positive interest in its own well-being. As a practical matter, you must be able to change your mind-set at any given instant between proactive intervention and preventive interaction or some combination of the two. Everything you learn in the other chapters in this book are now brought to bear.

Imagine your relationship-building process in three phases: networking, anchoring, and community integration.

Networking: Networking, at its core, is about building positive relationships based on trust. It is more than merely waving at or chatting with residents and getting to know the neighborhood, but also involves you introducing the neighborhood to itself again. Ideally, you are the one who leads the charge in getting residents involved in their own community through a variety of initiatives, such as participating in or organizing community events, being a positive role model, playing with children so they and their parents can enjoy the common areas and amenities, and encouraging residents to interact positively with one another, with you and your fellow officers, with local law enforcement, and with other community resources.

At this stage, residents see you as a resource. You are friendly, supportive, and encouraging in assisting them in addressing their challenges. You are aggressive and tireless in driving away the negative influences that have impacted the community in the past. This phase tends to see a lot of proactive intervention and preventive interaction, with you displaying an agile mind-set mastering both, as described above. Can you grasp the power of this sort of "experience" for the various users of your services yet? Do you see the positive cues?

Anchoring: As the community recognizes its own strengths and asserts itself positively in controlling its own destiny, you work to "anchor" the community. More of your efforts are spent in preventive interaction as you assist the community in building those skills necessary to maintain control. Relationships are built across the community to encourage long-term positive growth. Indeed, many who employ these sorts of community building tactics work to build very strong relationships with the parents in the community, which will assist greatly in managing the many juvenile issues that almost undoubtedly will arise.

Community Integration: As an extension of anchoring, you take the next step and reach out to the community as a whole, rather than as separate parts. You become an active participant in, or organizer of, community events specifically designed to further the community-building effort. These are often limited only by your creativity and initiative, as well as your organizational talents, and may appear as trash clean-up days, field days, cookouts, and so on. The security operation for which you work may even encourage you to coordinate such events and will ensure appropriate resources can be allocated to assist or participate.

Consider on your own how this paradigm for community building can be used in different settings, different strategies. What sorts of networking or anchoring might be fitting in an industrial setting? How can security personnel be active participants in community integration efforts in a professional building or luxury resort? Do not underestimate the value of this concept. Take some time and seriously consider how this may be used in the environments where you usually work (see Table 43-6).

The community-building concepts of networking, anchoring, and community integration can be applied to any setting, any environment. This table presents only a few ideas for the three environments sampled. How can your operation or you apply these concepts to the environment you serve?

As you think through the tactics inside community relations, keep in mind the various types of people you may encounter. Each one, each type, has some interest or stake in the community. We refer to these as "stakeholders." Your primary user, the person who contracted with you or who oversees your department certainly has an interest, and is thus a stakeholder. Executives or managers of the

TABLE 43-6 Community Relations in Other Environments

	Hospital Setting	Industrial Facility	Retail Environment
Stakeholders (examples): Each stakeholder will have a different interest.	• Doctors, nurses, orderlies, and other hospital staff • EMS personnel • Patients • Family members of patients	• Upper management • Line or floor employees • Contractors and vendors • EMS personnel responding to safety incidents	• Store manager • Store employees • Customers • Law enforcement personnel responding to thefts
Proactive Intervention	• Keep the public areas clean and uncluttered. • Use layered access control throughout the hospital. • Manage the ER and other waiting areas to prevent disturbances.	• Seek out and resolve safety issues. • Use layered access control throughout the facility.	• Be clear that thefts and shoplifting are prosecuted; use signage and visible camera systems. • Deploy loss prevention personnel. • Use visible security personnel to show a presence and remove problem customers.
Preventative Interaction	Build relationships and encourage the staff and others to take an interest in safety and security at the hospital.	Build relationships and encourage the workers and others to take an interest in safety and security at the facility.	Build relationships and encourage personnel, customers, and others to take an interest in safety and security at the store.
Networking	Interact proactively and professionally with staff and others. Ensure they see you as a resource.	Interact proactively and professionally with workers and others. Ensure they see you as a resource.	Interact proactively and professionally with store personnel and others. Ensure they see you as a resource.
Anchoring	• Use networking to develop relationships beyond those with whom you normally interact. • Encourage staff and others to take charge of their own environments.	• Use networking to develop relationships beyond those with whom you normally interact. • Encourage workers and others to take charge of their own environments.	• Use networking to develop relationships beyond those with whom you normally interact. • Encourage store personnel and others to take charge of their own environments.
Community Integration	Develop or coordinate training or awareness programs and initiatives.	Develop or coordinate training or awareness programs and initiatives.	Develop or coordinate training or awareness programs and initiatives.

facility, or the employers or residents, have interests. They are stakeholders too. Others may be visitors or vendors. Law enforcement or emergency fire and medical personnel are stakeholders, as are any other legitimate user of the property or area you are there to protect. Your efforts should be focused on creating a positive experience for each of these stakeholder groups, according to what they may need or expect from your operation and you. The security operation probably has protocols for interacting with each stakeholder group, how to interact, who may interact at what levels, and so on. Through your efforts, the protocols support the idea of building the community and doing so with substance.

Contact Protocols

Regardless of where any relationship is intended to go in the end, it begins somewhere. There is always a first contact. Your agency's contact protocols very likely include some reference to that first contact and require you to be professional, address everyone with a certain degree of formality (i.e., "Sir" or "Ma'am"), and perhaps even stand up or smile, depending on the particular environment. As the saying goes, you only get one chance to make a first impression. Many protocols require similar interactions all the time. Less common among agency rules, though, are protocols that address the rest of the relationship.

Many of us are already adept at building relationships. We do so with our friends and loved ones, after all. However, as part of a strategy to support the overall security effort, relationship building is a lot more focused and purposeful. To be sure, there is a considerable amount of sheer personality that comes into play, but guiding that relationship to support the security effort requires specific protocols. Protocols serve as rules for who in the security team should interact with whom on the client or business side. What types of issues are you expected and empowered to address on your own and which should you refer to someone else? How should the front line security officer interact with the line employee, plant manager, doctor or department head, member of the public, and so on?

Some security operations observe a very strict chain of command or supervisory hierarchy. An officer must be of a particular rank or position in order to speak or make a presentation to a client or business unit director. If you work in one of these types of organizations, you will probably be required to make any issues known to your supervisor and trust him/her to carry the matter forward. On the other hand, some operations encourage open communication among security officers and client or business points of contact. More likely than not, you work in an operation that falls somewhere in between. There are some people you are expected to contact regularly, with whom you should communicate openly, and others who only your supervisors should address. If not already clearly spelled out for you, your supervisor should be able to explain these particular protocols and where you fit in.

For those with whom you are expected to communicate regularly, you probably have protocols around what is or is not to be discussed. Certain types of security issues, such as blocked fire exits, exposed tools or valuables, or day-to-day operations of an access control point may be acceptable for you. The times of shift changes or the exact patrol routes or coverage areas may be reserved for your supervisors to discuss. Again, if you do not already have clear protocols available to you, ask your supervisors for guidance.

Whenever you do interact with others, regardless of who they may be, how you present yourself will go a long way to establishing what sort of relationship is built. You should consider your body language as a very important part of how you communicate with others. How is your posture? Is it straight and professional, or relaxed? Where are your hands? Are they at your sides or behind you, or are they in front of you as part of an "interview stance"? How do you position your feet? Are they square to your shoulders or are you angled slightly to the other person with your strong foot slightly behind you and ready to react? When you present a relaxed or lackadaisical image, people imagine this to be how you approach your work. When you present a crisp image and a commanding bearing, people will see you that way.

Similarly, how you speak to people and engage in conversation with them is an important part of building rapport and relationship. Do you speak in clear English or whatever language is most common for your environment? Or do you use slang terms and phrases? Do you treat other people with respect, or even deference if they are senior to you, or are you insulting or degrading? It can be a considerable challenge to be respectful to those who challenge you, be they malefactors, criminals, or otherwise decent people who are being redirected for some policy issue you have to enforce.

Sensitivity to the needs or issues of others in how we interact with them can be very important. Employees or residents, for example, generally have a right to be in the area doing whatever they do. Even when redirecting them, you should do so in a way that respects this. In some cases you will need to be very sensitive to race, gender, ethnic, political, or other issues. What you may say in one such setting may be wholly inappropriate in another. Even when the policy remains the same and your job is to ensure the safety and security of those people and assets you protect, how you interact with one person or group of people in a given situation may be very different from how you interact with another person or group of people in essentially the same scenario. We would like to believe we treat everyone similarly. In terms of holding them all to the standards of safety and security, or whatever rules we are charged to enforce, we do. However, everyone is different. Motivating different people to follow those rules or comply with your directives may require an awareness of those differences and considerable people skills on your part. Protocols from your operation and guidance from your supervisors can support you here.

What should you do when law enforcement or fire/EMS personnel are on site for some emergency? Are you required to call a supervisor, or are you empowered by your agency to manage your part of the incident without them? Under what conditions should you request law enforcement or fire/EMS? Are you able to make that request on your own, or must you defer to someone else?

Established protocols, written guidance as part of a policy manual, would be ideal for you as you determine your role in contact protocols and relationship building to support the overall security effort. You will know which client or business contacts you may approach directly and about what, and which should be reserved for your supervisors. You will know what sorts of issues are your responsibility to address and which should be referred to someone else. You will also have some guidance on what is acceptable interaction with various stakeholders you may encounter. If you do not have written guidance and you encounter others with any frequency, ask your supervisors how they want you to interact.

Remember, despite any apparent informality in interacting with others in the environment you protect, your role there is part of a greater strategy. Your job as a professional security practitioner is to recognize this and conduct yourself in a manner that supports that strategy.

Media relations is addressed elsewhere in this book. As a strategic tool, though, the media can be employed as powerful allies in community building. In-house operations may be able to use internal business media. Whether external or internal, positive stories with lots of background video or pictures can build the reputation of the security operation and its efforts in the minds of the stakeholders. Whenever a new and interesting deployment or event presents itself, the media should be invited to attend. Having dedicated personnel available to respond to any media inquiries not planned is a good idea too. Those personnel should have some media savvy and be able to field tough questions with dignity and class. Imagine the positive cues sent to your stakeholders when they see your agency presented well on the evening news; for that new contract or deployment, as subject matter experts on personal security in the workplace, or responding to a significant event like true professionals!

Complaints: Despite our best efforts, someone somewhere will still complain. Aside from what we have already mentioned about how complaints represent costs of quality, they should also be considered for what they are. Almost every complaint presents some opportunity for improvement. Some complainants do so because they express a genuine concern. Perhaps the complaint is about a real security risk. Maybe a point of contact called because an officer did not notice a key area was left unsecured the night before. That is an important matter and should be addressed decisively. The complaint presents an opportunity for the operation to review its systems and ensure they are built to prevent such things. Remember appraisal costs? Complaints like this inform the security operation of some liability exposure that needs to be managed. We should appreciate them as such.

Many times complainants just want to be heard. The substance of their complaint may not be such that it contains a material risk or any exposure. But it is important to them. As they are part of the community, we should make every effort to "hear" their complaint. Even if there is no reasonable resolution to be offered, more often than not, simply listening to the complaint, letting the complainant know that his concerns are important to us, and taking the time to talk with them and explain matters fully can go a long way to turning the negative cue of the complaint into a very positive cue of listening and relationship building.

THE TRANSFORMATION

So what happens when a focused strategy is determined, the brand established, the systems are in place to ensure positive experiences and manage total quality costs, and there is a community relations effort in place? What happens when you, similar to the janitor at NASA, can say, "I make sure people can sleep at night"?

With all of the techniques of modern security in the mix, and you bringing in the community of stakeholders as well, the entire process becomes unimaginably more powerful. When you bring them the tools, and people are taught how and encouraged to assume responsibility for the safety of their own communities or workplaces, or at least to play a more active role, complete transformations can be seen. Crime-ridden neighborhoods become places where children can play without worry, because the residents look out for each other. Workplaces with lots of machines and safety hazards around become safer because fellow employees pay more attention. High-security areas become less vulnerable to attack because those who work in and around them are more aware of threats and threat indicators.

Interestingly, Pine and Gilmore (1999) suggest the next type of economy, after the experience economy, will be the "transformation economy." People will buy because they want to become something else. They want to better themselves. As a competitive security operation, can you build a transformation strategy into your offering? As a security officer, can you play a role in transforming the community into a safer place? If so, then welcome. You are the professional practitioner of the future!

EMERGING TRENDS

Over the past several years, businesses have assumed more and more responsibility for the safety and security of their facilities. Part of this shift may be attributed to perceptions of new threats from which assets must be defended, and the recognition that law enforcement agencies simply cannot do it all. Part may be a reaction to an increasingly complex legal environment and an interest in mitigating liability exposures. Governments have also made efforts to privatize services where possible and have been reaching out to private security agencies and service providers. Whatever the cause, we have seen our industry grow quite a bit and it continues to do so.

As more is being asked of us, we rise to the challenge to ensure the needs of our clients or users are met. New technologies allow us to control access with greater certainty, monitor our areas of responsibility more efficiently, or detect intrusions or variances more effectively. Associations such as the International Foundation for Protection Officers and some regulatory authorities continue to develop and promote professional standards or regulations such as licensure and training requirements respectively. The days of "observe and report" are fading away and being replaced with an expectation to act, indeed even to be proactive.

As seductive as the technology is, however, it is significantly limited. Technology can be used well as a tool to supplement a security effort, but it must never be used to replace the decision-making component that necessarily comes with operating a "people business." A security officer in the area, even when supported by technology, simply serves many environments better.

The private security officer is becoming less and less the "night watchman" rarely seen by most of the public, or a figure behind a desk or discreetly making rounds and barely noticed by others in the area. The role is moving into a highly visible component of the security effort, where the officer interacts with others and makes decisions on the ground. As this continues, that officer will have to understand his role within the strategy of the agency or department for which he works and he will have to develop a strong set of "people skills" in order to be successful.

References

Campanella, J. (Ed.). (1999). *Principles of quality costs, principles, implementation and use* (3rd ed.). Milwaukee, WI: ASQ Quality Press.

Davidson, M. (1996). *The transformation of management.* Boston, MA: Butterworth-Heinemann.

Pine, J. B., & Gilmore, J. H. (1999). *The experience economy, work is theater and every business is a stage.* Boston, MA: Harvard Business School Press.

SECURITY QUIZ

1. The society that wants to buy what they buy based on the thrill derived from the item purchased is an example of which of the following types of economy:
   a. Agrarian economy
   b. Service economy
   c. Experience economy
   d. Credit-based economy

2. Creating a positive experience involves being effective in which of the following:
   a. The security officers must maintain an even temperament
   b. The security officers must be proactive when faced with problems or challenges
   c. The security officers must be liability conscious
   d. All the above

3. Total quality costs include all the following except:
   a. Prevention costs
   b. High Federal tax cost
   c. Failure costs
   d. Appraisal costs

4. In a service-related business, such as security, total quality costs can be significantly reduced by providing which of the following:
   a. A positive experience
   b. A relaxation of rules and regulations
   c. A self-inspection every five years
   d. All the above

5. The operation's brand is a function of all of the experiences, as we explored above, perceived by the various users of its services with whom the operation comes in contact. It is more than just a logo on a letterhead, it is also which of the following:
   a. The uniform
   b. The way the security officers present themselves
   c. The image of the operation at every touch point
   d. All the above

6. Branding is about the image of the operation at every touch point, at every single place anyone has any contact whatsoever with the operation.
   a. True
   b. False

7. Our account representative, our executives, even our officers should interact with our client or overseeing executive as though:
   a. We know security
   b. We are in this together
   c. We are in charge of the security effort
   d. All the above

8. Almost every complaint presents some:
   a. Opportunity for improvement
   b. Issue that must be corrected
   c. Threat to the relationship with the client
   d. Evidence that someone is not doing the job correctly
   e. Challenge that must be managed

9. The key to your success lies in your ability to build which of the following with the communities in which you serve. (Choose the one best answer.)
   a. A sense of profit for your company
   b. A strong coalition of police and security officers in the neighborhood
   c. Positive, meaningful relationships between the company and the neighbors
   d. Developing anti-crime strategies and perimeter security for the company

10. The next type of economy, after the experience economy, will be the transformation economy.
    a. True
    b. False

Networking and the Liaison Function

Brion P. Gilbride

CHAPTER OBJECTIVES

- Describe the various types of liaison and networking activities
- Provide scenarios describing interactions that present networking opportunities

The security professional is often the public face of an organization, whether working directly for that organization or under a contract assigned to it. Each day, security personnel deal with people, especially fellow company/client employees, management, law enforcement officials, emergency response personnel, and government inspectors or agents. Professional relationships with these people can potentially impact the security professional in a variety of positive ways. The best description of these relationships comes to us from the term "liaison." According to Reference.com, liaison is defined as "the contact or connection maintained by communications between units of the armed forces or of any other organization in order to ensure concerted action, cooperation, etc."

(Reference.com, 2009). Most people, however, refer to these relationships as "networking." Contacts made with other professionals can enhance both the security operation as a whole as well as the security professional working for it. Bear in mind that these liaison relationships can also come from membership in professional organizations, academic institutions, and even organizations that sponsor events such as the local Chamber of Commerce.

Although it may seem commonplace, the importance of networking cannot be overstated. As an employee in a proprietary security or public safety department, retail loss prevention operation, contract guard service, or law enforcement agency, the security officer is the guardian of the interests of the company that he/she serves; the security officer protects the company's assets, its personnel, its reputation, and its interests. It is also in the security professional's own interest to establish and maintain these relationships. For example, if a job requires a security practitioner to conduct a preliminary investigation into something—be it a fire alarm, shoplifting report, suspicious person, fake identification, or a stolen credit card—professional relationships can be key to providing timely and actionable information to the appropriate authorities or even resolving the situation entirely. Through professional success, one proves the value of maintaining the security operation. In a tight economy, this could mean the difference between walking on patrol versus walking the unemployment line.

Most important to the security professional will be the opportunities that liaison relationships may bring. With the post-9/11 and post-Katrina emphasis on the Incident Command System (FEMA, 2009) and the interchangeable roles involved, the security professional will likely be the first-on-scene presence at an incident, meaning that he/she will function at least temporarily as Incident Commander as other assets are called up. That will bring the security practitioner into contact with police, fire, EMS, local, state, and even federal officials as the response is organized. Contacts made in that situation could lead to proposing or even organizing a tabletop exercise among various entities for future responses. Such a gathering would likely be noticed by company management or possibly the local media, and in turn could lead to promotion, training opportunities, or a new position elsewhere. Although promotion or new positions also heavily depend on a security professional's performance, the networking possibilities and what they could offer are quite real.

Many liaison contacts will be formal professional relationships (i.e., those that are built through one organization interacting with the security team at a particular location). There are a multitude of scenarios through which these relationships could be built. For the purposes of this chapter we will examine five scenarios that could occur, irrespective of location or discipline within the security profession. Three of these scenarios are incidents: a fire, a vehicle break-in, and a special event such as a VIP factory tour. The fourth scenario involves normal security operations at a seaport facility. The fifth scenario is the installation of a central station

that combines access control, CCTV, fire control and suppression, and environmental monitoring systems.

FIRST SCENARIO: FIRE

A fire occurred at a manufacturing facility, on the manufacturing floor. Some equipment was damaged when the sprinkler system was activated and two employees were treated for smoke inhalation because it took several minutes to put the fire out. The responding security professionals did one or more of the following: assisted in moving injured people to safety, extinguished the fire, cleared and secured the area, or reported the incident to management. As a result, those security practitioners probably met with and assisted police, firefighters, and EMTs. If the manufacturing operation involved HAZMAT, the security practitioners may also have been in contact with the local HAZMAT unit or the company's internal HAZMAT-trained staff regarding possible dangers or containment scenarios. They may have written a report on the incident for presentation to the security manager or director. Because equipment was damaged and people were injured, a variety of entities will take an interest in the report and will likely want to interview the security professionals regarding the events. The corporate insurance company's representatives may be interested, as well as corporate counsel, OSHA or its state-level counterpart, local fire department investigators, and perhaps local code enforcement officials (see Figure 44-1). That is a sizeable group to be faced with as a security practitioner, especially over one incident.

Each one of these subsets is a potential contact, even if it might not seem so at the outset. Local law enforcement, firefighters, and EMTs are good contacts because security professionals are likely to see them more than once; accordingly they offer the best opportunity to form relationships. Their benefit to the security professional will be

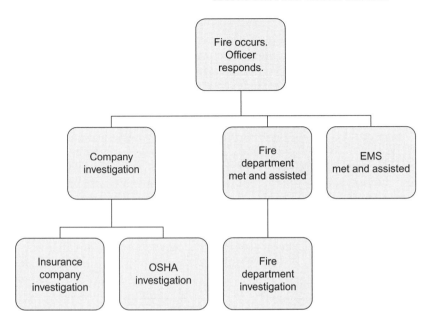

FIGURE 44-1 Investigation of a fire—networking possibilities.

one of familiarity—ideally the security practitioner will be recognized as competent and not prone to frivolous use of emergency response services. In turn, emergency response services personnel will recognize and pass on to their coworkers that a call from the security professional is likely to be legitimate. Whether this is morally appropriate is debatable; however, the company/client's interests are paramount here, and a quick and professional response from emergency services is in the company/client's best interest. The HAZMAT specialists are valuable resources for inquiries about specialized training or for information on responding to hazardous material issues in their absence or before they can be mobilized.

In a similar vein to the HAZMAT personnel, valuable networking contacts may be encountered after the incident. Positive meetings with internal company officials could lead to consideration for other career opportunities within the company. Doing well in front of those that make promotional decisions is important. The favorable opinion of representatives from the corporate insurance or legal departments could mean increased responsibility; the manager might task the security professional with addressing such incidents in the future or drafting/revising the company's Standard Operating Procedures for critical incidents. Such accomplishments might also lead to other opportunities within the company. Finally, contacts within OSHA could be valuable in terms of both potential training opportunities and information-sharing capabilities. Helping to address safety issues with knowledge of OSHA requirements can be a career enhancer, particularly if an inspection or audit is coming up. OSHA is a regulatory agency that seeks compliance; therefore OSHA contacts can provide critical information or referrals to other contacts who can answer questions or help resolve dilemmas.

SECOND SCENARIO: VEHICLE BREAK-IN

Consider another scenario that can occur at a large shopping mall with several parking garages. The mall security officers receive a report that a vehicle has been found with a smashed driver's side window and items appear to be missing from the car. The vehicle owner wants to file a report with the local police. The mall security officer will likely meet the responding police officer and share information for both the police officer and mall security's own internal report. The mall security officer may have secured the scene and interviewed the vehicle owner and/or potential witnesses. As with the fire scenario, mall security personnel are likely to encounter the responding police officer(s) on other occasions, hence forging positive relationships with them will help the mall security officer to do his/her job. For this incident, investigators from the police department may follow up on the complaint. Detectives might request surveillance camera footage, time-stamps on the time the vehicle entered the garage if it is a pay-to-park facility, information on other similar incidents in recent days that may not have generated a police report, or something else. A relationship with local investigators might lead to training opportunities or even participation in multiple-agency operations related to auto theft and similar crimes. Depending on the situation, the National Insurance Crime Bureau (NICB, 2009) may also be involved in an investigation. That entity deals with vehicle theft and fraud of all kinds, and contacts there could lead to training opportunities or beneficial information regarding theft and fraud issues.

THIRD SCENARIO: SPECIAL EVENT

The third scenario involves a state governor giving a speech at a large multifunction sports facility staffed by contract security guards. At the conclusion of opening remarks, the governor will give a 30-minute speech. The governor was recently the subject of an ethics investigation and in recent weeks has faced protests at every public appearance. In this situation there are numerous entities and individuals that are potential networking contacts. Let's begin with the smallest group and work outward.

The governor will likely have a protective detail—in this case they will be state police troopers on assignment. That protective detail will handle arrival and departure arrangements for the governor. They will have advance staff coming before the event to assess the best routes, the layout of the facility, entry and egress points, and other issues. Contract security guards may meet with these people, escort them throughout the facility, explain the security precautions normally in place, or assist in other ways. These individuals can be valuable connections for a variety of reasons—their experience in law enforcement, their experience as protective details, and their proximity to a senior government official. Aside from the governor's protective detail, there will be officials from the local and/or state police jurisdiction involved in a variety of functions—traffic control, crowd control, vetting functions, counterintelligence, and K-9 operations. Law enforcement officials have considerable training in these functions and have access to a wide spectrum of information. Networking relationships here could lead to potential training opportunities, access to open-source information systems not previously utilized, and contacts within the various disciplines. In addition, the fire department will be involved with capacity issues, fire safety and inspections, and other functions. Local EMS units will also be involved to determine staging and/or triage locations, the number of personnel necessary to cover the event, and other functions. As with the fire scenario mentioned earlier, working side-by-side with fire and EMS officials provides perspective as well as ideas for future trainings or multiple-agency operations. Company management officials will be involved at all levels, providing support and guidance. The contract guard company may

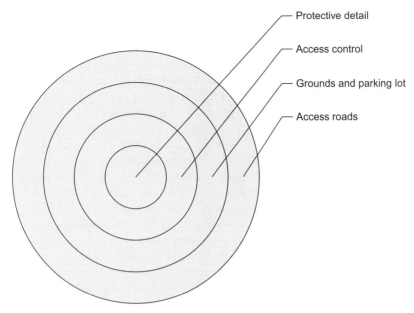

- Protective detail
- Access control
- Grounds and parking lot
- Access roads

FIGURE 44-2 Elements of VIP security scenario. Regardless of your role, these four rings represent the major roles that would be covered with regard to physical security in the event of a VIP visit at your location. Each of these rings represents a different skill set and different types of personnel/agencies involved, all of whom could be potential liaison contacts.

supplement existing security staffing by hiring additional staff for various duties, such as parking lot patrols, escort duties, access control at the doors, or other functions. The liaison possibilities in an event like this are tremendous (see Figure 44-2).

FOURTH SCENARIO: SEAPORT OPERATIONS

Even without an incident occurring, some security operations offer considerable networking opportunities by their very nature. Consider a port security officer working for a Port Authority. The port security officer's job is to provide security for the seaport and all of the various facilities within it. How many different entities could be encountered in a situation like that? Port Authority officials come

to mind first—the port security officer works directly for them. There are many networking opportunities there; seaports are always being toured or visited by the various agencies that work within it. There is usually a representative of the Port Authority involved during these events. Performing duties professionally when these representatives are in the area creates an opportunity for security personnel to be noticed. The Port Authority usually maintains business offices, warehousing facilities, transportation equipment, and other infrastructure involved in operating a seaport. The port security officer will deal with a variety of unique issues relating to warehouse security, containerized cargo, security seals, bonded warehouses, crew members detained on board their vessel, and other issues.

Beyond the Port Authority officials, a variety of agencies in the United States, for example, have jurisdiction over a seaport, particularly one receiving foreign-arriving vessels. With regard to the vessels themselves, two agencies have jurisdiction: the U.S. Coast Guard and U.S. Customs and Border Protection (CBP), both of whom are under the U.S. Department of Homeland Security. Their duties differ somewhat: the Coast Guard is more interested in vessel and port facility safety while CBP is more interested in the immigration and customs processing of the people and cargo onboard the vessel. CBP's interest also covers the warehouses operated by the Port Authority that receive the offloaded cargo. On the state level, most states have a Division of Waterways or Natural Resources or something similar. Those agencies will have an interest in the port facilities as well as the vessel and its cargo. These agencies have a diverse array of experience to draw from regarding everything from navigation laws, security bolt seals, container safety, confined space and HAZMAT training, law enforcement techniques, concealment methods, document fraud, knowledge of immigration laws relating to crew members, and more.

It is likely that in a seaport environment the port security official will encounter these state officials on a daily basis and will get to know them professionally. For those that are willing to share, there will be much for the port security officer and state official to learn from and teach each other. The utility in this type of networking is largely knowledge-based. It is doubtful that these individuals impact hiring decisions; however, what they can share is knowledge of the hiring processes, time frames, and qualifications involved should one seek a career change (see Figure 44-3).

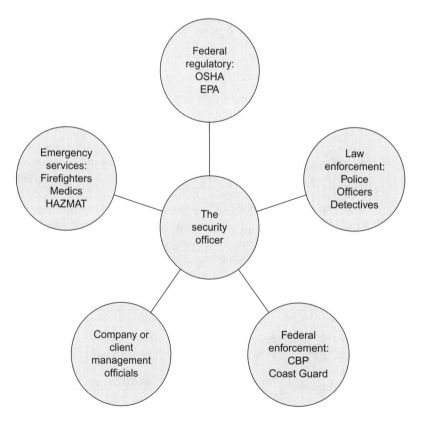

FIGURE 44-3 Relationship diagram—the security officer.

FIFTH SCENARIO: INSTALLING A CENTRAL STATION

The final scenario involves installation of a central security location at a big-box store. It will be equipped with computers and monitors for the proximity card access control system, a fire detection and suppression system, CCTV with digital storage and thermal printer, and an environmental monitoring system. This means that loss prevention agents at the store will need to be trained on using and maintaining this equipment. It is likely that a different company handles each system, meaning multiple training sessions, different troubleshooting techniques, and different contacts should a system malfunction.

In terms of networking, there is opportunity here. The technicians who install the equipment and/or set up monitoring systems to work with existing equipment will likely be the same people the loss prevention agents would call in the event of equipment malfunction or damage. Technicians may not come to the store for relatively minor problems, but will likely talk through minor equipment issues with the loss prevention agents. The more issues that can be resolved without a service call, the more money loss prevention agents could potentially save the organization. Those savings are usually quantifiable and therefore would likely be of benefit to the security operation as a whole.

The more knowledge loss prevention agents can obtain regarding how the equipment in their facility functions, the more valuable they will be in general. Someone who is only proficient with the CCTV equipment may not know what to do if the access control system requires security personnel to produce and issue security badges. Someone who is only proficient with the access control equipment may not know how to deal with a fire panel; knowing the difference between a ground fault and a legitimate alarm condition may be the difference between hundreds of dollars in minor damage versus tens of thousands in lost productivity. Someone who is not proficient with the CCTV equipment may not know that a still picture can be printed on the thermal printer of a particular frame of CCTV video, much less how to print it. That lack of knowledge could be the difference between a closed theft case versus an unsolved one. It is in the loss prevention agent's best interest to know as much about the equipment they use in their daily work as possible. The best people to explain what the various systems do are the people who install them.

PROFESSIONAL ORGANIZATIONS AND TRAINING

These five scenarios are not in any way an exhaustive list of opportunities for establishing networking relationships with outside individuals or groups. Professional development groups can also introduce a wide variety of professionals with whom a liaison-type relationship is beneficial. There are a variety of professional organizations out there for security officers. For example, there is the International Foundation for Protection Officers (IFPO, 2009), which specializes in entry-level and intermediate security officer training and certification. There is the American Society for Industrial Security (ASIS, 2009), which specializes in advanced training and certification for security officers. There is the International Association of Healthcare Safety & Security (IAHSS, 2009), which specializes in entry-level and intermediate security officer training and certification within the health care field.

Networking opportunities within these organizations are numerous. ASIS, for example, holds monthly chapter meetings in many locations. The meetings may include guest speakers or discussions on issues affecting the security profession. ASIS members, due to the advanced training the organization offers, are often former military or law enforcement officials and as such have a variety of contacts throughout the profession. The IFPO has numerous training offerings, culminating in the Certified Protection Officer (CPO) and Certified in Security Supervision and Management (CSSM) designations. The IFPO has instruction manuals for its programs that are written by authors from various disciplines throughout the security profession and are updated periodically to keep the material fresh and to keep up with the tremendous technological advances of the past 10–15 years. The IAHSS has regions and meetings as well as certification programs geared toward guard and officer positions or management, such as Certified Healthcare Security Officer (CHSO) and Certified Advanced Healthcare Security Officer (CAHSO).

In addition to professional organizations, there are a variety of educational institutions offering associate's, bachelor's, and even master's degrees in security-related disciplines. These degree programs, although considerably more expensive and time-consuming than a certification or training program, also offer networking opportunities. Many institutions employ instructors and professors in the security discipline that have had real-world experience in the field as security professionals, law enforcement, or prior military personnel. Many students also have diverse backgrounds that could provide networking possibilities. As with the professional organizations, these individuals will have diverse contacts as well as capabilities of their own that may positively impact one's career.

INDUSTRY REGULATION BY GOVERNMENT

In an increasing number of countries, the private security industry as a whole is subject to regulation by governmental or quasi-governmental bodies. Accordingly, the security professional, whether a mall security officer, loss prevention agent, contract security guard, armored car driver, night watchman, or even off-duty law enforcement officer, needs to be aware of the regulations pertaining to their work as well as those of the agencies and individuals who enforce them.

For example, in the United Kingdom the security industry is regulated by the Security Industry Authority (SIA). The SIA was established by the Private Security Industry Act of 2001 (SIA, 2009) and has subsequently been amended several times. The SIA deals primarily with the licensing of security industry employees working in the following job classifications: CCTV, close protection, door supervision, event security, key holding, private investigation, security consultancy, security guarding, and vehicle immobilizing. In addition, companies hiring personnel for these activities are able to check the license status of employees and/or job applicants. The SIA maintains a registry of current, revoked, and suspended licenses. Companies may apply for accreditation by the SIA as "Approved Contractors" by meeting certain standards. They must renew this designation periodically, are subject to independent assessment annually, and there exists a mechanism to report malpractice by an "Approved Contractor" (SIA, ACS, 2009).

Those regulated by the SIA are required to provide documents or information relating to any matter regulated by the SIA. Persons who are regulated by the SIA include security contractors and their employees, managers and supervisors of contract security providers, directors of companies and partners even if they do not carry out security functions themselves, and vehicle immobilizers as well as employers or managers of them. It should be noted that under the Private Security Act of 2001, proprietary staff, even if supervising contract employees, are generally not subject to licensure (SIA, License Requirements, 2009).

South Africa has a similar arrangement. Their licensing apparatus is maintained by the Private Security Industry Regulatory Authority (PSIRA). The PSIRA's mandate derives from the Private Security Industry Regulatory Act of 2001. Those regulations require that any person seeking to be a "security service provider" must apply for such a designation through the PSIRA. In doing so, the applicant must provide proof of South African citizenship or permanent residency, fingerprints, a clearance certificate regarding the applicant's criminal record, and documented proof that the applicant has completed security training courses recognized by the PSIRA. The PSIRA also requires that any applicant, if a former member of a military force, intelligence service, police, or security agency, must obtain a clearance certificate from that entity as well, if possible. Businesses providing security services must also be designated and must provide a list of shareholders or partners in the venture, tax clearance certification, trust deed, and information pertaining to the company's ability to provide a security service (Regulations Made ... 2001 2(1) through 2(8)).

The PSIRA, by virtue of their regulations under the Act, regulates the operation of security service providers in a variety of ways. Issues falling under their purview include infrastructure of regulated companies. This includes the physical facilities, telephone and facsimile equipment, sufficient security equipment, vehicles, and firearms (Regulations Made ... 2001 5(1) through 5(3)). Security service providers are required to provide information on the business and all of its subsidiaries and offices, employees, all applicable licenses, and all firearms permits held (Regulations Made ... 2001 6(1) and 6(2)). Record keeping is also covered, to include an electronic list of all security personnel, ID numbers, all wages and pay stubs, attendance records for all locations, duties performed at all locations, the names of personnel on duty at any location at any time, and any disciplinary actions taken against security staff (Regulations Made ... 2001 10(1) through 10(8)).

In the United States these arrangements are largely regulated on a state-by-state basis, if at all. For example, the state of Virginia has regulations enacted for security officers and providers. As with the previous examples, Virginia regulates both the employer and the employee and does so via the Department of Criminal Justice Services. A person applying for a position as a security officer (armed or not), private investigator, armored car operator, personal protection specialist, canine handler, or electronic security provider/technician must be 18 years of age at the time of application, must have proof of completion of the necessary training courses (to DCJS standards) for the type of application they seek, proof of U.S. citizenship or legal permanent resident status, and must submit fingerprints (Regulations Relating ... 6 VAC 20-171-120).

Security service providers in Virginia are regulated in a somewhat more stringent fashion than their personnel. To apply for a business license under any of the aforementioned positions, all principals and supervisors of the business must submit fingerprints, must obtain a $100,000 surety bond, a Virginia corporate identification number, proof of a physical location in Virginia, and they must designate a compliance agent (Regulations Relating ... 6 VAC 20-171-50). A security service provider in Virginia must maintain all documentation on any employee during that employee's entire tenure plus 3 years beyond the date they separate. Such information includes date of hire, any training documentation, proof of U.S. citizenship or legal permanent residence status, and proof of their fingerprint submission. If any principal, supervisor, or employee of a security service provider is found guilty, pleads guilty or *nolo contendere*, or is convicted of a misdemeanor or a felony, the provider must notify DCJS (Regulations Relating ... 6 VAC 20-171-220).

The security professional, the loss prevention agent, or the armored car operator are all impacted by the regulatory regime in whatever jurisdiction they work. It is also possible that local, state, or federal regulations overlap. Regardless, the security professional must make sure that he/she meets the necessary legal requirements to work in their chosen field. That will require compliance with the bureaucracy that oversees the field. Any relevant applications should be completed properly and submitted in a timely manner—it behooves the applicant to be sure everything is ready before submitting materials. All three examples of regulated security positions might be subject to an audit or a validation conducted by the licensing entity. A security officer could be tasked with assisting auditors, which provides potential networking opportunities. The security professional who has a good working relationship with the auditing agency or is knowledgeable about the process will be noticed. Any audit that is completed without problems is a successful one.

CONCLUSION

The liaison function, better understood as networking, is a critical part of day-to-day performance as a security professional, contract guard, loss prevention agent—any security practitioner. The relationships formed during the course of a security professional's work, from membership in professional organizations or due to academic interests, will sustain the security professional as well as his/her career for years to come. With the proliferation of social networking Web sites, e-mail, and technology in general, it is far easier to build and foster these relationships than it was in the past. However, nothing can substitute for face-to-face contact and a good reputation. Networking is just acknowledgment that everyone can use a little help.

References

Author Unknown. *Liaison*. (Dictionary.com, LLC). Available: <http://dictionary.reference.com/browse/Liaison>. Accessed June 23, 2009.

Author Unknown. *Incident Command System Overview* (Washington, DC: Federal Emergency Management Agency). Available: <http://www.fema.gov/emergency/nims/IncidentCommandSystem.shtm>. Accessed June 30, 2009.

Author Unknown. *National Insurance Crime Bureau* (Des Plaines, IL: National Insurance Crime Bureau). Available: <https://www.nicb.org/cps/rde/xchg/nicb/hs.xsl/index.htm>. Accessed June 30, 2009.

Author Unknown. *International Foundation for Protection Officers* (Naples, FL: International Foundation for Protection Officers). Available: <http://www.ifpo.org>. Accessed June 30, 2009.

Author Unknown. *American Society for Industrial Security* (Alexandria, VA: American Society for Industrial Security). Available: <http://www.asisonline.org>. Accessed June 30, 2009.

Author Unknown. *International Association of Healthcare Security & Safety* (Glendale Heights, IL: International Association of Healthcare Security & Safety). Available: <http://www.iahss.org>. Accessed June 30, 2009.

Author Unknown. *Welcome to the SIA* (London, UK: Security Industry Authority). Available: <http://www.the-sia.org.uk/home>. Accessed July 1, 2009.

Author Unknown. *License Requirements* (London, UK: Security Industry Authority). Available: <http://www.the-sia.org.uk/home/about_sia/legislation/psia_3-6.htm>. Accessed July 1, 2009.

SECURITY QUIZ

1. Contacts made outside your company with other professionals tend to enhance both the security operation as well as the security professional. Professional liaison relationships can come from all the following except:
   a. Taking classes in academic institutions
   b. Memberships in professional association
   c. Colleagues you work with on the job every day
   d. Organizations that sponsor events
2. The elements of VIP protection include protective detail, access control, armored limousines, and fire arms proficiency.
   a. True
   b. False
3. Performing duties professionally when VIPs are in the area creates an opportunity for security personnel to be noticed by some very influential observers.
   a. True
   b. False
4. When emergency situations occur, the first responding security officer is expected to take certain emergency steps. When public

assistance arrives, what they find can bring recognition for that first responding security officer. Which of the following is one of those recognition tasks:

a. Immediately move injured people to safety regardless of injuries

b. Immediately commence using emergency rescue equipment to reach victims

c. Clear the area of all non-emergency persons, secure the incident scene providing an unobstructed work area, and report conditions to management

d. None of the above

5. Which of the following are good contacts for the security professional to make contact with because they offer the best opportunity to form long lasting relationships with:

a. Local firefighters

b. Local law enforcement

c. Local EMTs

d. All the above

6. Networking relationships are valuable because they can lead to training opportunities.

a. True

b. False

7. As for fire emergencies, security personnel might be in a position to assist the responding police officers hence forging positive relationships with local law enforcement. Detectives from that same police department

may arrive asking for additional help providing even a further opportunity for valuable contact development. Which of the following are ways to be of assistance:

a. Providing surveillance camera footage to the investigators

b. Time-stamp information on garage parking

c. Incident reports from the past that did not generate a police report

d. All the above

8. A relationship with police investigators might lead to which of the following:

a. Participation in multi-agency operations

b. Training opportunities

c. Both a & b

d. None of the above

9. Professional development groups, like the IFPO and ASIS International, can also introduce a wide variety of professionals with whom a liaison-type relationship is beneficial.

a. True

b. False

10. Every large company in the United States employs instructors in the security discipline that have had real-world experience. This provides future opportunities for security professionals with good networking capabilities.

a. True

b. False

45

Ethics and Professionalism

Christopher A. Hertig

CHAPTER OBJECTIVES

- List and define key terms and concepts
- Provide a guide to ethical decision making
- Review ethical issues in protection
- Discuss reasons why unethical behavior occurs

The business realities of contemporary management require that security (asset protection) efforts provide protection for *all* of an organization's assets, including people, property, information, and image. Asset protection should incorporate Bottom and Kostanoski's WAECUP model in order to address these concerns. This model asserts that losses stem from waste, accident, error, crime, and unethical/unprofessional practices. Under unethical/unprofessional practices are dissemination of confidential information, lying to clients, discrimination, profanity in public, poor relations with law enforcement, EMS and other security organizations, and slovenly dress. Most of this loss relates to negative public/client image. Additionally, within

organizations that are stricken by serious scandal, there are legal costs, increased personnel turnover, and lowered efficiency by a demoralized workforce.

An additional concern regarding ethics and professionalism is the role that protection officers play for the public at large. As protection officers increase in number and take on an increasing array of functions that place them in contact with the public, it becomes readily apparent that there is an acute need for higher standards of professionalism. Consider the following trends:

- A steady increase in the number of security personnel, particularly in the contract service sector.
- Increased contact with the public. Contemporary protection officers are more commonly found in shopping centers, office buildings, and parks, than they are in the warehouses and industrial facilities that were guarded by their predessors.
- Gradual—yet often unrecognized—assumption of duties formerly performed by public entities, such as maintaining order at special events, transporting prisoners, and responding to alarms (privatization).

Obviously, the role played by security officers is changing. When one looks at future trends, it becomes apparent that:

The Greatest Issue in Public Safety Is Private Security

From a personal perspective, officers should realize that those individuals who are unethical and unprofessional do not have rewarding careers. They are snubbed by colleagues and superiors, passed over for promotion, and terminated from employment in the more serious cases. The most extreme cases result in revocation of licenses that the officer may possess, and civil and criminal liability.

Those Who Make the Wrong Choices Do Not Last

Protection officers must be equipped with the decision-making skills and professional knowledge to make the right choices. For too long, words such as "professional" have been used indiscriminately, without a complete examination of their meaning. Understanding what the terms represent is a necessary step toward adopting and implementing professional behavior.

KEY TERMS AND CONCEPTS

Ethics: the study of good and bad conduct within a profession. Ethics deals with the examination of moral philosophy, combined with the duties and obligations within a certain profession. Ethical behavior results when the correct ethical decisions have been made and carried out. The International Foundation for Protection Officers Code of Ethics is:

I. Respond to employer's professional needs.
II. Exhibit exemplary conduct.
III. Protect confidential information.
IV. Maintain a safe and secure workplace.

V. Dress to create professionalism.
VI. Enforce all lawful rules and regulations.
VII. Encourage liaison with public officers.
VIII. Develop good rapport within the profession.
IX. Strive to attain professional competence.
X. Encourage high standards of officer ethics.

Duty: a professional obligation to do a certain thing. Protection officers have a duty to protect the lives and property of employees, conduct professional investigations, maintain order, and assist visitors/employees/customers. Duties may be established by statute, custom, or contract.

Professionals Think in Terms of Their Duties and Obligations, Not Their Authority!

Professional: one who practices a profession; one who has special knowledge and skill that results from advanced training and education. Often, an apprenticeship is required, such as for the experience qualifications necessary for professional certification (Certified Protection Officer, Certified in Security Supervision and Management, Certified Protection Professional, and so on). Professions have professional codes of ethics and professional organizations to which members belong. A professional is loyal to his or her chosen profession. A true professional has the following:

1. Education relating to the profession.
2. Training for the tasks and duties that must be performed.
3. Experience within the profession. Sometimes, an apprenticeship or internship is served.
4. Collegiality with coworkers. This includes aiding and assisting those they work with; never demeaning colleagues.
5. Exclusivity. There are requirements that must be met to be a professional. Not just anyone can do it! These may be in the form

of a license, certification, or completion of challenging, professional development (education and training).

6. A *commitment* to the profession, marked by continuously striving for excellence.
7. Recognition from the public being served that the individual is a professional.

The acronym **PROFESSIONAL** outlines the attributes of a professional:

P—precise, exact, detailed
R—responsive to clients and the public
O—objective in thought, free of prejudice and preconceived notions
F—factual in all reporting processes, honest
E—ethical
S—sincere about doing the best job possible
S—striving for perfection by constantly trying to improve one's job performance
I—informed about events and trends within one's profession
O—observant of people and the work environment
N—neat and orderly in dress and work
A—accommodating and helpful to others
L—loyal to one's employer, clients, and profession

Deportment: how one carries oneself, bearing, outward manifestation of attitude, and image. A few things to bear in mind about deportment are:

- Dress should be neat, precise, and conservative.
- Shoes should match belt.
- No purses for women.
- Socks should always match the pants and cover the calf.
- Conservative ties, properly tied; silk is a good choice of material.
- Jewelry worn judiciously.
- "Less is more" with makeup and cologne.
- Uniforms should be worn uniformly. All officers should have the same placement of insignia and equipment.

The acronym **DEPORTMENT** provides additional insight into the meaning—and practical application—of the term.

D—dress as a representative of your employer and/or client.
E—efficient in performing both routine and emergency job duties.
P—precision. Ironed shirts, neatly combed hair; all buttons, zippers, and pins properly secured.
O—organized on the job.
R—responsive to customers, clients, visitors, and community members; approachable.
T—talk as a professional does, using proper English.
M—manners—respect for others—exhibited at all times.
E—edit and review interviews and notes before concluding these segments of an investigation.
N—nurture professional growth and development at all times; strive to learn!
T—timely; being on time is essential. "Fashionably late" is out of style in professional settings.

Manners: manners are simply accepted means of conducting oneself in public (i.e., politeness). They consist of *consideration* and *respect* for others. They are *social graces*. A few basic tenets of proper manners are:

- Allow people to talk and express their views; DO NOT INTERRUPT! Not only does this reflect good manners, but it is effective interviewing. The truly professional protection officer makes every conversation an interview.
- Be respectful of people's input. *Compliment rather than criticize.*
- Praise others when appropriate. Be genuine in doing so.
- Stand up to greet people entering the room, especially women, clients, or VIPs. This is a sign of respect and consideration. It is an opportunity to create a personal bond that no true professional can afford to pass up.

ETHICAL DECISION MAKING

Protection officers must be equipped with the ability to make *professional judgments*. They need to be proficient at decision making as it applies to ethics. Basic decision making involves problem solving. Problem solving consists of the following steps:

1. Identify the problem. There should be a descriptive definition of the problem. Inadequate problem definition often results in poor decisions being made.
2. Determine if a decision needs to be made immediately or if it can wait.
3. Research the various options that are available; *many poor decisions stem from a failure to fully explore all of the options.* Professional knowledge of law, technology, and organizational structure/chain of command is important in understanding all of the options.
4. Choose an option. Pick the one which seems best.
5. Implement the decision. Put it into effect.
6. Evaluate the decision and follow through. This means seeing how it works and reporting/documenting it. Keeping superiors informed is always important! Soliciting feedback from them is essential.

A practical, "real-world" method of dealing with ethical dilemmas can make use of simple, easy-to-remember acronyms. Once the problem has been identified, the ethical dilemma can be managed by use of the **PORT** acronym:

> **P**—problem—define and describe it. If possible, write a sentence or two describing it.
> **O**—options—what are they? Be sure to list all of them.
> **R**—responsibilities to employers, family, the public, the profession, and so on.
> **T**—time; the test of—"How will I feel about my decision in 20 years?"

Ethical decision making must be real. It must exist in everyday work situations. Using the PORT acronym can help to maintain ethical conduct by protection professionals.

ETHICAL ISSUES IN PROTECTION

There are a number of ethical issues that are pertinent to the protection of assets. These include the following.

Both police and security personnel have had a historic involvement in class struggles. These include labor disputes during the 19th and early 20th centuries (in North America). Today, both public law enforcement and private protection officers face the ethical issue of removing homeless persons looking for a place to sleep, often in areas under officer patrol.

Violation of privacy by using privileged information they have obtained from police. In some cases, people use their "networks" to tap into restricted databases. Private security and private investigative personnel may have contacts with public law enforcement personnel who provide them with restricted information. In other cases, public law enforcement personnel who are moonlighting use these databases to run their own investigative and security services.

Another information issue involves celebrities. Some protection officers exploit their position as Personal Protection Specialists (PPS) to acquire, and then divulge, confidential information. In a society that is obsessed with celebrities, this is difficult to control. Being able to trust someone to guard a principal and their family and not violate their privacy will be an increasing challenge. While the major risk is with close protection PPS personnel, there are also uniformed officers who guard the estates, offices, and dressing rooms of celebrities.

Another issue with celebrities and/or VIPs is when protection staff subjugate themselves to the principal or their family. They become more like servants than professionals. PPS personnel are not housekeepers or babysitters. They are protection professionals.

There is also abuse of force in protecting celebrities. It may be easy for a PPS or an event security staffer to use force liberally when in a crowd situation. Some celebrities actually may encourage such displays of aggression, and there may not be good witnesses to file civil or criminal charges against the protection staff that do this.

Covering up or facilitating the bad behavior of the principal. Some principals do things which are illegal or unethical. PPS must determine whether they can tolerate such conduct. Examples might include the rock star who uses drugs, or the CEO who has an extramarital affair that is overtly or covertly funded by the company. Protection staff may be asked to lie or even aid in the commission of such activities.

Abuse of force in restraining patients is another concern. In some instances, there is a great degree of legal leeway for using force when restraining patients—especially mental patients. Persons who have been involuntarily committed to an institution must be restrained in many cases. However, protection officers do not have moral license to abuse patients or use force when it is merely convenient, but not really necessary, to do so.

Public police may, in some cases, exploit their positions by getting involved in security functions. Police operating for profit always raises questions. This may occur either by individual officers moonlighting, or police departments charging fees for services that have been formerly offered for free, such as alarm response or traffic direction. Any time that a public servant generates a revenue stream due to their office, it must be questioned.

Civil recovery presents ethical questions. Obtaining payments from shoplifters through civil demand is intended to compensate the merchant for his loss. Criminal prosecution of shoplifters is expensive and time consuming; the stolen merchandise must be held as evidence, and so it cannot be sold. Criminal prosecution costs merchants money, so we have enacted laws in most states that enable a merchant to have a civil demand letter sent to a shoplifter. Collecting on the civil demand is a temptation for merchants. They may see this as a way to defray their loss prevention expenses, rather than as a means of making them whole when victimized by shoplifters.

WHY UNETHICAL BEHAVIOR OCCURS

It is important to understand why unethical and unprofessional behavior occurs so that it can be prevented. Some of the more common causes of ethical lapses are:

- Protection officers—or any other person in a position of trust—must possess good character. As past behavior is the most reliable indicator of future behavior, it is necessary to do a check of prior employment. There can be no substitute for screening!
- Taking the "path of least resistance." Unfortunately, doing what is easy does not always solve the problem. Taking a "short cut" usually means *problem avoidance,* where the person confronting the dilemma just hopes the problem will either go away or solve itself. It won't! Avoiding the problem almost always causes the problem to become larger and more damaging over time.
- Conflict with full-time and part-time employment. The practice of moonlighting, with its inherent division of loyalties between the full-time and part-time employers, can create a breeding ground for unethical conduct.
- Fatigue. People often make the wrong choices simply because they are tired. Fatigue and stress impede good decision making. This can set up a vicious cycle where poor decisions are made, and more

stress is the result. The world of asset protection is filled with shades of gray, so it is important to have your wits about you.

- "Traditionalism" and a resistance to change. Just because protection officers have not been trained in first-aid and CPR does not mean that the practice should continue. Just because protection officers have not had a full and complete orientation to the organization they are protecting does not mean that this should remain standard practice. A pertinent example of "traditionalism" is the practice of handcuffing. Handcuffs are rarely double-locked. Not doing so can cause the cuffs to cinch tightly on the subject's wrists, which can potentially cause permanent nerve damage. Another example is traffic control. Some organizations do not train their officers to direct and control traffic, in spite of the fact that this is a key safety issue, not to mention a crucial juncture in public relations.

CONCLUSION

Ethical and professional conduct by protection officers is necessary for all concerned—the officer, the organization they represent, and the public that they protect. Officers who wish to have long and fulfilling careers need to be above reproach. They need to be ethical. And they need to perform in a professional manner at all times.

Employers and clients benefit from ethical and professional behavior by being able to trust the protectors. They can have faith in them. They can be assured that those who protect them are acting in their best interest.

The employees, visitors, students, patients, patrons, or customers—the public that officers serve—place an extensive amount of trust in protection personnel. And professional protection officers both earn and deserve that trust.

EMERGING TRENDS

Protecting a society from the concerted actions of criminals and terrorists, as well as disasters, is a challenging undertaking. While respect for individual rights must be paramount in a free society, the common good must also be considered. Homeland security has ushered in an era of utilitarianism: we protect the greater good, even if individual rights are curtailed to a degree.

What is essential is that we respect individual rights and make every attempt to preserve them.

As an information-based economy becomes more firmly established, so, too, do concerns with how that information is handled. While adhering to the basic principle of "need to know" affords some protection against abuse, there is still an increasing potential for confidential and proprietary information to be disclosed. Recent advances in Internet communications

have made this even more so. One answer to this is ethics and respect for privacy.

Perhaps an adoption of an *ethics of care philosophy* is appropriate for those who protect. Ethics of care means being concerned with the welfare of others. It means having empathy, participating in other's feelings, and understanding how they view things. The ethics of care fits in with the community policing model to a significant degree. Care, concern, and partnering with a community to solve its crime-related problems are what community policing is all about.

An ethics of care philosophy helps to prevent an "us versus them" syndrome from occurring. As protection officers become better educated, they are becoming more sensitive to their ethical obligations. Ultimately, they will become more professional.

Resource

The National Institute of Ethics has been established to further integrity and ethics in America. The Institute offers a variety of seminars which can be customized to specific organizational needs. There is also an array of instructional materials available, as well as instructor certifications. Visit http://www.ethicsinstitute.com/.

SECURITY QUIZ

1. What is the greatest issue in public safety?
   a. Private investigation
   b. Policing
   c. Private security
   d. Animal control

2. _____ are how one carries themselves, conduct, and one's attitude of image.
   a. Manners
   b. Deportment
   c. Ethics
   d. Duty

3. Where do most poor decisions emerge from?
   a. Lack of commitment
   b. Misunderstanding of what is being asked of you
   c. Failure to explore all potential options
   d. Exposure to unethical behavior

4. There is substantial legal leeway concerning the amount of force that can be used to restrain a patient. This is an ethical issue in protection.
   a. True
   b. False

5. Professionals think in terms of their authority.
   a. True
   b. False

6. Using the _____ acronym can assist one in dealing with ethical dilemmas.
   a. PROFESSIONAL
   b. DEPORTMENT
   c. ETHICS
   d. PORT

7. _____ may be established by statute, custom, or contract.
   a. Rights
   b. Duties
   c. Choices
   d. Practices

8. Taking shortcuts are one reason why unethical behavior occurs.
   a. True
   b. False

9. "Traditionalism" is _____ to change.
   a. Devotion
   b. Willingness
   c. Resistance

10. The world of asset protection is black and white. There is no gray area.
    a. True
    b. False

Index